CUBA

CUBA

*Ted A. Henken, Miriam Celaya,
and Dimas Castellanos,
Editors*

 ABC-CLIO

Santa Barbara, California • Denver, Colorado • Oxford, England

Library of Congress Cataloging-in-Publication Data

Cuba / Ted A. Henken, Miriam Celaya, and Dimas Castellanos, Editors.
    pages cm. — (Latin America in Focus)
  Includes index.
  ISBN 978-1-61069-011-9 (hardback) — ISBN 978-1-61069-012-6 (ebook)
1. Cuba. I. Henken, Ted. II. Celaya, Miriam. III. Castellanos, Dimas.
  F1758.C94865   2013
  972.91—dc23   2013028917

ISBN: 978-1-61069-011-9
EISBN: 978-1-61069-012-6

17 16 15 14 13   1 2 3 4 5

This book is also available on the World Wide Web as an eBook.
Visit www.abc-clio.com for details.

ABC-CLIO, LLC
130 Cremona Drive, P.O. Box 1911
Santa Barbara, California 93116-1911

This book is printed on acid-free paper (∞)

Manufactured in the United States of America

Para Jack, amante de la libertad, que tu vuelo sea eterno.

Contents

Preface and Acknowledgments

Writing and coediting a comprehensive reference book on a country with such an intricate history and rich culture as Cuba has been both a challenge and a pleasure. Cuba is literally bursting with a diversity of voices and competing perspectives. However, the internal media monopoly and rigid ideological parameters regulating the island's writers, artists, intellectuals, and scholars often make it difficult for outsiders to hear or make sense of these many voices. Moreover, outside coverage of Cuba often deals in shallow stereotypes and wishful thinking, uninformed by serious, sustained examination of how life is actually lived on the island itself. Fortunately, this study has been prepared as the island undergoes an unprecedented period of change—coming both from above and below—challenging traditional limits on critical expression and creating more space for independent analysis.

In an effort to seize this special moment, the editors of this book (two of whom, Miriam Celaya and Dimas Castellanos, currently live in Cuba) recruited a dozen others to give their independent, internal voice to the many topics examined here. All of these authors are Cuban and nearly all continue to live and work on the island today. Most are also both experts and hands-on practitioners in the fields about which they write, including history, anthropology, law, politics, economics, migration, religion, racial and ethnic relations, class structure, literature, dance and music, theater, film, civil society, human rights, the media, and the Internet.

The editors would like to recognize these authors who—each from his or her particular point of view—took the risk of making their knowledge and analyses public. Given that their analyses are often at odds with both the "official story" promoted by the Cuban government and the often ill-informed one coming from abroad, their effort to show this other, often hidden face of Cuba while continuing to reside there is particularly valuable and commendable.

Writing a balanced, accurate, and original overview of this unique and fascinating island-nation has been a daunting task. How does one describe the innumerable ways in which Cubans have embraced and, indeed, internalized much of U.S. culture during the island's century of independent existence, while at the same time recognizing the fact that the United States has often wielded its power and influence in a manner ultimately harmful to Cuban sovereignty? Likewise, how does one do justice to the enormous initial popularity and impressive social achievements of the Cuban revolution, without ignoring the suffering endured by the Cuban people both on the island and in exile as a result of the Cuban government's internal rigidity, intolerance, and paternalism? As Cubans like to say, *No es fácil* (It ain't easy)!

Although writing and teaching about Cuba can be a political minefield of sorts, even for the most enterprising and sensitive of scholars, the country of Cuba, with its unique culture, and the people of Cuba, with their contagious charisma, passionate convictions, and gracious generosity of spirit, make the never-ending task of understanding the country and its people inestimably rewarding and enriching. This book is the fruit of more than five years of collaboration among its three coeditors and many authors, often thanks to our strategic use of the Internet and social media to share, edit, and translate the book's various chapters. Thanks are due to the Swedish, Dutch, and Swiss Embassies in Cuba for opening their doors to the Cuban coeditors, enabling the free flow of uncensored information back and forth between Havana and New York necessary to make this book a reality. We even managed to convince a few brave (and happily anonymous) souls to help us by spiriting author contracts and payments back and forth between Cuban and the United States. We thank them here as well.

The volume provides an up-to-date overview of historical, political, economic, and sociocultural development of Cuba from the pre-Columbian period to the present, with an emphasis on the Cuban revolution, U.S.-Cuban relations, Cuba's impressive cultural achievements, and the country's current socioeconomic reality. The book contains seven narrative chapters, on (1) geography, (2) history, (3) politics and government, (4) economy, (5) society, (6) culture, and (7) contemporary issues. Augmented by a total of 76 brief vignettes on various historical, political, cultural, or biographical topics of special interest or importance such as the Guantánamo Bay Naval Base, the Platt Amendment, the U.S. Embargo, the writer Reinaldo Arenas, the film director Tomás Gutiérrez Alea, the artist Wifredo Lam, or the human rights activists The Ladies in White. While the history chapter focuses almost exclusively on prerevolutionary Cuba, the bulk of the other chapters are dedicated to chronicling the economic, political, social, and cultural changes that have taken place in Cuban society since 1959 under the revolution.

The editors would like to give special thanks to our two intrepid student translators, Michael Prada Krakow and Natalia Pardo Becerra—both natives of Colombia. With key financial support from Baruch College's Weissman School of Arts and Sciences, Mike and Natalia worked together with the book's lead editor and translator—Ted A. Henken—for over a year rendering the various authors' original Spanish-language chapters into an English that would preserve the content of their ideas and the beauty of their language. We also thank Regina Anavy for stepping in at a key moment with her own expert, emergency, volunteer translation of a few sections of this book. It's readers will judge how well we succeeded.

The editors would also like to thank Archibald Ritter, Yoani Sánchez, and Reinaldo Escobar who first introduced us to one another physically. We also acknowledge M. J. Porter, Karen Chun, and Aurora Morera, whose intrepid, behind-the-scenes work setting up portals to host their blogs allowed us to more easily collaborate virtually. Baruch College professor and top-flight literary translator Esther Allen also deserves *nuestros más sinceros agradecimientos* (our most sincere thanks) as she was a key link in the translation chain at an early stage of this project. The writer, blogger, and photographer Orlando Luis Pardo Lazo also deserves our gratitude for graciously allowing us to raid his stunning trove of digital images of today's Cuba, 15 of which illustrate the book's pages. Queens-based graphic designer Rolando Pulido assisted with getting these photos camera-ready. Also, journalist Tracey Eaton, poet Uva de Aragón, and Cuban photographer Luzbely Escobar each generously contributed a wonderful photo of their own to the book.

Kaitlin Ciarmiello, ABC-CLIO's acquisitions editor for the Geography and World Cultures series was especially instrumental in shepherding what unexpectedly became an unwieldy coedited, dual-language, and multi-author project through various stages of completion. Likewise, both James Dare, the book's illustrations editor, and Valavil Lydia Shinoj, the book's project manager were exemplars of resourcefulness and professionalism. Finally, we would like to acknowledge the assistance of Cuban scholars Samuel Farber, Domingo Amuchástegui, and Eusebio Mujal-León, each of whom provided extensive comments on Chapter 3 "Politics and Government." Likewise, Dafnis Prieto, the virtuoso Cuban percussionist and MacArthur "Genius" grantee, performed a similar service by thoroughly reviewing the section on Cuban music. Archibald R. M. Ritter kindly did the same for Chapter 4 "Economy." We hope the published book reflects some of their extensive knowledge and editorial care. Of course, all errors, omissions, and oversights are our own.

Geography

Ted A. Henken and Miriam Celaya

Cuba is often referred to as being just "90 miles" (145 kilometers) south of Key West, Florida. However, just as important in the island's often turbulent history is the fact that it is also 130 miles (210 km) east of Mexico's Yucatan Peninsula, 87 miles (140 km) north of Jamaica, and 48 miles (77 km) west of the island of Hispaniola. Frequently and erroneously described as a "small island nation," Cuba is in fact a large island nation; far larger than any other single Caribbean island and roughly the same size (42,804 square miles; 110,862 square kilometers) as the rest of the Antilles combined.

Cuba's large size and strategic location at the confluence of the Gulf of Mexico, the Caribbean Sea, and the Atlantic Ocean—the crossroads of the Americas—have uniquely positioned it to absorb, transform, and reexport new ideas, technologies, and fashions throughout its history. This unique "situation" has also allowed it to play an important role in nearly every hemispheric and international craze and confrontation, from its founding as a Spanish colony at the dawn of "the age of empire" in 1511, to its use as a springboard in the rise of the United States as an imperial power during the so-called Spanish-American War in 1898, to its role as the first "communist beachhead" in the Western Hemisphere during the Cold War in the early 1960s, to the surprisingly pivotal if increasingly controversial position of the Guantánamo Bay Naval Base in today's "global war on terror."

GEOGRAPHICAL SITUATION—"CUBA IS THE KEY"

Geographers typically evaluate a city or nation's location based on two key variables: site and situation. While "site" refers to the actual physical, topographical, and climactic condition of a place, its "situation" refers to its location relative to other cities

1

and nations, and especially to adjacent bodies of water. Cuba's importance derives from its strategic situation at the center of the Western Hemisphere, straddling the trade winds of the Gulf Stream, in the very heart of the "American Mediterranean." In that key situation, throughout its long history Cuba has played the role of a geographical hub, linking the peoples, cultures, and economies surrounding it. It has also long been coveted as a military defense post, given its proximity to strategic landmasses and vital sea lanes. The island lies at the crossroads of every principal maritime passage in and out of the Caribbean. Both the Spanish and their many European rivals for predominance in the Caribbean knew this. Control of Cuba was key to supremacy in the New World.

Cuba's history is filled with vivid instances that highlight the importance of its geographic situation. For example, given the island's closeness to Miami and its burgeoning Cuban-American community, in 1980 the United States became the country of first refuge in a mass refugee migration for the first time. In a period of less than six months, 125,000 Cubans came to the United States, ferried across the waters in small boats by their Cuban-American relatives. Never before had the United States received so many immigrants in one place, at one time. This was possible primarily because of geographic proximity. Miami Cubans could simply rent a boat and go get their relatives. While not pleased with the open violation of its borders, the U.S. government was loath to arrest these supposedly heroic Cuban-Americans as smugglers or deny entry to Cubans as illegal immigrants.

Even now after the turn of the 21st century, Cuba's unique geography continues to give it a prominent place in international politics, landing it repeatedly in the

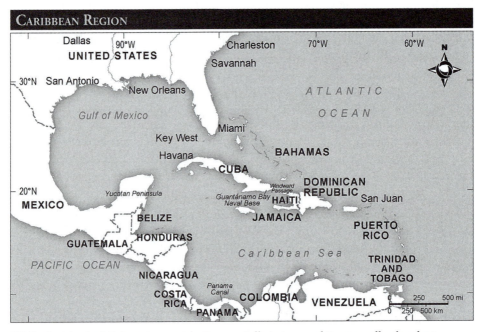

While the island of Cuba enjoys a rich site especially in terms of its unusually abundant endemic flora and fauna, it has a truly enviable situation lying between the peninsula and straits of Florida, the Yucatan Peninsula and Channel, the Windward Passage, the Gulf of Mexico, and the Isthmus of Central America. (ABC-CLIO)

GUANTÁNAMO BAY NAVAL BASE

Referred to by the U.S. military as "Gitmo," the U.S. Naval Base at Guantánamo Bay has straddled the entryway to the bay, 21 miles south of the city of Guantánamo itself, since February 19, 1903. The base's original purpose was to be a strategic bulwark protecting the eastern approach to the Panama Canal, the construction of which was begun in 1904. A 1903 treaty between Cuba and the United States stipulated that Cuba would lease the land to the United States in perpetuity for an annual fee of $2,000. The original base was expanded to its current size of 45 square miles in 1912, with the rent raised to $4,085. A later agreement in 1934, following the repeal of the Platt Amendment, changed the original indefinite U.S. lease to one with a 99-year expiration date like that on the Panama Canal. However, the new agreement continued to stipulate that the lease cannot expire without mutual consent. After 1960, Fidel Castro refused to cash the U.S.' annual lease checks to protest U.S. control of sovereign Cuban territory. Today, the base is home to 7,000 U.S. military personnel and their families, who enjoy access to five swimming pools, four outdoor move theaters, a golf course, and Cuba's only McDonald's. The base is also used as a temporary holding facility for Caribbean rafters rescued at sea by the U.S. Coast Guard and, more infamously, to indefinitely imprisoned enemy combatants in the U.S. war on terror.

headlines. For example, the Guantánamo Base was used as a "safe haven" for Cuban (and Haitian) rafters in 1994, when Fidel Castro once again called Washington's bluff by opening up his borders. More recently, part of the base was converted into a prison for "enemy combatants" conveniently located within U.S. military control but outside the bounds of U.S. territory, and thus beyond the reach of the most basic of U.S. legal guarantees. While as a presidential candidate Barack Obama promised to close the infamous prison during his first year in office, as president he has discovered that it is easier said than done, especially since it may involve a discussion of Cuba's continued sovereignty over the land the base occupies.

Each of these historical examples underlines the fact expressed most simply by the key that lies at the center of the Cuban national coat of arms: Cuba is the key that unlocks the "Indies," the Caribbean, and by extension the entire Western Hemisphere. Whoever controls Cuba will have leverage and influence throughout the Americas. The island's undeniably attractive *site* may have caused Columbus to famously call it, "The most beautiful land that human eyes have ever seen." However, it is Cuba's truly unparalleled geographic *situation* that has given it its outsized, and ongoing, importance throughout its history.

GEOGRAPHICAL FEATURES

Cuba is the largest and westernmost island of the Greater Antilles. Its total area is 42,804 square miles (110,862 sq. km), making it slightly smaller than Pennsylvania or about half the size of the United Kingdom. In fact, Cuba is not a single island but an archipelago with a total area that includes the mainland (40,520 sq. mi.; 104,946 sq. km), the Isle of Pines (renamed *Isla de la Juventud*, or Isle of Youth in 1976) to the southwest (850 sq. mi.; 2,202 sq. km), and literally thousands of small islets, keys, and coral reefs (1,434 sq. mi.; 3,714 sq km) most of which are located on the northeastern coast or east of the Isle of Youth in the Gulf of Batabanó.

Cuba's coastline measures 3,570 miles (5,764 km). By comparison, the coastline of Puerto Rico measures just 310 miles (501 km), making it about one-twelfth the size of Cuba. At its longest, measured from east to west, Cuba is 775 miles (1,250 km) long and varies between 19.3 miles (31 km) and 118 miles (191 km) wide, with an average width of 50 miles (80 km). As a comparison, the distance between Cabo de San Antonio in the west to Punta de Quemado (also known as Punta Maisí) in the east equals the distance from Miami to Nashville, or alternately from Paris to Budapest. The northern boundary of Cuba's territorial waters is framed by the Florida Straits and the Old Bahamas Channel. The eastern limit is the Windward Passage, which separates Cuba from the island of Hispaniola—shared by the nations of Haiti and the Dominican Republic. To the south, the archipelago is limited by the Caribbean Sea, and to the west by the Gulf of Mexico and the Yucatán Channel.

Cuba has a population of 11,241,161 inhabitants, who exhibit a high degree of *mestizaje*, or racial, ethnic, and cultural mixture. Spanish is the official language of the island, which has no autonomous regions or ethnic minorities. Cuba's ethnicity is comprised of two main component parts: the different Spanish conquistadores, colonists, and immigrant groups who came to the island throughout its 500-year history, and the various African groups from different sub-Saharan regions who were imported as slave labor mainly during the 19th century. Other elements that make up Cuba's particular ethnic *ajiaco* (stew) are the descendants of Cuba's various native

ONE ISLAND, MANY NAMES—CUBA'S ISLE OF YOUTH

Considered alone, the Isle of Youth is the sixth largest island in the Caribbean, after Cuba, Hispaniola, Jamaica, Puerto Rico, and Trinidad. Its large size and proximity to the Cuban mainland made it a perfect hideaway for pirates during the 16th and 17th centuries. First christened *La Evangelista* by Columbus, the island has been referred to colloquially by Cubans as both *Isla de Cotorras* ("Parrot Island") and *Isla de Tesoros* ("Treasure Island"). As such, the island and its legends of treasure, pirates, and crocodiles have fueled writers' imaginations, making it the inspiration for both Robert Louis Stevenson's *Treasure Island* and James Mathew Barrie's Neverland Island in the tale *Peter Pan* (Martínez-Fernández 2004: 2). More recently, the island has come to play a significant role in the mythology of the Cuban revolution itself. After Fidel Castro's failed raid on the Moncada Barracks in July 1953, the captured rebel leader was held in the island's Modelo Prison until his amnesty in 1955 under the dictatorship of Fulgencio Batista. Not long after assuming power, however, Castro himself used the prison to punish his own adversaries, including human rights activist Armando Valladares and former rebel *comandante* Huber Matos.

groups, as well as others of Amerindian descent brought as laborers from the Yucatan in the late 19th century, a small but significant remnant of the Chinese indentured laborers also contracted at that time, and small groups of Europeans of various nationalities, including a small but significant Jewish population.

Topography

Cuba's topography is mostly flat savanna interspersed with rolling plains, called *llanos*, which make up two-thirds of the island's territory. Roughly 60 percent of the total land area is used for agriculture, but only about 12 percent of that land is highly productive deep and permeable soil. Twenty-one percent of the land is used for grazing or left fallow, while roughly a quarter of the total land area is still forested (though only a small portion of that is tropical rain forest). Only 6.3 percent of the land is occupied by human settlements. The island also boasts more than 200 natural harbors. Some of these feature wide-open bays like those of Matanzas and Manzanillo, while others have deepwater ports well protected by bottleneck entrances (such as the "pocket bays" of Havana, Santiago de Cuba, and Nipe). The majority of these harbors are located on the northern coast, as are most of the island's more than 289 natural beaches.

The beaches on the northern coast tend to be longer and whiter, with breaking waves and rolling surf. However, they are more affected by northern cold fronts, making swimming occasionally unpleasant in the winter. Cuba's southern beaches tend to be warmer in the winter months but are less attractive for swimmers because of their rocky, swampy character and their abundance of sea urchins. Important exceptions are the attractive, popular destinations Playa Girón and Playa Ancón. The majority of the islands in Cuba's four archipelagos are also located off the northern coast, including "Los Colorados" north of the province of Pinar del Río and the "Sabana-Camagüey" archipelago located north of Matanzas, Villa Clara, Sancti Spíritus, Ciego de Ávila, and Camagüey provinces (Baker 2006; Stanley 2000).

The eastern extreme of the Sabana-Camagüey archipelago contains a group of keys (or "cayos" in Spanish) collectively known as the *Jardines del Rey* (King's Gardens), including Cayo Guillermo, Cayo Coco, and Cayo Romano, which have been extensively developed as exclusive and all-inclusive international tourist destinations. Cuba's two other archipelagos are the *Jardines de la Reina* (Queen's Gardens), south of Ciego de Ávila and Camagüey provinces, and *Los Canarreos*, east of the Isle of Youth and south of the mainland in the Gulf of Batabanó.

Despite being the least mountainous of the Greater Antilles, with an average elevation of less than 328 feet (100 meters), Cuba is home to three mountain systems (or *sierras*), the Sierra Maestra in the southeastern Oriente region (which is also home to the Nipe, Cristal, Purial sierras); the Guamuhaya (containing the Escambray range) in the south-central provinces of Cienfuegos, Villa Clara, and Sancti Spíritus (peaking at 3,740 feet; 1,140 m); and the Guaniguanico system in the western province Pinar del Río, which contains both the Rosario and Órganos ranges (neither of which is higher than 2,293 feet; 699 m). Pinar del Río is also home to the uniquely beautiful Viñales Valley, which features numerous underground limestone caves and high conical limestone hills, called *mogotes*, that rise abruptly from the valley floor.

Viñales Valley features Cuba's richest and most productive tobacco farms or vegas, as well as numerous underground limestone caves and high conical limestone hills, called mogotes, which rise abruptly from the valley floor. (Patrick Escudero/Hemis/Corbis)

The Sierra Maestra contains Cuba's highest point, Pico Turquino, which rises to 6,474 feet (1,974 m) above sea level. Pico Turquino is the Caribbean's second highest peak after Pico Duarte of the Dominican Republic, which towers 10,407 feet (3,170 m). Off the southern coast of Cuba, near the Sierra Maestra range, lies the Bartlett Trough or Cayman Trench, the lowest point in the Caribbean, which drops

---

THE *MOGOTES* AND CAVES OF VIÑALES VALLEY

Part of the oldest geological formation in Cuba, the *mogotes* of Viñales Valley make the region one of the island's most picturesque natural wonders. Together with the region's extensive underground caves, such as the *Gran Caverna de Santo Tomás*, these enormous, roughly hewn, skyscraper-high slabs are what is left of a great limestone plateau that climbed out of the sea more than 150 million years ago. The underground caves hidden below the *mogotes* were first home to Cuba's Siboney Indians, giving their name to the fascinating if tourist-laden *Cueva del Indio*, an underground river within a massive limestone cave. Later, some of these same caves were inhabited by Cuba's famed runaway slaves, called *cimarrones*. Atop these *mogotes* are unique ecosystems, complete with endemic plants, mollusks, and Cuba's ancient cork palm, found only in the Viñales region. The valley's economy is dominated by Cuba's rich tobacco, thanks to the ease with which the plant grows in the cool climate in the shadow of the *mogotes*.

precipitously 23,720 feet (7,230 m) below the sea floor between Cuba and Jamaica. This deep trench is the place where the North American and Caribbean tectonic plates meet, causing occasional earthquakes in the vicinity (Stanley 2000).

Cuba's rivers tend to be short, narrow, shallow, and non-navigable, making them of limited use as transportation channels in the history of the island's development. Because of the lack of major navigable rivers to aid in transportation and the extractive nature of most economic activity in the colonial period, most early passenger and cargo transportation was by ship from port to port. For that reason nearly all of Cuba's early settlements were on the coast or on bays that had openings to the sea, not on rivers. An unwritten colonial rule stipulated that no sugar estate should be more than 50 miles (80 km) from a port, since there were few serviceable roads in the interior. In fact, even though Cuba was the first Spanish-speaking country to develop a rail system, starting in 1837 (even before Spain), railroads were built to export sugar, not as a means of public transportation. The lesson, of course, is a key geographic one growing out of Cuba's economic history: major population centers grew naturally out of port towns, just as port towns grew from natural harbors (Pérez 1995).

The Cuban coastline's many keys and well-hidden and protected ports and bays allowed for the early development and dogged persistence of a ubiquitous contraband trade in sugar and slaves. Just as the wealth of natural harbors provided the opportunity for smuggling, Spain's attempt to monopolize trade necessitated it. Indeed, given the privileged position of the capital city of Havana, southeastern Cuba found itself both underpopulated and undeveloped (ibid.). Isolated from the rest of the island, parts of Oriente became important sanctuaries for communities of free blacks and *cimarrones* (escaped slaves) who formed their own communities (*palenques*) (Alvarado Ramos 1998).

THE SIERRA MAESTRA AND THE ESCAMBRAY MOUNTAIN RANGES

Most famous as the strategic hideout and occasional battleground for Castro's guerrilla fighters during late 1956 and 1957, the Sierra Maestra extends from Cabo Cruz east for 155 miles (250 km), dipping briefly at Santiago Bay, all the way to Guantánamo Bay. Throughout its history, it has suffered extensive deforestation from timbering, cattle ranching, and subsistence agriculture before being made a protected national park in 1980. The high altitude, cool climate, and rich soils make it ideal for coffee growing as fully half of Cuban coffee is grown on its slopes.

The much smaller Escambray mountain range measures just 50 by 25 miles (80 by 40 km) and is located almost exactly in the middle of the island, just north of the colonial city of Trinidad in Villa Clara and Sancti Spíritus provinces. It is famous for having been a base for anti-Batista guerrilla operations in the late 1950s and was used again later in the early 1960s by anti-communist guerrillas, some of whom were clandestinely supported by the CIA. As a result of this second clandestine operation, the area was cut off, its residents relocated, and the remaining rebels routed and definitively defeated by 1966.

Cuba's neglected Oriente was also home to many communities of small independent peasants, Cuba's *guajiros*. New immigrants often came to settle in the western provinces of Havana and Matanzas, but Oriente was always the most "Cuban" province on the island (Pérez 1995). Of course, "revolutionary Oriente," distant and scornful of authority, has also been the starting place for the great majority of the island's military conquests and revolutionary movements, including Velázquez's scorched-earth campaign against the Indians starting in 1511, both of Cuba's wars for independence (1868 and 1895), and the Cuban Revolution itself, which began in the foothills of the Sierra Maestra in December 1956.

Ironically, Cuban independence, prolonged U.S. influence, and even the onset of the revolution itself did nothing to alter the island's colonial administrative divisions. It was not until the First Congress of the Communist Party in 1976 that provincial divisions were reorganized. To facilitate more effective administration, many of the 407 original municipalities were eliminated, leaving just 169. The original 6 provinces were divided into 14, with the Isle of Pines renamed the Isle of Youth and designated a "special municipality." Thus, from 1976 to 2010, Cuba's 14 provinces (moving from west to east) were Pinar del Río, Havana Province, City of Havana Province, Matanzas, Villa Clara, Cienfuegos, Sancti Spíritus, Ciego de Ávila, Camagüey, Las Tunas, Granma, Holguín, Santiago de Cuba, and Guantánamo. More recently in 2010, Havana Province was divided into two, with the new Artemisa province to the west and Mayabeque province to the east. In the process, while the "City of Havana" province remained the same in size, it is now known simply as "Havana" province.

The capital of Cuba is Havana, a seaside city located on Havana Bay on the northwest coast of the island. It has been Cuba's principal commercial port since colonial times. As capital, Havana is the seat of the nation's government and has a population of over two million people. Havana itself is divided into 15 municipalities, or

In 1878, upon the close of the Ten Years' War, the Spanish Crown reorganized the island's political and administrative divisions establishing the island's six traditional provinces (from west to east): Pinar del Río, La Habana, Matanzas, Las Villas, Camagüey (known as Puerto Príncipe before 1902), and Oriente. (Lina0486/Dreamstime.com)

ORIENTE AND THE *ORIENTALES*

Despite the disappearance of *Oriente* as an official province in 1976, Cubans still speak of anyone from the eastern end of the island as an *oriental* (an easterner). That is often done by proud, urban(e) *habaneros*, who commonly disparage their more rural compatriots for their country ways, colloquial accents, and often darker complexions. It is even common to hear Havana residents derisively describe arrivals from the east as being *de provincia* (from the provinces) or even *palestinos* (Palestinians)! In fact, Cuba's leading dance band since the early 1970s, Los Van Van, once made a hit with a song that facetiously declared, *"La Habana no aguanta más"* ("Havana can't take any more"), indicating the extent to which overcrowding had become an issue in the capital city. Indeed, the government passed a migration law in 1997 denying housing and ration benefits to those unlawfully living in the capital and threatening them with deportation. Some even joke that Havana's two most famous *palestinos* are none other than Fidel and Raúl Castro, both of whom are from the town of Birán in *Oriente*, now part of Holguín province.

boroughs, which are themselves further subdivided into 105 *consejos populares* or wards. The island's second largest and most important city is Santiago de Cuba, located deep within Santiago Bay on the southeastern coast at the opposite extreme of the island from Havana. Other important cities include Pinar del Río, Matanzas, Santa Clara, Cienfuegos, Camagüey, Holguín, and Bayamo, all of which are the capitals of their respective provinces. Roughly 70 to 80 percent of the Cuban population is urban, with the principal population groups found in Havana and Santiago.

PROVINCES IN CUBA

Cuba's 15 provinces (moving from west to east) are Pinar del Río, Artemisa and Mayabeque (added in 2010), Havana, Matanzas, Villa Clara, Cienfuegos, Sancti Spíritus, Ciego de Ávila, Camagüey, and the five provinces carved out of Oriente after 1976: Las Tunas, Granma, Holguín, Santiago de Cuba, and Guantánamo. Isla de la Juventud is a special municipality. (Lina0486/Dreamstime.com)

Underlying these political and administrative divisions are Cuba's five major geographical subregions, each of which has played an important historical role in the social, demographic, and economic organization of the island. These are the Occidental region, the Central or Las Villas region, the vast savanna of Camagüey, the Oriental region, and the Isle of Youth. The Occidental region, which includes the provinces of Pinar del Río, Artemisa, Havana, Mayabeque, and Matanzas, is the location of the most significant cash crops, sugar and tobacco, which are grown abundantly in the region (Ortiz 1995). Other regions either have specialized in one agricultural or industrial activity, as did Camagüey in cattle ranching, or developed a diversified economic profile to match an equally diverse terrain, as did Oriente, which produces coffee, citrus, cacao, bananas, and sugar, as well as being home to its share of ranching and mining operations (Martínez-Fernández et al. 2002; Stanley 2000).

Geology and Mineral Deposits

Cuba is home to vast mineral diversity. Peat stands out as the most plentiful fuel resource on the island and can be found in large quantities in the Zapata Swamp and Peninsula in Matanzas Province. The most important mineral deposit with industrial potential is nickel, which is mined—often together with cobalt, iron, and laterite—in large deposits in Moa, Nicaro, and Pinares de Mayarí along the northeastern coast of Oriente. Deposits of other important minerals such as coal and phosphate are very limited. Significant petroleum reserves have also been detected along the northern coast of the island between Havana and Villa Clara. While these oilfields are closely linked with the production of asphalt due to the traditionally low grade of the crude, Cuba is currently undertaking a major drilling effort in these areas with significant foreign investment and technical assistance aimed at becoming a net oil producer—thus attempting to end its dependence on preferential petroleum trade from Venezuela.

Climate

Cuba's subtropical climate is moderated by the prevailing trade winds coming in from the northeast during winter and from the east-northeast in summer. Likewise, powerful warm ocean currents (known as the Gulf Stream) flow during the entire year along the north and south coasts of the island. An additional moderating factor to Cuba's climate is the cool air masses (*frentes fríos*) periodically pushed down from the North American continent. These factors have a crucial influence on the weather of Cuba. Yearly mean temperature is 77 degrees Fahrenheit (25°C) and varies little during the year, from an average high of 81 degrees (27°C) in the summer months to an average low of 70 degrees (21°C) in the winter. The hottest part of the island is southern Oriente, where temperatures can reach beyond 106 degrees Fahrenheit (41°C), especially in the lowlands of Guantánamo.

Rainfall fluctuates during the year between a summer rainy season (May to October) that normally brings in between 8 and 10 inches (20–26 centimeters) of precipitation each month, and a winter dry season (November–April) that sees just 1 to 4 inches (3.2–10 cm) per month, with an average of 96 rainy days each year. Almost two-thirds of the rainfall is concentrated in the wet season, in part because of the frequency of hurricanes during September and October. Central and western areas are occasionally known to endure a three- to five-month annual drought, known as *la seca*, and recently the eastern provinces of Holguín and Las Tunas have had extensive droughts of their own.

Easily Cuba's most significant climatic phenomena are the Atlantic hurricanes that chronically threaten the island (the word originates from the Spanish *huracán*, based on the Taíno god of wind and rain, Uracán). The Atlantic hurricane season lasts from June to November, with Cuba's coast, especially its far west, subject to hurricanes from August to November. In general, the country averages one hurricane landfall every other year. More than 150 recorded hurricanes have hit the island since 1498.

The 2008 hurricane season was unprecedented for Cuba, marking the only instance in recorded history where three major hurricanes, Gustav, Ike, and Paloma (and one tropical storm), made landfall on the island in a single season. Together, the three hurricanes caused massive damage to the island's agriculture, electric grid, and housing stock, especially on the Isle of Youth and in the western province of Pinar del Río with total reported losses valued at more than $5 billion (U.S.) (Cuba Hurricanes 2012). Taking place just after Raúl Castro took over as president and coinciding with the start of the global economic crisis, this series of catastrophic storms was his first major test as the island's new leader. Despite extensive infrastructural damage and economic fallout, Cuba fared well in terms of loss of life when compared to its similarly vulnerable Caribbean neighbors Haiti and the Dominican Republic. This is likely due to its uniquely effective system of civil defense.

Flora

Given its diversity of climatic zones, especially on its isolated keys, extensive coral reefs, mountainous regions, and in the unmatched natural habitat of the *Ciénaga de Zapata* (Zapata Swamp), Cuba enjoys a rich variety of plant (flora) and animal (fauna) species. More than 7,000 plant species are found on the island, many of which are found elsewhere in the hemisphere because the island was once attached to the continent. Still, nearly half of these (3,180) are endemic to the island with about 950 endangered. Such a high level of endemism is due to several factors which enhance the genetic distinctiveness of Cuban flora and its further development (including the emergence of new species and subspecies). Among these factors are Cuba's geographic insularity, the extension and variety of soil types found across the island, the characteristics and variations of Cuban topography, the island's ecological diversity, and the hybridization of the plant and animal species. Despite human intervention, local endemism can also be found in areas with a high population density or on large land holdings devoted to agriculture and cattle grazing. The mountainous *Oriente* region and especially the Moa area have the highest concentration of endemic plants on the island.

Prior to 1492, 90 percent of the island was covered with dense tropical forests. However, by 1900 Cuban forests had been reduced to just 54 percent of the island's total area, dropping to just under 14 percent by 1959 (Moreno Fraginals 1976).

A solitary palm tree grows tall in a small patio rising above the tiled rooftops of Old Havana.
(Uva de Aragón)

Today, 75 percent of the island is either savanna or plains, as a result of the uncontrolled expansion of the population of swine, the development of extensive cattle ranches, and the heavy exploitation of sugarcane, especially during the 19th century. To combat the loss of forest, in 1987 the government instituted Plan Manatí, which succeeded in planting as many as 3 billion trees and increasing the forested proportion of the island to almost 24 percent. Unfortunately, most of those plantings were of either firs or transplanted eucalyptus trees, not the mahogany, cedar, lignum vitae, or ebony that originally flourished across the Island (Baker 2006).

Just as human intervention aimed at the development of cash crops altered or destroyed local vegetation and completely transformed the island's once extensive tropical forests, the unwitting introduction of a number of invasive floral species has presented a major obstacle to current efforts to revamp Cuban agriculture under Raúl Castro. While Cuba's tropical climate and rich soils make crop cultivation relatively easy, they also enable the growth of many unwanted plant species. Perhaps the most tenacious and emblematic example of these invasive species is the infamous *marabú* plant (sicklebush or *Dichrostachys glomerata*). The marabú is a thorny bush of African origin that has become a veritable plague upon Cuban agriculture. Arable land in Cuba, which is government property in its majority, has been left in a state of neglect for so long that the invasive marabú plant has been allowed to virtually take over large tracts of potentially productive land. This has significantly driven up the cost of crop cultivation on the island because it is necessary to first dig up the marabú and completely remove its extensive root system to enable the growth of edible crops.

Although greatly depleted during the sugar boom in the 19th century, tree varieties still in existence include the palm, cedar, ebony, mahogany, oak, pine, and extensive coastal mangroves. Appropriately, Cuba's national tree is the royal palm (*Roystonea regia*), which is featured on the national coat of arms and can grow up to 130 feet (40 m) high. Unlike other, shorter palms, the towering royal palm has a smooth, marble-like gray trunk topped by a curious green bulb surrounded by a cascade of gracefully draped palm leaves. Apart from its majestic beauty, the tree has been very useful historically, with both the Taínos and Cuban Creoles exploiting different parts of the tree for a variety of uses.

For example, Cuba's famous thatched huts, called *bohíos* (still common in rural areas), were first engineered by the indigenous Taínos from the tree's palm fronds (called *pencas*). The sturdy bases of the fronds have been used as a naturally waterproof roofing and siding material. Also, palm honey and palm seeds have been used as animal feed, and the succulent heart of palm (*palmito*) is a highly sought after treat extracted from the center of the majestic trunk. Birds even feast on the tree's fruit, inadvertently helping to spread the seeds (*palmiches*) across the island and aiding in the tree's proliferation. Apart from other palm species, there are said to be as many as 20 million royal palms thriving across the expanse of the island today, almost double the island's human population (Baker 2006; Stanley 2000).

Two other palm trees of note are the rare, prehistoric cork palm and the rounded, belly palm, *palma barrigona*, easily recognized by its distinctive shape. Other trees characteristic to Cuba include the transplanted royal poinciana, known in Cuba by its colloquial name, *flamboyán*, because of its flamboyant orange and red blooms that appear in December and the *Jagüey*, a unique fig species that often grows on the

This photo of a royal palm taken in the town of Viñales in Pinar del Río province features an improvised orthopedic "brace" to honor Cuba's renowned orthopedic surgeon Rodrigo Álvarez Cambras. (Orlando Luis Pardo Lazo)

branches of other trees and sends its aerial roots like curtains down to the ground for support and sustenance, eventually enveloping and strangling the host tree. There is also the swollen *baobab*, which is often referred to as the "upside-down tree" since it seems to have its roots exposed to the air, and the wide-trunked *ceiba* or kapok (silk-cotton) tree, revered as sacred by Indian, African, and European cultures alike. Pine forests are most abundant in appropriately named Pinar del Río (Pine River) Province, as well as in eastern Holguín, central Guantánamo, and on the Isle of Youth (originally called Isle of Pines because of its once extensive pine forests).

Another tree variety that has proliferated in Cuba is the mangrove (*manglar*). Although not as majestic as the royal palm, mangroves are just as useful: they act as natural filters of water runoff, protect shorelines from erosion (and hurricane storm surges), and provide a nutrient-rich habitat for scores of small fish and birds. Though Cuba's mangroves are located in many of the island's coastal areas, they are most extensive in Cuba's massive Zapata Swamp on the southern coast of Matanzas Province, just west of the Bay of Pigs.

Cuba is also home to more than 300 species of wild orchid, with a number of sites dedicated to their cultivation, including an *orquideario* built in the 1940s in the western town of Soroa which cultivates many species not found in the wild. Orchids are Cuba's largest and most diverse family of flowering plants, with flowers that range from less than a millimeter in size to hanging orchids with petals more than half a meter long. Another flower of note is the butterfly jasmine, Cuba's national flower, called the *mariposa blanca*. Because of its deep whiteness, the flower became associated with the Cuban nationalist ideals of rebellion, independence, and purity during the island's 19th-century independence wars, when Cuban women sympathetic to the rebel cause would wear the flower in their hair to transport secret messages (Baker 2006). Perhaps the two most verdant locations on the island to find the richest diversity of Cuba's floral heritage are on the Isle of Youth and in the vast Zapata Swamp, the largest swampy wetland in the Caribbean. There are more than 750 botanical varieties in the swamp, 116 of them native to Cuba and 6 found only there.

Fauna

The floral richness of Cuba is best represented by Zapata Swamp, which is home to a truly spectacular variety of fauna, including amphibians and reptiles, marine turtles, fish and shellfish, offshore coral, mammals, bats, marine mammals, insects and butterflies, and many unique bird species. In fact, Cuba boasts 354 recorded species of birds including the parakeet, owl, woodpecker, *sinsonte* (mockingbird), *ruiseñor* (nightingale), flamingo, and the famous *tocororo*, the national bird. Almost half of these use the island primarily as a breeding or migration stopping point, while 21 are native to the archipelago. Cuba's remarkable diversity of birds is due to the island's being located along a natural corridor for many continental migratory species, some of which nest in Cuban territory. These migratory species often take shelter in the Zapata Swamp and Peninsula, as well as in the thousands of small keys and islets that surround the island. As a result, many of these areas have been declared protected by the government in an attempt to save the 37 bird species listed as threatened due to the destruction of their habitats (Baker 2006).

Among the migrant birds, pink flamingos stand out because they nest in flocks of thousands in Cuba's many shallow swamps, keys, or lagoons. They feed on the high-salinity and larval- and algae-rich water, which also contains carotenoid pigments, a microscopic substance that gives the birds their distinctive pink color. Because of this, Cuba's flamingos are born without their distinctive coloring and only gradually gain it as they grow to adulthood. One look at the *tocororo* (also called *tocoloro*), a Cuban trogon of the Quetzal family, makes clear why it was chosen as Cuba's national bird. It has a blue head, white chest, and red belly. Like its Central American cousin, it is also distinctive for its short wings and long, flowing tail. Apart from the bird's tricolored plume, its nationalist significance stems from the legend that it is unable to live in captivity (*¡patria o muerte!*).

Even more fascinating and unique than its multicolored avian relative is the diminutive ornithological gem, the *zunzuncito* (bee hummingbird), which is a subspecies of the hummingbird (*colibrí*). This amazing Cuban creature is the world's smallest bird. Resembling more a bumble bee or large insect than a winged creature of the air, the male of the species weighs just 2 grams (less than a penny) and is slightly larger than a grasshopper. Cuba is also home to other of the world's smallest animals, including a tiny tree froglet (*Sminthillus limbatus*, the world's smallest frog), a fly bat (*murciélago mosca*), a tiny tree rat (*jutía enana*), a pygmy owl called *sijucito* (or *Sijú platanero*), a Microtytus scorpion, and an 8-inch (20 cm) long pygmy boa found only in the caves of Viñales (Baker 2006; Stanley 2000).

At the opposite end of the spectrum, Cuba is home to relatively few large animals, including the *jutía*, a 2-foot-long Cuban tree rat found mostly on isolated keys among the mangroves. Given the nearness of the Cayman Islands, the Cayman Trench, and the fact that Cubans have even nicknamed their island *el caimán* (because of its elongated shape and its ability to endure), it is not surprising to find that the island is home to a number of important reptiles (80 percent of which are endemic), includ-

Cuba's national bird, the tocororo *or blue crowned Trogon, has a blue head, white chest, and red belly—the same colors as the Cuban flag. Apart from its tricolored plume, the* tocororo's *nationalist significance stems from the legend that it is unable to live in captivity* (¡patria o muerte!). *(Ra'id Khalil/Dreamstime.com)*

THE *ZUNZUNCITO*, CUBA'S BEE HUMMINGBIRD

Like its larger cousin the hummingbird, the *zunzuncito* can perform amazing acrobatics because of the unbelievable rapidity of its wings. Cuba has 16 different species of hummingbirds in all, each of whose wings beat faster than a naked eye can detect (up to 100 beats per second). Hummingbirds are unique in that they are the only species of bird that get lift from both their forward and backward wing strokes. This allows them to hover in place, turn upside down, and even fly sideways and backward. These abilities enable them to float as if by magic beside flowers as they extend their distinctive bills forward to extract nectar, simultaneously performing the symbiotic service of pollination for Cuba's flowers. Cuba's indigenous inhabitants revered these creatures as sacred, calling them *colibrí*, or "god bird." Even today, Cuban superstition has it that the best way to entrap prospective lovers is by having them drink a potion made from dried, ground-up hummingbirds (Stanley 2000; Baker 2006).

---

ing both the caimán (alligator) and its longer and more feisty cousin, the crocodile (*lagarto criollo*). The diminutive caimán measures less than 6.5 feet (2 m) long and is relatively common in Cuba's wet lowlands. The Cuban crocodile is found almost exclusively in the Zapata Swamp, where the government has worked over the past two decades to save them from extinction. There are now around 6,000 Cuban crocs living in the wild.

Unlike its continental brother, the American crocodile (*Cocodrilus acutus*), the Cuban crocodile (*Cocodrilus rombifer*) is an omnivore whose diet, though based on fish, also includes large mammals like wild boars, deer, and even the occasional unwitting birdwatcher. Both species of croc are endemic to Cuba and have a significant presence in the Zapata Swamp and other estuaries such as the Cauto River basin in the Guacanayabo Gulf (Baker 2006). Other common reptiles include iguanas, which are usually found in coastal areas, lizards, salamanders, marine turtles, and 15 species of nonpoisonous snakes, of which the nocturnal *maja* python is the largest, reaching 13 feet (4 m) long.

Cuba's native fauna has been diversified somewhat due to the introduction of alien species, some of which have adapted well to the tropical conditions of the island. As a result, it is possible to find deer and wild hogs (*puercos jíbaros*) in forest regions of Cuba. These hogs are a good example of the adaptation to wildlife of the domesticated pigs first introduced by Spaniards centuries ago. After escaping into the wild, they survived on the abundance of wild tubers, edible roots, and other such plant species. These wild hogs then bred and extended their presence through dense forest areas and other isolated zones such as the Zapata Swamp.

Cuba has coastal waters filled with more than 900 species of fish and crustaceans. Crabs, turtles, thirty-five species of shark, and tuna are the most common. One sea animal that is in great abundance just off the perimeter of much of the island is the coral. The coral reef that stretches along Cuba's northern coast is the world's second longest, after the Great Barrier Reef of Australia. This animal, often not thought of as an animal at all, is better known for its "shell," the huge reefs that are the product of millions of tiny individual corals secreting an external calcium carbonate skeleton. More amazing still is the hidden secret to the growth of coral reefs, which is in the symbiotic relationship that these organisms have with the zooxanthellea, a single-celled algae that live inside corals. Through a sunlight-induced process of photosynthesis, these algae produce oxygen and nutrients that enable the coral to live and grow. However, it is for this reason that coral reefs can grow only in shallow water that is exposed to sunlight, making the clear, shallow coasts of northern Cuba a perfect habitat (Baker 2006).

Apart from their beauty, intricate lifecycle, and complex structure, coral reefs function as a key growing ground for external algae and other plants that are the base of the marine food chain. Therefore, the loss of coral reefs is not simply an aesthetic matter. It also threatens the many fish and crustacean species that thrive in the coral habitat. Some of the marine life common in Cuba's coral-rich coastal waters, and often found on the tables of dollar-rich or well-connected Cubans, are shrimp, lobster, and the *caguama* (a protected but highly sought after loggerhead sea turtle). This and other species of Cuban marine turtle (such as the green turtle, *tortuga verde*, and the hawksbill turtle, *el carey*) take advantage of the island's many isolated beaches and keys as strategic points of spawning. The population decline of these turtle species is related to their indiscriminate capture for their highly valued meat and for the use of their beautiful shells in the making of crafts.

The diet of less affluent Cubans includes a variety of other abundant but less expensive fish, such as the *cherna* (grouper), swordfish, *pargo* (red snapper), *bonito* (stripped tuna), and *aguja* (gar or needlefish). Still, the majority of these marine products are destined for international export or internal consumption by foreign tourists. Instead, Cuban nationals are more likely to consume small fish of lesser quality such as the *jurel* (crevalle jack), *macarela* (mackerel), or *merluza* (hake).

A singular survivor of the geological past is the manjuarí (*Lepisosteus tristoechus*), a fish that can be found with luck in brackish waters of Cuba's eastern swamps and estuaries. The name given to this fish by the native inhabitants of the island is of Arawak origin and corresponds to its unique appearance: *manju* (means "many") *arí* (means "teeth"). A true living fossil, the manjuarí is Cuba's oldest freshwater species at approximately 270 million years old. Belonging to the gar family and known as the Cuban "alligator gar" as it seems part fish and part reptile, the manjuarí is likely among the most primitive of the earth's first vertebrates and is believed to have played an important role in the evolutionary transition between fish and mammals. A final notable but nonedible crustacean is the endangered and highly sought after *polimita* (polymite) snail. Popular for sale to tourists because of its colorful striped shell, the tiny *polimita* snail is found only in the Baracoa region of Cuba.

Endangered Species, Conservation, and Environmental Challenges

Prior to the European conquest, native species like the great sloth (*Megalognus rodens*) and the tropical seal (*Monachus tropicalis*) seem to have disappeared due to overhunting by aboriginal groups. Avian species like the macaw were already nearly extinct because their colorful feathers were highly prized by Taíno chiefs. The arrival of Europeans increased the exploitation of native species like the *jutía conga* (also known as the Cuban hutia (*Capromys pilorides*), marine and river turtles, manatees, and several species of birds. European conquest also set in motion the destruction of the native forest, with trees of precious woods such as mahogany, cedar, ebony, *dagame*, and *quebracho*, being systematically felled and sent to the capital to be used in shipbuilding, housing construction, and furniture manufacture. Much of this harvested fine wood was also sent back to Spain.

The loss of the natural habitat of many species in danger of extinction today began with the progressive loss of native forest in past centuries. Among these rare species, the *almiquí*, or Cuban solenodon (*Solenodon cubanus*), stands out. Endemic to Cuba and first discovered in 1861, it was thought extinct until the 1970s when a small number were captured. Unusual among mammals in that its saliva is venomous, the almiquí remains endangered and is very rarely encountered mainly because it is a nocturnal burrower and lives largely underground in the forests of western Oriente.

The biggest threat facing Cuba's rich variety of flora and fauna is also the island's latest and most promising economic strategy: tourism. Like sugarcane before it, tourism promises a highly lucrative but also economically vulnerable, marginally sustainable, and environmentally threatening economic development strategy. In its zeal to attract greater numbers of tourists to the island, the Cuban government has begun to develop its northern keys into exclusive international resorts. Apart from the environmental impact of new hotels and their associated facilities, the government has built a series of massive stone causeways (*pedraplenes*) to facilitate access to those remote and once-virgin keys. Such causeways do enormous damage to marine and coastal habitats, cutting wildlife off from food supplies and nesting sites, as has already happened at Cayo Coco and Cayo Guillermo.

Additionally, the construction and mineral extraction industries have led to the denuding of a number of natural areas, including the land surrounding the cement factory at Mariel and the nickel-mining operations at Moa in Holguín Province. Efforts have been made to clean up Havana's filthy harbor and reduce sulfur emissions from the many oil wells near Varadero, but there is still a long way to go (Stanley 2000). Cuba has few emission controls, but ironically the slow pace of development and chronic energy shortages have prevented extensive environmental destruction thus far. However, as Cuba recovers from the 1990s economic crisis, the government has few developmental options other than increased exploitation of its limited natural resources. The recent discovery of potentially large deposits of petroleum off Cuba's northwest coast is a case and point, both potentially lucrative and environmentally destructive. Thus, it is imperative for Cuba to develop effective environmental policies aimed at the conservation of the island's rich natural ecosystems and their many unique flora and fauna, currently under increasing threat by human intervention.

On the flip side, Cuba's economic crisis has forced it to implement a number of sustainable-development strategies, including using bagasse (a sugarcane waste) and other biomass fuels to fire some industries (as was commonly done prior to the revolution), developing a respectable organic farming industry, and reaching into its popular traditions to promote "green" medicine. Cuba's early implementation of such sustainable development practices was recognized in 1993 at the Rio Earth Summit where the island was one of only two countries in the world to receive an A+ rating. Since then, much gas-powered transport has been converted to human or animal power, leading to the return of oxen and donkeys for farm labor and public transportation in many provincial cities and towns.

Likewise, the once-ubiquitous automobile has given way in many places to the bicycle. Already in 1993, Havana had more than 700,000 bicycles, up from just 100,000 in 1990. These mostly Chinese-made bicycles are used by private citizens, and after a difficult learning curve for a culture once as wedded to the automobile as is the United States, many roads and street signs recognize cyclers' rights and seek to protect them. Inadvertently, that has worked to reduce air pollution and has given rise to a semi-legal sector of private bicycle repair and parking services. At the same time, the increased time and energy needed to commute and the drop in industrial and agricultural output resulting from the use of such antiquated technologies have taken a heavy economic toll (Baker 2006; Scarpaci and Hall 1995).

BIBLIOGRAPHY

Alvarado Ramos, Juan Antonio. 1998. *La Ruta del Esclavo en Cuba*. Havana: Fernando Ortiz Foundation.

Baker, Christopher P. 2006. *Moon Handbooks: Cuba* (fourth edition). Emeryville, CA: Avalon Travel Publishing.

Cuba Hurricanes 2012. http://www.cubahurricanes.org/index.php. Accessed May 6.

Martínez-Fernández, Luis. 2004. "Geography, Will It Absolve Cuba?" *History Compass* 2, no. 1: 1–21.

Martínez-Fernández, Luis, D. H. Figueredo, Louis A. Pérez, Jr., and Luis González, eds. 2002. *Encyclopedia of Cuba: People, History, Culture*. Two vols. Westport, CT: Greenwood Press.

Moreno Fraginals, Manuel. 1976. *The Sugarmill: The Socioeconomic Complex of Sugar in Cuba, 1760–1860*. New York: Monthly Review Press.

Ortiz, Fernando. 1995. *Cuban Counterpoint: Tobacco and Sugar*. Durham: Duke University Press.

Pérez, Louis A., Jr. 1995. *Cuba: Between Reform and Revolution* (second edition). New York: Oxford University Press.

Scarpaci, J., and Annie Z. Hall. 1995. "Cycling in Havana: 'Green' Transportation by Policy Default." *Sustainable Transport* 6 (Summer): 4–6.

Stanley, David. 2000. *Lonely Planet: Cuba* (second edition). Melbourne: Lonely Planet Publications.

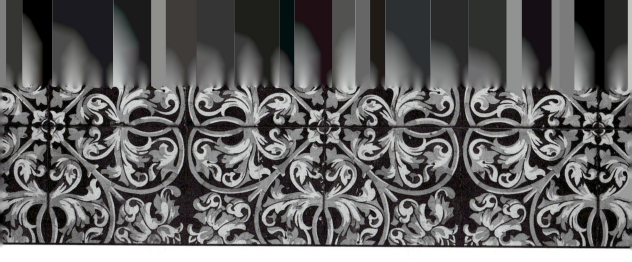

History

Dimas Castellanos, Ted A. Henken, and Miriam Celaya

CUBA BEFORE COLUMBUS

The European "discovery" of Cuba in October 1492, and the subsequent process of conquest begun by Spanish conquistador Diego Velázquez in 1511, marked the beginning of the end for the native cultures that existed on the island. The exact demography of the natives of Cuba is unknown. However, judging by the chronicles of the Indies penned by various conquistadors and by the archaeological record, they lived in significant numbers—perhaps as many as 100,000—throughout the Cuban archipelago at the time of the conquest, but were unable to resist Europe's "civilizing" impact. In a short time they were mostly wiped out by the system of slavery to which they were subjected, and the destruction of their social and family organizations. Moreover, the Spanish forced the native population to provide many young men as "tribute" to the conquistadors' continental expeditions in Mexico and Peru, a fact that contributed significantly to their decline and eventual disappearance as a people.

Those who managed to survive this initial culture shock were quickly assimilated, first by the waves of conquistadores who soon arrived on the island and later by the strong African population introduced as slave labor to replace the weak and dwindling native inhabitants. After only a few decades the native cultures perished, leaving only highly adulterated trace elements of their culture as part of Cuban oral and material (especially culinary) traditions. Still, a small number of specific geographic concentrations of their highly intermixed (both culturally and racially) descendants continue to exist in the far eastern villages and towns of Cuba's *Oriente*.

The island of Cuba was home to at least two major indigenous groups: the *Siboney* (sometimes spelled Ciboney) and the more advanced *Taíno*. A third group, known as the *Caribs*, who gave their name to the Caribbean (*el Caribe*, in Spanish), never actually set foot on the island of Cuba, though they were fierce challengers to the Taínos in many of the islands of the Lesser Antilles. What is certain is that the Taíno were the dominant and most populous group on the island when Spanish conquest began in the early 1500s.

THE CONQUEST AND COLONIZATION OF CUBA

Cuba's colonial history began in the first half of the 16th century (1500–1550). The *peninsulares*—Spaniards who hailed from the Iberian Peninsula—arrived in the Indies with the idea of making a quick fortune and then returning to their homeland. Thus, they devoted themselves to the search for precious metals and, to that end, subjugated the island's original inhabitants to a ruthless system of slavery. Despite the resistance offered by the natives (under the leadership of indigenous *caciques* or chiefs Hatuey and Guamá), the attempt to offer some protection by a number of Dominican friars, and the enactment of Spain's New Laws in 1542 (intended to regulate the treatment of the native peoples of the Indies) Spain's conquest and colonization of Cuba caused an irreversible demographic collapse.

Columbus arrived on the northeastern coast of Cuba on October 27, 1492. After this initial visit, the Spanish concentrated their efforts on colonizing the smaller island of Hayti to the east, which they renamed *La Española* (Hispaniola in English) after Queen Isabella of Spain. Rumors of abundant deposits of gold on the abandoned island turned attention back to Cuba when Columbus's son Diego was appointed governor of the Indies in 1508. Increasing disputes between Spanish conquistadors on Hispaniola over the dwindling tracts of available land and dwindling numbers of natives who could be forced to work also fueled the exodus. Hispaniola's governor

---

GIBARA, BARACOA, AND COLUMBUS' FIRST SIGHTING OF CUBA

There is some dispute as to whether Columbus originally landed at Baracoa (a Taíno word meaning "elevated land"), close to the far eastern tip of the island in Guantánamo Province, or in the town of Gibara (from the Taíno word *jiba*, a bush that is still found along the shore), in the far west of Holguín Province. It seems that Columbus did indeed disembark in both places on his first voyage in 1492, but each town lays claim to being "the most beautiful land that human eyes have ever seen," as Columbus famously described Cuba.

In either case, Columbus surveyed most of the coast between these two towns for over a month and lured 13 native Taínos onto his ship as trophies to take back to Spain. However, after the shipwreck of his own large vessel, the *Santa María*, and a mutiny led by Martín Alonzo Pinzón who abandoned Columbus and attempted to sail his own small caravel, the *Pinta*, back to Spain first, Columbus loaded everyone onto his only remaining caravel, the *Niña*, and set sail for Spain himself, finding none of the gold or spices for which he was looking.

Nicolás de Ovando (1502–1509) then sent Sebastián de Ocampo to Cuba in an attempt to circumnavigate and survey the island. Ocampo returned to confirm that Cuba was indeed an island. He also discovered numerous well-protected deepwater ports and brought news of gold deposits in the island's interior. Ovando reacted by entrusting a colonization campaign to his lieutenant, Diego Velázquez, who had already distinguished himself as a competent administrator, wealthy landowner, and stalwart soldier in early battles against Hispaniola's own band of Taínos.

Velázquez, Las Casas, and Hatuey

The conquest, colonization, and settlement of Cuba proceeded in two waves. First, Velázquez landed at the eastern tip of Cuba near Maisí in 1511 with 300 men and moved westward along the coast to establish Cuba's first small Spanish settlement at Baracoa in 1512. Velázquez was accompanied in Cuba by his young and dashing personal secretary Hernán Cortés, who was soon named mayor of Baracoa and later of the island's second capital, Santiago. However, Cortés quickly grew tired of civic administration and trying to "tame" Cuba's land and native population. Just seven years later, in 1519, he would violate Velázquez's direct orders and set sail on his own voyage of discovery and conquest—in Mexico (Thomas 1993).

The second wave of the conquest of Cuba was led by Pánfilo de Narváez, who arrived at Cuba's southern coast near the Gulf of Guacanayabo with a smaller expedition from Jamaica. Given past experiences, Cuba's natives knew exactly what to expect from the arriving Spanish forces and resisted them tenaciously from the start. Resistance, however, was futile, given the Spaniards' far superior weapons and technology (horses, dogs, guns, and iron swords), as well as their most lethal secret weapon (secret even to themselves)—disease. In 1512, Velázquez and Narváez reconnoitered in Oriente, subdued the Taíno forces there, which included capturing and putting to death the Taíno cacique Hatuey. They then enacted a scorched earth campaign to subdue and colonize the rest of the island.

Upon assuming the role of the first governor of Cuba in 1512, Velázquez had a bit of a contradictory aim: to continue to pacify the country while simultaneously ending the abuses against the Indians. Velázquez willingly accepted his duty of pacifying Cuba in the name of the king, but he sought to reign in his often brutal and murderous soldiers because the Indians would be needed later as laborers once the bloody task of conquest was completed. Perhaps Velázquez's most important, if unwitting ally in achieving these somewhat incongruous goals was a former *encomendero* (land grantee) from Hispaniola who had since become a Dominican friar in 1510 (the first priest so ordained in the new world), later becoming a staunch defender of the Indians. His name was Fray Bartolomé de Las Casas (1484–1566). Knowing from bloody experience the cost the Taínos would pay for resistance, Las Casas would often head off other Spaniards by arriving first into Cuba's remaining native villages, trying to convince them to cooperate with the conquistadors.

Of all the pages Las Casas wrote, perhaps the most legendary is his dramatic retelling of the resistance and eventual capture and execution of the Taíno *cacique*, Hatuey (?–1512). Hatuey and his followers thought that the Spaniards persecuted them because they wanted them to worship their God. Hoping to protect themselves, Hatuey and his followers proceeded to give honor to the Spanish God by dancing around a basket of gold and jewels, thinking that since the Spanish so lusted after these things they must be their God. Of course, these efforts failed to placate the Spaniards who eventually captured Hatuey and before burning him alive on February 2, 1512, as a punishment for leading the native resistance, offered him a Christian baptism. When made to understand that the flames of the stake were nothing compared to the flames of everlasting damnation, Hatuey asked, "Do all Christians go to Heaven?" When told yes, Hatuey declared that he preferred to go to Hell, so that he would never again have to endure the cruelty and wickedness of such Christians.

Extermination or Assimilation—What Happened to Cuba's Native People?

Unfortunately for the Spanish conquistadors, who came to Cuba hoping for more labor and better gold deposits than they had found on Hispaniola, neither the expected gold nor the desire of the natives to work as slaves ever panned out. Gold production peaked by 1519 and had all but ceased by the mid-1540s. Moreover, those natives not killed during the fierce and bloody battles of conquest rapidly succumbed to disease, committed suicide, or escaped into the mountains between 1516 and the mid-1540s, leaving the Spanish victors vanquished by their own brutality. These victorious conquistadors found themselves surrounded by vast tracts of fertile, virgin land, but left alone on an increasingly depopulated island. Although the bulk of natives on whom they had relied for labor were gone, the Spanish stubbornly refused to soil their hands by working the land like lowly farmers (Gott 2004).

The native population of Cuba upon Spanish arrival was roughly 112,000 (Pérez 1995). By the mid-1530s, it had been reduced to just 5,000–6,000, a catastrophic demographic loss of 95 percent. The causes of Taíno deaths were diverse and often cumulative. Cuban historian Juan Pérez de la Riva (2003) has estimated that war and massacres, as gruesome as they were, accounted for only about 12 percent of native deaths. Disease (25%) and suicide (35%) were much more significant. Finally, infant mortality (20%) and famines (8%) caused by the destruction of native plots rounded out this sad episode. However, the fact that Pérez de la Riva's numbers add up to a tidy 100 percent hints at his underlying assumption that Cuba's native population was completely wiped out. On the other hand, British historian Hugh Thomas indicates that even after the drastic demographic drop initially suffered by the Taíno, they probably still outnumbered Spaniards and African slaves as late as 1535. In that year, Cuba was home to approximately 300 Spaniards, 5,000 Indians, and 1,000 newly arrived African slaves (Thomas 1998).

What happened to those 5,000 remaining Indians? The answer lies in a final, as yet unmentioned factor. That is the supposition that those natives who did not succumb to the aforementioned depredations yielded instead to *mestizaje*—that is, they disappeared into Cuba's white Creole population over the next 350 years of colonial rule. Pérez de la Riva admits as much when he indicates that "[a]fter 1550, when the indigenous population had been reduced to some five or six thousand, *mestizaje* surely became the main cause of the extinction of the indigenous race" (Pérez de la

Riva 2003: 24–25). However, one wonders whether "extinction" is the best word to describe the outcome of a process of *mestizaje* (Barreiro 2003).

It is perhaps more accurate to say that Cuba's Indians were not eradicated so much as they were absorbed into its white Creole population very early on. Spaniards generally arrived without female companionship and so quickly began taking native women as their wives or concubines, making the majority of the first generation of native-born Cubans *mestizo* (the mixed offspring of native women and Spanish men). However, these children were not thought of as *indios* (Indians) or even as mestizos. Instead, they were raised and identified as white *criollos* (Creoles, meaning in this context, Spaniards born in Cuba as opposed to *peninsulares*, or Spaniards born in Spain itself), despite the fact that they were half Taíno (Thomas 1998). Still, after a series of ultimately unsuccessful experiments with different systems of labor and land grants (*encomiendas* and *repartimientos*), the Spanish Crown and Catholic Church decided to place the remaining Indians in *reducciones* (reservations): towns set apart exclusively for Indians.

Before the strategy of *reducciones* was implemented, many Taínos had already chosen their own spontaneous form of resistance by simply escaping into the woods, swamps, or mountains. There were at least two types of communities of Taíno escapees or "runaways." The earlier group was known as the *indios cayos* (keys Indians), a name based on their strategic use of Cuba's innumerable and isolated keys and islets, from which they would occasionally emerge to attack the Spaniards. A second, much longer-lasting type of isolated native community hid itself in Cuba's vast, forested interior.

The Spanish initially referred to this second group of escapees simply as *indios del monte* (mountain or wild Indians), but they became more commonly known as

---

THE *ENCOMIENDA* AND *REPARTIMIENTO* IN CUBA

During the early 16th century the Spanish were engaged in a feverish effort to extract as much gold from the island as possible, using the natives as virtual slaves under the Spanish land and labor system known as the *encomienda*. This system obliged land owners to Christianize and civilize native workers. In practice, however, the *encomienda* functioned as a way of rewarding Spanish conquistadors with large tracts of land and the labor with which to farm and mine it. Supposedly, native workers under the *encomienda* would become free once they had converted to Christianity. However, this only caused the *encomenderos* to wring all possible labor from their native workers by working them to death.

Cuba's governor Diego de Velázquez was made the island's official *repartidor* (supplier), which legally enabled him to provide between 40 and 300 of these native laborers to each *vecino* (land holder). As with the land itself, each *vecino* would subsequently divide up this labor allotment among various *encomenderos*. As a result, the infamous *encomienda* was combined with a novel mechanism, the *repartimiento* (a labor contracting system invented in the Indies) leading to the plunder of native lands and the enslavement of the natives.

ETYMOLOGIES POPULAR AND SCIENTIFIC—WHAT'S A *GUAJIRO*?

Recent anthropological research indicates that the Taíno did not simply disappear in the 1500s. In fact, the very region first colonized by Velázquez in 1512, the Baracoa-Maisí region of Oriente, is still home to many Cubans who trace their heritage and traditions as Cuban *guajiros* back to the Taíno-Arawak people, whom the Spanish priest and defender of the Indians Bartolomé de Las Casas called *cubeños*. These family nuclei (*caseríos*) still plant *yuca* fields (which they continue to call *conucos*), bake and eat *yuca* bread (*casabe*), and get together to share Cuba's Taíno stew, *ajiaco* (Barreiro 2003).

These Cubans continue to identify themselves as natives, using the common Cuban word *guajiro* to express that identity. "Guajiro" has its etymological origin in the Taíno/Antillean strain of the Arawak language. Thought to originally indicate a person of high esteem or rank among the Taíno, guajiro is used most commonly today as a synonym of *campesino*, or country farmer. Still, a competing—and very likely apocryphal—popular etymology has it that guajiro is an Hispanicization of the English term "war hero," absorbed into Cuban Spanish following the arrival of thousands of North American troops during the War for Cuban Independence of 1898.

---

cimarrones. A Spanish term meaning "wild" or "untamed," cimarron was first applied to animals like horses or pigs that had broken free and gone to live in the wild. Depending on the size, duration, and organization of these cimarron communities, they might be considered *palenques*, and the people who lived in them are called *apalencados*. Given the rapidity with which the Taíno population collapsed and the Spanish colonists' subsequent turn to African slaves to replace them, many of these "rebel" Indian communities soon began welcoming runaway African slaves into their midst.

DEPOPULATION AND ABANDONMENT, 1540–1760

In the decades following the conquest of Mexico by Cortés in 1521, Cuba quickly came to be seen as a vast, untamed backwater, compared with the unimaginable size and wealth of gold and Indian laborers in Mexico. Spanish conquistadors did not venture across the seas, risking their lives in battle to resume the lowly life of farmers. The conquistadors came to the Indies without the commitments of family and had little of the enduring patience of the religious refugees and yeoman farming families who would later settle in North America. Instead, they sought to become wealthy *hidalgos* (men of title), overseeing vast tracts of land and hundreds of workers. Realizing that such a future was rapidly becoming impossible for them in Cuba, many left for Mexico during the 16th century. This shift mirrored Spain's own goal of extracting mineral wealth from Mexico and later Peru. By the mid-16th century, Cuba entered a long lethargy in which it served Spanish interests mainly as a port. And it is through Cuba's ports, especially at Havana, that the next 200 years of Cuban history would be written.

The Beginnings of the Slave Trade

Before abandoning the island, Spanish colonists sought to replace their dwindling Indian workforce with a new imported labor force. Unwilling to take on the harsh work of digging mines and cultivating fields themselves, they first attempted to substitute the Taínos with Mayan and other Indians from Central America and the Yucatan. When that scheme failed, the colonists turned to what would later become the backbone of Cuba's labor force: African slaves. Intended to replace Indian labor, the first African slaves were brought to Cuba from the neighboring Spanish colony of Santo Domingo in 1522. One reason that they were chosen was the fact that they came originally from a place so distant that they would harbor no realistic hope of return. That was quite different from Cuba's Indians, who were made into virtual slaves on their own land and as such were always disappearing into the *manigua* (wilderness). Unfortunately for the Spaniards, the Africans were quick to learn this form of resistance from the Indians. However, African slaves had the advantage of being more resistant to the European diseases that had decimated the Taínos.

African slavery in the Spanish West Indies grew out of a labor system that had already existed in southern Spain since at least 1450, in which as many as 100,000 African slaves labored in agriculture, ports, and as personal servants by the early 16th century. Thus most slaves initially came to the Caribbean not to work in large-scale, export-oriented plantation agriculture, but as personal servants. When colonists began to realize that these initial slaves brought in from other parts of the Spanish empire were insufficient, they pleaded with the Crown for right to bring in African slaves directly from Africa in order to avoid economic "ruin." That right was granted as early as 1527, but it never came to fruition since colonists lacked the funds to pay for them.

Since sugarcane had yet to take on an economic importance in Cuba, the island rarely received more than 100 African slaves each year during the 16th century, a trend that continued until the final decade of the 18th century. During this period, life for Cuba's slaves was somewhat better than it became later under the strict drive for profit that characterized the 19th-century Cuban sugar boom. For example, the practice of *coartación* (manumission, or the purchase of one's own freedom) was within reach of many urban slaves. There were even occasions when masters would free their slaves after they had performed a number of years of service. Unlike in the United States, the children of slaves were not automatically slaves. Also, the lack of Spanish women in Cuba led to the rapid growth of a second generation of *mestizos* and mulattoes, who made the population of free coloreds quite sizable.

The opportunity for slaves to become "free people of color" added an important and influential class of free blacks to Cuban society. Although often ignored in practice, Spanish law provided both slaves and free coloreds with certain legal protections against arbitrary abuse, allowing them to marry and providing space for the formation of African associations. Thus, the peculiar combination of the protections of Spanish law, the paternalism of Spanish Catholicism, the island's underdeveloped economy, and the more lenient Spanish attitude toward sexual relationships with blacks led to a surprising level of black autonomy and racial integration in early colonial Cuban society.

The Pirates of the Caribbean and Havana's
Fortifications and Walls

For the next 200 years most of Spain's attention was focused on the colonial mainland, from which it extracted ever greater amounts of agricultural and especially mineral wealth. The shortage of precious metals or minerals on the island meant that almost every Cuban village dedicated itself to animal husbandry, establishing a ranching tradition in many principal interior cities such as Camagüey. Cuba was important to Spain only to the extent that it served the mercantilist policy of funneling products reaped from other lands back to the mother country—not because of the as yet untapped potential of its vast and fertile soils. Still, Spain came to realize that ignoring developments in Cuba, especially given the growing challenge from rival European powers, was not an option. Cuba may have been on the margins of empire, but its strategic position made its defense essential (Pérez 1995).

This realization led directly to the second major economic activity in Cuba at this time: the construction of a series of fortresses aimed at the military defense of the island. Concentrated around the narrow entry of the colony's twin harbors in Havana and Santiago, this complex defense system was intended to protect the uninterrupted flow of goods back to Spain and ensure its role as a gateway, pipeline, and strategic meeting point for the annual fleets of merchant ships. The construction of fortifications required the use of great numbers of slaves. All these edifications made the port of Havana the best defended stopping point in the maritime route between the Indies and the Spanish main. The port city's "key" importance is reflected in its coat of arms which depicts the city's first three fortresses and a key in a blue field, which represent its military defenses and its all-important role as a point of safe harbor and rendezvous. Thus, Cuba was converted into a roadhouse, weigh station, and stronghold of Spain's mainland booty, based on its advantageous location in the center of the Atlantic trade winds.

Because the Spanish were the first to establish colonies in the Caribbean, it was against Spain that France, Britain, and Holland fought to wrest control of these islands. However, those incursions were rarely carried out by the naval forces of the respective nations. Instead, the constant attacks at sea and raids on landed settlements were led by the legendary pirates of the Caribbean, the proto-bounty hunters, hired guns, and contrabandists of the age (alternately known as corsairs, privateers, freebooters, or buccaneers). Often working in cahoots with local Spanish officials and almost always licensed and paid by the royal family of one or more of Spain's rival European powers, the infamous privateers were outlaws in a time of frontier justice. Laws were often as arbitrary and unjust as they were unenforceable. Although detested by the Spanish Crown for constantly threatening their settlements and violating prohibitions against contraband, privateers were more often welcomed by desperate colonists who were used to getting fleeced by the Spanish monopoly on trade (Suchlicki 1997).

Cuban Coffee, Tobacco, and Sugar, and the Birth
of Creole Proto-Nationalism

By the end of the 17th century and during the first quarter of the 18th century, tobacco and coffee had come to dominate Cuba's economy. These two crops employed

HAVANA'S WALLS

The imposing city walls that once encircled colonial Havana are now all but a memory, with only tiny sections still extant hinting at their former glory. Funds for the construction were raised starting in 1674 by a tax levied on the treasure fleets coming out of Mexico as well as on every glass of wine sold in Havana's taverns. It took a crew of African slaves 23 years to complete the 10-meter (33-foot) high, 1.4-meter (4.5-feet) thick walls that ran the full 4,892 meters (just over 3 miles) of the city perimeter. Originally, there were just two gates that connected the city within the walls to the world outside, opened each morning and closed each night to the sound of a cannon blast. Furthermore, the walls held 9 defensive citadels, 180 cannons, and had barracks for up to 3,400 soldiers. Finally, in 1863 after years of petitioning the Crown, Havana's residents were able to breathe easier (literally) when they were allowed to begin the decades long process of dismantling the walls. The city had long outgrown its colonial confines and disease was often contained within the walled city, creating a noxious death-trap.

slave labor: tobacco partially and coffee fully. Thanks to the growing European demand for these products, Cuba became a veritable "factory" for these agricultural commodities. Yet, Cuba's relatively marginal use of slave labor at this time was only a shadow of its centrality in sugar production in the two centuries to come. The prominence of tobacco led Spain to establish a monopoly that forced planters to sell all of their production to the state at meager prices, prompting protests from *vegueros* (tobacco planters) that climaxed in 1723 when some 300 planters were attacked by the colonial army.

During this period a new social class arose in Havana: a Creole planter oligarchy from which the seeds of national identity and politics grew on the island. This emergent group's foremost ideologue was the historian José Martín Félix de Arrate y Acosta (1701–1764) who penned the famous polemic, *The Key to the New World, Bulwark of the West Indies: Havana Described, News from Its Foundation, Growth, and State*. Calling loudly for an increase in the colony's power and opportunities, this was the first work to make the Creole planter oligarchy's major political demands known. Given the period and political context in which it was written, the work was elitist, colonialist, proslavery, and racist. Already in 1760, the Creole oligarchy was determined to transform Cuba into the world's leading producer of sugar and coffee. However, this would not be possible until several internal and external factors converged between 1762 and 1803. The three determining developments were the brief capture of Havana by the British, the ruin of the French colony of Saint Domingue (today's Haiti), and the entrepreneurial skill and political vision of Cuba's Creole planters.

Tobacco, an indigenous crop, was originally kept at arm's length by Creole planters. In fact, it was first adopted by slaves and free coloreds who began to grow and successfully market it to Cuba's many visiting sailors. Only later did Creoles begin to see the economic potential in systematically cultivating tobacco, which they did mainly in the fertile lands south and west of Havana. Ironically, Creoles proceeded to pass laws that prohibited blacks from profiting from what had initially been considered *cosa del negro* (a black thing). Tobacco cultivation remained in Creole hands for most of the 16th and 17th centuries.

The Crown later turned the tables on the Creole planters in Pinar del Río. As the trade and profitability of tobacco cultivation grew, Spain placed increasingly complex regulations and taxes on the sale of the product (Pérez 1995). Then, in 1717, the government enacted the hated *factoría* system, which made the cultivation of tobacco an official monopoly for the next 100 years. Cuba's fiercely independent *vegueros* were forced to accept a new system whereby the Spanish Crown would advance them money with the requirement that they sell their harvest to the government at a fixed price (Suchlicki 1997: 27). Ironically, such an arrangement could just as easily describe the communist government's longtime relationship with Cuba's private farmers—necessitating current economic reforms.

By the end of the 18th century, Cuba's *vegueros* found themselves pressured to sell their land as its value shot up because of the growth of the much more profitable, but unstable and labor intensive crop, sugarcane. The Spanish Crown encouraged this shift, since the more lucrative sugar trade could provide greater revenue. Throughout the colonial period (and even after independence), there was little consideration of developing a local manufacturing economy or of diversifying Cuba's monocultural agricultural industry. In fact, over time Cuba became less, not more, agriculturally diversified. The Crown discouraged local entrepreneurship, preferring that the island depend upon it for the basics, allowing Cuba to continue to specialize as a producer of raw materials for Spain—the very definition of mercantilism.

Aiming to eliminate contraband trade and increase profits, the new Bourbon rulers of Spain moved decisively to check the growing political and economic power of Cuba's Creoles. Starting in 1740, the Crown began to implement a rigid and ambitious

---

THE *FACTORÍA* SYSTEM, THE *VEGUEROS'* REVOLT, AND *VUELTA ABAJO*

In 1717 the Spanish crown decreed a monopoly over the price and production of all Cuban tobacco appointing the *Factoría de Tobacos* (Royal Tobacco Factory) to enforce and manage the monopoly. If this weren't enough, producers were outraged by the fact that the Company was not required to purchase Cuban farmers' total output, but forbade the *vegueros* from selling any surplus tobacco on the open market. Cuban *vegueros* rose up in armed protest. On August 17, 1717, more than 500 of them marched on Havana in a show of force against the new policy. The *vegueros* initially succeeded in sending the new Governor Vicente Raja and his enforcement officials back to Spain, the first time Cuban Creoles forced the resignation of a Spanish governor.

The *vegueros'* revolt ended in 1723 when the colonial government captured and executed 11 of the main insurgents. However, remaining growers continued to resist the royal monopoly by relocating to faraway zones in Pinar del Río and continuing to market their product through contraband trade, giving rise to Cuba's most renowned tobacco cultivation areas in that province, especially along the banks of the Cuyaguateje river in a region that would become famously known as *Vuelta Abajo*.

commercial system aimed at exercising absolute control over Cuban trade, the *Real Compañía de Comercio de La Habana* (Royal Company of Commerce of Havana). This incongruous name highlights Spain's attempt to find an effective balance between notoriously corrupt and inept "royal" enterprises and the much more productive and efficient private "companies." The hope was that this new Royal Company could perform the royal task of funneling all production surpluses back to Spain (putting an end to smuggling, piracy, and contraband trade), while at the same time making the process of production, marketing, and sale more efficient and profitable. However, the *Real Compañía* met with only limited success before it was eventually abandoned after the British occupation of Havana in 1763.

The unpopularity and ultimate failure of the *Real Compañía* among Cuban residents owed in part to the fact that they were now paid a pittance by the company for products that they had previously sold (legally or through contraband) for much more. Even worse, the company now had an exclusive right to provide the island with all its imported manufactured goods, which were notoriously expensive given the company's monopoly on sales. On top of all that was a never-ending series of new taxes designed to transfer to Spain a greater portion of the colony's wealth, including an import tax (the *almojarifazgo*), a sales tax (the *alcabala*), and a fleet tax (*avería*), in addition to the church (*diezmo*) and mining taxes (*quinta*) already in place (Pérez 1995).

As with the factoría system, this trade arrangement put into place to prevent contraband and make production more efficient and profitable for Spain only provoked ever more contraband and smuggling. Also, the *Real Compañía* was established at a time when Cuban proto-nationalism was beginning to awake from its 200-year slumber, first signaled by the abortive *vegueros'* revolt of 1717. Other indications of the growing sense of Cuban identity included the establishment of the first printing press (1723), the founding of the University of Havana (1728), the recognition of Havana as an independent bishopric (1748), the building of the first Cuban post office (1754), and the incorporation of an association to promote national economic development, the *Sociedad Económica de Amigos del País* (The Economic Society of Friends of the Country 1792).

"LA PROSPERIDAD BRITÁNICA": THE BRITISH CAPTURE OF HAVANA, 1762–1763

Without underestimating the Bourbon reforms introduced by Charles III (1711–1788) and the progress made by the emerging Cuban Creole oligarchy, the changes that took place in Cuba in the coming years would have been impossible without the British occupation of Havana. From today's perspective, the invasion amounted to a major turning point in the socioeconomic life of the Spanish colony, splitting the island's history into the 250 years of Spanish colonialism preceding it (1512–1762) and the 250 years since (1763–2013) (Echerri 2012). In the Seven Years' War (1756–1763) between Britain and France, the Spanish Crown entered as an ally of the French. In response, the sails of the British Navy descended upon Havana—the naval, military, and communications center of the Spanish Empire—aiming with the capture of such a strategic and coveted location to achieve complete naval dominance in the

Caribbean. On the eve of the invasion, Havana's population of 30,000–40,000 made it the third largest city in the Western Hemisphere after Mexico City and Lima, but larger than both New York and Boston. Never before in the history of the Americas was there a military and naval mobilization of such magnitude and the *Castillo de los Tres Reyes del Morro* was its main stage.

Led by Lord Albemarle (George Keppel, 1724–1772), the British attack force was "the most formidable armada that had crossed the Atlantic Ocean up to that time," including 200 warships carrying more than 8,000 marines and 12,000 soldiers, representing more than half of all British naval forces in the Caribbean at the time. This formidable fighting force relied on the support by 2,000 black servants, 60 field medics, and reinforcements from the 13 British colonies to the north (Echerri 2012). Albemarle's strategy was to split Spanish defense forces with simultaneous attacks on *El Morro* Castle on the east side of Havana harbor and a diversionary force aimed at the entry to Almendares River, west of the city. Marshal Juan del Prado (1716–1770) led a doomed attempt to hold the besieged city with just 14 ships anchored in the bay, backed by the strength of Havana's defense system, and about 9,000 troops.

Instead of engaging the British fleet at sea, Prado decided to rely on Havana's extensive fortifications and simply sank three ships at the mouth of the harbor. While this action succeeded in preventing British ships from entering the harbor, it gave the British navy free reign of the sea by trapping all Spanish ships inside the port. The British attack began on June 7, 1762 and troops succeeded in storming *El Morro* on July 30, 1762. On August 10, Albemarle demanded that the city surrender and two

Spain enlisted the Roman military engineer Gian Battista Antonelli to design a pair of fortresses that straddle the mouth of Havana's harbor (pictured in the background of this photo). Built upon a crag of limestone rocks to the east of the harbor's entrance between 1590 and 1630, the Castillo de los Tres Santos Reyes Magos del Morro, *or simply* El Morro, *did not receive its signature lighthouse until 1845. In order to catch invaders in a crossfire, the Castillo de San Salvador de la Punta was built on the western point of the harbor's entrance directly opposite Havana's Morro Castle. (Orlando Luis Pardo Lazo)*

days later Prado capitulated. In retrospect, however, it is doubtful that British forces could have held out much longer. The 744 battle casualties suffered by the British were dwarfed by the 5,922 Brits lost to disease between early June and mid-October. However, it wasn't until almost a full year later in July 1763 that the Treaty of Paris was signed, signaling the British withdrawal from Havana in exchange for Florida.

It is estimated that during the 11-month British occupation (often referred to as simply *la prosperidad británica*), an unprecedented 900 merchant ships visited the port of Havana bringing in an estimated 10,000 slaves, a number equal to what would have normally arrived in 10 years (Pérez 1995). Meanwhile, the British occupation of the capital immediately led to a spike in trade between numerous neglected provincial outposts such as Santiago de Cuba and Bayamo in far away Oriente. The Spanish fleet stationed in the port of Cuba's second city turned readily to privateers from the nearby French Caribbean island colonies to procure food supplies. Moreover, planters in Bayamo and Santiago raised cattle for the coffee, indigo, and cotton producers on the adjacent island of Santo Domingo, thereby reducing the control that the Spanish colonial authorities in the capital had previously imposed on them. After exposure to the material benefits of freer trade under the British, there was no going back to the sclerotic status quo ante—a lethargic, unproductive, and fundamentally unfair Spanish institutional, administrative, and legal system.

Once the island was recovered, Charles III realized that the best way to keep it was to strengthen its defense system and to improve the quality of life of his subjects. He built the fortress of San Carlos de La Cabaña, abolished both the Royal Company of Commerce and the Royal Tobacco Factory, and initiated a public works program aimed at beautifying the capital. In 1765, Madrid ended the trade monopoly of Seville and Cádiz, allowing seven other Spanish ports to do business with Cuba. Trade was also initiated with other Spanish Caribbean islands, and all previous taxes and duties were replaced by a flat 7 percent ad valorem tax. Moreover, between 1778 and 1803 eight other Cuban port cities were authorized to trade directly with Spain and other Spanish colonies.

After a few years, Havana was filled with fountains, avenues, and palatial estates such as that of the Capitan General and the Segundo Cabo. The construction of Havana's Cathedral was also completed. In short, the British occupation allowed for Cuba's long-awaited escape from the backwaters of Spanish mercantilism and its entrance into Western civilization. Because of this more tolerant and enlightened context in political, legal, and religious matters, Cuba's inhabitants could finally begin to openly benefit from the island's privileged geographical situation for maritime trade.

Most importantly for the coming 19th century, after the British withdrawal the island's nascent sugar plantations entered into a period of rapid expansion. The necessary conditions for rapid economic development were finally in place: installed productive capacity, accumulated capital, and free access to slaves from British slave traders (see Table 2.1). This expansion of slave labor was accompanied by new markets for Cuban products, the most important of which were sugar and tobacco. In fact, this mutually reinforcing sugar-slave nexus, expanded under the British, would come to define Cuban society and link it in a dependent position to the world economy in the 19th and 20th centuries. At the time, however, few Creoles, recently relieved from the excessive restrictions of Spanish mercantilism, were concerned about overdependence on sugar and slave labor, or about the contradiction between free

TABLE 2.1 Estimated Cuban Slave Imports, 1512–1865

Years	Total Numbers	Average Annual Numbers
1512–1763 (251 years)	60,000	239
1763–1789 (26 years)	30,875	1,188
1790–1799 (10 years)	50,516	5,052
1800–1809 (10 years)	52,958	5,296
1810–1819 (10 years)	115,931	11,593
1820–1829 (10 years)	58,109	5,811
1830–1839 (10 years)	92,085	9,209
1840–1849 (10 years)	31,754	3,175
1850–1859 (10 years)	63,600	6,360
1860–1865 (6 years)	8,000	1,333
Totals (353 years)	**563,828**	**1,597**

Source: Thomas (1998).

trade and a captive labor force. They were more interested in finally being able to tap Cuba's formidable economic potential, which had so long been stymied by Spanish mercantilism (Syrett 1970).

The Cuban Creole Planters

The British occupation of Havana and the ruin of the French colony of Saint-Domingue allowed a new class of Cuban Creole sugarcane planters to emerge, without whom Cuba could not have replaced Haiti as the Caribbean's premier sugar producer and slave importer. Trained as a lawyer, Francisco de Arango y Parreño (1765–1837) was the Cuban Creole planter most responsible for convincing the Spanish Court to allow the open introduction of slaves into Cuba directly from the African coast. He immediately recognized the exceptional opportunity the Haitian revolution provided Cuba and vociferously advocated for the rapid modernization of Cuban agriculture before Haiti recovered. According to Arango, one must look at the neighboring island "not only with compassion but also with political eyes" (Ponte 1937: 27). With this goal in mind, he criticized Spain's absence in the slave trade, recommending absolute freedom of trade. These recommendations took shape in the 1789 Royal Decree that authorized the importation of blacks directly from Africa and exempted them from all duties. Arango was also the guiding force behind the formation of the *Sociedad Económica de Amigos del País* (1792) and the subsequent *Consulado Real de Agricultura, Industria y Comercio* (1794), as well as the island's first newspaper, the *Papel Periódico*, which together functioned as the voice of the white Creole elite and the vehicle they used to introduce the ideas of the European Enlightenment to Cuba (Gott 2004: 43). It was men like Arango, along with wealthy, influential Creole planters like Cristóbal Madan and Miguel Aldama who constituted a new type of plantation owner, possessing shrewd business sense, large amounts of capital, efficient exploitation of labor, enlightened use of modern technology, political savvy, proto-nationalist sentiment, and intellectual curiosity (Thomas 1998).

SUGAR AND SLAVERY IN CUBA DURING THE 19TH CENTURY

The great irony of Cuban slavery is that it experienced its greatest, most concentrated spurt of growth only after the slave trade had been officially outlawed by a treaty between Spain and Britain in 1820. In the entire 302 years between 1518 and 1820, Cuba received a total of 385,000 slaves, whereas 468,000 came in illegally during the 52 years between 1821 and the last recorded clandestine arrival in 1873. The explosive growth of slave labor contributed to the development of the island's economy and the wealth of sugar planters and especially slave merchants, who often acted as Cuba's only bankers providing essential credit to planters. However, the rapid growth of Cuba's slave population caused increasing alarm among Cuba's Creoles, who feared a repeat of the lopsided population distribution. Indeed, in 1841, Cuba's 436,000 slaves together with its 153,000 free people of color made up almost 60 percent of the island's population of 1 million. While this population distribution shifted back toward a white majority in the second half of the 19th century, there was relatively little white Spanish immigration during the early decades of the century.

Toward Independence and Emancipation: The Aponte and Escalera *Conspiracies*

Beginning as early as 1533, when several runaway slaves were brutally executed at the Jobabo mines in Oriente, escapes and rebellions took place daily. In 1724, the slaves of the Santiago del Prado copper mines revolted, and in 1795 Nicolás Morales was executed in Bayamo for leading another major revolt. The first movements for independence during the 19th century were led by Cuba's small community of educated free people of color sometimes in collaboration with progressive whites. The most significant of these was led by José Antonio Aponte y Ulbarra, a free man of color, artisan and amateur artist, and a corporal in a battalion of the *Batallones de Pardos y Morenos Leales* (Loyal Battalions of Browns and Blacks).

Aponte was perhaps the perfect protagonist of such a conspiracy given his connections among his fellow free colored tradesmen combined with his leadership of both his local Yoruba *cabildo de nación* and the underground Nigerian society *Shangó Tedum*. During this time, a growing number of blacks and free mulattos managed to acquire small properties and education, allowing them to develop a marked sense of *"cubanía"* (the consciousness of being Cuban and the sense of belonging to the culture of Cuba). These free people of color also began to establish a close relationship of solidarity with black slaves, an identification process that was based on what Cuban historian Ramiro Guerra has called "the double desire for civil liberty and social equality on the part of the slave and free black." All of this was cemented by the organization of the *cabildos de nación* and reinforced by the establishment of the *Batallones de Pardos y Morenos Leales*.

What became known as the "Aponte conspiracy" was anathema to both Spanish authority and the conservative white Cuban Creole elite, because its stated purpose was none other than "to abolish slavery and the slave trade, and to overthrow colonial tyranny, and to substitute the corrupt and feudal regime with another, Cuban in nature, and without odious discriminations" (quoted in Gott 2004: 50). Directly inspired by Haiti's revolutionary example of 1804 and supported from abroad by abolition-ists in Haiti, the United States, and Brazil, the dual goal of the Aponte conspiracy was political independence and emancipation from slavery. In the end, however, the conspiracy was betrayed just before it was to go into action in April of 1812, with its leaders, including Aponte, publicly hanged and beheaded by the colonial government. Their heads were displayed at the Havana's entrance as a warning to others.

In each of these conspiracies, as well as in the subsequent and equally unsuccessful conspiracy of the 1820s, *Soles y Rayos de Bolívar*, led by José Francisco Lemus, black conspirators were almost always brutally executed, while their white counterparts were more often imprisoned or exiled. One reason that these initial independence movements were unsuccessful and so harshly repressed is that they could always be portrayed by Spanish officials as aiming at the creation of a "black republic," follow-ing Haiti's example. Officials would unapologetically play the race card against white Cuban Creoles by reminding them that only Spain and its soldiers could protect them against the "African hordes" on the one hand, and ensure the profitability of their slavery-dependent sugar fortunes on the other (ibid.: 52).

The increase in Spanish repression, sustained attacks on Cuban slavery by British abolitionists, and a burgeoning slave population that had come to surpass Cuba's white population by 1841, led to rising expectations among Cuba's slaves followed by brutal, reactionary repression ordered by Captain General Leopoldo O'Donnell (1843–1848). Known as the *Escalera* conspiracy, the series of slave rebellions that began at the Matanzas sugar mill "La Conchita" in 1839 was the early 19th century's most significant challenge to colonial rule and a piece of Cuba's national history writ-ten almost exclusively by blacks (Aguirre 1974: 99). Captain General O'Donnell saw the rebellion as a golden opportunity to crack down on Cuba's leading white aboli-tionist intellectuals, including Domingo del Monte and José de la Luz y Caballero, teach Cuba's growing slave population some needed discipline, and finally have a pretext to deport a portion of Cuba's "subversive" free black immigrant population.

After the uprising was brutally put down between 1843 and 1844, O'Donnell granted his *Comisión Militar Ejecutiva* unchecked powers to unleash a macabre, months-long series of Inquisition-like interrogation sessions in which hundreds of blacks (slave and free alike) were literally tortured to death as the authorities sought more information about the conspiracy. It was these interrogations, conducted with prisoners strapped to wooden ladders (*escaleras*), that gave the episode its chilling name. More than a thousand people were imprisoned, and an almost equal number of free coloreds (many of them immigrant workers from nearby islands) were forced into permanent exile. To prevent future conspiracies, O'Donnell even banned the future immigration to Cuba of any emancipated slave or free person of color (Gott 2004).

The Slave Plantation

As a result of the often contradictory forces that structured the lives of Cuba's slaves, a significant free black and mulatto population developed on the island during the 19th century. The ability to purchase one's freedom, the frequency of mixed unions, and the fact that children were not normally kept as slaves, allowed the free blacks and mulattos to constitute as much as 15 percent of the Cuban population of 1 million by 1841. Moreover, a detailed code regulating the treatment of slaves slightly miti-gated the harshness and inhumanity of Cuban slavery as it spread across the island during the 19th century. Slaves were considered to have souls and given a place (albeit at the bottom) in the social and religious system. They were considered to be both moral and legal personalities in the sense that they could marry, hold property, and theoretically even use the courts if wronged (Thomas 1998).

Despite these legal protections, Cuban slaves imitated their native predecessors in devising numerous ways to resist and rebel. Suicide, escape, and rebellion were the three most common types of resistance, apart from the tactic of preserving their religious traditions by "hiding them in plain sight" in syncretic combination with Catholic saints and ritual (Sublette 2004). Urban slavery, with its relative autonomy stood in stark contrast to the brutal prison that was plantation slavery. Cut off from the outside world, plantations were prisons where blacks were subjugated for life. In them, human groups developed in which there were virtually no women. With rare exceptions, sugar plantations did not allow female slaves, and when they were al-lowed, the possibility of cohabitation was hampered. As a result the concept of family disappeared for blacks. Later, as the slave trade came to an end, planters turned to the breeding of slaves in much the same way farm animals were bred. This practice generated horrible consequences such as infanticide, where mothers sought to free their children from the horrors of slavery by killing them at birth.

The average annual mortality of Cuba's slave population during the 19th century has been estimated at between 8 and 10 percent, with the majority of deaths occurring during the harvest. Death came from overwork, accidents, epidemics, punishments, and outright murder. The advent of more modern plantations with steam-driven mills toward the end of the 19th century led to slaves being treated worse, inasmuch as they were more likely to be "regarded and treated as economic rather than human units" (ibid.: 176). As a result, slave uprisings became more common.

The constant fear of a slave rebellion injected a nearly ubiquitous tension into the lives of Cuba's sugar planters. Since slaves and equipment were often bought on credit, mill owners found themselves in a state of continual and absolute dependency on merchants and slave traders. Also, since Spain had officially outlawed the slave trade in 1820, Cuban planters were always anxious that they would have to give up their slaves because they were illegally obtained. Finally, planters feared that their slaves would rebel as they had done in Haiti. This difficult position forced most planters to continue to support both the slave system and the colonial domination that protected it.

The Intellectual Foundations of Abolition and Independence: Varela, Saco, Del Monte, and Luz

In the first decades of the 19th century—parallel to the advent of Cuba as a major sugar and coffee producer and slave importer—a new generation of proto-nationalist intellectuals emerged that led to a significant deepening in critical thought about the island's future. The most original, active, and influential of these men were Father Félix Varela y Morales (1778–1853), José Antonio Saco y López (1797–1879), Do-mingo Del Monte y Aponte (1804–1853), and José de la Luz y Caballero (1800–1862).

Varela taught at Havana's seminary of San Carlos, where he held the inaugural chair of Spanish Constitutional Studies. Varela developed two projects that he planned to discuss at a meeting of the Spanish parliament set for 1821. One was the subject of national autonomy, where for the first time the issue of expanding the rights of those born on the island—including blacks—was to be raised. The other project was the abolition of slavery. However, neither issue was ever breached at the meeting since parliament was dissolved. Varela was the first in Cuba to employ the concept "*patria*," or homeland, to refer to the entire territory of the island. He was also the first to celebrate education as the path to liberation, beginning a tradition in Cuban thought. He is still celebrated today alongside José Martí and Carlos Manuel de Céspedes as one of the main pioneers in demanding national independence. Much like Martí would do after him, Varela insisted on and exemplified the idea that those demanding change in Cuba in the future must do so out of convictions of conscience and virtue.

A star pupil of Varela's, José Antonio Saco emerged during the 19th century as the most influential political figure in the anti-annexationist reformist movement, an alternative to outright independence which sought to make the island a province of Spain instead. Saco was one of the leading figures of the *Sociedad Económica de Amigos del País* (Economic Society of Friends of the Country, SEAP). Founded in Cuba during the late 18th century, the SEAP aimed to forge a capitalist society out of the colonial reality. Because of this, SEAP members opposed the slave trade and advocated for the introduction of salaried labor. Unlike Varela, however, their motives were purely economic. For example, Saco was a lifelong advocate of "whitening" Cuba through greater Spanish immigration and returning African slaves to their homelands and thereby shifting Cuba's economic base away from plantation

---

FATHER FÉLIX VARELA Y MORALES (1787–1853)

Born in 1787 in the then Spanish city Saint Augustine, Florida, to a Cuban-Spanish military family, Félix Varela did not arrive in Cuba until age 14. Against his father's wishes—who wanted him to follow family tradition becoming a soldier—he was ordained a priest in 1811 in Havana. Thereafter, he became Cuba's leading educator, teaching philosophy, chemistry, physics, theology, and music at the University of Havana. Though his tenure was short in Cuba, his influence on later nationalist political and cultural leaders was unquestionable as his students included José Antonio Saco, Domingo del Monte, and José de la Luz y Caballero.

While attending government consultations in Spain 1823, his advocacy of abolition and independence led to a death sentence. Varela escaped to New York, arriving on December 17, 1823. He spent the rest of his life in the United States, ministering to and defending New York City's Irish Catholic immigrants. While in New York, Varela also worked tirelessly as a journalist, publishing the nationalist newspaper, *El Habanero*, which he sent into Cuba clandestinely. Varela died in his hometown, Saint Augustine, Florida, on February 25, 1853, the same year in which Cuban patriot José Martí was born.

agriculture toward small, rural family farms owned and operated by a white peasantry. The racist underpinnings of Saco's nationalist thinking are clear in the following declaration against annexation: "The Cuban nationality of which I spoke, and
the only one that any sensible man should contemplate, is formed by the white race,
which amounts to just over 400,000 individuals" (Saco 2002: 87).

Domingo Del Monte was the most prestigious literary mentor of the colony. Together with a group of young illustrious men—including Saco—he founded a literary committee within the SEAP and began to publish the *Revista Bimestre Cubana*
(Cuban Bimonthly Magazine) in 1831. In 1833, they managed to turn the committee
into an independent academy, through which they attacked the slave trade. However, strong opposition to them by slave traders, planters, and colonial authorities led
to the dissolution of the academy, the closing of the magazine, and the deportation
of Saco. Under such circumstances, Del Monte turned to holding a series of now
legendary *tertulias* (social, intellectual, and artistic gatherings) in his own home. At
these gatherings, friends would share and analyze their written work and discuss
political and social issues that were impossible to discuss in public due to colonial
repression. Although not totally identified with blacks—whom he defended in his
literature—Del Monte played a leading role in the abolitionist literary movement,
which is an indispensible reference when considering the end of Cuban slavery and
the birth of the movement for national independence.

José de la Luz joined the SEAP in 1831 and began collaborating with the *Revista
Bimestre Cubana*. He held the Chair of Philosophy at the Seminary of San Carlos and
founded the *El Salvador* preparatory school, where he actively spread the "liberationist" and often seditious educational ideas of his mentor Father Varela. Among
his most notable students was Rafael María de Mendive, the eventual mentor of José
Martí. His famous aphorism, "Anyone can instruct; but to truly educate one must
be a living gospel" (Sanguily 1962: 174), shows his high regard for critical thinking
in education. Luz understood that the processes of founding a people and a nation
must have as its basis the preparation of individual historical actors and the moral
foundations for its implementation. Without his contributions, the all-important
independence movements of 1868 and 1895—in which more than 200 of his disciples
took part—is impossible to understand.

Annexation and Rising U.S. Interest in Cuba

Parallel to the abolitionist and reformist movements, the first half of the 19th century
saw the rise of annexationism. In fact, though he later repudiated the idea, José Antonio Saco was one of the most strident advocates of Cuba becoming part of the United
States in the 1820s and 1830s as a way of modernizing the island both economically
and politically. For many Cuban Creoles, since the independence of the 13 North
American colonies in 1776, the United States had become a model for development
and democracy. Moreover, for economic reasons a sector of Cuban landowners who
were against the abolition of slavery, leaned toward the annexation of Cuba to the
United States as a way of preserving that "peculiar institution." A group of Creole
sugar planters and annexationists in Las Villas province even supported a military
invasion, led by the Venezuelan-born and New Orleans–based Narciso López, to

achieve annexation. However, after a series of unsuccessful filibustering attempts, the conspirators were captured with their leader and executed for treason against Spain in 1851.

U.S. policy toward colonial Cuba during the 19th century set the parameters that would influence relations between the United States and an independent Cuba in the 20th century. Perhaps the most telling summation of U.S. policy toward the island came from Secretary of State John Quincy Adams in 1823:

> There are laws of political as well as physical gravitation, and if an apple, severed by a tempest from its native tree, cannot chose but fall to the ground, Cuba, forcibly disjoined from its own unnatural connection with Spain, and incapable of self-support, can gravitate only toward the North American Union, which, by the same law of nature cannot cast her off from her bosom. (Quoted in Pérez 1995: 108)

This vivid declaration indicates that as early as the 1820s the United States already had designs on Cuba. Furthermore, Americans assumed that Cuba's connection with Spain was unnatural and that the island was incapable of existing as an independent, self-sustaining unit. Both of these assumptions would survive until the end of the 19th century and drive U.S. policy during the so-called Spanish-American War of 1898. The second assumption influenced the U.S. approach to a nominally independent Cuba and still influences American policy toward the island today.

Although former president Thomas Jefferson shared Monroe's inclination of making Cuba part of the American union, going so far as to offer to purchase the island from Spain in 1808, he understood that the United States could gain the island only through violent conquest, which he wanted to avoid at all costs. "I have no hesitation in abandoning my first wish [of annexation] to future chances," Jefferson wrote in an 1823 letter to then president James Monroe, "and accepting its independence . . . rather than its association, at the expense of war and her enmity" (quoted in Gott 2004: 58). Unfortunately, this wish to avoid the enmity of Cuban patriots and respect the island's sovereignty has not been shared by many subsequent U.S. lawmakers.

In fact, during the 19th century various factions both in the United States and in Cuba actively lobbied for Cuba's annexation to the United States. Whether Cuba could be added to the union as a new slave state was the driving reason for U.S. interest in the island during the 1840s and 1850s. Likewise, many increasingly disenfranchised Cuban Creoles felt that they would fare better under U.S. tutelage than as second-class citizens under Spanish rule. As a result of this annexationist fervor, the United States offered to buy the island outright from Spain on three different occasions in midcentury. Finally, the Ostend Manifesto of 1854, issued by U.S. ministers at an international meeting in Ostend, Belgium, defended U.S. designs on the island, warning Spain and other world powers: "We shall be justified in wresting it from Spain if we possess the power" (Pérez 1995: 110). In fact, that warning became a reality 44 years later, when the United States invaded the island, snatching victory and sovereignty—if not formal independence—out of the hands of Cuban revolutionaries and transforming a Cuban war of liberation into a war of U.S. conquest.

The Decline of the Plantation and the End
of Cuban Slavery, 1880–1886

While the outcome of the American Civil War put to rest the idea of Cuba's annexation as a way to preserve American slavery, it also led many Cuban planters to grudgingly accept the fact that the days of Cuban slavery were numbered. By this time, Cuba's clandestine slave trade had ended, with the last known slave arrival in 1873. Cuban planters began searching for new sources of labor to replace Cuban slaves. Also, some planters had begun to realize that the skyrocketing price of slaves made the institution of slavery economically obsolete. It was becoming preferable to consider using contract laborers from Spain (Galicia and the Canary Islands), Ireland, the Yucatan, and, most prominently, China, since they could be inexpensively employed for a period of eight years without long-term obligations or fears of violent rebellion. In fact, as many as 130,000 Chinese "coolies" arrived

TABLE 2.2 Chinese Imports to Cuba, 1847–1873

Years	Number of Vessels	Chinese Shipped	Chinese Died at Sea	Chinese Landed	Mortality Rate
1847	2	612	41	571	6.70
1853	15	5,150	843	4,307	16.37
1854	4	1,750	39	1,711	2.23
1855	6	3,130	145	2,985	4.63
1856	15	6,152	1,182	2,970	19.21
1857	28	10,101	1,554	8,547	15.38
1858	33	16,411	3,027	13,384	18.44
1859	16	8,539	1,332	7,207	15.60
1860	17	7,227	1,008	6,219	13.95
1861	16	7,212	290	6,922	4.02
1862	1	400	56	344	14.00
1863	3	1,045	94	951	9.00
1864	7	2,664	532	2,132	19.97
1865	20	6,810	407	6,403	5.98
1866	43	14,169	1,126	13,043	7.95
1867	42	15,661	1,247	14,414	7.96
1868	21	8,400	732	7,668	8.71
1869	19	7,340	1,475	5,864	20.10
1870	3	1,312	63	1,249	4.80
1871	5	1,827	178	1,649	9.74
1872	20	8,914	766	8,148	8.60
1873	6	3,330	209	3,121	6.28
Totals	**342**	**138,156**	**16,346**	**121,810**	**11.83**

Source: Thomas (1998).

in Cuba between 1847 and 1873 (Table 2.2) (Dana 2003; Guanche Pérez 1999; Thomas 1998).

Given the harsh treatment endured by Cuba's new contract laborers, it is clear that the end of slavery in Cuba had little to do with a change of heart on the part of Cuban planters. It is likely that living and labor conditions for both emancipated slaves and those freed through the *patronato* (a system of gradual emancipation between 1880 and 1886), as well as for contract laborers, were actually worse than those of slaves, since planters had no obligation or financial incentive to feed, clothe, or house these workers properly. In fact, many planters freed their slaves or turned to Asian contract workers since those new groups had no status and therefore no legal protections, nor did they provoke the same condemnation as did the institution of slavery.

The increase in technical innovation on Cuba's sugar plantations in the late 19th century further undermined the economic logic of slavery. The introduction of new technology tended to push out smaller planters because of the prohibitive costs of new equipment. Also, as a result of the illegality of the slave trade after 1820 and Britain's stepped-up enforcement thereafter, the price of newly arrived slaves continued to rise, placing them out of reach of most small planters. Only those planters with sufficient capital benefited from innovation, simultaneously reducing the number of *ingenios* and increasing the size of those that remained. Finally, technical innovations mechanized the harvesting and refinement process and allowed production to skyrocket, while reducing the need for slave labor on many plantations.

The age-old Cuban *ingenio* was transformed in the 1880s and 1890s into the massive *central*, an enormous factory in the field that was completely mechanized and used only free labor. Cuban *centrales* typically subcontracted the growing and harvesting of sugarcane to dependent *colonos* (tenant sugar farmers), who worked on the fields surrounding the centrally located and capital-intensive sugar mills (thus, the name *central*). While *central* owners paid *colonos* for producing and harvesting the cane, they normally owned both the land itself and the extensive network of railroads that were used to transport it to the mill and later to Cuba's ports. The increase in mechanization and the end of slave labor actually increased stratification and placed more power in the hands of fewer owners, who were increasingly likely to be foreigners.

THE LONG STRUGGLE FOR INDEPENDENCE AND ITS AFTERMATH, 1868–1901

The Ten Years' War

Cuba's first full-fledged war aimed at independence from Spain, known as the Ten Years' War, began in 1868 with the *Grito de Yara* (Cry of Yara). Led by the prosperous plantation and slave owner, Carlos Manuel de Céspedes, the war was largely fought in Oriente. Trouble on the Spanish throne sparked Céspedes to free his slaves, declare Cuban independence, and commence the war on October 10 (a date still celebrated in Cuba today). After taking the town of Bayamo, the rebels formed a government-in-arms and commenced publishing *El Cubano Libre* (The Free Cuban), the newspaper of the independence movement. They also raised the same flag first used in 1850 by Narciso López; the composer Pedro Figueredo premiered *La Bay-amesa*, a melody inspired by France's *La Marseillaise*, which was later adopted as Cuba's national anthem in 1902.

Although there was disagreement within the revolutionary coalition over the issue of slavery, Céspedes freed his own slaves making them soldiers in the cause for independence. Although celebrated today—with José Martí—as the "father of the Cuban nation," Céspedes was in fact impeached by the more conservative members of his government-in-arms on October 27, 1873, accused of being dictatorial. Many also took issue with his unwavering commitment to total independence, staunch opposition to any negotiation with Spain, and distrust of Cuban annexationists.

Ostensibly aimed at Cuban independence, the Ten Years' War was more than a simple struggle between Cuban revolutionaries and Spanish troops. Internal conflict among the Cuban-born Creole elite, many of whom sought independence as a means of economic self-determination, weakened the rebel cause. Furthermore, while some powerful Cuban landowners continued to favor independence via annexation by the United States so as to preserve their economic position, others sought absolute independence leading to an immediate end to slavery and the establishment of a representative democracy on the island. These issues divided the rebel forces and poisoned the eventual peace treaty that closed the war. After the war started, Céspedes declared that once the independence was achieved, one of the first acts of the government would be the abolition of slavery. To reconcile this statement with the interests of slave owners, he issued an order to the revolutionary leaders to certify the ownership of the slaves who were being used in the war effort, so that the owners could be compensated later. It should be made clear that Céspedes' decision, and the decision of other planters to free their slaves so they could employ them as soldiers, does not mean that black and mulattos lacked the will and the reasons to participate

---

CARLOS MANUEL DE CÉSPEDES (1819–1874)

Born in Bayamo on April 18, 1819, Carlos Manuel de Céspedes became caught up in politics in the 1850s when Spain refused to grant Cuba even limited autonomy. He began to organize a war for independence under the cover of his membership in a Masonic lodge. Céspedes declared Cuban independence on October 10, 1868, when he assembled his supporters as well as his slaves at his own sugar plantation, *La Demajagua*, near the town of Yara, and proclaimed Cuba's sovereignty in the "Grito de Yara."

Soon thereafter he freed his slaves, adding them as foot soldiers in his growing rebel army and took the town of Bayamo. Calling for universal suffrage, complete independence from Spain, and the liberation of all of Cuba's slaves, Céspedes met resistance from his more conservative supporters who favored annexation to the United States. Céspedes also antagonized the more liberal members of his coalition by hedging on the immediate freedom for all of Cuba's slaves and assuming near absolute civil and military control of the independence movement. He was deposed in 1873 and killed a year later by Spanish troops. He is remembered today as the "Father of the Cuban Nation."

in the fight. They had been fighting for their freedom for many centuries, and the only new thing was the overlap of their struggle for abolition with the struggle for independence, which generated common interests between masters and slaves.

Ending less in defeat of the rebels than in mutual exhaustion, the war concluded in 1878 with the Pact of Zanjón, signed on February 10 by the rebel's committee in charge of peace negotiations. Though the agreement split the rebel forces into various factions, it also highlighted the fact that the failure to win the war resulted more from the internal dissention, lack of discipline, and contradictory goals of the rebels themselves than from the superior military force of the Spanish. As José Martí would later express, it was a war "that nobody took out of our hands, but one that we ourselves let fall."

Antonio Maceo, the Protest of Baraguá, and the Fruitful Truce

Antonio Maceo (1845–1896), a distinguished mulatto lieutenant colonel from Santiago de Cuba, refused to accept the terms of the peace treaty. Among the first free men of color to join Céspedes' uprising in October 1868, Maceo was just 24 years old at the time yet became a field commander after just five months and was soon promoted to lieutenant colonel. However, because of his intelligence and growing popularity among the *mambises* (the largely black and mulatto insurgents of the Liberation Army), some of the more conservative members of the liberation army accused him of seeking to establish a "black republic" modeled after Haiti. Though he vociferously denied any such aims, this jealousy and dissention contributed to the failure of the war in 1878.

Refusing the terms of the armistice, Maceo staged what has since become known as the protest of Baraguá held in the town of Mangos de Baraguá on March 15, 1878. Meeting personally with Spanish General Arsenio Martínez Campos, Maceo rejected the Zanjón treaty since it failed to recognize Cuban independence and freed only those slaves who had fought as *mambises*. Maceo's protest cannot be understood without considering that the war, which was initially led by wealthy white Creole planters, ended with a strong leadership of poor blacks, mulattos, and whites. This was an established sociological reality since the bulk of Maceo's troops were natives of Santiago and Guantánamo two regions where blacks predominated and that were home to a considerable number of poor peasants.

Although the Ten Years' War never reached the country's capital, Havana, the city was not a stranger to the struggle for liberation. In May of 1869, a successful coup was carried out against the liberal Captain General Domingo Dulce. He was replaced by the hardliner General Francisco Lersundi Hormaechea, who revitalized the Volunteer Corps—a feared paramilitary organization infamous for its vigilante attacks on anyone sympathetic to the cause of independence. In this context, the figure of José Martí emerged, who—imbued with the ideas of his mentor, Rafael María de Mendive—published the newsletters *El Diablo Cojuelo* and then *La Patria Libre*, which in its only issue published Martí's poem *Abdala*. In October of 1869 at the age of just 16, Martí was indicted along with Fermín Valdés Domínguez for having written a letter in which they criticized a schoolmate who had enlisted as a volunteer in the Spanish army. Martí was convicted, imprisoned, and deported to Spain.

There, in 1871 he published, "*The Political Prison in Cuba*," a shocking account of the horrors he witnessed during his confinement. In 1873 he followed up with "*The Spanish Republic and the Cuban Revolution*," a critical analysis of the incoherent and damaging policies that sought greater liberties in Spain, while maintaining Cuba under oppression.

In compliance with the Pact of Zanjón, between 1879 and 1886 laws dealing with freedom of the press, assembly, and association—endorsed by article 13 of the Spanish Constitution—were implemented in Cuba. As a consequence, news outlets and economic, cultural, fraternal, educational, and recreational associations were created. Trade unions, associations against racial discrimination, and the first political parties were also established. For example, in 1886 the *Directorio de las Razas de Color* (Board of Colored Races) was founded. After just six years it was able to bring together 75 independent colored associations from across the island. In addition, thanks to the amnesty that was granted as part of the Pact of Zanjón, José Martí, Juan Gualberto Gómez, Antonio Maceo, and Calixto García—among many others—were able to briefly return to their homeland. The results speak for themselves: when Martí later secretly sent his lieutenants to the island to lay the groundwork for a new uprising, there was already a well-organized independence movement in many provinces.

Slavery was abolished in 1886 and replaced by wage labor. Cuba became the first country to produce one million tons of sugar, and to export 90 percent of its harvest to the United States. This allowed Cuba's northern neighbor to impose on Spain a reciprocity treaty—known as the McKinley Bill—which established the free entry of Cuban sugar to that nation with the reciprocal entry of U.S. products into Cuba duty-free. This led to a high concentration of land ownership, especially by American companies. Despite still being a Spanish colony politically, Cuba became economically dependent on the United States with its economy reliant on a single product and largely one market. This generated a structural socioeconomic deformation and a highly skewed distribution of wealth, which was reflected in the miserable plight of workers, poor peasants, and freed slaves. These political, economic, and social transformations—all related in one way or another to the Pact of Zanjón and the deepening relations with the United States—created a new context for the continued struggle for independence.

The Little War, the Autonomists, and José Martí's Cuban Revolutionary Party (PRC)

The period between the end of the Ten Years' War in 1878 and the start of the second Cuban War of Independence that began in 1895 was marked by three major developments: the *Guerra Chiquita*, or "Little War" (1879–1880), the rise and decline of Cuba's Autonomist Party, and the founding and growth of José Martí's Cuban Revolutionary Party (PRC) in exile. The *Guerra Chiquita* occurred largely because of the bad peace made by the Pact of Zanjón in 1878. In compliance with the agreements of Zanjón, General Calixto García was released from prison in 1878. He became the chair of the Revolutionary Committee of Cuban Emigration, which clandestinely helped insurgents who continued to fight on the island, and to lead the

Guerra Chiquita, which began in the eastern part of Cuba under the leadership of the black Brigadier General Guillermón Moncada. However, from its very beginning in August of 1879, fatigue, frustration, and the same ills that led to Zanjón, condemned the war to failure. Moncada was captured and made prisoner, and soon thereafter in May of 1880 when General Calixto García landed in Cuba, he was immediately arrested with the rest of his forces.

The formation of the Autonomist Party was a liberal response to the Zanjón armistice. While not seeking immediate, absolute independence, the party advocated self-rule for Cuba while remaining a colony of Spain. This gradualist approach gained significant support from an embattled public because of its rejection of violent revolt after a decade of bloody warfare, the end of slavery between 1880 and 1886, and nominal Spanish reforms. Lasting for 20 years (1878–1898), the Autonomist movement eventually lost momentum as a result of its inability to reduce inequalities between Creoles and *peninsulares* (those of Spanish birth) or gain any significant and lasting reforms from Spain. Although autonomy was formally declared by Spain in the early days of 1898, Cuban rebels saw it as a treasonous ploy aimed at preventing their eminent victory, refusing even to consider it as an option (Ramírez Cañedo and Rosario Grasso 2008: 133).

Stepping into this void and picking up the mantle of the Ten Years' War were José Martí and his intrepid Cuban Revolutionary Party. Though largely unknown inside the island because of a life lived in exile, Martí quickly gained predominance in the independence movement on account of his deep analysis of the mistakes made in the previous war, his knowledge of politics, and his close relations with key political parties in Spain and the Americas. All this allowed him to found a new party

Universally considered by Cubans to be their national hero, José Martí was a poet, journalist, and charismatic orator who founded the Cuban Revolutionary Party in the early 1890s in the United States and led the fight for independence from Spain. He was killed in the battle with Spanish troops in 1895. (Library of Congress)

to act as the organizing, controlling, and consciousness raising institution of the independence movement. This institution, the Cuban Revolutionary Party (PRC), was established at the beginning of 1892, with the expressed purpose of "founding in the frank and cordial exercise of man's legitimate capacities, a new, truly democratic nation, capable of overcoming, through the order of real work and the balance of social forces, the dangers of sudden freedom in a society created for slavery" (Martí 2000, III: 26). In his writings and speeches of the time, Martí was at pains to emphasize his belief—not shared by all members of the movement—that the military apparatus needed to win the war must be subordinate to the civilian leadership during the war, so that "in the conquest of independence today, we carry the seeds of tomorrow's definitive independence" (Martí 2000, III: 99). For Martí, the Republic was the destination while the war and the party constituted the necessary steps on the path to get there.

Martí stood out from his Cuban contemporaries for his uncompromising yet inclusive and convincing stand for Cuba's absolute independence from Spain (as opposed to the many at the time who favored some kind of autonomy or self-rule under Spain). He also vehemently rejected the idea that Cuba's future lie in annexation to the United States. In fact, he spent the most extended, 15-year period of his life living, working, and planning revolution in New York City and in the process developed an intimate knowledge of American society, respect for its institutions, principles, and progress, and healthy fear of its growing materialism and expansionism. In short, in his fight for Cuban independence, Martí aimed to avoid the enmity of his Spanish enemies and the greed of his American friends.

Despite Martí's admiration for American democracy and economic progress, perhaps Martí's greatest fear was that a protracted battle would give the United States an excuse for intervention and eventual annexation of the island. In fact, that was

---

JOSÉ MARTÍ (1853–1895)

Born on January 28, 1853, in Havana, Martí was the son of Spanish immigrants; his father a first sergeant in the Spanish army. In the 160 years since his birth, he has come to embody all that is pure, just, and right in Cuba's long-frustrated nationalist cause. If George Washington, Thomas Paine, Abraham Lincoln, and Walt Whitman were rolled into a single individual then we might have some idea of the importance that this man, reverently referred to by Cubans on both sides of the Straits of Florida as "*el apóstol*," has for the divided and long-suffering Cuban nation.

Martí was deported from Cuba by the Spanish government for his separatist views when he was still just a teenager. He lived the rest of his life in itinerant exile returning briefly to his homeland just three times, lastly in 1895 to lead the final War of Independence where he would meet his death. Martí is best remembered today for a group of interrelated causes that sprung from the single unifying goal of his life: to see his beloved *patria* (homeland) free from Spanish domination, American imperialism, and Cuban despotism—in short, the achievement of *Cuba libre* (a free Cuba).

exactly his state of mind when he sat down to write what would turn out to be his final letter, addressed to his Mexican friend and politician, Manuel Mercado:

> Every day now I am in danger of giving my life for my country and my duty— since I understand it and have the spirit to carry it out—in order to prevent, by the timely independence of Cuba, the United States from extending its hold across the Antilles and falling with all the greater force on the lands of our America. All I have done up to now and all I will do is for that. (Martí 2002: 347)

Later in the letter, Martí makes the famous declaration, "I lived in the monster," referring to his time in New York City, "and I know its entrails—and my sling is the sling of David" (ibid.). Coming from any other Cuban political or military leader, this declaration might sound demagogic. However, coming from the unblemished and single-minded Martí and given the subsequent history of U.S. deep penetration of Cuba's social, economic, and political life, such a statement sounds more like a sadly accurate prophecy than a politician's scheming bombast.

As critical Martí was of the United States' imperialist designs on the Cuban nation, he reserved his harshest condemnation for the ambitious military leaders among his fellow Cuban rebels who would "bring a regime of personal despotism to my land, [and] take advantage of a great idea to serve [their] own personal hopes for glory or power" (ibid.: 259). Martí had hoped to fight a quick war, fearing that a drawn-out confrontation with Spain would lead to great loss of life and massive destruction of Cuba's infrastructure and productive capacity. He was also deeply troubled that a protracted war against Spain would marginalize the PRC's civilian leadership, ceding unchecked power to military leaders, led by Generals Antonio Maceo and Máximo Gómez.

In fact, although less well known than the letter he wrote to Mercado the day before his death in 1895, Martí also penned an equally prophetic, impassioned letter to his comrade-in-arms General Máximo Gómez more than 10 years earlier. In it he expressed the fear that Cuba's independence could just as easily be undermined by the very soldiers who fought so bravely to achieve it. Constantly in conflict with Gómez over civil-military relations, Martí reluctantly withdrew from the independence movement in 1884 out of fear that Gómez harbored dictatorial designs. Announcing his resignation to Gómez in the letter, Martí asked, "Are we the heroic, modest servants of an idea, or are we bold and fortune-favored *caudillos* who prepare to bring war to a nation in order to take possession of it for ourselves?" Then he famously reminded Gómez, "A nation is not founded, General, as a military camp is commanded" (ibid.: 258–259).

From the War of Independence of 1895 to the "Spanish-American War" of 1898

Martí's hopes for a quick and decisive war were dealt a critical blow when, on the eve of the attack, the U.S. government seized the majority of the rebels' ships and supplies in Fernandina, Florida, early in 1895. Going ahead with the plan, Martí and Gómez met in the Dominican Republic, where they jointly signed the Montecristi Manifesto as the respective civil and military heads of the independence movement.

Just prior to this declaration of principles, rebels on the island issued their own *Grito de Baire* (Cry of Baire) on February 24, 1895, signaling the start of the war.

During March and April, José Martí, Máximo Gómez, Antonio Maceo, and Calixto García, all landed clandestinely on the far eastern end of the island together with their troops. Rendezvousing in the town of La Mejorana, Martí, Gómez, and Maceo attempted once again to clarify the details of the insurrection and the crucial push toward the West. Despite 15 years of effort, the disagreements that ruined the Ten Years' War returned. On May 5, 1895, Martí lamented in his campaign diary—recovered from his body by the Spanish after he fell in battle—"Maceo has another philosophy of government [than I do]: A military *junta* with generals in command, [. . .]. The *patria* (homeland), therefore, and all the positions therein, will arise from and be inspired by the army [. . .]" (Martí 2000, III: 544). Just two weeks later, on May 19, at a place known as Dos Ríos, the civilian head of the Cuban Revolutionary Party was killed in combat.

Despite the devastating loss of Martí, the Rebel Army managed to spread their revolt west across the island and into all six provinces by 1897. However, General Maceo was also killed during the war, leaving Gómez as the commander-in-chief, while civilian control fell to a weak and unknown school teacher (and U.S. citizen), Tomás Estrada Palma, back in New York. It had perhaps been suicidal for Martí, a middle-aged writer in failing health with no military training, to join the rebels in Cuba. However, he was likely trying to prove his mettle to the military leadership, counterbalance their ambition with his own selfless example, and deflect the criticism that he always ended up "giving the Cuban emigrants lessons in patriotism under the shadow of the American flag" while others were dying for the cause of Cuban liberation on Cuban battlefields (Martí 2002: 335).

Developing their own style of guerilla warfare designed to defeat the Spanish by destroying the country's productive capacity, the *mambises* took control of most of the island, leaving only the major cities in the hands of the disease-stricken and

CUBA'S *MAMBISES*

The term *mambises* (*mambí* in the singular) refers to the guerrilla insurgents of the Cuban liberation army who fought against Spain in the either Ten Years' War (1868–1878) or the later War of Independence (1895–1898). The origin of the term can be traced to Juan Ethnnius Mamby (known colloquially in Cuba as "Eutimio Mambí"), a black Spanish military officer who deserted from the Spanish army in the 1840s while serving in Santo Domingo, taking up arms with the rebels there against the Spanish.

The Spanish soldiers used the term in Santo Domingo as a derogatory way to refer to black insurgents, whom they called "the men of Mamby" or "mambises." When some of these surviving Spanish soldiers were stationed in Cuba after the outbreak of the Ten Years' War in 1868, they took note of the similar guerrilla tactic of the feared machete charge that the Cuban insurgents systematically employed, applying the same term to them. While meant as a racial slur, the term was taken up by the Cuban insurgents both during the war and in later years by veterans as an honored title of bravery and national sacrifice.

demoralized Spanish troops. This turn of events led to a sharp decline in the island's economy and the resignation of Captain General Arsenio Martínez Campos on January 22, 1896, who had directed Spanish military operations until then. In response, Spain turned to the brutally effective General Valeriano Weyler, who arrived in Cuba on February 11, 1896, and rapidly put into place his infamous strategy of *reconcentración*. Weyler's plan was to reduce the insurgents' supply bases in the countryside by concentrating the peasantry in a handful of fortified towns. However, these "reconcentration camps" were not equipped to handle hundreds of thousands of displaced civilians leading to a famine that killed almost a third of the country's rural population. Shifting strategies again, the Spanish Crown removed Weyler in late 1897 to quell rising protests, even though his ruthless tactics were the only thing that seemed to work against the determined Cuban rebels.

"Remember the Maine, to Hell with Spain!": The United States Enters the War

In the final months of 1897 and early months of 1898, four developments unalterably changed the nature and direction of the war, leading to the intervention of the United States. First, the assassination of the Spanish prime minister in 1897, Antonio Cánovas del Castillo, led to the return of the Liberals to power in Spain allowing the Autonomist Party to reassert its influence in Cuba. The new Liberal Spanish government replaced the brutal if effective Valeriano Weyler, appointed General Ramón Blanco in his place, and approved a project of autonomy for Cuba. The Autonomists took control of the colonial administration of the island and attempted to placate the rebels, but it was far too late.

Second, in response to Weyler's ruthless reconcentration policy, U.S. newspapers such as William Randolph Hearst's *New York Journal* and Joseph Pulitzer's *New York World* began to print sensational stories trumpeting Spanish atrocities and fanning war fever among the U.S. public. This circulation battle between New York's leading newspapers, forever since referred to as "yellow journalism," gave rise to Hearst's legendary (and perhaps apocryphal) directive, "You give me the pictures, I'll give you the war," when war correspondent Richard Harding Davis and artist Frederic Remington complained that they could find no battles to report (Cluster and Hernández 2006: 101; DePalma 2006).

Then, in the second week of February, two events combined to draw the United States irrevocably into the war against Spain. First, a U.S. paper published a letter from Dupuy de Lôme, the Spanish diplomatic chargé d'affaires in Washington, deriding President McKinley. Members of the Cuban Junta (exiled supporters of the rebel cause) intercepted the letter and leaked it to the press, trying to end U.S. neutrality, if not provoke direct intervention on the side of the rebels. Added to that insult was the tragic and mysterious explosion on February 15, 1898, of the U.S. warship USS *Maine*, which had been sent into the Havana harbor ostensibly to protect "American lives and property" during unrest in the city. Although investigations were inconclusive at the time, this catastrophe took the lives of 266 servicemen and was used by U.S. expansionists to justify intervention, with the implication that Spain was responsible for the explosion.

THE EXPLOSION OF THE USS *MAINE* (1898)

The USS *Maine* was an American battleship sent to Havana harbor in the winter of 1898. On the evening of February 15 the battleship exploded killing 266 American soldiers, nearly all those aboard. It was clear that the ship's own five tons of powder charges had exploded. What was unclear is how the charges ignited. Was the explosion caused by heat from coal on the inside of the vessel or from an external source like a Spanish mine? A U.S. Naval inquiry quickly determined that a naval mine had caused the explosion, making it an act of war. The United States soon declared war against Spain, with the rallying cry, "Remember the *Maine*, to Hell with Spain!" Later studies concluded that the tragedy was more likely self-inflicted, caused by a fire in the coal bunker. Some of the remaining cannons from the ship were melted down and used to construct the *Maine* memorial that is located at the southwest corner of Central Park in New York City, just adjacent to Columbus Circle. Two other cannons from the ship also grace the memorial on Havana's seaside *malecón* (without the bronze bald eagle that once topped it).

The presence of the USS *Maine* in Havana's harbor was a direct result of Spain's previous decision to placate the Autonomists in Cuba. When the Autonomist Constitution was published in Cuba in December of 1897, the pro-Spanish parties opposed to any negotiation with the rebels and any change in Cuba's status as a Spanish colony staged a demonstration outside the *Diario de la Marina* newspaper, praising the demoted Weyler and insulting the new Autonomist Captain General Ramón Blanco. Similar protests were staged the following month, obliging the government to use force to restore order (Ramírez Cañedo and Rosario Grasso 2008: 124–126). The United States reacted by dispatching the battleship USS *Maine* to Cuban waters on January 25, 1898, aimed at protecting American lives and property.

Three weeks later—on February 15—the ship exploded, leading directly to the March 25 U.S. ultimatum that Spain enact an armistice with the insurgents. On April 19, the U.S. Congress passed its joint resolution authorizing the use of force in Cuba and plainly stating: "The people of the Island of Cuba are, and of right ought to be, free and independent." Despite this language and given the broad support in the United States at the time for *Cuba libre* (a free Cuba), it is ironic that the congressional resolution authorizing President McKinley to intervene in Cuba did not grant formal recognition to the Cuban rebel forces. In fact, despite the widespread belief that the United States went to Cuba to win the island's independence, the resolution was not officially a declaration of war against Spain but merely an authorization of the use of force to end the Cuban conflict.

In the debate that preceded the final resolution, President McKinley argued against language that would recognize the Cuban Rebel Army, as it would restrict U.S. movement on the island and subordinate U.S. troops to Cuban generals. He also opposed any statement that would recognize Cuban independence, as that would limit U.S. options after the war. Still, support for a free and independent Cuba was strong enough in Congress to have the so-called Teller Amendment added to the joint resolution, stipulating that the United States "disclaims any intention to exercise sovereignty or control" over Cuba and would "leave the government and control of the island to its people." On April 22, U.S. ships began to enact a blockade of the island. Three days later the U.S. declared war on Spain; a war that was decided in the naval battle of Santiago de Cuba.

The Naval Battle of Santiago and the U.S. Occupation

The Battle of Santiago Bay began when Spanish Captain General Ramón Blanco ordered Captain Cervera to leave the bay with all his ships in order to confront the American warships at sea. However, the U.S. forces under General Shafter had already arrived and simply waited for the Spanish armada to try to run the impossible gauntlet through the bottleneck exit of Santiago Bay. On the morning of July 3, the Spanish fleet did just that in an act of pure sacrifice. The American fleet, having a strategic advantage and superior numbers and technology, turned the once powerful Spanish armada into a smoking hulk of blood and fire. At two in the afternoon on that same day, after just five hours of lopsided fighting, it was all over. The outcome of the battle for Spain was devastating: 350 killed, 160 seriously wounded, 1,700 prisoners of war, and all 6 of its ships destroyed. The United States lost but a single man, Yeoman George Henry Ellis.

On July 10, the ground war resumed but the Spanish artillery was soon knocked out. Negotiations for Spanish capitulation began on July 12 and the city of Santiago surrendered on July 14. On July 16, under a copious ceiba tree, the basis of the armistice that ended five centuries of political domination of Spain was signed.

Begun in 1638, Santiago's Morro Castle (pictured here) sits at the eastern entrance to the city's harbor. It had to be rebuilt in 1664 after Welsh privateer Captain Henry Morgan made child's play of its defenses. It was along Cuba's mountainous southern coast visible here in the background that the Spanish Armada was routed by American warships in 1898. (Ted Henken)

However, as a sign of things to come, Cuban general Calixto García and his rebel army were barred from entering Santiago. The Cubans were also forced out of the formal handover of the city from the Spanish to the Americans—not to the Cuban rebels—on July 17, 1898, ostensibly to protect Spanish officials from Cuban reprisals. In late July, an insulted García penned an outraged letter to General Shafter expressing his incredulity that the Americans had left the unelected Spanish authorities in control of Santiago, but refused his men entry to the city.

The ultimate insult to Cuban independence was added months later at the signing of the Treaty of Paris on December 10, 1898. While the United States and Spanish forces were represented, the Cuban rebels were not even invited. In a supremely ironic and symbolic coincidence, General García died suddenly of a massive stroke the next day in Washington, D.C., while awaiting news of the terms of the transfer of Cuban sovereignty to the Americans. At the same time, General Máximo Gómez refused to attend the ceremony for the raising of the U.S. (not Cuban) flag at Morro Castle in Havana. "Ours," he wrote, "is the Cuban flag, the one for which so many tears and blood have been shed. We must keep united in order to bring to an end this unjustified military occupation" (Sierra 2006).

With the U.S. banner waving in El Castillo del Morro and the government house, the Cuban liberation efforts of the 19th century ended. It was a political and military defeat for Spain, which in turn heralded the beginning of a new and

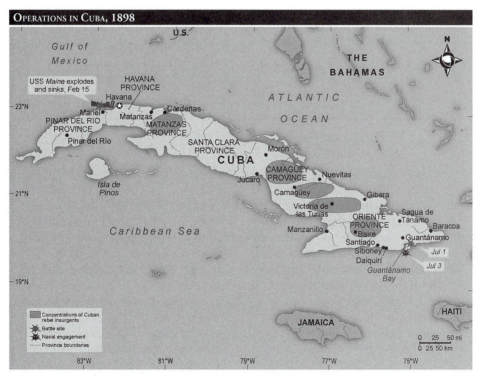

On May 19, 1898, the Spanish fleet arrived in Santiago de Cuba under Admiral Cervera, setting the stage for the final act of Cuba's War for Independence. Ironically, the two principal players in the war were Spain and the United States, with the Cuban rebels sidelined to a supporting role at best. (ABC-CLIO)

difficult phase in the struggle of the Cubans, who saw their independence spoiled after 30 years of war. Inadvertently, U.S. president McKinley captured the great and contradictory predicament now facing the soon-to-be independent nation of Cuba in his message of December 5, 1899, when he said: "The new Cuba yet to arise from the ashes of the past must needs be bound to us by ties of singular intimacy and strength."

A four-year U.S. military occupation of Cuba followed (1898–1902). The Spanish captain-general was replaced by a U.S. military governor, and more U.S. troops arrived in Cuba to enforce the occupation than had come to fight the war (Cluster and Hernández 2006: 104). The frustrated Cuban Rebel Army was disbanded and Martí's PRC dissolved. True to the letter, if not the spirit, of the Teller Amendment, the U.S. military government left control of the island to the Cubans after Cuban representatives passed a new constitution in 1901. However, U.S. insistence on the addition of the Platt Amendment to the constitution caused deep resentment among Cubans and undermined any real possibility for self-rule. Essentially, Cuban representatives were forced to choose between a "protected republic or no republic at all."

The Platt Amendment fatally undermined Cuba's hard-won independence, granting the United States the right to intervene in the future to "preserve Cuban independence." Over the next three decades, the new Cuban republic lived out the dire consequences of U.S. occupation. In the postwar period, U.S. penetration of the island went far beyond its previous economic engagement, to include political, military, and cultural aspects that had largely been absent prior to the war. Also, the existence of the Platt Amendment, especially the article granting the United States the right (and obligation) to intervene whenever Cuban sovereignty was threatened, acted as a major obstacle for Cuban politicians to control their own political affairs or to learn by trial and error the imperfect art of democratic governance.

THE PLATT AMENDMENT, 1902–1934

Originally conceived by U.S. secretary of war Elihu Root as a means of giving United States hegemony in Cuba a legal guarantee, the Platt Amendment was proposed to Congress by Senator Orville H. Platt and enacted by the U.S. Congress in 1901. Its major provision was, "That the government of Cuba consents that the United States may exercise the right to intervene for the preservation of Cuban independence, the maintenance of a government adequate for the protection of life, property, and individual liberty" (Roosevelt 2003: 148).

The amendment also proposed that "the government of Cuba shall never enter into any treaty or other compact with any foreign power or powers which will impair or tend to impair the independence of Cuba, or permit any foreign power or powers to obtain by colonization any portion of said island" (ibid.: 147). The text of the amendment also stipulated that "the government of Cuba will sell or lease to the United States land necessary for coaling or naval stations" on the island "to enable the United States to maintain the independence of Cuba, and to protect the people thereof" (ibid.: 148), which soon became the infamous Guantánamo Bay Naval Base.

THE PLATTIST REPUBLIC, 1899–1934

The Platt Amendment: An Occupation without Occupiers

Once Spain had been defeated and the Treaty of Paris signed, the occupying forces called on the people of Cuba to hold elections to appoint delegates to a constitutional convention. In his opening remarks, Leonard Wood—the U.S. military governor of the island—said to the delegates: "It will be your duty, first to draft and adopt a constitution for Cuba and, once that is completed, to determine what should be, in your judgment, the nature of the relationship between Cuba and the United States" (Pichardo 1980, II: 72). When the convention ended and delegates signed the final text of the new constitution in February of 1901, a special commission was established to formalize the bilateral relationship. In their deliberations, delegates were asked to take into account a set of recommendations shared with them by U.S. authorities; a set of recommendations that—once formalized—would become known as the "Platt Amendment." When analyzed, however, the commission concluded that some recommendations were unacceptable because they undermined Cuban sovereignty. Having completed its work on February 26, 1901, the commission communicated the result to General Wood, but the resulting constitution without inclusion of the amendments was unacceptable to the U.S. government.

Meanwhile the U.S. Congress was debating its own amendment to a bill establishing bilateral relations with Cuba, modeled on the recommendations the secretary of state had sent to the military governor of Cuba. In part, the text stated that "under no circumstances, would the United States allow any foreign power, other than Spain, to ever acquire possession of Cuba" (Roig de Leuchsenring 1973: 38–39). Once approved and signed by the president of the United States, the Platt Amendment was given to the constitutional convention for its inclusion in the constitution, effectively overturning the Teller Amendment to the joint resolution of 1898 that recognized the Cuban people's "right to be free and independent."

In March of 1901, delegates received the text of the amendment in the form of a U.S. law, resumed deliberations, and reached a defined position. The Cuban commission went to Washington to explain the reasons for their opposition, but failed to alter the decision of the United States. On June 5, the amendment was passed by the constitutional assembly by 15 votes to 14, but with objections, so this agreement was also rejected. Days later, the convention received a report signed by the U.S. secretary of war Elihu Root, stating that as a statute passed by the legislature, the president of the United States was obligated to execute it as written. Root added that as a condition of ending the U.S. military occupation: "You cannot change it, alter it, add to it, or take away from it" (Roig de Leuchsenring 1973: 160). Finally, having exhausted all possibilities, the Cubans approved the amendment to their nascent constitution by 16 votes to 11.

Cuban Electoral Politics, 1902–1925

After the constitution was approved and a dozen political parties were created, the first presidential elections were held with two former presidents of the Republic-in-Arms running against each other: Bartolomé Masó and Tomás Estrada Palma. The latter came out on top. On May 20, 1902—a date still celebrated today by many Cuban exiles in the United States but not recognized by the current Cuban government—the Cuban flag finally replaced the American one at the Castillo de del Morro and at all government institutions. Estrada Palma focused his administration on austerity measures for the management of public goods, but during his tenure the passage of legislation was extremely difficult because it required the presence of two-thirds of the members of congress, whose attendance was not mandatory. This situation was exploited by the rival Liberal and Moderate parties to obstruct unwanted legislation. Facing such a situation, President Estrada Palma—who until then had refused to join any existing party—decided to join the Moderates in order to be able to obtain the necessary legislative quorum.

Although reelection was endorsed in article 96 of the 1901 Constitution, Estrada Palma's attempt to stay in power for a second term proved disastrous. In his attempt at reelection, the president created the "Combat Cabinet," using the full coercive force of the government, including fraud, to prevail and thereby provoking the Liberal uprising of 1906. *La Guerrita de Agosto* (The August Little War, as the uprising was known) caused heavy damage and loss of life, including the assassination of the only surviving general to have served in each of the three wars of independence, Quintín Banderas.

In the lawlessness that followed, Estrada Palma sought the intervention of the United States. On September 28—along with the vice president and all the members of his cabinet—Estrada Palma resigned from office, leaving the country under a provisional government headed by the new U.S. secretary of war (and future U.S. president), William H. Taft. This constituted the second U.S. military intervention of Cuba; one that was actually made necessary by Cubans themselves. During the military government of Charles E. Magoon—who replaced Taft—sewage and garbage collection services were instituted, a census took place, new political parties were created, a civil war was avoided, and new elections were convened, which were won by the Liberals in 1909. In order to avoid a repeat of the conflict that had precipitated the second U.S. occupation, Magoon distributed privileges known as "*botellas*" (bottles), favoring the use of public office for personal gain. Thus, the U.S. intervention strengthened the culture of dependency and corruption, further damaged Cubans' self-esteem, and reinforced a "Plattist mentality" among Cuba's political class.

Throughout Cuba's republican period leading up to the revolution of 1959, political life on the island had little to do with ideology or party loyalty. Instead, Cuban politicians skillfully used the currency of corruption to garner and sustain support, transforming politics into a deeply balkanized exercise in personal power. Politicians owed their popularity not to their ideas or accomplishments, but to the patronage that they could dole out to their supporters. Likewise, the populace came to identify with and support different leaders not because of any unifying nationalist vision but simply because this or that politician had developed a personal reputation of providing his supporters with jobs, kickbacks, and public works projects, all looted from the public till.

In the elections of 1909, a Major General of the war of independence, José Miguel Gómez (1858–1921), was elected. Even though exports increased during his administration, political and administrative corruption prevailed. Gómez distinguished himself as especially adept at making politics profitable (in part by reintroducing cock fighting and the national lottery). Nicknamed "*El Tiburón*" (The Shark) for his high-profile political corruption and for harnessing the lottery as an efficient machine of political patronage, Gómez stepped down as a rich man in 1913 (Aguilar 1993: 43). In fact, given his skill at doling out political patronage to his supporters, Gómez was popularly known by the phrase: "*El Tiburón se baña, pero salpica*" (The shark bathes, but splashes), meaning that he may have been corrupt, but at least he shared the wealth.

Gómez's almost total lack of attention to the most serious issue of social justice during his administration—that of racial discrimination—led to a bloody and infamous episode. Blacks, who in the first half of the 19th century revolted against their masters and in the second half participated in the three wars of independence, ended up being treated under the republic simply as "blacks," that is, second-class citizens. The agenda of equality and social justice for which they had fought continued to be unresolved, and their interests were not represented by any existing political party.

Making use of the 1901 constitution, a group of Afro-Cubans led by the former slave and Independence War veteran Evaristo Estenoz founded the *Agrupación Independiente de Color* (Independent Colored Group) in 1907, later renamed the *Partido Independiente de Color* (PIC) (Independent Colored Party). The PIC was the first black political party in Cuba and, for that matter, anywhere in the entire hemisphere. Its goal was to demand an end racial discrimination and to call for employment opportunities for Afro-Cubans proportional to their presence in the population. In 1910, the PIC was outlawed by a constitutional amendment introduced by Senator Martín Morúa Delgado (Afro-Cuban himself), which prohibited the formation of political parties of exclusive racial groups. In its fight to repeal the amendment in 1912, the PIC used the slogan: "War or down with the Morúa Law." Never did they imagine that instead of repealing the act, they would be targeted in a bloody massacre.

Fearing renewed unrest in Cuba, the U.S. government sent in a small contingent of marines once again. Anticipating another all-out occupation, the Gómez administration suspended constitutional guarantees, declared a state of war, and unleashed a wave of repression against Afro-Cubans across the country. Thousands of blacks were murdered in what was one of the worst crimes perpetrated in Cuban history. After all, unlike the brutal wars of independence, this bloodletting was enacted by one group of Cubans against another. Cuba's historic fear of a race war—and a "black republic" a la Haiti—had not died with the end of slavery and Spanish colonialism. Indeed, the twin issues of Cuban race relations and U.S. intervention would influence politics for the next 50 years. The repression of the 1912 revolt also served to dampen black political participation in the years to come (Gott 2004).

In the elections of 1913, General Mario García Menocal (1866–1941)—popularly known as "*El Mayoral*" since he was the former administrator of Cuba's largest sugar mill—was elected. During his tenure, political and administrative corruption continued. Although he publically criticized gambling and the lottery, he privately used them as a means of personal enrichment. At the same time, thanks to increased demand for sugar during World War I, the sugar industry expanded and many new ambitious public works projects were undertaken. Initially, Menocal decided against seeking a second term, but when he changed his mind and began to run for reelection during 1917, he provoked a new uprising by the Liberals and a third round of U.S. intervention (but not invasion).

Led by former president Gómez and Liberal candidate Zayas, the Liberal Party sought to use the U.S. military to force Menocal out. However, their cause was dealt a serious blow when a diplomatic cable from the U.S. State Department to its Havana envoy William González declared support for "legally established governments only." Instead of being provoked by Liberal claims of electoral fraud (800,000 votes were cast by 500,000 eligible voters, for example), the United States decided to throw its full diplomatic weight behind Menocal, quickly selling him arms that allowed him to defeat the Liberal uprising. In the future, Cubans would often refer to *las notas de Mr. González* as evidence of the constant threat of U.S. intervention and the inability of any Cuban president to rule without its blessing (Aguilar 1993: 45–46).

To ensure stability during Menocal's second term, the United States appointed General Enoch Crowder as Cuba's "controller." Under his leadership a new electoral code was approved in 1919, known as Crowder Code. That same year, the huge amounts of sugar sold to the United States created a financial bonanza known as the "Dance of the Millions." However, this time of prosperity, or "*vacas gordas*" (fat cows), was immediately followed by the depression of 1921, which is remembered in Cuba as the time of "*vacas flacas*" (skinny cows). Due to the worsening of living conditions, social conflict increased, creating a strong civic and nationalist movement. The economic crisis that erupted during his second term forced Menocal to come to an agreement with opposition candidate Alfredo Zayas in the lead up to the 1920 elections. To that end, the National League (a union of Menocal's Conservative Party and Zayas People's Party) was formed.

In December 1920, U.S. president Woodrow Wilson ordered General Enoch Crowder to Havana as his personal representative without the prior approval or even a request by the Cuban Government. Arriving in January aboard the battleship *Minnesota*, Crowder was sent to Cuba to monitor the upcoming elections and to clean up Cuba's endemic corruption. Upon arrival, he set March 15, 1921, as the date of the vote and Alfredo Zayas—popularly known as "*El Chino Zayas*" (the Chinese Zayas) and "*El Pesetero*" (tightfisted)—was elected. A year later, Crowder infamously forced the notoriously corrupt Zayas to install an "honest cabinet" made up of individuals that Crowder himself handpicked. Crowder even issued a series of memos to Zayas, which the president was forced to present publically as his own. When news of Crowder's meddling leaked, Cuban congress adopted a resolution condemning foreign intervention in Cuban affairs.

By 1922, the Zayas administration was strengthened by the increase in sugar prices and foreign loans. Distancing itself from Crowder's interventionism, and buoyed by an outpouring of nationalist support, Zayas openly dismantled Crowder's cabinet and proceeded to fill the government with his cronies. However, now that Crowder had been formally named the first U.S. ambassador to Cuba, he was forced to remain neutral. He never seemed to understand, as Dwight Morrow once tried to explain to him, that "Good government is no substitute for self-government" (Aguilar 1993: 49).

The Movement for National Renewal

As Zayas took office in the midst of this economic crisis in 1921, the economic shock awakened Cuba's sleeping nationalism and led to calls for national reform and renovation. Economic legislation that would put Cuban interests and workers first, a demand for public honesty, a departure from sugar monoculture, and resistance to doing the bidding of the U.S. government all became national issues (Aguilar 1993).

Having experienced firsthand the many wrenching contradictions of a monocultural, export-oriented, dependent sugar economy during the "dance of the millions," Cubans of all classes and political persuasions were beginning to reassess their supposedly protective relationship with the United States. Thus, as Cubans became aware that the effects of U.S. "protection" were not unambiguously positive, they began to call for a fundamental change in politics as usual (Thomas 1998).

The crucial decade of the 1920s saw the emergence of nationalistic and increasingly anti-imperialist political, cultural, and intellectual movements that would begin to constitute an emergent Cuban civil society. Most prominent among these were the National Association of Veterans and Patriots; the more radical Anti-Imperialist League (formed by Julio Antonio Mella); the Cuban Communist Party, which was founded in 1925 (also with Mella's participation); the right-wing *Falange de Acción Cubana* (Cuban Action Falange), the *Universidad Popular José Martí* (José Martí Popular University), the *Confederación Nacional Obrera de Cuba* (National Workers Federation of Cuba), and several women's associations. A group of young intellectuals calling themselves *Los Trece* (The Thirteen) also emerged by publishing a devastating political manifesto that protested against the rampant corruption of the Zayas regime and condemned the entire Cuban political system (Aguilar 1993: 49–50).

On the cultural front, Cuba saw the rise of the periodical *Cuba contemporánea* (1913–1927), which led the charge to revisit the life, work, and patriotic vision of José Martí. Also influential during these years was the *Grupo Minorista*, which included intellectual, artistic, and political luminaries such as Alejo Carpentier, Rubén Martínez Villena, Juan Marinello, Emilio Roig de Leuchsenring, and Jorge Mañach, and which was responsible for publishing the important magazine *Revista de Avance*. Many members of this group were also involved in the artistic renaissance known as *Afrocubanismo*, which sought ways of challenging the complacency of Cuba's Creole bourgeoisie and to celebrate the unique elements of homegrown Afro-Cuban culture and art that could constitute a national culture.

Perhaps most prominent among these groups was the *Junta Cubana de Renovación Nacional* (Cuban Association of National Renewal), founded in 1923 by the widely respected Cuban anthropologist Fernando Ortiz. Typical of this movement's goals and criticisms was Ortiz's complaint, expressed later in his famous book *Cuban Counterpoint*, that "Cuba will never really be independent until it can free itself from the coils of the serpent of colonial economy that fattens on its soil but strangles its inhabitants and winds itself about the palm tree of our republican coat of arms, converting it into the sign of the Yankee dollar" (Ortiz 1995: 65). This movement reflected a growing disgust with U.S. influence and a rise in Cuban nationalism. Their program called for the protection of national industry through a renegotiation of the U.S. reciprocal trade agreement; demanded labor, educational, and health reforms; and advocated for an end to the graft and corruption endemic to Cuban politics (Pérez 1995: 229–247).

The Machadato, *1925–1933*

The multiplying contradictions and nationalist frustrations of the early Cuban republic came to a climax during the Machado incumbency (1925–1933). Another former independence war general, Gerardo Machado (1871–1939) won the 1925 elections by a landslide on a populist platform of nationalist reform and public works with the slogan: "water, roads, and schools." He began his first term on a positive note by instituting a series of nationalist reforms, including an increase in government oversight of the economy, limits on U.S. access to the economy, the expansion of public education, recognition of trade unions, and restructuring of Cuba's ineffective and arbitrary party system (Domínguez 1978). He also implemented a comprehensive plan of public works that included the construction of Cuba's central highway, an extension of Havana's seaside promenade known as *el Malecón*, the massive signature stairway at the University of Havana known as *la Escalinata*, the Capitol building, and the *Parque de la Fraternidad*, among others. He also instituted a tariff policy based on modern theoretical concepts to stimulate domestic production.

Although widely popular at first, these reforms could not endure in the face of the near collapse of Cuba's economy during the Great Depression. When first elected Machado had declared that he would "not aspire in any way for reelection" (Pichardo 1980, III: 360). However, once in power he pursued the totalitarian dream of unifying all parties into one: his own. In the face of increasing instability, in 1928 Machado forced congress to accept his own unconstitutional reelection and lengthened presidential terms from four to six years beginning with his own second term in 1929. To remain in power, he turned to violent repression to deal with the social unrest brought about by economic collapse and his own illegitimacy. The response from mobilized university students was immediate. They wrote the *Manifiesto al Pueblo de Cuba* (Manifesto to the Cuban People) and organized a series of public marches, which the government repressed resulting in the first martyr in the coming revolution of 1933: the student Rafael Trejo, who was killed by police during a march.

Ironically, many of the same nationalist voices calling for a change in the U.S.-Cuban relationship found themselves demanding U.S. intervention as Machado altered the constitution and began to protect his illegitimate rule with brutality and corruption. As early as 1927, leading nationalist intellectual Fernando Ortiz petitioned the State Department to intervene, reminding the United States that the Platt Amendment gave it the moral obligation to ensure "good government" in Cuba (Pérez 1995: 259). By 1931, when Carlos Mendieta appealed for U.S. intervention, such calls had become as commonplace as they were fruitless. Inadvertently, the United States exhibited its approval of the Cuban president when President Coolidge accepted Machado's invitation to attend the opening of the sixth Pan-American Conference in Havana in 1927. Emboldened by U.S. support, Machado responded to his opponents' demands for outside intervention by passing a law against any Cuban found seeking outside interference in Cuban development.

As Cuba began to suffer from the economic aftershocks of the Great Depression, the fundamental dilemma of a history of Plattist intervention became clear. The election of Franklin D. Roosevelt in 1932 and the institution of his Good Neighbor Policy made intervention in Latin America off limits, even as Cuban nationalists saw such heralded nonintervention as tacit support of the murder and political assassination associated with the Machado regime. One infamous example of Machado's brutal policies was the so-called *ley de fuga*, whereby Cuban police would murder suspected subversives in custody, washing their hands of the crime by explaining that the suspects had "died while trying to escape."

During this period, the *Directorio Estudiantil Universitario de 1930* (University Student Directorate of 1930) (DEU) was founded. Several other associations—mostly of radicalized university students—were also formed, such as the *Unión Nacionalista* (Nationalist Union), the *Ala Izquierda Estudiantil* (Student Left Wing), the *Directorio Estudiantil Revolucionario* (Revolutionary Student's Directorate), and the ABC. While ideologically diverse, these groups shared a palpable nationalist outrage that the ideals of Martí had been forgotten, as had the fact that Cuba was a Latin American nation and not an Anglo-Saxon colony (Thomas 1998: 599–602). In their mobilization, they set off a spiral that began with peaceful street demonstrations, but ended with bombs, government repression and murder, and armed uprisings, all leading to an attempted military revolt against Machado in 1930. Strikes became more common culminating in the general strike of August 5, 1933, which shut down the country and forced Machado out. Although he had confidently declared that no strike would last more than 24 hours while he was in power, Machado himself was ousted by the most successful strike in the history of the Cuban labor union movement.

The Revolution of 1933 and the Rise of Fulgencio Batista

President Roosevelt dispatched U.S. diplomat Sumner Welles to Havana in the summer of 1933 to mediate between Machado and the rising opposition. While much criticized later for his arrogant king-making in Cuba, Welles clearly understood the implications of the no-win situation years of Plattist policy had placed the United States in:

> To President Roosevelt two facts were clear. First, that while the existing treaty with Cuba gave this country the right to intervene, any such intervention would be contrary to the general line of inter-American policy which he had set for himself. Second, that a state of affairs where governmental murder and clandestine assassination had become matters of daily occurrence must be ended. (Quoted in Aguilar 1972: 129)

Disembarking in Havana on May 7, 1933, Welles stepped directly into a situation where the United States would be accused of irresponsibility by respecting the Good Neighbor Policy and *not* sending in the Marines. "Each declaration of the Roosevelt administration reaffirming the Good Neighbor Policy and the desire of nonintervention in Latin America," Aguilar notes of the months leading up to Welles's arrival, "was hailed as a triumph for Machado and a setback for his 'anti-Cuban' enemies" (ibid.: 128). This alternating "Yankee-go-home; Yankee-come-back-please" posture, called the "Plattist mentality" by Cuban historians, characterized the history of the first Cuban republic from its inception in 1902 to its apogee in 1933, to its final replacement in 1940 by a new constitution. This same mentality also characterized the complex and rapidly unfolding developments during the second half of 1933, a period known in Cuba as the "Revolution of 1933" (also called the "government of the one-hundred days" since it lasted just over three months).

On August 12, Machado fled the country and Welles negotiated the appointment of the provisional president Carlos Manuel de Céspedes—colonel of the war

Following the September 1933 sergeant's revolt, Fulgencio Batista emerged as the de facto leader of the Cuban Army. He is pictured here wearing a colonel's uniform in late 1933, shortly before his coup against the government of President Ramón Grau San Martín. (Bettmann/Corbis)

of independence, and the son of the man known to Cubans as the "Father of the Nation." Congress was dissolved, and the constitutional statutes of 1928 repealed. On September 4, the "sergeants' revolt" took place, led by Pablo Rodríguez, Fulgencio Batista, Eleuterio Pedraza, and others who formed the *Junta de los Ocho* (Board of Eight), which together with the DEU (University Student Directorate) and other associations released the "Proclamation to the People of Cuba." Céspedes resigned from office and the movement led by the military junta appointed a *Pentarquía* (five-man ruling coalition) composed of Sergio Carbó, Guillermo Portela, Ramón Grau San Martín, Miguel Irrisarri, and Porfirio Franca. Four days later, the *Pentarquía* appointed Batista chief of the army, promoted him to colonel, and named Grau president of the republic. On September 10, a military insurrection led by Batista dissolved the *Pentarquía*, and Grau was named provisional president of the government of 100 days.

The presence of Antonio Guiteras as head of the Secretariat of Governance of the new government of 100 days gave it a decidedly radical character, despite the fact that the much more conservative Batista continued as the head of the army. In just over three months the new administration promulgated a series of unprecedented socio-economic policies including university autonomy, the eight-hour work day, the right to form trade unions, the granting of unused agricultural land to small farmers, and a decree that required at least 50 percent of all workers in industry, commerce, and agriculture to be Cuban citizens (Pérez 1993: 70). It also issued a decree lowering utility rates by 45 percent, established a minimum wage for the harvesting of sugarcane, and granted women the right to vote. The Platt Amendment was unilaterally abrogated and all political parties that had participated in Machado's government were dissolved. The Grau/Guiteras government even briefly took over the Electric Company and called on the U.S. government to withdraw Ambassador Sumner Welles. In response to the changes, the displaced military officers briefly occupied the *Hotel Nacional*, but were forcibly removed the following month. In November, another abortive military conspiracy attempted to seize control of Havana's principal military bases, *Campo Columbia* and the *Castillo de Atarés*.

In the roughly 100 days between September 1933 and January 1934, Welles met with both the civilian (Ramón Grau San Martín) and military (Fulgencio Batista) leaders of this new government, but consistently refused to recommend that the United States recognize the revolutionary government based on his estimation that it lacked popular support and had not succeeded in stabilizing the country. Welles was replaced in December by Ambassador Jefferson Caffery who generally shared his conviction that effective diplomacy meant protecting the interests of American businesses, which were threatened by the Grau/Guiteras government. Following Welles lead, Caffery supported Batista's eventual ouster of Grau in January 1934.

Events continued to unfold at a dizzying pace. After getting assurances from the business and military sectors of the country, on January 14, 1934, Batista carried out a second coup, withdrawing military support from Grau's government of 100 days. Without a way to defend his rule Grau's resistance was short-lived, and he fled into exile on January 17, leaving Batista behind as kingmaker. Batista then appointed the secretary of agriculture, Carlos Hevia, to the presidency, who quickly resigned after failing to form a government. Three days later, Manuel Márquez Sterling was named provisional president, and he formed the Board of Revolutionary Sectors, which appointed Colonel Carlos Mendieta as president. Just five days later, on January 23, Welles's replacement, U.S. ambassador Jefferson Caffery, extended to Mendieta Washington's official diplomatic recognition.

Among the memorable actions of Mendieta's government was the signing of a Reciprocal Trade Agreement with the United States in 1934, which finally repealed the now clearly counterproductive and obsolete Platt Amendment. He also enacted the constitutional statutes of 1934 and called for elections to form a constitutional convention. This last measure was frustrated by the opposition and by the March 1935 general strike, which led to Mendieta's resignation. Then, José A. Barnet provisionally assumed the presidency, until Miguel Mariano Gómez was elected in 1936.

For his part, Antonio Guiteras went underground and created the paramilitary organization *TNT* in March, 1934. TNT soon dissolved to give way—in October of that same year—to *La Joven Cuba* (Young Cuba), a clandestine revolutionary organization named in honor of *La Joven Turquía* (Young Turkey), which had recently overthrown the Turkish monarchy. *La Joven Cuba* sought to overthrow Batista's government and form in its place a democratic, anti-imperialist, revolutionary government of national liberation. On May 8, 1935, while attempting to flee the country to organize an insurrection from abroad in Mexico—just as another would-be revolutionary, Fidel Castro, would do in 1955—Guiteras was gunned down along with the Venezuelan revolutionary Carlos Aponte in the port town of Morrillo, Matanzas.

ANTONIO GUITERAS (1906–1935)

The revolutionary government set up in September 1933 was not only divided between civilian Ramón Grau San Martín and military Fulgencio Batista. It was also internally divided between moderates from the Student Directorate and the more radical members of the *Unión Revolucionaria* led by Antonio Guiteras. It was Guiteras' revolutionary program that was quickly put into place in the short-lived 100 days of Grau's incumbency. Guiteras gave a political direction to the administration, serving in positions that allowed him nominal civilian control over the country's armed forces. However, it was also Guiteras' radical goals that caused Sumner Welles to refuse the rebel government's American recognition.

As a political leader, Guiteras had a single-minded, austere style, especially enamored of using direct violent action where electoral politics itself was thinly veiled gangsterism. Though not a Communist, Guiteras was perhaps Cuba's most radical political leader between Julio Antonio Mella of the 1920s and Fidel Castro after the 1950s. After fleeing into exile when the revolutionary government of 1933 was overthrown by Batista, Guiteras returned clandestinely and founded a new political movement that he named *La Joven Cuba*. In the end, Guiteras was ambushed while trying to escape into exile once again in 1935.

Miguel Mariano Gómez—son of general and former president José Miguel Gómez—won the presidential election of 1936. However, due to pressure exerted by Batista, he was dismissed and replaced by yet another colonel of the war of independence, Federico Laredo Bru. As president, Laredo Bru mediated between competing political forces to convene a constitutional convention and restore constitutional order. To that end, he granted political amnesty to more than 3,000 prisoners, allowed for the return of exiles, and—in April of 1938—issued Decree 798, which was the most important labor legislation of the republican period.

This decree included rights and benefits ranging from the 8-hour day to paid holidays and sick leave, in line with the provisions of the International Labour Organization. Its contents were later included in 27 articles of the 1940 constitution. The normalization of the country between 1934 and 1939 permitted trade unions to pursue their interests through binding arbitration. In late-January 1939, the National Workers Confederation of Cuba (CNOC) was dissolved to make way for the birth of the *Central de Trabajadores de Cuba* (Cuban Workers' Union) (CTC), and in 1940 the republican constitution included both individual and collective labor rights.

In the six years between 1934 and 1940, Batista successfully managed to unify the army and the government into a single force with the window dressing of a series of mostly ineffectual puppet presidents controlled by him. As in the past, these governments were the country's major source of public employment and political patronage, except that now these goods were administered and redistributed through Batista's army. After solidifying his relationship with the United States and coming to an accommodation with the Communist Party–controlled labor union at home, Batista felt confident enough to seek to fully legitimize his de facto rule by allowing

Congress to call a constitutional convention aimed at writing a new constitution and to make arrangements for a new election, for which Batista himself declared his candidacy.

YEARS OF HOPE AND BETRAYAL, 1940–1952

The Constitution of 1940

Although the revolution of 1933 was ultimately unsuccessful, the 100-day revolutionary experiment led to a fundamental shift both in Cuba's domestic politics and in its relationship with the United States. "The revolutionary episode of 1933," writes Aguilar, "was for Cuba a step forward, but only one step, and a step fraught with frustration and disillusionment" (1972: 239). Soon afterward, new political parties emerged, a massive labor organization (the CTC) was founded, and economic nationalism expanded with growth in the number and proportion of Cuban-owned sugar mills and banks. Between the years 1940 and 1952, there was also progress toward the establishment of democracy on the island. Two major positive developments associated with this period (and directly related to the dashed hopes of 1933) were the passage of the progressive 1940 Constitution and the peaceful transition in 1944 from Batista to his democratically elected successor, the opposition candidate Grau San Martín—the same man he had ousted only 10 years earlier.

Ten political parties—representing three ideological tendencies—participated in the elections for delegates to the constitutional convention held on November 15, 1939. The Liberals advocated free markets, individual rights, and a minimal state role in the economy; the Communists, in contrast, emphasized social justice, strong unions, and state regulation of the economy; the Social Democrats favored a middle path that rejected both extremes. The sessions were held from February 9 to June 8, 1940, with the resulting text signed in Guaimaro on July 1 and presented at the University of Havana on the fifth. The Constitution of 1940—the last one passed in democratic Cuba—entered into force on October 10, 1940.

The value of the 1940 Constitution emanates from its provisions. It granted universal suffrage, abolished the death penalty, and provided social protections for women, children, and workers. Racial and sexual discrimination in the workplace was outlawed, and public education was made free and mandatory. Article 37 legalized the formation and existence of oppositional political parties and organizations. Article 40 enshrined the protection of individual rights; an article invoked by Fidel Castro himself during his trial for the assault on the Moncada barracks in 1953. Article 87 recognized the legitimacy of private property and article 90 banned large agricultural estates (*latifundia*).

One major problem with the constitution was that many of its articles were more goals to be achieved than mandates for immediate implementation. Still, it would act as an important symbol in coming years, simultaneously serving as the embodiment of many of the radical goals of the thwarted revolution of 1933 and as a manifestation of the highest ideals of a clean, socially conscious, democratic Cuba. Thanks in part to this constitution the Cuban middle class grew, state intervention in the economy was complemented by private entrepreneurship, two-thirds of the island's sugar mills were owned by Cubans, and Cuba became one of the three Latin American and Caribbean countries with the highest standard of living.

The Cuban Democratic Experiment, 1940–1952

In the presidential elections of July 1940, Fulgencio Batista was elected as the candidate of the Social Democratic Coalition—composed of the traditional parties in alliance with the Communist Party. They prevailed over a coalition headed by Grau San Martín. Batista's triumph had much to do with support from the peasants, thanks to several rural social programs that he had promoted since 1936. Among these were rural literacy, which created 1,000 rural schools, and the Triennial Plan, which benefited thousands of small sugar cane farmers. During Batista's administration (1940–1944), he demonstrated an unwavering support for the United States as it entered World War II. He allowed the United States to construct airfields on the island, use Cuban ports for reconnaissance, and patrol the Cuban coast as a way to keep German submarines out of the Western Hemisphere. This strong alliance with the Americans in the war against European fascism helped to mute past expressions of Cuban anti-imperialism aimed at the United States.

In the lead-up to the 1944 election, Batista's preferred candidate, Carlos Saladrigas, found himself in a tough battle against Grau, who had returned from exile. Grau promised to achieve the nationalist goals set out in the heady days of 1933. Piquing the hopes of the populace, he won in a landslide. The smooth transition from Batista's government to the opposition was a positive sign. Moreover, it now seemed that the progressive, nationalist promise of the 1940 constitution would be fulfilled. Indeed, while in exile Grau had sought to rekindle Cuba's frustrated nationalism by naming his new party after the one founded (also in exile) by Cuban patriot José Martí half-a-century earlier in 1892—the Cuban Revolutionary Party (PRC). However, given the betrayal of Martí's democratic vision by a long series of Cuban politicians claiming to govern in his name, Grau wanted to symbolically rescue the authenticity of Martí's hopes for Cuba by adding the nickname, *Los Auténticos* (or the Authentic Cuban Revolutionary Party, PRC-A).

Over the next eight years Grau, his party, and his successor, Carlos Prío Socarrás (1903–1977), went on to violate nearly every principle of good government in a fashion that would bring shame perhaps even to the utterly venal and corrupt politicians of Cuba's first republic. Instead of using their opportunity to make good on the frustrated hopes denied an entire generation, the *Auténticos* used their incumbency as a way to make good on their long-denied birthright as Cuban politicians: to quickly and lavishly enrich themselves. The great hope embodied in the Authentic Revolutionary movement turned out to be a disillusioning disappointment that was neither authentic nor revolutionary (Pérez 1993: 79). Even more disturbing was the fact that after setting hopes so high upon gaining power, the *Auténticos* fall from grace was that much more detrimental to the legitimacy of Cuban electoral politics. This debasement of electoral politics and the later usurping of the entire democratic system by Batista would be the two main reasons that future revolutionaries would turn to armed struggle as their only option.

The fact that these were boom years in the Cuban economy mitigated the public reaction to the Grau administration's increasing corruption, allowing him to pass power to his *Auténtico* successor, Carlos Prío Socarrás. In fact, Prío's anticlimactic election in 1948 was Cuba's last direct presidential election in its history as an independent nation. With the United States buying the 1945, 1946, and 1947 sugar harvest en masse in order to feed a Europe recovering from war, the cash flow allowed those controlling the purse strings of the Cuban economy to become masters of corruption. Another dangerous development during these years was the transformation of political debate into violent *gangsterismo*. Since political competition led to opportunities for personal enrichment, the battle over political positions and access to government sinecures often turned into violent gang wars worthy of Hollywood played out on the streets of Havana (Farber 2003, 2006).

When former *Auténtico* stalwart Eduardo Chibás became aware of the depth and breadth of *Auténtico* corruption, he made it his personal mission to investigate, expose, and publicize every last detail of it over the airwaves in his famous Sunday afternoon news broadcasts. In May 1947, Chibás also founded a new splinter party to give an organizational home to his campaign of criticism. Called the Orthodox Party (*Partido del Pueblo Cubano—Ortodoxo*), Chibás's party sought to make a "clean sweep" of *Auténtico* corruption with its broom logo and resounding slogan, *Vergüenza contra Dinero* ("shame against money").

On August 5, 1951, just a year shy of a national presidential election in which he was the leading candidate, Chibás vociferously denounced the corruption of *Auténtico* education minister Aurelio Sánchez Arango on his radio show. However, unable to produce definitive proof of his accusation, Chibás may have concluded that he had committed an unpardonable error. He then shouted what would be his last words as his radio address ended dramatically:

> Comrades of Orthodoxy, let us move forward! For economic independence, political freedom, and social justice! Sweep the thieves from the government! People of Cuba, rise up, and move forward! People of Cuba, wake up! This is my last call! (Chibás 2003: 299)

As he uttered these words, Chibás shot himself in the stomach, hoping that the sound of the shot would resound over the airwaves in a powerful, symbolic suicide attempt. Chibás's death days later and subsequent massive funeral acted as a symbolic burial of Cuban democracy itself.

Staggering toward the planned 1952 election without Cuba's most popular and charismatic public figure and after almost a decade of endemic graft and corruption, Cuban political life never arrived at that date with destiny. Instead, running a distant third in the coming election, Batista staged a bloodless coup ousting outgoing president Prío on March 10, 1952. Batista's coup—his third—was facilitated by the fact that he was but delivering "the *coup de grâce* to a moribund regime" (Pérez 1993: 83). He quickly suspended the 1940 constitution, dissolved congress, instituted a provisional government, and promised elections for the next year. Eight years of corruption made the *Auténticos* indefensible, and the death of Chibás had left the *Ortodoxos* defenseless. Mexican intellectual José Vasconcelos pronounced what is perhaps the best epitaph for the fall of Prío's presidency: "Prío fell like a rotten fruit, almost of its own weight" (Thomas 1998: 775). Such an epitaph could serve just as well for the entire Cuban democratic experiment from 1940 to 1952.

The fact that the planned 1952 election never took place frustrated a great many Cubans. One of those whose first run for a local elected office was upended by Batista's coup was a young, brilliant, ambitious, and exceedingly eloquent member of Chibás's Ortodoxo Party, who took the lesson of the coup to heart. He would never again run in an open, direct election, nor would he ever need to. A little more than a year later, living under Batista's unconstitutional dictatorship, he would take up arms instead. His name was Fidel Castro Ruz.

THE CUBAN INSURGENCY, 1953–1958: THE RISE OF FIDEL CASTRO

From Moncada to Granma, 1953–1955

Fidel Castro's dramatic entry into Cuban politics came just a year after Batista's 1952 coup. As fate would have it, this was also the centenary of Martí's birth in 1853. Castro's plan was to stage an audacious assault on the country's second most important army headquarters, the Moncada barracks in the far eastern city of Santiago de Cuba. Castro chose the city of Santiago and the date of July 26, 1953, for both strategic and symbolic reasons. Since July 26 marked the culmination of the weeklong carnival celebration in Cuba's second city, it was likely that the barracks would be left unguarded—or that any guards on duty would be either asleep or still drunk from the previous night's revelry. Furthermore, Castro knew that a revolt would have a much better chance of success if it began in the insular and historically neglected eastern province of Oriente. Having come of age in the province and studied as a boy in Santiago, Castro knew that his small band of guerrillas could beat a quick retreat into the fastness of the nearby Sierra Maestra mountains if necessary.

The 150 members of the attack force recruited by Castro were drawn, like their charismatic leader, from the youth wing of the Ortodoxo Party. Only two members of his force were or had ever been Communist Party members: Castro's younger brother Raúl and one other. The rest were likely motivated by their rejection of Batista's illegitimate rule and by the progressive nationalist ideals of the Ortodoxo Party: social justice and anticorruption, but also anticommunism. Castro did not believe that his handful of men could win a war against the much larger and better equipped Cuban Army. However, he hoped that such an audacious attack, if successful, could inspire a nationwide uprising against the dictator and lead to the regime's eventual downfall (Szulc 1986: 241).

Castro's plan was to take Moncada and then broadcast Chibás's "Last Call" over the city's radio stations. However, it was not his victory at Moncada that electrified the Cuban people, leading to mass rebellion and eventual revolution, but his defeat. This was no ordinary defeat. Batista's brutality in putting down the uprising and murdering most captured rebels afterward, combined with Castro's "spectacularly defiant stance afterward" (ibid.: 242), ignited the indignation of the Cuban people and led to an outpouring of support for the rebel cause and its charismatic leader.

After the attack, Batista declared that his brave soldiers had successfully repelled the rebels, most of whom were supposedly killed in battle. However, in the four days after the attack, 61 men were captured and then assassinated, most of them being first horribly tortured. Only eight rebels had actually died in combat. Castro was able to turn this brutality and duplicity into a powerful weapon with which he could expose Batista as a tyrant before the Cuban public. When Cuba's newspapers began to publish graphic pictures of bloody, dismembered, and mutilated bodies of scores of young Cuban men, the public discovered that Batista had not only ordered his army to brutalize and execute these brave young men but had then lied about it, trying to paint his own soldiers as brave defenders of the homeland.

A licensed lawyer and charismatic speaker, Castro refused the aid of Santiago's public defender and took on the task of his own defense. Batista moved to muffle the coverage of Castro's trial by holding the proceedings in the tiny examination room of a civilian hospital. However, the young journalist Marta Rojas, who sympathized with the rebels, took it upon herself to scribble down as much of Castro's mesmerizing speech as possible. Knowing that his guilt was predetermined and that the trial was aimed only at giving an impression of judicial impartiality, Castro decided not to defend his innocence. Instead, he used the trial as a public forum in which to meticulously and devastatingly indict the Batista regime itself.

Subsequently, Castro's defense speech became the expansive if conveniently vague political platform for his new movement, announcing his goals to the nation and exposing Batista's tyranny and hypocrisy. However, few Cubans heard Castro's message, given the new controls over the press. Because of that, over the next few months an embellished version of his speech was clandestinely distributed across the island in thousands of mimeographed copies. When Cubans read the words of this daring, charismatic figure, what they found was not only a litany of indictments against Batista's illegitimate regime but also a serious political program for national regeneration.

For example, Castro indicated that had his attack been successful, he would have immediately decreed "five revolutionary laws": the restoration of the 1940 Constitution; agrarian reform; 30 percent profit sharing for workers in large enterprises;

MONCADA AND CASTRO'S "HISTORY WILL ABSOLVE ME" SPEECH

Taking place at the close of Santiago de Cuba's carnival celebration and exactly 100 years after the birth of José Martí, Fidel Castro's attack on the Moncada military barracks was as audacious as it was disastrous. The 83-man attack force was immediately divided and most fighters were killed in the firefight or hunted down over the next few days. However, Batista's brutality came to Castro's aid when it became public that only eight rebels were killed in combat while another 61 were in fact murdered in captivity. With this public relations victory in hand, Castro wisely turned his own trial a few months later into an unreal public indictment of the Batista regime. First, he listed the many needed reforms that his group would have enacted had they been successful, and then he meticulously outlined the crimes of the Batista regime ending his defense with the ringing declaration, "Condemn me. It does not matter. History will absolve me."

entitlement to a share of 55 percent of the profits of Cuba's powerful sugar mills for Cuba's *colonos*; and the confiscation of all property obtained through corruption. Additionally, Castro reassured the Cuban public that he intended to maintain a policy "of close solidarity with the democratic peoples of this continent." Finally, he promised to address the intractable socioeconomic problems common to under-developed countries like Cuba: "The problem of the land, the problem of industri-alization, the problem of housing, the problem of unemployment, the problem of education, and the problem of people's health" (Castro 2003: 314).

Throughout his speech, Castro was also at pains to pledge that these new revolu-tionary laws and many ambitious goals would be accomplished together "with the restoration of civil liberties and political democracy." He concluded with the rousing declaration: "Condemn me. It does not matter. History will absolve me." Upon the close of the trial, Castro and his followers were sentenced to 15 years in prison on the Isle of Pines. They served less than two (Bardach and Conte Agüero 2007).

After the failed assault on the Moncada barracks, Batista called for elections in 1954, in an attempt to legitimize his unconstitutional rule. In those elections he was ratified as president. His main opponent was once again Grau San Martín. How-ever, because he did not want to legitimize a clearly flawed and unfair contest, Grau dropped out of the campaign two days before the election. Upon taking office in February 1955, Batista ended martial law, restored the 1940 Constitution, allowed for the freedom of the press, and granted amnesty to political prisoners, including the rebels who attacked the Moncada barracks. He then tried to consolidate his il-legitimate regime by instituting a program of economic development, which—along with stabilizing of the world price of sugar—did achieve many of its economic aims. However, Batista's continued opposition to political dialogue with his opponents ruined any chance of a negotiated settlement to the constitutional impasse.

Castro was freed along with his entire rebel force at noon on Sunday, May 15, 1955. Upon release, he quickly organized his group of followers into the *Movimiento 26 de Julio* (26th of July Movement, M-26-7). Realizing that Batista had effectively co-opted the legal opposition, Castro decided that clandestine armed struggle was his only option. On July 7, Castro left for exile in Mexico, knowing that he was a marked man in Cuba. Upon his departure, the magazine *Bohemia*, his ally in public relations in the wake of the Moncada debacle two years earlier, published his defiant parting message to the Cuban people: "From trips such as this, one does not return or else one returns with the tyranny beheaded at one's feet" (Quoted in Szulc 1986).

After just 15 months of fundraising, training, and coordination with the move-ment's growing clandestine wing back on the island, Castro and 81 of his fellow would-be revolutionaries set sail from Mexico for Cuba. The group departed from the small port town of Tuxpan, near Veracruz, in late November 1956 aboard the *Granma*, a yacht purchased from an American expatriate and named, presumably, after his grandmother. The small yacht was far too small to comfortably hold the 82 rebels, more than three times its capacity of 25 passengers. Overcrowded as the yacht was, things could have been much worse, since as many as 50 other rebels had to remain behind in Mexico.

The group's planned arrival at Playa Las Coloradas on the southwestern tip of Oriente was delayed for two days on account of bad weather. During the unantici-pated seven days at sea, most of the men became seasick, one fell overboard, and

---

ERNESTO GUEVARA DE LA SERNA BECOMES "EL CHE"

Soon after arriving in Mexico City, at a party celebrating the second anniversary of the Moncada attack, Castro met an Argentine doctor named Ernesto Guevara de la Serna with whom he shared an immediate sympathy. Guevara exposed Castro to a more radical political ideology than he had perhaps up to then contemplated, and Castro gave Guevara exactly the revolutionary cause for which he had been traveling across half the continent to find. Returning home in the morning after a marathon 10-hour conversation with Castro, Guevara told his then wife, Hilda, that he had met "a great political leader, . . . a master of great tenacity and firmness. . . . If anything has happened in Cuba since Martí, it is Fidel Castro: He will make the revolution. We agreed profoundly. . . . Only a person like him would I be disposed to help in everything" (Szulc 1986: 336). Guevara joined Castro's guerrilla movement as a doctor. He later opted for the role of a soldier and quickly became known to his fellows as "*El Che*," based on his habit of addressing everyone he met in Argentine slang, "*¡Che!*"

---

most supplies ran out. Just before dawn on December 2, 1956, the *Granma* suddenly became lodged in a mud bank more than a mile from the beach at Las Coloradas.

The crew was forced to leave the ship and most of their supplies behind and wade ashore. As they made their way through the maze of submerged tree roots, razor sharp sticks and vines, and swarms of ravenous mosquitoes, they were detected, and a merciless military bombardment began. The attack force of 82 was quickly reduced to just 18 fighters who managed to regroup in the Sierra Maestra (though revolutionary tradition dictates that there were an apostolic 12). Despite such an inauspicious beginning, Castro had been true to his pledge to return to Cuba to resume the insurrection before the end of 1956.

The Long Road from the Sierra Maestra to Havana, 1956–1958

After regrouping with his handful of men now relatively safely hidden in the fastness of the mountains, Castro realized that they needed only to survive, since their very existence within Cuba constituted a challenge to the regime. Despite losing more than 80 percent of his fighting force, nearly all of Castro's leadership structure remained intact, including most of those who later became *comandantes* during the war: Che Guevara, Raúl Castro, Juan Almeida, Ramiro Valdés, and Camilo Cienfuegos. For his part, Batista aimed to finish off the survivors of Castro's party, ordering his soldiers to remove peasants forcibly from the foothills of the Sierra Maestra, much as Spanish General Weyler had done 60 years before. However, as with Weyler, this policy backfired, because it only enlarged the rebels' "liberated" territory and made it easier for them to strike and then disappear into the forest.

In order to maximize the impact of his tiny rebel force, Castro and his followers developed two strategies that would help them defeat Batista's 40,000-member military: guerrilla warfare and propaganda. Used successfully 60 years earlier by

Cuba's revered *mambises*, guerrilla warfare was a strategic attempt to transform the liabilities of small numbers and weak firepower into assets by mastering the environment and effectively utilizing a hit-and-run strategy. In his many writings on irregular military tactics, Che Guevara coined the term *foco* (focus) to describe this method of warfare. Guevara also emphasized what he touted as the greatest asset of the irregular rebel army in the Sierra Maestra, which was that poor peasants, especially in isolated rural areas, could constitute a "tremendous potential revolutionary force" if presented with the right tactics and leadership.

By early 1957, the arrival of Castro's forces had become common knowledge in Cuba and was on the verge of becoming international news. However, Batista had ordered a news blackout within Cuba censoring anything about the survival of the rebel forces. In fact, Batista faltered in trying to project an image of absolute confidence in his military, making the mistake of insisting to an expectant press that he had defeated the rebels and that Fidel Castro was among the dead. Seizing this golden propaganda opportunity, the urban leadership of the M-26-7 in Havana approached the bureau chief of *The New York Times*, Ruby Hart Phillips, to request that a reporter be sent to the Sierra Maestra to interview Castro. Reluctant to go herself since she made her home on the island, Phillips contacted Herbert Matthews, a veteran war correspondent and respected member of the editorial board of *The New York Times*.

This photo, filed June 1957, is believed to be the only existing one of Fidel Castro, leader of Cuba's 26th of July Movement, with his top commanders made at a secret base near the coast. The group includes the entire top group of "comandantes" of the guerilla army. From right are Capt. Juan Almeida, Capt. George Sotus, Fidel Castro, Capt. Raúl Castro, the leader's younger brother (kneeling in the foreground), Capt. Guillermo García (wearing helmet at left), Lt. Universo Sánchez, Castro's adjutant (third from left), and Ernesto "Che" Guevara (second from left). (Bettmann/Corbis)

Thus was born Castro's second major public relations coup following his Moncada turnabout four years earlier. This time his audience would be global, and he was ready (DePalma 2006; Phillips 1959).

Matthews traveled to the Sierra from Havana in mid-February, feigning a holiday with his wife. After a legendary interview with Castro in the foothills of the Sierra in the early dawn of February 17, 1957, Matthews published the first of three articles a week later on Sunday, February 24. Projecting an image of military strength and popular support, Castro led Matthews to believe that he had a large number of men under arms. Casually mentioning the existence of two other guerrilla camps, Castro had a fellow soldier interrupt him with the news that a liaison from "column number two" had just arrived (Szulc 1986: 409). In fact, at the time of the interview there were still just 18 men in Castro's force.

Captivated, Matthews described the sharp political mind and "overwhelming personality" of a man he glowingly characterized as "a powerful six-footer, olive-skinned, full-faced, with a straggly beard." He added, "It is easy to see that his men adored him and also to see why he has caught the imagination of the youth of Cuba all over the island. Here was an educated, dedicated fanatic, a man of ideals, of courage, and of remarkable qualities of leadership" (Matthews 2003: 329). Matthews also noted Castro's criticism of the sale of U.S. military equipment to Batista, which he was illegally using against the guerrillas. Finally, Castro indicated that his revolt was motivated only by democratic, pro-American goals, hoping to positively influence public opinion and quell any doubts about his commitment to democracy or desire for friendly relations with the United States.

After this laudatory report from within the Sierra Maestra, a place supposedly under tight military control, Batista exacerbated his problems by having his defense minister publicly assert that the article was a fabrication. However, the lies, brutality, and incompetence of his administration were exposed once again when *The New York Times* published a follow-up article featuring a grainy photo of Matthews standing beside a very alive Fidel Castro, each man sporting a heavy coat, cap, and signature Cuban cigar (De Palma 2006).

Over the next year, the Sierra rebel force gained momentum as Castro gradually distinguished himself as the most important opposition leader. On March 13, 1957, the student-led Revolutionary Directorate (DR) carried out an audacious attack on the presidential palace in Havana, with 100 men attempting to break past the guards and blast their way up into the third-floor presidential apartments where Batista was hiding. Despite successfully breaking into the palace and making it to the interior presidential offices, the assassination force could not penetrate to the third floor, since it was accessible only by a single elevator. Thirty-five rebels were killed in the attack, with only three managing to escape. Worse still, in the bloodbath that followed, most of the DR's leadership including its figurehead, José Antonio Echeverría, was killed.

While the attack made Echeverría into a martyr, it left the DR significantly weakened while greatly strengthening both Batista's base and Castro's position as head of the opposition. In the days following the attack, Batista received visits from a parade of powerful well-wishers who assured him of their continued support. Repression against student activists increased thereafter under the guise of investigating the attack. "Had the attack succeeded," reasons Szulc, "it would have left Fidel Castro in his mountains as a suddenly irrelevant factor in the revolutionary equation" (1986: 417). However, the first significant rebel victory against the army in the hamlet of El Uvero in the Sierra took place soon after the failed DR attack. As a result, "Castro's rivals had all been severely weakened or destroyed by the middle of 1957, and his tiny guerrilla army in the Sierra—still with only a hundred men in May—was now the only viable insurgent force on the island" (Gott 2004: 160).

Castro's forces grew and split up in order to bring the revolution across the entire expanse of eastern Cuba. By March 1958, Raúl Castro's 65-man Second Front had established a foothold in the northeastern Sierra Cristal, while Juan Almeida managed to open another front north of Santiago. Likewise, Camilo Cienfuegos and Che Guevara departed the Sierra in mid-1958 to penetrate the west. As victory followed victory, Batista's government was forced to concede ever greater areas of "liberated territory" to the rebels. Batista was also faced with a series of new uprisings within the military, the most important of which was the successful takeover of the naval base at Cienfuegos. Although Batista's army was able to crush the revolt using B-26 bombers provided by the United States, this illegal use of U.S. weaponry provoked a U.S. arms embargo.

Batista launched a massive offensive against the rebels in the summer of 1958. However, the rebels managed to fend off repeated attacks against their mountain positions, outlasting the much larger and better equipped Cuban Army. The offensive ended on August 6, 1958. Just 321 men had held out against thousands of Cuban soldiers, who suffered as many as 1,000 casualties and lost scores of soldiers to rebel capture. The guerrillas' success was the last major turning point in the guerrilla phase of the revolution. In July and August, Castro began to implement an invasion of western Cuba. Guevara set out for Las Villas province, where he would score an important victory in Santa Clara. Camilo Cienfuegos was sent to Pinar del Río by way of the Escambray Mountains to assert control over a group of independent guerrillas there.

Two things were now clear. Batista's days were numbered, and under Castro's leadership the M-26-7 had achieved clear hegemony over all other revolutionary factions. Batista tried to hold on in the waning months of 1958 with a last-ditch election that fooled no one. Seeing the writing on the wall, the United States sent a secret emissary to plead with Batista to hand power over to a moderate junta, so as to prevent the looming victory of the unpredictable Castro. Batista stubbornly refused, and Guevara's decisive victory in Santa Clara in December of 1959 sealed his fate. He reluctantly boarded a plane on December 31, leaving the country in the hands of Castro's bearded rebels as a new year, and a new era, dawned over the island.

A Peak behind the Insurrectionary Curtain

During the fight against Batista, a series of important political negotiations unfolded within the broad insurrectional coalition. Understanding them helps explain the ultimate turn the Cuban revolution took away from the democratic and popular process toward the current totalitarian system. Resistance to Batista's coup arose from main two quarters: insurrectional and civic. While they agreed on the need to denounce Batista's breach of the 1940 Constitution, they parted ways over strategy and leadership. The insurrectional group prioritized revolutionary violence against Batista's regime while the civic group favored negotiations with it. The first approach was famously debuted on July 26, 1953, with Castro's dramatic, suicidal assault on Moncada. The second took shape in January, 1954, with the formation of the Civic Resistance Movement led by José Miró Cardona, president of the National Bar Association and a member of the *Sociedad Amigos de la República* (Society of Friends of the Republic, SAR).

During the spring of 1957, Frank País (1934–1957)—a founding member of the 26th of July Movement—proposed that Castro form a provisional government together with the leading figures of the civic movement (Buch 2002). To this end, a meeting was held in the Sierra Maestra in July 1957, between leaders of the M-26-7 and José Miró Cardona, Raúl Chibás—president of the Orthodox Party and brother of the late Eduardo Chibás—and Felipe Pazos, former president of the Cuban National Bank. The meeting produced the jointly signed agreement *Manifiesto al pueblo de Cuba* (Manifesto to the Cuban people). Chibás and Pazos then traveled to the United States and, in October 1957, signed the Pact of Miami with other civic associations in exile. Because this second agreement did not correspond to the ideas set forth in the first, it was rejected by the M-26-7 leadership. Another meeting was held in Venezuela, where the appropriately named "Revolutionary-Civic Front" was created under the Pact of Caracas. This agreement designated José Miró Cardona as the Front's Coordinator, and approved Manuel Urrutia Lleó as Cuba's provisional president. This is the same man who, as chief justice of Santiago de Cuba's criminal court, issued a brave dissenting vote of acquittal in the case against Fidel Castro for his assault on Moncada.

On a parallel front, in February 1958 Cuba's bishops called for a ceasefire and proposed a Commission of Conciliation, which was rejected by Castro. In March 1958, 43 civic associations headed by José Miró Cardona demanded the resignation of Batista, the dissolution of Congress, and the formation of a provisional government. The answer of the M-26-7 to these and other civic efforts came in a May 1958 meeting held in the Sierra Maestra, in which Castro was appointed executive secretary general of the M-26-7 and commander-in-chief of all revolutionary forces—thus establishing a policy of unified command centralized in his person.

Of course, on January 1, 1959, it was the insurrectional—not the civic—line which triumphed. Still, Urrutia assumed the presidency and on January 2, he publicly appointed Fidel Castro commander-in-chief of the Revolutionary Armed Forces. On the following day, the first cabinet was formed, made up jointly of civic and revolutionary figures, with Miró Cardona serving as prime minister. Then, at Castro's insistence, the 1940 Constitution was changed instead of being restored—without a popular referendum—to confer the role of Head of Government on the prime minister, and bestow the functions of Congress on the newly created Council of Ministers. Ironically, this amendment was very similar to the one Batista himself had implemented after carrying out his coup in 1952.

A few days after the constitutional modification, disagreements between Urrutia and Miró Cardona led Castro to step in as prime minister, thereby legally concentrating almost all state power in his hands. Once the government was under his control— and parallel to the first widely popular and democratic revolutionary decrees—there began a slow but sure process of dismantling the civil framework that had been slowly built up since the Pact of Zanjón in 1878, concentrating all property in the hands of the state.

"THE REVOLUTION BEGINS NOW": 1959–1961

Observers unacquainted with the complexities of the first three years of the Cuban Revolution often assume that Castro marched into Havana on January 8, 1959, a confirmed communist and a committed enemy of the United States. However, Castro's political ideology and foreign policy remained quite ambiguous, if increasingly radical, during his first years in power. In fact, socialist and anti-American rhetoric was much more important in consolidating a revolution under attack *after* January 1959 than it had been *during* the movement to overthrow Batista (Domínguez 1978). In January, Castro took up residence in Havana and declared his desire to remain the head of the military only. He moved quickly to create a new, rather moderate cabinet of ministers made up of leading liberal professionals who had opposed Batista but who were neither bearded guerrillas nor members of the Communist Party.

On the other hand, it was immediately clear that Castro's ambitions were not limited simply to removing Batista from power. He rejected the possibility of a military junta or a new round of U.S. intervention as had occurred in 1898 and again in 1933. To prevent either eventuality, he called for a general strike that would paralyze the country and allow his guerrilla forces the time to rally the population and converge on Havana. This time, the strike was absolute. "The history of 1898 will not be repeated," declared Castro over the radio on January 1, referring to how the U.S. occupying force had not allowed Cuban rebels to enter Santiago following Spain's defeat. Upon arriving in Cuba's second city on January 2, Castro marched into the Moncada barracks with wild crowds celebrating as he symbolically took possession of the fortress where he had begun the armed struggle five years earlier.

That evening, Castro spoke to a delirious throng of supporters, indicating that the real revolution was only now just beginning. "The revolution begins now," he announced. "This time, luckily for Cuba, the Revolution will truly come into power. It will not be like in 1898, when the North Americans came and made themselves the masters of our country" (Szulc 1986: 459). Surprisingly, the United States responded by recognizing the new Cuban government almost immediately. However, the revolutionary honeymoon would be over almost before it started and by 1961 U.S.-Cuba relations would end in a bitter, acrimonious, and seemingly irrevocable divorce.

The Dismantling of Civil Society

In January 1959, the public mandates of governors, mayors, and city council members were extinguished; the courts dissolved; magistrates and judges removed from office; and the key democratic principle of the division of powers abolished. The new ministers from the civic resistance movement, who formed part of the first cabinet in 1959, were replaced. A few days later, Castro publicly announced his resignation as prime minister—reasoning that constant conflicts with President Urrutia made it impossible for him to continue. In fact, Castro's public denunciation undermined Urrutia's already weak base so much that it was he who ended up resigning. Osvaldo

Dorticós Torrado was then appointed as president, and on July 26, 1959, Castro returned as prime minister.

After the traditional parties disappeared, the *Directorio Revolucionario 13 de Marzo* (March 13 Revolutionary Directorate, DR-13-M)—a key insurgent group often at odds with M-26-7—took over the presidential palace, the University of Havana, and the military base at San Antonio de los Baños. Unable to hold these strategic posts for very long, the DR disintegrated as an armed force and was unable to challenge the M-26-7's dominance. After holding its Sixth National Congress in August 1960, the *Partido Socialista Popular* (Popular Socialist Party, PSP)—the only other surviving insurgent group with the capability of challenging M-26-7—also stood on the verge of disintegration. In March 1962, both groups were merged with the M-26-7, to form the *Organizaciones Revolucionarias Integradas* (Integrated Revolutionary Organizations, ORI), which after the substitution of Anibal Escalante as organizing secretary, had its leadership taken over by Castro.

In January 1963, the ORI was briefly renamed the *Partido Unido de la Revolución Socialista* (United Party of the Socialist Revolution, PURS), and in October 1965, it became the *Partido Comunista de Cuba* (Cuba Communist Party, PCC), with Castro as its secretary general. From that moment on—completing a masterful and inexorable cycle of purging, merging, and unifying the revolution under his uncontested leadership—Castro served simultaneously as the leader of the revolution, the commander-in-chief of the armed forces, prime minister, and secretary general of the PCC. Only the presidency—formally held by the pliable Dorticós—remained out of his reach.

The success of the general strike called by Castro on January 1, 1959—to avoid being cheated out of his victory—made controlling the union movement a decisive factor in the revolution's consolidation. On January 22, 1959, the preexistent CTC was dissolved and replaced by a new Revolutionary CTC. The second blow came at the CTC's Tenth Congress in November, 1959. When Secretary General David Salvador Manso was asked to explain the interests and projects of the workers, he simply and emphatically replied: "Whatever the *Comandante* [Fidel Castro] says," indicating the degree to which the CTC had become beholden to political power. Finally, at the Eleventh Congress in 1960, a single candidate was proposed for each position removing any real democratic choice for union members, and the elected leadership proceeded to give away almost all their historic achievements in terms of autonomy and benefits. A once fierce and powerful Cuban labor movement had fallen completely under state control with the CTC transformed into an arm of the government, not an independent bulwark that would defend the interests of workers.

In the same way, all youth associations disappeared to be replaced first by the *Asociación de Jóvenes Rebeldes* (Young Rebels Association), and later by the *Unión de Jóvenes Comunistas* (Young Communists Union). Cuba's numerous women's organizations were also eliminated to give birth to the single, unified, and state controlled *Federación de Mujeres Cubanas* (Federation of Cuban Women) directed for nearly all of its history by Raúl Castro's wife, Vilma Espín. Peasant associations, such as the *Cosecheros de Tabaco* (Tobacco Harvesters) and the *Asociación Nacional Campesina* (National Peasants' Association) were replaced in January 1961 by the *Asociación Nacional de Colonos* (National Settlers Association), which was later renamed the *Asociación Nacional de Agricultores Pequeños* (National Association of

Small Farmers). As for business associations, in one stroke 44 of them were eliminated. The rest disappeared, or were subordinated to the objectives of the state. University autonomy, guaranteed in article 53 of the 1940 constitution, also ceased to exist. The press, radio, and television, Cuba's vast, modern network of cinemas, and publishing and cultural institutions, all came under the control of the Cuban Communist Party, which gradually unified them under the watchful eye of the state and transformed them—with rare exceptions—into organs of propaganda.

The damage caused by the elimination of civil society—which can be defined as the range of associations, institutions, and public spaces for interaction, debate, and citizen participation independent of, though not necessarily in opposition to, the state—is revealed by Castro's own words at his 1952 trial for the assault on Moncada, where he described pre-Batista Cuba, saying:

> I am going to tell you a story. There was once a republic. It had its constitution, its laws, its liberties, a president, a congress, and courts; everyone could meet, associate, speak, and write freely. The government did not satisfy the people, but the people could change it. . . . There was a respected and heeded public opinion, and all problems of common interest were freely discussed. There were political parties, radio shows representing different political tendencies, polemical TV programs, and public demonstrations . . . (Castro 2008)

Castro was asking his listeners to imagine a society without any of the mentioned characteristics; just the kind of society that subsequently emerged under his version of the revolution.

The Concentration of Ownership

Parallel to the dismantling of civil society, the concentration of property in state hands began. The first step was the "recovery of misappropriated assets"—an expropriation of the assets of officials of the deposed Batista regime. Then in May 1959, the first agrarian reform law was decreed. Its stated purpose was to eliminate *latifundia* (large estates), and give ownership of the land to those who worked it. The law limited the size of agricultural holdings to 30 *caballerías* (a *caballería* is equal to 13.4 hectares or 33 acres) and mainly impacted foreign and national interests with much greater holdings. In 1960, all American companies on the island were nationalized, followed by large national companies. In 1962, the second agrarian reform law was issued, and it reduced the maximum size from 30 to just 5 caballerías. Finally, the process to eliminate all forms of private property reached its climax in March 1968, with the so-called Revolutionary Offensive, which eliminated in a single stroke the more than 50,000 remaining independent retail outlets, corner stores, bodegas, bars, night clubs, and family run businesses.

The revolution's ability to successfully orchestrate such a rapid and complete concentration of property and power in the hands of the state was made possible by the weakness of the institutions of Cuban civil society after the corruption of the *Auténtico* years and the repression and illegitimacy of the Batista regime. The turn toward totalitarianism was also possible because it took place against the tense backdrop of the Cold War and the battle between the great powers of the United States and the Soviet Union. The often arrogant approach with which successive U.S. administrations dealt with Cuba exacerbated the deterioration of bilateral relations, with external conflicts tending to weaken internal ones. The Castro regime has skillfully taken advantage of this ongoing dispute to further eliminate civil society and independent civic spaces with the justification that "*En una plaza sitiada, desentir es tración*" (In a state of siege, to dissent is treason). Opposition parties or any such political organizations are illegal and dissent is criminalized. Even today, more than 50 years later, to publicly criticize the revolution or to stand squarely outside of it—while living on the island—is to risk being labeled an "anti-Cuban mercenary" or a "lackey of U.S. imperialism" and suffer the consequences. So negative has been the outcome that Cuba—which had been a regional leader in enshrining progressive civil and political rights in its 1940 Constitution—has receded to a state of civil liberties similar to that which existed under Spanish colonialism.

In 1960, Washington responded to Cuba's nationalizations by authorizing the president to cut the sugar quota and secretly prepare an expeditionary force of exiles. In January 1961, the United States broke off diplomatic relations with Cuba, and sponsored the abortive landing at the Bay of Pigs in April of that year. In 1962, it engineered Cuba's expulsion from the Organization of American States, tightened the partial trade embargo that had been put in place in 1960, and ordered a naval blockade in response to the installation of Soviet missiles in Cuba in October 1962. Between 1961 and 1965, the United States provided material support to thousands of opponents who took up arms in the Escambray mountains and other regions around the country aiming to mount another revolution—this time against Fidel Castro. These measures—along with others added later such as the 1996 Helms-Burton Act and the 2003 creation of the "Commission for Assistance to a Free Cuba"—are contrary to the norms of international relations, and therefore illegitimate in matter of international law. For its part, three days after the United States reduced its sugar quota in 1960, Cuba expropriated all U.S. companies on the island and proudly proclaimed the socialist character of the revolution. "What the imperialists cannot forgive us for," declared Castro to a massive crowd in April 1961 on the eve of the Bay of Pigs invasion, "is that we have made a socialist revolution under the nose of the United States."

BIBLIOGRAPHY

Aguilar, Luis E. 1972. *Cuba, 1933: Prologue to Revolution*. Ithaca: Cornell University Press.

Aguilar, Luis E. 1993. "Cuba, c. 1860–1930." In Leslie Bethell, ed., *Cuba: A Short History*. Cambridge: Cambridge University Press.

Aguirre, Sergio. 1974. *Eco de Caminos*. Havana: Editorial de Ciencias Sociales.

Barcia, María del Carmen, Gloria García, and Eduardo Torres-Cuevas. 1996. *Las luchas por la independencia nacional y las transformaciones estructurales 1868–1898*. Havana: Editora Política.

Barcia Zequeira, María del Carmen. 2003. *La otra familia. Parientes, redes y descendencia de los esclavos en Cuba*. Havana: Casa de las Américas.

Bardach, Ann Louise, and Luis Conte Agüero. 2007. *The Prison Letters of Fidel Castro*. New York: Nation Books.

Barreiro, José. 2003. "Survival Stories." In Aviva Chomsky, Barry Car, and Pamela Maria Smorkaloff, eds., *The Cuba Reader: History, Culture, Politics*. Durham: Duke University Press.

Benjamin, Jules. 1990. *The United States and the Origins of the Cuban Revolution: An Empire of Liberty in an Age of National Liberation*. Princeton: Princeton University Press.

Buch Rodríguez, Luis M. 1999. *Gobierno Revolucionario Cubano: génesis y primeros pasos*. Havana: Editorial de Ciencias Sociales.

Buch Rodríguez, Luis M. 2002. *Otros pasos del gobierno revolucionario*. Havana: Editorial de Ciencias Sociales.

Castro Fernández, Silvio. 2002. *La masacre de los independientes de color en 1912*. Havana: Editorial de Ciencias Sociales.

Castro, Fidel. 2003. "History Will Absolve Me." In Aviva Chomsky, Barry Car, and Pamela Maria Smorkaloff, eds., *The Cuba Reader: History, Culture, Politics*. Durham: Duke University Press.

Castro, Fidel. 2008. *La historia me absolverá*. Annotated edition. Havana: Oficina del Consejo de Estado.

Chibás, Eduardo A. 2003. "The Last Call." In Aviva Chomsky, Barry Car, and Pamela Maria Smorkaloff, eds., *The Cuba Reader: History, Culture, Politics.* Durham: Duke University Press.

Cluster, Dick, and Rafael Hernández. 2006. *History of Havana*. New York: Palgrave Macmillan.

Córdova, Efrén. 1995. *Clase trabajadora y movimiento sindical en Cuba*. Florida: Ediciones Universal.

Córdova, Efrén. 2000. "Política laboral y legislación del trabajo." *Encuentro de la Cultura Cuba* no. 24 (Spring): 212–222.

Crespo Roque, Nelson. 2005. *El pensamiento fundacional de la nación cubana en el siglo XIX*. (Compilación de las memorias del encuentro "El pensamiento fundacional de la nación cubana en el siglo XIX.") Havana: Equipo de Reflexión y Servicio del Arzobispado de La Habana, May.

Dana, Richard. 2003. "The Trade in Chinese Laborers." In Aviva Chomsky, Barry Car, and Pamela Maria Smorkaloff, eds., *The Cuba Reader: History, Culture, Politics*. Durham: Duke University Press

De Céspedes, Carlos Manuel. 2003. *Señal en la noche*. Santiago de Cuba: Editorial Oriente.

De la Fuente, Alejandro. 2000. *Una nación para todos. Raza, desigualad y política en Cuba. 1900–2000*. Madrid: Editorial Colibrí.

DePalma, Anthony. 2006. *The Man Who Invented Fidel: Castro, Cuba, and Herbert L. Matthews of the New York Times*. New York: Public Affairs.

Departamento de Orientación Revolucionaria del CC del PCC. 1976. *Constitución de la República de Cuba*. Havana.

Díaz, Duanel. 2003. *Mañach o la República*. Havana: Editorial Letras Cubanas.

Domínguez, Jorge I. 1993. "Cuba since 1959." In Leslie Bethell, ed. *Cuba: A Short History*. Cambridge: Cambridge University Press.

Domínguez, Jorge I. 1978. *Cuba: Order and Revolution*. Cambridge: Harvard University Press.

Echerri, Vicente. 2012 "Los ingleses en La Habana," August 14. http://www.penultimosdias.com/2012/08/14/los-ingleses-en-la-habana. *Accessed August 14, 2012.*

Farber, Samuel. 2003. "The Political Gangster." In Aviva Chomsky, Barry Car, and Pamela Maria Smorkaloff, eds., *The Cuba Reader: History, Culture, Politics*. Durham: Duke University Press.

Farber, Samuel. 2006. *The Origins of the Cuban Revolution Reconsidered*. Chapel Hill: University of North Carolina Press.

Fernández Robaina, Tomás. 1994. *El negro en Cuba, 1902–1958*. Havana: Editorial de Ciencias Sociales.

*Gaceta Oficial de la República de Cuba.*1992. No. 7. Havana, Saturday, August 1.

Gott, Richard. 2004. *Cuba: A New History*. New Haven: Yale University Press.

Guanche Pérez, Jesús. 1999. *Chinese Presence in Cuba*. Havana: Ediciones GEO.

Guerra, Ramiro. 1970. *Azúcar y Población en las Antillas*. Havana: Editorial de Ciencias Sociales.

Guerra, Ramiro and José María Pérez Cabrera. 1952. *Historia de la nación cubana. Tomo I: Culturas primitivas, descubrimiento, conquista y colonización*. Havana: Editorial Historia de la Nación Cubana, S.A

Guerra, Ramiro et al. 1962. *Manual de historia de Cuba. Economía, Sociedad y Política desde su descubrimiento hasta 1868 y un apéndice con la historia contemporánea*. Havana: Consejo Nacional de Cultura.

Guevara, Ernesto. 1969. "Guerrilla Warfare: A Method." In Rolando E. Bonachea and Nelson P. Valdés, eds., *Che: Selected Works of Ernesto Guevara*, pp. 89–103. Cambridge: MIT Press.

Ibarra Cuesta, Jorge. 2004. *Varela el precursor, un estudio de época*. Havana: Editorial de Ciencias Sociales.

Ichaso, Francisco. 1957. "Los presidentes de Cuba Libre." *Diario de La Marina*. Special 125th anniversary edition. September.

Kuethe, Allan J. 1986. *Cuba, 1753–1815: Crown, Military, and Society*. Knoxville: University of Tennessee Press.

López Sánchez, Tomás. 1964. *Tomás Romay y el origen de la ciencia en Cuba*. Havana: Academia de Ciencias.

Martí, José. 1963. *Obras completas. Tomo 8*. Havana: Editorial Nacional de Cuba.

Martí, José. 2000. *Obras escogidas en tres tomos*. Havana: Editorial de Ciencias Sociales.

Martí, José. 2002. *José Martí: Selected Writings*. Edited and translated by Esther Allen. New York: Penguin Books.

Martínez, Urbano. 1997. *Domingo del Monte y su tiempo*. Havana: Ediciones Unión.

Matthews, Herbert. 2003. "The Cuban Story in *The New York Times*." In Aviva Chomsky, Barry Car, and Pamela Maria Smorkaloff, eds., *The Cuba Reader: History, Culture, Politics*. Durham: Duke University Press.

Moreno Fraginals, Manuel. 1978. *El ingenio*. Havana: Editorial de Ciencias Sociales.

Moreno Fraginals, Manuel. 1995. *Cuba/España, España/Cuba. Historia Común*. Barcelona: Grijalbo Mondadori.

Ortiz, Fernando. 1943. "Por la integración cubana de blancos y negros." *Tomado de la Revista Ultra* (Havana) 13, no. 77 (January): 69–76.

Ortiz, Fernando. 1991. *Estudios etnológicos*. Havana: Editorial de Ciencias Sociales.

Ortiz, Fernando. 1995. *Cuban Counterpoint: Tobacco and Sugar*. Durham: Duke University Press.

Ortiz, Fernando. 1996. *Los negros esclavos*. Havana: Editorial de Ciencias Sociales.

Partido Comunista de Cuba. 1976. *Constitución de la República de Cuba. Tesis y Resoluciones*. Havana: Departamento de Orientación Revolucionaria del Partido Comunista de Cuba.

Pérez, Louis A., Jr. 1993. "Cuba, c. 1930–1959." In Leslie Bethell, ed., *Cuba: A Short History*. New York: Cambridge University Press.

Pérez, Louis A., Jr. 1995. *Cuba: Between Reform and Revolution* (second edition). New York: Oxford University Press.

Pérez, Louis A., Jr. 1998. *The War of 1898: The United States and Cuba in History and Historiography*. Chapel Hill: University of North Carolina Press.

Pérez, Louis A. 2005. *Política, campesinos y gente de color: la "Guerra de Razas" de 1912 en Cuba*. Havana: Editorial de Ciencias Sociales.

Pérez de la Riva, Juan. 2003. "A World Destroyed." In Aviva Chomsky, Barry Car, and Pamela Maria Smorkaloff, eds., *The Cuba Reader: History, Culture, Politics*. Durham: Duke University Press.

Pérez Landa, Rufino. 1957. *Vida pública de Martín Morúa Delgado*. Havana: Academia de Historia.

Pérez-Stable, Marifeli. 1999. *The Cuban Revolution: Origins, Course, and Legacy* (second edition). New York: Oxford University Press.

Phillips, Ruby Hart. 1935. *Cuban Sideshow*. Havana: Cuban Press.

Phillips, Ruby Hart. 1959. *Cuba: Island of Paradox*. New York: McDowell Obolensky.

Pichardo, Hortensia. 1980. *Documentos para la historia de Cuba*. Havana: Editorial de Ciencias Sociales.

Pittaluga, Gustavo. 1999. *Diálogos sobre el destino*. Havana: Editorial Félix Varela.

Ponte, Domingo. 1937. *Arango y Parreño estadista colonial cubano*. Havana: Edición del Centenario.

Ramírez Cañedo, Elier, and Carlos Joane Rosario Grasso. 2008. *El autonomismo en las horas cruciales de la nación cubana*. Havana: Editorial de Ciencias Sociales.

Rodríguez, Carlos Rafael. 1962. "La Reforma Universitaria." *Cuba Socialista* no. 6, February.

Roig de Leuchsenring, Emilio. 1973. *Historia de la Enmienda Platt*. Havana: Editorial de Ciencias Sociales.

Roosevelt, Theodore. 2003. "The Platt Amendment." In Aviva Chomsky, Barry Car, and Pamela Maria Smorkaloff, eds., *The Cuba Reader: History, Culture, Politics*. Durham: Duke University Press.

Saco, José Antonio. 1982. *Acerca de la esclavitud y su historia*. Selection and introduction by Eduardo Torres Cuevas and Arturo Sorheguí. Havana: Editorial de Ciencias Sociales.

Saco, José Antonio. 2002. *Obras*. Havana: Biblioteca de clásicos cubanos, Imagen Contemporánea.

Saco, José Antonio. 2002. *Historia de la esclavitud*, vol. I. Havana: Biblioteca de clásicos cubanos. Ediciones Imágenes Contemporáneas.

Sanguily, Manuel. 1949. *Discursos y conferencias*. Havana: Publicaciones del Ministerio de Educación. Dirección de Cultura.

Sanguily, Manuel. 1962. *José de la Luz y Caballero; estudio crítico*. Havana: Consejo Nacional de Cultura.

Santovenia, E. 1949. *Cosmé de la Torriente, Estadista. Colección de Ensayos*. Havana.

Schlesinger, Stephen, and Stephen Kinzer. 1999. *Bitter Fruit: The Story of the American Coup in Guatemala* (expanded edition). Cambridge: David Rockefeller Center for Latin American Studies, Harvard University Press.

Scott, Rebecca. 1987. *La emancipación de los esclavos en Cuba: la transición al trabajo libre, 1860–1899*. Havana: Editorial de Ciencias Sociales.

Sierra, J.A. 2006. "History of Cuba. 1898." http://www.historyofcuba.com/cuba.htm. Accessed November 26.

Sublette, Ned. 2004. *Cuba and Its Music: From the First Drum to the Mambo*. Chicago: Chicago Review Press.

Suchlicki, Jaime. 1997. *Cuba: From Columbus to Castro and Beyond* (fourth edition). Washington DC: Brassey's.

Syrett, David, ed. 1970. *The Siege and Capture of Havana*. London: Navy Records Society.

Szulc, Tad. 1986. *Fidel: A Critical Portrait*. New York: Avon Books.

Thomas, Hugh. 1993. *Conquest: Montezuma, Cortés, and the Fall of Old Mexico*. New York: Touchstone.

Thomas, Hugh. 1998. *Cuba or the Pursuit of Freedom* (updated edition). New York: Da Capo Press.

Torras, Jacinto. 1984. *La Constituyente y la Economía Nacional. Obras Escogidas*, vol. I, p. 16. Havana: Editora Política.

Torres Cuevas, Eduardo. 2004. *Historia del pensamiento cubano*, vol. I. Havana: Editorial de Ciencias Sociales.

Torres Cuevas, Eduardo, and Oscar Loyola Vega. 2001. *Historia de Cuba 1492–1898, Formación y liberación de la nación*. Havana: Editorial Pueblo y Educación.

Varela, Félix. 1977. *Escritos políticos*. Havana: Editorial de Ciencias Sociales.

Varona, Enrique José. 1999. *Política y Sociedad*. Havana: Editorial de Ciencias Sociales.

Viñalet, Ricardo. 2001. *Fernando Ortiz ante las secuelas del 98, un regeneracionismo transculturado*. Havana: Fundación Fernando Ortiz.

Politics and Government

Wilfredo Vallín and Ted A. Henken

INTRODUCTION

This chapter describes the origins and functioning of the Cuban government and political system. Specifically, it covers three distinct stages during the last half-century, beginning with a *charismatic* stage of government (1959–1970). During that time, while the Cuban Communist Party (PCC) was consolidated and many mass organizations were created to channel and control popular participation, state institutions were relatively weak and the revolution's "maximum leader," Fidel Castro, exercised unmitigated authority through his unique charismatic style of leadership. The *institutional* stage (1971–1989) saw the creation of the formal institutions of politics and government, including a new Constitution, the Party's Central Committee and Politburo, the Council of State, the Council of Ministers, and the National Assembly of People's Power (Cuba's Parliament).

The most recent *emergent* stage of governance began in 1990 and is characterized by a relative weakening of state institutions, a slight opening of public space, and the growth of civil society. This opening has not been one freely chosen by the Cuban leadership. Instead, it has been necessitated by two major and ongoing challenges to the longevity of the socialist system: the economic crisis that began with the collapse of the Soviet Union in 1990 and the shift in political power from Fidel to Raúl Castro that began with the elder Castro's life-threatening illness in mid-2006 and culminated in Raúl's ascension to the presidency in early 2008. This part of the chapter describes recent constitutional and economic reforms, address the issues of human rights, political prisoners, and dissident movements, and discuss the elusive concept of "civil society" as new social, economic, and political actors and movements have emerged since 1990.

CONSOLIDATION, RADICALIZATION, AND CHARISMATIC LEADERSHIP, 1959–1970

The brutality of the Batista dictatorship during the bloody two-year revolutionary war (1957–1958) culminated in the triumph of a loose coalition of rebel forces headed by Castro's 26th of July Movement. This left the old generation of Cuban political leaders discredited, along with their institutions and political parties. In fact, the constitutional democracy reestablished in 1940 had proven deeply corrupt and easily gave way when Batista returned to the presidency in 1952, this time as a usurper and dictator. Thus, when Castro marched into Havana in January 1959 as the unmistakable leader of the future, he represented the long-frustrated aspirations of a new generation of Cubans (Domínguez 1993). Castro also benefited from the ideological and institutional vacuum left behind by the collapse of the Batista regime. Almost immediately, his virtually unchallenged ascendancy revealed new rules of the game of Cuban politics.

First of all, the Cuban military was both discredited and destroyed, along with the political class in whose interests it had exercised its authority. Second, since Castro's movement was not a political party, it was not indebted to any established institutional interests when it gained power. Thus, upon victory the revolution easily swept aside all previous parties except the Popular Socialist Party (communist), which had quietly begun to collaborate with Castro's movement during the last year of the guerrilla struggle. Third, Castro's refusal to seek approval from Uncle Sam for his political decisions, or financial aid for his economic projects, broke with a long tradition of Cuban dependency on U.S. approval and economic largess. Fourth, Castro quickly responded to the power vacuum by creating a series of new decrees, laws, and institutions that could both channel the rising revolutionary effervescence of the people and stimulate social integration and national mobilization that would give weight to the meaning of revolution (Pérez 2002: 243). Finally, for many of its progressive supporters around the world, the Cuban revolution represented an inspiring break with the bureaucratic and antidemocratic socialism that had become institutionalized by then in the Soviet Union. "It's difficult to remember today, when Havana itself is run by a wrinkled oligarchy of old Communist gargoyles," wrote the late, brilliant polemicist Christopher Hitchens in his 2010 memoir *Hitch-22*, "but in the 1960s there was a dramatic contrast between the waxworks in the Kremlin and the young, informal, spontaneous, and even somewhat sexy leadership in Havana" (2010: 110–111).

Early Revolutionary Decrees

The new government's first major decree came in May 1959 with the announcement of the first Agrarian Reform Law. The law reduced individual land holdings to a maximum of 1,000 acres but extended exceptions in the key areas of sugar, rice, and livestock holdings, which were allowed to remain at a maximum of 3,333 acres. Despite the fact that the law was not as radical as many expected, it turned the U.S. government against Castro (Farber 2006). Along with the law, a vast, powerful state institution, the National Institute of Agrarian Reform (INRA), was created. The

INRA had the authority to resolve labor–management disputes and grew to exercise extensive control over the entire economy during the first half of the 1960s.

The first nine months of 1959 saw as many as 1,500 revolutionary decrees, lowering postage, pharmaceutical, telephone, electricity, and tax rates. After agrarian reform, perhaps the most far-reaching reform measure was the Urban Reform Law enacted through a series of decrees between 1959 and 1960. That law reduced rents by up to 50 percent, gradually allowing renters to purchase their homes (Pérez 2002: 243). The law also socialized all commercially owned property, virtually eliminating the private real estate market (Domínguez 1993: 104). These first acts struck a balance between the rising demands of the people and the practical need to create order out of revolution (ibid.: 95). However, just as these new measures provided relief from inequality and injustice and won the new government broad-based popular support, they also provoked powerful domestic and international enemies whose interests were directly affected by reforms (Pérez 2002: 243).

Although relatively modest in scope and in line with Castro's declared intentions in his programmatic defense speech of 1953, the May 1959 Agrarian Reform Law was interpreted as an assault on large-scale private property by the Cuban bourgeoisie, leading to a crisis in the revolutionary government's first moderate cabinet (Farber 2006). In June 1959, most of these moderates left the government. Prime Minister José Miró Cardona resigned in February, Pedro Luís Díaz Lanz, the head of the Cuban Air Force, left in June, and President Manuel Urrutia was forced out in July after publicly questioning the rising influence of communists in the government. He was replaced by Osvaldo Dorticós, who would serve until 1976. Perhaps most tragically, the respected commander Huber Matos publicly resigned in October 1959 to protest rising communist influence in the revolution. Matos, however, paid a heavy price for his public break with Castro. He was quickly convicted of "treason and sedition" and spent the next 20 years in prison before being released into exile in 1979.

For these exiting moderates, the issue of communism and what they saw as an emerging *caudillismo* (strongman rule) were crucial. However, Castro would have to continue to orchestrate a delicate balance of power between the communists (whom he secretly favored but attempted to control) and the many noncommunist members of the Rebel Army who now were becoming institutionalized as the new Cuban Revolutionary Armed Forces. In fact, while the communists were ultimately ascendant in politics, the military achieved a significant and lasting independence from the party early on. Their relative autonomy was enhanced by their greater legitimacy achieved during the war and by the leadership of the capable Raúl Castro, who was made Cuba's defense minister in October 1959 based on his distinguished service in the clandestine war. Over the next 30 years, he would create Cuba's single most coherent and effective revolutionary organization (Domínguez 1993: 104).

In late November 1959, two other prominent moderates were forced out of the cabinet, the minister of public works, Manuel Ray, and the president of the National Bank, Felipe Pazos. Thus, out of a total of 21 government ministers appointed at the start of the year, 12 had resigned their posts or been forced out by the close of 1959, signaling the beginning of an institutional shift toward the radical consolidation of the revolution. Four more ministers would leave during 1960 (ibid.: 105). Despite this wave of defections, for an entire generation of Cubans 1959 was the best year of their lives. The vast majority saw themselves as active participants in an epoch-making event: the long-awaited fruition a broad-based movement for national regeneration that both fed on and evoked an outpouring of human solidarity, humanistic altruism, and revolutionary effervescence.

If 1959 was the revolution's honeymoon, then 1960 started with increasing marital trouble and ended with an emphatic divorce as the United States cut diplomatic relations in January 1961. In fact, 1960 was the crucial year that defined the radical direction of the revolution, as well as the year in which the United States gave up on diplomacy and began preparing a military solution to its "Cuba problem." In February, the Soviet foreign minister, Anastas Mikoyan, paid a courtesy visit to Cuba accompanying a trade exhibition that had previously appeared in Mexico. The visit, quite ominous for the United States, resulted in the reestablishment of diplomatic relations between the two countries. Next, counterrevolutionary sabotage was suspected when the French freighter *La Coubre* exploded in March while delivering military equipment in Havana's harbor. Castro responded by pointing an accusing finger at the United States. Also in March, President Eisenhower secretly authorized the CIA to begin planning Castro's overthrow, what would become Kennedy's most infamous fiasco—the April 1961 Bay of Pigs invasion.

Economic warfare between the two countries began in the summer, when two U.S.-owned petroleum refineries followed State Department instructions, refusing to refine the Soviet crude purchased by the Cuban government. Cuba quickly responded by nationalizing the two refineries. It is likely, however, that this whole episode was set in motion by Che Guevara, who accurately anticipated that the U.S. refineries would refuse to accept the Soviet crude even before he arranged to have it sent from the Soviet Union. Guevara knew that Washington would never tolerate the imposition of a radical socioeconomic experiment in its erstwhile economic colony. Much less would it sit idly by and watch its Cold War rival openly support such an experiment. Guevara also knew that a hostile U.S. reaction would facilitate the subsequent consolidation of the revolution under the socialism that he advocated.

When the United States eliminated Cuba's long-standing sugar quota in July, the USSR offered to purchase the balance of the quota and pledged to make a similar purchase the following year. In the waning months of 1960, economic warfare heated up again with the Cuban nationalization of all remaining U.S. properties and businesses, including utilities, sugar mills, banks, railroads, and factories. The United States responded by imposing the first elements of its now infamous trade embargo and recalling its ambassador, Philip Bonsal. Now clearly under threat from the United States, the revolution began to establish a series of mass organizations that would provide for national defense, promote mass mobilization, and effectively control all future political participation.

Mass Organizations

Although the revolution would not become fully institutionalized until the mid-1970s, the deepening rift with the United States, combined with other international and internal crises, led the government to begin to develop an incipient defensive, organizational, and institutional apparatus between 1960 and 1962. As a result, citizen participation in civic and political life became institutionalized under a number of formal mass organizations. While very popular during the early 1960s and sometimes described as "socialist civil society," these organizations are better understood as corporate control mechanisms used to channel popular mobilization into activities explicitly supportive of the government. Likewise, mass organizations seldom function as "interest groups" representing and promoting members' needs. Instead, they aim to subordinate members' interests to nationally defined goals, seeking to avoid conflict and enlist support for regime policies that affect members' lives.

While membership reaches well into the millions for the larger mass organizations, participation does not translate into effective influence or restraint on the behavior of the country's political leadership. While the popularity and effectiveness of mass organizations have waxed and waned over time, most Cubans participate to some degree in them, either because they freely choose to or because the cost of nonparticipation can be high. However, perhaps 20 percent of the adult population refuses to have anything to do with mass organizations, regardless of the consequences (Domínguez 2002).

The four most prominent mass organizations in terms of size, revolutionary integration, and external vigilance and internal control are the Committees for the Defense of the Revolution (CDR), founded in September 1960; the Federation of Cuban Women (FMC), first established in August of the same year; the Union of Young Communists (UJC), formed in 1962; and the Cuban Workers Federation (CTC), originally founded in the 1930s and reorganized under the revolution in 1959. Also a citizen militia with 300,000 members was created in 1960 to help defend the revolution from external attack. Peasant associations, such as the *Cosecheros de Tabaco* and the *Asociación Nacional Campesina*, were replaced after 1959 by the *Asociación Nacional de Colonos*, which in turn became the *Asociación Nacional de Agricultores Pequeños* (National Association of Small Farmers, ANAP), in 1961. Finally, Cuba's National Union of Writers and Artists (UNEAC) was founded in 1961.

The CDRs are neighborhood-based organizations that span the entire breadth of the island. Under the joint jurisdiction of the National Revolutionary Police (PNR) and the Ministry of the Interior, each CDR serves a variety of formal and informal functions, the most important of which is to stimulate political participation of neighborhood residents and guard against subversion of revolutionary principles. Led by a president who is popularly elected by all neighborhood residents based on his or her "revolutionary integration and commitment," each CDR maintains files on neighborhood residents and convenes monthly meetings aimed at political socialization in which revolutionary sloganeering, citizen complaint, and popular feedback on local issues take place. Though the "bright" side of the CDRs such as their work in vaccinating infants or collecting blood donations is often heralded, they are primarily intended to be instruments of "vigilance and repression" (Farber 2011: 17). As such, the CDRs monitor potential dissidents and pass information on to state security, further consolidating governmental power by turning the entire population into informants. In the very speech in which he announced their creation in 1960, Fidel himself openly emphasized the purpose of the CDRs:

We are going to establish, against imperialist campaigns of aggression, a system of revolutionary collective surveillance where everybody will know who lives on their block, what each person who lives on the block does, who they meet with, and what relations they have with the tyranny. (Ibid.: 17; Sánchez 2012)

The CDRs play a key role in stimulating mass participation in rallies and revolutionary mobilizations. They are also instrumental in effectively responding to natural disasters, such as rapid, coordinated evacuations during Cuba's frequent hurricanes. One regrettable example of the political function of the CDRs took place during the 1980 Mariel boatlift, when members were encouraged to participate in *mítines de repudio* ("repudiation actions") against those who had chosen to emigrate. Those public shaming sessions often included young school children and involved vicious insults, the throwing of eggs and tomatoes, and occasionally ended in violence. Such violent attacks are still selectively carried out today against regime opponents. "All Cubans were required to participate in the CDRs, regardless of age or employment," writes political scientist Samuel Farber. "Failure to do so was interpreted as unwillingness or resistance to being 'integrated' into the revolutionary process, which carried serious educational and employment repercussions" (2011: 17).

Other important functions of the CDR include drawing attention to needed neighborhood repairs, sponsoring community self-help missions, participating in government-initiated campaigns in the area of literacy and immunization, ensuring universal local participation in Cuban elections, as well as monitoring the activities of neighborhood residents. For example, despite the economic crisis of the 1990s and the general weakening of the role of the mass organizations since the start of the special period, the CDRs were a key element in combating selective and blank voting and ensuring that nearly 90 percent of voters approved of the official unity slate in the 1998 National Assembly elections. CDR members also take turns performing nighttime vigilance (*guardia*) of their building or neighborhood. Likewise, when neighborhood residents change residence, run for elected office, or apply for university admission, membership in other mass organizations such as the UJC or the party, promotions, special positions, or licenses (such as a self-employment license), other CDR members are questioned about that resident's proper revolutionary attitude and behavior.

The Federation of Cuban Women (FMC) was founded in 1960 and actually began by merging as many as 40 previously existing women's organizations. Thereafter it rapidly increased its membership from just 17,000 in 1961 to 240,000 by 1962. The *federadas*, as members are known, had been led since the organization's inception by a single president, Vilma Espín, member of the party's Central Committee, Rebel Army coordinator during the 1950s, and estranged wife of Raúl Castro. Espín died in 2007. By the 1990s, membership, which is virtually mandatory for all adult women, reached some 3.2 million women, or 81 percent of the female population over 14. Officially formed as a *feminine* organization (that is non*feminist* organization, officially considered an anachronistic, capitalist term), the FMC works to integrate women into the revolutionary process and labor force. The organization has also been recognized for improving living conditions for rural women and children and for defending the right of women to pursue higher education and ensuring their equitable treatment in the workplace. The FMC also runs an extensive network of daycare centers, called *círculos infantiles*, that function to allow women with children to enter the labor force. Sending one's children to these daycare centers is one of the privileges of FMC membership.

In the fall of 1960, the Association of Rebel Youth (AJR) was formed by collapsing the youth wings of the three most prominent revolutionary organizations—the old Popular Socialist Party (PSP), the Revolutionary Directorate (DR), and the 26th of July Movement. It would later become the Union of Young Communists (UJC). Like the FMC, this organization's goal is to promote revolutionary indoctrination among its members and to channel its activities toward the formation of new socialist men and women.

Members of the UJC must be under 30 years of age and are drawn from all sectors of society. In the early years of the revolution, noncommunists who had come into the UJC through the consolidation of previously existing organizations were expelled and membership dropped from 100,000 to just 18,000. There was also criticism in the early 1970s that the UJC had focused on recruiting students and young professionals at the expense of urban workers and agricultural laborers. However, the UJC was eventually placed directly under the control of the Cuban Communist Party, and membership grew after the major institutional reorganization of the mid-1970s. The UJC eventually established its own newspaper, *Juventud Rebelde* (*Rebel Youth*), and holds sway over Cuba's three student organizations: the elementary school "Pioneers" (*Organización de Pioneros José Martí*, OPJM), the Federation of Middle School Students (FEEM), and the Federation of University Students (FEU). The UJC is an important grooming organization for ambitious and talented youth

Cuban young women pass in front of a huge Havana mural depicting the logo of the Communist Youth League (UJC) on April 4, 2007 on the day commemorating the 45th anniversary of its creation by Fidel Castro in 1962. The logo features Julio Antonio Mella, Camilo Cienfuegos, and Che Guevara emblazoned with the motto, "Study, Work, Rifle." (AFP/Getty Images)

who hope to fill leadership positions as adults. While not a prerequisite, membership in the UJC strengthens one's candidacy for party membership after the age of 30.

Unlike unions in most countries, the Cuban Workers Federation (CTC) is not organized based on trades or professions but according to sectors of economic activity. Likewise, the role of the CTC is more that of assuring that labor discipline and the achievement of production goals are in line with government priorities than that of defending workers' interests. Strikes, for example, have been unknown in Cuba since the early 1960s. This does not mean, however, that workers have not developed an arsenal of resistance strategies. Absenteeism, off-the-books and after-hours work, and pilfering resources from one's state job for resale on the black market are a few of the many ways in which Cuban workers assert their autonomy. On the other hand, the revolution won workers a series of significant benefits including health care, periodic vacations, pension coverage, and a gradual increase in the role of material rewards (greater pay) over moral incentives.

The CTC also maintains a labor file on each worker that indicates occupational status, labor history, absenteeism, merits, special skills, and participation in voluntary labor brigades. These labor files are linked to the identity cards that each Cuban must always carry and produce upon request. Thus many Cubans seek to maintain an occupation not necessarily because of their need for a peso income (increasingly meager after 1990) but to gain access to state goods or out of the need to avoid the stigma that accompanies unemployment in a worker's state.

The 1990s saw a slight increase in the autonomy of the CTC. On a number of occasions the federation has defended workers from proposed economic legislation interpreted to be harmful to their interests. For example, the CTC stalled a new law that sought to remove recalcitrant workers to other jobs, resisted the implementation of stricter sanctions on absenteeism, and objected to the increased use of material incentives that would lead to income inequality. The CTC also successfully modified legislation that would have included salaried workers in a new income tax law aimed at the self-employed (del Águila 1994; Díaz-Briquets 2002; Domínguez 1993, 2002). However, as the next chapter on the Cuban economy describes, it was through an announcement penned by the CTC leadership itself and published in *Granma* on September 13, 2010, that Cuban state workers learned of the impending layoffs of more than a half-a-million workers.

The very concept of "mass organizations" indicates their lack of autonomy. These institutions were created starting in 1959 as part of the revolution's strategy to dismantle the wide range of voluntary civic associations that had existed in Cuba up to that moment. This would allow for their replacement by explicitly revolutionary groupings organized around socialist priorities. For example, Article 7 of the 1976 Constitution describes these new associations as follows: "The Cuban socialist state recognizes and encourages the mass and social organizations that have emerged in the historic process of our people's struggles, which gather together different sectors of the population, represent their specific interests, and incorporate them into the tasks of the construction, consolidation, and defense of socialist society."

Official state publications refer to the mass organizations as the institutions civil society that—without being part either of the state or of the Communist Party—make up the country's political system. However, in practice they function as mere transmission belts to roll out and implement the policies that emanate from the

Party above. These policies are often aimed at raising members' social and political consciousness and encouraging them to participate in the building, consolidation, and defense of the socialist state.

The Consolidation and Radicalization of the Revolution

A number of major domestic and international events between 1959 and 1962 enabled Castro to consolidate and radicalize Cuba's nationalist uprising into an overtly anti-American, communist revolution. In the months following Batista's fall in December 1958, it became incumbent upon the rebels—now in government—to establish the rule of law in their punishments of the old guard in order to be seen as legitimate and democratic by the Cuban people. However, the trials of those accused of "war crimes" provoked an immediate conflict between the liberal values of fairness and moderation, and the need for the new regime to enact "revolutionary justice" in response to the rising demands from an emboldened and traumatized populace (Domínguez 1993: 97). Castro reacted angrily to what he saw as hypocritical criticisms in the U.S. press—which had begun referring to the dramatic public trials as "kangaroo courts"—of the punishments after they had turned a deaf ear to years of abuse under Batista. He further flaunted U.S. concerns by holding trials in a huge sports arena and showing them to the anxious masses on live television. Despite this early confrontation, Castro paid an unofficial visit to the United States in April 1959, surprising officials by refusing to request any economic aid for his new government.

Signaling his growing preference for revolutionary unity under communist leadership, Castro intervened in the fall of 1959 in the first postrevolutionary elections in two of the most important prerevolutionary institutions of civil society, the University Student Federation (FEU) and Confederation of Cuban Workers (CTC), Cuba's principal labor union. Although both institutions had already been thoroughly politicized before the revolution, Castro's open intervention on the side of what he called the "unity candidates" led to the victory in both cases of the less popular slate aligned with the PSP (the communist party) and the loss of the coalition that grew out of Castro's 26th of July Movement. Castro argued that the defense of the revolution required unity above all. Thus, he catapulted the communists into positions of authority and undercut the cadres of his own movement, with the goal of preventing the 26th of July Movement from congealing into a real organization (ibid.: 104–105; Farber 2011).

During the two-year revolutionary war that preceded the triumph of 1959, the PSP refused active participation in the armed struggle until mid-1958. In fact, the communists had criticized Castro's attack on the Moncada Barracks in 1953 as a pointless putsch, referring to it as "a crazy adventure coming out of university classrooms." However, starting January 1959, Castro would use the relations between the PSP and Soviet communist party to facilitate a gradual rapprochement between Cuba and the USSR. In fact, with all former political parties abolished, only the three revolutionary groups that participated in the fight against Batista remained as political organizations with any power, authority, and popular following. These were Castro's 26th of July Movement—divided between the radical guerrillas who had fought in the mountains and the movement's more moderate urban wing—the March 13 Revolutionary Directorate, which had grown out of the University of Havana's Student Federation, and the PSP (Popular Socialist Party), Cuba's traditional, Soviet-aligned communist party. Ironically, though the PSP was the organization least involved in the armed struggle, its proven organizational capacity, clear political program and ideological grounding, and international links to Moscow made it an especially attractive vehicle for consolidating power and defending the revolution in the tense geopolitical atmosphere of the Cold War.

In July 1961, Castro merged these three groups into a single new unified political party, to which he gave the name Integrated Revolutionary Organizations (ORI), signaling its role as *the* party of the revolution. However, this was an "integrated" party only in name, since both the 26th of July Movement and the Revolutionary Directorate had all but ceased to exist as organically independent groups. Castro reorganized the ORI once again in January 1963 renaming it the United Party of the Socialist Revolution (PURS). Its name was changed one final time to the Cuban Communist Party (PCC)—with Fidel Castro as its general secretary—in 1965. Thus, by repeatedly dissolving and reconstituting the PSP during the first half of the 1960s, Castro was able to purge its ambitious leaders, convert them along with most of the country into *Fidelistas*, and create a new Cuban Communist Party (PCC) under his unquestioned leadership and vision. From that moment forward, Castro simultaneously occupied the positions of commander-in-chief of the Armed Forces, prime minister, and first secretary of the Communist Party.

Also in 1965, Cuba's three semi-independent daily newspapers, *Revolución* (published by the 26th of July Movement), *Hoy* (published by the PSP), and *Combate* (published by the Revolutionary Directorate), were all closed down and replaced by a single daily, *Granma*, the official organ of the new PCC. The principle of university autonomy—enshrined in Article 53 of the 1940 Constitution—also ceased to exist. Likewise, Cuba's rich and diverse mass media—print journalism, all radio and television stations, the island's vast network of movie theaters, as well as all publishing houses and other cultural institutions—were summarily taken over by the PCC. With the elimination of these essential elements of civil society and as noncommunists and anticommunists were gradually removed from the government between 1959 and 1962, the way was paved for the complete transformation of Cuba's internal government and political institutions under centralized and authoritarian communist rule.

Still, a trigger was needed to justify such a move to a nationalistic but still traditionally anticommunist populace. The effect of the U.S.-backed invasion in April 1961 in this process cannot be overestimated. This watershed event in the radical consolidation of the revolution had the effect of undermining the position of the few moderates still left in positions of influence on the island, while simultaneously strengthening the hand of the communists (Linger 1999). In the aftermath of the failed invasion, Castro could easily justify increased repression and stepped-up security measures, implanting a siege mentality in the country. Many moderates were jailed or fled the country, making space for the most radical elements of the revolutionary coalition, such as Che Guevara, to fill. Therefore, by 1962, power had been consolidated under socialist revolution, with Castro as the county's undeniable leader.

FIDEL CASTRO (1926–)

Born on August 13, 1926, Fidel Castro has become a political figure of mythic proportions as an inspiration for the anticapitalist struggles of the 20th century. Castro's iron hand has often been enveloped in a velvet glove permitting him to rule with Machiavellian cunning, spellbinding charisma, and brute force. He has also benefited from the powerful nationalism of the Cuban people, the U.S. threat to Cuban sovereignty, and the enactment of an ambitious program of social justice. Originally from the town of Birán in *Oriente*, Castro studied in Jesuit schools and exhibited a work ethic, fierce competitive streak, and almost egomaniacal confidence that would serve him well in the years to come.

Castro organized an unsuccessful raid on the Moncada Barracks on July 26, 1953. Amnestied from prison in 1955, he regrouped abroad, clandestinely invaded Cuba at the end of 1956, and two years later, marched triumphantly into Havana. Initially taking on the post of commander-in-chief of the Armed Forces in January 1959, Castro soon became prime minister and first secretary of the Communist Party. He was named president in 1976. Until a life-threatening illness forced him to step down in July 2006, Castro served as president of the Councils of State and of Ministers. While his rule has been characterized by human rights abuses and economic incompetence, Castro has distinguished himself as a consummate political operator on the world stage.

BUREAUCRATIC AUTHORITY, INSTITUTIONALIZATION, AND PEOPLE'S POWER, 1970–1989

Because of the charismatic nature of his authority, upon victory and consolidation of the revolution, Castro faced the danger of becoming obsolete. However, in the late 1960s he made the creation of a new selfless, socialist man and the achievement of all-or-nothing economic goals the new battles around which to rally the nation. Continued U.S. hostility also provided him with a threatening Goliath against which to call for revolutionary unity and focus nationalist resistance. From 1959 to 1976, no national elections took place in Cuba. Instead, Castro's legitimacy as Cuba's maximum leader (though hardly unquestioned) stemmed from the four pillars of personal charisma, political deliverance, economic redistribution, and fervent nationalism (Domínguez 1993: 126).

However, the failure of the 10-million-ton sugar harvest in 1970 called that arrangement into question. Built as it was on Castro's charismatic preaching, his all-encompassing faith in the new man, and the revolutionary consciousness of the masses, the failure of the *Gran Zafra* signaled the bankruptcy of personal charisma and revolutionary consciousness as the basis for long-term institutionalization of the revolution. Starting in 1970 and culminating in the First Congress of the Cuban Communist Party (PCC) in 1975 and the subsequent constitution approved by popular referendum in 1976, Castro reluctantly moved toward the institutionalization of the revolution. In July 1972, Cuba became a member of the

Soviet bloc's Council of Mutual Economic Aid (CMEA) and initiated a process of fashioning Cuban government institutions in the image of the Soviet Union. In November 1972, Cuba's Council of Ministers was reorganized to create an executive committee, headed by a prime minister and composed of a handful of deputy ministers who oversaw the various state ministries. This change made the executive committee of the Council of Ministers the government's central decision-making body (Blanco and Benjamin 2003; González 1974; Guillermoprieto 2004; Halperin 1972, 1981, 1994).

Cuba's Constitution and Legal System

Cuba's legal system is composed of a strict hierarchy of laws and courts. The ascending hierarchy of authority of the laws begins with regulations, which are dictated by various state institutions, and resolutions, which are the domain of the Council of Ministers. Decree-laws are issued by the Council of State during the months in between the twice-yearly weeklong sessions of the National Assembly of People's Power—which must in turn ratify them. Then there are laws, which are passed by the National Assembly. In theory, the supreme law of the land—reigning over and above these lesser and more transitory laws—is the Constitution.

Nevertheless, this formal hierarchy is violated in the daily practice of Cuban jurisprudence where laws, decree-laws, and even administrative resolutions are often issued in direct contradiction to what is written in the Constitution. For example, until Raúl Castro repealed it in 2008, a special disposition long prohibited Cuban nationals from staying in the island's tourist hotels, which were reserved for the exclusive use of dollar-paying foreigners. Likewise, a special law on internal migration outlawed Cubans who lived in the island's eastern provinces from coming to reside in Havana, even if they were moving to the homes of their relatives. Both of these special dispositions, along with many others like them, were and are absolutely unconstitutional, given that Article 43 of the 1976 Constitution had always plainly stated: "The state consecrates the right conquered by the Revolution of all citizens, without distinction . . . to reside in any sector, zone, or area of the [nation's] cities and to stay in any hotel."

Introducing a number of significant elements from the island's constitutional history can help explain Cuban constitutional law. The seeds of this history are found in the *Proyecto de Gobierno Autonómico para Cuba*, proposed by Father José Agustín Caballero in 1811. This document represented the claims of autonomy of the island's emerging Creole planter class. In 1812, the Bayamo lawyer Joaquín Infante prepared his own draft constitution, which was aimed at full independence (Castellanos 2011: 124). Then in 1823, Father Félix Varela presented another proto-constitution to the Spanish Courts with the aim of winning Cuban autonomy. Varela's document was more advanced than that of Caballero, since it went beyond claiming political rights for white Creoles only (Ibarra Cuesta 2004: 72). Additionally, Varela's project was the first of its kind to call for the abolition of slavery.

Various constitutions were issued by the rebel governments-in-arms during Cuba's wars for independence in the second half of the 19th century. These are also important antecedents in Cuban legal history. First was the Constitution of Guáimaro, which was approved on April 10, 1869. Applying to the rebel occupied territories, this Constitution included 29 articles and laid out a classic separation of powers between legislative, executive, and judicial branches of government. The document also included important restrictions on state power, preventing the government-in-arms from infringing on citizens' freedom of religion, the press, peaceful assembly, education, and right to an address of their grievances. Similarly, the Constitutions of Baraguá (1878), Jimaguayú (1895), and Yaya (1897) each guaranteed a set of inalienable citizen rights, made a clear delineation between civil and military powers, and placed ultimate governmental power in civilian—not military—hands (Castellanos 2011: 125–126). Referring to the Guáimaro Constitution's democratic principles and recognition of individual rights, Carlos Manuel de Céspedes, the then president of the Republic-in-Arms, wrote the following words to Cuba's representative in the United States:

> The Cuban Republic has been constituted based on the most purely democratic principles. We have recognized as inalienable the rights of petition, freedom of religion, speech, and the press, with no restrictions on these last two except those arising from the exceptional circumstances in which we find ourselves. (Ibid.: 125)

At the close of the war in 1898, Cuba fell under the provisional control of the United States through a military occupation that remained until 1902. During these years the Constitution of 1898 was in force, which was little more than a list of regulations issued by Leonard Wood, the U.S. military governor at the time. On May 20, 1902, in the Morro Castle at the mouth of Havana Bay, Gen. Máximo Gómez lowered American flag and raised the Cuban one, thus bringing to a close the foreign military occupation of Cuba and transferring political power to the first national government in the island's history. The Republic of "*Cuba libre*" was born. However, as indicated in Chapter 2, the ostensibly sovereign nation was born under a bad sign since its new 1901 Constitution included the numerous restrictions of the Platt Amendment. Still, the new supreme law of the land represented continuity with the previous wartime constitutions as it expanded the previous individual rights and liberties to now include the freedom of movement, the right of citizens to leave and return to the country, the inviolability of the home and of correspondence, and the right to own property (Castellanos 2011: 126–127).

The 1940 Constitution eliminated the Platt Amendment—which had already been abrogated in 1934—but retained all the individual rights recognized in the 1901 Constitution. However, as indicated in chapter two, the 1940 Constitution stands out for its pioneering recognition and enumeration of a host of socioeconomic rights, many of which made the document into a model of democratic legislation for the rest of the continent. Some of these include university autonomy, universal suffrage (now to include women), mandatory free public education, and the right to march and form oppositional political parties. The 1940 Constitution was especially progressive in its recognition of labor rights including a minimum wage, paid time off, and maternity leave, with workers granted the right to strike and form unions (Bernal 1984; Castellanos 2011: 127; Marril Rivero 1989).

The Cuban Constitution of 1976 recognizes many of these same rights and liberties, such as equality before the law, universal suffrage, and freedom of speech, the press, assembly, association, and demonstration. It also guarantees many economic and social rights including access to employment, health care, education, food, clothing, culture, and sports. Furthermore, it states that the economy is based on "socialist ownership by all the people," which is irreversibly established for all means of production and natural resources. The fundamental difference from previous constitutions, however, lies in the fact that all these rights are subordinated to Article 5, which explicitly names the Communist Party as "the organized vanguard of the Cuban nation and the superior directing force of both society and the State . . . for the construction of socialism and the advancement toward communism." Such subordination of the legal order to a political party has no precedent in Cuban constitutional history (Castellanos 2011: 127–128).

This socialist Constitution has been modified twice since 1976, first in 1992 and again in 2002. The 1992 reform granted religious freedom and the right of small farmers to form associations, while the 2002 change made socialism "irrevocable." Thus was abolished the necessary future adaptation of the highest law of the land to changes that constantly take place in every society. As amended, the Constitution has been converted into a rigid, unchanging document, precisely in an age of globalization and new flows of information and communications, anchoring the country in the past and alienating the people from their own sovereignty. As the brief constitutional history outlined earlier demonstrates, the 1976 Constitution amounts to a giant step backward. This is clear when we remember that nearly all the rights included in the Universal Declaration of Human Rights (UDHR) of 1948 were already enshrined in the 1901 and 1940 Cuban Constitutions. It was not by coincidence that the first draft of the UDHR submitted to the Economic and Social Council of the United Nations was presented by the Cuban delegation. This fact underlines the importance that the concept of human rights had acquired in Cuba during the first half of the 20th century (Castellanos 2011: 128).

Because the Constitution occupies the apex of Cuba's legal hierarchy, it is presumed to be the ultimate source of law from which the authority of the rest of the national legal system emanates. For that reason, it cannot be contravened or undermined by any provision of lower legal authority. When this occurs, proper legal procedure is to consider the lesser statute null and void. However, in actual practice the socialist Constitution has been systematically violated by the routine application of lesser laws that clearly contradict it. For example, though Article 51 reads, "Everyone has the right to an education," for decades ideological criteria have been used to deny a higher education to some under the de facto slogan: "The university is reserved for revolutionaries."

In fact, a significant number of people have been expelled from Cuba's universities for having voiced opinions at odds with official state dogma. There are even cases of students being punished for carrying copies of the Universal Declaration of Human Rights on campus. These purges have even targeted college professors, who have been expelled from their jobs for similar acts of "indiscipline." On the other hand, for over 30 years the university curriculum included a series of required courses designed to reinforce Marxist ideology. That is to say that the State, from the very start of the revolution, granted itself the right to subject students to a thoroughgoing ideological indoctrination at all levels of the educational system. This practice was inaugurated most prominently in the baldly political content of the primers used in the literacy campaign of 1961.

The 1976 Constitution enshrines the following rights as fundamental guarantees:

- Article 53: Citizens have freedom of speech and of the press in keeping with the objectives of socialist society. . . . The press, radio, television, film, and other organs of the mass media are State or social property and can never be private property . . .
- Article 55: The state . . . recognizes, respects, and guarantees freedom of conscience and of religion . . .
- Article 56: The home is inviolable . . .
- Article 57: Mail is inviolable. . . . The same principle is to be applied in the case of cable, telegraph, and telephone communications.
- Article 58: Freedom and inviolability of persons is assured to all those who live in the country. Nobody can be detained, except in the manner and with the guarantees indicated by law. Those detained or in prison are inviolable in their person.
- Article 59: Nobody can be tried or sentenced except by the competent court by virtue of laws which existed prior to the crime and with the formalities and guarantees that the laws establish. Every accused person has the right to a defense. No violence or coercion of any kind can be used against people to force them to confess or testify . . .

Nevertheless, all the freedoms discussed earlier come to naught when we consider that Article 62 of the same Constitution stipulates:

None of the freedoms recognized for citizens can be exercised contrary to what is established in the Constitution and by law, or contrary to the existence and objectives of the socialist state, or against the decision of the Cuban people to build socialism and communism. Violations of this principle are punishable by law. (ConstitutionNet 1976; CubaNet 1992; CubaVerdad 1992)

Moreover, crucial future amendments to this most fundamental of Cuba's legal documents have been summarily blocked by the previously mentioned "Special Disposition," which modified the Constitution in 2002 enshrining the socialist regime in perpetuity. Given its important consequences, we reproduce part of the text of this amendment here:

Socialism and the revolutionary political and social system established in the Constitution and proven through years of heroic resistance to all kinds of aggression and economic warfare waged by successive administrations of the mightiest imperialistic power that has ever existed, and having demonstrated their capacity to transform the country and create an entirely new and just society, are irrevocable. Cuba will never again return to capitalism. (CubaVerdad 2002)

THE VARELA PROJECT

Engineered by the late Cuban dissident leader Oswaldo Payá and his *Movimiento Cristiano Liberación* (Christian Liberation Movement), the Varela Project took advantage of an obscure provision of the 1976 constitution that allowed citizens to propose new legislation provided they could come up with 10,000 signatures. The main goal of the petition was to call for direct elections of the head of state and a referendum on the country's one-party system. It also demanded amnesty for political prisoners, the establishment of freedom of speech, assembly, and association, and the allowance of a private sector.

Payá delivered his petition to Cuba's National Assembly in May 2002, just before former U.S. president Jimmy Carter's plane touched down in Havana. Despite Carter's laudatory remarks about the Project—delivered in Spanish on Cuban national television and reprinted in *Granma* the next day—Castro mobilized his considerable state security apparatus to crush the petition drive by harassing and jailing the activists and invalidating the petitions. Failing at that, Castro orchestrated a successful Constitutional referendum of his own later in the year that resulted in declaring the socialist nature of the revolution "irrevocable."

Cuba's System of Government: The National Assembly, the Council of State, and the Council of Ministers

The organizational structure of the current Cuban government cannot be classified among the two traditionally known models: parliamentary and presidential. Instead, the Cuban model of government continues to closely mirror the characteristics of the now-defunct socialist bloc. The concepts of "socialist democracy" and "democratic centralism" continue to predominate. In essence, this means the complete subordination of all lower levels of government to higher ones. Additionally, the principle of unity of power reigns, which means that the unicameral National Assembly simultaneously exercises both legislative and executive powers. There is also a judicial branch of government, which is theoretically independent. However, in practice both the National Assembly and the judiciary are subordinated to the all-powerful Council of State.

The political system that results from such an arrangement fits perfectly within what political scientist Felipe Isasi Cayo has labeled "authoritarian":

> Socialist dictatorships are based on the domination of a single party, which operates under a constitutional system where the assembly is formed through monolithic elections, supported by the collective ownership of the means of production, and inspired by a Marxist ideology. . . . Competitive multi-party elections, political pluralism, and legal opposition are banned. These are replaced by referendum elections with single candidates or by the complete absence of elections. The principle of the separation of powers is replaced by the concentration of authority in the hands of one man or one party, and the absence or illusory nature of public freedoms and their guarantees. (Isasi Cayo 1989: 107)

Given such a structure, three institutions are the most important foundations of the Cuban government: the National Assembly, the Council of State, and the Council of Ministers.

The creation of the National Assembly of People's Power (NAPP) in 1976 coincided with the political and geographical reorganization of the island that transformed the 6 traditional provinces into 14 (with the Isle of Pines, renamed the Isle of Youth, made a special municipality). Old municipal divisions were abolished, and 169 new municipalities were created in their place. At the same time, provincial and municipal governments (Assemblies of People's Power) were established through elections within each province and municipality for the first time. Elections for Municipal Assembly delegates are held every two-and-a-half years while Provincial Assembly elections take place every five years. While these local and regional Assemblies are the bodies from which the power of the state emanates, in practice their role is reduced to the simple transmission of complaints from the local population upward. They lack real power, material resources, or the capacity to make decisions or solve the problems of their constituents. The National Assembly is made up of deputies (currently there are 614) elected by a "free, secret, and direct vote of electors, in the proportion and according to the procedure determined by the law" (Article 71 of the Constitution). In socialist Cuba, however, these deputies are understood to be representatives of the nation as a whole and not of the local or regional body that elected them. Thus, deputies do not have to obtain the consent of the voters to validate their positions.

Deputies are elected for periods of five years. Upon the seating of each new legislature, the National Assembly elects from among its members a president, vice president, and secretary.

The NAPP also elects from among its members those who will serve on the Council of State, including its president (the head of state), a first vice president, five other vice presidents, a secretary, and 23 other members. It elects the Council of Ministers as well, including a prime minister, and the judges of the People's Supreme Court. The Assembly holds two sessions each year, normally in early August and late December. Each session lasts about a week.

The 1976 Constitution formally vested the NAPP with legislative powers, naming it the ultimate repository of all power and authority in the socialist state; that is, of both its popular and national sovereignty. It constitutes a unicameral parliament that aims to "represent and express the sovereign will of all the people" (Article 69). It is the only body with constitutional and legislative power in the country. These functions had been exercised exclusively by the Council of Ministers before 1976. Theoretically, the National Assembly represents the people in lawmaking and governance, has the power to declare war, ratify peace treaties, amend the Constitution, make all international policies, and initiate, approve, modify, and repeal laws.

In practice, however, since the NAPP meets for brief periods and rarely initiates original legislation, most day-to-day legislative power and policy-making authority (which includes all of the aforementioned functions) is relegated to the Council of State. In fact, the Council of State is the real decision-making institution in the Cuban government, ruling largely through decree laws that are invariably later ratified unanimously and perfunctorily by the National Assembly.

While constitutional principle dictates that "the permanent representative body [the Council of State] cannot alter, modify, or repeal the normative dispositions approved by the National Assembly," we find that "the practice has been adopted whereby decree-laws [from the Council of State] can indeed modify laws approved by the National Assembly" (Prieto n.d.). That is, laws of lesser constitutional authority can override those of greater authority. This fact demonstrates more than anything else the totalitarian and vertical nature of the Cuban state, where the dominant political elite, the Council of State, modifies or annuls the decisions and laws dictated by the National Assembly, which is the supposed representative of the popular will. Thus, the unique character of the Cuban political system rests on the legal incapacity of the Assembly to invest true authority in the laws it approves. In fact, from its creation in 1976, it has never once repealed a single decree-law or rejected a proposal set forth by the Council of State.

Thus, in the mid-1970s, Cuba's institutions of governance formally passed from the exclusive realm of Castro's personalistic charisma to various representative and administrative bodies. The new constitution formally separated the powers of Cuba's three institutional branches of government. The 27-member Council of State stood in for the National Assembly when the latter was not in session (legislative branch). The 10-member executive committee of the Council of Ministers led the government (executive branch) as its maximum executive and administrative body, directing economic, monetary, and credit policy, drawing up the national budget, crafting foreign policy, engaging in international trade, providing for national defense and internal security, and protecting citizen rights, all duties theoretically subject to periodic review by the National Assembly.

While Cuba's Supreme Court is the country's foremost judicial unit, it does not in fact constitute an independent branch of government, with the leverage and autonomy to act as a check on potential excesses of the legislative and executive branches, or the 15-member Politburo of the Communist Party. Such "adversarial" relations among different branches of government are a threat to the overriding principle of national unity. In short, Cuban courts are not designed to limit the power of the government and protect individual rights and liberties (del Águila 1994: 165). Likewise, the formal separation of powers and the investing of legal, institutional preeminence to the National Assembly cannot hide the fact that it does not exercise de facto rule. For example, until February 2013 when José Ramón Machado Ventura was replaced by the much younger Miguel Díaz-Canel Bermúdez, the same three men, Raúl Castro, Machado Ventura, and Ramiro Valdés, held the top three positions in the Council of State, the Council of Ministers, and the Politburo (see Figure 3.1).

Thus, the delegation of some responsibility to incipient institutions did not fundamentally change the oligarchic character of Cuban state institutions. A small group of two or three dozen trusted, historic leaders made up the majority of members of the Council of State, the Council of Ministers, and the Politburo well into the 1990s. By law, the head of government (the prime minister of the Council of Ministers) and the head of state (the president of the Council of State) are the same individual. In Cuba, this individual's reach and power is vast, especially since he—Fidel Castro until 2006 and his younger brother Raúl thereafter—also holds the post of first secretary of the Communist Party (Domínguez 1993).

While some rejuvenation and diversity has indeed been achieved in these governing bodies in the 20 years between 1992 and 2013—with a greater representation of cadres in their 50s, women, and Afro-Cubans—there has also been a simultaneous

Raúl Castro
Commander-in-Chief
President of the Council of State
Prime Minister of the Council of Ministers
First Secretary of the Central Committee of PCC
∧

Miguel Díaz-Canel Bermúdez
First Vice President of the Council of State and the Council of Ministers
José Ramón Machado Ventura, Second Secretary of the Central Committee of PCC
Gen. Leopoldo Cintra Frías, Minister of the Armed Forces
∧

POLITBURO (14)

∧	∧	∧	∧
GOVERNMENT ADMINISTRATION	**POLITICAL LEADERSHIP**	**LEGISLATIVE**	**JUDICIARY**
∧	∧	∧	∧
Executive Committee (10)	Central Committee (105)	Council of State (27)	∧
∧	∧	∧	∧
Council of Ministries (27)	Organization Secretariat Departments	National Assembly of People's Power (614)	Supreme People's Court
∧	∧	∧	∧
Provincial Governments (15)	Provincial Committees (15)	Provincial Assemblies (15)	Provincial Courts (15)
∧	∧	∧	∧
Municipal Governments (169)	Municipal Committees (169)	Municipal Assemblies (169)	Municipal Courts (169)
∧	∧	∧	
Public Enterprises	Party Committees	Local Delegates	
	∧	∧	
	Party Core Members	Voters	
	∧	∧	

"Militantes del Partido" (PCC)   *"Unión de Jóvenes Comunistas"* (UJC)

MASS ∧
ORGANIZATIONS

∧	∧	∧	∧	∧	∧
Committees for the Defense of the Revolution **(CDR)**	Federation of Cuban Women **(FMC)**	National Association of Small Farmers **(ANAP)**	Confederation of Cuban Workers **(CTC)**	Federation of Secondary Students **(FEEM)**	Federation of University Students **(FEU)**

FIGURE 3.1 *Organizational Structure of the Cuban Government.*
Sources: Domínguez (2002); Sagás (2002); Cuban Transition Project (2012); Amuchástegui (2012).

and systematic purging of a series of once-trusted young cadres as they fell into disfavor. It is important to note that nearly all members of this group owed their rapid rise to prominence directly to Fidel Castro, being members of his private (and now defunct) "Coordination and Support Group." Despite their relative youth, this loose group of young leaders was often referred to as *los talibanes* given their "hard-line views and enthusiastic participation in the 'battle of ideas' that Fidel Castro had launched" (Mujal-León 2011: 156). The most prominent members of this group were former foreign ministers Roberto Robaina, 56, and Felipe Pérez Roque, 47, as well as former vice president Carlos Lage, 61, and former head of the UJC and ousted chief of Civil Aeronautics, Luis Orlando Domínguez, 67 (Amuchástegui 2012).

Since his ascension to the presidency in 2008, Raúl Castro has refused to passively assume the role of a mere caretaker president. Instead, he has aimed to shrink size and scope of paternalistic state, turn state enterprises into autonomous holding companies, and expand opportunities for private employment in order to provide jobs to those laid off from the state sector. Only time will tell if this ambitious program of economic reforms will succeed. However, Raúl has also sought to lay the groundwork for the orderly transfer of power from the still ruling remnants of Cuba's gerontocracy (often referred to as the "revolutionary generation" or "*históricos*") to "a 'successor generation' of military elites and party provincial secretaries" (Mujal-León 2011: 150). He has introduced term limits (two terms of five years each), leadership rotation, the separation of party and state functions, and demanded that

Cuba's president Raúl Castro, center, waves to people attending a May Day march. Accompanying him are Armed Forces Minister Guillermo García Frias, left, and Interior Minister Abelardo Colomé Ibarra. They stand in front of the José Martí monument in Revolution Square in Havana on May 1, 2013. (AP Photo/Ramon Espinosa)

party membership no longer be a prerequisite for state or government posts (ibid.: 149, 158).

Indeed, Raúl's rise to power has further facilitated the advancement of the military into commanding government positions (Cuban Transition Project 2012). Many of these emerging military elites have honed capitalist management techniques in military enterprises, which now act as a model for the entire economy. Others are military-technocratic entrepreneurs associated with the holding company GAESA (*Grupo de Administración Empresarial, S.A.*) (Mujal-León 2011: 153). The changes in the Politburo following the Sixth Party Congress in April 2011 indicate the military dominance among Cuba's new leadership. For example, while many younger cadres were removed from the Politburo between 2002 and 2010, almost an equal number of older *históricos* were not reelected in 2011 (or have died since as was the case of Julio Casas Regueiro or refused to stand for office as was the case with Fidel Castro).

Eight of the 15 new Politburo members elected in 2011 have military backgrounds and 30 percent of the 115-member Central Committee are members of Cuba's Armed Forces (Mujal-León 2011: 158–160). The "up-and-coming" group of military leaders includes the 54-year-old Division General Onelio Aguilera Bermúdez, recently promoted to Chief of Cuba's Eastern Army; Marino Murillo Jorge, 51, a government vice president and FAR technocrat who was named in March 2011 the chairman of the Economic Policy Commission of the PCC and charged with implementing Cuba's economic reforms; Gen. Alvaro López Miera, 69, the newly appointed first vice minister of the Armed Forces, as well as a member of Politburo and the Council of State; and politburo member Gen. Adel Yzquierdo Rodríguez, 66. Nonmilitary members of this "successor generation" include Lázara Mercedes López Acea, 48, first secretary of the Provincial Committee of Havana's PCC and member of the Politburo and Central Committee; and the recently appointed first vice president Miguel Díaz-Canel Bermúdez, 53, a former provincial party first secretary and minister of higher education who is also a member of the Politburo and Central Committee (see Figure 3.2) (Amuchástegui 2012; Mujal-León 2011: 159, 167).

Despite the rejuvenation of some sectors of the governing coalition, the cross-cutting, interlocking membership pattern between the party (and especially the Politburo) and the top posts in governmental institutions and ministries ensures a commanding role in policy-making and governance to a small group of leaders. These leaders are often two or three steps removed from having to face voters directly, despite the existence of an institutionalized system of representative government known as *Poder Popular*, or "People's Power." Despite its name, many Cubans have long concluded that as currently organized, the system of popular power is in fact neither "popular" nor very "powerful" (Bengelsdorf 1994).

The Cuban Communist Party (PCC)

From the end of the 19th century, European socialist ideas were periodically introduced to Cuba. The major socialist influence began within the island's workers' movement. The victory of the Socialist Revolution in Russia in October 1917—which led to the creation of the first proletarian state based on the idea that the dictatorship of the proletariat would free the working class from capitalist oppression—had a

Name	Council of State	Background	Year of Birth (Age)
Raúl Castro	President	REV	1931 (82)
José Ramón Machado Ventura*	VP	REV	1930 (83)
Ramiro Valdés	VP	REV	1932 (80)
Abelardo Colomé Ibarra	VP	FAR	1939 (73)
Esteban Lazo Hernández	VP	PCC	1944 (68)
Ricardo Alarcón de Quesada*	–	PCC	1937 (76)
Miguel Díaz-Canel Bermúdez*	First VP	PCC	1960 (53)
Leopoldo Cintra Frías	Member	FAR	1941 (71)
Ramón Espinosa Martín	–	FAR	1939 (73)
Alvaro López Miera	Member	FAR	1943 (69)
Salvador Mesa Valdés	Member	PCC	1941 (71)
Lázara Mercedes López Acea	–	PCC	1964 (48)
Marino Murillo Jorge	VP	FAR-TECH	1961 (51)
Adel Yzquierdo Rodríguez	–	FAR	1946 (66)

Key: VP = Vice President; REV = Revolutionary Generation; FAR = Military;
PCC = Cuban Communist Party; FAR-TECH = Military Technocrat.

* In February 2013, the 83-year-old Machado Ventura was replaced as Cuba's first vice president by the 53 year-old Díaz-Canel. In July, 2013, Ricardo Alarcón was also relieved of his positions in both the Politburo and the Central Committee of the Communist Party.

FIGURE 3.2 *Politburo Members with Appointments to the Council of State, September.*
Source: Mujal-Leon (2011: 161); García 2013.

major influence on the rise of the first Cuban Communist Party (PCC) in 1925. This first PCC was affiliated with Commitern (the Communist International). In 1937, the PCC joined the Revolutionary Union which was made up of left-wing intellectuals and adopted the name of Communist Revolutionary Union (URC). In 1944, now as a legal party, it changed its name to the Popular Socialist Party (PSP) the Cuban People's Party (*Ortodoxos*), and Republican Action.

During the early 1940s, Cuba was home to a wide spectrum of ideological tendencies such as liberal, social democratic, communist, and conservative. These crystallized in a wide variety of political parties active between the 1930s and 1950s, including the Liberal Party, the Nationalist Union, the Democratic Republican Party, the Cuban Revolutionary Party (*Auténticos*)—which held power from 1944 to 1952—the National Democratic Coalition, the Popular Cuban Agrarian Party, the ABC, National Revolutionary Movement (*Realistas*), the Popular Socialist Party, and Republican Action. However, parties at this time were more often vehicles of charismatic or military leaders than of commonly held ideological convictions. Thus, Batista won election to the presidency in 1940 under the banner of a Democratic-Socialist coalition which included support from the PSP (the Communists), a number of whose members served in his cabinet. In fact, Communists allied with Batista attacked opposition parties such as Grau's *Auténticos* as "fascists" and "reactionaries" (Domínguez 1978). Upon his coup in 1952, Batista rejected any future association with the PSP.

Of the three leading insurgent organizations—the 26th of July Movement, the Revolutionary Directorate, and the PSP—only the PSP had experience as a capable party organization with international connections. This, coupled with Fidel Castro's staunch support, allowed it to become the first among equals when the three revolutionary organizations were merged in 1961 to form Cuba's first unified revolutionary party, "*las ORI*" (the Integrated Revolutionary Organizations), which—once socialism was revealed as the revolution's guiding ideology—became the United Party of the Socialist Revolution (PURS) in 1963 and the Cuban Communist Party (PCC) in 1965. However, it was not until the First Congress of the PCC, held a decade later in 1975, that the party began to exercise a central institutional role in governing. For the first time, party members worked together to draft platforms affecting national policy. Specifically, the party helped to draft the new 1976 Constitution (which was largely modeled after the Soviet Constitution of 1936) and approved the first five-year plan, as well as other economic policies (del Águila 1994). The new Constitution also designated the party as the "guiding force of society and the state," leading the effort to build socialism.

While powers of governance are formally separated among the PCC, the Council of Ministers, and the Council of State (which represents the supposedly all-powerful National Assembly), as described earlier the top leadership of all three of these institutions is largely the same. Moreover, the PCC exercises great informal power through party cells, which are found at all levels of society. For example, the First Party Congress set up party committees in each of the country's 15 provinces and all 169 municipalities, with formal party representation in all military units, schools, neighborhoods, and workplaces. Furthermore, because municipal elected officials in Cuba have little effective clout, the party has focused its influence on the selection process of appointed officials. Thus, while the PCC does screen electoral candidates for the national and provincial assemblies, all appointed officials, as well as central government agency heads, state enterprise managers, hospital administrators, and military leaders, must be cleared and endorsed by party commissions (Domínguez 1993).

At the time of the first Congress, in 1975, the Central Committee was expanded to 112 members. The party's more exclusive Political Bureau was also vested with new authorities. Party membership gradually increased from 15,000 in 1962, to 50,000 in 1965 when its name was changed, to about 100,000 in 1970, reaching 203,000 on the eve of the First Congress in 1975. After the institutionalization of the party in 1975, membership shot up to more than 400,000 by 1980, reaching beyond 500,000 by the third Congress in 1986. Since party membership provides preferential access to some material goods, membership actually grew during the economic crisis of the early 1990s, reaching 780,000 by 1997 (Domínguez 2002). This growth was aided by the decision to drop the longtime ban on religious believers becoming party members and to shorten the waiting period for UJC members to apply for consideration from three to two years. Not all who desire to become *militantes del partido* (party "militants," or members) can do so. Membership must be requested, and there are typically two paths to consideration for membership: having been selected as a "vanguard worker" or having distinguished oneself previously in the UJC.

The PCC is organized in a strictly hierarchical structure, with the periodic party congresses formally governing its decisions and policies. However, given the unwieldy nature of large organizations and the long period that typically passes between congresses (though slated for every 5 years, 14 years passed between the fifth Congress of 1997 and the sixth one in 2011), the Central Committee's much smaller and more exclusive Political Bureau actually holds effective power and makes day-to-day decisions. The Central Committee meets annually, and its size increased from just over 100 members in 1975 to 225 after the Fourth Party Congress in 1991. However, by 1997 the Political Bureau decided to shrink the Central Committee to just 150 members, ending the experiment of making it broadly representative of the population.

In contrast to the Central Committee, the 14-member Politburo meets weekly and is composed of Cuba's most powerful leaders. It has been presided over by the same three men since its inception in 1965 until the mid-2000s: First Secretary Fidel Castro, Second Secretary Raúl Castro, and chief of party discipline Juan Almeida. In the 15 years between 1965 and 1980, it doubled in size, growing from 8 to 16 members. At the time of the Fourth Congress in 1991, however, the PB dropped 6 members (through death or retirement), adding a total of 17 new members, increasing total membership in this elite group to 25. By 1997 it had dropped to 24 members, but apart from José Ramón Machado Ventura, who joined in 1975, and Abelardo Colomé Ibarra and Esteban Lazo who joined in 1986, 18 others had joined in the 1990s, rejuvenating Cuba's top decision-making organ during the nation's most difficult time (ibid.; Corrales 2004). Most recently in 2006, after having been abolished decades earlier, the party Secretariat was reconstituted, signaling the party's emergence as Cuba's central power base, as Fidel Castro receded in prominence.

In Socialist Cuba, the Communist Party penetrates every aspect of the state and society, including its most minimal details. The Party governs all aspects of the political system and it issues the guidelines for the work and direction of the nation. These guidelines are oriented toward achieving a socialist society in the medium term and a communist society in the long term. In theory, the Party's guidelines and recommendations are constitutionally protected and as such should be strictly implemented. However, many of its guidelines are not carried out in practice. The absence of alternative proposals and the inability of the population to take an active part in decision making has led to a permanent state of crisis that prevents the country from overcoming the difficulties it currently faces. Today, Cuban society is physically and morally exhausted with a single political party enthroned in power for more than half-a-century. A large part of the population lacks any faith in either the Party or its current leaders. As a response to this chronic economic and political crisis, the government has begun a process of timid and insufficient economic reforms in an attempt to avoid at all costs a necessary and inevitable political opening.

The Cuban Electoral System and the Assemblies of People's Power

Upon the triumph of the revolution in January 1959, Cuba's traditional political parties were defunct. In one of his first speeches, Fidel Castro posed a rhetorical question that has since become quite historic and not a little ironic: "Elections," he asked, "what for?" Ever since then Cuba's official history has attempted to interpret this phrase to mean that there was no sense in holding formal elections, given the great popularity and support the rebel triumph initially enjoyed. Others, however, saw this statement as the first manifestation of Castro's intention to remain in power indefinitely brushing aside the democratic institution of periodic elections.

According to official historiography, the gradual institutionalization of the revolution came about as a natural result of the increasing complexity of governmental tasks. However, the real impetus for this shift was the need for Cuba to join the Council for Mutual Economic Assistance (COMECON or CAME) in 1972, following the economic disaster brought about by the failure of the 10-million-ton sugar harvest of 1970. The Soviet Union was also keen on creating a legal foundation in Cuba that would permit a better fit with the legal norms of the socialist bloc. Because of this, when the 1976 Cuban Constitution was written, many of its principles and much of its verbiage were copied from the Soviets.

According to Article 131 of the Constitution, all citizens have the right to be heard at the highest level of the state, either directly or through elected representatives in the Assemblies of People's Power. Citizens also have the right to participate in periodic elections and popular referendums through a free, equal, and secret vote, with each elector afforded a single vote. Suffrage is universal for those over 16 years of age, except for those legally declared mentally unfit or convicted of a crime. Furthermore, all citizens have the right to be elected, but must be over 18 to serve in the National Assembly. This right to vote and be elected is extended to members of all branches of the armed forces.

Elections for the 614 National Assembly deputies take place every five years simultaneously with Provincial Assembly elections, while midterm elections for Municipal Assemblies occur every two-and-a-half years. Victory is based on simple majority. Voting is by secret ballot but is not mandatory. However, since voting is considered a fundamental revolutionary duty, failing to do so repeatedly can brand a citizen politically suspect and impact his or her social standing and career aspirations. However, term limits for top officials were instituted for the first time only in 2012–2013.

Between 1976 and the electoral and constitutional reforms of 1992 (discussed later), only the members of Municipal Assemblies were directly elected by the voters. Those elected as delegates to these Assemblies became empowered to then elect the delegates for each Provincial Assembly and the deputies who would serve in the National Assembly. However, these municipal delegates do not freely elect those who serve on the Provincial or National Assemblies. Instead, lists of candidates (along with alternates) are drawn up by candidacy commissions after consultation with mass organizations, and then these lists are presented to municipal delegates for approval (Roman 1993, 2003, 2006).

While the new Constitution of 1976 created a new system of People's Power, the new electoral law, passed in the same year, placed significant obstacles on the flexibility, strength, and autonomy of the Assemblies of People's Power. For example, all nominations for candidates for Municipal Assemblies take place at public gatherings where those present can nominate others who reside in the local area for the post of municipal delegate. Previous campaigning and electioneering is outlawed and elections do not include the discussion or debate of national issues or information about competing candidates' positions on any issues. This is because plans that impact the socioeconomic and political life of the country are designed at a much higher level than that of the municipal delegate. Such delegates have no ability to change plans or policies made at higher levels or to propose alternatives to them. In this sense, delegates are reduced to mere intermediaries between the local area from which they were elected and the Municipal Assembly that instructs them on how to respond to their electors.

A proposed candidate must agree to be nominated. While those present at the public meetings can share their opinions about the qualifications of the nominee, the law does not allow voters the chance to ask direct questions to the candidates during the nomination process. Once candidates are selected, the party and government simply publish candidate photos and biographies that highlight their revolutionary accomplishments, to which candidates have no input (Domínguez 1993). The method of voting for nominees at the municipal level is through a show of hands. Electors can vote for only a single nominee and each local area can put forth between two and eight candidates for election to the Municipal Assembly.

The electoral law of 1976 indirectly strengthened the power of the party over popularly elected representatives, since Candidacy Commissions led by party representatives prepared lists of nominees for provincial delegates, municipal and provincial executives, and national deputies (ibid.). Also, prior to 1992, National Assembly candidates had to be approved by the party's Central Committee before they could stand for election. Consultation in drawing up these lists was greatly broadened after 1992 to include input from all the major mass organizations (CTC, CDR, FMC, ANAP, FEU, FEEM, etc.), except the PCC and the UJC, which were removed from formal consultation (Roman 1993, 2006).

These Candidacy Commissions put together lists with an eye to assuring that at least 50 percent of the candidates for the Provincial Assemblies and the National Assembly are drawn from the previously elected delegates of the Municipal Assemblies, while the rest are chosen directly by the Candidacy Commissions. For example, in order to complete the candidate list of the more than 600 deputies who will serve in the National Assembly, roughly 300 are taken from the approximately 15,000 previously elected municipal delegates across the country, while another 300 are people with relevant social achievements or positions as determined by the Candidacy Commissions. This process allows these Commissions to easily circumvent undesirable or untrustworthy municipal delegates guaranteeing that no one who does not represent the interests of the reigning political system will make it beyond the local level and into the Provincial or National Assemblies.

While elected officials need not belong to the party, in practice these procedures resulted in more than 90 percent of National Assembly members being party members in the 1976 elections. While slightly over half of those elected to the first 1976 National Assembly had indeed been previously elected directly by the voters to their own municipal assemblies, more than 40 percent of the National Assembly was nominated for office by party-controlled nominating committees without ever having gone before the voters in direct elections. Also, there are no direct elections for the offices of president and vice president in Cuba. Instead, in Cuba those offices are filled by internal, indirect, noncompetitive elections within the National Assembly itself. Likewise, all top officers of the National Assembly, as well as the leadership cadre of the Council of State and the Council of Ministers, are elected by the National Assembly, not by popular vote. Furthermore, as with president and vice president, all candidates for these top posts are preselected by the party leadership. Thus, unlike elections at the municipal level, internal elections in the National Assembly provide deputies no choice among candidates (Roman 1993: 19).

Cuban authorities openly admit that only municipal elections are open and competitive, in the sense that candidates are chosen by constituents at neighborhood meetings and voters have a choice among two to eight different candidates at election time. However, even after the 1992 electoral and constitutional reforms, which made elections for National Assembly also direct, elections for both the Provincial and National Assemblies remained closed and noncompetitive. Voters now vote directly for their National Assembly deputies (who do not have to live in or be from the district they represent), but they are presented with a closed list of preselected candidates and encouraged to vote for the entire slate rather than for individuals. Thus, the number of candidates is equal to the number of posts to be filled: nomination is the equivalent to being elected, since there is just one candidate per post (Roman 2003, 2006). Voters do not choose between one or another candidate, but either approve or disapprove of those listed on the ballot, with the government encouraging voters to "*votar por todos*," that is, to endorse the entire slate listed as a symbolic show of unity and support. As a result of these structural conditions, no candidate who ran for office in the 1993, 1998, 2003, or 2008 National Assembly elections failed to be elected (Domínguez 2002: 243). Still as we will see later, an increasing proportion of Cuban voters have either refused to vote or refused to vote in the manner requested.

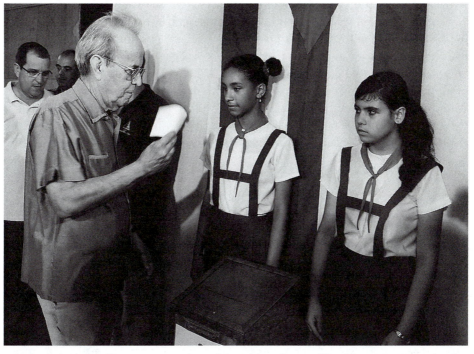

Former diplomat and long-time president of the National Assembly of People's Power of Cuba (NAPP) Ricardo Alarcón (left) casts his ballot, at a polling station in Havana, on April 25, 2010, during municipal elections. He was not reelected NAPP president in the subsequent 2012 elections and was removed from the Party's Politburo and Central Committee in the summer of 2013. (Adalberto Roque/AFP/Getty)

Former National Assembly president Ricardo Alarcón has explained that these procedures are a way to ensure "pluralistic" representation in the National Assembly. Thus, while the 1992 electoral reforms stipulate that up to 50 percent of National Assembly delegates must be previously elected in open, competitive elections at the municipal level, the rest are selected by candidacy commissions to ensure the election of those who already hold important government or party jobs, as well as to promote the representation of all sectors of society (women, youth, religious leaders, workers, doctors, farmers, teachers, etc.). Thus, unlike municipal elections in which voters are given a ballot of competing candidates, National Assembly elections feature a ballot with a list of preapproved candidates. Voters can approve of the candidates as an entire slate, choose individual candidates, or vote "blank" in protest (Roman 1993, 2003, 2006).

The inability of the Assemblies of People's Power and their delegates to resolve local problems and the failure of even high-placed leaders to respond effectively to the deepening crisis that threatens the country have provoked an increasing apathy toward participating in recent elections. This apathy is especially pronounced among young people who lack faith in government institutions. Many of them turn out on the day of election only to comply with a formal duty, while increasing numbers of them simply annul their ballots. Voting in Cuba is not a political act that reflects a citizen right but instead a survival mechanism for the population in the face of a system of near total governmental control. This growing apathy and dissent were on display in the results of the national elections held on January 20, 2008, as compared to the previous national vote five years earlier in 2003 (see Table 3.1).

Despite the patent lack of electoral alternatives and a strong campaign rolled out in the state media in favor of a "united vote," the 2008 elections showed a decrease in overall turnout and an increase in defiant votes. The sum of abstentions, selective votes, and invalidated ballots came to 1,370,725 electors, or more than 16 percent of all voters. This is a clear signal of the existence, permanence, and growth of a sector of the electorate that refuses to conform to government dictates and that will sooner or later demand a political space. They are Cuban citizens who lack the right to freely associate and to participate in creating a future for the nation (Castellanos 2008).

TABLE 3.1   Recent Growth in Abstentions, Selective, and Invalidated Votes

	2003	%	2008	%	Difference
1. Total number of electors	8,310,512	100	8,495,577	100	185,065
2. Total number who voted	8,115,215	97.65	8,231,365	96.89	116,150
3. Abstentions	193,306	2.35	264,212	3.11	70,906
4. Valid votes	7,803,893	96.16	7,839,358	95.24	35,465
5. United slate vote	7,128,856	91.34	7,125,752	90.89	−3,104
6. Selective vote	660,990	8.66	713,606	9.11	52,616
7. Invalidated ballots	313,247	3.76	392,907	8.16	79,660
8. The sum of 3 + 6 + 7	**1,167,543**	**14.04**	**1,370,725**	**16.13**	**203,182**

Cuba's International Relations

The foreign policies of states are often closely related to their domestic policies. Following this trend, after the revolution that began on January 1, 1959, Cuba's foreign policy was characterized by two fundamental elements: confrontation with the United States and solidarity with the world's socialist countries, chief among them the Soviet Union—at least until it ceased to exist after 1991.

As described earlier, Castro's ascension to power was immediately followed by a radicalization of Cuba's domestic policies, which led to an irreparable fracture in its close, historic, and dependent relationship with the United States. In 1960, after a number of U.S.-owned oil refineries in Cuba refused to process petroleum purchased from the Soviet Union, the Cuban government nationalized them. Outgoing U.S. president Eisenhower reacted by cutting Cuba's vital sugar quota to zero. The Soviet Union was only too happy to step in to purchase all of the remaining quota, as it would do systematically thereafter for the next 30 years. In January 1961, the United States severed its diplomatic relations with Cuba and sponsored an armed invasion force of Cuban exiles at the Bay of Pigs in April. In 1962, the United States engineered the expulsion of Cuba from the Organization of American States (OAS), intensified its trade embargo that had been first put in place in 1960, and in October 1962—now under orders from President John F. Kennedy—imposed a naval blockade of the island in response to the discovery that the USSR had been secretly installing nuclear missiles there. Also, between 1961 and 1965, the United States aided thousands of guerrillas who opposed the new Castro government and attempted to start a rebellion in the Escambray Mountains and in other regions of the country.

By the time Washington had severed its diplomatic relations with Cuba in January 1961, hundreds of thousands of Cubans had already fled to the United States. The

---

THE ORIGINS OF THE U.S. EMBARGO

At the direction of the U.S. State Department, in the fall of 1960, U.S. oil refineries refused to process Soviet crude. That was followed by Cuba's nationalization of the refineries, which was followed in turn by the suspension of the U.S. sugar quota. Sealing the acrimonious relationship was Cuba's announcement of the nationalization of all remaining U.S. properties and companies. After that precipitous decline, U.S. Ambassador Phillip Bonsal was recalled to Washington in late October with diplomatic relations broken off as 1961 dawned over a new Cuba.

On October 19, 1960, the first elements of what would become the infamous U.S. embargo, always referred to as the *bloqueo* ("blockade") by the Cuban government, were put in place. Starting on that day, the Eisenhower administration prohibited all U.S. exports to the island except for nonsubsidized food, medicine, and medical supplies. A little over a year later, President John F. Kennedy made the embargo total, by prohibiting all exports and imports, with exceptions requiring a special license. By May of 1964 the U.S. Commerce Department had instituted an unofficial policy of henceforth denying all such requests, including for food and medicine (Schwab 1999: 54).

Cuban exile invasion force that would attempt to oust Castro at the Bay of Pigs later that spring, Brigade 2506, drew its membership from that first group of exiles. Also among the exiles were the members of the Cuban Revolutionary Council, including its president, José Miró Cardona, revolutionary Cuba's first prime minister. The council was set up in late March 1961 by Richard Bissell, deputy director of the CIA. Organized just three weeks prior to the planned invasion, the council was expected to form the provisional government of Cuba once the Castro regime had been ousted.

The Cuban invasion was expected to proceed with the same ease that CIA-backed Guatemalan exiles had overthrown Guatemalan president Jacobo Árbenz and his reform government seven years earlier in Central America. However, CIA planners drastically underestimated the nationalist resolve and revolutionary commitment of the Cuban people. Unlike the counterintelligence and subterfuge successfully used against the Guatemalans in 1954, the CIA based its strategy in Cuba largely on wishful thinking and bad intelligence from biased sources within Cuba. They also misjudged Castro, who, unlike the indecisive and fatalistic Árbenz acted with re-sourcefulness and tenacity. Finally, Castro's deputy, Che Guevara, had witnessed the fall of Guatemala in 1954 first hand, steeling Cuban resolve to call Washington's bluff this time around (Schlesinger and Kinzer 1999).

On April 15, two days prior to the invasion, U.S. planes camouflaged as Cuban fighters and flown by exile pilots strafed various Cuban airports and military installations. Attempting to cripple the Cuban Air Force, the strikes only succeeded in killing several civilians, alerting the Cuban government to the imminent invasion, and provoking the ire of the Cuban people. During the massive state funeral for the dead that followed, Castro made a rousing speech in which he paraphrased Abraham

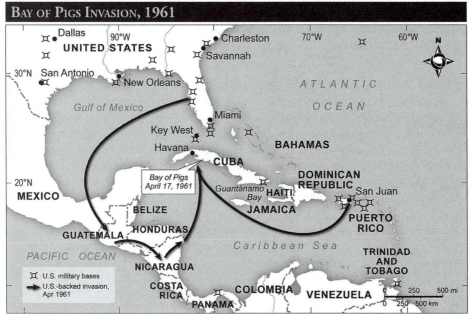

Often described as a perfect "fiasco," the failed U.S.-sponsored invasion of Cuba at the Bay of Pigs in April 1961 was carried out by Cuban exiles and only succeeded in helping to radicalize and consolidate the revolution. (ABC-CLIO)

Lincoln, calling his a revolution "of the humble, by the humble, and for the humble" (Cluster and Hernández 2006). Castro then wisely sized this opportune moment of national unity and publicly declared the revolution a socialist one for the first time.

"What the imperialists cannot forgive us for," he roared, "is that we have made a socialist revolution under the nose of the United States." This audacious statement implicitly connected socialism to the defense of the Cuban nation, transforming the previously taboo socialist ideology into the revolution's guiding light and primary means of consolidation. Under attack from the American-supported exiles, the majority of the Cuban people seemed to rally to Castro's call. At the same time, Castro ordered the roundup and imprisonment of as many as 100,000 suspected sympathizers and collaborators in the counterrevolutionary movement.

On April 17, the exile invasion began at Girón Beach near the Bay of Pigs on Cuba's south coast. However, Brigade 2506 could make little headway beyond the shallow coral reef that protected the beach. Once ashore, their advance was stymied by the large and inaccessible Zapata Swamp. Like the *Granma* guerrillas only five years before, the *brigadistas* had to jump into the water and wade ashore, where they were quickly defeated. Survivors were taken prisoner and later ransomed to the United States in exchange for $53 million in food and medical supplies.

Designed to achieve the feat of overthrowing the revolution, while at the same time ensuring "plausible deniability" to President Kennedy, the Cuban invasion was a complete failure. Kennedy had inherited a plan originally hatched by Eisenhower and so was never fully committed to supporting it. Despite tough anticommunist rhetoric in his presidential debates against Richard Nixon the year before, Kennedy refused to allow any direct U.S. military involvement in the invasion. However, CIA planners deluded themselves into believing that Kennedy would change his tune once the invasion was afoot. Such wishful thinking and miscalculation doomed the invasion from the start. In the end, the failed invasion facilitated exactly the outcome that it was designed to prevent. The revolution was both radicalized and consolidated, allowing Castro to disqualify all remaining moderates and purge the country with impunity. Also, this early attempt to overthrow the revolution justified Cuba's fear of subsequent invasion attempts, leading directly to the Cuban Missile Crisis.

"If the making of a radical revolution in Cuba required a break with the United States," writes Jorge Domínguez, "the defense of a radical revolution in the face of U.S. attack demanded support from the Soviet Union" (1993: 102). Known in Cuba as *La crisis de octubre* (the October crisis), what became known in the United States as the Cuban Missile Crisis began as a result of the continued threat of U.S. invasion after the failure of the Bay of Pigs 18 months earlier. Seeking out protection, Castro suggested that the Soviets sign a public military pact with Cuba as a way to keep the Americans at bay. However, when the Soviets proposed to back up such a public pact with the secret placing of Soviet nuclear missiles on the island, Castro agreed. Still, Castro was concerned that accepting the missiles might compromise Cuban independence, since they would be under exclusive Soviet control. He also preferred a public military pact, fearing what might happen if the Soviet missiles were discovered before they were fully operational.

These fears were confirmed when a U-2 spy plane detected the missile sites in the final stages of construction in mid-October 1962. Kicking off a famous "thirteen days" of calculated threats and intense negotiations, Kennedy announced to the world on October 22 that the United States had discovered the missiles. He demanded that the Soviets remove them and ordered a U.S. Navy "quarantine" of the island. While projecting a tough image, Kennedy also wanted to give Khrushchev the ability to respond to his demands without losing face. For that reason he labeled what was an illegal U.S. "blockade" of an independent country, a preventative "quarantine," refusing his generals' requests to authorize a military strike on the island.

As the world held its breath riveted on the verge of a potential nuclear holocaust, Kennedy projected a surprising toughness and poise in tense, sometimes cryptic negotiations with the Soviets, contrasting sharply with his previous missteps at the Bay of Pigs. For many exiles, however, Kennedy's earlier "betrayal" of Brigade 2506 was exacerbated when he helped to diffuse this new crisis by secretly promising not to invade Cuba. Khrushchev showed his own negotiating skill by successfully using backdoor communications to diffuse the crisis over the objections of Soviet hardliners. However, when he removed the missiles without consulting Cuba, Castro was furious.

While the Kennedy–Khrushchev agreement included a U.S. pledge not to invade Cuba, it also indicated that the fate of Cuba would again be decided by outsiders. The episode taught Castro that he could not fully trust his new Soviet sponsors. In fact, he would spend the remainder of the decade experimenting with insurgent subversion abroad and radical economic experimentation at home in defiance of Soviet advice. He would not reach out to them again until these radical experiments proved ruinous with Guevara's death in Bolivia in 1967 and Cuba's failed 10-million-ton sugar harvest of 1970.

The ongoing dispute with the United States (chronicled later) favored an eventual ideological rapprochement between the USSR and Cuba. Despite the resentments that continued to brew over the withdrawal of the Soviet missiles in 1962 and the Cuba's insistence on exporting armed rebellion to other Latin American countries, Fidel Castro left no doubt as to where his loyalties lay when he declared his staunch support of the Soviet invasion of Czechoslovakia during the Prague spring of 1968. Of course, this process of rapprochement accelerated after the economic crisis that engulfed Cuba at the end of the 1960s. Upon the centenary of Lenin's birth on April 22, 1970, when it was already clear that the Castro's wild plan to produce 10 million tons of sugar was unattainable, Cuba's maximum leader delivered a rousing speech praising the USSR. As a result, within two years Cuba signed several agreements that guaranteed financial assistance, trade, the postponement of debt payments, and Cuba's entry into the Council for Mutual Economic Assistance (Comecon).

Then in 1975—a full 17 years after the triumph of the revolution—the institutionalization of the state in the image of the USSR began. As described earlier, in that year the first Congress of the PCC took place, followed a year later by the adoption of a new Constitution, which declared the PCC to be the vanguard of society in the building socialism. More surprising was the fact that the Constitution's preamble specifically celebrated the need for socialist "internationalism" and strong relations with the USSR, something so absurd in constitutional history that it had no precedent even when Cuba was under American military occupation in 1901. Other milestones which marked improving relations between Havana and Moscow were the visit of Soviet premier Leniod Brezhnev in the mid-1970s and Comecon's announcement in 1977 of the building of a nuclear plant in Cuba along with the signing of an agreement to complement that plant with the construction of a center for nuclear research on the island.

Relations took on a new, more circumspect tone in April 1989 when Havana received a visit by the general secretary of the Communist Party of the Soviet Union, Mikhail Gorbachev. This man was the architect of the twin reforms that inadvertently led to the disintegration of the Soviet Union, *perestroika* (restructuring) and *glasnost* (openness). Even though Castro rejected the implementation of any such reforms in Cuba, upon the visit, the two countries signed a friendship pact for the coming 25 years. Gorbachev's Soviet opening contrasted sharply with the spirit of retrenchment that had prevailed at the third Congress of the PCC held in February 1986, where it launched the "Rectification of Errors and Negative Tendencies," a mobilization aimed at curbing the influence of perestroika in Cuba. As part of this effort, in 1989 the PCC prohibited the circulation of Soviet newspapers and magazines such as *Novelties of Moscow* and *Sputnik*, under the justification that they had begun to promote the false values of bourgeois democracy and the American lifestyle. This was followed shortly thereafter by the suspension of all economic trade with Cuba, food shortages and blackouts, the eventual withdrawal of Soviet troops, and an end to $2 billion annual economic subsidy that Moscow had long granted Havana.

Tensions between the United States and Cuba have waxed and waned since the negotiated settlement between the United States and the USSR that diffused the Cuban Missile Crisis in 1962. One cause of ongoing conflict was Cuba's military incursions in several Latin American countries. This was followed by its increasing presence in African countries including Algeria, the Congo, Guinea-Bissau, Somalia, and most importantly, Angola. These and other events were clear manifestations of the Cuban

As part of Soviet president Mikhail Gorbachev's first visit to Cuba in April 1989, he meets for a summit with Cuban president Fidel Castro (left). Within a year the Soviet Union would begin to collapse and as a result Cuba would enter the "special period." (AP Photo)

government's position that armed struggle was the only way for the countries of the Third World to liberate themselves once and for all from American imperialism. In this vein, Havana played host to the 1966 Tri-Continental Conference, which was attended by representatives from revolutionary groups in countries around the world. Similarly, ill-fated Cuban military expeditions were dispatched to Venezuela and— most infamously and disastrously—to Bolivia under the leadership of Che Guevara. This belief in armed struggle was reinforced after the failure of the Popular Front in Uruguay and a U.S.-supported military coup put an end to Salvador Allende's democratic socialism in Chile in 1973.

The only regional victory of the Cuban government in exporting armed revolution was in Nicaragua, where the Sandinistas overthrew the dictator Anastasio Somoza in 1979. Another major military victory for the Cuban policy of armed struggle took place between 1975 and 1989 in Africa. Starting 1975, Cuban soldiers fought in Angola and Ethiopia with logistical support from the Soviets. The United States interpreted this deployment as a manifestation of illegitimate communist infiltration and expansionism in the region. In 1980, relations deteriorated further when the U.S. government accused Cuba of aiding left-wing rebels in El Salvador. This was exacerbated in 1983 when the United States invaded Granada, whose own revolutionary government had received Cuban support.

Cuba has steadfastly rejected attempts by any figure, foreign country, or nongovernmental organization or institution attempting to include Cuba in international agreements that would require the restoration of civil society on the island. This may have been behind the events of February 1996, when a number of opposition figures gathered under the banner of the *Concilio Cubano* (Cuban Council) were arrested. Just a few days later, Cuban fighters armed with air-to-air missiles shot down two light civilian aircraft belonging to the Miami-based exile group Brothers to the Rescue,

THE CARTER THAW AND THE MARIEL BOATLIFT, 1978–1980

In the mid-1970s some Cuban-Americans initiated a dialogue with the Cuban government aimed at allowing family visits and wining the release of more than 3,000 political prisoners (Levine 2002; Ojito 2005). The Carter administration eventually won the release of the prisoners and more than 100,000 Cuban-Americans made family visits in 1978 and 1979. The governments also set up "interests sections" in each other's capitals to enable diplomatic representation. However, rapprochement was derailed by Cuba's military incursions in Africa and the refugee crisis known as the Mariel boatlift.

Ironically, the exodus of 125,000 people from the port of Mariel in the summer of 1980 was provoked in part by the demonstration effect of Cuban-American visits. Many islanders asked themselves why continue to sacrifice for a revolution that had been unable to provide a standard of living equal to that achieved in the United States by their relatives. While many Cubans gained the opportunity to start over in the United States through Mariel, it also contributed to Carter's loss in the 1080 elections. This threw U.S.–Cuban relations into a deep freeze and gave *Marielitos* both a black eye and a "scarred face," based on their negative portrayal in the U.S. media.

leaving four dead. As a result, President Bill Clinton quickly signed the Helms–Burton Law scuttling any hope of improved relations. Similarly, in 2003, just as Cuba sought membership in the Cotonu Accords—economic cooperation agreements between the European Union (EU) and the countries of Africa, the Caribbean, and the Pacific—the island's government imprisoned 75 nonviolent dissidents and executed three young adults who had attempted to hijack a ferry in order to flee the country. In response, Cuba's application to Cotonu was denied and the EU adopted a "Common Position" of economic sanctions against the Cuban government. Then, in 2009, the Cuban authorities rejected an historic invitation to rejoin the OAS. While Havana justified its position by saying that the organization was "dead" and an "instrument of U.S. imperialism," its refusal may have had more to do with the condition that it follow the Inter-American Democratic Charter adopted on 2001, which demands that all members respect the human rights and fundamental freedoms of its citizens. Thus, in its rejection of the invitation Cuba excluded itself from the OAS.

ECONOMIC CRISIS, REFORM, AND EMERGENT CIVIL SOCIETY, 1990–2013

The 1990s were years of major transformations in Cuban social and economic life. The economic crisis that began in the late 1980s led to a series of economic reforms, including the promotion of foreign investment and international tourism and the allowance of domestic microenterprise and exile remittances. Such reforms are best understood as calculated adjustments *within* the existing socialist political system aimed at ensuring its survival, not changes of the system itself necessarily leading to transition or regime change (Domínguez 1997). Still, reforms led to the emergence of new domestic and international dynamics that directly affected the way state institutions had traditionally interacted with Cuban society.

Specifically, the economic crisis allowed the emergence of a host of new civil, cultural, intellectual, and economic actors. The presence of these actors has indirectly and unintentionally challenged the hegemony of existing revolutionary state institutions. Likewise, the presence of new national and especially international NGOs, the renewed profile and presence of organized religion—especially the Catholic Church—and the boom in both exile visits and emigration have affected Cuban society in important ways. In short, the vast array of civil, political, and cultural institutions originally created by the Cuban government in the 1960s and 1970s to serve and promote, as well as to channel, coerce, and control, the broad-based revolutionary consensus of the Cuban population were confronted by a new economic and sociopolitical environment, challenging their effectiveness and legitimacy as representatives of the Cuban people.

The Fourth Party Congress of 1991 and the Constitutional Revisions of 1992

One major result of the collapse of the Soviet Union was the series of institutional adjustments proposed during the Fourth Congress of the PCC in 1991, most of which were approved as part of the revised Constitution in July 1992. Party leadership underlined its desire to make no ideological concessions and rejected outright the errors of openness and restructuring (*glasnost* and *perestroika*) that had led to the "political disaster" in the communist regimes of Europe. Still, the Congress ratified the repatriation of Cuban troops from Africa and sought to work within the UN system in the future. Likewise, while it reiterated the socialist nature of the revolution under the principles of Marxism–Leninism, it also recognized that ideology "should not be applied dogmatically" (Domínguez 2002: 246) and that the nationalism of José Martí was as important to the revolution as the socialism of Karl Marx.

This ambivalent opening to the realities of a changing world was exemplified by the often contradictory policies approved of by the Fourth Congress and later added to the revised Constitution. For example, the Congress endorsed the development of an international tourism industry, the liberalization of self-employment, and the promotion of foreign investment. It also committed itself to real dialogue with Cuba's various religious denominations and permitted believers to join the rank and file of the party for the first time. However, the main thrust of the 1991 Congress was to resist any far-reaching political change and preserve the socialist character of the revolution at all costs.

Similarly, while the party issued a call for open discussion and debate in the run-up to the Congress and subsequent constitutional revisions, final changes were tightly controlled by party and National Assembly committees, and the final text was never submitted to a national plebiscite. Still, a few changes in the constitution and the functioning of the institutions of governance are noteworthy. First, all references to the Soviet Union and to Cuba's membership in the "socialist community" of nations were removed from the Constitution and replaced with a greater emphasis on the nation's "solidarity" with its Latin American and Caribbean neighbors. Second, the declared commitment to advocate and support "internationalist" missions and wars of national liberation was stricken from the constitution.

Third, the open advocacy of a "scientific materialist conception of the universe" was replaced by a new emphasis on the freedom of religion. In fact, the PCC's requirement that all members be strictly "atheist or agnostic" was replaced by a declaration of the party's "secular" orientation. This change indicated that religious belief and revolutionary commitment were no longer incompatible, presaging a religious revival in Cuba during the 1990s. Fourth, the ineffective National Assembly was brought back to life through the appointment of rising star and Castro confidant Ricardo Alarcón as its new president. Included in the renovation of the National Assembly was the initiation of the first ever direct elections for its deputies (mentioned earlier). Finally, the constitution limited state ownership to the "fundamental" means of production, theoretically opening the economy to limited forms of foreign investment, privatization, and private entrepreneurship (Pérez Milán 1992).

Despite these formal constitutional changes, few far-reaching economic reforms and no real political liberalization took place after initial adjustments proved sufficient in ensuring regime survival. In fact, privatization never took place; private entrepreneurship was regulated almost out of existence (or driven underground) by the end of the decade and foreign investment dropped off significantly after 2000. The character of the Cuban government continues to be deeply authoritarian, with a single legal political party and extensive limits on the exercise of most civil liberties and political freedoms. Despite the emergence of a lively and at times vigorous intellectual, social, and cultural debate and criticism in the arts, in popular music, in cinematic production, in some semi-independent think tanks, and in the pages of specialized journals and some magazines, all mass media (radio, television, and newspapers) remain under strict state control. Indeed, mass media comes across like a series of government press releases and remains a tool of the party, faithfully performing a clearly propagandistic, cheerleading function.

The U.S. Embargo Today

After the onset of the "special period," the Cuban government legalized the possession of dollars. Cuban exiles responded by sending millions in remittances to their relatives in Cuba. Around that time, Cuba's official news media began to refer to the Cuban-American community in more neutral terms, calling them simply *la comunidad* ("the community"), in place of the more derogatory *gusanos* ("worms") or *traidores* ("traitors") that had been standard previously. Cubans joke that this change in rhetoric was the result of the fact that these *gusanos* had now become all-important *mariposas* ("butterflies") flying back to Cuba with money that could be used to keep the revolution alive. In other words, the *traidores* ("traitors") of old had been transformed into *trae-dolares* ("dollar bringers") of the special period.

On top of that contradiction is the irony that the single most important group of organized and vocal supporters of the U.S. embargo against Cuba (Cuban-Americans) are the very same people who most consistently violate the spirit, purpose, and effectiveness of the embargo by sending upward of as much as $2.6 billion each year to their struggling relatives on the island with another $2.5 billion sent in the form of care packages of food, medicine, electronics, etc. (Morales 2013). However, on an individual level most exiles can easily reconcile supporting an economic strike against the Castro government, while at the same time making sure that their relatives live marginally better during material scarcity and growing inequality of the interminable special period.

Prior to this much needed injection of hard currency from Cuban-Americans, the U.S. government (influenced by the powerful Cuban-American lobby) had sought to strengthen the stalemated embargo by passing the Torricelli Act (also known as the Cuban Democracy Act) in 1992. Prohibiting subsidiaries of U.S. companies from trading with Cuba and refusing U.S. docking rights to ships that had recently docked in Cuba, the Act sought to make it harder for companies to thwart the embargo by working through a third party (Jatar-Hausmann 1999: 133). The Torricelli Act also included a "Track II" stipulation that promoted increased cultural and scholarly exchange with Cuba with the controversial aim of promoting change and "democracy building efforts" on the island. While many students, journalists, and scholars were able to travel to the island as a result of this stipulation, the Act was taken advantage of as a boondoggle by some exile organizations in Miami and attacked by the Cuban government as the equivalent of formalized spying (Raúl Castro 1996).

Combined with the catastrophic impact of the fall of the USSR, the Torricelli Act seemed to provoke just the chaos and desperation it was designed to create. In early August 1994, the government endured its first ever crisis-induced riots along

Havana's Malecón, as unsafe departures on flimsy rafts exploded across the island. Forced to the bargaining table in order to put an end to the rafter crisis, the U.S. and Cuban governments eventually agreed to a migration accord that would allow a minimum of 20,000 Cuban immigrants per year to enter the United States, while future rafters would be returned to Cuba. Such an unexpected change in policy infuriated many exile leaders who emboldened their efforts to ratchet up the embargo through the Helms–Burton Act (Mesa-Lago and Pérez-López 2005: 17; Uriarte 2002: 30).

Helms–Burton, officially christened the Libertad (Liberty) Act, was essentially a 39-page law written by the elected political leaders of the Cuban-American community (Ileana Ros-Lehtinen and Lincoln Díaz-Balart of Florida, and Robert Menéndez of New Jersey) with a little help from their friends at the Cuban American National Foundation (CANF). The law's four titles required the United States to (1) oppose the admission of Cuba to any international lending organizations and revoke aid to any former republic of the USSR that provided economic assistance to Cuba, (2) draw up an assistance plan for a transition government that specifically did not include the Castro brothers and ensure the return of confiscated properties to Cuban-Americans, (3) allow these former property owners to sue third country parties who "traffic" in or profit from this property, and (4) deny U.S. visas to officers of any of those foreign companies and their family members. Given the unprecedented harshness of these measures, few expected the bill ever to become law. However, when the Cuban Air Force made good on its warnings to shoot down two exile-piloted Brothers to the Rescue planes in the spring of 1996, Clinton quickly signed the bill into law in a bid to outflank Bob Dole in the coming presidential elections.

Given the controversy surrounding the extraterritoriality of title 3, Clinton, George W. Bush, and Obama have each consistently waived its application, as it imperils economic relations with many of the major trading partners of the United States. Apart from throwing a bone to the politically important Cuban-American lobby, Helms–Burton seems to have had little practical effect in Cuba. In fact, it has only served to further alienate U.S. policy toward Cuba in the eyes of the world, providing Castro another tool with which to rally a fearful Cuban population against the United States.

Ironically, while "democracy" and "*libertad*" are the code words used to name these acts, the fact is that the majority of the articles contained in them have more to do with recovering the lost property of exiles and dictating to Cuba what form its future government should take, than actually promoting democracy or liberty on the island (Jatar-Hausmann 1999: 131–147). Perhaps Castro was indicating his preference for a politically useful enemy when he ordered the shoot down of two planes in an election year, all but ensuring that Clinton would sign Helms–Burton.

Since 1996 a major movement by a host of grassroots organizations and a collection of U.S. businesses has attempted to weaken the embargo. They scored a major victory in 2000 in the passage of the Trade Sanctions Reform and Export Enhancement Act (TSRA), which led to the first ever sales of U.S. food and agricultural products to Cuba since the revolution. Direct sales of these products continue to be fully legal, provided that they are conducted on a cash-only basis. Although rejected at first by a proud Fidel Castro, he decided to purchase these products starting in 2001 after a slump in tourism and the destruction caused by Hurricane Michelle. Since then Cuba has gradually increased its food imports from the United States from $4.4 million in 2001 to $470 million in 2005, making the island the 25th largest agricultural export market of the United States that year and making the United States Cuba's fourth most important supplier of imports after Venezuela, China, and Spain (Mesa-Lago and Pérez-López 2005: 38; Pérez-López 2006).

After being the target of considerable criticism from an expectant exile lobby, the Bush administration announced limits on the flow of foreign currencies into Cuba in May 2004, with the recommendations of the Commission for Assistance to a Free Cuba (CAFC). Realizing that remittances were neutralizing the effectiveness of the embargo, the commission targeted Cuban-American remittances and family visits. The various recommendations, accepted in their entirety by President Bush on June 30, 2004, confirmed the remittance limit of $300 per quarter, restricted the kinds of family members who could legally receive remittances, limited family visits to once every three years for a maximum of two weeks, and severely restricted the amount of luggage and money one could bring to the island (Mesa-Lago 2004).

Fidel Castro responded by raising prices in dollar stores across the island, instituting the equivalent of a 20 percent tax on anyone changing dollars into convertible pesos, and removing U.S. dollars from national circulation (Mesa-Lago and Pérez-López 2005: 38, 188). Then, in the summer of 2006, CAFC issued a second report that reiterated its refusal to accept a Cuban succession upon the death of Fidel Castro and included a secret annex that has given rise to much speculation. At the same time, a November 2006 GAO report criticized the USAID and many exile organizations for their inadequate oversight and misuse of some of the monies allocated by CAFC to spur the Cuban transition (GAO 2006; Ruiz 2006). Moreover, unlike the EU sanctions imposed in 2003, U.S. measures like Helms–Burton and CAFC include extraterritorial punishments of third countries and seek to unilaterally dictate the terms of any future Cuban transition, putting them in direct conflict with accepted norms of international relations and making them illegitimate under international law.

During his first term, President Barack Obama fulfilled his campaign promise to do away with much of the Bush-era restrictions on travel and remittances. In fact, most Cuban-Americans can now send remittances and travel to Cuba at will. Moreover, the Obama administration has pushed through changes that allow for much greater access to U.S. visas for Cuban academics, intellectuals, and artists wanting to visit the United States. Additionally, despite the fact that a general travel ban is still in place for the U.S. population as a whole, opportunities for legal, academic, religious, and cultural people-to-people travel to Cuba have greatly expanded. On the Cuban side, the rising expectation that Raúl Castro's economic reforms would also include a major liberalization of his government's own extensive restrictions on the international travel of its own citizens was met with the January 2013 migration reform, which did away with the exit visa requirement.

Another major stumbling block to improved relations is the imprisonment of U.S. contractor Alan Gross, who was sentenced to 15 years in prison in 2010 for distributing equipment among Cuba's tiny Jewish community to enable independent access to the Internet. At the same time, Cuba continues to demand the release and return of five agents who—as members of an extensive clandestine "wasp network" in South Florida—had infiltrated a number of exile groups in the mid-1990s. While one of the five was recently released on probation and returned to Cuba, the four others continue to serve long sentences in U.S. federal prison.

THE TWO EMBARGOS

The U.S. embargo against the Cuban government obscures the other, more tangible embargo endured by the Cuban people. This is the embargo the Cuban government imposes *internally* upon the creativity, entrepreneurship, and ambition of the Cuban people. The biggest irony and tragedy behind the continuance of the external U.S. embargo is that the threat it poses to the current Cuban government (both real and exaggerated) has made it easy for the Castro brothers to justify their continued internal embargo against any further economic or political reforms that might threaten the current government's vice-like grip on power. It is in this sense that the strengthening of the U.S. embargo under Helms–Burton and CAFC has only helped to entrench and embolden the regime it is presumably designed to weaken. Moreover, in practice, the embargo functions much like a new version of the hated Platt Amendment, dictating Cuba's future from abroad and arrogantly seeking to protect Cubans from themselves. Also like Platt, the embargo serves as the perfect imperialist symbol against which the Cuban government can easily rally nationalist unity and support.

Human Rights, Political Prisoners, and Opposition Groups

As has been explained, the existence of other political parties in Cuba is legally prohibited and the Communist Party is constitutionally recognized as sole political, economic, and social guide of Cuban society. Still, Cuba is home to various parties and groupings from across the political spectrum, including libertarian-socialists, liberals, republicans, social-democrats, and Christian-democrats, among others. While of diverse ideological tendencies, these groups share a nonviolent approach, an insistence on independence, and demands for opening the political system to multiparty elections, releasing all political prisoners, enforcing the rule of law, reforming the economy, and ending the age-old U.S.-Cuba dispute. However, these groups—together with various human rights groups and opposition organizations—"remain isolated, weak, and subject to constant harassment" (Mujal-León 2009: 30). They do not have large membership nor have they succeeded in promoting a clear political alternative or program appealing enough to take root among the population. Of course, apart from the internal challenges that all such groups face, the regime's repressive nature, the lack of effective freedom of assembly, the state monopoly over the mass media, and severe restrictions on access to the Internet have all contributed to this situation.

The creation of any independent association in Cuba requires official recognition from the Ministry of Justice. This requirement constitutes a serious obstacle because any association without such legal certification is considered illegal, and thus, vulnerable to legal prosecution, with its members risking arrest and long prison sentences. Additionally, the palpable fear typically found among the population of totalitarian states is also present in Cuba. This fear hobbles the growth of these small political groups and prevents an informed and objective appraisal of their programs—if they exist—by other Cuban citizens.

Despite the initial broad-based popular support for the revolution, active opposition existed from the very beginning. However, in the aftermath of the Bay of Pigs fiasco (April 1961) and the eventual routing of the remaining armed opposition groups by the mid-1960s, most significant antigovernment activity was organized from abroad and thus had little impact or resonance with the Cuban people. Those who openly criticized the direction that the revolution took were routinely sentenced to long prison terms. Many who criticized the regime but were unwilling or unable to fight sought to emigrate in one of the many exile waves since 1959. In short, with the unwitting help of the United States in welcoming exiles "with open arms," the Cuban government succeeded in controlling internal dissent by externalizing it.

In fact, many of Cuba's most prominent political prisoners have been released on the condition that they immediately leave the country. Such was the case of most of the 3,600 political prisoners released from Cuban prisons after the tireless efforts of some Cuban-Americans working in conjunction with the Carter administration in 1979. This was also the case with the vast majority of the 166 political prisoners who were released between July 2010 and March 2011 as a result of negotiations between the Cuban authorities, the Catholic Church, and Spanish government. Only 12 remained in Cuba under parole (Freedom House 2012). Those who oppose the regime but cannot go into *exilio* ("exile") often resign themselves to living in what Cubans call *insilio* ("internal exile," or "insile"). That is, these citizens opt to unplug as much as possible from public life and develop a strategic double personality or duplicity (*doble moral*), wearing one false face in public and another more authentic face in private.

However, the economic, moral, and existential crisis of the special period during the last two decades (1990–2013) has made it more difficult for all Cubans to maintain such a delicate ideological balance. This new environment has led to the strengthening of an increasingly vigorous and legitimate opposition movement from within the island's alienated professional middle class. That movement had begun to emerge at the end of the 1970s under leaders such as Ricardo Bofill and the brothers Gustavo and Sebastián Arcos Bergnes, who advocated nonviolent change from within. Unlike early counterrevolutionaries who saw socialism as a betrayal and used violence and often terrorism to undermine and overthrow the revolution, most emerging dissidents had been lifelong revolutionaries and thus directed their objections against the widespread lack of intellectual freedom, authoritarian centralism of state power, and absence of any real opportunity for internal debate. As such they have generally rejected solutions coming from Washington or Miami, including the embargo, and instead have attempted to work within the socialist structure to bring about nonviolent change and national reconciliation (Sánchez Santacruz 2003).

The first significant dissident movement of the 1990s to provoke repression from the Cuban government and gain international recognition was a coalition of more than 140 tiny opposition groups led by Leonel Morejón. This *Concilio Cubano* (Cuban Council), as the group called itself, was founded in October 1995 and called for amnesty for political prisoners, respect for the current Socialist Constitution, respect for all human rights as recognized by the UN, freer markets and ownership rights, and a more open and direct electoral system. However, before the group could hold its first major meeting, the government unleashed a wave of repression against it, jailing its leaders and banning any future meetings.

The second high-profile effort to bring about nonviolent changes from within was led by a small nucleus of four economic specialists, one of whom, Vladimiro Roca, is the son of a founder of Cuba's Communist Party. Known as Internal Dissidents' Working Group, this group published a scathing critique of the government's economic strategy and political system, entitled "*La patria es de todos*" (The Fatherland Belongs to Us All), demanding that the government go beyond tentative economic reforms and embrace a full democratic opening. Criticizing the total lack of space in which to develop an authentic civil society where alternative voices, policies, and visions could be developed, the declaration argued, "The Cuban government ignores the word 'opposition.' Those of us who do not share its political stance, or who just simply don't support it, are considered enemies" (Bonné Carcasses et al. 1997). The government responded by arresting the declaration's four authors and holding them without a trial for almost two years. Finally, they were charged with sedition and endangering the national economy in September 1998 and were tried and convicted in March 1999.

Perhaps the most well-known effort to widen the political playing field and bring about major changes in the country's constitution and political structure grew out of the lay-Catholic organization *Movimiento Cristiano de Liberación* (Christian Liberation Movement, MCL), which was led until his untimely death in the summer of 2012 by the longtime dissident Oswaldo Payá. Named the Varela Project, after the famous 19th-century Cuban priest and independence advocate Félix Varela, this movement aimed to change the socialist system from within using nonviolent constitutional means. Although Payá was awarded the Sakharov Prize in 2002 as a recognition for his pro-democracy work, he often worked in obscurity within Cuba and faced a for-

This May 14, 2002, photo shows Cuban dissident Oswaldo Payá speaking in Havana. During his lifetime, Payá was nominated for the Nobel Peace Prize for his leadership of the pro-democracy Varela Project. He died in a tragic auto crash on July 22, 2012 under mysterious circumstances. (Jorge Uzon/AFP/Getty Images)

midable foe in the unbending and repressive socialist regime. In fact, after effectively quashing the Varela Project—even after former president Jimmy Carter lauded it during his historic May 2002 visit to the island—Fidel Castro engineered a constitutional reform of his own that made socialism an "irrevocable" and constitutionally protected part of the island's character. He followed this a year later with an unprecedented crackdown on Cuba's dissident movement.

In the spring of 2003, with the world's attention focused on the U.S. invasion of Iraq, Castro stoked the nationalist fear of a simultaneous invasion of Cuba. He used this popular anxiety to justify harsh measures against dissidents. With the help of a number of well-placed Cuban agents who had infiltrated the opposition, including Manuel David Orrio, who had become a well-known independent journalist and frequent visitor to the home of James Cason, the chief of the U.S. interest section in Havana, a total of 75 opposition leaders, economists, and independent journalists were arrested in what became known as the "black spring." Convicted of collaborating with the country's "enemies" against Cuban independence, these activists were sentenced to prison terms averaging 20 years each. These dissidents joined the roughly 350 political prisoners already in Cuba's jails, according to Elizardo Sánchez Santacruz, the leader of the island-based Cuban Committee for Human Rights and National Reconciliation. As a result of this episode and other similar incidents over the past 45 years, Cuba's poor record in upholding universally recognized civil and political freedoms continues to be condemned by the leading human rights organizations around the world, including Amnesty International, Human Rights Watch, Freedom House, and the United Nations.

LAURA POLLÁN AND *LAS DAMAS DE BLANCO* (THE LADIES IN WHITE)

Two weeks after the imprisonment of 75 dissidents during the "black spring" of 2003, Laura Pollán—whose husband Héctor Maseda was among the prisoners—led a group to Havana's Santa Rita Catholic Church. Dressed in white and bearing photos of the imprisoned, these women prayed together for their release. After repeating this on a number of successive Sundays, the women began a public procession from the church to a nearby park after Mass. Now carrying pink gladiolas and chanting "*Libertad!*" (freedom) as they walked, the women's silent prayers quickly became a public protest.

Not content to merely ask Saint Rita for her divine intercession, these "*Damas de Blanco*" (Ladies in White)—as they soon became known—simultaneously demanded freedom for their loved ones and boldly exercised their right to freedom of expression and association. Casting aside the anonymity of the domestic sphere and consciously occupying public space provoked the ire of Cuba's "rapid response brigades" who verbally and sometimes physically abused the women. Although the last of "the 75" were released in 2011 and despite the tragic death of Pollán in October of that year, the *Damas* continue their Sunday processions now demanding the release of all political prisoners (García Freyre 2008).

The Emergence of Civil Society

Exiled Cuban political sociologist Haroldo Dilla has argued that the economic crisis of the 1990s has "accelerated the bankruptcy of the state socialist economic-growth model" (Dilla and Oxhorn 2002: 16). As a result, the vertically integrated and highly centralized system of state institutions has begun to erode, ceding space to a wide variety of new actors and organizations, which together constitute an emergent civil society. This civil society includes the strictly private fraternal, cultural, and sports associations, which have little political impact or social profile beyond the local level. Cuba's many religious institutions are also an important and increasingly dynamic element of Cuban civil society. One might also include Cuba's many state-sanctioned mass organizations themselves, given their embeddedness in many people's lives.

Raúl Castro declared as much in a March 1996 speech to the party's Central Committee. "Our concept of civil society is not the same as the one they refer to in the United States," he explained. "Rather, it is our own Cuban socialist civil society, encompassing our strong mass organizations, namely the CTC, the CDRs, the FMC, the ANAP, the FEU, the FEEM, and the Pioneers" (Gunn 1995; Raúl Castro 1996). However, the limited autonomy of these government-operated nongovernmental organizations normally prevents them from successfully resisting subordination to the state. Indeed, with rare exceptions, they normally function as mere consultation and "transmission belts" for top-down state policies.

Civil society can be defined as "the social fabric formed by a multiplicity of self-constituted, territorially based units which peacefully coexist and collectively *resist subordination* to the state, at the same time that they *demand inclusion* into national political structures" (Dilla and Oxhorn 2002: 11, emphasis in the original). By this definition, institutions of civil society need not be absolutely independent from the state, nor have an antistate agenda. However, they must exercise significant autonomy from the state, have some organic base, derive from elements within the national territory, seek to impact national issues, and accept nonviolent coexistence with other civil and political organizations. While such criteria clearly exclude some, it would also include a wide spectrum of actors and organizations that make up the emergent civil society of today's Cuba.

This group is constituted by a variety of churches and religious congregations, including the many traditional Afro-Cuban communities of faith, the Catholic Church and its many lay organizations, Cuba's many mainline and evangelical Protestant denominations, as well as a small but vibrant Jewish community. There are also a series of community-based social movements clustered around environmental and self-help issues. Furthermore, Cuba's many new economic actors, including the members of cooperatives and farmer's markets, the foreign and domestic technocratic-entrepreneurial sector, and the more than 400,000 registered self-employed workers (along with their perhaps more numerous underground counterparts) are likely the domestic leaders in transforming their growing economic power and independence into civic and social influence, if not yet into a formal political presence (Dilla 2000, 2001, 2003, 2005, 2006; Dilla and Oxhorn 2002).

An assortment of domestic and international magazines, websites, think tanks, and nongovernmental organizations (NGOs) make up an important part of this emergent civil society. Official Catholic Church publications such as *Espacio Laical* (http://www.espaciolaical.org/) and *Palabra Nueva* (http://www.palabranueva.net/) have been instrumental in creating a space for vital dialogue and debate of national issues outside the control of the PCC and its official media. The semiofficial journal *Temas* (published in Havana since 1995 and directed by Rafael Hernández) has also played a role in fostering constructive and critical debate. Likewise, the Madrid-based websites, *Cuba Encuentro* (http://www.cubaencuentro.com/) and *Diario de Cuba* (http://www.diariodecuba.com/) have functioned as welcome antidotes to the lethargic and uninformative state media, as have an assortment of blogs and blogger platforms written from both within Cuba—such as *Havana Times* (http://www.havanatimes.org/), *La Joven Cuba* (http://jovencuba.com/), *Observatorio Crítico* (http://observatoriocriticodesdecuba.wordpress.com/), and the *Voces Cubanas* portal (http://vocescubanas.com/), which hosts Yoani Sánchez's *Generation Y* (http://www.desdecuba.com/generationy/)—and abroad—including the Barcelona-based blog *Penúltimos Días* (http://www.penultimosdias.com/) and the Miami news site *Café Fuerte* (http://cafefuerte.com/).

The organized internal opposition (described in this chapter) is perhaps a leading element of civil society, except that it still is internally divided and continues to suffer from the problem of invisibility on account of its total lack of access to the mass media. While this situation has improved slightly in recent years due to the emergence of blogging, Twitter, and other social media on the island since 2007, the extremely slow speed, high cost, and low rate of penetration of the Internet in Cuba is a continuing obstacle. The government holds that this opposition is illegitimate, arguing that members join only in order to qualify for U.S. refugee status so that they can emigrate. Another common accusation is that dissidents are merely "lackeys of imperialism" whose nationalist aims are compromised by the financial support they supposedly receive from the U.S. government. Furthermore, the government claims that they lack any internal following or organic popular support.

While these criticisms are indeed true of some of the more opportunistic elements of the opposition, most dissidents and other independent activists actually oppose the U.S. embargo and maintain a political line quite independent from that promoted by Washington. Furthermore, the only real difference between their opinions and those held by the population at large is that they have decided to cease being silent (and complicit) in a system with which they have fundamental disagreements. They bravely overcome their considerable and legitimate fears of state retribution, seeking to exercise their rights as citizens to share their opinions openly about the significant issues that face their embattled homeland.

Some of the leaders in creating independent, alternative spaces for creative dialogue and critical debate in recent years include the *Convivencia* (http://convivenciacuba.es/) project in Pinar del Río headed by the lay Catholic catechist Dagoberto Valdés, the Cuban art and poetry group *Omni-Zona Franca* (http://omnifestivalpoesiasinfin.blogspot.com/), The Cuban Lawyers' Association (http://ajudicuba.wordpress.com/) the Cubalex Legal Information Center (http://jurisconsultocuba.wordpress.com/) started by a group of young independent Afro-Cuban lawyers such as Laritza Diversent, Yaremis Flores, and Veizant Boloy, and the TED Talk-like organization "*Estado de SATS*" (http://www.estadodesats.com/) created by Antonio G. Rodiles and Ailer González. These emergent civil society groups and projects make intensive use of new information and communication technologies (NITCs) such as Internet,

ESTADO DE SATS AND *OMNI-ZONA FRANCA*

Estado de SATS and *Omni-Zona Franca* are two of Cuba's most unique and innovative autonomous sociocultural projects. Founded by Antonio G. Rodiles, *Estado de SATS* seeks to create a pluralistic space where open and frank debate can take place. The project sponsors panel discussions, forums, technology seminars, and other events that are filmed and broadcast via the Internet. *Omni-Zona Franca* is a multidisciplinary art and poetry collective started in the drab and isolated housing project east of Havana known as Alamar. Their work has a spiritual orientation and is a unique blend of performance, music, poetry, spoken-word, rap, visual art, graffiti, video, and public art. Working together since 1997, the many members of the group have collaboratively produced several music/poetry CDs and videos, including the CD *Alamar Express* and the recent video *Protesto!* They also put on an annual independent poetry festival called *Poesía Sin Fin* (Endless Poetry) in Havana. While tolerated, given their critical and independent stance, both projects have been subject to periodic harassment and kept under strict surveillance by Cuba's state security.

blogs, Twitter, flash drives, digital video and music, DVDs, and cell phones in order to break the state monopoly on information and promote public debate among free citizens. They tend to avoid drawing rigid ideological boundaries, favoring instead a united resistance against a vertical, top-down, and totalitarian civic culture and a collective insistence upon an inclusive, horizontal project of civic formation fully cognizant of their rights and responsibilities as citizens (Mujal-León 2009: 22, 30).

BIBLIOGRAPHY

Amuchástegui, Domingo. 2012. "The Cuban Leadership Ten Years Down the Road." Unpublished paper provided by the author.

Bengelsdorf, Carollee. 1994. *The Problem of Democracy in Cuba: Between Vision and Reality.* New York: Oxford University Press.

Bernal, Beatriz. 1984. *Cuba: Fundamentos de la democracia; antología del pensamiento liberal cubano desde fines del siglo VXIII hasta fines del siglo XIX.* Madrid: Fundación Liberal José Martí.

Blanco, Juan Antonio, and Madea Benjamin. 2003. "From Utopianism to Institutionalization." In Aviva Chomsky, Barry Carr, and Pamela Maria Smorkaloff, eds., *The Cuba Reader*, pp. 433–442. Durham: Duke University Press.

Bonné Carcasses, Félix Antonio, René Gómez Manzano, Vladimiro Roca Antúnez, and Martha Beatriz Roque Cabello. 1997. "The Homeland Belongs to Us All," Havana, June 27. http://www.cubanet.org/CNews/y97/jul97/homdoc.htm.

Castellanos Martí, Dimas Cecilio. 2008. "Elecciones y pluripartidismo." *Consenso Digital Magazine.* February.

Castellanos Martí, Dimas Cecilio. 2011. *Desentrañando claves.* Unpublished manuscript.

Castro, Fidel. 2008. *La Historia me absolverá*. Edición anotada. La Habana: Oficina del Consejo de Estado.

Castro, Raúl. 1996. "General of the Army Raúl Castro Ruz to the Central Committee of the Communist Party of Cuba," March 23. http://www.marxmail.org/Raúl_castro.htm.

Cluster, Dick, and Rafael Hernández. 2006. *History of Havana*. New York: Palgrave Macmillan.

Constitución de la República de Cuba. Ministry of Justice. Havana: Política Editions, 2004.

Constituciones de Cuba, 1869–1940. Havana, Política Editions, 1978.

ConstitutionNet. "The Constitution of the Republic of Cuba, 1976 (as Amended to 2002)." http://www.constitutionnet.org/files/Cuba%20Constitution.pdf.

Corrales, Javier. 2004. "The Gatekeeper State: Limited Economic Reforms and Regime Survival in Cuba, 1989–2002." *Latin American Research Review* 39, no. 2: 35–65.

CubaNet. 1992. "Constitution of the Republic of Cuba, 1992." http://www.cubanet.org/ref/dis/const_92_e.htm.

Cuban Transition Project. 2012. Institute for Cuban and Cuban-American Studies. Organizational Charts. http://ctp.iccas.miami.edu/main.htm.

CubaVerdad. 1992. "English Translation of the 1992 Constitution Excluding the 2002 Amendment." http://www.cubaverdad.net/cuban_constitution_english.htm.

CubaVerdad. 2002. "2002 Constitutional Amendment." http://www.cubaverdad.net/2002_constitutional_amendment.htm.

del Águila, Juan M. 1994. *Cuba: Dilemmas of a Revolution* (third edition). Boulder, CO: Westview Press.

Díaz-Briquets, Sergio. 2002. "The Society and Its Environment." In Rex Hudson, ed., *Cuba: A Country Study* (fourth edition). Washington, DC: Federal Research Division, Library of Congress.

Dilla Alfonso, Haroldo. 2000. "The Cuban Experiment: Economic Reform, Social Restructuring, and Politics." *Latin American Perspectives* 27, no. 1 (January): 33–44.

Dilla Alfonso, Haroldo. 2001. "Local Government and Economic and Social Change in Cuba." Ottawa, ON: FOCAL Background Briefing (Canadian Foundation for the Americas, RFC-01–1).

Dilla Alfonso, Haroldo. 2003. "Civil Society." In Aviva Chomsky, Barry Carr, and Pamela Maria Smorkaloff, eds., *The Cuba Reader*, pp. 650–659. Durham: Duke University Press.

Dilla Alfonso, Haroldo. 2005. "Larval Actors, Uncertain Scenarios, and Cryptic Scripts: Where Is Cuban Society Headed?" In Joseph S. Tulchin, Liliam Bobea, Mayra P. Espina Prieto, and Rafael Hernandez, eds., *Changes in Cuban Society since the Nineties*, pp. 35–50. Washington, DC: Woodrow Wilson Center Report on the Americas #15.

Dilla Alfonso, Haroldo. 2006. "Cuban Civil Society: II. Future Directions and Challenges." *NACLA Report on the Americas* 39, no. 4 (January/February): 37–42.

Dilla Alfonso, Haroldo, and Philip Oxhorn. 2002. "The Virtues and Misfortunes of Civil Society in Cuba." *Latin American Perspectives* 29, no. 4 (July): 11–30.

Domínguez, Jorge I. 1978. *Cuba: Order and Revolution*. Cambridge: Belknap Press.

Domínguez, Jorge I. 1993. "Cuba since 1959." In Leslie Bethell, ed., *Cuba: A Short History*. Cambridge: Cambridge University Press.

Domínguez, Jorge I. 1997. "¿Comienza una transición hacia el autoritarismo en Cuba?" *Encuentro de la cultura cubana* 6, no. 7 (Fall/Winter): 7–23.

Domínguez, Jorge I. 2002. "Government and Politics." In Rex Hudson, ed., *Cuba: A Country Study* (fourth edition). Washington, DC: Federal Research Division, Library of Congress.

Engels, Frederich. 1979. *El Origen de la Familia, la Propiedad Privada y el Estado*. Havana: Progreso Publishers.

Farber, Samuel. 2006. *The Origins of the Cuban Revolution Reconsidered*. Chapel Hill: University of North Carolina Press.

Farber, Samuel. 2011. *Cuba since the Revolution of 1959: A Critical Assessment*. Chicago: Haymarket Books.

Fernández Bulté, Julio. 1971. *Historia del Estado y el Derecho en la Antigüedad*, vol. I, Havana: Revolutionary Editions.

Freedom House. 2012. "Cuba: Freedom in the World, 2012." http://www.freedomhouse.org/report/freedom-world/2012/cuba-0

GAO (U.S. Government Accountability Office). 2006. "US Democracy Assistance for Cuba Needs Better Management and Oversight." November. http://www.gao.gov/new.items/d07147.pdf.

García, Anne-Marie. 2013. "Ricardo Alarcón es removido del Buró Político del Partido Comunista de Cuba," *El Nuevo Herald*, July 3. http://www.elnuevoherald.com/2013/07/02/1513664/alarcon-deja-cargo-en-la-conduccion.html.

García Freyre, Laura. 2008. "De la iglesia a la plaza: Las Damas de Blanco y la lucha por el espacio público en La Habana," *Cuba in Transition*, vol. 18, pp. 284–292. Washington, DC: Association for the Study of the Cuban Economy. http://www.ascecuba.org/publications/proceedings/volume18/pdfs/garciafreyre.pdf.

González, Edward. 1974. *Cuban under Castro: The Limits of Charisma*. Boston: Houghton Mifflin Company.

Guillermoprieto, Alma. 2004. *Dancing with Cuba: A Memoir of the Revolution*. Translated by Esther Allen. New York: Pantheon Books.

Gunn, Gillian. 1995. *Cuba's NGOs: Government Puppets or Seeds of Civil Society?* Washington, DC: Georgetown University Caribbean Project, Briefing Paper #7, February. http://www.trinitydc.edu/academics/depts/Interdisc/International/caribbean%20briefings/Cubas_NGOs.pdf.

Halperin, Maurice. 1972. *The Rise and Decline of Fidel Castro: An Essay in Contemporary History*. Berkeley, CA: University of California Press.

Halperin, Maurice. 1981. *The Taming of Fidel Castro*. Berkeley, CA: University of California Press.

Halperin, Maurice. 1994. *Return to Havana: The Decline of Cuban Society under Castro*. Nashville: Vanderbilt University Press.

Hitchens, Christopher. 2010. *Hitch-22: A Memoir*. New York: Twelve, Hachette Book Group.

Ibarra Cuesta, Jorge. 2004. *Varela el precursor, un estudio de época*. Havana: Ciencias Sociales Editions.

Isasi Cayo, Felipe. 1989. *Elementos de Cultura Política*. Lima: Publicaciones de la Universidad de Lima.

Jatar-Hausmann, Ana Julia. 1999. *The Cuban Way: Communism, Capitalism, and Confrontation*. West Harford, CT: Kumarian Press.

Levine, Robert M. 2002. *Secret Missions to Cuba: Fidel Castro, Bernardo Benes, and Cuban Miami*. New York: Palgrave Macmillan.

Ministerio de Justicia. 1987. *Ley de Procedimiento Penal*. Havana: Pueblo y Educación Editions.

Linger, Eloise. 1999. "From Social Movement to State in Cuba, 1952–1966." Unpublished Ph.D. dissertation, New School for Social Research, New York.

Marril Rivero, Emilio. 1989. *La Constitución Cubana*. Havana: Ciencias Sociales Editions.

Mesa-Lago, Carmelo. 2004. "El reinado de la doble moral." *Encuentro en al red*, July 21. http://arch1.cubaencuentro.com/sociedad/20040719/2a9420b525724927fe988fa580cb5 81a/1.html.

Mesa-Lago, Carmelo, and Jorge Pérez-López. 2005. *Cuba's Aborted Reform: Socioeconomic Effects, International Comparisons, and Transition Policies*. Gainesville, FL: University Press of Florida.

Morales, Emilio. 2013. "Remesas a Cuba: $2,605 millones en el 2012," *Café Fuerte*, June 8. http://cafefuerte.com/miami/noticias-de-miami/economia-y-negocios/2915-remesas-a-cuba-alcanzaron-los-2605-millones-en-el-2012.

Mujal-León, Eusebio. 2009. "Can Cuba Change? Tensions in the Regime." *Journal of Democracy* 20, no. 1 (January): 20–35.

Mujal-León, Eusebio. 2011. "Survival, Adaptation and Uncertainty: The Case of Cuba." *Journal of International Affairs*, 65, no. 1 (Fall/Winter): 149–168.

Ojito, Mirta. 2005. *Finding Mañana: A Memoir of a Cuban Exodus*. New York: Penguin.

Pérez Milán, F. 1992. "Motivos para una reforma." *Revista Cubana de Derecho* No. 7, National Union of Cuban Jurists.

Pérez, Louis A., Jr. 2002. "The Cuban Revolution." In Luis Martínez-Fernández, D.H. Figueredo, Louis A. Pérez, Jr., and Luis González, eds., *Encyclopedia of Cuba: People, History, Culture*. Two vols, pp. 242–246. Westport, CT: Greenwood Press, 2002.

Pérez-López, Jorge. 2006. "The Cuban Economy in 2005–2006: The End of the Special Period?" *Cuba in Transition* 16, pp. 1–13. Washington, DC: Association for the Study of the Cuban Economy.

Prieto, M. n.d. *El estado cubano. Su caracterización general. Programas lectivos sobre Derecho Constitucional*. University of Havana.

Roman, Peter. 1993. "Representative Government in Socialist Cuba." *Latin American Perspectives* 20, no. 1 (Winter): 7–27.

Roman, Peter. 1995. "Worker's Parliaments in Cuba." *Latin American Perspectives* 22, no. 4 (Autumn): 43–58.

Roman, Peter. 2003. *People's Power: Cuba's Experience with Representative Government*. Revised edition. Lanham: Rowman and Littlefield Publishers.

Roman, Peter. 2005. "The Lawmaking Process in Cuba: Debating the Bill on Agricultural Cooperatives." *Socialism and Democracy* 19, no. 2 (July): 1–20.

Roman, Peter. 2006. "Electing Cuba's National Assembly Deputies: Proposals, Selections, Nominations, and Campaigns." Paper presented at the Latin American Studies Association Conference, San Juan, Puerto Rico, March 15–18.

Ruiz, Albor. 2006. "US Fights Fidel—with Chocolates?" *New York Daily News*, November 26.

Sagás, Ernesto. 2002. "Government Structure." In Luis Martínez-Fernández, D. H. Figueredo, Louis A. Pérez, Jr., and Luis González, eds., *Encyclopedia of Cuba: People, History, Culture*. Two vols, pp. 224–226. Westport, CT: Greenwood Press.

Sánchez, Yoani. 2012. "Fidel's 'Revolutionary Collective Surveillance' Neighborhood Spies Create Social Violence and Hatred." *Huffington Post*, September 28. http://www.huffing tonpost.com/yoani-sanchez/fidels-revolutionary-coll_b_1921751.html; also published as: "CDR: Citizen Representation or Political Control?" *Translating Cuba*, September 27, 2012. http://translatingcuba.com/cdr-citizen-representation-or-political-control-yoani-sanchez.

Sánchez Santacruz, Elizardo. 2003. "A Dissident Speaks Out." In Aviva Chomsky, Barry Carr, and Pamela Maria Smorkaloff, eds., *The Cuba Reader.* pp. 664–665. Durham: Duke University Press.

Schlesinger, Stephen, and Stephen Kinzer. 1999. *Bitter Fruit: The Story of the American Coup in Guatemala* (expanded edition). Cambridge: David Rockefeller Center for Latin American Studies, Harvard University Press.

Schwab, Peter. 1999. *Cuba: Confronting the U.S. Embargo.* New York: St. Martin's Griffin.

Uriarte, Miren. 2002. "Cuba—Social Policy at the Crossroads: Maintaining Priorities, Transforming Practice." Boston, MA: Oxfam America. http://scholarworks.umb.edu/cgi/view-content.cgi?article=1114&context=gaston_pubs

Economy

Oscar Espinosa Chepe and Ted A. Henken

INTRODUCTION

Like most subjects related to contemporary Cuba, accurate and unbiased data on Cuba's economy is hard to come by. Insiders are often hesitant to show poor performance, and outsiders are often reluctant to believe positive results. A significant but ultimately unknowable portion of the economy operates underground and exists off the books. Moreover, the government's ideological rhetoric and the sometimes drastic changes in its economic policies can be confusing to outsiders not armed with a healthy sense of nuance, complexity, and apparent contradiction (Mesa-Lago 2000). Indeed, like many other areas of contemporary Cuban life, nothing concerning the Cuban economy is as simple and straightforward as it at first may seem.

A common joke heard on the streets of today's Cuba vividly illustrates the ironic and contradictory nature of many of the revolution's accomplishments. "What are the three greatest achievements of the revolution?" asks a curious foreigner of a Cuban national. "Universal access to education, a world class system of public health, and the defense of the homeland," responds the proud Cuban. However, when the inquisitive visitor asks about the revolution's three most prominent failures, the same Cuban sarcastically responds, "Breakfast, lunch, and dinner!" This bitterly humorous anecdote highlights the fact that the revolution's economic development policies have always been much more successful at redistributing the country's wealth and ensuring egalitarian access to basic social services than it has at creating wealth or implementing development policies that achieve economic growth.

This anecdote also reveals the fundamental contradiction in revolutionary Cuba's economic policies. On the one hand, one of the revolution's top priorities has always been the leveling of the economic inequalities that plagued 1950s Cuba. Cuba has also successfully guaranteed universal access to many social services, including health care, education, and social security, as well as chipping away at the age-old inequities based on region and race. Although already a regional leader in the provision of social services before 1959, Cuba's laudable commitment to universal access to a wide array of social services allowed for the achievement of enviable levels of social welfare between 1960 and 1990. On the other hand, these social gains have been achieved at the expense of economic growth, through the sacrifice of many civil and political liberties, and predicated on overdependence on the Soviet Union. Moreover, after the collapse of the USSR and the loss of its economic support, the island began to experience the precipitous erosion of many of its social achievements, not to mention the drastic contraction of its already poor profile in the area of economic growth, efficiency, and productivity.

This chapter provides a critical analysis of the Cuban government's changing economic development strategy over the last half-century (1959–2012). After describing the economic profile of prerevolutionary Cuba, we trace a number of stages in the revolutionary government's economic policy. The first stage culminated in the eradication of the private sector and an unsuccessful drive at economic independence symbolized by the failure to harvest 10 million tons of sugarcane in 1970. This was followed by the gradual reintroduction of the market, including the allowance of small-scale private enterprise between 1971 and 1985. However, in reaction to the Soviet Union's reform policies of perestroika and glasnost, between 1986 and 1989 Cuba's already tiny private sector was reigned in once again as part of the "rectification of errors and negative tendencies."

The economic crisis brought about by the fall of the USSR between 1989 and 1991 forced the Cuban government to grudgingly enact a series of economic reforms, which included the search for foreign investment, the rapid development of a tourism industry, and the reemergence of a domestic private sector (in both its clandestine and legal manifestations) during the first years of the "special period" (1990–1996). However, starting in 1996 and increasingly thereafter, economic reforms stalled, and the incipient growth of private enterprise was gradually scaled back in favor of ever greater economic centralization, crackdowns on corruption and the "new rich"—as part of Fidel Castro's "battle of ideas"—and a newfound reliance on international tourism, nickel export, oil exploration, and increased aid and trade from China and especially Venezuela (1996–2006).

The bulk of our chapter, however, is a critical description and analysis of the significant but as yet insufficient economic reforms introduced by Raúl Castro since 2006. Taking over as acting head-of-state upon his elder brother's illness in August of that year, Raúl Castro has attempted to remake the Cuban economy—and save the revolution—by eliminating many state subsidies, streamlining nonproductive state firms, and drastically reducing the numbers of people with state jobs. He has simultaneously demanded that remaining state enterprises and workers become more efficient and productive, famously declaring that Cuba can no longer afford "to be the only country in the world where people can live without working." The ideal of "egalitarianism"—long trumpeted by Fidel Castro—has become a dirty word. Raúl openly rejects the notion that everyone can or should be equal, emphasizing the revolution's commitment to equality of opportunity only.

In order to absorb laid-off workers, reduce the size of the black market, and jumpstart job creation and the provision of goods and services, in October 2010 the government allowed for an unprecedented expansion in Cuba's microenterprise sector. By August 2013, the numbers of licensed self-employed entrepreneurs - including privately contracted employees for the first time - had grown almost three-fold to 436,000 from roughly 150,000 three years earlier. Cooperative small- and medium-sized businesses were added in the second half of 2013. Within limits, Cubans can now also buy and sell property—including their homes and automobiles—on the open (if not fully free) market. Raúl promises to continue to move forward with these and related economic changes "without haste but also without pause" as a way of "updating" socialism and ensuring the survival of the revolution. We attempt to evaluate the degree of his success to date in this chapter.

CUBA'S ECONOMIC HISTORY AND THE SOCIOECONOMIC PROBLEMS OF THE 1950s

Historically, Cuba has long suffered under a classic form of economic dependence first on Spain and then on the United States. The island was first developed by the Spanish as a roadhouse for gold coming from the Spanish Main and then, after the British occupation of 1762, as a factory for sugar. As a result, Cuba became an archetypically extractive monocultural, slave-based, export-oriented, agricultural economy that understood "economic development" as plunder of the island's natural resources. By the second half of the 19th century Cuba came face to face with the central contradiction of all economic colonies: the Creole bourgeoisie found itself increasingly torn between a rising sense of nationalism and continued reliance on Spain for economic viability and social order.

This contradiction was exacerbated by the rapidly rising importance of the United States as the island's main trading partner leading up to eventual independence. In fact, over the course of the 19th century, the proportion of Cuban exports going to the United States grew from 27 percent in the late 1820s to 84 percent in the early 1890s. During this same period, sugar grew from comprising just 35 percent of Cuban exports to the United States in the early 1820s to making up almost 80 percent of exports in the early 1890s (Fraginals 2001). Tragically, the result of U.S.-sponsored independence in 1901–1902 under the Platt amendment was renewed economic dependence (now almost exclusively on the U.S. market) and insertion into the world economy as a monocultural sugar producer ruled by systematically corrupt and often illegitimate governments. The central economic contradiction of Cuba's republican period (1902–1958), then, was ostensible political independence coupled with the deep penetration of the Cuban economy by U.S. investors and its organization for the benefit of U.S. interests linked with a small, powerful native oligarchy (Warren 2005: 4–5).

Despite the ongoing debate over the socialist path eventually taken by the revolution after 1959, there is general agreement about the island's key socioeconomic problems during the 1940s and 1950s. Paradoxically, on the eve of what would prove to be Latin America's most far-reaching revolution, Cuba ranked among the top two to three countries in the region in most aggregate social and economic development indicators. However, the island's economy was still characterized by an ongoing (if decreasing) economic dependence on sugar exports to the United States. Hopes of political independence, stable economic growth, and social equality had given way to increasing economic insecurity and a growing sense of national frustration (Pérez 1999). This frustration was rooted in a series of domestic imbalances that were all too clear to many Cubans, yet often overlooked by outsiders, especially by those in the U.S. government.

Cuba's Close but Dependent Relationship with the United States

The first imbalance was the fact that while Cuba remained near the top of regional socioeconomic rankings, it had all but ceased comparing itself with its Latin American neighbors, having become fully incorporated into the U.S. sociocultural orbit (Pérez 1995, 1999). Thus, while standards of comparison were extremely high, Cuba lacked the domestic economic base to live up to such high expectations. Indeed, a report prepared in 1958 by the British development agency, the Royal Institute of International Affairs (RIIA), captured this fundamental paradox by uncovering that while Cuba's standard of living was higher than that of any other "tropical" country, and among the highest in the hemisphere, it was just one third that of the American Southeast (Mississippi, Alabama, Georgia, etc.), traditionally the poorest region of the United States (RIIA 1958: 22).

Dependent economic relations with the United States compounded this sense of frustration. For example, between 1955 and 1958, 64 percent of Cuban exports went to the United States, and 73 percent of its imports came from there. The asymmetrical nature of this relationship was highlighted by the fact that only 3.2 percent of U.S. trade was with Cuba. Thus, while many middle- and upper-class Cubans liked to think of themselves as the equal partners of their northern neighbors, the fact was that Cuba was completely dispensable to the United States, while the United States was all but indispensable for Cuba. Consequently, the economic costs of a break in such a lopsided relationship would be inestimably huge for Cuba, but relatively negligible for the United States (Ritter 1974: 51, 55–56).

Despite some efforts at economic diversification—tobacco, nickel, and fresh fruits and vegetables—in the 1940s and 1950s, the Cuban economy was still highly dependent on the monocultural production and export of unrefined sugarcane. This product and its derivatives accounted for over 80 percent of the island's total exports and were sent primarily to the United States, which was in turn the source of most imports. This trade took place through a series of reciprocal treaties with the United States based on a system of preferences for Cuban sugar at guaranteed prices, usually higher than the international market rate. However, this arrangement limited the development of domestic sugar production due to the fact that U.S. purchases of Cuban products were made under a strict quota system. In return, Cuba guaranteed tariff preferences to American products, hindering the development of national manufacturing and of a number of agricultural products. Thus, the terms of such "reciprocity" were chronically unfavorable to the island, requiring Cuba to seek trade surpluses with the rest of the world in order to achieve an overall balance of trade.

Because Cuba was so dependent on a single product—sugar—the health of its economy was largely determined by the notoriously unstable world market price of this commodity. When prices were high, an economic bonanza would follow—

famously known as the time of *las vacas gordas* (the fat cows). However, when prices fell the island would suffer the economic bust of lean years of depression and misery— *las vacas flacas*. This vicious economic cycle of boom and bust was accompanied by Cuba's annual employment cycle where the early, employment-rich three to four months of sugar harvest would be followed by eight to nine months characterized by a sharp rise in unemployment known as the *tiempo muerto* (dead time). According to surveys carried out by Cuba's National Office of Demographics, in the early months of 1958 unemployment was just 7 percent, while by August—the *tiempo muerto* of that same year—it had almost doubled to 13.2 percent.

The dependence on one export product and a single market was compounded by another serious problem: the high concentration of land in the hands of a few owners. According to the 1946 Census, nearly 80 percent of all farms were smaller than 27 hectares but held just 15 percent of the island's arable land. In contrast, just 3 percent of Cuba's farms were larger than 400 hectares but held almost 57 percent of the available land. In addition, 63 percent of existing farms were worked by tenants, subtenants, sharecroppers, or squatters—who did not own the land—while the remaining 37 percent were operated by their owners or managers, but comprised 58 percent of the agricultural land. This data reveals that Cuban agriculture was characterized by large estates (*latifundio*) and absenteeism, root causes of its low productivity. In the *latifundia* system, owners of vast tracts of land are not motivated to intensively harness their land's productive potential given the low costs of labor and the large areas of uncultivated land *latifundistas* (owners of large tracts of land) hold in reserve. For their part, neither tenants nor sharecroppers favor the intensive exploitation of land since any investment in the land's productivity would benefit absentee landlords, not the workers themselves.

The 1950s also saw intensified efforts to more consciously develop the island's potential as an international tourism destination. On the positive side, this effort led to the construction of many large, modern hotels and related urban infrastructure, providing employment and income to many. At the same time, the rapid expansion of the tourism industry was based on the combination of political corruption, the spread of gambling, and the participation of kingpins in the international underworld—such as Santo Trafficante and Meyer Lansky—who worked hand in glove with the Batista dictatorship.

The Urban-Rural Divide

Another major domestic imbalance, hidden by high aggregate socioeconomic indicators, was the concentration of Cuba's great wealth and substantial middle class in Havana, with little of that success managing to "trickle down" to lower income groups or out to rural areas (Warren 2005: 5–6). Essentially, Cuba was one nation with two distinct socioeconomic realities. Skilled, urban, industrial workers benefited from high wages and were well protected by Cuba's strong labor unions, while isolated, rural, agricultural workers suffered from extremely low wages and chronic unemployment (Mesa-Lago 2000). Housing, health, and educational services, advanced for urbanites and especially so for those who could afford Havana's many private schools and hospitals, were absent from most rural areas.

Homes such as this one pictured in a June 1959 photo, standing beside the trail to La Plata in the heart of the Sierra Maestra mountains, were the rule in rural Cuba at the time. Called a "bohío," it has wooden walls, a thatched roof made of palm fronds, and a dirt floor. There are no sanitary facilities and drinking water comes from a nearby stream. A national survey conducted at the time indicated that more than 60 percent of rural homes were of this type with its occupants typically living in abject poverty. (AP Photo)

According to the 1953 Census, over 70 percent of rural homes had dirt floors and were built of palm fronds (dried palm leaves) and rustic wood. Moreover, 54 percent of these dwellings lacked toilets or latrines; 90 percent had no showers or baths and were lighted by kerosene. The nutritional situation was not much better. According to a survey published in 1957 by the Catholic University Organization, 4 percent of the agricultural workers interviewed regularly ate meat, just 1 percent ate fish, and only 11 percent drank milk—indicating an epidemic of malnutrition for Cuba's rural population at the time. Parasites and other gastrointestinal diseases were common afflictions for the rural population, most of whom faced great barriers in accessing health care.

Similarly, the 1953 Census reflected a relatively low national illiteracy rate of 23.6 percent. However, rates were 3.6 times higher in rural than in urban areas (41.7% vs. 11.6%). In terms of access to education, a full 31 percent of the population of six years and over had no schooling whatsoever, another 58 percent had completed between just one and six years of primary school, while only 11 percent had studied beyond the sixth grade. Such chronic regional inequities led to an increase in rural-urban migration during the decade. However, the insufficient growth of urban employment combined with high barriers to entry into skilled, unionized jobs transformed many urban migrants into shantytown dwellers and informal workers (Mesa-Lago 2000: 172).

In conclusion, we reproduce here the closing section of the executive summary of the 1951 "Truslow Report." Entitled "The Choice Before Cuba," these few brief paragraphs of the *Report on Cuba* reflect the findings and recommendations of a World Bank economic and technical mission provided to the then president of Cuba, Carlos Prío. The mission, headed by Francis A. Truslow, presented its more than 1,000-page report to Prío on July 12, 1951, less than a year before Batista's coup:

> The choice before the people of Cuba is clear-cut. They may take advantage of their present opportunity to start to substitute a growing, dynamic and diversified economy for the present static one, with its single crop dependence. This may be a long and arduous task. It will involve great effort and some sacrifice of tradition and comfort. But it can diminish present risks and instabilities and it can prepare the economy to meet a reduced demand and price for sugar and increasing competition in its production.
>
> The choice is plain; and the Mission believes that failure to choose the dynamic alternative can bring to Cuba consequences of the utmost seriousness.
>
> War prosperity has created new standards of living for many of Cuba's people. If her economy cannot maintain these—at least in some reasonable degree—in less prosperous times, it will be subject to great political strains.
>
> If leaders have neglected to prepare Cuba for this, they will be held to blame by the people. And, if that should happen, control may well pass into subversive but specious hands—as it has done in other countries whose leaders have ignored the trends of the times. (Truslow 1951: 13)

Prophetic words, written 62 years ago, which were not heeded leading to a fateful outcome for the Cuban nation from which it is still suffering today.

ECONOMIC EXPERIMENTATION, COLLECTIVIZATION, AND INSTITUTIONALIZATION, 1959–1990

Batista's bloodless coup of March 1952—carried out just two months before the general elections scheduled for June 1—closed off the possibilities of implementing reforms that could address the obstacles to economic development in a democratic environment. Batista repeated the same stubborn behavior seen throughout Cuban history. Just as the Spanish colonists and the dictator Machado before him, his intention to retain power at all costs left the Cuban people no other viable option than armed struggle. And, as predicted by Truslow, this tragic turn of events was used by ambitious leaders employing deceptive means to take and keep power for themselves.

Thus triumphed the Cuban revolution on January 1, 1959, with broad popular support of a kind perhaps never before seen in the history of Latin America. From the start, the new revolutionary government sought to achieve the ambitious economic goals of reducing income inequality, eradicating unemployment, raising the standard of living for all, ending chronic economic dependence on a single crop and a single market, and promoting the democratization of society through the broad integration and participation of the populace in the revolution through the creation of a "new man" (Ritter 1974). Following the implementation of economic measures that would give meaning to the word "revolution"—such as the Agrarian Reform Law of May 17, 1959, the Urban Reform Law, the Literacy Campaign, and the adoption of an independent foreign policy—the vast majority of the Cuban population, but particularly the poorest sectors, showed their increased faith in the revolution by giving it their active support.

However, the country's political leadership quickly took advantage of this impressive reserve of political capital only to cement themselves in power in perpetuity. They abandoned their repeated promises to democratize society and chose to rule autocratically. As a result, the promise to hold free elections was violated and all media was gradually taken over by the new revolutionary state. Between 1959 and 1963 the revolution was consolidated politically and Soviet-style central planning aimed at diversification and industrialization were instituted. As justification for imposing absolute control over society, Fidel Castro cultivated among the population a fervent nationalism and proud defiance of the United States, which reacted with heightened confrontation playing directly into Castro's hands. This, in turn, facilitated the very argument that Cuba had no choice but to double down on a path of intolerance and dogma if it intended to preserve its young revolution.

A sharp change in development strategy (a return to sugar specialization) took place after mid-1963 and lasted until 1970, along with renewed debate and experimentation over just which kind of socialism would be built in Cuba. Finally, between 1966 and 1970, Cuba strove to achieve full collectivization. It threw all its force behind Che Guevara's radical vision of a new society peopled by selfless "new men," seasoned with an extreme voluntarism that the Soviets themselves often criticized. In the process, the last remnants of the private sector were subsumed under the "revolutionary offensive" of 1968 and all the country's dwindling resources were thrown behind the failed effort to harvest a record 10 million tons of sugarcane in 1970; an all-or-nothing project as arbitrary and as it was quixotic.

The State Takeover of the Economy and Implementation of the Central Plan, 1959–1963

Between May 17, 1959, and October 3, 1963, the new government—under the de facto rule of Fidel Castro—implemented an ambitious policy of economic nationalization, which rapidly confiscated nearly all of Cuba's productive forces. Specifically, seven laws were enacted that placed the Cuban economy under rigid state control. While large foreign and national enterprises were the initial target of these expropriations, they eventually included artisans and small traders, inhibiting individual entrepreneurial initiative by Cubans themselves. The seven laws were the First Agrarian Reform Law (May 17, 1959); the First Nationalization Act of August 6, 1960—which took over 26 U.S. companies—a Second Nationalization Act (October 13, 1960); the Bank Nationalization Law (October 13, 1960); the Urban Reform Law (October 14, 1960); the Nationalization of Education Law (June 6, 1961); and the Second Agrarian Reform Law (October 3, 1963).

The First Agrarian Reform Law fulfilled the long denied hopes and dreams of peasants and farmworkers to have access to land. In its first article, *latifundia* was outlawed and 402.6 hectares was established as the maximum possible holdings of any one entity (1 hectare is equivalent to 2.47 acres). The law also declared in its final section that "the adequate redistribution of land among a large number of owners and farmers . . . [is] of social utility and in the public interest." This initial agrarian reform law was also characterized by a rational flexibility aimed at ensuring production. For example, in Article 2, a concession was made so that sugarcane, rice, or livestock producers—who required more land than the previously established ceiling in order to maintain their yields—be allowed to possess up to 1,342 hectares.

Article 16 established a "vital minimum" (or poverty line) of 26.84 hectares of fertile land for a peasant family of five. Moreover, Article 18 stipulated that land under private ownership cultivated by settlers (*colonos*), tenants (*arrendatarios*), sharecroppers, or squatters would be awarded free of charge to those who already worked it provided it did not exceed the "vital minimum" in size. When such workers possessed plots of land smaller than the "vital minimum," they would be awarded additional land at no cost so that they would have enough land to work and live off of—provided such land was available. Finally, if the lands under cultivation exceeded the "vital minimum"—but as long as they were not more than 5 hectares over the limit—its tenants would be provided two additional *caballerías* (a caballería is roughly equivalent to 13.42 hectares) free of charge, prior to the land's expropriation by the National Institute of Agrarian Reform (INRA). In this manner, titles of ownership to land that was already de facto home to thousands of peasants were granted.

At the same time, a substantial portion of the *latifundia* land expropriated was transformed into large state farms, as was the case with the *Granjas del Pueblo* (People's Farms) and the *Cooperativas Cañeras* (Sugarcane Cooperatives). However, the central ideas of the First Agrarian Reform Law—putting an end to *latifundia* and granting ownership and control of land to dispossessed peasants—were soon subsumed under statist policies. Instead of distributing land, power, and control to the people, as promised, real power lie in the hands of a giant state bureaucracy, the National Institute of Agrarian Reform (INRA). And the INRA, with its centralizing methods, gradually drained away the peasants' initiative and motivation to work and make the land productive.

On October 3, 1963, the Second Agrarian Reform Law was issued. It further reduced the maximum land tenure to just 67.1 hectares, repealing the flexible aspects of the first law. It deepened the centralization of Cuban agriculture by creating state monopolies, which acted as the sole purchasers of agricultural harvests as well as the sole providers of seeds, supplies, and farm equipment, which were sold to farmworkers under unilaterally fixed prices and conditions. In order to ensure the political control of private farmers the National Association of Small Farmers (ANAP) was created, as were the Credit and Service Cooperatives (CCS). The Organization of State Farms was also formed, which originated out of the lands confiscated—often for political reasons—from small- and medium-sized farms, which were later subsumed by other state agencies.

While the initial Agrarian Reform Law had positive elements and provided for the long-awaited distribution of land to Cuban farmers, it was never implemented. Instead, the Second Agrarian Reform Law was adopted, which simply transformed the old private estates into enormous state-run *latifundia*. Moreover, these state farms were never able to diversify and break Cuba's dependence on sugarcane. They were highly bureaucratic, centralized agricultural enterprises which were even more difficult to manage given their unwieldy size. As a long-term result, the countryside has become deserted and Cuba has only deepened its dependence on a single crop—now under notoriously inefficient management. As we will discuss in greater detail later, since the onset of the "special period" in 1990, Cuba's once mighty and defining sugar industry has all but disappeared. At the same time, the fertile tropical island has become increasingly dependent for its food on external sources, which at times provide more than 80 percent of the total.

While the full collectivization of agriculture would take some time, the seizure of major industry, utilities, banks, schools, apartment buildings, and department and wholesale stores were made quickly, most taking place in a period of less than three months between August 6 and October 14, 1960. This process began with the so-called Law of Nationalization of 26 U.S. companies, among which were the utility, oil, and import-export firms the Cuban Electric Company, the Cuban Telephone Company, Esso Standard Oil, the Texas West Indies Co., the Sinclair Cuba Oil Co., and the Cuban Trading Company. The remaining expropriated U.S. companies were all large sugar enterprises.

The subsequent Nationalization Act was announced on October 13, 1960. It had a much greater reach as it included the nationalization of property belonging to Cuban citizens themselves. It constituted, as expressed in its first Article, "a forced expropriation of all industrial and commercial enterprises, as well as factories, warehouses, depots, and other property." The nationalization of banks was also announced on October 13. On that date, Cuba's 44 private banks as well as its 5 credit unions passed into state hands. At the same time, the National Bank of Cuba was declared the sole authority and surrogate of all formerly private banks. This measure was preceded by a resolution adopted days earlier through which the U.S. banks the First National City Bank of New York, the First National Bank of Boston, and the Chase Manhattan Bank were confiscated together with all their branches in the country.

This was followed the next day by the Urban Reform Law, which legalized the massive confiscation of urban real estate, lowered rents by half, and allowed former renters to gradually become owners of their apartments (without the right to resell their newly acquired property). A year later, on June 6, 1961, came the Nationalization of Education Law, which made all educational facilities public and free. This was accomplished through the state seizure of all private and religious educational institutions along with all their rights, materials, and assets. This seizure was justified by the need to place at the disposal of the revolution all instructional facilities to facilitate the "construction of the new man," a project that has resulted in a colossal failure in the long term.

The rationing of foodstuffs and articles of clothing, through a "ration card," was adopted on March 12, 1962. While it assured access to a basic level of necessary products for all Cubans for many years, the rationing system has also led to major economic distortions and disincentives and, in particular, has functioned in practice as a key source of corruption. As a system of food distribution, the rationing system continues operating today though the government of Raúl Castro has promised to eliminate it and replace it with a system that targets only those with demonstrated need. This change is necessary because the rationing system had gradually lost its ability to provide quality foodstuffs to the population in sufficient amounts, while at the same time acting as a major drain on state resources.

A worker delivers plantains, a Cuban staple, to a state run store at O'Reilly and Obispo Streets in Old Havana. Popularly known as "bodegas,' these stores offer limited amounts of basic items at subsidized prices. This system of rationed distribution is set to be gradually phased out during Raúl Castro's final term as president between 2013 and 2018. (Orlando Luis Pardo Lazo)

The aforementioned series of nationalizations placed the fundamental elements of the Cuban economy under strict state control. This allowed central planning to begin in earnest with the February 1961 creation of the Central Planning Board, the agency responsible for coordinating short-, medium-, and long-term economic plans.

THE RATION BOOKLET—A CUBAN STAPLE NO MORE?

During the 1960s, the monthly ration per person included 3 pounds of meat, 1 pound of fish, 6 pounds of rice, 1.5 pounds of beans, 14 pounds of tubers, 2 pounds of oil, a dozen eggs, 1 pound of coffee, and 6 liters of milk. Other items included sugar, bread, gas, detergent, soap, toilet paper, toothpaste, and even cigarettes, cigars, and beer. After the "special period" began in 1990, 28 new foodstuffs and 180 consumer goods were added to the ration booklet. Other items simply disappeared from government *bodegas* altogether. Still, the government managed to provide pregnant women and children under seven with a liter of fresh milk daily (Mesa-Lago 2000: 186, 387).

Since taking over in February 2008, President Raúl Castro has repeatedly declared that the rationing system's days are numbered, arguing that the state can no longer afford to subsidize it, especially given that almost 80 percent of the island's food is imported, at an annual cost of $1.5 billion. He insists future food aid should target only those in need since general rationing amounts to a form of "paternalism," disincentivizing work and promoting the waste of limited goods (Miroff 2010; Peters 2012a: 22–23).

In fact, the following year, 1962, was ceremonially christened the "Year of Planning." Despite having managed to gain control over the key levers of the Cuban economy, the revolutionary leadership continued to demonstrate its desire for an even more absolute power over society. Thus were nationalized thousands of Cuban-owned clothing, hardware, and shoe stores, on December 5, 1962, under Law 1076. This was followed on January 7, 1963, by a new decree, which subsumed all private medical clinics, mutual aid societies, and hospitals under the bureaucratic control of the newly created Ministry of Public Health.

Cuba's New International Economic Relations with the Soviet Bloc

Following the triumph of the revolution, Cuba's international economic relations also underwent a radical change. Dependence on the United States was quickly replaced by an even greater reliance on the USSR and the other nations that made up the Soviet bloc. While Cuba broke free of U.S. hegemony, it also lost out on the modernizing influence of the technical advances of its northern neighbor, which was replaced by the technological backwardness of Eastern Europe. If before 1959, trade with the USSR was limited to marginal sales of Cuban sugar; afterward trade with the Soviet bloc came to dominate the Cuban economy. On average, over the period 1959–1970, 56 percent of all trade was with Eastern Europe while the other 44 percent was with the USSR. This trend continued during the 1970s and 1980s, with dependence on the Soviet Union deepening further. By 1989, for example, trade with the USSR had come to comprise 65 percent of Cuba's total foreign trade.

Commercial cooperation with these countries—based on a political-ideological affinity—had a number of positive impacts for Cuba. For sugar alone, the USSR and its allies paid an estimated 1.6 billion pesos between 1962 and 1974 well beyond the prices that Cuba could get exporting to market economies. This amount subsequently increased substantially when Cuba joined the Council for Mutual Economic Aid (CEMA) in the mid-1970s and partner nations significantly increased the prices paid for sugar and other Cuban export products like nickel and citrus.

As for imports, prices were generally favorable, established under agreements aimed at giving support to the Cuban economy. However, as noted the technological characteristics of Soviet bloc machinery and equipment were relatively rudimentary and inefficient, especially that coming from the USSR. A common strategy was to provide needed fuel and lubricants to Cuba at prices far below that on the international market. This allowed Cuba to reexport Soviet oil to third countries thereby earning substantial hard currency income. Given its large size, these third country sales made up Cuba's main hard currency income, especially during the 1980s.

Another key benefit the closer relations with the Soviet bloc provided was extensive educational, scientific, and technical cooperation. It was through such cooperation that thousands of university level specialists were educated. Many others received specialized training and had previous degrees updated. Moreover, between the 1960s and the 1980s Cuba played host to thousands of Soviet bloc technicians and consultants in virtually all sectors of the economy, in sports, and, of course, in the military—including specialists in counterintelligence and surveillance and repression. This policy of "aid" to Cuba, which took a huge economic toll on the USSR and several of its Eastern European allies—especially East Germany, Czechoslova-kia, and Bulgaria—had as its objective the creation of a Soviet sphere of political influence in Latin America and a strategic military presence just 90 miles from the United States.

Despite the fact that the supplies Cuba received during these years were not the most advanced technologically, the fact remains that trade and aid from the Soviet bloc represented an immense material resource for economic development. More-over, the Cuban population was already one with a high cultural and educational level relative to other developing countries. The big question, then, is why with such extensive human and material resources at their disposal was Cuba? unable to achieve better economic results. In fact, low productivity, economic inefficiency, and the waste of resources became such chronic features of the Cuban landscape that it became impossible to break the cycle of dependency and transform the old eco-nomic structure the revolution had inherited. The reason behind this failure lies in the wholesale adoption of a dysfunctional economic model from the Soviets. This model was built on bureaucratic centralization and the dogmatic implementation of rigid and unrealistic economic plans. Political patronage was rewarded and promoted as official doctrine, while critical thinking and individual initiative were punished. Rational economic analysis was replaced with ideological posturing and unchecked voluntarism—exemplified, above all, by Fidel Castro and his many spontaneous agricultural projects that often ended in costly failures amounting to little more than flights of economic fancy.

It should be recognized, however, that the 1960–1990 period saw important so-cial achievements, principally in education, public health, and social security. These advances were due in part to Cuba's relatively high level of social development prior to 1959 especially in the cases of education and health. Undoubtedly, the substantial foreign subsidies Cuba received during these years also facilitated these achieve-ments. As for social security, the revolution introduced a universal pension system that allowed the population to live in secure if austere material conditions thanks in part to the existence of the rationing system. At the same time, the revolution pur-sued policies aimed at achieving full employment. However, in order to achieve this goal, state enterprises routinely hired far more workers than it needed, exacerbating chronic problems of inefficiency, low productivity, absenteeism, loafing, and low worker morale. This also fueled the informal sector as underpaid and unmotivated workers would often show up not to perform a job but to gain access to supplies that they could steal and later resell.

Che Guevara, the "New Man," and the Great Debate

The Argentine doctor turned revolutionary, Ernesto "Che" Guevara, played a key role in building the new economic base of socialism in Cuba. After achieving the rank of *Comandante* in the war, Guevara was named the director of Cuba's National Bank in 1959, and later head of the industrial department of the National Institute of Agrarian Reform (INRA). From those two powerful posts, Guevara strove to implant in Cuba a new set of socialist values and a "new (socialist) man" who could embody them. Guevara feared resorting to capitalist methods of individualism and material incentives in the building of socialism and argued against the capitalist idea of work as a means to personal enrichment, professional advancement, and social prestige. As idealistic as it sounds today, Guevara believed that only moral incentives could engender what he considered to be the ultimate, socialist values of humanity: selflessness, altruism, sacrifice for the greater good, human solidarity, dedication to a cause, and a sense of duty—in short, a new revolutionary consciousness, what he and Fidel called simply, *conciencia*. Unfortunately for the Cuban economy of the 1960s, in practice, the ideals of moral incentives, work as a social duty, noncoercive voluntary labor—the three pillars of the consciousness of the "new man"—often resulted in dramatic economic failures on a national scale.

Because Cuba's initial attempt to establish central planning and industrialize its economy faltered, the Cuban leadership decided to shift its priorities back to sugar production, starting in 1964 (Mesa-Lago and Pérez-López 2005; Ritter 1974: 167). This return to sugar was quite ironic, since monocultural dependence had long been blamed for Cuba's weak position vis-à-vis its international trading partners prior to the revolution. However, the costs of producing cane sugar in Cuba for its fraternal allies in the Soviet bloc were much lower than those incurred in Eastern Europe's beet sugar production. Furthermore, the very low input costs and high earnings that were ensured by access to large markets with stable prices, combined with the increase in world free market sugar prices at the time, convinced the leadership to return to sugar-centered development (Ritter 1974: 167). Thus, in a few short years revolutionary Cuba's development strategy shifted from rejecting sugar dependence as an obstacle to embracing it as a solution.

This change of direction was also a reaction to the economic difficulties brought on by the rigidity of the system introduced after 1959. In fact, some of Cuba's leading

This photo of a billboard featuring Che Guevara pushing a wheelbarrow was taken in Santiago de Cuba during that city's famed carnival celebrations in July 2003. Celebrating Guevara's promotion of the "new socialist man," the billboard encourages Cubans to be "Present in Voluntary Labor." (Ted Henken)

CHE GUEVARA'S NEW MAN

Largely a myth to the children (and grandchildren) of the revolution and a vaguely rebellious commercialized image to most of the rest of the Western world, Ernesto "Che" Guevara was one of the Cuban Revolution's most important and influential economic thinkers. In the early 1960s, Guevara was one of the main planners and protagonists in setting the economic goals and building the economic institutions of Cuban socialism. His most seductive and influential idea was the concept of the "new man." Essentially, Guevara believed that the heroic self-sacrifice and moral motivation that was essential to the success of revolutionary triumph could be rekindled and powerfully applied to the day-to-day economic tasks of the new socialist society in the making. As he declared in his famous 1965 essay "Socialism and Man in Cuba," the challenge was "to find the formula to perpetuate in day-to-day life the heroic attitude of the revolutionary struggle," because "in the attitude of our fighters, we could glimpse the man of the future" (Guevara 1997).

---

economists and policy makers began to call for major changes in the management of state companies and in the overall operation of the economy. Thus was born Cuba's mid-decade "great debate" over the character and depth that these changes should take. While all parties agreed on the preservation of socialism, the state ownership of the means of production, and central planning, they differed over the extent to which Cuba's nominally socialist economy should incorporate elements of the market, capitalist accounting methods, and material incentives.

Before he was to renounce his Cuban citizenship and depart the island to spread the revolution to other lands, Che Guevara led the domestic fight for the creation of a radical form of socialism that had at its base the belief in the malleability of human nature. In Marxian terms, he and his followers held that "subjective conditions" (the ideas, consciousness, and social morality of the "new man") could overcome Cuba's "objective conditions" of low natural resource endowments, weak productive forces, and lack of infrastructure. In Guevara's thinking, the transformation of consciousness would be achieved by consciousness-raising, voluntary work, labor mobilization, and reeducation on a massive scale, with patriotism and solidarity replacing greed and self-interest as motivating factors (Mesa-Lago 2000: 195–196). On the material and institutional level, the market and pricing would be abolished completely and replaced by full collectivization, highly centralized planning, and the rationed allocation of consumer goods (ibid.; Martínez Heredia 2003). Finally, in order to "strengthen" the revolutionary consciousness of workers, moral incentives were prioritized over material ones. Vanguard workers would be publicly celebrated but would not be "corrupted" by extra pay for extra work, bonuses, and the like.

Staunchly opposed to the "Guevarist" model was a group of communists loyal to Soviet-style pragmatism and socialist self-management led by economist Carlos Rafael Rodríguez, an early member of Cuba's Communist Party from the mid-1930s (later renamed the Popular Socialist Party in the 1940s). Essentially, these pragmatists argued that Cuba, an underdeveloped country sorely lacking in the material conditions necessary for the immediate achievement of communism, must first develop a material base before embarking on the creation of the "new man." Toward that end, Rodríguez favored the implementation of a reform-minded market socialism that made selective use of capitalist mechanisms and material incentives in the construction of Cuba's new socialist society (Mesa-Lago 2000: 196). Somewhat influenced by the reformist currents then circulating in some of the countries of Eastern Europe—particularly Poland, Czechoslovakia, and Hungary—this group opposed full collectivization of the means of production, arguing that the premature elimination of all markets and the private sector would only lead to popular resentment and economic stagnation.

Rodríguez and his supporters advocated the distribution of goods based on work and were willing to accept a degree of inequality, which they considered the only way to enhance productivity and efficiency. The group pushed for a model of economic self-management that would allow a greater degree of decentralization under the plan. Enterprise managers would be granted the autonomy to make their own financial decisions, retain some profits within the firm, and reward workers for the quality and quantity of the work performed, while still complying with their obligations to the state. Finally, they defended the use of financial instruments common in market economies, such as bank credits and tax payments. In practice, however, such market mechanisms would have limited impact given the straightjacket that the central plan imposed on all state enterprises.

One historical anomaly of this important mid-decade debate over alternative socialist models—which took place incidentally not in the party controlled mass media but in the pages of specialized highbrow journals—is the fact that Fidel Castro maintained a total silence, showing no preference for either side. In short order, however,

---

ERNESTO "CHE" GUEVARA (1928–1967)

Ernesto Guevara de la Serna—better known simply as "Che"—was born in Rosario, Argentina in 1928. As a child, he developed an iron willpower to overcome his asthma. Forced to spend long hours in bed, he took refuge in books. While a medical student, he traveled widely in Latin America and—after graduating in 1953—surprised his family by embarking on a life of travel and revolutionary adventure. One night in Mexico City in 1955, Guevara was introduced to Fidel Castro, with whom he spent the rest of the evening engaged in a marathon political discussion. By morning, he had agreed to join Castro's guerrilla group as its medic.

In November 1956, he departed Mexico for Cuba. Over the next two years, Guevara distinguished himself as a brave and loyal member of the guerrilla force, being named a *Comandante*. After the triumph of the revolution in January 1959, he helped consolidate the revolution under communism. However, after 1964, eager to spread the success of the revolution to other lands, he left Cuba. Guevara ended up in Bolivia where his small guerrilla force became disoriented and divided. He was captured on October 7, 1967, and executed the next morning.

he threw his full authority behind the radical Guevarists and their arguments for full collectivization and total elimination of the market. He even began to lodge criticisms against a number of "insufficiently revolutionary" European socialist countries, including the USSR, which were said to be permeated by capitalism. Ironically, by mid-1966, when Castro publicly embraced Guevara's radical economic policies, both Rodríguez and Guevara had already renounced their posts and no longer had any direct influence on policy making.

The Radical Experiment, the "Revolutionary Offensive," and the Gran Zafra, *1966–1970*

In the summer of 1966, after the departure of Che Guevara—who left Cuba with the mission to, in his own words, "create two, three . . . many Vietnams"—Castro announced a new "radical experiment" for revolutionary Cuba. This experiment was an attempt to establish greater economic independence from the Soviets, while reintroducing the all-important element of *conciencia* (revolutionary consciousness) into the economy. Over the next four years, Castro took Guevara's economic model and implemented it in a more radical and idealistic fashion than even Guevara had contemplated. As a result, the Cuban economy began to operate both beyond market principles and outside any bureaucratic central plan. Instead, as with the against-all-odds guerrilla victory against Batista, economic decisions were based almost entirely on Castro's fervent belief in the passionate application of revolutionary faith, struggle, and *conciencia* (Domínguez 1993: 108–109; Mesa-Lago 2000: 209–211).

The radical experiment prioritized political objectives over and above economic realities. This led to an all out struggle against capitalist influence in Cuban society, ranging from economics to culture. Economic management was turned upside down, with the elimination of financial exchanges between state firms. Under the guise of a "campaign against bureaucracy," economic controls were dismantled within state enterprises leading to the final destruction of Cuba's rich prerevolutionary traditions of accounting and business administration. Numerous bank branches were shuttered and interest payments for savings accounts were labeled "remnants from the past" and eliminated. With voluntary work prioritized, thousands of Cubans were dispatched to the countryside to labor in agriculture, while factories introduced the so-called *horarios de conciencia*, or "consciousness schedule"—which extended the work day to well over 8 hours—and the *jornadas guerrilleras*, or "guerrilla shift"—which required several consecutive days of work. In most cases, such volunteer brigades were both disorganized and unproductive, and not truly voluntary.

In the revolutionary clamor of the time, even Christmas was eliminated on the grounds that it constituted an obstacle to the sugar harvest. The celebration was drained of any religious significance and moved to July 26 to commemorate Fidel Castro's attack on the Moncada Barracks in 1953. While private Christmas celebrations were allowed once again beginning in the late 1990s, July 26 has remained revolutionary Cuba's "high holy day." There was even an aborted attempt to eliminate money altogether and replace it with a program of egalitarian distribution. Rules restricting rural-to-urban migration were strengthened, and excess urban employees were dismissed and reassigned to work in the countryside (Mesa-Lago

2000: 203). Voluntary weekend agricultural labor—termed *Domingo rojo*, or "red Sunday"—as well as the use of students, soldiers, and convicts in the sugar harvest, became commonplace. Furthermore, starting in 1965 the infamous UMAP (Unidades Militares de Ayuda a la Producción) work camps were set up in an effort to reeducate "antisocial" elements through hard agricultural labor. Loafers, dissidents, religious believers, political prisoners, homosexuals, as well as youths who had decided to drop out of school or society were forcibly assigned to these camps (Pérez-López 1995: 72).

At the heart of the radical experiment lay two specific labor-related campaigns. Perhaps because it was such a colossal failure and led to the "taming" of the revolution during the 1970s, the best known of these is the *Gran Zafra*, an effort to harvest 10 million tons sugar in 1970. In his ad hoc, charismatic style, Castro declared—quite arbitrarily—that producing anything less than 10 million tons of sugar would be tantamount to a "moral defeat" of the revolution (Mesa-Lago 2000: 213). Consequently, 1969 was officially christened *El año del esfuerzo decisivo* ("the year of the decisive struggle"), while 1970 was baptized *El año de los diez millones* ("the year of the 10 million"). For a period of 18 months (folding part of the 1969 totals into 1970), every resource available was recklessly diverted toward the singular goal of achieving *los diez millones*. Tens of thousands of workers who knew nothing about sugarcane were sent to the fields to wield machetes leaving many urban areas paralyzed for lack of workers.

However, Castro's attempt to free Cuba from economic dependency and political fealty to the Soviet Union and thus gain some economic freedom and

As part of the failed effort to reach a record 10 million tons of harvested sugarcane, the crop is loaded on wagons after being cut by hand in a photo from 1969 near Havana. (AP Photo)

maneuverability in the midst of the ideologically polarized Cold War was unsuccessful. Although a record 8.5 million tons of sugarcane was harvested, the elusive 10-million-ton goal was not achieved. The failure of this massive undertaking caused a major shift in Cuban socialism, leading to the institutionalization of a more strictly Soviet economic model in the country, with important implications for Cuban life during the 1970s. Despite the failure of the *esfuerzo decisivo* and the economic dislocation it caused, Cubans refused to be outdone by Fidel's constant mobilizations and revolutionary rhetoric. Instead, they quietly rechristened the whole abortive effort, *El año del esfuerzo de si vivo* ("the year of the struggle to see if I'll survive") (Guillermoprieto 2004).

Coming during the lead-up to the push for a 10-million-ton sugar harvest in 1970 was a lesser-known economic campaign called the "Revolutionary Offensive." Taking place in March and April 1968 (just before Castro's endorsement of the Soviet's suppression of the Prague Spring), this offensive against the last remnants of private trade made crystal clear the Cuban government's antagonistic attitude toward the remnants of private enterprise. The stated objectives of the campaign were: "to eradicate completely the individualism, selfishness, and antisocial behavior engendered by private ownership, to eliminate alienation and exploitation, to destroy the consumption privileges obtained by the private operators" (Ritter 1974: 237). In a single legislative act, the Cuban government banned self-employment, confiscated the country's still remaining 58,000 small private businesses, and eliminated farmer's markets and family gardens on state farms (Acosta 2003; Mesa-Lago 1969; Mesa-Lago and Pérez-López 2005: 10; Pérez-López 1995: 37–38; Ritter 1974: 238).

While the offensive was justified partly with the aim of improving the overall quality of services and lowering their prices, often the services eliminated were simply lost for good. Small producers and service providers, in many cases simple artisans without employees—cobblers, butchers, barbers, carpenters, tailors, plumbers, etc.—were brutally deprived of their livelihoods. An estimated two thirds of the roughly 58,000 stores and businesses shut down continued operation under new state management—with the former owner often asked to stay on now as a state employee (Pérez-López 1995: 44). The elimination of the more than 3,700 street vendors in urban areas did away with exactly the kind of efficient, service-oriented, niche activity for which the already overtaxed state service sector was not prepared to substitute. As a result, consumers suffered from the lack of food provisions and increased queuing (Ritter 1974). In the end, the overall result of the revolutionary offensive was seriously damaging to the overall production of goods and services.

The radical experiment failed because human nature was not as malleable as the Cuban leadership had hoped. The failure to achieve economic independence, create the "new man," and reach the 10-million-ton goal originated in the government's belief that self-interest could or even should be eliminated. The labor mobilization system put in place was one of absolutes. The capitalist man was eliminated and replaced by the "new (communist) man." There was no room for compromise.

Part of the failure in achieving many of the stated goals of the radical experiment was the result of the autocratic and coercive methods of labor mobilization utilized. As it became increasingly apparent that *conciencia* alone was not enough to motivate Cuban workers, militarization of the labor force was used to fill the void.

THE REVOLUTIONARY OFFENSIVE, APRIL 1968

On April 7, 1968, the newspaper *Granma* published a list of the remaining 58,000 private Cuban businesses that would be nationalized in the "Revolutionary Offensive." They included 17,000 food retailers, 2,500 sellers of industrial products, 11,300 bars and restaurants, 14,000 barbers, laundries, and repair shops, and 9,600 small-scale workshops (Pérez-López 1995: 37–38; Ritter 1974: 238). Ironically, the elimination of these many diverse, niche operations hurt the government itself since the state had been one of the private sector's primary customers (Mesa-Lago 1969, 2000). Another irony is the fact that more than half of these enterprises were established after 1961 (Pérez-Stable 1999: 118). The revolutionary offensive also had a devastating impact on Cuba's music scene. The small private businesses eliminated included all privately owned clubs. Even worse, according to Cuban musicologist Leonardo Acosta (2003), the havoc caused by the revolutionary offensive—together with the U.S. embargo—disrupted the transnational flow of exchange and innovation between Cuba and the United States that had been so essential in musical creation, making 1968 the single most devastating year in the history of Cuban popular music during the 20th century.

Conscripts, students, prisoners, declared emigrants, weekend volunteers, and "social undesirables"—such as homosexuals, hippies, and the religious—were all put to work under militarized labor arrangements (Pérez-Stable 1999). The "new man" was to be created in a schematic fourfold process that included political reeducation, the supervised practice of hard labor, following the example of the leadership, and working with the support of the party and the mass organizations (Ritter 1974).

Despite massive reeducation campaigns and government control of schooling and the mass media, Guevara's dream of transforming the Cuban population into a loyal cadre of new men and women bore little fruit. "Voluntary" manual work in agriculture for 45 days a year became a duty for all true revolutionaries as part of their consciousness training. This same hard work—combined with political education—was also seen as a cure for all types of "antisocial behavior," including homosexuality, laziness, and decadent Western youth culture, exemplified by long hair, blue jeans, and rock and roll. In the end, however, such methods tended to exacerbate antisocial and unproductive behaviors such as absenteeism, black market activities, loafing, and a general cynicism and distrust toward the revolution—the polar opposite of *conciencia*. Conceiving of the creation of the "new man" as an all-or-nothing project, in which individual self-interest and "the good of society" are necessarily mutually exclusive, led to a fundamental breakdown in Cuba's economic system. As a result, in the years to come Cuba would introduce a moderate Soviet model that made strategic use of the market and, especially after 1980, the private sector in self-employment, food markets, and housing construction. Indeed, after the catastrophic performance of the previous economic development model, the revolutionary government was left with little choice.

Soviet Institutionalization and the Taming
of Fidel Castro, 1970–1985

To cope with the bankruptcy of the Guevarist radical experiment and the symbolic failure of the *Gran Zafra*, the government reorganized the economy once again in the 1970s, now embracing the less adventurist and more pragmatic market socialism of the USSR. This amounted to a taming of sorts of Fidel Castro's economic practices and the institutionalization of the revolution under the first Communist Party Congress in 1975. The adoption of the Constitution in 1976 was important in this process of institutionalization, even if it was thoroughly permeated by Soviet influence. For example, Article 5 of the Constitution defines the role of Cuba's Communist Party as: "the organized vanguard of the Cuban nation; the superior force of society and the Cuban state, which organizes and orients the common effort toward the honored goals of building socialism and advancement toward a socialist society."

In this context, Raúl Castro took on a role beyond that of being minister of the Armed Forces, such that the Communist Party and various highly qualified individuals were placed in strategic positions of economic authority. The central plan was reintroduced as the guiding force behind the economy, taking into account elements of the market and granting some flexibility and autonomy in the management of state enterprises. Agricultural Production Cooperatives (CPAs) were also created through the union of private farms, and they were empowered with command of a limited amount of state resources. A limited expansion took place in private self-employment in the late 1970s, allowing artisans to market their products and services once again. Likewise, farmers' markets (*mercados libres campesinos*, MLCs) appeared and were allowed to sell produce to the public at market prices (Mesa-Lago 2000: 246–247).

Despite this small opening, these economic reforms were stymied by the government's repeated criticisms that lumped legal operators together with illegal profiteers (ibid.: 230). In 1982, the government raised taxes and initiated a crackdown on self-employment, sending confusing signals to potential entrepreneurs. Although both

---

THE BRIEF LIFE OF FREE FARMERS' MARKETS
(*MERCADOS LIBRES CAMPESINOS*)

The legalization of self-employment in 1978 was followed on April 5, 1980, by Decree-Law 66, which opened private agricultural markets, the so-called free farmer's markets (*mercados libres campesinos*, MLCs). The MLC law allowed all private agricultural producers (private farmers and members of agricultural cooperatives) to set up retail agricultural markets throughout the island. Products like sugar, tobacco, coffee, and beef, thought to be vital in the state sector, were prohibited from these markets. Likewise, private farmers were first required to meet their quota obligations to the state (*acopio*) before being allowed to sell their surplus in these free markets. Finally, farmers were restricted to their local markets and prohibited from using intermediaries or hiring non-state trucks to transport their produce (Marshall 1998; Pérez-López 1995; Rosenberg 1992).

the legalization of self-employment and the establishment of the MLCs were carried out with Castro's approval, these reforms never had his active support and continued to be viewed as anachronistic and somewhat illegitimate, despite their legality.

Already by 1982, private entrepreneurs were being accused of using state stores as sales points for their own products, secretly and illegally setting up their own shops, diverting raw materials from the state sector, hiring employees and middlemen, selling goods for which they had no authorization and in places that were prohibited, and making exorbitant profits (Mesa-Lago 1988: 78–81). As a result of these criticisms many self-employed workers were arrested, and raids were carried out against many workers in the MLCs. Finally, in 1986 the increasingly moribund private sector finally received its coup de grace. That year saw a new crackdown on self-employment and the MLCs that all but eliminated private economic activity from Cuba once again.

The Rectification Process, 1986–1989

Fidel Castro personally ended the liberalization process in 1986 with his "Rectification of Errors and Negative Tendencies" campaign. First announced publicly by Castro at the February 1986 inauguration of the Third Party Congress, the rectification process definitively eliminated the few small private sector spaces that had opened up during the previous 15 years, particularly the MLCs, artisan markets, and self-employment. Trends that had decentralized the economy to some extent were reversed with the abolition of most market mechanisms that had been functioning within and between state firms. Moral rewards were prioritized once again over material incentives. However, it is important to note—especially given his current role as Cuban president—that Raúl Castro managed to protect the growing business operations of the Armed Forces from the rectification process. In fact, he was not only able to maintain the Armed Forces' more rational mechanisms of economic governance and management but even expand and deepen them at this time; successfully positioning them for an even greater—some say commanding—role in the Cuban economy during the 1990s and beyond.

Apparently, the new crackdown undertaken by Fidel Castro was due to the fear coming from the most hard-line sector of the Cuban government in the face of the advent of Perestroika and Glasnost in the Soviet Union. It was evident that these openings in the USSR were encouraging reformist ideas among some cadres and the Cuban people in general. Cuban political leaders were well aware of the close relationship between economic and political freedom, especially in a country where the traditions of multiple political parties and freedom of expression have existed since colonial times, despite constraints. Added to this is the entrepreneurial nature of the Cuban people, influenced by the cultural impact of the United States, which could not be erased by totalitarianism. However, as a result of the return of centralization and restrictions on economic freedom, economic growth plummeted in the second half of the 1980s, with the Gross Social Product (GSP) falling 3.8 percent in 1987 and another 3.6 percent in 1990. With the demise of Eastern European socialist bloc, Cuba's huge subsidies and preferential trade arrangements evaporated overnight, provoking an economic crisis—known as the "Special Period"—of a severity never before experienced in Cuba's modern history and that has lasted until today.

FROM REFORM TO RETRENCHMENT: CUBA CONFRONTS THE "SPECIAL PERIOD," 1990–1996

As a result of the collapse of the Soviet Union, Cuba's gross domestic product (GDP) declined an amazing 34 percent between 1989 and 1993. This precipitous drop had a devastating impact on living standards and was felt in virtually every sector of society. Between those same years overall foreign trade fell by 77 percent and fuel became virtually unavailable. This brought the island's transportation to a standstill and made hours-long blackouts a feature of daily life. Many factories and service centers were shuttered for lack of power and raw materials, sending workers home with just a fraction of their salaries.

Food shortages and the scarcity of all kinds of products reached epidemic levels. Retail trade decreased by 44 percent between 1989 and 1993, while the use of public buses fell by 75 percent causing a virtual collapse of the sector. In turn, an under-nourished populace was forced en masse to travel to work and school each day atop bulky bicycles imported by the thousands from China. Domestic finances suffered a disastrous free fall as well. The 1993 budget deficit amounted to 34 percent of GDP, with a more than doubling of regular savings and excess currency in circulation leading to an inflation rate of 183 percent. By 1994 the unofficial exchange rate of the Cuban peso to the U.S. dollar rose to 130 to 1, and at times even higher, while the official rate remained 1 to 1. In real terms, this meant that the value of a Cuban's average monthly wage shrank to from 188 pesos in 1989 to just 19 in 1993 (Vidal 2009).

In response to this series of shocks, President Fidel Castro declared a "special period in peacetime" (*período especial en tiempo de paz*) to begin on August 30, 1990. Essentially a Faustian bargain, the temporary reform measures enacted between 1990 and 1995 amounted to using elements of capitalism to save socialism. With his traditional pragmatism, the minister of the Armed Forces Raúl Castro emphasized the urgent need for an economic opening—while remaining within the socialist system—under the slogan: "Beans are more important than cannons." Among these pro-market reforms were a new foreign investment law, the reopening private farmers' and artisan markets, an allowance of foreign remittances, the legalization of the possession and use of the U.S. dollar, and the licensing self-employment. In 1993, the Basic Units of Cooperative Production (UBPCs) were created. These were agricultural cooperatives on paper, but experience has since shown that they never functioned as genuine cooperatives and in practice operated much like the unproductive and bureaucratic state farms.

At the same time, Cuba turned once again to the intensive exploitation of its excellent natural conditions for international tourism, intentionally pushed aside since the early 1960s for fear of ideological contamination. Ironically, the defiant nation that had once scoffed at foreign investment and decadent tourism from the capitalist West now found itself forced to compete vigorously for hard-currency investment and to aggressively seek out partners for joint ventures in tourism. "Who would have thought," Castro asked in the summer of 1993, "that we, so doctrinaire, we who fought foreign investment, would one day view foreign investment as an urgent need?" (Pérez 1995: 404). At the same time, the harnessing of tourism-led development in the context of extreme scarcity and supposed socialist egalitarianism has forced Cuba to confront many social contradictions, including ubiquitous

Due to its historical, architectural, and commercial significance, Habana Vieja or Old Havana has been designated a UNESCO world heritage site and as such has been gradually refurbished as one of Cuba's hottest tourist spots since 1990 under the direction of City Historian and unofficial mayor of Old Havana, Eusebio Leal. This photo shows the transformation of Plaza Vieja with a new elegant fountain and a completely restored historical building. (Orlando Luis Pardo Lazo)

prostitution and hustling, jarring inequalities, claims of "tourist apartheid," the cheap commodification of culture, and environmental degradation.

The dominant state sector of the economy saw the beginning of a process of corporate governance reform, known as the *Sistema de Perfeccionamiento Empresarial*

TOURISM

Tourism has rapidly become the island's number one "export" during the special period, outpacing both sugar and remittances. Visits have grown 10-fold from a mere 275,000 in 1989 to more than 2.7 million in 2011. The number of hotel rooms also jumped from 5,000 in 1987 to almost 65,000 in 2010. There was a brief two-year decline in tourist arrivals between 2005 and 2007 due to hurricane damage and the worldwide economic recession. However, the industry rebounded thereafter with record numbers of arrivals in each year since 2008 (Pérez-López and Díaz-Briquets 2011: 318).

Canada is the leading source of Cuba's tourists with more than a third of 2010's visitors arriving from that country (945,300 out of 2.5 million). Other important sending nations include the United Kingdom, Italy, and Spain, each of which sent between 100,000 and 200,000 visitors to the island every year from 2005 to 2010. Another surprising source of Cuba's tourists is the United States. While official numbers for 2010 were only 63,100, industry insiders estimate that as many as 400,000 Americans—and especially Cuban-Americans—visited in 2011 as a result of the Obama administration's new travel rules (Burnett 2011).

(System of Enterprise Improvement). To a large degree, this experiment applied the successful military business model developed in the 1980s to other branches of the state sector. This model called for greater decentralization and decision making in production and service units, as well as closer linkages between the work performed and the pay received in order to stimulate greater productivity, efficiency, and growth. This limited set of reforms applied in a country with enormous underutilized productive potential managed to pull Cuba out of its economic tailspin in 1994, achieving modest growth by 1995. This turnaround demonstrated that the key factors in achieving economic development are those related to enabling citizens to deploy their own entrepreneurial ideas and initiatives in an atmosphere of freedom and trust that facilitate labor motivation.

ECONOMIC RETRENCHMENT, RECENTRALIZATION, AND THE EXIT OF FIDEL CASTRO: 1996–2006

Although not new on the scene, Cuba's non-state sector, or "second economy," expanded significantly during the special period. In fact, there is a consensus among government officials, analysts on the island, and scholars abroad that as the official, first economy entered a major crisis, the unregulated second economy exploded in scope and size (Pérez-López 1995). An indicator of the growing economic importance of Cuba's second economy is the government's attempts to legalize and incorporate it into the official, first economy through the expansion of legal self-employment (*trabajo por cuenta propia*) during the first half of the 1990s (Henken 2002; Peters 2006; Peters and Scarpaci 1998; Ritter 2004). For example, the size of the official self-employed sector grew from 70,000 in December 1993 (just months after it was legalized) to 140,000 by May 1994 (Jatar-Hausmann 1999; Peters and Scarpaci 1998; Smith 1999: 49).

The government's unofficial policy of alternately encouraging, repressing, and regulating self-employment since then has produced significant fluctuations in its size and composition. Although the sector reached its zenith in January 1996 with 209,606 licensed operators, it shrank considerably thereafter as a result of the institution of a quota-based, personal income tax later that same year. Likewise, the government's awareness that many of the self-employed either worked without licenses or routinely "cut corners" to stay in business caused the state to impose a law-and-order approach to the private sector during these years. For example, in a March 1996 speech to the Party's Central Committee Raúl Castro observed:

> More than 200,000 citizens now engage in . . . self-employment. . . . It is evident that the real figure is much higher, since there are thousands more who engage in self-employment of some kind or another without the necessary authorization. . . . These [legal] self-employed workers should be the first to want to eradicate the new crop of speculators, thieves, and violators of tax laws or health regulations—that is, those who wish to get rich off of the people's needs and hardships arising from the special period. . . . Severe punishment of those who break the law should serve to make everyone understand that crime has no future in a socialist country. (Raúl Castro 1996)

After 1996, reforms were slowly scaled back and spaces that had been opened up to private enterprise were closed off. Self-employment—which had played a major role in reanimating the provision of goods and services and provided tens of thousands of Cubans a legal way to earn a living—languished due to increased restrictions and prohibitions. By April 1997 official numbers of the self-employed sector dropped to 180,919, falling further to 165,438 by April 1998 (Jatar-Hausmann 1999; Peters 1997). Since then numbers continued to drop, with the government marching out new offensives and obstacles to their growth and survival between 2003 and 2005 (Resolución No. 11, 2004). Numbers had fallen to 153,800 by early 2001 (Espinosa Chepe 2002; National Office of Statistics 2001: 116), reaching 149,990 by 2003.

Likewise, Cuba's famed speakeasy eateries, known as *paladares*, the one true example of private microenterprise allowed on the island, dwindled from a peak of 1,500 in 1996 to just 150 by 2003 (Jackiewicz and Bolster 2003; Mesa-Lago and Pérez-López 2005: 52; Peters 2006). Interviews with both legal and clandestine *paladar* operators in Havana and Santiago between 2003 and 2006 confirm this downward trend. In fact, by April 2006, there were just 98 remaining licensed *paladares* in all of Havana.

In 2005, the Cuban government moved to increase the minimum wage and pensions and began an ideological mobilization known as the "Battle of Ideas," which included raising the prices of electricity and cracking down on corruption, theft, pilfering, and the "new rich." In a November 17 speech delivered upon the 60th anniversary of his own entry into the University of Havana, Fidel Castro attacked the self-employed whom he considered part of the "new rich," singling out taxi drivers, bed and breakfast operators, and especially *paladar* operators. "In this battle against vice, nobody will be spared. Either we will defeat all these deviations and make our revolution strong, or we die," he declared. He called for a return to an egalitarian society and hinted that the "total renewal" of Cuban society would include drastic moves to eliminate rising difference between Cuba's haves and have-nots (Fidel Castro 2005).

On balance, the economic results of the reforms enacted between 1990 and 1996 were clearly positive. While commitments to equality and full employment were affected negatively, the growth rate rebounded, inflation fell sharply, the fiscal deficit contracted, and both exports and imports grew (Mesa-Lago and Pérez-López 2005). However, because of two unacceptable side effects further economic reforms were halted and many later reversed. First, the growth in inequality and the expansion of unemployment (along with other jarring social contradictions) were signs of the failure to uphold socialist egalitarian ideology. More important, on the political front, the economic reforms provided increased economic independence to a new class of state enterprise managers, private farmers, and self-employed workers (among others) to whom the state felt it was losing economic control. Essentially, the fear that economic independence inevitably leads to political independence caused the leadership to begin a slow rollback of reforms starting in 1996.

The reversal of the reform process was also associated with the emergence between 1998 and 2000 of Hugo Chávez's Bolivarian Revolution in Venezuela, leading to major subsidies for the Cuban economy. This permitted a new recentralization of the Cuban economy, which lasted through the end of 2006. Also during these years, a series of positive—if short-lived—economic developments lessened the urgency that initially made the reforms necessary. Cuba became adept at welcoming increasing numbers of foreign tourists and attracting hard currency remittances from Cuban-Americans. It was also able to recentralize its economy while simultaneously courting new, economically and politically strategic foreign partners, including a booming China and an oil-rich Venezuela (Corrales, Erikson, and Falcoff 2005). Finally, Cuba benefited during this time from the booming international market price of nickel, one of its leading mineral exports (Pérez-López 2006).

This reversal indicated that the reforms implemented in the mid-1990s were intended to achieve the survival of the socialist regime by making certain, limited concessions to the market, but not by making any substantial changes to the existing socialist model. However, as we will see later, with Fidel indefinitely convalescing and not being able to set the economic agenda after 2006, Raúl Castro—under new international and domestic pressures—changed his approach to self-employment after becoming president in 2008. In fact, starting in October 2010, Cuba's long-suffering private, non-state sector went once again from being considered a necessary evil to being embraced as the island's economic salvation. Even the normally hard-line Communist Party national newspaper *Granma* celebrated the 2010 return of self-employment as a way "to increase levels of productivity and efficiency" and "provide workers with another way to feel useful with their personal effort." Going even further, the newspaper openly repudiated the past policies enacted under Fidel—without directly naming him, of course—saying: We must "distance ourselves from those policies that condemned self-employment to near extinction and stigmatized those who decided to join its ranks legally in the decade of the 90s."

THE RISE OF RAÚL CASTRO, 2006–2013

The rise of Raúl Castro, sparked by the sudden illness of his elder brother Fidel in late July 2006, raised hopes on the island for change. During his time as second secretary of Cuba's Communist Party and minister of the Revolutionary Armed Forces, the younger Castro distinguished himself as a relatively pragmatic and realistic manager. Although he is far from being a democrat, he has shown himself more inclined to listen to others' opinions than was the habit of his brother. Moreover, he has generally avoided public presentations and long speeches, preferring to focus on organized labor instead. These differences in his governing style could be noted from the very beginning of his time as acting president, even if he has made no changes in the foundations of the socialist system. Fidel's never ending political mobilizations and lengthy public events were phased out immediately with brevity reigning at the few public events Raúl has been party to.

While state propaganda and the systematic manipulation of news have continued to predominate in the Cuban media, a modest opening to debate is evident relative to the absolute unilateralism that had been the rule in the past. Even Cuban television—notorious for its constant interruptions of a political nature, such as Fidel's long speeches or guest appearances by Venezuelan President Hugo Chávez—has begun to stick to its schedule. The prospects for change were given a boost on July 26, 2007, when Raúl Castro—nearing the close of his first year as acting president—assured his listeners that "structural and conceptual changes" were in the works. In the same

Cuban president Fidel Castro, left, and his brother, Minister of Defense Raúl Castro, attend a Cuban Parliament session at the Palace of Conventions on July 1, 2004 in Havana. After spending more than a year fighting for his life, the ailing elder Castro resigned as Cuba's president on Feb. 19, 2008, saying in a letter published in the official media that he would not accept a new term. Raúl was elected Cuba's new president a few days later. (AP Photo/Cristobal Herrera)

speech, he was harshly critical of Cuban agricultural performance, lambasting managers for allowing large tracts of undeveloped land to become choked with weeds, while the government was forced to spend its precious resources on importing ever greater amounts of foodstuffs that could be grown on the island.

The final resignation of Fidel Castro and the confirmation of Raúl as Cuba's new president on February 24, 2008, seemed to open the way to deeper reforms that could begin to tap Cuba's pent up productive forces. On February 2, just three weeks before Raúl's inauguration, the Ministry of Labor and Social Security issued Resolution No. 9, which allowed greater pay for higher quality work and removed arbitrary salary caps. While this resolution has been difficult to put into practice due to insufficient autonomy in most state enterprises, it was an indication of the new president's pragmatic economic goals. Raúl's first move as president was to eliminate a series of what he himself referred to as "absurd prohibitions." Consequently, just weeks after his inauguration he authorized the sale of computers, DVD players, and other high-priced and much sought after electronic equipment. Consumer items as simple as bicycles, electric cookers, and cell phones were now available for purchase by those who could afford them. Additionally, the prohibition against Cubans staying in hotels was removed, as were restrictions against car rentals and the sale of certain medicines.

Agricultural Reforms and Their Limits

As part of Raúl's reforms, Decree-Laws No. 259 and 282 on the distribution of vacant land were enacted in the summer of 2008. The goal was to make productive more than a million hectares of idle land, thus counteracting the need to import nearly 80 percent of the island's food, bought in recent years mainly—and ironically—from the United States. Landless peasants could receive usufruct rights (nonownership rights to cultivate crops) on a maximum of 1.42 hectares of idle land, while those already owning land could receive up to 40.26 hectares, provided they could demonstrate that the lands they already possessed were being used productively. However, usufruct rights to the land were granted only for a period of 10 years with the possibility of another 10-year extension for private producers. In contrast, the law extended use rights for 25 years for "legal persons" (that is, state entities), renewable for another 25 years, thereby discriminating against private producers. This is without taking into consideration the fact that the later 2010 Decree-Law No. 273 extended land leases to foreign companies—for tourism developments such as golf courses and luxury marinas—for a period of 99 years, thus granting foreigners more rights than either private Cuban farmers or state entities.

Decree-Law 259 is stymied by many other restrictions indicating that, while a step forward, it has not been able to give agricultural production the jumpstart it urgently needs, nor has it succeeded in reducing Cuba's high level of dependence on food imports. Originally, the law omitted key details such as the freedom of its beneficiaries to grow and sell their products on the open market. Growers' obligation to sell a set amount of their harvest to the state at prices and conditions set unilaterally by the state (known as *acopio*) continued in force. These gaps were later partially corrected in November 2011 by the allowance of direct sales to the tourism sector.

The 10-year usufruct periods discourage potential beneficiaries from entering the program since such short terms rule out the cultivation of long-term crops and raising cattle. This is exacerbated by the prohibition against building housing or similar installations on the land under cultivation—a prohibition that was also later rescinded. Moreover, much of the idle land being distributed is overrun by weeds, especially a particularly invasive, thorny shrub known as *marabú*. Initially, the state provided only very limited access to tools with which peasants could uproot the weed and at often exorbitant prices. Fortunately, this deficiency was addressed in August 2011 with prices of such equipment slashed by up to 60 percent. Still, while there has been some improvement in the provision of resources, the continued difficulty in obtaining proper inputs remains a significant obstacle to increasing agricultural production.

As with the rest of the economy, agricultural production also suffers from a severe decapitalization, with limited access to modern farm machinery. Over the past 20 years, tractors have been progressively replaced by oxen, hoes, and machetes; and fertilizers, pesticides, herbicides, and fuel are extremely hard to come by. For all of these reasons, the distribution of land for use by private farmers has not only not yielded the expected results, but has even provoked a drop of 2.8 percent in agricultural production in 2010, only accentuating Cuba's severe dependence on food imports. Between September and November 2008, several hurricanes made landfall on the island, causing enormous losses to the economy and inflicting extraordinary agricultural damage. Cuba's often outdated and weathered infrastructure was also seriously impacted with damage to 647,110 homes, 84,737 of which were completely destroyed. These natural disasters coincided with the global financial crisis. Occurring simultaneously, these factors only exacerbated the crisis that had already been ravaging the Cuban economy for 20 years. This led in turn to a crisis of liquidity, preventing the government from paying its debts to foreign companies operating in the country. Worse still, in order to prevent a foreign capital from fleeing the country, these companies were temporarily prevented from exchanging the Cuban convertible pesos (CUCs) they had earned in Cuba for foreign exchange, essentially trapping their assets within the country. Although this situation has improved since then, the distrust it generated in Cuba's foreign partners in the ability of the country to pay its debts and allow the free flow of financing has lingered.

Pilot Privatization Programs and the Start of State Sector Layoffs

In 2009, Raúl's government began to quietly put into practice a number of pilot semiprivatization programs called "new formulas to release productive potential." Among them was the authorization of farmers in eastern Cuba to sell fruits and vegetables directly to consumers. This successful experience was soon expanded throughout the entire country. At the same time, new licenses were issued to food vendors and the government began to study the possible establishment of small service and production cooperatives. Subsequently, thousands of cafeterias located at work places all across the country were closed with the justification that they had become economically unsustainable. Instead, workers would be given cash stipends and expected to either bring their own food to work or buy lunch in one of the many flourishing private cafeterias nearby.

These small experiments expanded in April 2010 to include three service sector innovations. Certain state employed taxi drivers and small-scale barbers and beauticians began to operate as legal private entrepreneurs—a practice many had been engaging in on the sly for years. Instead of being employed by and receiving a salary from the government, henceforth they would rent their cars and places of business from the state, pay taxes, and be responsible for covering the costs of gas, repairs, and other supplies out of pocket. In turn, they would be allowed to charge more realistic market prices for their services and retain their profits. That said, they could also now fail to turn a profit and be forced to go out of business for the first time. In conjunction, the state eased regulations for the construction and repair of homes, and in June expanded sales of building materials in to the public in pesos. Beginning in August, the sale of fruits and vegetables along Cuba's rural highways—another practice long done clandestinely—was made legal.

Of particular importance that year was Raúl Castro's speech on August 1 addressing National Assembly delegates. He announced the long-awaited expansion of self-employment with the unprecedented allowance for them to hire employees. The removal of the taboo on the hiring of labor is particularly significant, as it lays the potential groundwork for the establishment of small- and medium-sized enterprises (SMEs) in the future. This would be an important source of jobs, goods, and services, provide a needed flexibility to the economy, and contribute to the national budget through taxes. Nevertheless, this measure has not yet yielded all its potential benefits given that the initial tax system regulating the hiring of labor actually discourages growth by taxing those with more workers at a higher rate.

In that same speech, the president made a second, even more shocking announcement: a "rationalization" program for surplus state employees, which projected the layoffs of as many as 1.3 million people, approximately 25 percent of Cuba's workforce. Raúl Castro explained that in the first phase of this major restructuring of the state enterprise sector, the central government would iron out details of deciding which workers would be "rationalized" and the levels of severance pay they would receive. Still, he left no doubt as to his intentions, saying that Cuba must: "suppress paternalistic policies that undermine the need to work to live, thereby reducing nonproductive expenditures: wages that are the same no matter the number of years worked and guaranteed salaries for long periods for people who don't work." He justified these cuts as a way to simulate greater efficiency and productivity in state enterprises. Without that, he reasoned, "it is impossible to raise salaries, increase exports and replace imports, expand the production of foodstuffs and in point of fact, to sustain the enormous social spending of our socialist system."

Intending to reassure the increasingly nervous Cuban population, the Cuban state media led the following day, August 2, with a headline taken directly from Raúl's speech: "No one will be abandoned to his fate." However, Cuba's new president intended to make crystal clear that the social safety net would be henceforth intended only for those "who really are unable to work." Most Cubans got the hint, as did the international press which tended to emphasize another line from his speech. "The notion that Cuba is the only country in the world where you can live without working," Raúl soberly reminded his listeners, "must be erased forever" (Siegelbaum 2010). Just over month later, in September 2010, the state-controlled workers union, the *Central de Trabajadores de Cuba* (CTC), issued a statement reprinted in all Cuban newspapers formally announcing the layoffs and outlining the procedure for the dismissal of workers ("Announcement . . ." 2010). Similarly, the new law outlining the layoff procedures placed the onus of deciding who is "expendable" on workers themselves—through the election of 5–7 member "expert commissions in each workplace—when such a decision is a clear responsibility of management (Gaceta Oficial 2010b).

Although a half-a-million state employees were to be let go in the six months between October 2010 and April 2011, such a rapid transition proved impossible to achieve and has since been postponed until 2015. At a meeting of the Council of Ministers in late February 2011, Raúl reasoned that "updating the [socialist] model is not a single day's task, nor even one that can be accomplished in a single year. Given its complexity, it will require no less than five years to complete."

The Return of Self-Employment: Once More with Feeling?

October 2010 saw the publication of the new laws that would expand self-employment and shortly thereafter—on November 8—it was announced that the Sixth Congress of the Communist Party (PCC) would be held in April 2011. Neither the new self-employment regulations nor the draft *"Lineamientos"*—a set of economic policy guidelines aimed at preparing the country for the upcoming Party Congress—have been sufficient to the task of confronting Cuba's deepening economic and demographic crisis. Both have been subsequently amended. While positive steps in the right direction, the documents made clear that Raúl's aim was to change enough to overcome the current crisis—more acute with each passing day—without jeopardizing the total control that virtually the same group of people have maintained over Cuban society for more than half a century.

The new self-employment regulations, for example, did in fact "distance [Raúl's policies] from those [of Fidel] that condemned self-employment to near extinction" in the 1990s, as *Granma* so succinctly put it ("Mucho más . . ." 2010). After a long drought, licenses were now made easily available in 178 occupations. For the first time since 1968, microenterprises would be permitted to hire employees in 83 occupations (later permitted for all 178). While the previous incarnation of self-employment allowed only retirees and those holding down a state job to become self-employed, this time around anyone could do so. Furthermore, a single person could be licensed in more than one occupation. Homes and other spaces could now be rented out to others so that they could run businesses out of them. Finally, many of the prohibitions impeding the growth of Cuba's famed private "*paladar*" restaurants—such as the limit of 12 chairs and the ban on beef and shellfish—were rescinded (Gaceta Oficial 2010a; "Mucho más . . ." 2010; Peters 2010a; Ritter 2010).

Centrally located near the University of Havana, this large, open-air, private restaurant - named "La Moraleja" (The Moral) - is one of the most successful new "paladar" eateries to open up following Raúl Castro's 2010 reversal of past policies that had stigmatized selfemployment. (Ted Henken)

These clearly positive steps were undermined by a deep and lingering distrust of potential Cuban entrepreneurs. A raft of cumbersome and unnecessary restrictions, taxes, and safeguards were deployed to prevent anyone from growing too wealthy or too successful. Likewise, a number of fundamental oversights in the launching of self-employment—a lack of access to credit and wholesale supply markets, a continued prohibition against professionals becoming self-employed in their own areas, an often arbitrary tax system, and basic contradictions to the existing Constitution—have prevented it from reaching its full potential (Martínez Hernández and Puig Meneses 2010). The height of the lack of preparation behind the rollout of the self-employment regulations is perhaps their clear violation of the Cuban Constitution, which has still not been reformed. For example, the laudable measure allowing for the hiring of labor contradicts Article 21 of the Constitution, which "guarantees ownership of the means and instruments of personal or family labor, which cannot be used for the generation of income from the exploitation of the work of others." Likewise, the announcement to lay off 500,000 people, without any guarantee of fallback employment, conflicts with Article 45, which states: "Work in socialist society is a right . . . guaranteed by the socialist economic system, which fosters economic and social development, without crisis, and has thus eliminated unemployment."

The *Lineamientos* made clear Cuban authorities' intent to avoid "the concentration of ownership," so as to prevent citizens from achieving greater economic freedom with which they could advocate for more political freedom. This intention is evident in the introduction of a steep system of taxation for the emerging self-employed sector; one much more severe and restrictive than that which applies to either existing state-owned enterprises or joint ventures with foreign companies. On the positive side, the new tax regime significantly increases tax deductions, allowing the self-employed to deduct up to 40 percent from income for the cost of supplies, compared to just 10 percent under the old regime in place between 1993 and 2010. However, the new system includes many more taxes than the old and comes with a warning of stiffer enforcement and punishment for tax evasion (Frank 2010; Peters 2010b).

Additionally, private enterprises must pay a special tax for each worker they employ, equivalent to 25 percent of that worker's salary. The legal base salary used for this tax calculation is the average monthly wage plus an additional 50 percent. If between 10 and 15 workers are hired, the base upon which the 25 percent tax is calculated increases to two full average monthly wages; and those employing more than 15 workers have a base of three monthly wages. Of course, taxing the businesses that provide employment to greater number of people at a higher rate than their smaller competitors undermines the goal of harnessing self-employment as a way to absorb the ever greater numbers of workers laid off from their state jobs (Gaceta Oficial 2010b). The government seems divided between a desire to encourage the development of a larger private sector and tax policies openly aimed at limiting the growth of that sector. "This tax is regulatory in character to avoid concentrations of wealth and indiscriminate use of labor," the Party newspaper *Granma* explained. "The more labor hired the more severe the tax" (Frank 2010; Martínez Hernández and Puig Meneses 2010).

Another example of the intent to limit individual initiative is the way individual income tax rates are calculated. After deducting one's expenses and the monthly

TABLE 4.1   Tax-Rates for Self-Employment, 2010

Annual Net Income (in Pesos)	Tax Rate (%)
Up to 5,000	Exempt
Between 5,000 and 10,000	25
Between 10,000 and 20,000	30
Between 20,000 and 30,000	35
Between 30,000 and 50,000	40
More than 50,000	50

taxes already paid from the sum of all income earned, one's tax rate is determined according to the following sliding scale (see Table 4.1; Gaceta Oficial 2010b: 155).

As is evident from Table 4.1, those with annual incomes above 50,000 pesos (US$2,500) face an effective tax rate (defined as the taxes payable as a percentage of true net income) of over 50 percent, and one that in some cases could exceed 100 percent (Ritter 2011). Coupled with the existing tax payment for the use of labor, this system of personal income tax makes it practically impossible for new businesses to earn enough to ensure survival, much less growth. (Partially recognizing the burden imposed by the sliding scale in Table 4.1 the National Assembly exempted from taxes personal income up to 10,000 pesos in its sessions on December 23, 2011).

To these taxes was added a mandatory monthly social security contribution for all self-employed. While the creation of an economic safety net for private workers is positive in principle, making it mandatory is questionable, especially with the private sector still in its infancy (Gaceta Oficial 2010a). Canadian economist Arch Ritter zeros in on the remaining problems of Cuba's new tax regime for micro-entrepreneurs, describing the reform as moving in "the right direction," while also describing it as "still onerous and stultifying."

> The overall tax level is punitive. The sum of the income tax, employee hiring tax, and public service surtax is high and . . . can help create effective tax rates exceeding 100%. . . . This will continue to promote non-compliance. It will discourage underground enterprises from becoming legal. The establishment of new enterprises will be discouraged. (Ritter 2011)

As mentioned earlier, the self-employed sector was launched without first creating wholesale markets or assuring access to credit. Therefore, business owners have no place to turn where they can purchase inputs or obtain loans under reasonable conditions. Instead, they are forced by the circumstances to rely on expensive hard currency stores (originally intended for dollar-rich foreigners) or the black market for inputs, and relatives or loan sharks for credit. Of course, the black market will surely expand to meet this new demand in the absence of an affordable, legal alternative.

Likewise, the government made a strategic and ideological choice to err on the side of control when it decided to reignite self-employment by publishing a list of just 178 permissible occupations. As it stands, the list of 178 occupations—later expanded to 181, and again to 187—is far from sufficient as it excludes many professions. The list is also plagued by many specific jobs such as "book binder," "piñata maker/seller," "party clown," "dandy," "button upholsterer," "maker/seller of crowns of flowers," or "door-to-door knife and scissors sharpener" that have limited economic or occupational significance.

By the end of January 2011, official figures showed that 113,618 new self-employment licenses had been granted in addition to the roughly 145,000 licenses already in operation as of October 2010. However, nearly 70 percent of these new licenses were issued to people previously unemployed. This indicates that the private sector opening has functioned in practice more as a path of legalization for preexisting informal operations than as a way to absorb workers recently laid off from state jobs, as intended. This is to say nothing of the many entrepreneurs who have already thrown in the towel and returned their licenses either because of high taxes, problems obtaining affordable supplies, or due to some of the other obstacles described earlier.

It is clearer than ever that the process of restructuring Cuba's state enterprise sector and labor system is highly dependent on the success of creating a dynamic and welcoming environment for the private, non-state sector. However, the sector is still weighed down by outdated dogmas and bureaucratic difficulties of all kinds, making the necessary reorganization of the state sector and relocation of as many as 1.3 million workers in the coming three to five years extremely difficult.

The *"Lineamientos"* and Preparations for the Sixth Party Congress

The Sixth Congress of the Communist Party was announced by President Raúl Castro on November 8, 2010. In theory, party congresses take place every five years. However, the previous Congress was convened more than 10 years earlier in October 1997. Raúl indicated that this long-delayed Congress would be held in mid-April 2011 with the intervening months dedicated to hammering out an agenda based on the so-called *"Lineamientos"* (draft guidelines), which were also released to the public on November 8. According to Raúl, between December 1, 2010, and February 28, 2011, these guidelines would be submitted to the public for a broad discussion. He stressed that the Congress "would be an event of the entire Party membership and all the people," and that all opinions shared during the three-month discussion period would be analyzed and taken into account when preparing the final document adopted at the Congress.

Significantly, after giving Fidel the first copy of the *"Lineamientos"* document, Raúl ceremoniously presented a second copy to visiting Venezuelan president Hugo Chávez. Moreover, Raúl's November 8th announcement of the April Congress was made at the ceremony commemorating the 10th anniversary of the Comprehensive Cuba-Venezuela Cooperation Agreement with Chávez in attendance. This put in stark relief Cuba's deepening ties with and increasing economic dependence on Chávez Venezuela against the background of a worsening economy and deepening crisis in virtually all areas of Cuban society. In convening the event, President Castro said: "The Congress will focus on solving Cuba's economic problems and on the fundamental decisions needed to update the Cuban economic model. It will adopt the draft guidelines of economic and social policy of the Party and of the Revolution." He added that the April Congress would be followed by a first-ever National Party Conference in January 2012 aimed at "confronting other internal Party matters not addressed at the Congress but that also require updating in the light of the experience of the past 50 years."

The strategy was clear. Raúl was using the "*Lineamientos*" and the upcoming Party Congress in an attempt to update an absolutely irreparable economic model. This was to be accomplished through policy band-aids and solutions leading the country into uncharted territory, all in a bald attempt to preserve power. The draft guidelines were full of partial reforms, massive layoffs, and significant cuts in social spending, but refused to give the Cuban people the necessary freedom to earn an honest living or even address the need for any political reforms. Furthermore, they continued to lay the main blame for Cuba's economic problems on external forces, such as the global recession and the U.S. embargo. Absent was any mention that the United States is now Cuba's fifth largest trading partner, its number one food supplier, the undisputed leader in remittances—one of Cuba's main sources of foreign exchange—and now the second largest source of foreign visitors (after Canada)—given the Obama Administration's recent changes in its travel policy.

The draft guidelines only dedicated two brief sections to Cuba's internal problems, citing "low efficiency, the decapitalization of the productive base and infrastructure, an aging population, and stagnant population growth." However, all of these problems—along with many others not mentioned—are the consequence of a model that it is impossible to update or reform. With this mask, the document once again attempted to sweep under the rug transcendent domestic realities that have been repeatedly shown to be at the root of the country's current social, economic, and political woes. Cuba's most serious problems are not rooted abroad. Nor can they be solved by outsiders. They arise from internal causes and can only be addressed by replacing Cuba's economic and political system.

The draft guidelines clearly stipulate that the central plan will continue to predominate over the market. In the second section, the document states: "the socialist state enterprise . . . is the principal motor of the national economy," adding in section three that, "the concentration of property . . . will not be allowed in the new non-state sectors of the economy." Thus, the document that is to guide Cuba's economic modernization does not mention the concept of "private property," doubling down on a policy that willfully blocks the growth of individual entrepreneurial initiative. Announced as a plan for the future, the "*Lineamientos*" only ratify the continued bureaucratization of society under rigid centralization, which prevents the flexibility required for productive and efficient economic activity.

THE SIXTH CONGRESS OF THE CUBAN COMMUNIST PARTY, APRIL 2011

As expected, the Sixth Congress of the Communist Party, held in April 2011, approved the "Guidelines of Economic and Social Policy," which will govern the destiny of Cuba over the next five years, serving as a blueprint for removing the country from the economic crisis in which it finds itself. The original draft guidelines were expanded from 291 to 313 sections in the final approved document. Nevertheless, the original outdated concept of socialist planning remained at the heart of the guidelines, with only a slight nod to the market "as a factor influencing the plan."

Furthermore, state enterprise remains the principal motor of the economy, while the document recognizes the supplementary role of foreign investment and other forms of ownership, such as cooperatives, small private and usufruct farms, and self-employment, among other "non-state" entities. Still, concentrations of wealth and property remain prohibited for private individuals and entities.

The "*Lineamientos*" aims to "update" Cuba's demonstrably dysfunctional socialist economic system, which in fact needs to be radically replaced by another system. Moreover, completely absent from the final document were vital political issues—which are intricately interconnected with the economy and society—such as political and civil liberties, democracy, respect for human rights, access to the Internet, and a legal system that offers guarantees and equal protection to foreign investment and what the document insists on calling the "non-state sector of the economy." The final document also fails to address many issues related to international travel and relations with the Cuban diaspora, such as establishing the clear right for all Cubans to travel abroad and return freely to their country of origin without having to ask permission from the government, setting up a more flexible policy for Cubans to work abroad under contract (as in the case of athletes), and improving diplomatic relations with the United States and strengthening links with the Cuban community abroad. Finally, there is no mention of the urgent need to regain membership in international financial institutions, such as the World Bank, the International Monetary Fund (IMF), and the Inter-American Development Bank (IDB), which could be a source of financial advice and support in reviving the Cuban economy.

A Cuban boy stands atop the oldest section of Havana's famed Malecón seawall and promenade adjacent to Centro Habana near Galiano Street begun in 1901. He watches as a cargo ship loaded down with containers nears the entrance to the Port of Havana. (Orlando Luis Pardo Lazo)

The Triumph of Raúl Castro and the Armed Forces

With the approval of the "*Lineamientos*," Raúl Castro and the military class consolidated their hold on power, bringing to a close the chapter which begun in late July 2006 when Fidel's illness suddenly catapulted the long-time head of the armed forces to the helm of the nation as provisional leader. Despite its many limitations, the final document produced by the Sixth Party Congress contains many pragmatic policies—long-incubated within the armed forces—for reforming the island's economic system. However, it is worth repeating that these reforms have never been aimed at regime change, but instead at making the socialist system more efficient and productive in order to preserve it. Still, even these timid reforms were long roundly rejected by the hard-line elements of the Party and government. As part of the April 2011 Congress, however, the vast majority of these more conservative elements within the Political Bureau and the Central Committee of the Party were replaced by active duty military leaders and others clearly identified with President Raúl Castro's more pragmatic economic ideas. The triumph of Raúl and his followers is evident in the final version of the "*Lineamientos*," which featured a new section 15 that read: "The System of Enterprise Improvement [*El Perfeccionamiento Empresarial*] (originally created in the Ministry of the Armed Forces) will be integrated into the policies of the economic model, with the goal of making state firms more efficient and competitive."

The slightly expanded final draft of the "*Lineamientos*" included other similar additions due to the worsening economic situation of the country—"on the brink of a precipice," as Raúl Castro himself described it in December 2010. The methods employed by military enterprises have conferred a greater degree of autonomy and decision making on their managers, a comparatively greater degree of administrative flexibility, and some worker participation, which stimulates increased productivity. Nevertheless, this experience was carried out in a limited context with levels of organization, discipline, incentives, and labor recruitment that do not exist in the rest of the economy, and, most importantly, with material guarantees completely different from those prevailing in the civilian sector of the economy, which is dominated by instability and the lack of supplies and material incentives. As a result, when the System of Enterprise Improvement has been implemented in state firms, in most cases the results have not been the best because those firms are not equipped with even the minimum necessary conditions—including a reliable system of accounting—to make them work successfully.

As a consequence, the methods used in the armed forces will have to be radically altered before they can be successfully applied to the economy as a whole. And this will be impractical if private enterprises are not allowed to participate on a broad scale and with sufficient guarantees. In the same way, the market must be given a greater role and recognized as an objective economic category. This should not imply the elimination of the state as an economic regulator and as a sometime participant in certain sectors of the economy, nor that planning cannot play an orienting role guiding the decisions of both public and private economic entities.

Despite its uncertainties and limitations, the "*Lineamientos*" are a step forward over what existed before in that they reflect a more rational approach to important economic issues. They have even already recognized the lack of sufficient depth in a number of previous reforms, which have fallen far short of achieving their goals. This has been the case, for example, with Decree-Law 259 on the distribution of vacant land, which has failed in its objective of increasing agricultural production. Section 189 of the final document amends the original Decree-Law, as does Section 183, which "address the possibility that the producer be able to sell his or her products directly on the market." Furthermore, just days after the Congress ended, Orlando Lugo Fonte, president of Cuba's National Association of Small Farmers (ANAP), in an interview with the newspaper *Juventud Rebelde*, spoke favorably about granting farmers permanent usufruct rights. He also expressed support for the right of these farmers to become more fully established on their land, building houses and other facilities for protect their property and granting their children inheritance rights to the land. Finally, he underlined his support for Section 183 of the "*Lineamientos*," cited earlier, reasoning that "if private and diversified production exists in Cuba, you can't have monopolized markets."

Modifications to the Self-Employment Regulations, May 2011

In May 2011, a similar conclusion was reached "to continue facilitating self-employment," when it became evident that initial reforms in that important sector were insufficient to spark the levels of productivity and job creation originally envisioned. The announced dismissal of as many as 500,000 state sector workers by April 2011 had to be indefinitely postponed given the lack of sufficient private sector employment opportunities. In this context, on May 14, 2011, the Council of Ministers agreed to extend the right to hire workers to all 178 self-employed occupational categories (which had previously applied to only 83). Then, in early September, the number of occupational categories was increased to 181, reaching 187 by 2012. May 2011 also saw the announcement of a tax holiday for the hiring of employees—for those businesses with less than six employees—for the remainder of 2011.

Businesses would also be allowed to "more easily close for repairs and for longer periods, suspending their licenses and their tax obligations." Perhaps most interestingly, some state enterprises will be identified, "primarily in food service," where business is slow and "where the premises can be better utilized by renting to the self-employed" ("Continuar . . ." 2011; Peters 2011). Finally, a handful of other timid openings of little overall economic significance were made, including increasing the maximum capacity for private "*paladar*" restaurants from 20 to 50 seats and a reduction (of 25% to 150 pesos) of the mandatory monthly payment imposed on Cuba's bed and breakfast operations.

Future Reforms, Current Crises, and U.S.-Cuban Relations

The "*Lineamientos*" also announced the government's intention of eliminating rationing, in force since March 1962, and the dual currency system, which has characterized Cuba's domestic economy since the early 1990s. However, no timetables were announced nor was a plan shared of how either of these complex but necessary reforms would be carried out. Also hinted at was the upcoming publication of laws allowing the sale of cars and houses, discussed later. Another particularly important reform was obliquely referred to in section 265, which stated the government's intention "to study a policy that would allow Cubans residing in the country to travel abroad as tourists." Regardless of the obvious benefits that such a measure would have for Cuba—finally coming into compliance with Article 13 of the Universal Declaration of Human Rights—this issue is quite complicated in the current context of a growing frustration and hopelessness about the future of the nation. While implementing such a measure would restore a fundamental human right to the Cuban people, it could also lead to a mass exodus of people—especially the young—who would leave in search of a better life abroad. Such a possibility - combined with other major social, political, and economic consequences of a reform in migration policy - long delayed the anticipated migration reform despite rising expectations of a pending announcement. Finally, in October 2012 a new migration law was published, taking effect in January 2013. While it eliminated the exit visa requirement, the new law failed to restore the key rights of return or investment to members of the extensive Cuban diaspora.

In four of the last five years, the Cuban population has declined in absolute terms, with a relative increase of those over 60 years of age to 17.8 percent of the total population in 2010. It is estimated that the over-60 proportion of the population could reach 22 percent in 2020, 30.8 percent in 2030, and 34.0 percent in 2035. This is provided Cuba retains its current low annual fertility rate (1.6%) and continues its veritable exodus of citizens, which resulted in a net loss of 332,356 people—particularly the young—between 2000 and 2009, a number nearly equal to three times the annual number of births in recent years. Demographically, this situation is unsustainable, especially for a nation with such a low level of productivity, immersed in a seemingly irreversible process of decapitalization and a chronic colossal technological lag, with no ability to meet current expenses, much less make the future investments that such a lopsided age-structure will increasingly demand.

Sections 145 to 153 of the "*Lineamientos*" address education and definitively abandon the policies of schools in the countryside, emergent and integral teachers, the contempt for technical education (*técnicos medios*) and skilled labor, and the excessive priority given to the humanities—still delivered with a high degree of "ideological" instruction. Damage has already been done to both the education and health care systems, areas where important achievements had been made. As a result, it will take time to fix them, especially given the lack of a sustainable economic model that can allocate the considerable resources necessary for the recovery and normal functioning of these important services.

By focusing the April Congress almost exclusively on the economy, the government left many other pressing issues out, including its continued refusal to allow open access to the Internet. This self-defeating policy deprives the Cuban people of a basic tool for cultural development. Furthermore, students and professionals are denied access to an important source of scientific and technical knowledge. Worse still, in order to avoid breaching this crucial issue, the "*Lineamientos*" does not include any section where the current state and future development of telecommunications is addressed. Cubans had waited with growing exasperation for word of broadband access after the much-celebrated ALBA-1 fiber optic cable connected the island to the World Wide Web via Chávez's Venezuela. Finally, in June, 2013, 118 cybercafés were opened to the public. However, as with the positive but limited migration

Taken next to Havana's famed Parque Central (Central Park) on the border between Centro Habana and Habana Vieja, this photo features an ultramodern Chinese Yutong bus carting foreign tourists around the city. Thousands of such buses began to appear in Cuba during the mid 2000s imported from China for use both in Cuba's expanding tourism industry and as replacements for the island's aging stock of public buses. (Orlando Luis Pardo Lazo)

reforms, these new Internet access points remain hobbled by their high cost, monopoly control, and easy surveillance via the state telecom company Etecsa.

Another key issue is the urgent need to normalize relations with the United States. Apart from its obvious political ramifications, restoring diplomatic relations is vital to Cuba's future economic development in a number of areas from tourism to potential joint oil exploration in Cuba's Gulf waters. U.S. companies—especially those run by Cuban-Americans—are an obvious potential spring of foreign investment and source of cutting-edge technology. The "*Lineamientos*" also overlooked the enormous importance for the future of the Cuban nation of the island's ties with its diaspora, particularly with the major portion of it in the United States, which has already surpassed 1.8 million people according to the 2010 U.S. Census. With their experience, resources, and prestige developed over many decades as émigrés, they could become a vital conduit for key economic and social links between Cuba and the United States.

Cuban authorities are failing to take advantage of positive gestures from President Obama that can benefit the Cuban people. The recent series of repressive crackdowns and sentences of several years in prison against peaceful dissidents combined with the pariah status of a number of renowned artists such as Pedro Pablo Oliva who have dared to express themselves freely do not bode well for Cuba's inclusion as a member in good standing of the community of nations. Nor does it help improve relations with the United States and the European Union. A particularly troubling development in U.S.-Cuban relations is the rigid and incomprehensible attitude of Cuban authorities in sending down a 15-year prison sentence against U.S. contractor Alan Gross. While international migration, demography, education, Internet, and bilateral relations are essentially noneconomic issues, they do have an extraordinary weight in the full and necessary international integration of Cuba. It will be impossible to find willing economic partners and desperately needed resources if the lack of freedom and democracy and the routine violation of human rights persist. The complexity and plurality of an increasingly globalized world makes it increasingly necessary to develop a robust culture of civilized debate based on the free flow of information that can enable the nation to freely choose the best path of development. Without these conditions, peaceful progress of Cuban society becomes virtually impossible.

Conclusion: *The Deepening of Raúl's Reforms, September 2011*

The slow implementation of Raúl's reforms seemed to pick up pace in September 2011 with the adoption of several new measures. While still incomplete and lacking in depth and comprehensiveness, the new reforms have positive and encouraging elements that, if complemented by additional steps toward a more open economy, may lay the groundwork for progress. The most significant measures taken were:

- Private car sales: The authorization of the buying and selling (or donation) of motor vehicles built after 1959 (Decree No. 292 of the Council of Ministers, September 20).
- Private housing sales: The lifting of the ban on the buying and selling, swapping, donation, or award—through a divorce, death, or emigration of the owner—of housing between private individuals residing on the island (Cuban citizens or foreign residents) (Decree-Law No. 288 of the Council of State, October 30).
- Direct tourism sales: Permission to produce and market one's goods and services directly to the tourism sector as a wholesaler, and also to sell goods directly to Agricultural Production Cooperatives (CPA), Credit and Services Cooperatives (CCS), and the Basic Units of Cooperative Production (UBPC), as well as to organic farms belonging to state entities. The goods are authorized to provide industrial raw agricultural products, rice and charcoal consumption, setting prices in Cuban pesos (CUP) with the agreement (Resolution No. 122 of the Ministries of Finance and Prices, and Tourism, November 14).
- Credit for the private sector: The extension of credit to the self-employed, small farmers, persons licensed to practice other forms of non-state enterprise, and to buy building materials or pay labor to be used in construction (Decree-Law No. 289 of the State Council, November 16).

The measures taken since September 2011 have innovative and positive aspects, but are still limited and insufficient. This is evident in the fact that the liberalization of the sale of cars only applies to used cars, such as the famed prerevolutionary American models—called *almendrones* in Cuba due to their typically round and elongated shape—and the usually well over 20-year-old Soviet Ladas and Moskovich models, which manage to continue to operate through the ingenuity of their owners. New cars, however, are a state monopoly and will only be sold to persons "who have obtained the funds . . . as a result of their job, in duties assigned by the state and in the state's interests." Thus, the government will continue its segregationist and exclusionary policy aimed at promoting (and rewarding) political commitment (Haven 2011; Sánchez 2011).

The situation with housing is much better with 52 years of prohibitions broken in one fell swoop, allowing private housing to be bought and sold, exchanged (swapped), donated, or awarded through the divorce, death, or emigration of the owner. The state will not mediate these transactions and prices will be set freely between private parties. Of singular importance is the fact that the homes of people who choose to emigrate will no longer automatically be forfeited to the state as they were in the past. However, the law only applies to Cubans residing in the country and to foreigners who are permanent residents, excluding those Cubans who do not have permission to reside abroad (PRE). Likewise, it will remain illegal to own more than two residences, one as a permanent residence and another for vacation.

Perhaps the most economically beneficial new measure is that which extends sorely needed credit to the private sector. This will come in multiple possible forms such as IOUs, bills of exchange, pledges, and some types of checks. Equally important is the end to the virtual ban on trade between the state sector and private sector. Up until now, such exchanges were severely limited to a maximum of just 100 pesos ($4 U.S.), which effectively prevented state firms from contracting the services or purchasing the goods of private entities. This change will have a ripple effect on the economy as a whole, as state enterprises will not have to have to possess enormous and costly labor reserves and supply lines. Nor will they have to endure endless bureaucracy to acquire needed goods and services since they can now buy them directly from the private sector, which will get an economic boost of its own as a result.

REFERENCES

Acosta, Leonardo. 2003. *Cubano Be, Cubano Bop: One Hundred Years of Jazz in Cuba*. Translated by Daniel S. Whitesell. Washington, DC: Smithsonian Books.

"Announcement of the *Central de Trabajadores de Cuba*." *Granma*, September 13, 2010.

Buch, Luis M., and Reinaldo Suárez. 2004. *Gobierno Revolucionario Cubano*. Havana: Ciencias Sociales Publishers.

Burnett, Victoria. 2011. "An airlift, family by family, bolsters Cuba's economy." *The New York Times*, June 11.

Cantón Navarro, José, and Martín Duarte Hurtado. 2001. *Cuba: 42 años de revolución. Cronología Histórica*, vol. I, 1959–1982 and vol. II, 1983–2000. Havana: Ciencias Sociales Publishers.

Castro, Fidel. 2005. "Discurso pronunciado por Fidel Castro Ruz en el acto por el aniversario 60 de su ingreso a la universidad," Havana, November 17. http://www.cuba.cu/gobierno/discursos/2005/ing/f171105i.html.

Castro, Raúl. 1996. "Informe del Buró Político al Comité Central." *Encuentro de la cultura cubana*, vol. 1, pp. 18–24. http://www.marxmail.org/raul_castro.htm.

CEPAL (Economic Commission for Latin America). 2000. *La Economía Cubana. Reformas Estructurales y Desempeño en los Noventa*.

CEPAL. 2010. *Anuario Estadístico de América Latina y el Caribe*.

CEPAL. 2011. *Balance Preliminar de las Economías de América Latina y el Caribe 2011*. Informe sobre Desarrollo Humano (IDH), 2011.

Constitución de la República de Cuba de 1967, con sus posteriores modificaciones.

"Continuar el proceso de flexibilización del trabajo por cuenta propia." *Granma*, May 27, 2011. http://www.granma.cubaweb.cu/2011/05/27/nacional/artic01.html.

Corrales, Javier, Dan Erikson, and Mark Falcoff. 2005. *Cuba, Venezuela, and the Americas: A Changing Landscape.* Cuba Forum Working Paper, Inter-American Dialogue, Washington, DC, and the Cuban Research Institute, Florida International University, Miami, Florida. December, 2005. http://www.thedialogue.org/publications/2005/winter/cuba_venez.pdf.

Documentos de la Revolución Cubana. 1959, 1960, 1961, and 1962 editions. Havana: Ciencias Sociales Publishers.

Domínguez, Jorge I. 1993. "Cuba since 1959." In *Cuba: A Short History*. Leslie Bethell, ed. Cambridge: Cambridge University Press.

Economist Intelligence Unit (EIU). Reports from 2008 to 2011.

Encuesta de Trabajadores Rurales 1956–1957. Agrupación Católica Universitaria, 1957.

Espinosa Chepe, Oscar. 2002. "Ofensiva contra el cuentapropismo en Cuba." Mimeographed article provided by the author. Havana, December 2.

Espinosa Chepe, Oscar. 2007. *Cuba ¿Revolución o Involución?* Valencia: Aduana Vieja Publishers.

Espinosa Chepe, Oscar. 2011. "Cambios en Cuba: Pocos, Limitados y Tardíos," Havana. http://reconciliacioncubana.files.wordpress.com/2011/03/cambios-en-cuba.pdf.

Fraginals, Manuel Moreno. 1978. *El Ingenio, Complejo Económico-Social Cubano del Azúcar.* Havana: Ciencias Sociales Publishers.

Fraginals, Manuel Moreno. 2001. *El ingenio* [The Sugarmill]. Barcelona: Crítica.

Frank, Marc. 2005. "Cuba's Painful Transition from Sugar Economy." *Reuters*, August 17.

Frank, Marc. 2010. "Cuba Unveils New Tax Code for Small Business." *Reuters*, October 22. http://www.reuters.com/article/2010/10/22/us-cuba-reform-taxes-idUSTRE69L3WY20101022.

Frank, Marc. 2011. "Cuba Closes Once Powerful Sugar Ministry." *Reuters*, September 29. http://www.reuters.com/article/2011/09/29/food-cuba-sugar-idUSS1E78S0AG20110929.

Gaceta Oficial de la República de Cuba. 2010a. Ministry of Justice, Special Edition, No. 11, Decree-Laws Nos. 274/10 through 278/10 and Decree 284/10, 17 pp., October 1.

Gaceta Oficial de la República de Cuba. 2010b. Ministry of Justice, Special Edition, No. 12, Resolutions Nos. 32/10–36/10, 98/10, 285/10–289/10, 305/10, 399/10, 750/10, 81 pp., October 8.

Guevara, Ernesto Che. 1997. "Socialism and Man in Cuba." In David Deutschmann, ed., *Che Guevara Reader: Writings on Guerilla Strategy, Politics, and Revolution*, pp. 197–214. Melbourne: Ocean Press.

Guillermoprieto, Alma. 2004. *Dancing with Cuba: A Memoir of the Revolution.* Translated by Esther Allen. New York: Pantheon Books.

Haven, Paul. 2011. "Car Sales Legalized." *Associated Press*, September 28. http://www.huffingtonpost.com/2011/09/28/cuba-car-sales_n_985829.html.

Henken, Ted. 2002. "Condemned to Informality: Cuba's Experiments with Self-employment during the Special Period (The Case of the Bed and Breakfasts)." *Cuban Studies* 33: 1–29.

Informe Económico del Banco Nacional de Cuba. August, 1982.

Informe del Ministerio de Economía y Planificación a la Asamblea Nacional del Poder Popular. December 23, 2011. Havana, Cuba.

Jackiewicz, Edward L., and Todd Bolster. 2003. "The Working World of the Paladar: The Production of Contradictory Space during Cuba's Period of Fragmentation." *ProfessionalGeographer* 55, no. 3 (August): 372–382.

Jatar-Hausmann, Ana Julia. 1999. *The Cuban Way: Communism, Capitalism, and Confrontation*. West Harford, CT: Kumarian Press.

"Lineamientos de la Política Económica y Social del Partido y la Revolución." Aprobados en el VI Congreso del Partido Comunista de Cuba. April 2011.

Marshall, Jeffery H. 1998. "The Political Viability of Free Market Experimentation in Cuba: Evidence from *Los Mercados Agropecuarios*." *World Development* 26, no. 2: 277–288.

Martínez Heredia, Fernando. 2003. "El Che y el gran debate sobre la economía en Cuba." Commentary upon the presentation of the book *Ernesto Che Guevara: El gran debate. Sobre la economía en Cuba en 1963–64*. Havana: Ocean Press, Centro de Estudios Che Guevara. http://www.nodo50.org/cubasigloXXI/economia/heredia_301104.htm.

Martínez Hernández, Leticia, and Yaima Puig Meneses. 2010. "Más valen las cuentas claras." *Granma*, October 22. http://www.granma.cu/espanol/cuba/22octu-mas-valen.html.

Mesa-Lago, Carmelo. 1969. "The Revolutionary Offensive." *Trans-Action* 6, no. 6 (April): 22–29, 62.

Mesa-Lago, Carmelo. 1983. *La Economía en Cuba Socialista. Una Evaluación de Dos Décadas*. The University of New Mexico.

Mesa-Lago, Carmelo. 1988. "The Cuban Economy in the 1980s: The Return of Ideology." In Sergio G. Roca, ed., *Socialist Cuba: Past Interpretations and Future Challenges*. Boulder, CO: Westview Press.

Mesa-Lago, Carmelo. 1994. *Are Economic Reforms Propelling Cuba to the Market?* Miami: University of Miami, North-South Center.

Mesa-Lago, Carmelo. 2000. *Market, Socialist, and Mixed Economies: Comparative Policy and Performance—Chile, Cuba, and Costa Rica*. Baltimore, MD: Johns Hopkins University Press.

Mesa-Lago, Carmelo. 2005. "The Cuban Economy in 2004–2005." *Cuba in Transition*, vol. 15, pp. 1–18. Washington, DC: Association for the Study of the Cuban Economy.

Mesa-Lago, Carmelo. 2011. "Reformas de Raúl, el VI Congreso del PCC y resultados." *Cubaencuentro*, December.

Mesa-Lago, Carmelo, and Jorge Pérez-López. 2005. *Cuba's Aborted Reform: Socioeconomic Effects, International Comparisons, and Transition Policies*. Gainesville, FL: University Press of Florida.

Miroff, Nick. 2010. "Amid Reforms, Cubans Fret over Food Rations Fate." Morning Edition, *National Public Radio*, October 22. http://www.npr.org/templates/story/story.php?storyId=130700949.

"Mucho más que una alternativa." *Granma*, September 24, 2010. http://granma.co.cu/2010/09/24/nacional/artic10.html.

National Office of Statistics (Oficina Nacional de Estadísticas, ONE). 2001. *Anuario Estadístico de Cuba, 2000*. Havana.

National Office of Statistics (ONE) and State Committee of Statistics, 2005, 2010, and 2011. *Anuario Estadístico de Cuba*. http://www.cubagob.cu/ingles/otras_info/estadisticas.htm

Nuestra Industria Magazine. Various editions from 1963 to 1964.

Oficina Nacional de Estadística (ONE). 2011. "Panorama Económico y Social, Cuba 2010." January.

Pérez, Louis A., Jr. 1995. *Cuba: Between Reform and Revolution* (second edition). New York: Oxford University Press.

Pérez, Louis A., Jr. 1999. *On Becoming Cuban: Identity, Nationality, and Culture*. Chapel Hill, NC: University of North Carolina Press.

Pérez-López, Jorge. 1995. *Cuba's Second Economy: From Behind the Scenes to Center Stage*. New Brunswick: Transaction.

Pérez-López, Jorge. 2006. "The Cuban Economy in 2005–2006: The End of the Special Period?" *Cuba in Transition*, vol. 16, pp. 1–13. Washington, DC: Association for the Study of the Cuban Economy.

Pérez-López, Jorge. 2011. "The Global Financial Crisis and Cuba's External Sector." In José Raúl Perales, ed., *The Cuban Economy: Recent Trends*, pp. 31–49. Washington, DC: Woodrow Wilson Center Reports on the Americas, No. 28, Woodrow Wilson Center for Scholars, Latin America Program, July. http://www.wilsoncenter.org/sites/default/files/WWC_LAP_RoA_%2328.pdf.

Pérez-López, Jorge, and Sergio Díaz-Briquets. 2011. "The Diaspora and Cuba's Tourism Sector." *Cuba in Transition*, vol. 21, pp. 314–325. http://www.ascecuba.org/publications/proceedings/volume21/pdfs/perezlopezdiazbriquets.pdf.

Pérez-Stable, Marifeli. 1999. *The Cuban Revolution: Origins, Development, and Legacy* (second edition). New York: Oxford University Press.

Pérez Villanueva, Omar Everleny, ed. 2009. *Cincuenta Años de la Economía Cubana*. Havana: Ciencias Sociales Publishers.

Peters, Philip. 1997. "Islands of Enterprise: Cuba's Emerging Small Business Sector." Arlington, VA: Alexis de Tocqueville Institution. http://adti.net/html_files/cuba/curpteml.htm.

Peters, Philip. 2002a. "International Tourism: The New Engine of the Cuban Economy." Lexington Institute, December.

Peters, Philip. 2002b. "Survival Story: Cuba's Economy in the Post-Soviet Decade." Lexington Institute, May. http://lexington.server278.com/docs/cuba4.pdf.

Peters, Philip. 2003. "Cutting Losses: Cuba Downsizes Its Sugar Industry." Lexington Institute, December. http://lexington.server278.com/docs/cuba1.pdf.

Peters, Philip. 2006. "Cuba's Small Entrepreneurs: Down but Not Out." Lexington Institute, September 30. http://lexingtoninstitute.org/docs/cubas_small_entrepreneurs.pdf.

Peters, Philip. 2010a. "Looking Like a Small Business Sector." *The Cuban Triangle*, September 24. http://cubantriangle.blogspot.com/2010/09/looking-like-small-business-sector.html.

Peters, Philip. 2010b. "The New Tax System." *The Cuban Triangle*, October 22. http://cubantriangle.blogspot.com/2010/10/new-tax-system.html.

Peters, Philip. 2011. "314, 538 Entrepreneurs." *The Cuban Triangle*, June 16. http://cubantriangle.blogspot.com/2011/06/314538-entrepreneurs.html.

Peters, Philip. 2012a. "A Viewer's Guide to Cuba's Economic Reform." Arlington, TX: Lexington Institute.

Peters, Philip. 2012b. "Cuba's Entrepreneurs: Foundation of a New Private Sector." Arlington, TX: Lexington Institute.

Peters, Philip, and Joseph L. Scarpaci. 1998 "Cuba's New Entrepreneurs: Five Years of Small-Scale Capitalism." *Alexis de Tocqueville Institution*. http://adti.net/html_files/cuba/TCPSAVE.htm.

"Pocket World in Figures." *The Economist*, 2009, 2010, and 2011 editions.

Problemas de la Nueva Cuba. Colectivo de Autores. Informe presentado al gobierno cubano por una comisión de expertos norteamericanos. Edición 1935.

Proyecto de Documento Base para la Primera Conferencia Nacional del PCC. 2011.

Resolución No. 11. 2004. "Reglamento sobre el trabajo por cuenta propia." May 11.

RIIA (Royal Institute of International Affairs). 1958. *Cuba: A Brief Political and Economic Survey*. London: Chatham House Memoranda, Information Department, Oxford University Press, September.

Ritter, Archibald R. M. 1974. *The Economic Development of Revolutionary Cuba: Strategy and Performance*. New York: Praeger Publishers.

Ritter, Archibald R. M. 1998. "Entrepreneurship, Micro-enterprise, and Public Policy in Cuba: Promotion, Containment, or Asphyxiation?" *Journal of International Studies and World Affairs* 40, no. 2 (Summer): 63–94.

Ritter, Archibald R. M. 2000. "El regimen impositivo para la microempresa en Cuba." *Revista de la CEPAL* 71 (August): 145–162.

Ritter, Archibald R. M. 2004. "The Taxation of Microenterprise." In Archibald R. M. Ritter, ed., *The Cuban Economy*, pp. 121–145. Pittsburgh, PA: University of Pittsburgh Press.

Ritter, Archibald R. M. 2006. "Cuba's Economic Re-Orientation." Paper presented at the Bildner Center conference, "Cuba: In Transition? Pathways to Renewal, Long-Term Development and Global Reintegration." March 30–31. http://web.gc.cuny.edu/bildner-center/cuba/documents/CITBookFMpdfbychapter_000.pdf.

Ritter, Archibald R. M. 2010. "Raúl Castro and Policy Towards Self-Employment: Promising Apertura or False Start?" *The Cuban Economy*, August 4. http://thecubaneconomy.com/articles/2010/08/raul-castro-and-policy-towards-self-employment-promising-apertura-or-false-start/.

Ritter, Archibald R. M. 2011. "Micro-enterprise Tax Reform, 2010: The Right Direction but Still Onerous and Stultifying." *The Cuban Economy*, January 10. http://thecubaneconomy.com/articles/2011/01/micro-enterprise-tax-reform-2010-the-right-direction-but-still-onerous-and-stultifying/.

Rosenberg, Jonathan. 1992. "Cuba's Free Market Experiment." *Latin American Research Review* 27, no. 3: 51–89.

Sánchez, Yoani. 2011. "Cuba Allows Car Sales: Cars Over 15 Years Old for Us, Newer Cars Only for the Party Faithful." *Huffington Post*, September 30. http://www.huffingtonpost.com/yoani-sanchez/cuba-allows-car-sales-car_b_989149.html.

Siegelbaum, Portia. 2010. "Raúl Castro Says Cuban Economy Will Be Tweaked but Remain Socialist." CBS News, August 1. http://www.cbsnews.com/8301-503543_162-20012303-503543.html.

Smith, Benjamin. 1999. "The Self-Employed in Cuba: A Street Level View." In *Cuba in Transition*, vol 9, pp. 49–59. Washington, DC: Association for the Study of the Cuban Economy.

Truslow, Francis A. 1951. *Report on Cuba: Findings and Recommendations of an Economic and Technical Mission*. Baltimore, MD: International Bank for Reconstruction and Development (World Bank) and The Johns Hopkins Press.

Vidal Alejandro, Pavel. 2009. "Política Monetaria y Doble Moneda." *Miradas a la Economía Cubana*. Havana: Ciencias Sociales Publishers.

Warren, Cristina. 2005. "Governance and Social Justice in Cuba: Past, Present and Future—Policy Brief: Lessons for Cuba from the Latin American Experience." Miami: Cuban Research Institute, FLACSO-Mexico, and FOCAL (the Canadian Foundation for the Americas). http://www.focal.ca/pdf/cuba_brief.pdf.

Society

Religion and Thought

Rogelio Fabio Hurtado and Ted A. Henken

INTRODUCTION

Religious Syncretism and National Identity

Religion in Cuba is characterized by paradox. To different degrees, Cubans engage in a wide variety of informal religious and spiritual practices yet are notorious for their reluctance to participate in formal, organized religious institutions. This contradiction arises in part from the revolution's past repression of religion. However, Cubans' failure to internalize religious formalism predates socialism and is rooted in the long history of a weak, elite-oriented Catholic Church in both colonial and republican Cuba. Although Cuba is often considered the "most Spanish" of all Latin American countries, it is simultaneously one of the "most African," leading to a syncretic mixing of formal Spanish Catholicism with a wide array of less rigid spiritual practices introduced by African slaves. This mixture produced what is popularly referred to as *Santería*, a diverse group of Afro-Cuban religious beliefs and rituals that has essentially become the popular religion of today's Cuba.

Cuba is perhaps the most secular of all Latin American and Caribbean countries due to the shallow penetration of organized religion during the island's history. Also, given the militant anticlerical orientation of the revolution, organized religion faded from public view after 1959, with the older generation either rejecting its practice or practicing it in secrecy and the new generation being socialized as if organized religion simply did not exist. However, many Cubans on the island (even if they have never been inside a church) exhibit a deep cultural spirituality that manifests itself in the practice of different forms and degrees of syncretic religion.

In today's Cuba, organized religion plays a relatively minuscule role in the public sphere and focuses most of its energy on nonconfrontational evangelical and social welfare activities. Unlike the role of organized religion in other national contexts, where it has often become wedded to nationalism (as in Poland or Colombia), in Cuba, Catholicism was long associated with Spanish colonialism and later in the republican period with urban middle-class whites, while Protestantism was associated with the United States.

To the extent that Cubans are religious, they have creatively hedged their (religious) bets by rejecting the typical Western "either-or" approach to organized religion. Instead of highlighting religious exclusivity, Cubans have typically embraced a wide spectrum of inclusive "both-and" religious beliefs, spiritual practices, and Afro-Hispanic cultural traditions. As Ned Sublette has wisely observed in his recent history of Cuban music, "You do not have to disavow Catholicism to practice *Santería*, though the priest might tell you that you must disavow *Santería* to be a Christian" (Sublette 2004: 213). Even before the revolution, religion was understood as more personal than institutional. For example, a 1954 survey carried out by a group of Catholic university students revealed that while 96.5 percent of those Catholics polled claimed to believe in God, just 17 percent of them actually attended church regularly (Fernández 2002: 526).

Despite a long history of repression from church and state officials, African religion, African deities (orishas), and especially African-influenced musical forms survived during the 400-year colonial Spanish-Catholic period of Cuba's history by "hiding in plain sight" under the catchall term *Santería* (literally, the worship of the saints) (Sublette 2004). In order to avoid detection and harsh punishment, African slaves and their descendants in Cuba would mimic and feign fealty to Catholic symbols and saints, when in fact they were keeping their long-repressed traditions and beliefs alive. However, after hundreds of years of simulation, few Cubans today know (or care) where Catholicism starts and *Santería* begins. Moreover, the Catholic Church typically neglected its religious obligation to instruct Africans in the faith, rarely going beyond baptizing them and providing them with a Christian name (Thomas 1998).

Such neglect, however, opened the door for both slaves and free coloreds alike to blend their varied and rich traditional beliefs with Spanish Catholicism. The need to hide one's religious practices in a context of repression and violence certainly motivated slaves to quickly adapt a feigning and duplicitous display for their masters and priests, while secretly preserving authentic traditions. However, over time it is likely that many Africans and certainly their descendants could think of themselves as Christian while continuing to worship and pay homage to African deities. Indeed, Cuba's blacks could easily reconcile being adherents of two or more belief systems at once. Take, for example, Cuban novelist Alejo Carpentier's description of religious syncretism in Cuba:

From the outset, the Christian church exercised a powerful attraction for the blacks brought to the Americas. . . . Deep down, of course, it did not mean that the ancient gods of Africa were renounced. Ogún, Changó, Elegguá, Obatalá, and many others continued thriving in the hearts of many. . . . But the African transplanted to the New World never believed that these two worlds, Catholic and African, could not be shared in admirable harmony. . . . In this fashion, Saint Lazarus became Babalú-Ayé; the Virgin of Regla is Yemayá; Saint Barbara is associated with Changó; and so forth. (Carpentier 2001: 81–82)

CATHOLICISM

From the very beginning of the conquest, the Christian cross supported the efforts of the colonizers, even to the point of justifying the excesses committed by the Spanish sword. Despite the constructive efforts of the Dominican friar Bartolomé de las Casas, who became renowned for his role as protector of the native peoples and whose suffering at the hands of the Spanish he repeatedly denounced to the Spanish crown, the cross and sword were partners in the conquest of Cuba. During four centuries of colonial rule, Cuba's Catholic clergy was of Spanish origin. Because the island was part of Spain, the relations of the Cuban Church and the Vatican's Holy See were routed through Spain. As a result, many religious orders prevented Cuban-born Creoles from becoming members of the clergy. Even half-a-century after independence, Cuba's first black priest, Father Arencibia, continued to face countless obstacles to his legitimacy, which Monsignor Carlos Manuel de Céspedes has tried to attribute to Arencibia's own cultural deficiencies.

As a result, both the Church hierarchy—appointed by the Spanish crown—and the vast majority of the island's clergy were hostile to independence. Sermons and church documents issued during the second half of the 19th century are rife with critical, even insulting references to independence leaders like José Martí, Antonio Maceo, and Máximo Gómez. Still, there were exceptional cases like that of Bishop Antonio María Claret, who openly defended a group of condemned revolutionaries in 1851, requesting that his own life be taken in substitute for theirs.

Despite the fact that the Catholic Church's virtual religious monopoly was increasingly challenged after the turn of the century, first by the Masons and later by a variety of Protestant denominations, its influence was felt well into the republican period. Cuba's small towns were typically home to at least one Catholic school, while the country's larger cities had many. There were also two Catholic institutions of higher learning in Cuba, Marist University (now the notorious prison *Villa Marista*) and the University of Villanueva—both in Havana. By 1955, there were 212 Catholic schools in Cuba with 62,000 students.

During the insurrectional phase of the revolution of 1959, a group of clergy joined the rebel troops in the fight against Batista. A notable case was that of father Guillermo Sardiñas Menéndez, the parish priest of Nueva Gerona on the Isle of Pines. He even journeyed to the Sierra Maestra with the permission of the Archdiocese of Havana in order to meet with the rebels where he eventually became the first chaplain of the Rebel Army and attained the rank of *comandante*. His influence is reflected in the fact that when the *barbudos* (bearded ones) came down victorious from the mountains, almost all—including Fidel Castro—donned Santajuana seed necklaces, Our Lady of Charity medals, crucifixes, scapulars, or rosaries.

The Church of Impassioned Confrontation

Following the triumph of the revolution in January 1959, relations between the Catholic Church and Cuba's increasingly totalitarian government passed through three successive stages: impassioned confrontation, silence, and dialogue. An impassioned confrontation characterized the Church's approach to the new government between the second half of 1959 and the spring of 1962. Many priests and bishops were imprisoned, including Monsignor Enrique Pérez Serantes, despite the fact that he had previously interceded on behalf of the Moncada rebels, saving the life of Fidel Castro in 1953. In February 1959, the *Ley Once* (Law #11) was enacted, which unilaterally annulled all degrees awarded by private universities after November 1956, including those from the University of Villanueva. The imposition of communism and the nationalization of education in 1961 saw the Church stripped of its 350 private schools, losing its main means of social influence. Many Catholic churches were closed and some 255 charitable institutions were taken over by the state or shuttered altogether. Hundreds of priests and nuns were expelled from the island, which together with those members of the clergy who chose to leave Cuba imperiled the continuity of the Catholic Church on the island.

The Church of Silence

After the Cuban Missile Crisis in October 1962, the Church entered a long period of protective silence. The Holy See appointed Monsignor Zacchi as the new Apostolic Pro-Nuncio. The Italian cleric was able to strike up a surprising friendship with Fidel Castro, but was unable to parlay that relationship into greater space or autonomy for the Church. These were years in which the Ministry of the Interior (MININT) coordinated the capture of the hijacker of a *Cubana de Aviación* flight who had been hiding out inside the Church of San Francisco in Old Havana. Both Father Loredo, a young Franciscan priest, and his elderly superior Father Serafín Ajuria collaborated in the capture. Less dramatic, but more frequent, were discriminatory practices against Catholic students which often resulted in their expulsion from the university. The creation of the so-called *Unidades Militares de Ayuda a la Producción* (Military Units to Aid Production, UMAP) in 1966 led to the internment of many priests, including the current Cuban Cardinal, Father Jaime Ortega (Fabio Hurtado 2003).

Also in 1966, the Ministry of Education issued Resolution #13, which led to the firing of many teachers who continued to exhibit religious practice or belief. Students were henceforth prevented from wearing religious medals or crucifixes. Outdoor Masses, processions, catechism classes, and all other religious activities that took place outside the Church itself were prohibited. The traditional celebration of religious holidays such as Easter, Christmas, and Three Kings Day was abolished, and any products related to these holy days disappeared from stores.

The Office of Religious Affairs of the Central Committee of the Cuban Communist Party (PCC) directed the superficial relations with the Church that remained during the 1960s and 1970s. However, this inertia was broken during the unrest surrounding the Mariel boatlift of 1980. Provoked by the bombastic and overconfident actions of Fidel Castro himself, this massive exodus was an opportunity for many to break publicly with their past facade of conformity and openly express their determination to leave the country. Others—seeing their efforts to emigrate frustrated—sought solace in the social space the Church provided. Over the course of the 1980s the slow recovery of the Catholic Church continued, culminating in the 1986 celebration of the First National Cuban Ecclesial Encounter (*Primer Encuentro Nacional Eclesial Cubano*, ENEC) in Havana. Lay persons of the stature of Dagoberto Valdés, Oswaldo Payá, Joaquín Bello, and Eduardo Mesa began to acquire a public profile as leaders during the event, which also marked the entrance onto the public stage of Monsignor Jaime Ortega, already the Archbishop of Havana.

The Church of Dialogue

So began the third stage, that of dialogue, which only its totalitarian interlocutor—the government—pretended not to hear. These were times of rising hope in Cuba in reaction to the unexpected pace of change in the USSR, with glasnost and perestroika. At the same time, an open, peaceful dissident movement emerged on the island to remain. And though it was tiny and thus almost inaudible, it distinguished itself in its willingness to challenge the monologue of the self-styled "Maximum Leader" of the nation, Fidel Castro.

For example, the emergence of the *Comité Cubano de Derechos Humanos* (Cuban Committee for Human Rights)—also in 1986—took place during a Mass at the Church of the Convent of *San Juan de Letrán* in the Vedado neighborhood of Havana. With the consent of the Dominican Fathers, Ricardo Bofill, Elizardo Sánchez Santacruz, Adolfo Rivero Caro, and Reynaldo Bragado issued a manifesto, which became the "birth certificate" of today's dissident movement. Subsequently, Bofill established Sunday Mass at the Church of *La Caridad* as the central meeting point for his collaborators. Later, Indamiro Restano and in 2003 the *Damas de Blanco* (Ladies in White) would repeat the strategy of using the sacred space of the Church as a launching pad for political opposition, this time in the Church of *Santa Rita* in Havana's Miramar district.

In September 1993, the Cuban Conference of Catholic Bishops issued a pastoral letter entitled, "*El Amor Todo lo Espera*" (Love Hopes for All Things), which was read in all Sunday Masses across the country. The government responded with the threat to circulate a statement rejecting the bishops in all schools, requiring all children to sign it. Priests warned Catholic families about the initiative so that their children would resist being forced to sign it. As a result, many brave souls—Catholics and non-Catholics alike—lined up on the sidewalk outside the Palace of the Archdiocese to express their solidarity with the prelates. Emphasizing the different context of the 1990s where Catholic activists could overcome their fears with bold, collective action, the auxiliary bishop of Havana, Monsignor Alfredo Petit Vergel, said in a homily: "This will not be like it was in the 1960s, when the temples were left empty." He then repeated a children's saying to reassure his listeners that they should not be afraid: "*¡El que tenga miedo que se compre un perro!*" (He who is afraid should buy himself a dog!).

Aware of the bishops' willingness to put up a fight, the regime halted its campaign and answered the bishops' challenge with silence. The bishops agreed to the truce, which seemed to them like a victory. Nevertheless, the leader of the revolution immediately put into motion a long-term maneuver, calculated with his proverbial political savvy. From that moment on, instead of infiltrating Churches with informants, he flooded them with revolutionary "believers" full of Catholic enthusiasm. Since 1993, this massive influx of converts also reached other Christian denominations, including the orthodox Jehovah's Witnesses (discussed later), who for the first two decades of the revolution had been among its most bitter adversaries. On the other hand, an official state policy of rapprochement with the Vatican was also put into motion. This culminated in the visit of Fidel Castro himself to the Vatican for an audience with Pope John Paul II in January 1997, leading in turn to that Pope's historic visit to Cuba in 1998 (Castellanos 2004).

During the special period that began in 1990, Cuba underwent what can only be described as a spiritual revival. Many Cubans, especially the young, found themselves confronted with a moral crisis as the institutions and beliefs that had sustained them for three decades began to disintegrate. Family and community solidarity began to erode, provoking a sense of alienation in many youth (Crahan 2003). As a result, churches of many faiths became more popular than ever. During the decade, many Cubans joined Protestant and Catholic churches, sought to rediscover their long-forgotten Jewish roots by visiting the island's few remaining synagogues, and deepened their practice of Afro-Cuban rituals in search of answers to spiritual questions. For many Cubans, this quest was mixed with a more immediate search for accessing the material goods that many churches and synagogues could provide. Also, since spiritual belief and the public practice of religion had long been punished by the government and associated with counterrevolutionary attitudes, some people joined churches to make explicit their rejection of what they saw as the bankrupt values on which the revolution was predicated.

It was within this context that Castro extended an invitation to Pope John Paul II to visit Cuba, which he accepted in February 1998. Among the many repercussions of the late Pope's visit to Cuba was his call for "the world to open up to Cuba and Cuba to the world," hinting at his rejection of the U.S. embargo. This statement was a crucial turning point for many Cuban-American Catholics who felt called by their religious leader to set aside their pain and resentment and work toward reconciliation (de Aragón 1998). Also, Protestant churches, both mainstream and evangelical, began to attract greater numbers of believers, reflecting the explosive growth of evangelical sects throughout Latin America. In fact, a year and a half after the John Paul II's historic visit to Cuba, 100,000 Protestants turned out for a massive public religious service in the Plaza of the Revolution.

One of the most important spaces won by the Church is the network of Catholic publications that now acts as a vital part of Cuba's emergent civil society. Among these are the Pinar de Río magazine originally founded by Dagoberto Valdés, *Vitral* (Stained Glass); Valdés' new online publication, *Convivencia* (Living Together); the magazine of the Archdiocese of Havana, *Palabra Nueva* (New Word); and *Espacios* (Spaces), which was later renamed *Espacio Laical* (Lay Space), is co-edited by Roberto Viega and Lenier González, and has emerged as perhaps the island's leading freely circulated publication with a critical and independent perspective (Miroff 2011). Other Church activities have become increasingly important in Cuban public life, such as the "Pedagogical Week," which is held annually in Havana, along with Church-sponsored conferences—such as those held each month at *San Juan Letrán* in Havana—and a variety of courses taught across the country, including ones in computer science and business administration. Moreover, the ascendance of Raúl Castro to the presidency in the summer of 2006 seems to have begun a new era in Church-state relations, with the Church hierarchy engaging in unprecedented cooperation and negotiation with the government (an issue addressed in Chapter 7 on Contemporary Issues).

AFRICAN RELIGIONS

In Cuba, African slaves were organized into various *Cabildos de Nación* (national councils) with members sharing the same ethnic and geographic origin. This allowed them to more easily preserve their religious traditions. Once communication with their places of origin in Africa was cut off, their traditions—practices and ceremonies as well as beliefs—were gradually adapted to fit the new context, evolving to the point that today they can be considered genuinely Cuban. While generally grouped under the catchall term *Santería*, there are in fact a handful of distinct African-derived religions practiced in Cuba today. The first of these is popularly known as *Santería*, but more properly called *Regla de Ochá*. This religious group is perhaps the most widespread throughout the island and has been the most adept at absorbing new influences and syncretizing itself with Catholicism. Ethnically, practitioners of *Santería* were originally known to Europeans as *Lucumí* (apparently from the Yoruba greeting *Oluku mi*, meaning, "my friend") and hailed from the great African civilization of Oyó in what is now Nigeria. Today, the term *Lucumí* has lost prominence to the more general term *Yoruba* to describe not only the language but also the people and their religion, though *Santería* is more commonly used to describe the religion.

The second Afro-Cuban religion is of Bantu origin and is known as *Palo* (*Palo Monte* or *Palo Mayombe*). Its adherents are referred to as *Paleros* (a religious designation) or *Congos* (a more general ethnic term). The term *Congo* is used due to the fact that *Palo* originated in central and southwestern Africa in what is today the Democratic Republic of the Congo (formerly Zaire) and Angola. Today, the *Palo* divisions of *Mayombe*, *Quimbisa*, *Briyumba*, and *Santo Cristo del Buen Viaje* have members in almost all of Cuba's rural areas with the greatest presence in the east. The third major religion is a secret society called *Abakuá*, which descends from the Nigerian Leopard Societies. Its practitioners are known as *Ñáñigos* or, alternately, *Carabalí*. It originated in a region of Africa once called the Calabar, but divided today between Nigeria and Cameroon. Three other, less widely dispersed or practiced Afro-Cuban rites are the Dahomeyan tradition known as *Arará*, the transplanted Haitian religion *Vodú* (Voodoo—similar in many ways to *Palo*), and the legacy of the blacks who came to Cuba directly from Spain, known in colonial times as the *negros curros* (Sublette 2004: 171–172, 207).

The Orishas

Although Cuban slaves originated from many different African "nations" and thus brought a diverse array of gods and beliefs with them on the slave ships, they generally shared animistic belief systems that endowed natural objects with supernatural power and meaning. They also brought with them their own pantheon of orishas, each of which possesses a particular personality. Though often called *santos* (saints) in Spanish, these orishas are not particularly saintly and, indeed, can frequently act quite deviously. Each orisha also has favorite foods, songs, rhythms, dances, an earthly realm, special symbolism (colors, vestments, etc.), and sacrificial animals.

Each practitioner of *Santería* is connected to a particular orisha, who in turn serves the believer as the equivalent of a guardian angel. Initiates are distinguished by dressing all in white for an entire year prior to their acceptance as practitioners, a process known as *hacerse el santo* (making saint) that includes the performance of many costly rites and rituals. As an orisha's "son" or "daughter," an initiate will frequently make an offering of the blood of a sacrificed animal in order to contribute to the life force, or *aché*, of the orisha. In this sense, the orishas are not the dead saints of old but alive today, constantly intervening in the lives and affairs of human beings. As such, these orishas are frequently consulted for knowledge about the past or future through a process of divination usually involving the reading of cowry shells by a *babalao*. Of course, these many rituals gave themselves easily to mixing with Spanish Catholicism, which has always had an elaborate tapestry of processions, rituals, idols, stories, signs, omens, and saints of its own (Luis 2001: 27–32; Sublette 2004: 213).

As a social phenomenon, *Santería* and its most common external manifestation of syncretism are fundamental parts of Cuban identity. On the other hand, its components and foundations remain purely African. According to the Ifá priest, Víctor Omolófaoro, the *Regla de Ochá* represents only beliefs imported by *Lukumís*, while the *Santería* religion is the result of crossbreeding between four basic systems: the *Regla de Ochá* and the *Regla de Palo Monte* (which are its two main pillars), and Christianity and Kardecian Spiritism (described later). After 1959, African religions were suppressed, although with less intensity than other religions. The revolutionary leadership assumed that a *santero* would never be as bothersome as a Protestant or a Catholic. Of course, it must also be added that the Cuban government had to protect important political interests in Africa. Moreover, practitioners of *Santería* do not have the support of a structured international organization, as is the case with other world religions practiced on the island.

In any case, religious practices of African origin became clandestine, and the folkloric *toques* of *bembé*—the main liturgical celebration of Afro-Cuban religion—disappeared. While a law banning the *toques* was never passed, since they constituted public events that required a permit that would never be granted, they were *de facto* illegal. At the same time, the Ministry of the Interior had its own Department for the Prevention of Criminality (*Departamento de Lacras y Prevención Social*), which dealt with prostitutes, alcoholics, thieves, pimps, drug addicts, and priests and religious practitioners. For these and other reasons, many practitioners of Afro-Cuban religions emigrated from Cuba and spread their beliefs to other countries, explaining why Cuban religions of African origin are more important today and more widely dispersed than the original African Yoruba religion itself.

Despite the closed nature of many of these traditions—making their political penetration and exploitation difficult—Cuba's political police managed to infiltrate some of them and turn some priests to their cause. It seems that this is what happened to *Ifá ayer, Ifá hoy, Ifá mañana* (Ifa yesterday, Ifa today, Ifa tomorrow), an association that won the government's blessing. Its name was changed to *Asociación Cultural Yoruba de Cuba* (Yoruba Cultural Association of Cuba, ACYC) and was awarded with a spacious and centrally located new headquarters just opposite the *Parque de la Fraternidad* in Havana. Cuba's current economic crisis and the resulting hopelessness have sparked a notable growth in the appeal of Afro-Cuban religion. Today on the streets of any Cuban city it is easy to find a white-clad *Iyawó* (a believer performing the rite of initiation known as "making saint"). There are also many people who make a living from the collection, manufacture, and sale of religious items used in various Afro-Cuban rites. By the end of 2006, there were an estimated 5,000 Ifá priests in Cuba.

The Abakuá

The kingdom of Calabar in southeastern Nigeria had a port from which slaves were sent to the New World. The slaves who departed from that port became known as *Carabalís*. A number of their descendants worked on the docks of the ports of Havana and Matanzas, where they organized a system of work squads, which were feared for their almost military discipline and mutual defense. Their shared economic hardship and an interest in preserving their customs led them to organize into groups to continue their religious and cultural practices based on mutual support and solidarity, similar to the Leopard societies that existed in the Calabar region. In this way, by 1836 there emerged in the port town of Regla the first *Abakuá* societies, which constitute a singular phenomenon in the Americas.

The characteristics of the *Abakuá*—apart from the fact that they admit no women or homosexuals—include industry, cheerfulness, rebelliousness in the face of injustice, loyalty to the moral code established by one's ancestors, fraternity, and being a good father, son, brother, and friend. Members of the brotherhood have a special place called *el baroko* where initiation rites and cultural events take place. In Cuba, there are over 120 *barokos*, most commonly found in Havana and Matanzas, and their internal organizational structure features 13 hierarchically arranged ranks. Like Cuba's Masons (described later), beginning in the 1860s the *Abakuá* allowed white men as well as individuals who did not work on the docks into their ranks. Among the cultural contributions of the *Abakuá* are the *iremes*—or *diablitos* (little devils)— and the *ekue* or the drum (a word also found among the songs of black Peru and that makes up part of the title, *Ecue-Yamba-O*, of a famous novel by the renowned Cuban writer Alejo Carpentier). Indicating the often overlooked power and influence of the *Abakuá* in Cuba today is the fact that on the eve of Pope John Paul II's visit to Cuba in 1998, the first secretary of the PCC in Havana and the official in charge of the Office of Religious Affairs of the PCC attended the celebration of the 160th anniversary of the foundation of Cuba's *Abakuá* society.

PROTESTANTISM

Protestantism arose between the 15th and 16th centuries as the result of reforms within and "protests" against the Roman Catholic Church by its members. It made its first appearance in Cuba during the capture of Havana by the British (1762–1763).

It later became popular among Cuban émigrés in the late 19th century because American pastors who sympathized with the movement for Cuban independence opened their churches to Cuban immigrants in the United States. As a result, this branch of Christianity was reintroduced onto the island itself by some of these same pastors and former émigrés, in the last decades of the nineteenth century, coming from the United States. Unlike the monolithic, centralized, and rigidly hierarchical Catholicism, Protestantism is much more internally diffuse, independent, and "horizontal." It can further be divided between "mainline" historic denominations such as the Presbyterian, Episcopalian, Lutheran, Baptist, Methodist, and Quaker churches and later "evangelical" churches, such as Pentecostals, Seventh Day Adventists, the Church of the Nazarene, and the Salvation Army (Castillo Téllez 2003; Hernández Suárez 2010; Pigeaud n.d.).

During the Republican period (1902–1958), Protestantism boasted a prestigious nationwide system of schools. Among these were Prinson College, Buenavista, and Candler College, all located in Havana; the renowned Baptist International Schools of Christ in Bayamo; the Episcopal School of Guantánamo; and the "Friends" Quaker schools of Holguín and Banes. This Protestant network of schools disappeared with the nationalization of education in June 1961, when the government seized about 100 of them. This loss was followed by the exodus of some 225 foreign missionaries who—because of their American citizenship—could no longer work as teachers in Cuba. In the 1960s, 70 percent of the Baptist pastors left, whereas 40 of the country's total 44 Methodist ministers fled the country in 1962, as did two-thirds of the Presbyterian clergy. Some Protestant pastors were even executed. Such was the fate of Rev. Alonso González of the Episcopal Church who tried to infiltrate the country after fleeing in order to take up arms against the revolutionary government. During these years a number of Methodist churches were raided, with shipments of Bibles from Canada and Mexico confiscated and destroyed. As a result, the membership of Cuba's Protestant churches decreased considerably.

In 1959 Cuban Protestant church membership stood at about 60,000 people. Of these, approximately 66 percent were members of the mainline branches, which—when compared to the country's six million residents at the time—accounted for just 0.6 percent of the total population. By the mid-1980s the number of Protestants on the island had fallen to about 50,000, with the mainline branches losing almost half of their members, coming to represent just 0.2 percent of the population. At the same time, Pentecostalism and other more evangelical denominations began their ascendancy. As has been the case in the rest of Latin American and the Caribbean, the newer Pentecostal branch of Protestantism appealed to Cubans in part due to its open, democratic character, a strict moral code of behavior, and its spontaneous liturgical style characterized by demonstrative praise and an emphasis on emotional expression. At this time, Pentecostals accounted for roughly 25 percent of Cuba's Protestants (numbering 10,000–15,000 members), with another 25 percent spread among other evangelical denominations.

In the 1980s Protestants began to enjoy greater official tolerance. The visit of Rev. Jesse Jackson during these years contributed to a rapprochement between them and the government. Between the late 1980s and early 1990s, two tendencies within Cuban Pentecostalism became evident. One existed outside of the revolutionary project (without necessarily being opposed to it), while another featured leaders and lay people who openly identified with the revolution. The government took advantage of this split offering privileges to those who considered themselves *within* the revolution. One such privilege was the ability of some of these Protestant pastors to travel abroad under the authority of the Ecumenical Council, which was in turn overseen by the Office of Religious Affairs of the Central Committee. In 1990 an important meeting took place between Fidel Castro and 75 Protestant leaders. At the gathering, Castro recognized the existence of religious discrimination and even spoke of "atheism arising from imported manuals," thereby undercutting concepts foundational to Marxism-Leninism. Pastors who submitted to the regime's authority have been rewarded with seats in the National Assembly. Moreover, with government support some pastors have even managed to be elected to important positions in international organizations, which are used as platforms for revolutionary propaganda.

In recent years Cuba and its Protestant churches have received help from "Pastors for Peace," a U.S.-based progressive group of Protestant ministers—founded by the late Baptist pastor Lucius Walker—who oppose the U.S. embargo and carry out humanitarian missions in Cuba in open violation of U.S. law. Given the scarcity of Protestant churches and the lack of resources to build them, during the 1990s the government also authorized the opening of home-based temples (*casas-culto*) led by pastors and marginally trained lay people. There are now more than 3,000 of these temples and between 1993 and 1998 more than 700 new evangelical congregations were authorized. Since the end of the 1990s, evangelical congregations have steadily grown on the island, exceeding half-a-million members by 2007. There are 9 seminaries dedicated to pastoral formation and over a thousand pastors, of which about 50 are currently studying or serving abroad (Berges 1997).

Cuban Protestantism has its own publications such as the Presbyterian *Heraldo Cristiano* (Christian Herald) and *La Voz Bautista* (The Baptist Voice). There is an ecumenical printing press in Matanzas that maintains ties with foreign Protestant publishers. Nevertheless, their influence on society at large is still quite limited due to continued government restrictions on their activities. Protestant churches that follow the government line accept the prohibition against religious schools. They contend that "the government takes care of that," revealing their clear subordination to the state. In the areas of higher education, the Ecumenical Council of Cuban Churches has the *Instituto Superior de Enseñanza Bíblica y Teológica* (Advanced Institute of Biblical and Theological Education, ISEBIT), which is the equivalent of a private religious university. While the ISEBIT employs a moderate approach that seeks collaboration and understanding rather than open conflict with the state, the institution has recently begun to address social issues considered taboo by the authorities leading to greater government control.

JEHOVAH'S WITNESSES

This Christian denomination emerged in the mid-19th century in the United States and arrived in Cuba in the mid-20th century, alongside its masthead publication *The Watchtower*. Jehovah's Witnesses preach the imminent end of the world (Armageddon) and the urgency to convert and accept the word of Jehovah (their name for god). In 1959, the Witnesses were no more than a curious presence in the sidewalks and doorways of Havana and other towns around the country, offering their *Watchtower* Bible and preaching with it in hand. Until then, it was unthinkable that these handful of believers could embarrass or threaten the government. However, consistent with their end-of-days doctrine that rejects the taint of participation in many worldly, political, and cultural affairs, the Witnesses soon became the most disconcerting religious group for the Cuban socialist state. This was due both to their strict other-worldly doctrines and practices and their rapid growth among the population.

Unlike previous governments whose leaders worried more about accumulating personal wealth than the religious beliefs of their citizens, Fidel Castro's ambitions were much more "total." His government demanded that all citizens become active revolutionaries and exhibit an almost religious selflessness and unlimited loyalty to the socialist cause. While many willingly heeded this all-encompassing call, others did so with hopeless resignation. The Witnesses, however, openly and almost joyfully refused to cooperate (Castro Figueroa 2008).

Directed from the United States, Jehovah's Witnesses focused their evangelization on the segment of the population who had been forcibly displaced by the revolution: sectors of the working class, soldiers, and military police officers who had served under the previous government. Since these families had no hope of ever being integrated into the newly formed, pro-government mass organizations, they found their "promised land" in the *Kingdom Halls of Jehovah*, which began to flourish in all the neighborhoods of Havana and in the major provincial cities during the 1960s. These diminutive *Halls*—tiny family homes or shops converted into temples—could not handle the demand from the newly converted. If at first they offered religious services just once or twice a week, many communities eventually began to hold services on an almost daily basis.

Although their preaching was absolutely peaceful, the Jehovah's Witnesses preached disobedience to compulsory military service, refused to wear military uniforms, to carry firearms, to sing the national anthem, or to recognize and respect the national symbols. While such behavior has long been standard practice for Witnesses in countries around the world, it was a shock to the newly nationalistic Cuban authorities, especially in schools where the national anthem was sung and the Cuban flag saluted as an obligation each morning. More shocking still was the fact that some children, encouraged by their parents, proselytized in the classroom. Cuba's hospitals also became trenches of ideological/religious warfare, as believers obeyed a Bible verse that commanded them to "abstain from blood," that is, to refuse blood transfusions. At the same time, the Witnesses were well prepared to base their rejection on purely medical grounds since they agreed to accept transfusions of plasma.

In the 1970s, the authorities withdrew their protection from the *Kingdom Halls*, which were often attacked with stones and Molotov cocktails in the provinces. A decree was also passed, which threatened parents with fines and even prison time for baptizing their children in the *Halls*, accusing them—in the official parlance of the system—of "threatening the proper formation of children." Because of the attacks against the *Halls*, the Witnesses demanded police protection which was denied to them. As a result, the Witnesses' National Council of Elders made the drastic decision to shutter their *Halls* and continue to practice their religion more inconspicuously. No Jehovah's Witness would hide his or her religious affiliation, nor would they cease to evangelize and give testimonials. They would only discontinue meeting in public.

The struggle between the government and the Jehovah's Witnesses continued well into the 1980s. Witnesses' homes were routinely raided under the assumption that unauthorized Bible studies were taking place. Elders were punished with fines, the confiscation of their Bibles, and even jail sentences. If any religion suffered systematic persecution in Cuba, it was the Jehovah's Witnesses. However, they refused to cede to the government repression or give up their evangelical zeal. By the early 1990s, the government began negotiations, which led to the reopening of the *Kingdom Halls* and the end of open persecution, both material and ideological. Today, Witnesses preach in Cuba's streets and celebrate their activities undisturbed.

JUDAISM

The first Jews to set foot in Cuba came with Columbus, fleeing the Spanish Inquisition. However, there is no historical continuity between them and those who immigrated to the island later. The Cuban Jewish community that exists today began to form after the 1895 War of Independence, when some Cuban Jews residing in Florida were among the most active supporters of José Martí. Later, a group of American Jews settled on the island and founded the United Hebrew Congregation synagogue in 1904, acquiring a cemetery two years later. In 1914 the community organization *Chevet Ahim* was born. Then in January 1919, thanks to the tireless efforts of David Blis, a Russian-Cuban Zionist and founder of Israeli Center of Cuba, the Cuban Senate passed a resolution in favor of the so-called Balfour Declaration, which supported the establishment of a Jewish state in Palestine. By 1924, some 4,000 Jews had arrived in Cuba from Eastern Europe. Thus, the Cuban Jewish community was composed of three main groups: about 100 families that came from the United States, the earlier Sephardic Jews who trace their origins to Spain and the larger Mediterranean area, and the more recently arrived Ashkenazi from Eastern Europe in the 1920s.

Although Cuba's few synagogues were to be found only in the country's larger cities, other Jewish traditions were kept alive in more isolated precincts such as the preparation of *criandillas*, a traditional dish made with lamb testicles. In Pinar del Río lived a Jewish family of Turkish origin with the last name Ruz, from which descended Fidel Castro's mother, Lina Ruz González. The meeting at which Cuba's first Communist Party was founded in 1925, took place in the *Centro Popular Hebreo de la Habana* (People's Hebrew Center of Havana). Among the delegates at the meeting were the Jews Salomón Mayer and Abraham Zimkowich, who was better known under the name Fabio Grobart. In 1939, the Central Committee of Jewish Organization was reorganized and recognized by the authorities as the official representative body for all sectors of the Jewish community.

As a result of religious repression, after 1959 Cuba experienced a large Jewish exodus. Already by 1962, more than half of the Jewish population had gone into exile. Then, during the Revolutionary Offensive of 1968—which nationalized all remaining small-scale retail operations—most of the rest of Cuba's Jewish community that still resided on the island emigrated. Since then, only a tiny remnant of the once thriving Cuban Jewish remained on the island. This remnant has been able to survive ideological and antireligious mobilizations due to the network of mutual solidarity that existed among them and because of the material support they received from abroad.

In 1999, Fidel Castro visited Havana's main Jewish synagogue, Temple Beth Shalom, during the celebration of the Sabbath, marking the beginning of a rapprochement. Currently, there is a Sunday school that teaches Hebrew and Jewish tradition and culture. The community's library holds over 13,000 volumes on Jewish history, life, and thought—including books in Yiddish—all of which are available to the public. There is a pharmacy that provides medicines for all the Jewish communities in the country, with access for non-Jews as well. Given the fact that the community receives so much outside support, it also engages in social services such as the distribution of food and clothing to the needy. On Saturdays a meal is served to all members of the congregation with food provided by friends from other countries. There are two other synagogues in Havana that perform similar activities on a smaller scale, but without a significant impact on larger Cuban society. These are the Orthodox *Adath Israel* and the *Sephardic Hebrew Center of Cuba*.

ISLAM

In 1990, there were only about 10 Muslims in Cuba, a figure that has grown significantly, if discreetly, since then. Starting in 1991, the Prayer Hall of the *Casa Museo del Arabe* (Arabic Museum House) was used as a place of Islamic prayer and congregation, thanks to the intercession of the Nigerian ambassador and other Muslim diplomats. This was done with the approval of Eusebio Leal Spengler, the City Historian. In 1994, a small number of Cuban Muslims received paid invitations to visit Qatar. The invitations were extended so that Cubans could spend some time getting to know the language and country, while better familiarizing themselves with Islam. However, only one Cuban was able to make the trip.

In the mid-1990s, there was also an attempt to create a Muslim Association, requiring official authorization. However, on October 22, 1996, the petitioners received notice that as long as they did not legalize their situation, they could not continue to pray in the area they had used until then. In response, the members drafted a constitution for the association. Nevertheless, when they had finally met all legal requirements, they were informed that petitions would no longer be accepted and that the legalization of their group would have to wait for promulgation of the *Ley de Cultos* (Religions Act). Since then, this small group of organized Muslims has periodically met in the homes of different believers where they perform their rituals and prayers, without being persecuted for doing so (González Quiroga 2004).

Cuba's Muslims have also been invited to take part in the most challenging of Islam's five pillars, making the pilgrimage of Hajj. However, these trips have not yet materialized. One major obstacle for any Cuban to travel to Mecca—apart from the cost—is the fact that there is no Saudi embassy in Cuba. Thus, the visa process would have to be done through a third country. Several efforts have also been made to obtain permission to build a mosque, but these have been unsuccessful. Cuba's Islamic community currently numbers about 550 people, with the majority in Havana. Within this young community, a division already exists between Sunni and Shia, although most are Sunni.

As with all who profess the Islamic faith, Cuban Muslims recognize the Quran as the primary guide to human behavior followed by the Sunnahs, or the traditional sayings and teachings of the Prophet Mohammed not contained in the holy book. Community consensus is also a powerful source of authority in Islam. To that end,

Cuba's Muslims have recently focused their attention on the position of women, since females have been denied a protagonist role in Islamic tradition. In this regard, the community agreed to promote a greater participation of women in its activities and create more space for women's concerns. As a result of this push, the Committee of Cuban Women Converts to Islam was established in 2002, which meets the fourth Sunday of each month.

THE FREEMASONS

The term "mason" was originally used to refer to German master builder associations and their apprentices who passed on their knowledge and customs to English guilds. Between the late 16th and early 17th centuries, the admission of new people into these guilds who had no connection to the building industry began a process of transformation that ultimately led to the current form of Freemasonry. Freemasons formed small secret groups called lodges, which were based on fraternity, equality, peace, and the use of symbols recognizable only to the initiated. They adopted a symbolic philosophy and believed in the perfectibility of the human being. Several such lodges came together in 1717 to form the Grand Lodge of England, the mother of modern Freemasonry.

During the capture of Havana by the British, the military lodge 218—attached to one of the regiments of Irish troops—worked in Cuba as part of the occupation army. Then, in 1793 with the French immigration from Haiti, the Masonic lodges *Perseverance* and *Concorde* arrived in Santiago de Cuba. Likewise, between 1802 and 1803 the lodges *Amitié* and *Benefique Concorde* were established in Havana. The first distinctly Cuban lodge—the *Templo de las Virtudes Teologales* (Temple of the Theological Virtues)—was founded in 1804, out of which grew a relationship with North American Freemasonry. In 1822, two parallel bodies—the Grand Spanish Lodge of the York Rite and the Grand Spanish Lodge of Freemasons of the York Rite—united under the name *Gran Logia de Francmasones del Rito de York en la Isla de Cuba* (Grand Lodge of Freemasons of the York Rite in the Island of Cuba). Later, in December 1859, the Grand Lodge of Columbus was founded in Santiago de Cuba. This in turn gave birth to the present Grand Lodge of Cuba, which was established in 1891 as the sole and sovereign symbolic Masonic body, and in 1892 became part of the Supreme Council to govern the higher degrees of Freemasonry.

Freemasonry was welcomed in Cuba primarily by men, especially those who felt that Catholicism was a thing for women. They were also drawn in by the brotherhood and rationalism that predominated in the lodges. The lodges' quasi-religious rituals, the social function of the organization, and the relative secrecy of their rites and ceremonies offered a perfect setting for Cubans unhappy with colonialism to come together, identify with one another, and conspire against the status quo.

Beginning with Cuba's first pro-independence conspiracy in 1809 up through the Independence War of 1895, freemasonry played a key role in the island's history. The rebellion that started the Ten Years' War that began in 1868 was planned in the Grand Orient of Cuba and the Antilles (GOCA) lodge. The leadership of the Tropical Star of Bayamo lodge was made up of the same three Cuban patriots who founded the Revolutionary Committee of that city. The architect of the uprising, Carlos Manuel de Céspedes, was appointed Venerable Master of the lodge of *Buena Fe* in Manzanillo. And in Puerto Principe, 72 of the 76 rebels who rose up in the town of Las Clavellinas were members of the lodge *Tínima*. Major figures such as Antonio Maceo, Máximo Gómez, Calixto García, Guillermón Moncada, José Maceo, Quintín Banderas, Juan Gualberto Gómez, and José Martí were all Freemasons, and the design of the national flag was based on the Masonic symbols of the triangle and star.

When the colonial period ended, Cuban Freemasons helped create orphanages for children and nursing homes for the elderly. They set up almshouses, helped the relatives of deceased Freemasons, founded institutions to fund public schools and low-income families, and created the Masonic University of José Martí. In 1936, they organized the Association of Young Fraternal Hope (AJEF) to ensure the young people's moral, physical, and intellectual development. In 1933 they sent a letter to President Gerardo Machado, who was himself a Freemason, which declared that Cuba no longer wanted him as president and requested that he step down. After the coup of 1952, Freemasons drew up a plan for free elections and presented it to Batista, insisting that the coup plotters—including Batista himself—not be allowed to participate.

On January 1, 1959, the Freemasons' Grand Master addressed the Cuban people "condemning any abuses perpetrated by those responsible for maintaining order under the pretext of restoring it." From that very moment, a number of lodges were closed and several floors of the building of the Grand Lodge that had been inaugurated in 1955 were taken over. The AJEF disappeared and the Freemasons were forced to surrender their university and schools to the state. As a result of these revolutionary measures, many Freemasons went into exile. Those who remained were marginalized and subjected to all kinds of pressures for the next three decades. During those years Freemasonry was debilitated and had to go underground in order to survive into the 1980s, when it began to recover.

In the 1990s, the José Martí Association of Liberty, Equality, and Fraternity (AMLIF) was created. The Ministry of the Interior reacted by unleashing a campaign of infiltration and destabilization, intending to outlaw Freemasonry because of the supposed threat posed by the AMLIF. As a result, AMLIF members were brought up on charges before the Supreme Court of Masonic Justice with the defendants' rights as Freemasons suspended for up to a year. This was followed by a more open persecution against dissident Freemasons. By 1997, with the addition of more than 2,000 new members, Cuban Freemasonry had again become the largest Masonic order proportionally in the Western Hemisphere. However, it still has not recouped its prerevolution membership. In Cienfuegos in 1999, Freemasons held an unauthorized public procession, and a year later, on January 28, 2000, about 100 Master Freemasons from 37 different lodges staged a march from the Payret Cinema to the José Martí Monument located in Havana's Central Park, carrying Cuban and Masonic flags to commemorate the 147th anniversary of Martí's birth. It was a brief, but unprecedented act.

ESPIRITISMO

Like parallel traditions in Puerto Rico and Brazil, Cuban *Espiritismo*, is often mixed together with spiritual and ritualistic elements of African origin. As such, it constitutes one of the most widespread religious practices in Cuba. *Espiritismo* in Cuba is organized through groups of followers who gather in house-temples or other common places to perform their rituals. Among its functions, it gives believers the possibility of channeling through rituals the problems that affect them in their daily lives. Because of the working class background of most of its adherents, it is often referred to as a "popular" religion. Lacking a unified and hierarchical structure, *Espiritismo*'s leaders organically emerge from religious practice not through formal education or training. Its theoretical development is found within the daily religious consciousness of its practitioners and its followers believe in the existence of spirits and their reincarnation.

In his book, *Ecaí, Shangó and Yemayá*, Juan Luis Martín posits that *Espiritismo* first came to Cuba in 1856 through the teachings of the French Christian theologian Allan Kardec. Following that, the Spiritist National Confederation of Cuba was created, which led to the blossoming of Spiritist manifestations in different regions of the island. Of the different variants that exist on the island today, it is Kardec's so-called *espiritismo científico* (scientific spiritism) that serves as a reference for all other groups. Characterized by the strong presence of Christian ethics and the attempt to give the theology a scientific basis, this Kardecian Spiritism has an empirical basis and a practical utilitarian sense. Apart from the common tendency to cling to Kardecian literature, Cuban *Espiritismo* has unique variants, which are highly influenced by other cultures and religious traditions. Among these is *Espiritismo Cruzado* from the town of Palma Soriano, which combines elements of Catholicism, *Santería*, *Palo Monte*, and Haitian voodoo. There is also *Espiritismo de Cordón*, which is strongest in Bayamo, Manzanillo, and Camagüey.

The following words of Darius Filiberto Reyes Arias, the director of the Center for Spiritist Studies *Más Luz* in the city of Bayamo, capture the syncretic character and pseudoscientific jargon of Cuban *Espiritismo*:

> After the revelations of Moses and Jesus Christ, *Espiritismo* is the third revelation of God; a revelation intended to teach us where we come from, where we are, and where we are going. It is a doctrine that teaches the improvement and progress of humanity. It is a science and moral philosophy that has come to teach how everyone at birth both incarnates and disincarnates in order to achieve light and progress through the Law of Reincarnation; the law of cause and effect. *Espiritismo* is all the love and kindness that, when studied, understood, and put into practice leads to the improvement of all human beings. Mediumship is one of the means of communication between the spiritual world and the material world. A means that provides us with the realization that with death, with desincarnation, not everything finishes and that the spirit is eternal. (Reyes Arias 2007)

BIBLIOGRAPHY

Berges, Juana. 1997. "El protestantismo cubano en los caminos del crecimiento." *Caminos*, Cuban magazine of Socio-theological Thought, no. 6.

Carpentier, Alejo. 2001. *Music in Cuba*. Minneapolis, MN: University of Minnesota Press.

Castellanos, Dimas. "Notes from the Lecture Series '*Espiritualidad y Sociedad: el reto de la modernización*'," given in the Social-Democratic Club of Havana, between October, 2003 and February, 2004 (unpublished manuscript).

Castillo Téllez, Calixto. 2003. *La Iglesia protestante en las luchas por la independencia de Cuba (1868–1895)*. Havana: Social Science Publishers.

Castro Figueroa, Abel R. 2008. *Las religiones en Cuba, un recorrido por la revolución*. México: Instituto Teconológico y de Estudios Superiores de Occidente.

Crahan, Margaret E. 2003. "Whither Cuba? The Role of Religion." Woodrow Wilson Center Update on the Americas No. 14, October.

De Aragón, Uva. 1998. "Winds of Change: Cuban-Americans in the Post-Papal Era." *Hemisphere* 8, no. 3 (Fall): 6–7.

Fabio Hurtado, Rogelio. 2003. *Orden Hospitalaria de San Juan de Dios. 400 años en Cuba*. Bogotá: Kimpres Publishers, Ltd.

Fernández, Damián. 2002. "Religion under Castro." In Luis Martínez-Fernández, D.H. Figueredo, Louis A. Pérez, Jr., and Luis González, eds., *Encyclopedia of Cuba: People, History, Culture*. Westport, CT: Greenwood Press.

González Quiroga, Mario. 2004. "El Islam en Cuba: Un fenómeno nuevo," in Religious Globalization and Neoliberalism, paper given at the Third International Encounter of Socio-Religious Studies, Havana, Cuba.

Hernández Suárez, Yoana. 2010. *Iglesias cristianas en Cuba entre la independencia y la intervención*. Havana: Cuban Institute of History.

Luis, William. 2001. *Culture and Customs of Cuba*. Westport, CT: Greenwood Press.

Miroff, Nick. 2011. "Cuba's Hot Publishing House? A House of God." *Global Post*, July 5. http://www.globalpost.com/dispatch/news/regions/americas/cuba/110701/publishing-house-god-church-magazines.

Pigeaud, Olivier. n.d. *El protestantismo*. Madrid: The Spanish Evangelical Church.

Reyes Arias, Darío Filiberto. 2007. "Tengo muchas pruebas, muchas comprobaciones." Interview conducted by Dimas Castellanos, published in the digital magazine *Consenso*, no. 6.

Sublette, Ned. 2004. *Cuba and Its Music: From the First Drum to the Mambo*. Chicago: Chicago Review Press.

Thomas, Hugh. 1998. *Cuba or the Pursuit of Freedom*. New York: DaCapo Press.

Ethnicity and Race, Class Structure, and Inequality

Dimas Castellanos and Ted A. Henken

ETHNICITY AND RACE

Cuba's geographical location at the entrance of the Gulf of Mexico, between North and South America, facilitated the arrival to the island of a diverse array of ethnicities, which have subsequently become quite intermixed. This process of ethno-racial mixture is a defining characteristic of Cuban culture and is often referred to as *mestizaje,* with the terms *mestizo* or *mestiza* used to refer to someone of mixed ethnic or racial ancestry. Following the arrival of the Spanish colonizers in the early

16th century, the native Arawak/Taino population fell into a drastic decline and never recovered. Survivors grouped together in a handful of towns such as Jiguaní in Granma, Guanabacoa in Havana, and Yateras in Guantánamo. Because of this demographic devastation, the indigenous contribution to the island's subsequent ethnic mixture—while present—is actually quite small.

Together with the Spanish migration and settlement of Cuba between the 16th and 19th centuries came the forced migration of Africans who were enslaved to replace the disappearing indigenous workforce. These two ethnic groups—white Europeans from Spain and black Africans from Nigeria, Angola, and the Congo—very slowly became fused together to form the foundation of a new and distinctly "Cuban" culture and ethnicity different from that of their ancestors in Spain and Africa. However, each of these two groups was internally diverse when they arrived in Cuba, already containing within them many different regional, ethnic, and language groups (Guanche Pérez 1990). When the ethno-racial mixture is between European and African ancestries—as is most often the case in Cuba—the term "mulatto" is used. While a bit antiquated and even derogatory in English, the terms *mulato* (for males) and *mulata* (for females) carry no such negative connotation in Cuban Spanish and are still commonly used today.

To this ethnic foundation were added Asian and Middle Eastern components starting in the mid-19th century. Both Chinese and Filipino contract laborers were brought in to gradually replace the dwindling supply of slaves, as were roughly 34,000 Lebanese, Syrians, and Palestinians who arrived after 1850 (Jiménez Pastrana 1963). An earlier wave of 30,000 French Caribbean immigrants arrived at the turn of the 18th century fleeing the Haitian Revolution. Finally, about 250,000 Haitian and Jamaican guest workers were brought to the island to work as cane cutters in the sugar harvests during the first quarter of the 20th century. They arrived at the same time as thousands of Spanish and other European immigrants. In fact, it is likely that more Spaniards arrived in Cuba in the 40 years *after* it became independent from Spain than had come during the entire almost 400-year colonial period.

Studies carried out in a dozen Cuban parish archives during the colonial period show that mixed marriages between Europeans and Cuban Creoles (the term Creole or *criollo* in Spanish refers those born on the island) were common. Moreover, in 95 percent of recorded cases the male partner was European, while the female was *criolla* (Creole). This peculiar type of gendered "cross pollination" was also true for African women and their female black and *mulata* Creole descendants—a marriage practice that accelerated the interracial and intercultural mixing. This indicates that the predominantly male immigrants to Cuba established conjugal relationships with Cuban Creole women, allowing for the easy transmission of Creole cultural traits and traditions due to the active role of the mother in childrearing and education (Medina Rensoli 2008).

This emergent ethnic formation of *Cubanía* (Cubanness) was accelerated by the "deculturation" of many African slaves, whereby their languages, ethnic bonds, and spiritual traditions were stripped from them in order to facilitate their exploitation as cheap, unskilled labor (Moreno Fraginals 2002). Because it is impossible to completely eradicate all the cultural values of an ethnic group and since the slave masters aimed to eliminate only those traits that they considered obstacles to maximum exploitation, the partial "deculturation" and assimilation of Africans was accompanied by a simultaneous "transculturation" (cultural exchange) between Africans and Europeans which furthered the development of an emergent Cuban ethnicity (Ortiz 1995a). Factors such as a sense of territorial belonging and the widespread use of Spanish by all islanders—enriched with many toponyms, hydronyms, and other words of both Arawak and African origin—played a role in the formation of a new ethnicity independent of that brought to Cuba by the islanders' diverse ancestors (see the "Language and Literature" section of Chapter 6 for examples of such words). This emergent ethnicity—though not without its own internal cleavages—often overshadowed the significant anthropological differences among the population.

An ethnic group is a community of people that emerges as the result of a historical process of adaptation and coexistence in a specific geographical area. Such a group typically shares a set of distinctive cultural practices and traditions, such as language, religion, music, dress, and cuisine. At times, ethnic groups also share common phonotypical traits, such as skin color, body shape, facial features, and stature. However, these more biological elements are commonly thought of as racial, not ethnic features (Díaz Artiga 2002; González 2003). Given the long process of cultural fusion—or "transculturation"—described earlier, Cuba can be said to have become largely mono-ethnic by the late 19th century. And though Cubans share many ethnic elements, especially their distinct way of speaking Spanish, they can still be separated into three somewhat distinct racial groups: white, mulatto/mestizo, and black. Thus, Cuba is mono-ethnic but remains a multiracial society due to the complex, contradictory, and very gradual process of *mestizaje* that has taken place there since colonial times.

The Racial Problem

Race, conceived as a cluster of inherited characteristics, lacks a scientific basis. The Swedish ethnologist Carolus Linnaeus (1707–1778), Frenchman Georges Louis Leclerc (1707–1788), and the German Johann Friedrich Blumenbach (1752–1840), believed that humans were part of the natural world and, as such, were naturally subdivided into three or five races or breeds, each a distinct variety of the human species. The fact that different scientists of the time could never seem to agree on exactly how many supposedly natural races existed hinted at the dubiousness of the science behind the concept. Later, others, like the Frenchman Joseph Arthur de Gobineau (1816–1882)—often described as the father of modern racism—divided human beings into just three races—white, black, and yellow—placing the black race in a clearly inferior position due to its supposedly animal nature, lack of morality, and emotional instability. Such notions as racial superiority or inferiority, as well as the pseudoscientific claim that races exist as distinct branches of the single human species, are rejected by modern science. Instead, the concept of race is a social construction and one with demonstrably negative effects on human dignity (Castoriadis 1985; Giddens n.d.).

The mixture of races is one of the characteristic features of Cuban society and, since one of the most common ethnic distinctions is that based on race, any study of Cuban society must take into account the close relationship between race and ethnicity. Although Cuban racial groups are not limited to black and white, we will focus primarily on them given their social salience. Blacks or "Afro-Cubans" have been a part of Cuban society since the early 16th century. However, it was not until the late 18th century when they arrived on the island en masse as slaves that their presence transformed not only the ethnic composition of the population, but also the economy, history, culture, and social structure of the entire country. Today, their contribution to Cuban society can scarcely be overestimated despite the fact that much of the 20th century was spent attempting to minimize or outright deny the ubiquitous African elements that make up Cuban culture.

Transculturation, the One-Drop Rule, and the Myth of Racial Democracy

As has been the case in other Caribbean countries with a strong African ethno-racial element—such as the Dominican Republic—many Cuban historians and ethnologists working at the turn of the nineteenth century sought to actively erase Cuba's African roots by replacing them with the brave, proud, but often apocryphal, exploits of the now conveniently dead and gone indigenous Taíno or Siboney groups. An important corrective to this willful historical amnesia was the all-important work of eminent Cuban jurist, historian, and anthropologist Fernando Ortiz. Although he began his long and influential career by writing a series of papers that equated blackness with criminality and *brujería* (black magic), Ortiz eventually rejected this simplistic, racist view becoming the leading authority celebrating the rich, complex, and diverse Afro-Cuban elements in Cuban culture. Forty years after the publication of his first book, *Los negros brujos* (The Black Sorcerers), Ortiz made the following frank admission about his own earlier ignorance. "I began to research," he wrote, "but I soon understood that, like all Cubans, I was confused." He went on to make the following masterful observation about the "chaotic transplantation" of culture that took place between Africa and the Americas:

> Not only did I encounter the curious phenomenon of a black Masonry [*i.e.,* Abakuá], but a complex tangle of religious survivals proceeding from different distant cultures, and with them various lineages, tongues, musics, instruments, dances, songs, traditions, legends, arts, games, and folkloric philosophies; that is, all the immensity of the African cultures that were brought to Cuba, fully unknown by the men of science. And all these were presented here in the most intricate form possible because they were transferred from one to the other side of the Atlantic, not in systematic reseedings but in a chaotic transplantation, as if during four centuries the slave-trading pirates had been burning and chopping down the forests of black humanity and had thrown onto the lands of Cuba, uncountable boatloads of branches, roots, flowers and seeds ripped out of all the jungles of Africa, mixed together and confused. (Ortiz 1995b [1906]: 8, quoted in Sublette 2004: 315)

Due in no small part to the pioneering work of Ortiz, during the 20th century Cuba gradually redefined itself as a "transculturized" nation that combines both Spanish and African elements. Coined in the 1940s by Ortiz, transculturation celebrates Cuban national identity as a unique meld of a number of diverse cultural

FERNANDO ORTIZ (1881–1969)

Sometimes referred to as Cuba's "third discoverer" after Christopher Columbus and Alexander von Humboldt, Fernando Ortiz was Cuba's leading anthropologist of 20th century and easily one of the most influential scholars of his generation. Ortiz is most famous for his reconceptualization of Cuban national identity as a rich mixture of African and European elements, likening it to the *ajiaco*, a traditional stew that derives its flavor from its variety of ingredients. He coined the term "transculturation" to describe the complex process when various cultures come together to form something new. Apart from revalorizing the African cultural elements in Cuban culture, Ortiz's other major accomplishment was his 1940 book on the impact of sugar and tobacco on the Cuban nation, *Contrapunteo cubano del tabaco y azúcar* (Cuban Counterpoint: Tobacco and Sugar). He also authored many ethnographic studies of "Afro-Cuban" culture—another term he coined—including *Hampa afrocubana* (The Afro-Cuban Underworld, 1905), *Los negros curros* (The Flamboyant Blacks, 1995), *Los negros brujos* (Black Magicians, 1906), and *El engaño de las razas* (The Fraud of Race, 1946).

elements similar to the American notion of the "melting pot." However, the Cuban version of this melting pot, known as the *ajiaco* (a tropical stew), is not based on the dominance of a single mainstream group (whether white, Anglo-Saxon Protestant or white, Spanish Catholic). Instead, the Cuban *ajiaco* reflects a more fully transculturized national identity that recognizes both African and European (as well as Indian, Chinese, Jewish, English, French, and American) cultural elements as co-contributors to national identity, without claiming any single one as the mainstream.

Unfortunately, the notion of a shared, transculturized national identity has often been cynically co-opted in practice to support the simplistic belief that Cuba is a "racial democracy" where racism is rare and racial discrimination has been mild (Pérez Sarduy and Stubs 1993, 2000). On the positive side, the ideal of racial equality has been employed by blacks as a way to claim full and equal rights as *Cubans*. On the negative side, however, the myth of racial democracy has made it less likely that those with Afro-Cuban ancestry will identify as *blacks*, making it more difficult, in turn, for those who have suffered from systematic discrimination to mobilize under a common banner of black solidarity or black pride (De la Fuente 2001). This historic dilemma was exacerbated by the well-meaning but often idealistic writings on race by Cuban patriot and independence leader José Martí.

Urban versus Plantation Slavery

While life for Cuba's slaves was often short and brutal, urban slavery was a world apart from rural, plantation slavery. Urban slaves were often rented out for municipal construction projects by their owners, allowing them to enjoy a superior range of individual liberty such that some were able to freely hire themselves out and even engage the services of other slaves. Some were able to establish their own businesses, develop trades, and live apart from their owners. This form of slavery led over time to the emergence of an artisan class of free people of color—blacks and mulattoes alike—who at the dawn of the 19th century dominated almost every form of trade and artistic endeavor, especially music. For example, the black violinist José Claudio Brindis de Salas was one of the most outstanding musical figures of the 19th century.

On sugar plantations, however, black slaves were almost completely cut off from the outside world and condemned for life to slavery. They had no legal mechanisms to acquire their freedom or the opportunity to learn trades. Out of these conditions came an irrepressible rebelliousness, which manifested itself in the figure of the *cimarrón* (the runaway slave), the *palenque* (a runaway slave community), and periodic revolts, the most notorious of which was the so-called Escalera Conspiracy in 1844. While it was met with brutal repression after being prematurely discovered, this revolt was particularly significant because it was led by free blacks and mulattoes who had been able to acquire small holdings and a certain level of culture. This allowed them to interact directly with whites, while also maintaining close bonds of solidarity with slaves. This intermediate civic and social position allowed Cuba's free black community to act as a conduit for what Cuban historian Ramiro Guerra has called the "dual desire for civil liberty and social equality" on the part of slaves and free people of color alike.

Given free blacks' unequal position relative to whites, as they developed their own sense of Creoleness they did so with a different set of priorities than did white Creoles. To paraphrase the prominent Cuban intellectual Jorge Mañach, Cuban blacks and whites were unable to find a common purpose that could transcend their differences. For example, when the Ten Years' War began in 1868, white planters joined the cause out of an aspiration for greater economic and political freedom, while blacks joined to continue their longtime struggle for the abolition of slavery.

The Myths of Legal Equality and Black Inferiority

This argument can be illustrated by a number of subsequent historical developments. For example, shortly after the abolition of slavery in Cuba—which took place in 1886—Juan Gualberto Gómez outlined several "civil rights" principles that would be at the heart of Martin Luther King, Jr.'s struggle for racial integration six decades later in the United States. First, racial prejudice must be confronted directly by Afro-Cubans themselves, with a forceful rejection of discrimination and denouncement of racism. Second, actions by blacks and mulattoes on behalf of racial justice could not and should not replace one form of discrimination (white against black) with another (black against white), but should instead seek to unify whites and blacks in a common struggle against all forms of discrimination. And third, the just aspirations of blacks were not to be separated from the general aspirations of the Cuban nation, of which blacks are a part (Aguirre 1997: 13). Imbued with these principles Gualberto Gómez founded the Central Directorate of Societies of Color in 1892, out of which thousands of blacks mobilized to demand equal treatment under the law. Step by step, with resistance and character in the face of humiliation, a whole generation of Afro-Cubans harnessed the law to gain access to public spaces and facilities previously unknown to them, from stadium seats and orchestra boxes to access to 700 public school classrooms that had previously been reserved for white children only.

During the Independence War of 1895, due to the expertise of blacks in mounting machete charges and at surviving the rough life of a guerrilla soldier in the wild, equality and solidarity prevailed over racial prejudice. However, upon the arrival of the Republic in 1902, in a context where such martial skills were useless, the equality they had previously achieved under arms quickly eroded in peacetime. While the eminent Cuban historian Moreno Fraginals has argued that "the national synthesis was hastened in Cuba as compared to other Caribbean countries," that does not mean that such a synthesis was fully achieved. As Aline Helg observed of the vulnerable situation of Afro-Cubans upon the birth of the Republic: "blacks remained what they had always been, '*negros*.' Unable to read or write, landless, with scant culture and victims of racial prejudice" (2000).

U.S. intervention and the subsequent American economic domination of the island helped exacerbate racial differences. According to the 1899 census, only 16.4 percent of soldiers and police were black, while this already low proportion dropped further to 14.3 percent by 1907—this in a country where fully 60 percent of the *mambises* (rebel fighters) in the Liberation Army had been black. Most public positions in trade, banking, insurance, communications, and transportation (with the exception of the railroad), were occupied by whites. Of the 504 workers employed in cigar factories at the time, just 70 were Cuban and only one of these was black. The plain fact was that the supposed national unity achieved during the war "was not understood to be a physical or cultural union, but the product of an interracial revolutionary alliance" (Ferrer 2002: 21; Martínez Heredia 2002), helping explain the fragility of the process of racial integration and its subsequent backsliding.

In the newly independent Cuban Republic, suffrage was limited to literate males who owned property of a minimum value of 250 pesos, making it impossible for more than a handful of blacks—even those who had been soldiers and generals in the War of Independence—to vote. This also made it impossible for any of the black generals to occupy a prominent position in the new government. One of the most illustrious of these, Quintín Banderas—who had served as a general in all three wars of independence—was not only denied a job as a doorman, but was also viciously murdered in a machete attack by Cuba's rural guard in 1906 at the age of 69. What we are faced with then is the coexistence of two competing, simplistic myths: that of legal equality and that of black inferiority. The first was written into the 1901 Constitution while the second was preserved in people's minds.

During the first half of the 20th century, the Cuban republic mostly betrayed the egalitarian ideology of Martí. First, a mixed-race liberation army was replaced by an exclusively white U.S.-organized police force and rural guard. In response to this and other discriminations, in 1908 the Independent Party of Color (PIC) was founded. Their leader, Evaristo Estenoz, justified the need for such an organization with these words:

> Cuba's colored race can expect nothing from the procedures followed thus far by the existing political parties because they have done nothing for us. . . . We will demonstrate this by nominating only black candidates, none of whom belong to the existing political parties. However small the elected minority that results from

such a strategy, no one can deny that the outcome will always be greater than that achieved to date . . . (Fernández Robaina 1994: 61)

In response to the rise of the PIC, the Afro-Cuban Senator Martín Morúa Delgado proposed a constitutional amendment prohibiting the formation of associations or political parties restricted to individuals of a single race. In the Senate debates, Morúa predicted that a political organization composed of blacks alone would automatically provoke its opposite, a parallel organization composed solely of whites, which was precisely the eventuality his bill was intended to prevent.

Protesting against this so-called Morúa Amendment, in May 1912 members of the PIC took up arms under the slogan: "Down with the Morúa Amendment or war!" The government of President José Miguel Gómez responded by calling their bluff. War is what they were given. The full military weight of the state was unleashed on them with scores of PIC members massacred in the name of the "nation" defending itself against "the inferior race." This "nationwide extermination of Blacks of quasi-genocidal proportions" had the long-term effect of eliminating the leadership of Cuba's Afro-Cuban community, leading to a generation of black underrepresentation in politics and systematic occupational discrimination (Casal 1989: 474). As a result, discrimination against Afro-Cubans as second-class citizens during the first half of the 20th century was the norm. Civil and social rights taken for granted by white, urban Cubans were systematically denied to blacks. Discrimination was especially egregious in access to housing, education, health care, and employment. Needless to say, such an outcome further delayed the formation of a common national identity and destiny that could transcend racial divisions.

In the 1930s the nascent interracial Cuban labor movement played an important role against discrimination. While progress was slow, it bore tangible fruits. As part of an artistic movement known as *Afrocubanismo* (very similar to the Harlem Renaissance), a significant number of media outlets, radio stations, and leading figures in Cuban politics and culture came out publically against racism, helping the social and cultural valorization and integration of blacks as part of a common national identity (Moore 1997). One result of this was the 1940 Constitution, which included a legal principle vital to the promotion of equality between blacks and whites. "All discrimination based on race, color, or class, or any other cause detrimental to human dignity," declared the document, "is illegal and punishable by law" (Fernández Robaina 1994: 144). Nevertheless, in actual practice this principle was left pending as part of the never enacted complementary criminal law against discrimination.

Race and Revolution

In response to the desperate economic and social situation of Afro-Cubans on the eve of the revolution, the new government made the eradication of racial discrimination one of its highest priorities. On March 22, 1959, Castro specifically threw down the gauntlet over the issue of racial discrimination, singling out the routine discrimination that took place at work centers and in the social sphere. In an open assault on the structures of institutionalized racial discrimination, the revolution opened up Afro-Cuban access to employment and integrated most of the previously segregated clubs, parks, and beaches. These policies legitimized Afro-Cubans' claims about the pervasiveness of racism and discrimination and had the effect of making racial discrimination tantamount to a counterrevolutionary act (Morales Domínguez 2008: 96).

While these egalitarian and redistributive moves made a point never to single out blacks as their exclusive beneficiaries, such measures benefited blacks the most since they were the most oppressed sector in prerevolutionary Cuba. Also, Castro's very public declarations against racism and discrimination led to a sea change in the perception of such attitudes. Now, not only was discrimination illegal, but it was also considered anti-Cuban. Thus, while old racist attitudes, habits, and preferences would take a long time to die out, even among the most ardent of revolutionaries, now racists would have to pay a tremendous price when expressing such attitudes publicly. Moreover, given the rapid efforts to eradicate all legal forms of discrimination, it became much more difficult for an individual's private prejudices to translate into systematic institutional discrimination (Casal 1989; De la Fuente 2001).

After 1962, however, the rapid and effective initial efforts of the revolutionary government to do away with racial discrimination were followed by a shift in tone, which "declared the problem of racism solved" and "the topic officially sealed" (Morales Domínguez 2008: 96). The government simultaneously outlawed all previously established Afro-Cuban organizations. While the government did not specifically target these black cultural, civic, or religious organizations, all such independent associations (black or white, civic or political, cultural or religious) were now subsumed under new revolutionary organizations that stressed national unity under socialism above all else. In fact, the insistence upon revolutionary unity had the effect of demobilizing any independent activity on the part of blacks themselves. Under the assumption that Cuba's traditional racial divisions had been solved by decree, the new government tended to view Afro-Cuban leaders who continued to raise the issues of racism or discrimination as ungrateful malcontents whose revelations of ongoing racial problems served only to divide a nation under siege. Alejandro de la Fuente, one of the leading scholars of race relations in Cuba, sums up this paradoxical impact of the revolution on racism, indicating that "the ultimate irony is that the same government that did the most to eliminate racism also did the most to silence the discussion about its persistence" (De la Fuente 2001: 338).

Cuban sociologist Esteban Morales has echoed this critical line of thought in his recent attempts to directly address an issue within Cuba that had been officially off limits for decades (Farber 2011; Morales Domínguez 2008). In his essay, "Challenges of the Racial Problem in Cuba," published in the Cuban journal *Temas* in 2008, Morales throws down his own gauntlet with the declaration:

> Converting the topic [of racism] into a taboo and removing any reference to it from all social and political spaces generated a social atmosphere that made it impossible to address it. Those who brought it up were ideologically and politically repressed. . . . For someone to attempt to analyze it critically in the midst of the political confrontation of those years, . . . was to risk being seen as sewing social division among Cubans and labeled racist or diversionary, or both simultaneously. (Morales Domínguez 2008: 96)

Expelled from public areas or open discussion, racism did not disappear but only went underground taking refuge in people's minds; "maintaining itself in the family, in individual subjectivity, and in some institutions; and now threatening to once again insert itself into the consciousness of Cuban society" (ibid.: 96). When Cuba's economic crisis that began in 1990 forced the socialist economy to open up to foreign investment, remittances from Cuban-Americans, and international tourism, many Cubans began to feel relegated to second-class citizenship in their own country once again. As dollars flooded parts of the socialist economy, inequality expanded. However, this new inequality emerged with a marked racial profile, leading to renewed social tensions and accusations of racial discrimination (ibid.). Blacks who had decided against emigrating for ample historical reasons found themselves excluded from much sought after family remittances. Because roughly 85 percent of Cuban-Americans are white, few blacks on the island receive remittances. This fact helps explain the significant presence of blacks during the mass rafter exodus of August 1994.

Likewise, Afro-Cubans are often indirectly (but not accidentally) excluded from jobs in the booming tourism industry under the requirement that potential employees possess a "pleasant aspect" (i.e., white skin). Effectively excluded from the most lucrative sector of the economy, many Afro-Cubans have turned to the island's ubiquitous underground economy for survival. Commenting on the bitter resentment felt by many Cuban youths (blacks and whites alike), Spanish anthropologist Isabel Holgado Fernández has written:

> One of the facts that has caused the most resentment among the Cuban population, especially among the youth, has been the impossibility of gaining access to areas of tourism and entertainment. . . . The development of tourism and the corresponding exclusion of Cubans from the enjoyment of its infrastructure contradicted the revolutionary axiom of social egalitarianism. Cubans had the bitter sensation that they were being demoted to second-class citizenship in their own country: Foreigners had access to beaches, hotels, restaurants, nightclubs, to all

---

"EL TEMBA"—A SUGAR DADDY, WITH A LOT OF CASH

The wildly popular Cuban timba group *La Charanga Habanera* came out with a song entitled "El Temba" (The Sugar daddy) in the mid-1990s that poked fun at Nicolás Guillén's 1964 poem, "Tengo," an ode to what Cubans "have" because of the revolution. Given the fact that many young Cuban women were then actively seeking out foreigners as boyfriends in order to gain access to material goods (or to emigrate), the song advises its young female listeners to "Look for a sugar daddy who can maintain you; So that you can enjoy, so that you can have [things]" (*Búscate un temba que te mantenga; Pa' que tú goces pa' que tú tengas*). Building on this ironic use of the words "maintain" (*mantenga*) and "have" (*tenga*), the song closes with a repeated chorus that directly mocks the signature line in Guillén's famous poem: "So that you have, what you had to have; A sugar daddy, with a lot of cash" (*Pa' que tengas, lo que tenías que tener; Un papirriqui, con güaniquiqui*) (K. Moore 2001; R. Moore 2006).

those places where they, the builders and beneficiaries by right of all that exportable paradise, could not even touch with their Cuban pesos. (Holgado Fernández 2000: 208)

In summary, throughout Cuban history the problem of racism and discrimination has never received the comprehensive treatment that a phenomenon of such complexity requires, and therefore it remains a significant problem in Cuban society.

CLASS STRUCTURE

Just as Cuba's ethnic distinctions are related to its racial ones, so too are race relations deeply connected to the island's social class hierarchy. "Nothing can be done," observed the Marxist Cuban historian Moreno Fraginals, "if we forget that black Africans were brought to Cuba as producers of surplus value and that their descendants have continued to be exploited under that same logic" (2002). For this reason any analysis of racial discrimination in Cuba must take the island's class structure into account. The analysis of the following three historical case studies will help illustrate how Cuba's class structure has changed over time: the slave-dominated, feudalist, but increasingly capitalist economy of the colonial period; the highly unequal, foreign-dominated, dependent capitalism of the Republican period; and the failed attempt to achieve socialist egalitarianism under a decidedly statist and authoritarian revolution.

The Colonial Class Structure

In colonial times, Cuba's class structure was determined by the coexistence of three distinct but overlapping relations of production: slavery, feudal land tenure, and capitalism. Out of that coexistence emerged a class structure composed of slaves and slave owners, peasants and landlords, and workers and employers. Of course, slavery was characterized by a strictly hierarchical, even bipolar relationship between the slave and slave owner, with the differentiation between them expressed as much by their distinct social positions as by the color of their skin.

The contradictory relations between Cuba's peasants and landowners is based more than anything else on the enormous tracts of land (*latifundio*) granted by the Spanish government to the first settlers on the island. The original grantees used this land to raise livestock, with small portions of the land later given over to small farmers to facilitate subsistence agricultural production. However, the coexistence between the *latifundistas* (large landowners) and the later *colonos* (squatters or small farmers) was short lived, coming to a head with the Royal Decree of July 1819, which confirmed the former as the legitimate and sole owners of the land. This forced the peasants to begin paying rent, become sharecroppers, or leave. The construction of Cuba's railways during the 19th century, coupled with the expansion of sugar, coffee, and cattle production, led to the forced expulsion of thousands of these now dispossessed peasants, which heightened class conflict in the countryside. Meanwhile, relations between urban workers and their employers in Cuba took on their modern shape from the start of the second half of the 19th century, when slave labor was rapidly replaced by wage labor. This explains the fact that by 1899 there were already 350,517 urban day laborers and manual workers in Cuba (Pittaluga 1999: 177; Roca 1961).

Dependent Capitalism

The political, economic, and social developments that transformed the island at the end of the 19th century were manifested in the peculiar "Plattist," externally dependent Republic born in 1902. The prevailing capitalist relations of production led to a domestic class structure dominated by a multitiered bourgeoisie made up of financial, trade, industrial, sugar, agricultural, and petty bourgeoisie elements. The growth and strength experienced by this social class is reflected not only in its internal contradictions and the struggle against the proletariat, but also in the unstable but increasingly domestically controlled nature of the Cuban economy. For example, after long being dominated by foreign—especially North American—planters, 75 percent of Cuba's sugar mills—which ground two-thirds of the island's sugar cane—was held by the domestic bourgeoisie by 1950. Sugar production exceeded seven million tons reaching its highest level ever recorded, while the gross national product (GNP) doubled. Moreover, Cuba's per capita income became the fourth highest in Latin America and United Nations figures placed Cuba among the top three countries in the region in several indicators.

The working class, composed of employees in industry and agriculture, achieved a high standard of living reflected in the formation of trade unions that fought for the eight-hour workday and wage increases. To that end, from the early years of the Republic, Cuba's unions held periodic strikes, which resulted in significant benefits. For example, during the sugar harvest of 1932 strikes temporarily paralyzed 25 mills and shut down more than 100 sugarcane farms. Likewise, the general strike of 1933—declared by the trade union movement—succeeded in ousting authoritarian president Gerardo Machado. Legal victories for the working class included the eight-hour day, the minimum wage for sugar workers, the right to strike, as well as other freedoms in line with the recommendations of the International Labour Organization (ILO). These developments peaked with the enactment of Decree-Law 798 in April 1938, which clearly defined—perhaps for the first time—the rights and responsibilities of labor and management in labor contracts. All this culminated in 1939 with the founding of Cuba's powerful unified labor union, the *Central de Trabajadores de Cuba* (CTC) and the subsequent progressive and pro-labor Constitution of 1940 (described in Chapters 2 and 3).

At the same time, most agricultural land was concentrated in just a few hands—both foreign and domestic—while hundreds of thousands of peasant families went landless. This resulted in the polarization of the countryside into two main groups: large and medium *latifundistas* and mid-sized and poor peasants. The concentration of ownership was exacerbated by land evictions. For example, in the 1890s, toward the end of the War of Independence 40,000 small farmers were evicted from lands taken over by American companies. During the great expansion of sugarcane between 1918 and 1924, there were violent expulsions of thousands more peasants, which explains the rise in the fight against further evictions during the 1930s.

The result of this process can be found in the 1946 census, which recorded that 89 percent of the island's 142,385 farmers held five *caballerías* of land or less. Moreover, the holdings of this 89 percent constituted only 24 percent of agricultural land. On the other hand, the 18,573 owners who made up the agrarian bourgeoisie—*latifundistas* and foreign companies—held the other 76 percent of the land. This lopsided distribution of the island's agricultural land resulted in the systematic exploitation of landless wage laborers by the large foreign and domestic landowners, while these *latifundistas* were themselves exploited by the mill owners and banks. The poor, in turn, were divided into tenants, sharecroppers, and squatters. Tenants paid rent to landowners in cash, sharecroppers paid in kind with their agricultural produce, and squatters—lacking any legal contract or rights—occupied mainly state lands and paid nothing, but were also the most vulnerable of all landless peasants to eviction (Mayo 1980; Regalado 1974).

The severity of the problem of land tenure in Cuba could not be ignored by the government, which was forced to periodically intervene. A January 1904 law provided for the sale of uncultivated public lands to veterans of the War of Independence. In June 1906, credits amounting to one million pesos were made available to farmers wanting to settle on and develop state lands. In June 1911, Decree-Law 492 made one *caballería* of land available to peasant families. (Ironically, this is very similar to the current effort under Raúl Castro to provide lands to small farmers, with the difference that the 1911 law included ownership rights, not simply those of usufruct.)

The Constitution of 1940 outlawed large estates, limited the ability of foreign companies to acquire new lands, and took steps to return the land to Cuban ownership. However, as in the area of race, the government never enacted the necessary legislation to enforce these high-minded goals and instead put in place a moratorium on land evictions for two years. President Fulgencio Batista (1940–1944), enacted Decree-Law 247, which enabled squatters to sign contracts and begin to pay rent, handing over more than 1000 *caballerías* of land to a group of families in the Sierra Maestra mountains. Many of these families decided to leave the area, however, since they were provided no access to credit to begin to make the land productive (also similar to the present Decree-Law 259, recently enacted as part of Raúl Castro's economic "updating"). For his part, President Grau San Martín (1944–1948) budgeted three million pesos for the purchase and distribution of the Ventas de Casanova lands as part of a failed effort to create a model agricultural experiment. The limited nature of these measures explains why the problem of land ownership in Cuba went unanswered during both the colonial and Republican periods.

¡Viva el socialismo! *Or Is It State Capitalism?*

In his famous speech, "History Will Absolve Me," given at his defense trial in 1953, Fidel Castro proposed granting ownership rights to all peasants who occupied parcels of five or fewer *caballerías* (Castro 1967). That proposal became law in the Sierra Maestra in October 1958 with the distribution of property, in areas controlled by the rebel army, to those who occupied less than five *caballerías*. After 1959, the revolutionary government enacted the first Agrarian Reform Law, by which all properties in excess of 30 *caballerías* were confiscated, with land titles granted to

100,000 peasants who had previously occupied and owned up to five *caballerías*. The remaining confiscated property became state property. In October 1963, with the Second Agrarian Reform Law, the government expropriated 10,000 farms larger than five *caballerías* so that state ownership of land suddenly rose to 70 percent of the country's land, a proportion almost exactly the same as that owned by the agrarian bourgeoisie, *latifundistas*, and foreign companies before the 1959.

The consolidation of the state's control over the economy was reflected in the fact that the proportion of workers employed by the state rose from 87 percent in 1970 to 92 percent in 1981, reaching an amazing 94 percent by 1988 (Noguera 2004). This new social structure, composed for 30 years of a largely homogeneous group of proletarians—the working class, small farmers, and a tiny sector of urban nonstate workers—with a thin layer of intellectual workers and a vanguard of political cadres at the top, was dealt a harsh blow with the collapse of socialism in Eastern Europe starting in 1989. This drastic contextual shift forced the government to enact an initial round of unprecedented economic reforms in the early 1990s, including the lease of state land to new agricultural cooperatives and an expansion in self-employment, both of which increased the number of private workers in Cuba's state-dominated class structure.

These changes, together with those currently being implemented under Raúl Castro since 2008, have expanded the number of Cubans working in the private sector and of those who—for the first time since 1968—are able to hire private employees. If just 41,400 persons were self-employed in 1988, by 1995 there were 208,346. After a long counterreform enacted by Fidel Castro between 1996 and 2006, the number of these so-called *cuentapropistas* (self-employed workers or microentrepreneurs) has nearly tripled from roughly 150,000 in October 2010 to more than 436,000 by August 2013. This—together with other similar developments such as the beginnings of massive layoffs in the state sector and the gradual elimination of the universal rationing system—has destroyed the basis of class "homogeneity" described earlier and created a new and much more complex and differentiated class structure.

Even the value of egalitarianism, once celebrated as a major goal and accomplishment of the revolution, has been publicly abandoned, with President Raúl Castro declaring repeatedly that socialism does *not* mean egalitarianism. Instead, under the new understanding of Cuba's political economy and class structure outlined in the 2010 *Lineamientos* document that set the stage for the long-delayed Sixth Party Congress that took place in April 2011, "socialism is equality of rights and opportunities for all citizens, not egalitarianism. Work is simultaneously a right and a duty, a motivation for personal realization for each citizen, and should be rewarded according to its quantity and quality." Raúl has even said that "egalitarianism is in itself a form of exploitation: exploitation of the good workers by those who are less productive and lazy" (Castro 2008).

One's position in this emergent, stratified class structure is determined by one's access to sources of hard currency, such as private-sector employment, foreign and tourism enterprises operating on the island, corruption, and remittances from abroad. This stratification is exacerbated by the constant increase in retail prices and resulting reduction in real wages. Ariel Terrero—an economist often featured on Cuban television—recently indicated that the new economic measures, while pushing up the prices of commodities, has divided Cuban society into four strata very similar to those present in Cuba before the revolution: the lower class, the middle class, the upper-middle class, and the high class (Terrero 2012).

Inequality, Poverty, and Social Contradictions in Today's Cuba

The economic crisis and off-again, on-again reforms of the past 20 years have ushered in the social problems of income inequality, poverty, and unemployment as well as an increase in economic crime and various forms of hustling and prostitution (Espina Prieto 2005; Espina Prieto et al. 1998). During the 1980s, Cuba had likely become one of the most egalitarian societies in the world. However, by all measures income inequality has risen precipitously since the crisis began in 1990. Cuba's Gini coefficient (a standard international measure of income inequality, with 0.0 being perfect equality and 1.0 denoting total inequality) rose from 0.22 in 1986 to 0.55 in 1995 by one estimate, while other measures have indicated a less significant but still substantial increase to 0.42 by late 2004 (Romanò 2012). Likewise, real wages in the state sector experienced a sharp decrease between 1989 and 2000, falling by 40 percent from 131 to 78 pesos ($19–$5) per month. Added to that is a simultaneous increase in wages in the small but significant private sector (Mesa-Lago and Pérez-López 2005: 72–73).

The eminent Cuban-American economist Carmelo Mesa-Lago has compiled an estimate of various wage rates based on interviews conducted with recent Cuban émigrés. For 1995, he estimated a wide differential of monthly wage rates (in U.S. dollars) for various state- and private-sector occupations in Cuba including minimum wage worker ($4), average state worker ($6), teacher ($8–$9), doctor or college professor ($11–$12), driver of tourist taxi ($100–$467), private farmer ($187–$311), and *paladar* owner ($2,500–$5,000). This range has only continued to widen since then, with the ratio of the highest- to the lowest-paid occupation jumping from 4.5 to 1 in 1989, to 829 to 1 in 1995, reaching 12,500 to 1 by 2002 (ibid.: 73–75; Mesa-Lago 2000).

As the preceding list of occupations demonstrates, income inequality in Cuba arises mainly from the wide disparity between state and nonstate sectors, leading to the underutilization of talented and highly educated workers who follow the money into the tourism sector and underground economy. Many others have also chosen to emigrate to gain a return on their educational investment, make ends meet, and support family left behind in Cuba. This misuse of skills also provokes low worker morale, high labor turnover, low productivity, and disrespect for state-sector rules against theft, as well as acting as a disincentive to staying in school. Neutralizing such a perverse incentive structure is one of the expressed goals of the economic plan being gradually put into place under Raúl Castro.

Given the extent of free or heavily subsidized social services available to all Cubans even today (housing, education, health care, rations, etc.), understandings of poverty and even uses of the word to describe Cubans who have limited access to certain goods must be qualified relative to measures of poverty elsewhere (Warren 2005: 1, 6–7). That said, poverty does exist in Cuba and, if defined as the "population at risk of not meeting some essential need," as is normally done by Cuban social scientists, it has been on the rise over the past two decades. Studies carried out by Cuban researchers estimate that the "at risk" population has risen from just 6 percent in 1988 to 14.7 percent in 1996, reaching 20 percent by 2000. Other econometric measures used in Cuban studies place the poverty incidence much higher, at between 61 and 67 percent, with surveys showing that between 41 and 54 percent of Havana's population considers themselves poor or nearly poor (Togores González and García 2004).

The dual currency system and the resulting severe disconnect between wages earned in Cuban pesos (CUPs) and the increasing number of consumer products available only in convertible Cuban pesos (CUCs) at the equivalent of dollar prices acts as a disincentive for Cubans to perform low-paid formal state-sector work since it is no longer the fundamental source of family income. It takes roughly 26 CUPs to purchase a single CUC, making the recent increase in the average monthly wage from 330 CUPs in 2005 (roughly equivalent to $12.69) to 458 CUPs in 2011 ($17.62) clearly insufficient. During that same period the average monthly pension rose from 179.36 CUPs ($6.90) to 255 CUPs ($9.81). These stark numbers help explain the rise in a number of disturbing social problems, including unemployment, lowered productivity, brain drain (the emigration of Cuba's young and talented), and an increasing tendency for Cubans to turn to informal, unregulated labor arrangements and black market sources for consumer goods (Carranza Valdés 2001).

This development has been coupled with a rise in prostitution, street hustling, high-level corruption, and small-time but systematic economic crimes (Díaz-Briquets and Pérez-López 2006). In fact, the first new regulation approved under President Raúl Castro was aimed at reducing absenteeism and increasing productivity in state enterprises through a more rigorous vigilance of work schedules and time off (Encuentro 2006). Since then, the younger Castro has introduced much deeper and wide ranging pro-market reforms aimed at remaking Cuba's socialist economy (described in detail in Chapter 4). These are bound to have a direct impact on Cuba's class structure, as well as on levels of unemployment, inequality, and poverty.

BIBLIOGRAPHY

Aguirre, Sergio. 1990. *Nacionalidad y nación en el siglo XIX cubano*. Havana: Social Science Publishers.

Aguirre, Sergio. 1997. *Un gran olvidado, Juan Gualberto Gómez*. Havana: Social Science Publishers.

Anthony Giddens. n.d. "Etnicidad y raza." www.cholonautas.edu.pe / Biblioteca Virtual de Ciencias Sociales.

Barberia, Lorena, Xavier de Souza Briggs, and Miren Uriarte. 2004. "Commentary: The End of Egalitarianism? Economic Inequality and the Future of Social Policy in Cuba." In Jorge I. Domínguez, Omar Everleny Pérez Villanueva, and Lorena Barberia, eds., *The Cuban Economy at the Start of the Twenty-First Century*, pp. 297–316. Cambridge: David Rockefeller Center for Latin American Studies, Harvard University.

Carranza Valdés, Julio. 2001. "La economía cubana: Balance breve de una década crítica." Mimeograph provided by the author of a paper presented at the "Facing the Challenges of the Global Economy" workshop. University of London Institute of Latin American Studies, January 25–26.

Casal, Lourdes. 1989. "Race Relations in Contemporary Cuba." In Philip Brenner, William M. LeoGrande, Donna Rich, and Daniel Siegel, eds., *The Cuba Reader: The Making of a Revolutionary Society*. New York: Grove Press.

Castoriadis, Cornelius. 1985. "Reflexiones en torno al racismo." Memories from the Coloquium "Inconsciente y cambio social," of the Association pour la Recherche et l'Intervention Psichologiques, France, March.

Castro, Fidel. 1967. *History Will Absolve Me*. Havana: Guairas Publishing.

Castro, Fidel. 2005. "Discurso pronunciado por Fidel Castro Ruz en el acto por el aniversario 60 de su ingreso a la universidad." Havana, November 17. Available online in English http://www.cuba.cu/gobierno/discursos/2005/ing/f171105i.html.

Castro, Raúl. 2008. "Socialismo significa justicia social e igualdad, pero igualdad no es igualitarismo." *Cuba Socialista*, July 11. http://www.cubasocialista.cu/index.php?q=social ismo-significa-justicia-social-e-igualdad-pero-igualdad-no-es-igualitarismo.

De la Fuente, Alejandro. 2001. A *Nation for All: Race, Inequality, and Politics in Twentieth-Century Cuba*. Chapel Hill, NC: University of North Carolina Press.

Díaz Artiga, Mayarí. 2002. "Etnicidad y racismo." Guatemala: Universidad de San Carlos. http://www.naya.org.ar/congreso2002/ponencias/mayari_diaz_artiga.htm.

Díaz-Briquets, Sergio, and Jorge Pérez-López. 2006. *Corruption in Cuba: Castro and Beyond*. Austin, TX: University of Texas Press.

Encuentro. 2006. "El gobierno introducirá una severa norma contra el absentismo laboral." *Cubaencuentro.com*, December 12.

Espina Prieto, Mayra Paula. 2004. "Social Effects of Economic Adjustment: Equality, Inequality and Trends toward Greater Complexity in Cuban Society." In Jorge I. Domínguez, Omar Everleny Pérez Villanueva, and Lorena Barberia, eds., *The Cuban Economy at the Start of the Twenty-First Century*, pp. 209–243. Cambridge: David Rockefeller Center for Latin American Studies, Harvard University.

Espina Prieto, Mayra Paula. 2005. "Structural Changes since the Nineties and New Research Topics on Cuban Society." In Joseph S. Tulchin et al., ed., *Changes in Cuban Society since the Nineties*. Washington, DC: Woodrow Wilson International Center for Scholars.

Espina Prieto, Mayra Paula, Lucy Martín Posada, and Lilia Núñez Moreno. 1998. "Componentes y tendencias socioestructurales de la sociedad cubana actual—resumen ejecutivo." Havana: Centro de Investigación Psicológica y Sociológica, March.

Farber, Samuel. 2011. *Cuba since the Revolution of 1959: A Critical Assessment*. Chicago: Haymarket Books.

Ferrer, Ada. 2002. "Cuba insurgente; raza, nación y revolución, 1868–1898." *Caminos, revista de pensamiento socioteológico* no. 24–25.

Fernández Robaina, Tomás. 1994. *El negro en Cuba, 1902–1958*. Havana: Social Science Publishers.

González, Mario. 2003. *Los árabes*. Havana: Editorial de Ciencias Sociales.

Guanche Pérez, Jesús. 1990. "Etnicidad cubana y seres míticos populares" (unpublished manuscript). http://www.slideshare.net/mase_lobe/1-etnicidad-cubana-y-seres-mticos-populares.

Helg, Aline. 2000. *Lo que nos corresponde. La lucha de los negros y mulatos por la igualdad en Cuba 1886–1912*. Havana: Ediciones Imagen Contemporánea.

Holgado Fernández, Isabel. 2000. *Mujeres cubanas y la crisis revolucionaria*. Barcelona: Antrazyt.

Jiménez Pastrana, Juan. 1963. *Los chinos en las luchas por la liberación cubana (1847–1930)*. Havana: Instituto de Historia.

Martí, José. 2002. *Selected Writings*. Translated by Esther Allen. New York: Penguin.

Martínez Heredia, Fernando. 2002. "La cuestión racial en Cuba y este número de Caminos." *Caminos, revista de pensamiento socioteológico*, no. 24–25.

Mayo, José. 1980. *Dos décadas de lucha contra el latifundio. Breve historia de la Asociación Nacional Campesina.* Havana: Editora Política.

Medina Rensoli, Rolando J. 2008. *Nación Cubana: Etnos y sociedad cuatro temas y un enfoque histórico.* Havana: Ediciones Extramuros.

Mesa-Lago, Carmelo. 2000. *Market, Socialist, and Mixed Economies: Comparative Policy and Performance—Chile, Cuba, and Costa Rica.* Baltimore, MD: Johns Hopkins University Press.

Mesa-Lago, Carmelo, and Jorge Pérez-López. 2005. *Cuba's Aborted Reform: Socioeconomic Effects, International Comparisons, and Transition Policies.* Gainesville, FL: University Press of Florida.

Moore, Kevin. 2001. "Artists: Charanga Habanera." http://www.timba.com

Moore, Robin D. 1997. *Nationalizing Blackness: Afrocubanismo and Artistic Revolution in Havana, 1920–1940.* Pittsburgh, PA: University of Pittsburgh Press.

Moore, Robin D. 2006. *Music and Revolution: Cultural Change in Socialist Cuba.* Berkeley, CA: University of California Press.

Morales Domínguez, Esteban. 2008. "Desafios de la problemática racial en Cuba." *Temas* no. 56 (October–December): 95–99. http://www.temas.cult.cu/revistas/56/10%20Esteban.pdf.

Moreno Fraginals, Manuel. 2002. "Aportes culturales y deculturación." *Caminos, revista de pensamiento socioteológico* no. 24–25: 6–18.

Noguera, Albert. 2004. "Estructura social e igualdad en la Cuba actual: La reforma de los noventa y los cambios en la estructura de clases cubana." *Revista Europea de Estudios Latinoamericanos y del Caribe* 76 (April): 45–59. http://www.cedla.uva.nl/50_publications/pdf/revista/76RevistaEuropea/76Noguera.pdf.

Ojito, Mirta. 2000. "Best of Friends, Worlds Apart." *The New York Times*, June 5.

Ortiz, Fernando. 1995a. *Cuban Counterpoint: Tobacco and Sugar.* Durham: Duke University Press.

Ortiz, Fernando. 1995b. *Los negros brujos.* Havana: Social Sciences Publishers. (original edition published in 1906).

Pérez-López, Jorge. 2004. "Corruption and the Cuban Transition." In Archibald R. M. Ritter, ed., *The Cuban Economy*, pp. 195–217. Pittsburgh, PA: University of Pittsburgh Press.

Pérez Sarduy, Pedro, and Jean Stubs, eds. 1993. *AfroCuba: An Anthology of Cuban Writing on Race, Politics, and Culture.* Melbourne: Ocean Press.

Pérez Sarduy, Pedro, and Jean Stubs, eds. 2000. *Afro-Cuban Voices: On Race and Identity in Contemporary Cuba.* Gainesville, FL: University Press of Florida.

Peters, Philip. 2006. "Who's to Blame for Corruption?" *Cuba Policy Report E-Newsletter #22*, Lexington Institute, October 22. http://lexingtoninstitute.org/1011.shtml.

Pittaluga, Gustavo. 1999. *Diálogos sobre el destino.* Havana: Félix Varela Editions.

Regalado, Antero. 1974. "Las luchas campesinas en Cuba." Havana: Department of Revolutionary Orientation of the Cuban Communist Party.

Roca, Blas. 1961. *Los fundamentos del socialismo en Cuba.* Havana: Ediciones Populares.

Romanò, Sara. 2012. "Commercial Circuits and Economic Inequality." In Alberto Gabriele, ed., *The Economy of Cuba after the VI Party Congress.* Geneva: Nova Publishers.

Sublette, Ned. 2004. *Cuba and Its Music: From the First Drum to the Mambo.* Chicago: Chicago Review Press.

Terrero Ariel. 2012. "Resurgen las clases sociales en Cuba." *Ciudadanos Cuba, Diario en Linea*, February 9. http://ciudadanoscuba.org/index.php/cuba/economia/economia-estatal/10683-resurgen-las-clases-sociales-en-cuba.html.

Togores González, Viviana, and Anicia García. 2004. "Consumption, Markets, and Monetary Duality in Cuba." In Jorge I. Domínguez, Omar Everleny Pérez Villanueva, and Lorena Barberia, eds., *The Cuban Economy at the Start of the Twenty-First Century,* pp. 245–295. Cambridge: David Rockefeller Center for Latin American Studies, Harvard University.

Warren, Cristina. 2005. "Governance and Social Justice in Cuba: Past, Present and Future— Policy Brief: Lessons for Cuba from the Latin American Experience." Miami: Cuban Research Institute, FLACSO-Mexico, and FOCAL (the Canadian Foundation for the Americas). http://www.focal.ca/pdf/cuba_brief.pdf.

Family, Gender, and Sexuality

Miriam Celaya and Ted A. Henken

INTRODUCTION

Women benefited greatly from the many socioeconomic achievements of the Cuban Revolution. This was especially so in the early years, when legal discrimination was abolished and the institutional mechanisms of sexism were destroyed. However, because women's groups were never empowered to advocate for their own liberation as women—the situation for Afro-Cubans and homosexuals being even worse—their liberation (to the extent that it has existed and still exists) has always been channeled through and contingent upon their acceptance of and incorporation into the larger project of top-down state socialism. Specifically, the revolutionary mass organizations described in Chapter 3 have been the means for Cuban women to participate in society and build socialism—always under the guidance (and control) of the government.

This has been the case for at least four reasons. First, as a revolution that has prioritized the goals of economic equality, social justice, and national sovereignty, Cuban socialism has consistently pursued its goals through an approach that sees class exploitation and foreign imperialism as the root causes of injustice. Other discriminatory practices against women or Afro-Cubans (discrimination against homosexuals was never targeted as a problem to be solved) were considered to derive from capitalism and would disappear when class privilege was eradicated. Likewise, the constant threat of U.S. invasion created a siege-like mentality among the Cuban leadership that prioritized revolutionary unity above the claims of any particular subordinated group. Indeed, under the ideal of national revolutionary unity the socialist government has consistently avoided the implementation of any "affirmative action" policies to equalize opportunities for specific aggrieved groups (women, blacks, sexual minorities, etc.). Instead, the eradication of the private economic sphere permitted the government to enact policies that would uplift all members of previously oppressed classes, regardless of gender, race, or sexual orientation (Casal 1989).

Second, Cuban culture is imbued with a deep machismo that celebrates male virility, aggressiveness, and fearlessness, while simultaneously devaluing women and men who cannot or will not live up to the macho stereotype—foremost among those being homosexuals. By extension, in revolutionary Cuba there was very little space in which homosexuals could participate in the socialist project as homosexuals, since their very homosexuality was often considered a decadent perversion or sickness, anathema to the ideal of the new socialist man. Most were faced with a stark choice: remain closeted as most had been under the previous system, disengage from society and become a nonperson, or go into exile.

Third, and perhaps most important, from the start the revolutionary leadership sought to achieve its often laudable and popular goals in a classically paternalist manner. This top-down command structure had the benefit of establishing an effective government apparatus that accomplished more in the first five years for Cuba's dispossessed and disenfranchised than had been achieved over many preceding decades. However, after those unprecedented efforts by the new government to eradicate past sexual and racial discriminatory practices, any further debate on the issues of sexism and racism (not to mention homophobia) quickly became taboo, since the problems were deemed already to have been solved. The lack of discussion of these issues as ongoing social problems made it impossible to go beyond the eradication of institutionalized discrimination and begin to address the more intractable racist, sexist, and homophobic attitudes and orientations rooted in Cuban culture.

This difficulty has been exacerbated by the outlawing of any autonomous organizations that aimed at the self-empowerment of these social groups. In most Western states, subordinated groups are controlled through their marginalization from the centers of power. However, in Cuba, women and Afro-Cubans have been controlled through their very incorporation. While their inclusion in the revolutionary project has brought them many benefits as Cubans, in practice it has also served to demobilize them as autonomous political or social interest groups, with the expectation that they feel forever indebted to the revolution for having given them their freedom. A good example of one of the negative side effects of this paternalistic approach to women's liberation is abortion. While the revolution has made abortion legal and readily available to all women regardless of class, it has completely failed to educate women (or men) about the risks of unprotected sex or empower them with contraceptive knowledge. As a result, condom use is rare, contraception is considered a women's problem, and abortion is routinely used as a form of birth control.

FAMILY

As with religion, family relations in Cuba exhibit a deep paradox. The Cuban family is beset by extremely high rates of divorce—comparable to or higher than those in the United States and Western Europe. Many children have been educated in countryside boarding schools, spending long, often traumatic, periods of their youth away from their parents. Others were sent into exile without their parents so as to "save" them from the revolution as part of the controversial *Pedro Pan* program run by the Catholic Church with collaboration from the U.S. government (Conde 2000; de la Campa 2000). Other families have struggled with the trauma of separation, sacrifice, and struggle, as parents often gave themselves and all their free time over to the never-ending task of building (or fighting against) the revolution. Moreover, many families have been tragically divided between the United States and Cuba by the politics of the revolution, as well as by the bureaucratic, intractable, and often inhumane orientation of each country's migration laws.

Nonetheless, the family is truly the heart of daily life in Cuba and in Cuba's extensive diaspora, often regardless of the distances between one's family members or the orientation of one's politics. While North Americans like to claim that American society is based on "family values," the fact is that in the United States family constitutes one's roots (where one comes from), not normally the essence of one's intimate daily activities (what one lives for). For Cubans, however, family is often one's very *raison d'etre*. That is, for most Cubans, the members of the extended family (including not only one's parents, siblings, and children but also one's cousins, aunts and uncles, grandparents and great-grandparents, nieces and nephews, and grandchildren, as well as one's many in-laws) constitute a network of the most intimate, heartfelt, and consuming relationships in life.

That is not to say that Cuban families are uniformly happy and well adjusted. On the contrary, highly charged emotions, disagreements, and conflicts are often aired openly, loudly, and passionately among family members. Still, family unity and solidarity normally override individual privacy and independence, and family loyalties are often stronger than all others. Decisions that would be personal and individual elsewhere are in Cuba endlessly discussed and debated among family members. Indeed, because of U.S. restrictions on travel to the island during the George W. Bush administration, many recent Cuban immigrants were forced to endure a minimum of three long years without seeing their families in Cuba. For those unable to share in their family's daily struggles and joys combined with the difficulty of maintaining such a close, intimate relationship from afar amounts to *el amor que te mata* ("the love that kills you").

Of course, the Cuban government's restrictions on the right of its citizens to travel freely have long been much worse, requiring them to apply for an "exit visa" before being allowed to emigrate or leave the country for a short visit abroad. There are also high costs and restrictions on the ability of émigrés to return home. However, some U.S. restrictions were recently eased under the Obama administration and Havana recently announced a major overhaul of its own antiquated and unjust migration controls. Still, as is often the case in these bureaucratic changes, the devil is in the details. For example, the laudable changes in Cuba's migration laws - including the elimination of the exit visa - that took effect in January 2013, remain incomplete since they continue to treat migration not as a human right but as a privilege awarded by the state. (The book's final chapter on "Contemporary Issues" includes a brief section describing the depth and scope of the new migration law.)

As the basic unity of society, the Cuban family is conditioned by many complex and dynamic factors, including those of historical, social, political, and religious natures. Thus, in Cuba there is no single family model, but instead a variety of family patterns depending on one's social class, standard of living, economic interests, and ownership of property. Also important are the values and norms one inherits from the previous generation, including ideas about gender roles; the rights, duties, and authority afforded to different family members; and legal standards regarding child custody, labor rights, and household obligations. Finally, considerations of a biological, legal, and cultural nature—including fertility rates, access to birth control, expectations about family size, and the sexual orientation of family members—all establish specific features within family structures.

Cuba is influenced by patterns inherited from diverse cultures, all of which have shaped the idiosyncrasies of the Cuban family. Therefore, the European family structure, which prioritizes the nuclear family (father-mother-children), has been modified over time by other influences. These include those introduced by the many African-origin groups, which came originally as slaves from almost the beginning of the island's colonization. In this case, family relationships often extend well beyond blood ties to include relations of "fictive kinship." Other influences include those of Asian-origin where grandparents, uncles, cousins, and other blood relatives are included in the family model.

Demography becomes particularly important when trying to give a clear and inclusive definition of the concept of family. This is the case because the term family is often paired with the idea of "home" or—demographically speaking—"household," which constitutes an "adequate space for the family's development and well-being, functioning to center its activities" (Benítez 2003: 3). This definition considers the basic element of the home (*"hogar"*) to be shared residency and a common budget among members. However, the concept of family in Cuba extends far beyond the physical space of a particular home—and even at times the criteria of blood ties—being a much more extensive and complex social structure.

Gender roles and sexuality are important variables in any family acting as important factors in its social configuration. Gender and sexuality are also conditioned by traditions and culture. In the Cuban case, this is a culture that is deeply male chauvinist and sexist (*machista-sexista*) that subordinates the female members to male control; a trait transmitted over generations and even by females.

Tradition has shaped the guidelines for behavior of each sex. The ideology of *machismo* (masculinity) teaches that the natural, proper, socially accepted role for men is that of the strong, tough, stubborn individual, predetermined to lead, who controls the family economy, makes all major decisions, and whose space of dominance and movement extends to the "street." Meanwhile, the feminine ideal (sometimes referred to as *marianismo*, or like the Virgin Mary, aka, *María*) is that of the sweet and obedient individual who is an exemplary mother, economically and socially subordinated to the male, and ready to satisfy the sexual needs of her partner and fulfill the domestic chores with abnegation and self-sacrifice. Of course, such an ideal limits the movement of the female to the private space of the "home," excluding the male-dominated public space of the "street." As a result, there has been an historical rejection of anything that violates these cultural patterns, including male or female homosexuality and any manifestation of female independence.

In actual social practice, this "ideal" structure has been gradually modified giving way to a relatively high-level autonomy for Cuban women, especially relative to that experienced by women in the rest of Latin America and the Caribbean. However, at the family level many of these patterns stubbornly remain in place, especially in the area of expectations about household chores, duties, and obligations. That is, while Cuban women have enjoyed great advances in legal and social equality—especially after the triumph of the revolution—the high levels of education and entry en masse into the labor force and professions has not corresponded with a lightening of their burden at home. Males benefit from this double standard, while women often suffer from a double work day. Similarly, marital infidelity is a widely accepted characteristic in males, while it is considered a serious flaw in females.

The Cuban Family Today

In the past half-century, a succession of dramatic socioeconomic and political transformations have taken place that have had important impacts on the structure and composition of the Cuban family. The establishment of a new social order in January 1959 initially brought with it a series of populist measures which, on the one hand, enabled undeniable achievements including the incorporation of women into the labor force, the virtual elimination of unemployment, and an increase in the creation of a skilled workforce, among other gains. On the other hand, this new revolutionary order imposed other changes to Cuban society including a radical upending of previous relations of property and politics, resulting in a continuous process of emigration. This loss of population—comprising nearly 20 percent of the island's population and hailing from different sectors of society for a variety of reasons over time—has fragmented many families, resulting in their reconfiguration.

The 1960s and 1970s were years of increase in the birth rate and a subsequent demographic boom. Guaranteed legal protections for mothers together with the creation and development of a nationwide program of free government daycare centers for the children of working women helped them become incorporated into the labor force. Because of a simultaneous expansion in access to education, many women were also able to find employment in areas where they had previously little or no access. This was a time of confrontation between Cuba's age-old patterns of *machismo*—still predominant in many areas of the population—and a surge in progressive ideas about women's liberation. Despite demonstrable gains the ideas of full independence and equality for women have still not achieved a definitive triumph.

From a legal standpoint, the norms established in 1975's historic Family Code—still in place today—were truly revolutionary in that they specifically required both partners to take responsibility for household chores and childcare, regardless of whether or not one or both of them work outside the home. Clause 24 of the Family Code, defined marriage as being "constituted on the basis of equal rights and duties of both partners." Then, Clause 27, clarified what this principle would mean in practice:

Both spouses are obligated to contribute toward satisfying the needs of faculties and economic capacities. Nevertheless, if one of the spouses contributes only through his or her work in the home and child-care, the other spouse must provide full economic support *without this meaning that he or she be relieved of the obligations of cooperating with the housework and child-care.* (Family Code 1975: 25, emphasis added)

At the same time, the Family Code defined the socialist concept of the family as:

"an entity in which social and personal interests are both present and intimately interrelated. This is the case because—as basic building block of society—the family contributes to social development and serves important functions in the formation of new generations. Furthermore, as the center for the formation of life's relationships, shared by a woman and man, along with their children, and all their relatives, the family satisfies deep human, emotional, and social interests of each person. (Family Code 1975: 6–7)

As this quotation makes clear, such a legal definition of family responds directly to the interests of the socialist ideology in power (with the mention of the "formation of new generations," for example), while also maintaining the patriarchal father-mother-children structure as the foundation of society and the legal structure of the family. Here, the "formation of new generations" means that raising children in the image of Che Guevara's "new man" is given priority and the force of law.

Two contradictory trends occurred during the following decades which directly affected family values. First, during the 1980s, women became incorporated into the labor force and universities at their highest levels in history. Then, during the 1990s, following the collapse of socialism in Eastern Europe, previous gains eroded as an unprecedented economic crisis forcefully brought back to the surface past ills once considered obsolete: prostitution and corruption became survival mechanisms, both of which encouraged women to quit their jobs and abandon their studies.

In general, there is a pronounced tendency for couples to begin living together from a very early age. Additionally, legal marriage constitutes the most prevalent form of union, fundamentally in urban areas. However, there is a high rate of divorce that has increased since the 1970s (Benítez 2003). Moreover, juvenile marriages, early pregnancy, and elective abortions have also occurred at very high rates. To all this must be added young couples' lack of preparation for marriage and life as a couple. On top of this are the difficulties of running a stable household in the midst of a chronic economic crisis and an anemic housing situation where it is not uncommon to find three generations of a family forced to share the same house. All these challenges cannot but affect marital stability and—in the long run—the strength of the Cuban family structure itself. Abortion is free and legal in Cuba. This allows women to freely control their fertility. However, among the young the use of contraceptives is not common, leading directly to a higher abortion rate as many women use abortion as a substitute for contraceptives. Sex education continues to be sorely lacking in most educational programs and discussing sex openly is still a taboo within many Cuban families, especially in rural areas. Finally, deciding and dealing with the potential conception of a child is still something left up to young women, with little input from their partner or family.

Marked characteristics of the contemporary Cuban family—in line with global trends—are the reduced number of children, the aging of its members, and the preeminence of its nuclear structure. There is also a rise in the proportion of female-headed households even while male-headed households continue to be in the majority. Another contemporary trend, also in line with wider global trends, is the growth of free unions and common-law marriages. However, in Cuba this phenomenon is more than a simple matter of the exercise of a couple's freewill or a way to give a legal marriage a "test run." Instead, these free unions are more often a practical solution to chronic material difficulties and marital instability.

GENDER

When discussing gender, a usual reference is made to the women's movement for equal rights, gender rights, and against discrimination, since those struggles are all interrelated. There is indeed a long history of women's participation in the political and social movements for change in Cuba. However, that activism has almost always been characterized by the subordination of women to defined, traditional roles, within organizations headed by men. The 20th century struggles for women's rights in Cuba have precedents going back to the 19th century struggle for emancipation and independence. During those struggles, a number of upper- and middle-class female intellectuals—some of whom were educated in Europe—transgressed the traditional norms long established for women. Some of these women—the most notable example of whom was the proto-feminist writer Gertrudis Gómez de Avellaneda (1814–1873)—were able to express their convictions about freedom and equality through literature. Others participated in the independence wars of the second half of the nineteenth century as spies, messengers, nurses, soldiers, or by donating their personal fortunes to the cause. Ana Betancourt, who participated in the first Constituent Assembly in arms of 1969, was the first Cuban woman to speak out in favor of women's liberation from a legal point of view when she proposed that it be recognized by the laws of the Republic.

In the second Cuban War of Independence (1895–1898) women played an ever greater and more direct role. For example, the Cuban Revolutionary Party (PRC) founded in 1892 by José Martí to organize and lead the war, had 49 women's clubs by 1897 making up 25 percent of the total PRC membership. However, the delegates representing these clubs were always men (Stoner 2003: 44–47). Other women of the time distinguished themselves by bringing the ideas of Cuban nationalism and women's liberation into the field of education. Such was the case of the teacher María Luisa Dolz, who is considered the first modern Cuban feminist (González Pages 2003). However, Cuba's history books tend to emphasize the role these women played as "heroic mothers" who gave their children for the cause freedom or as selfless wives who followed the example of their husbands—the true protagonists of history—into the rigors of life on the battlefront (Caballero 1982). Thus, Cuban women arrived in the Republican period at the start of the 20th century without many great achievements. Their subordination to male decisions continued, but having shown their mettle alongside their male counterparts during the war, many women entered the new century having also gained an awareness of their own capabilities. This prepared the ground for the struggle for women's rights to come.

Advances for Women during the Republic

In contrast to the feminist movements that developed during the 20th century in countries like the United States—where greater emphasis was given to women's political mobilization and participation—struggles for women's rights in Cuba tended to focus on the importance of motherhood and the woman's role within the family. The aims of the women's movement in Cuba were not predicated on gaining the same rights and social roles as men, but on attaining greater social space, work opportunities, and social security for mothers, as well as advocating for the implementation of poverty reduction programs (Stoner 2003). Far from disputing the traditional dominance of men in certain social spaces, Cuban feminists aspired to widen and improve the spaces traditionally associated with women. Nevertheless, between 1923 and 1940, Cuban feminist groups prevailed upon the island's political leaders to support legislation in favor of greater women's rights. Already in 1919, Cuban women had achieved the same literacy rate as men. Then, during the 1920s an equal proportion of women graduated from Cuban universities as did women in the United States—a global leader in women's liberation (ibid.: 184).

As in the 19th century, middle- and upper-class women were the leaders of Cuba's feminist movement during the Republic. They also founded many different associations and publications to advance the interests of women. Some of these groups were established with the purpose of affecting deep social reforms, others limited their focus to winning women the right to vote, and still others stand out for their mainly cultural and intellectual orientation. These latter groups tended to argue that it was impossible to affect radical changes in women's place in society without first raising their level of education and culture. One prominent organization was the *Unión Laborista de Mujeres* (Women's Labor Confederation), an association that placed the struggle for better labor rights and protections for Cuba's working-class women above the fight to win women the right to vote (Castellanos 2011).

In this period, there was an increase in women's activism directed at influencing Cuban legislation. There was also an outpouring of activity on many fronts in pursuit of legal, labor, health, and educational rights. For example, alliances were established with an array of groups headed by men, street demonstrations for suffrage took place, and women spread their ideas in newspapers and took to the airwaves of Cuba's many radio stations to advance their cause. Additionally, women mobilized to demand that obstetrics clinics be built, night classes offered, and special health programs developed—all to meet women's needs. Cuba's feminist groups also made formal contacts with their counterparts abroad (ibid.). All this activity culminated in 1914, when debates began about the possibility of establishing the legal right to divorce in Cuba. In 1916, a bill guaranteeing married women the right to control their property was presented. It was approved two years later in May 1918—the same year in which divorce was legalized.

Despite all this, during this time the great legislative victories on women's rights were driven more by the economic and political interests of those in power rather than by feminist groups' own fight for emancipation or as a result of the existence of a social consciousness about the need for women's rights. Laws were modified under the premise of separating the Catholic Church from the state. This came about primarily due to economic interests related to property and inheritance rights which, until then, women had lost upon marriage. Still, the mobilizations organized by feminist activists helped to modify both civil and property laws, which would now give legal force to women's position within the family. All this amounted to a significant advance in Cuban women's rights as compared to the situation in other countries in the region.

In 1923, the First National Congress of Women was celebrated with representatives from 31 women's associations across the island. The event's objectives were the creation of new opportunities for women and to debate problems that had a particular impact on the family, society, and nation. Once again, the meeting's agenda did not include a frontal assault on patriarchy (male dominance of society) as the origin of women's oppression, continuing to limit the discussion to women's traditional role as wife and mother in order to achieve their goals. The most important of these goals was "the general recognition that motherhood was women's divine right and that it justified their exercising political authority in nationalist Cuba" (Stoner 2003: 29). In 1925, women celebrated their Second National Congress—this time with the participation of 71 associations.

The big achievement of this gathering was the promise by then recently elected president Gerardo Machado to extend the right to vote to women during his presidency (ibid.: 102–103). Once in power, however, Machado broke his promise and the issue of female suffrage was added to the political agenda of the political opposition. The Congress was also noteworthy as it produced a rift between an accommodationist tendency and a group of women who made more radical demands. In sum, the political goal of winning the right to vote—favored by one part of the feminist movement—became the bargaining chip that would keep in check the more radical demands of full justice and equality, thus allowing the political interests of powerful male-headed groups to prevail.

Nevertheless, in spite of the limitations imposed on women by their age-old subjugation to the wishes of men, this was a period in which women "were capable of articulating a new model for social relations that would afford more authority and respect to women, and they were in a position to project an image of the emancipated woman" (ibid.: 123). As a result, new movements and women's groups emerged in the following years claiming important civil rights such as the eight-hour workday and paid maternity leave.

In 1933, after President Gerardo Machado was ousted, women's organizations began to pressurize the revolutionary Grau-Guiteras government for the right to vote that had been a legislative dead letter ever since Ana Betancourt first proposed it in the 19th century. In 1934, a provisional constitution was approved, which finally formally recognized women's suffrage. Article 38 of this draft Constitution declared: "All Cubans of both sexes have the right to vote according to conditions and exceptions as determined by law." In 1939, upon the celebration of the Third National Congress of Women the group demanded "a Constitutional guarantee for equal rights of women"—essentially a Cuban version of the U.S. Equal Rights Amendment but coming 30 years before the U.S. movement of the 1970s (Stoner 2003: 259). This demand was discussed during the Constituent Assembly of that year and finally recognized in Article 97 of the 1940 Constitution: "Universal, equal, and secret suffrage is established as a right, duty, and function of all Cuban citizens" (Pichardo 1980: 349). In contrast to the normally conservative nature of the island's feminist movement, Cuban women had attained the vote and the right to be elected for public office before their North American counterparts.

Even though the 1940 Constitution declared the equality of all Cubans before Law, with Article 20 stating that "any discrimination by reason of sex, race, color, or class and any other kind of discrimination destructive of human dignity, is declared illegal and punishable," no complementary bills were enacted to implement these principles. Thus, these legal rights attained on paper represented the final goal of the Cuban feminist movement, supposedly guaranteeing gender equality. However, Cuban women continued to suffer from a state of profound economic and social subordination to men, in whose hands remained all political and judicial power. The theoretical "equality" of the sexes guaranteed by the Constitution amounted to little more than window dressing on a dead letter in the face of the demands and priorities of a traditionally *machista* society.

From that moment forward, the majority of Cuba's feminist clubs and organizations put aside any political demands in order to dedicate themselves to social assistance programs that addressed the daily needs of women, children, and charity institutions. After women achieved the vote, "capturing that vote in successive elections became a priority for all of Cuba's political parties, which henceforth included women's demands in their political programs in an often cynical attempt to tip the electoral balance against their rivals at the polls" (Holgado Fernández 2000: 263). The relative autonomy that characterized the feminist movement during previous years was replaced with subordination to the interests of male-dominated political parties, resulting in a loss of feminist consciousness and a step backward in the movement for gender equality. Still, despite these losses and the failure to implement the positive language of the Constitution, Cuba's Republican period witnessed important advances in the struggle for full equality, including the right to vote, to own and control property, and to paid maternity leave (even if it specifically excluded domestic workers and farm workers); the recognition of the rights of "illegitimate" children; and a gradual increase in women's labor rights.

The 1959 Revolution and the End of the Cuban Feminist Movement

A brief look at the revolutionary movement which seized power in 1959 reveals that from the very beginning and throughout its entire process, women remained in a subordinate position vis-à-vis the male leadership. In its initial programs, the revolution did not include any proposal that specifically favored women's emancipation. Indeed, no women participated in devising the revolution's policies, nor was there a demand from women that the revolution prioritize the social objectives and aspirations of women. This is true despite the fact that by that point women had already achieved significant representation in the workplace and educational institutions, including in Cuban universities. By the end of the armed struggle—in which many females participated—not a single woman had achieved the rank of *comandante* (major). This contrasts with the high ranks and prestige enjoyed by many of the females who participated in the 19th-century wars of independence (Castellanos 2011).

The female presence in the Sierra Maestra only followed the traditional—and extremely sexist—established patterns. Women were subordinated to the decisions of the overwhelmingly male revolutionary leadership and were typically relegated to roles that echoed the patriarchal model, with women performing domestic functions and submitting to male decisions, only this time in the context of a military camp. This paternalistic and patriarchal dynamic was maintained once the rebels took state power. No woman was appointed to a senior administrative position in the new government, nor has any been entrusted with major political responsibilities during the past half-century, up to and including the current government of Raúl Castro. This is the case even though female revolutionaries took part in the armed struggle and played a key role in the urban resistance in support of the armed resistance in the mountains.

The massive mobilization of women—20,000 signatures were collected and presented to the Senate—to demand the release of the imprisoned rebels who had attacked the Moncada Barracks in 1953 proved crucial in the Batista government's eventual decision to grant them amnesty. Fidel Castro perfectly understood the power of enlisting the active support and participation of women in the revolutionary struggle. That is why a female front within the 26th of July Movement—the so-called Mariana Grajales Female Battalion—was created in 1958. However, it was headed not by a woman, but by Castro himself. Of course, there had long been a small group of female protagonists within the 26th of July Movement, led by Haydée Santamaría, Celia Sánchez, and Vilma Espín. However, despite the bravery and intelligence they demonstrated both during and after the war, none of these three women had any power or authority independent from the male-dominated revolutionary leadership. In fact, the power and authority that each did enjoy was largely derived from their intimate relationships with the leading men and martyrs of the revolution. Haydée Santamaría was the sister of the fallen Abel Santamaría; Celia Sánchez was Fidel's confidante and intimate; and Vilma Espín eventually became Raúl Castro's wife.

Following the rebel victory, the *Unión Femenina Revolucionaria* (Women's Revolutionary Union) was created, later renamed the Federation of Cuban Women (FMC, described in Chapter 3). From its very creation—through a decree by Fidel Castro—the principal objective of the FMC was to encourage the participation of women in the political, economic, and social life of the country, always under the condition of fealty toward the revolution and the new socialist ideology. "The FMC has described itself as a 'feminine,' not a 'feminist' organization," writes the Spanish anthropologist Isabel Holgado Fernández, "given that feminism was considered to be a social movement that distracted effort and attention away from the revolutionary struggle, apart from being an ideology of the 'idle bourgeoisie'" (Holgado Fernández 2000: 269). At the same time, all preexisting women's organizations were *de*-mobilized and dismantled to undercut interest group autonomy and deactivate any political tendencies that differed from those established by the new political leadership. No women, including ones who had held prominent positions during the war, were considered for important, decision-making posts in the new government. Only one woman briefly held the office of minister of education, and Vilma Espín, Raúl Castro's new wife and therefore Fidel Castro's sister-in-law, was tapped to head the FMC, a post she held from the organization's creation until her death in 2007.

The revolution aimed to achieve the massive incorporation of virtually all Cuban women into the FMC. However, this aspiration quickly met with the resistance of supposedly revolutionary men who continued to insist that a woman's proper place was in the private sphere of the home, in front of the stove and taking care of her husband and children; not in the street's public sphere. Nevertheless, the majority of Cuban women eventually became members and by 1995 the organization could boast 3.5 million "*federadas*," 82 percent of Cuba's female population.

Although in the beginning the FMC's members were indeed motivated by their sympathy with the revolution and its goals, their support for the organization and of the revolution itself has gradually become more of a formality; an obligatory public lip-service that rarely reflects their true feelings or priorities. Membership has also been attributed to the fear of subtle punishments for refusing to participate, while opportunism also plays a role. To the extent that membership in the FMC implies the acceptance of the status quo—public identification as a "revolutionary woman"—it also affords members access to certain jobs and other small advantages such as ensuring a place for one's children in a free, state-run child care facility. At the same time, membership is not always elective since many women are automatically enlisted as members upon their 14th birthday without their consent. Over time, however, membership has become more restrictive, providing benefits only to those who pay their monthly dues. These women are rewarded, in turn, with positive evaluations when it comes to applying for a certain job, entering a particular course of study, or joining other organizations of power, such as the Communist Party.

Thus, the possibility of an autonomous women's movement became engulfed in the supposed collective ideology of the revolution, with women's priorities subordinated to the political interests of the government and subject to the male-dominated system enthroned in power. Once the institutions of civil society that developed during the Republic were done away with, women found themselves at the mercy of the will of the state, which in its paternalist, *machista* fashion transformed them into a social transmission belt for its ideology. It remains ironic that, while women's organizations lost all political autonomy, by the turn of the century women held more than 60 percent of the country's technical and professional jobs. On the other hand, nearly every position of political leadership is occupied by a man.

As much as anything else, this illustrates the continued dominance of an ideology of *machismo* that continues to discriminate against women giving the lie to the supposed "achievements" of women under the revolution. These gains have always been paternalistically granted to women by men in power. In this sense, there remains a long road ahead until the achievement of the true liberation and full social equality of Cuban women. Despite their supposed emancipation by the revolution, the fact is that Cuban women continue to be subject to a hidden but no less powerful form of discrimination under the slogan of a false egalitarianism (Astelarra 2005).

Since the start of a series of economic reforms under the government of Raúl Castro that legalized the small-scale private sector in fits and starts after 2008, it has become evident that men far outnumber women as the owners and entrepreneurs behind these microenterprises. This trend illustrates the continued disadvantage faced by women in this emerging business sector. So far, there are no public policies aimed at ensuring equal opportunities for women in this sector. Furthermore, with the absence of a true feminist movement, Cuban women find themselves among those with the greatest civil vulnerability. There is no autonomy without democracy, especially in the midst of poverty and destitution. The full emancipation of women also demands full civic responsibility. The large number of females within the ranks of Cuban dissidents and among the groups that make up Cuba's emergent, alternative civil society (described in Chapters 3 and 7) hints at a greater consciousness of the need for gender equality in the future. However, only the restoration of democracy can enable the emergence of a vital and independent women's movement in the future.

BIBLIOGRAPHY

Astelarra, Judith. 2005. *¿Libres e iguales? Sociedad y política desde el feminismo.* Havana: Editorial Ciencias Sociales.

Benítez, María E. 2003. *La familia cubana en la segunda mitad del siglo XX. Cambios sociodemográficos.* Havana: Colección Sociología, Editorial Ciencias Sociales.

Caballero, Armando O. 1982. *La mujer en el '95.* Havana: Editorial Gente Nueva.

Casal, Lourdes. 1989. "Race Relations in Contemporary Cuba." In Philip Brenner, William M. LeoGrande, Donna Rich, and Daniel Siegel, eds., *The Cuba Reader: The Making of a Revolutionary Society*. New York: Grove Press.

Castelanos, Dimas Cecilio. 2011. *Desentrañando claves* (unpublished manuscript). Havana.

Conde, Yvonne. 2000. *Operation Pedro Pan: The Untold Exodus of 14,048 Cuban Children*. New York: Routledge.

De la Campa, Román. 2000. *Cuba on My Mind: Journeys to a Severed Nation*. New York: Verso.

Family Code (Código de Familia de la República de Cuba). 1987. Ministry of Justice. In effect from March 8, 1975, with annotations by the Ministry of Justice, October 15.

González Pagés, Julio César. 2003. *En busca de un espacio: Historia de mujeres en Cuba*. Havana: Pinos Nuevos, Ediciones de Ciencias Sociales.

Holgado Fernández, Isabel. 2000. *¡No es fácil! Mujeres cubanas y la crisis revolucionaria*. Barcelona: Editorial Icaria-Antrazyt.

Pichardo, Hortensia. 1980. *Documentos para la historia de Cuba*, vol. IV, part II. Havana: Editorial de Ciencias Sociales.

Sobre el pleno ejercicio de la igualdad de la mujer. Tesis y Resoluciones. 1975. Havana: Primer Congreso del PCC.

Stoner, K. Lynn. 2003. *De la casa a la calle. El movimiento cubano de la mujer en favor de la reforma legar (1898–1940)*. Madrid: Editorial Colibrí.

Education

Miriam Celaya

HISTORICAL ANTECEDENTS

A full analysis of education in Cuba must begin with a brief reference to its historical antecedents. The origins of Cuban pedagogy (educational instruction) go back to the turn of the 18th century, years closely related to the formation of Cuban cultural identity and thought. This began when European Enlightenment ideas—reinterpreted within the insular context of Cuba by the island's leading Creole thinkers of the time—definitively transformed the island's educational system and philosophy. This change laid the groundwork for what would later become a solid culture of pedagogy aimed decisively at the consolidation of *cubanidad* (Cubanness). The most celebrated foundational pillars of this culture of pedagogy—which would continue to resonate well into the 20th century—were a group of intuitions that included the *Sociedad Económica de Amigos del País* (Economic Society of Friends of the Country), the Patriotic Society, the University of Saint Jerome in Havana, and the Seminary of Saint Charles and Saint Ambrose (the final two of which were Catholic institutions operating under royal Spanish license). Working at these institutions, as well as at the University of Havana itself, were an important group of educational innovators including the priests José Agustín Caballero and Félix Varela, and the educator and philosopher José de la Luz y Caballero (to clarify, José Agustín Caballero is a different person than José de la Luz y Caballero).

As early as the late 18th century, José Agustín Caballero was already promoting a program of educational reform that included such advances as the universalization of free elementary education and educational access for women. For his part, Father Félix Varela was the first Cuban to use the word *patria* (homeland) when referring to Cuba with a sense of rootedness and belonging; as a community with shared interests and a common national spirit. He was also a supporter of independence and an abolitionist, who consciously "chose education as the path to liberation, tracing his own route in Cuban thought and, in turn, striving to teach us to think. He was the one who introduced ethical considerations into scientific, social, and political studies (Castellanos 2011: 28). Finally, José de la Luz y Caballero is considered the father of Cuban pedagogy. He placed Cuban education on par with the most advanced humanist and universal thinking of his time. He saw education as a necessary path toward the achievement of civic virtues. He considered the vocation of teaching one of the highest and most honored, which he expressed in the following often quoted aphorism: "*Instruir puede cualquiera; educar sólo quien sea un evangelio vivo*" (Anyone can instruct; but only those who are a living gospel can educate).

EDUCATION DURING THE REPUBLICAN PERIOD: GREAT ACHIEVEMENTS AND GREAT INEQUALITY

Already during the first years of the Republican period (1902–1958), Enrique José Varona, an educator and politician, led an important series of educational reforms. His work in the Department of Public Education during the first American intervention (1898–1902) was focused on totally reinventing the Cuban educational system from the elementary level up to the universities. In his educational philosophy, he rejected revolutionary violence as a method to address social ills and considered the university an autonomous civic space that should act as a forge for national democracy. Partly as a result of Varona's work, public education gradually became widespread, and as it extended the kinds of instruction diversified. A large number of schools that focused on general education emerged, as did teaching schools. For example, Cuba's so-called Normal Schools produced primary school teachers after a four-year course of study, while teachers at higher levels were required to take pedagogical courses at the university level. There were also both secular and religious vocational-technological and business schools. Apart from the over 100-year-old University of Havana, two new Cuban universities were founded during this time: the University of Oriente located in Santiago de Cuba and Santa Clara's Marta Abreu Central University.

By the mid-1940s numerous public and private educational institutions had emerged on the island. Still, there continued to be a marked imbalance in educational quality and access in urban areas relative to rural ones. Most schools were located in cities, with a majority in the country's capital, Havana. Despite these chronic inequities, by the end of the 1950s Cuba had one of the lowest illiteracy indexes in the Western Hemisphere. In fact, Cuba's 1953 illiteracy rate of 23.6 percent placed it above Spain and many other countries that are among the most developed in the world today. Of course, rural areas were in a considerably less favorable position, with a 42 percent illiteracy rate. This contrasted starkly with the 12 percent rate in urban areas. In fact, 31 percent of those six years of age or older who could read and write had never attended school at all, while another 58 percent had completed between one and six years of schooling. Only 11 percent of Cuba's literate population had attended school for seven years or more (Espinosa Chepe and Henken 2013, this volume; Mesa-Lago 2011). Finally, within Cuba's classrooms there was a high rate of educational lag, which meant that many students were two or more years beyond the intended age for the grade they were in. This resulted in a high dropout rate among these students, including those still in primary school. This educational lag and school desertion was also influenced by the pressure for the children of poor families to join the workforce to help support their families.

Moreover, the prerevolutionary educational system produced an imbalance in which available training did not respond to the labor needs of the country. Administrative corruption had also become chronic. For example, in the 1940s and 1950s, administrative costs absorbed as much as 20 percent of the educational budget, while only 4 percent was set aside for vocational and technical training. Additionally, in 1956, despite pouring 23 percent of the national budget into education, only 6 percent of the population received a secondary education and just 2 percent had attended college. In the mid-1950s, more than half of the population had less than a fourth-grade education, and just 1 percent held a university degree. Finally, among those with degrees, there was a vast overemphasis on law, while training in scientific, technical, and engineering fields was neglected. In fact, the 1953 census counted just 309 engineers, 355 veterinarians, and 294 agronomists, while the country was flooded with 6,500 lawyers (Ripton 2002: 279).

EDUCATION DURING THE REVOLUTIONARY PERIOD: INSTITUTIONALIZED VOLUNTARISM

When the revolution took power in January 1959, it brought with it a radical transformation of the educational system. Among the most far-reaching measures taken by the new government was the Nationalization of Education Law (June 6, 1961), which outlawed all forms of private and religious education and established a free, nationwide public education system in their place. Scores of foreign teachers were deported, especially the many Spanish priests and nuns who had taught at the country's parochial schools. Moreover, all institutions of private education, including their properties, equipment, and assets, were taken over by the state, which has exercised absolute control over all teaching and educational programs ever since. With the goal of open access in mind, at least 1,100 new schools were built and training programs established to prepare new teachers for a new kind of pedagogy (described later). As a result of these and other reforms, between 1959 and 1971 primary school enrollment jumped from 811,000 to 1.7 million. More startling was the jump in the badly neglected secondary and higher educational enrollments. Between 1959 and 1986, secondary enrollment grew from just 88,000 to 1.2 million. Likewise, university enrollment grew from 26,000 in 1966 to 269,000 by 1986 (Díaz-Briquets 2002: 145).

The 1961 Literacy Campaign

In 1961, the revolutionary government organized a massive literacy campaign aimed at eradicating illiteracy in Cuba once and for all. To achieve this ambitious goal, tens of thousands of young people from all educational levels, regions, and walks of life were mobilized to bring literacy to the country's neglected areas, including even the most humble, remote, and hardest to access corners of the island. Many of these young people, barely adolescents themselves, left their homes usually in urban areas for the first time to teach mostly rural families to read and write, sharing their rustic living conditions and arduous workdays. According to Armando Hart, the secretary of education in those days, perhaps 300,000 *brigadistas* (literacy instructors) took part in the campaign, more than half of whom were women, with a total of 120,000 adolescents.

The manual used by the *brigadistas* to teach their students to read and write was intended to serve instructors as both a "technical and political guide." Meanwhile, the primer used by the students contained "24 subjects related to basic revolutionary matters, including the definitions of the key words to be used" (García Galló 1961: 69–81). In other words, beyond the genuine altruism that motivated most *brigadistas* to—in the words of state propaganda at the time—"bring the light of teaching to the most isolated corners of Cuba," the literacy campaign had as its central objective the

On April 16, 2011, as part of the 50th anniversary of Cuba's victory against U.S.-backed Cuban exile forces at the Bay of Pigs, Cuba also celebrated the 50th anniversary of its 1961 literacy campaign. This young Cuban parader proudly wears a commemorative uniform of the Conrado Benítez Literacy Brigade. (Ted Henken)

THE 1961 LITERACY CAMPAIGN AND ITS *BRIGADISTAS*

Perhaps the most significant and certainly the most symbolic educational achievement in the revolution's early years was the literacy campaign of 1961. The mass mobilization began in December 1960, when the new government announced an all-out "War on Illiteracy," officially christening 1961 the "Year of Education." Although as optimistic as President Johnson's similarly named "War on Poverty," Cuba's literacy campaign truly captured the imagination of the country's youth. By April of 1961, as many as 120,000 young, idealistic literacy workers, known as *brigadistas*, began to penetrate the long-neglected reaches of the island, armed with the catechism of reading and writing. These literacy volunteers wore uniforms and carried with them signature blue and red oil lamps to light their way through the countryside, chanting the campaign's slogan, *Alfabetizando Venceremos* ("through literacy we shall overcome"). As pro-revolutionary influences on their peasant pupils, *brigadistas* encouraged their newly literate students to pen "Dear Fidel" letters to the revolution's *comandante en jefe*, thanking him personally with their newly acquired literacy skills.

pro-government political indoctrination of the great mass of Cuba's working class and peasant population, not to mention that of the *brigadistas* themselves.

If judged based on available statistics on literacy, however, the campaign can be said to have been an unmitigated success. While the previously cited 1953 literacy rate of 23.6 percent had already begun to fall, reaching 21 percent by 1959, by 1970 it had dropped again almost by half to 12.9 percent. This is the case even if the government got ahead of itself claiming to have virtually "eradicated" illiteracy in the 1961 campaign, supposedly reducing it to 3.9 percent. By 1989, 30 years after the start of the revolution, Cuba had indeed just about reached that number with the island's illiteracy rate reduced to just 4 percent. The latest figures from 2005 report a steady march toward virtual eradication of illiteracy indeed, with the adult literacy rate reaching 99.8 percent (Mesa-Lago 2011: 52, 59).

Mass Mobilization Campaigns and Educational Experiments: Education or Indoctrination?

The literacy campaign was only the first—and easily the most popular—in a long series of mass mobilizations promoted by the new government. It earned the revolutionary leadership a great reserve of political capital, even if it had great economic and social costs, the magnitude of which has still not been full calculated. This marked the beginning of a fateful experience that would repeat itself again and again in the future given the chronic insufficiency of educators: improvised teachers prepared through crash courses who went to work without receiving the necessary pedagogical training. Moreover, during the 1960s, the ideological bent that would characterize the Cuban educational system in the coming years became increasingly evident. Because the number of teachers was insufficient to meet rising demand, the government responded with the attempt to create a new kind of teacher. This would be someone capable of responding to the revolutionary government's ideological need to promote the birth of a "new man" after the image of the brave guerrillas who fought in the Sierra Maestra during the armed struggle. This, in turn, led to the creation of rugged, militaristic pedagogical schools, some of which were located—for both symbolic and practical reasons—in the isolated reaches of the Sierra Maestra itself (Ferrer 1963).

Among the government's first pedagogical experiments was the gathering of student teachers—its future revolutionary teachers—in new schools in mountainous areas after the closure of the Normal Schools of the 1950s (Hart 1963). These new schools for elementary teachers were designed to inculcate a new crop of teachers with revolutionary plans and programs. They were purposely built far away from city centers and under the strict regimen of a boarding school. Students would first study for a year at Minas del Frío, in the middle of the Sierra Maestra, followed by four more years at Topes de Collantes, in the Escambray mountain range, all under nearly *guerrilla* conditions. These students were trained not only in classroom pedagogy, but also through hard physical conditioning. Such training included overcoming the privations of long mountain marches and facing the rigors of inclement weather, all while living away from their families as if in a military camp. Teachers were expected to be as tenacious and tough as *guerrilla* fighters, and to inculcate the same martial spirit in their students.

At the same time, the first plans for the training of a new contingent of emergent teachers were created. Known as "*Maestros Voluntarios*" (voluntary teachers), the idea was that these elementary teachers could be trained in just four months in camps also located in the Sierra Maestra. In urban areas, a different plan was put into place for the training of these so-called *Maestros Populares* (popular teachers), which envisioned creating elementary school teachers out of young recruits with just six years of education themselves. Later on, plans were put into place for the improvement and recertification of these teachers, thus allowing for a gradual rise in the professional level of these teachers who had been first trained under the urgent conditions of the "emergent" programs. Despite these deficiencies, between 1960 and 1963 the revolutionary government had achieved an amazing feat: a guaranteed elementary education up to the sixth grade to the entire Cuban school-age population. UNESCO has estimated that under normal conditions the achievement of such an ambitious goal would take a period of at least 10 years.

During the 1970s, more specialized teaching schools arose but always conceived in the martial spirit of fighting "battles" and fielding "contingents" that has been the trademark of the educational programs promoted by the government. For example, the "Manuel Ascunce" Pedagogical Contingent and the "Salvador Allende" School for the Formation of Primary Teachers were intended for the training of high-school and middle-school teachers, respectively. The "Enrique José Varona" Advanced Pedagogical Institute was established at the end of the 1970s to train teachers with a higher educational level, receiving specialized training in all branches of instruction. With the help of subsidies and scientific, technical, and educational cooperation agreements with the Soviet Union and the other countries of the former Communist Bloc, thousands of specialists were trained both in Cuba and abroad at the technical or university level. Additionally, thousands of technicians and foreign

---

LAS ESCUELAS AL CAMPO AND OPERATION "PEDRO PAN"

The Cuban educational system has sought to ensure universal access, erase socioeconomic distinctions, and combine work and study. As such, countryside boarding schools (*escuelas al campo*) were set up for children to be sent for 30 to 45 days each year to perform agricultural labor. Boarding or "scholarship" schools (*la beca*) were also established where children would spend the entire school year, allowing their parents to dedicate their free time to the revolution. Since the educational priorities of the revolution emphasized both social justice and political indoctrination, Cuban families reacted differently to them. Some embraced the new educational opportunities while others feared that the government would socialize their children in communism and divide their families. These parents saw the new boarding school system as an attack on their parental rights. They also feared that Castro would ship Cuban children off to be educated in the Soviet Union. Some parents reacted by sending their children into exile in the United States with help from the Catholic Church and the U.S. government (Díaz-Briquets 2002: 146; Torres 2003). Dubbed Operation *Pedro Pan*, after the storybook character Peter Pan, more than 14,000 unaccompanied children were sent into exile in the early 1960s under this program (Conde 2000; de la Campa 2000).

---

specialists visited Cuba to impart their expertise, helping raise the qualifications of Cuban professionals.

The radical renovation of the Cuban educational system was aimed above all at the creation of the so-called new man. This fascist-inspired idea assumed the moral superiority of the man formed under socialism over that produced by capitalism, who was seen as intrinsically "alienated and dehumanized." To this end, the principle of combining study and work led to the implementation of the Countryside Boarding School Plan (*Plan La Escuela al Campo*) starting in the 1960s. This program required all students at the basic secondary, technical, and preuniversity levels to spend two months each year in agricultural camps where they would work and study. Though this period was later reduced and fixed at 45 days, what began in the 1960s as a voluntary show of revolutionary commitment had become an obligation for all students by the 1971–1972 school year.

At the start of the 1970s, the first full-year boarding schools—often referred to colloquially as *la beca* (the scholarship)—were created. This expanded boarding school system became commonplace for students in secondary, preuniversity, and other technological educational specialties. The first experimental school in this system was named "*Vanguardias de La Habana*" (The Havana Vanguard) and was built between 1971 and 1972 not in Havana but on the far-away Isle of Youth (previously known as the Isle of Pines). As a sign of the extreme voluntarism that guided education at this time, in the following years the Isle of Youth was designated personally by Fidel Castro as the "first communist territory in Cuba." Dozens of other schools were built for both Cubans and international scholarship students from fellow developing nations. It was this concentration of young students that gave the island its new revolutionary name.

The student body of *Vanguardias de La Habana* was made up of high-school students from the capital, serving as the model for an experiment that would soon be spread to the entire country. As with the *escuelas al campo*, these full-year "*beca*" schools began as voluntary opportunities for particularly adventurous, independent, or mature students. However, by the end of the 1980s, attendance became obligatory for students who hoped to continue with preuniversity studies and eventually attend college. Even more so than regular day schools, these boarding schools included the implicit, permanent, and systematic indoctrination of new generations of students in Marxist-Leninist ideas.

This allowed the state to become the new tutor of Cuba's young people, with more authority than their own parents. To facilitate this, new home-schools were built and Cuba's national history was reinvented: the past was done away with and only the revolutionary present could legitimize any sense of justice or rights for Cubans. According to these principles, adolescents were removed from their families and were educated far from the direct attention and influence of their parents. In many cases, this experiment caused an irrevocable rupture between these young people and their families, with a concomitant loss of the values traditionally passed from one generation to the next; from parents to their children. In the same way, the extreme politicization of education, the forced incorporation of young students into these boarding schools, and their obligation to adhere to communist ideology as prerequisites for admission to the university, all nurtured a deep duplicity (*doble moral*) and generalized hypocrisy in Cuban society. As a result, today falseness, feigning, and falsehood have become a fundamental part of the cultural heritage of many generations of Cubans. Such loss of values stands in ironic contrast to the high levels of education reported in official statistics.

Between Quality and Quantity

During the 1980s, many institutions of higher education were established in all of Cuba's provinces. In addition to the three universities that already existed in 1959, many other university satellite campuses, departments, and subsidiaries have been set up in every province as part of the national system of higher education. Nevertheless, Havana continues to be the principal destination for university students on the island today. It is also the place with the most renowned teachers and specialized expertise in Cuba. Apart from the main campus of the University of Havana located at the end of San Lázaro Street on the well-known *Colina Universitaria* (University Hill), between the end of the 1960s and the late 1970s a number of other institutions of higher education were built in the capital to satisfy the increasing demand for advanced and specialized study that characterized the first decades of the revolutionary process. Examples of these new educational centers include the Advanced Institute of Art (ISA) in Cubanacán; the breathtakingly beautiful, but largely abandoned and partially ruined National Schools of Art (ENA) also in Cubanacán; the Polytechnic University (known as CUJAE, or the *Institutio Superior Politécnico José Antonio Echeverría*); a new School of Medicine; and the Advanced Institute of Agricultural Sciences of Havana, as well as the previously mentioned "Enrique José Varona" Advanced Pedagogical Institute.

By the late 1980s, free and mandatory education up to the ninth grade had been extended to every municipality and corner of the island, allowing Cuba to achieve record numbers of university and technical college graduates. However, starting at the end of that decade and worsening since there has been a gradual deterioration in the quality of education, especially at the elementary level. Save for special cases, the repeated implementation of improvised courses for "emergent" teachers without the necessary qualifications combined with the push to sacrifice the quality of education for an ever greater number of graduates has led to a gradual loss of qualifications and expertise among Cuban professionals and technicians in comparison to their counterparts around the world. This tendency has become more evident in recent years as major advances in computer science as well as in information and communications technologies and other scientific and technical innovations around the world have far outpaced Cuba's capabilities placing them out of reach for the vast majority of Cuban students. Despite these limitations, Cuba's educational system managed to provide access to all sectors of its population, especially prioritizing access for historically marginalized social groups (Afro-Cubans, women, the poor, etc.), thereby fostering the belief in education as a right for all, not a privilege for the few.

During the 1990s, after the fall of the Soviet Union and the disappearance of the Communist bloc, the generous subsidies that supported Cuba's educational system vanished. School conditions, especially in rural boarding schools, deteriorated precipitously. The economic crisis that followed led to unprecedented student dropouts and the exodus of teachers in search of more economically viable occupations. For example, the government was forced to cut the state education budget by 38 percent between 1989 and 1997, leading to a severe scarcity in school equipment and materials, as well as the postponing of necessary investments and maintenance. Many students were also discouraged from attending school due to the reduction in transportation and school food. While primary school enrollment declined only slightly during this period, secondary school enrollment fell from 88 percent to 74.5 percent with that of Cuba's universities falling even more precipitously from 23 percent to 12 percent (Mesa-Lago 2011: 52). Scores of countryside boarding and scholarship schools that had been built to foster the creation of the "new man" were closed down and are today in a state of total neglect. The arrival of the so-called special period, the deepest and longest lasting economic crisis in Cuba's history, also put a resounding end to one of the greatest educational experiments ever conceived of by the official megalomania: making Cuba "the most educated country in the world." And this, despite lacking the economic base to sustain such a pharaonic undertaking and while remaining a virtual Soviet protectorate.

EDUCATION IN CUBA TODAY

The current structure of the Cuban educational system is essentially the same as the one established more than five decades ago. Elementary education (grades 1–6) and secondary education (grades 7–9) are obligatory. There is also preuniversity (high-school) education (grades 10–12), vocational, technical, and professional education (three to four years depending on the specialty), special education (for students with physical or mental limitations), special schools for sports, and higher education (which is normally five years). Access to different schools depends on one's rank as achieved at municipal and provincial levels and is based on academic achievement. Admission to vocational schools in each province that specialize in exact sciences is gained through competitive entrance examinations. Some intermediate and advanced specializations—as is the case with the fine and performing arts—require applicants to pass an aptitude test. Meanwhile, a number of courses of study such as journalism, law, and computer science at university level only accept students who are proven "revolutionaries." This means that over and above any academic requirements, accepted students must support the party and government position on all political issues.

Facing the collapse of what was once a solid and well-developed educational system, the government is reaping the consequences of the systematic application of misguided policies, which continue to produce new errors. In recent years, the educational crisis has forced the government to establish new courses for emergent teachers that enable rapid, but often inadequate training. Despite being a problem with enormous social significance, the public has quietly criticized this strategy as fundamentally flawed, mocking the graduates in *sotto voce* as "instantaneous teachers."

Added to the system's inherent limitations is the flawed assumption that the education of an entire country is best dealt with as if it were a series of military battles and campaigns. Another chronic difficulty that prevents a return to past levels of high educational quality and achievement is the permanent emigration of thousands of professionals and technicians who once formed the foundation of the training of new students. For example, it is estimated that in the last 30 years close to 15,000 doctors, more than 10,000 engineers, and over 25,000 college graduates in various fields have emigrated, together with numerous skilled workers and technicians. Cuba

This breathtaking photo captures a pair of iconic symbols of the University of Havana following a rainstorm: The grand 88-step staircase or "escalinata" leading up to the Greco-Roman columns that frame the open-armed Alma Mater statuette. Inspired by the Greek Parthenon, this formal entrance to the university is quite reminiscent of Columbia University's main quad. Alma Mater, the bronze seated statuette created in 1919 by Czech sculptor Mario Korbel, holds open her arms as a welcome to students. (Orlando Luis Pardo Lazo)

offers these people few occupational options and little economic incentive to remain in the country. This loss of human capital depletes the potential pedagogical base from which new professionals are drawn. Furthermore, the government itself has diverted tens of thousands of teachers and other Cuban educational professionals to serve in the training programs of the so-called Bolivarian Alliance for the Americas (ALBA). Those programs, grouped together in a new, continent-wide literacy campaign called, "*Yo, sí puedo*" (Yes, I can), have left hundreds of Cuban students without the expertise of the island's most qualified teachers. The classrooms that these "internationalist" teachers have left behind have been given over to Cuba's new crop of "emergent teachers" who are often hardly literate themselves, with serious consequences for the quality of education on the island.

The Return of Religious and Private Education?

In the midst of the educational system's structural crisis, there has been no lack of proposals seeking to address—however partially—some of the profound challenges. For example, various religious leaders have publicly suggested that Cuba's various faith communities be allowed to operate schools for their faithful once again. This initiative, defended by groups within the Catholic church and which pose no threat to the state system of secular, public education, has been rejected out-of-hand by the government. In fact, the issue has never been publicly debated in the state-controlled mass media and is therefore unknown to most Cubans.

Despite the enormous cost of supporting a free, nationwide system of public education—from daycare centers and elementary schools to technical colleges and universities—the government has also staunchly refused to open legal space for private schools. Still, with the gradual deterioration of the public school system, a large semi-clandestine network of private professors and tutors has emerged over the past 10–15 years. These tutors are available in a variety of subjects for students whose parents are able to pay for their services. Finally, in the past two to three years (2010–2013) as part of the package of reforms being implemented under the presidency of Raúl Castro, the existence of these underground tutors has been officially recognized. One of the 180-odd legalized self-employment occupations is that of a *repasador* (reviewer or tutor). In fact, many of these private tutors are actually qualified teachers who have already retired from the public education system. There are perhaps hundreds of these freelance teachers who earn the right to work by paying taxes to the state each month.

The superior test results of students whose parents have hired these so-called *repasadores* demonstrate the quality and efficiency that a private educational sector could bring to the moribund state of the government's education monopoly. This success also puts in stark relief the government's inability to solve the problem of Cuba's teacher shortage and the related disaster of the educational system. The reappearance of these "informal" routes of education mark a turning point that takes the island back once again to the start of the revolution—a time when a network of private schools coexisted alongside a public educational system designed for all. The emergence of this semi-legal system of private education also helps shatter the illusion of an official but false equality, which outlawed private education on the one hand, but in turn created a situation whereby only students from high-income families and/or with political connections had access to these private tutors.

Today, middle- and high-school students have returned from the countryside boarding schools to urban areas. Unfortunately, this newfound pragmatism does not indicate an end to the extreme politicization of education. Instead, Cuba's precarious economic condition will simply no longer allow it to bear the huge costs associated with bodily supporting tens of thousands of students in boarding schools. Apart from maintaining the facilities and paying the teaching personnel, those costs included food, accommodations, and transportation for all students who attended free of charge. At the same time, as the emergent teacher program was phased out, a specialized four-year course of training for elementary teachers has been reintroduced; virtually identical to the Normal Schools that trained Cuba's teachers before 1959. In fact, the very same campus used for this purpose in Havana in the 1950s has been recently restored for use once again in training elementary teachers. Still, deeper reforms are needed before the Cuban education system shows any real signs of recovery. Of course, a major investment of resources is also necessary.

BIBLIOGRAPHY

Castellanos Martí, Dimas C. 2011. *Desentrañando claves* (unpublished manuscript). Havana, 28 pages.

Conde, Yvonne. 2000. *Operation Pedro Pan: The Untold Exodus of 14,048 Cuban Children.* New York: Routledge.

De la Campa, Román. 2000. *Cuba on My Mind: Journeys to a Severed Nation.* New York: Verso.

Díaz-Briquets, Sergio. 2002 "The Society and Its Environment." In Rex Hudson, ed., *Cuba: A Country Study* (fourth edition). Washington, DC: Federal Research Division, Library of Congress.

Espinosa Chepe, Oscar and Ted A. Henken. 2013. "Economy." *Cuba.* Santa Barbara: ABC-CLIO Publishers, Inc.

Ferrer, Raúl. 1963. "Avances de la educación obrera y campesina en Cuba." *Cuba Socialista,* no. 23, year III, July.

Freire, Paulo. 2010. *Pedagogía de la autonomía y otros textos.* Havana: Caminos Publishers.

García Galló, Gaspar J. 1961. "La lucha contra el analfabetismo en Cuba." *Cuba Socialista,* no. 2, year I, July.

Hart, Armando. 1963. "El desarrollo de la educación en el período revolucionario." *Cuba Socialista,* no. 17, year III, January.

Mesa-Lago, Carmelo. 2011 "Social Services in Cuba: Antecedents, Quality, Financial Sustainability, and Policies for the Future." In José Raúl Perales, ed., *The Cuban Economy: Recent Trends.* Washington, DC: Woodrow Wilson Center Reports on the Americas, No. 28, Woodrow Wilson Center for Scholars, Latin America Program, July. http://www.wilsoncenter.org/sites/default/files/WWC_LAP_RoA_%2328.pdf.

Ripton, John. 2002. "Education in Cuba." In Luís Martínez-Fernández, D. H. Figueredo, Louis A. Pérez, Jr., and Luís González, eds., *Encyclopedia of Cuba: People, History, Culture.* Two vols, pp. 279–280. Westport, CT: Greenwood Press.

Torres, María de las Ángeles. 2003. *The Lost Apple: Operation Pedro Pan, Cuban Children in the U.S., and the Promise of a Better Future.* New York: Beacon Press.

Migration and Diaspora

Dimas Castellanos and Ted A. Henken

INTRODUCTION

Human migration is a form of geographic readjustment that occurs when natural, social, or political conditions in a place make it impossible for its inhabitants to meet their needs or guarantee the preservation of their lives. In Cuba the loss of civil and political rights after 1959, wages that are insufficient compared with cost of living (especially since 1990), and the ongoing dispute with the United States, reversed the historic immigration into Cuba and turned it into out migration (or emigration) leading to the formation of an extensive Cuban diaspora around the world, especially in the United States. The term "diaspora"—which originated in botany—means dispersal, and is used to describe ethnic, religious, or national groups (such as the African, Jewish, or Chinese diasporas) that have had to leave their ancestral homelands and relocate, becoming dispersed across the world (Blanco et al. 2011; Sheffer 1986).

Throughout Cuba's history—beginning with the first settlers who arrived through the islands of the Antillean Arc—the island has experienced various waves of immigration without which its formation as a people is inexplicable. As early as September 1501, and parallel to the migration of Europeans to colonize the Americas, the Catholic Monarchs issued the *Primera Instrucción Real* (First Royal Directive) for the entry of black slaves to the New World. That decree authorized the forced migration of Africans to Cuba as slaves, following the virtual enslavement and eventual extermination of the island's native inhabitants under the Spanish labor system known *la encomienda*. From the 16th to the 19th centuries, the immigration of Africans, Europeans, and Asians to Cuba was determined by the island's demand for a work force.

IMMIGRATION TO CUBA DURING THE COLONIAL PERIOD

According to the 19th century Havana-born writer and world traveler known as the Countess of Merlín (née María de las Mercedes Santa Cruz y Montalvo, 1789–1852), in 1521 the Flemish brought a contingent of African slaves to Cuba, authorized by King Charles I of Spain (Merlín 1841: 14–15). Calculations made by Alexander von Humboldt—another important travel writer with links to Cuba's 19th century history—indicate that from 1521 to 1763 (the year the British occupied Havana) some 60,000 slaves were brought to Cuba (Ortiz 1987: 90). In the next 27 years until 1790, the slave trade boomed in Cuba with the arrival of another 30,875 African slaves. In 1789 the head of Havana's city council, Francisco de Arango y Parreño, issued a report on the need for more slaves. This report was used later that same year as the basis for the issuance of the *Real Cédula* (royal decree), which eliminated many restrictions on the slave trade. This provision was followed by a series of other royal decrees issued until 1804, all of which further facilitated Cuba's importation of African slaves.

As a result, between 1790 and 1820 a total of 236,599 slaves passed through the Havana customs house. To this number should be added those slaves smuggled into the island clandestinely, bringing the total to perhaps 385,000 (ibid.: 61).

Between 1842 and 1873, another 221,000 Africans slaves together with 124,800 Chinese "coolies" or indentured laborers arrived in Cuba. This migratory movement continued despite the 1815 Declaration of Vienna, the 1835 London-Madrid Treaty, and the 1862 Anglo-American Treaty, all of which were international agreements outlawing the slave trade. During the early 19th century more than 30,000 French planters settled in Cuba, fleeing the Haitian Revolution (1791–1804). There were also more than 700,000 Spaniards (many hailing from the Canary Islands) who arrived in Cuba between 1868 and 1894, more than 290,000 of whom came as soldiers and officers to fight to preserve Cuba's colonial status. Tens of thousands of others continued to arrive on the island until the war ended in 1898 (Moreno Fraginals 2005).

IMMIGRATION DURING THE REPUBLIC

With the goal of preventing the entry of cheap labor that could affect American sugar producers (Pichardo 1980, II: 199–201), the U.S. military government that occupied the island extended the jurisdiction of U.S. immigration laws to Cuba from 1898 to 1902. Nevertheless, after taking over political control in 1902, the island's successive Republican governments promoted immigration—especially from neighboring Caribbean islands like Haiti and Jamaica—as a source of cheap labor for Cuba's sugar companies. To that end, in July 1906, President Tomás Estrada Palma issued the Immigration and Colonization Law to attract farmers from Europe and the Canary Islands. Next, President José Miguel Gómez issued a decree in January of 1913 that authorized the Nipe Bay Company to bring in 1,000 workers from neighboring islands (ibid.: 369–370). Finally, in 1917 President Mario García Menocal issued a new Immigration Law authorizing the import of contract laborers that lasted until two years after the end of World War I (ibid.: 421–422). Because of these provisions, and thanks to the fact that Cuba became the largest producer of sugar for the Allies during the War, the immigration of West Indians and others from the Caribbean greatly expanded. Additionally, between 1910 and 1925 Cuba absorbed a third of all Spanish emigrants who left for the Americas. An example of this growth is the fact that 11,986 immigrants entered Cuba in 1902, while that figure had ballooned more than 10-fold to 174,221 by 1920.

After the War, due to the fall in sugar prices and the rise of economic nationalism on the island, Cuba's immigration policy began to change. In 1921, President Alfredo Zayas issued a decree demanding the immediate deportation of Caribbean laborers back to their countries of origin, arguing that "the work in the fields had decreased considerably" (Pichardo 1980, III: 22–23). Simultaneously, due to heavy immigration to the United States in the first two decades of the 20th century, the U.S. Congress passed the National Origins Quotas Laws of 1921 and 1924, severely limiting the number of foreigners—especially those of Southern and Eastern European origin—admitted annually. As a result, many European immigrants who had been hoping to settle in North America stopped over in Cuba with the intention of continuing their journey to the United States—thus avoiding the European Quotas

Law, which did not apply to Latin America and the Caribbean. Despite this, Cuba experienced a notable decline in immigration. Between 1923 and 1924, only 87,509 Spaniards and 43,031 Haitians and Jamaicans arrived in Cuba. As many of them did so unlawfully, upon taking office in 1925 President Gerardo Machado issued Decree 1601 on the expulsion of aliens (ibid.: 280–283). After 1925, immigration continued to decline precipitously until 1932, when only 976 Spanish and 77 Caribbean islanders immigrated to Cuba.

In 1930, President Gerardo Machado drafted a new bill—mirroring the restrictive 1924 U.S. Quotas Law—that prohibited the entry of Caribbean and Chinese immigrants into Cuba. Anyone without work or a profession, as well as those suspected of subversive activities that could threaten the government, were ruled inadmissible. However, the final decline of Cuban immigration was triggered by Decree 2232 (Pichardo 1980, IV: 80–82), issued in 1933 by the government of Ramón Grau San Martín, which ordered the "forced repatriation of foreigners without work or resources." According to data cited by Margalit Bejarano (1993; National Archives 1934), in the 29 years between 1902 and 1931, almost 1.3 million immigrants came to Cuba. However, between 1946 and 1958 immigration to Cuba from the Caribbean disappeared with the number of Spanish arrivals declining precipitously as well (González and Aguilera, 2002).

CUBAN EMIGRATION TO THE UNITED STATES AND THE CREATION OF THE CUBAN DIASPORA AFTER 1959

The existence of a diasporic Cuban community in the United States dates back to the 19th century when a succession of prominent political exiles including Father Félix Varela, filibusterer Narciso López, and patriot José Martí all came to live in the United States for extended periods. Likewise, the first 60 years of the 20th century saw small but significant Cuban immigrant communities develop in Key West, Tampa (Ybor City), New Orleans, and New York (Pérez 2000). During this time, a small portion of these Cubans came as political exiles fleeing the repression of the Machado (1925–1933) and Batista (1952–1958) dictatorships. Ironically, even Fidel Castro himself toured the United States during the mid-1950s in search of support from the then very small Cuban-American community.

Despite this rich transnational history, it was not until the revolution of 1959 that Cubans began to come to the United States in large numbers. Upon the revolutionary victory, many new émigrés began to descend upon Miami and New York crossing paths with those already in exile from the Batista dictatorship who began to return to Cuba in the early months of 1959. Originally, these newcomers saw their stay in America as temporary. For these émigrés, their sojourn abroad was an emergency measure that would end only when the political crisis that necessitated it also ended. In short, these new arrivals did not think of themselves as immigrants at all, but as *exiles*.

Both sides in the ideological war between Cuba and the United States have attempted to manipulate the meanings and identities of post-1959 Cuban émigrés in line with their own geopolitical interests. On the one hand, between the 1960s and 1980s, the Cuban government consistently sought to control and politicize emigration as a threat to the revolution and stigmatize emigrants as "worms" (*gusanos*) or "traitors" (*traidores*). However, in response to economic need, during the 1990s (and occasionally before then) the Cuban government began to give nuance to its image of Cuban-Americans. While some exiles were labeled members of the "Miami mafia," the émigré group as a whole was often referred to as the Cuban "*comunidad*" abroad. It seems that the Castro regime realized that the "*gusanos*" of old had been magically transformed into today's valued "*mariposas*" (butterflies). That is, instead of being stigmatized as "*traidores*" (traitors), Cuban-Americans are now counted on to be the "*trae-dolares*" (dollar-bringers) whose remittances help maintain the Cuban economy—even if they continue to lose many of their rights on the island when they emigrate, including the right of return.

U.S. federal, state, and local governments have a similarly schizophrenic, love-hate relationship with Cuban-Americans. The first waves of Cuban émigrés were initially given wide welcome as freedom-loving "exiles," "heroes," and "refugees from Communism." Essentially, the United States sought to use this exodus to fulfill its strategic goal of overthrowing the regime (draining off its professional class and enlisting them in an invasion attempt) and its ideological goal of embarrassing Castro by welcoming Cuban émigrés who were ostensibly "voting with their feet" against the regime by leaving (Domínguez 1992). However, such a strategy had the unintended consequence of actually helping Castro consolidate his rule by allowing him to externalize dissent. Subsequent waves, however, beginning most notably with the Mariel boatlift of 1980, have often been portrayed as unsavory criminal elements and social charges; Castro's bullets aimed at Miami. As such, new Cuban arrivals are increasingly treated as just another group of unwanted and unwelcome immigrants—notwithstanding the fact that virtually any Cuban who manages to put a "dry foot" upon U.S. soil is allowed to stay legally due to the 1966 Cuban Adjustment Act and the related post-1995 "wet foot/dry foot" immigration policy (described later).

The Beginnings of Emigration Controls

Starting as early as 1959, the government began to establish certain controls over emigration. On January 9, 1959, Law No. 2 was issued to prevent officials of the previous regime—especially those who had committed abuses and war crimes—from leaving the country to evade justice (Zayas 2012). That initial provision was amended by Law No. 18, which stipulated that anyone who already had a passport intending to go abroad must first obtain "authorization for that purpose, which will be granted by the National Police Chief." After the sudden exile of several prominent members of the government and the 26th of July Movement—including President Manuel Urrutia—on September 29, 1961, the Ministry of the Interior issued for the first time the infamous "exit permit" decree, which henceforth required all Cubans to obtain expressed permission before leaving the country and even regulated the length of time migrants could remain abroad "in good standing"—that is, without losing the right to return or any of their rights and possessions on the island. In that same vein, on December 5, 1961, the government enacted Law No. 989 which regulated "the measures to be taken regarding the belongings, real estate, or anything of value of those who abandon the national territory with unforgivable disdain."

Later in September 1976, as Cuba's first socialist Constitution was enacted, Law 1312 was also passed, which further codified the exit permit requirement. However, as subsequent history has vividly and at times dramatically demonstrated, since the main cause of emigration has been the chronic lack of civil and political liberties together with the island's economic crisis, none of these laws has been able to prevent emigration. Wave after wave of émigrés has departed the island in search of a better life abroad. Finally, after a long and frustrating wait of over 50 years, in October 2012 the Cuban government put an end to the detested exit permit and announced that starting in January 2013 most (but not all) Cubans would be able to travel abroad with a passport and a valid foreign visa. (This reform is discussed in greater detail in Chapter 7 on "Contemporary Issues".)

The Golden Exiles, Operation Peter Pan, Camarioca, and the "Freedom Flights"

When the revolution came to power in 1959, the United States could count 124,000 Cuban-Americans—a number that has grown 15-fold since then, reaching 1.8 million in 2010. Despite early exiles' expectation of a rapid return to their homeland, they remained in the United States and were joined by four successive waves of new arrivals, each of which would gradually alter the overall orientation and identity of the émigré community at large. Typically, these five waves of Cuban émigrés are grouped into cohorts based on time of exit/arrival and their common social extraction (Pedraza 2002). First, there are the so-called golden exiles who arrived in the United States between 1959 and 1961. Pedraza has characterized this group as "those who wait" in the sense that they were made up largely of Cuba's pre-revolutionary elite who came to the United States awaiting a regime change back to the status quo ante back home. Comparatively, there has been no other system of refugee resettlement in the U.S. history more generous and accommodating than the *Cuban Refugee Program* (CRP) set up to receive this first wave of Cuban exiles.

After the revolution entered a new, more radical phase and Cuba was attacked by the United States at the Bay of Pigs in April 1961, there ensued a new phase of emigration characterized by "those who escape." This cohort was more middle class in social composition, included families, the 13,000 unaccompanied children who left as part of Operation Peter Pan (1960–1962), and others who resorted to escaping the island on boats and rafts when exit flights from Cuba were discontinued after the October 1962 missile crisis.

This first wave of exiles shared a number of characteristics that both distinguished them from other Latinos in the United States and enabled them to achieve unprecedented socioeconomic mobility and political influence in the United States. First of all, these Cubans were not simply a new ethnic minority in the American mosaic nor were they just another group of impoverished refugees. Instead, they were "the displaced elites of their former country with considerable resources of education, organizational skills, and entrepreneurship" (Portes 2005: 189). As such, many of them came with business skills, managerial experience, and, occasionally, financial capital. Many were also already knowledgeable about America from having previously attended U.S. colleges or worked with American firms. Finally, their common experience of dispossession, expulsion, and (to their minds) betrayal turned them into implacable anticommunists and helped them create strong bonds of social solidarity that were quickly utilized in the formation of a powerful ethnic enclave (Portes 1998, 2005).

Once the civil war that took place in Cuba between 1959 and 1965 had finished and the revolution had consolidated and radicalized its rule under Communism, the lack of freedom and the worsening of the economy spurred an increase in emigration. Facing this crisis, Fidel Castro convened a mass rally in 1965 in the *Plaza de la Revolución* and ordered the opening of the port of Camarioca for anyone who wished to leave. U.S. president Lyndon Johnson responded with "open arms and an open heart" to any Cubans who could reach U.S. shores. Between October 7, 1965, when the first group of Cubans arrived in Key West, and November 3 of that same year, when the last boat departed from Camarioca, a total of 2,979 Cubans had emigrated, leaving another 2,104 still waiting.

Given the seriousness of the situation, the Cuban and U.S. governments came to the table—with the mediation of the Swiss Embassy in Havana—and agreed to regularize the mass exodus by setting up an airlift. First, the remaining émigrés still left waiting were able to leave in ships chartered by the United States. However, many more left Cuba for the United States over the next eight years via the so-called freedom flights from Varadero, reaching a figure of 260,000 in April 1973 when the airlift was suspended by the Cubans. Pedraza has labeled this cohort "those who search" (2002) in the sense that it was neither easy nor automatic to get permission to leave the country through this airlift. Most potential émigrés had to be claimed by relatives already living in the United States. After being approved for emigration by the Cuban authorities, many were required to perform undesirable labor in the countryside and endure the humiliating experience of being stigmatized and discriminated against before leaving. This new group of a quarter-million exiles joined the arrivals of the early 1960s, driving the Cuban-American population over 665,000 by 1977.

The Mariel Boatlift

In April 1980, a group of Cubans hijacked a bus and rammed it through the fence of Havana's Peruvian embassy, where the occupants requested refuge. After the Peruvian ambassador refused to turn over the gatecrashers, Castro removed the Cuban guards from the embassy and announced that any other "*gusanos*" (worms) were welcome to join them. In a matter of hours, the grounds of the embassy were filled with more than 10,000 expectant Cubans hoping to leave the island. The Cuban government responded by organizing the massive May Day *Marcha del Pueblo Combatiente* (March of Combatant People) in order to show the supposed deserters and the entire world that the majority of the population "overwhelmingly supported the revolution" (Castro 1980). This series of dramatic events led Castro and U.S. president Carter to engage in a dangerous game of rhetorical one-upmanship, resulting in the historic exodus of more than 125,000 refugees through the port of Mariel during a six-month period that summer.

On the part of the Cuban government, there was a systematic attempt to portray those wanting to leave as the worst elements of Cuban society, with insulting labels

This image from 1980 shows the arrival to Key West of a boatload of Cuban refugees, known as Marielitos, *who fled the island from the port of Mariel over a six-month period during the summer of that year. Small leisure and fishing craft like the Miami, Florida registered boat "El Rigor" pictured here were often called into spontaneous service by Cuban-Americans desperate to go to Cuba to retrieve their relatives. Often they were forced to return with other, unknown refugees as well. (Getty Images)*

like *escoria* (scum) and *gusanos* (worms)—not to mention raw eggs hurled at them. The Cuban government directed all potential emigrants to the Port of Mariel, west of Havana, where they could rendezvous with their relatives. Unbeknownst to the boat captains, the government also allowed many convicted criminals out of prison with the understanding that they too would emigrate. Though they made up a very small proportion of the overall number of "*Marielitos*" (as the emigrants later became known), this criminal element tainted the overall image of the arrivals in the United States. Moreover, many of those who wanted to leave were forced to first "prove" that they were antisocial, homosexual, or counterrevolutionaries.

Given the magnitude of the exodus, the government also devised a macabre strategy to deter and publicly ridicule potential émigrés': acts of repudiation (*actos de repudio*). These were mob-style attacks, organized by the government designed to publicly and violently punish émigrés. These "rejection rallies" often included school children who were encouraged to pelt émigrés with rocks and raw eggs and chant slogans such as "*¡Pim, pom, fuera, abajo la gusanera!*" (down with the worms), "*¡Que se vayan las escorias!*" (out with the scum), and "*¡Que se vayan todos los que no quieren trabajar!*" (out with all who refuse to work) (Castro 1980). These mob scenes were a barbaric assault on the dignity of Cubans who aspired to a future unattainable on the island and have left a dark scar on the conscience of the Cuban nation. Despite all these obstacles, 125,000 Cubans left the island in the six months between April and October, 1980 (Ojito 2005). Given that the *Marielitos* who began to pour out of Cuba in 1980 were largely young, single males of working-class origins (veritable children of the revolution with a more marked Afro-Cuban component than ever before), Pedraza has labeled them "those who hope" (2002). Also, given the fact that they were by and large formed by the revolution, their social composition and mix of motivations to leave began to more closely reflect that of traditional immigrants rather than that of their exile forbearers making a warm reception from their compatriots in Miami unlikely (Pérez-Rey 2004).

The Balsero *Crisis*

During the decade following the Mariel boatlift, the United States allowed only a small amount of legal immigration from Cuba, while it readily accepted migrants who arrived illegally aboard hastily assembled makeshift rafts (*balsas*). Then, as Cuba began to feel the pinch of the Soviet Union's collapse between 1989 and 1991, the *balsero* crisis exploded, reaching alarming proportions in the summer of 1994. In the years leading up to 1994, the U.S. Coast Guard began to notice a marked increase in the numbers of rafters attempting to make it to the United States. Those intercepted at sea grew from 2,203 in 1991 to 3,656 in 1993. Then, in just the first

In this August 24, 1994 photo, Cuban refugees stranded on a makeshift raft float in the open sea halfway between Key West, Florida, and Cuba. The "balsero" exodus continued despite a reversal in U.S. immigration policy. (AP Photo/Hans Deryk)

seven months of 1994, another 4,731 rafters were intercepted. At this time, however, virtually all of these maritime migrants were brought to the United States after being detained, not returned to Cuba as would have been the case had they been coming from Haiti or the Dominican Republic.

Given the worsening economic crisis on the island, between May and August of 1994, Cubans began breaking into foreign embassies, consulates, and even the homes of ambassadors, while there were several boat hijackings—all with the intent to leave the country. On August 5 of that year, after a brief but unprecedented antigovernment riot on the streets of downtown Havana, Castro accused the United States of promoting illegal immigration to provoke an uprising. He then repeated a strategy he had used in both 1965 and 1980, announcing to an expectant and increasingly desperate public: "We will not prevent people from leaving nor will we hinder those who come to look for their relatives." As a result, the almost 5,000 rafters that had already departed in the first half of the year were joined by approximately 33,000 more in August and September.

President Clinton responded with the announcement that Cubans would no longer be permitted to enter the United States directly. Any future rafters intercepted at sea by the U.S. Coast Guard would be indefinitely detained in a "safe-haven" at the U.S. Naval Base at Guantánamo Bay (Gitmo) on the southeastern end of the island. This decision represented a reversal of a 35-year policy of automatically welcoming Cubans as refugees. While an initial group of *balseros* was able to make it to the United States, another 31,000 were held at Gitmo. They waited there in limbo until the United States paroled the vast majority into the country following secret migration talks between the two governments in 1995. However, the agreement also stipulated that unauthorized Cubans trying to enter the United States by sea in the future would be repatriated to Cuba. At the same time, the United States granted Cuba a minimum of 20,000 annual immigrant visas assuring that the Cuban population in the United States would continue to expand significantly into the 21st century.

THE SINKING OF THE TUGBOAT *13 DE MARZO*

During Cuba's three massive emigration crises, Camarioca, Mariel, and Guantánamo, an unknown number of tragic deaths took place. Conservative estimates suggest that at least 25 percent of Cuba's *balseros* (rafters) perished at sea, while many others suffered unspeakable trauma. One of the most tragic cases is that of the tugboat *13 de Marzo*. On July 13, 1994, a group of Cubans attempted to flee the island by diverting the tug. However, seven miles north of Havana the tug sank after the Cuban Coast Guard repeatedly rammed it and sprayed its passengers with high-pressure water hoses, resulting in the drowning deaths of 41 of the 72 passengers (some of whom were children). While the Cuban government maintains that the sinking and deaths were accidental, the OAS Inter-American Commission on Human Rights ruled that "The evidence clearly shows that the sinking of the tug was not an accident but rather a premeditated, intentional act" (LeoGrande 1995; OAS, 1996).

NEW ROUTES OF EXIT AND ENTRY:
BALSEROS, BOTEROS, EL BOMBO, AND *EL TRAMPOLÍN*

Because this newest cohort of Cuban émigrés began leaving the island on makeshift rafts due to the socioeconomic upheaval that resulted from the collapse of the Soviet Union—officially labeled the "special period" by President Castro in 1990—they have been characterized as "those who despair" (Pedraza 2002). However, while desperation may be an apt term to capture the complex and contradictory motivations of this cohort, Cuban immigration since 1995 has actually been composed of a number of different, complimentary streams. While the late 1980s and early 1990s saw upward of 30,000–40,000 Cuban rafters (*balseros*) arrive in the United States, after the 1994–1995 bilateral migration accords between the two governments, this stream has since split into a number of different migration paths.

First, since 1995 a record number of Cubans have benefited from the guaranteed minimum yearly quota of 20,000 immigrant visas (the bulk of which are granted through a visa lottery) as stipulated by the accords (Zayas 2012). As a result, the number of Cubans becoming legal permanent residents in the United States has skyrocketed over the past 15 years, reaching between 40,000 and 50,000 in some years. In fact, despite lacking any dramatic exodus of the likes of Camarioca, Mariel, or Guantánamo, the first decade of the 21st century saw the single greatest 10-year growth in the U.S. Cuban population, which expanded by 543,862 (or 44%) from 1,241,685 in 2000 to 1,785,547 in 2010 (Ennis, Ríos-Vargas, and Albert 2011; Leyva Martínez 2011). Then there is the little-known stipulation of the 1995 bilateral migration talks that allowed the United States to begin in-country refugee processing in Cuba. Since then, Cubans have been able to apply for admission to the United States as refugees if they qualify as human rights activists, former political prisoners, or their relatives. While the number of Cuban refugee arrivals in this program has fluctuated over time, it has normally been between 2,000 and 3,000 each year since 1995.

Unable to "win" one of these much sought-after visas or qualify as a refugee, a rising number of Cubans has resorted to irregular means of immigrating to the United States. One group has taken to sea once again as a means of exit, while another has attempted to use Mexico or Central America as a "trampoline" from which to cross into the United States. The first group of *balseros*, however, has largely abandoned the dangerous and unreliable method of coming on rafts and instead have opted for the more reliable method of emigrating as *boteros* (boaters) on speedboats. Elián González is the most prominent example of the more than 40,000 Cubans who have attempted to emigrate from Cuba by irregular maritime means since 1995. Some are interdicted at sea and—true to the letter of the 1995 migration accords—are returned to Cuba by the U.S. Coast Guard (numbering between 500 and 3,000 each year since 1996). Others, however, have managed to successfully run the gauntlet and arrive undetected on U.S. shores (typically numbering between 1,000 and 4,000 each year) (Chardy 2012; Chardy and Tamayo 2011, 2012; Wasem 2009).

Although Cuban migrants have traditionally attempted to reach the United States by crossing north over the proverbial "90 miles" of the Florida Straits, a new two-step stream of maritime migration has migrants heading west to Mexico's Yucatan

---

THE ELIÁN GONZÁLEZ AFFAIR (1999–2000)

Elián González was the only child of Elizabet Brotóns and Juan Miguel González. Following his parents' divorce, Brotóns developed a relationship with a Miami-based migrant smuggler named Rafa. In November 1999, Rafa loaded a group of 14 passengers onto a motorboat and set off for Florida. The boat capsized and all but three passengers drowned, including Brotóns and Rafa. On Thanksgiving Day, the 5-year-old Elián was discovered floating on a piece of wreckage and brought to Miami to recover. He was then placed in the temporary custody of his Miami relatives.

Over the next six months, an international custody dispute raged between the boy's Miami relatives, who wanted him to stay in the United States, and his father and grandparents who wanted him returned to Cuba. While both governments eventually supported the father, the ambivalence of the U.S. government in the year preceding a presidential election turned Elián's case into a dramatic cause célèbre. On April 22, 2000, U.S. federal agents raided the home where the boy was staying after his Miami relatives refused to release him. Elián's father came to the United States in the summer of 2000 to retrieve him, and they returned together to Cuba on June 28.

Peninsula, eventually making their way north over the U.S. border. In fact, in each year between 2006 and 2008 between 8,000 and 11,000 Cubans presented themselves at Texas ports of entry, the vast majority of whom lacked any valid immigration documents. After a lull in Texas arrivals between 2009 and 2011—when they averaged around 6,000 per year—the number of Cubans crossing the U.S.-Mexico border shot back up over 10,000 in the fiscal year that ended on September 30, 2012 (Chardy 2012). Cubans have begun using this alternative route in part to avoid stepped-up Coast Guard interdiction at sea. However, they are also well aware that once in the custody of the U.S. Border Patrol they will not be deported since these ports of entry are on U.S. soil. They are routinely paroled into the United States and able to gain legal residency after a year (Wasem 2009).

Thus, both the *boteros* and those using this "trampoline" alternative, take conscious advantage of a now-infamous loophole in U.S. immigration law, often referred to as the "wet-foot, dry-foot" policy. Passed in 1966 in order to help Cuban exiles regularize their murky immigration status, the Cuban Adjustment Act has remained on the books indefinitely, allowing any Cuban physically present in the United States to claim residency after one year. Although the 1995 bilateral migration agreement stipulated that Cubans intercepted at sea would be repatriated—ending the past policy of allowing them entry—it remained silent about those apprehended on land. As a result, the U.S. Coast Guard continues to interdict and repatriate most Cubans caught at sea (wet-foot), while the U.S. Border Patrol grants parole to those who successfully make it to the U.S. shores (dry-foot)—allowing them to eventually obtain permanent residency (Ackerman 2005; Duany 2005; Henken 2005; Masud-Piloto 2005).

THE CUBAN DIASPORA IN THE 21ST CENTURY

A Profile of the Cuban-American Population Today

The most recent U.S. Census reported that the Latino population reached a record 50.5 million in 2010. This makes up 16 percent of the nation's 308.7 million inhabitants, a growth of 15.2 million (or 43%) over the 35.3 million Latinos counted in 2000. Moreover, while slowing slightly toward the end of the decade, this 43-percent growth rate is more than four times the rate of growth for the overall U.S. population. And while Latinos now account for one-sixth of the nation's population overall, those under 18 make up nearly one-fourth (23.1%) of the U.S. minor population. Of course, Mexico sends the largest number of immigrants to the United States, making up nearly 63 percent (32 million) of the country's 50.5 million Latinos. Mexicans are followed by Puerto Ricans (4.6 million, or 9%, not including the other 3.7 million Puerto Ricans who live in Puerto Rico itself). Cubans are the nation's third largest group of Latinos with 1.8 million, or 3.5 percent of the Latino total (Ennis, Ríos-Vargas, and Albert 2011; Leyva Martínez 2011). While the number of Cubans is dwarfed by that of Mexicans, in recent years the island of Cuba with a mere 11.2 million inhabitants has consistently ranked among the United States' top 10 migrant sending countries. In fact, in fiscal year 2008, the 49,500 legal permanent residents of Cuban descent placed Cubans in fifth place after Mexico, China, India, and the Philippines, four countries whose populations are exponentially larger than Cuba's (Wasem 2009).

The Cuban-American population is also exceptional demographically relative to other Latin American and Caribbean immigrant groups in the United States. For example, there is a striking difference between how Cubans identify racially and how the members of other Latino groups do. Simply put, Cubans are by far the most likely of all Latinos to self-identify as white, with 85.4 percent doing so as compared to just 53 percent of Latinos overall. Likewise, just 9.5 percent of Cubans opted for one of the Census' two more open-ended racial categories of "some other race" (5.8%) or "two or more races" (3.7%) (the lowest proportion of all Latinos). In contrast, a full 43 percent of all Latinos chose one of these two alternate categories (37% and 6%, respectively), indicating their greater dissatisfaction with rigid notions of a single and mutually exclusive racial or ethnic heritage (Ennis, Ríos-Vargas, and Albert 2011).

Cubans also stand out demographically for their relatively high median age (40 years vs. 27 for all Latinos), greater likelihood to be foreign-born (59% vs. 37%), high educational attainment (24% have at least a college degree vs. 13% for all Latinos) average annual incomes ($26,400 vs. $21,400), and rates of home-ownership (57% vs. 46%), and low poverty rate (15% vs. 23%) (Pew Hispanic 2011). Apart from Puerto Ricans who are U.S. citizens by birth, Cubans also exhibit the highest rate of U.S. citizenship (74%) among all Latinos, despite the fact that more than half of them (52%) arrived in 1990 or after (Motel and Patten 2012a). A final distinguishing demographic feature of the Cuban-American community is that it is a diaspora that has refused to disperse. That is, instead of spreading out over time and assimilating geographically into the so-called vanilla suburbs, Cubans have defied tradition and actually become more geographically concentrated the longer they are in the

United States, redoubling the inordinate political, economic, and cultural influence that emanates from their unique ethnic enclave in South Florida. Cuban-Americans are heavily concentrated in Florida, with a full 68 percent living in the state. Of the 1.8 million Cuban-Americans, 1.2 million reside in Florida (almost half of whom, 48%, live in Miami-Dade County). In fact, Cubans are by far the most heavily concentrated Latino ethnic group in the United States. While Miami-Dade county is home to 856,007 Cubans (48% of the U.S. total), the Latino group with the next highest rate of concentration are Salvadorans with 358,825—or 22 percent of all Salvadoran-Americans—calling Los Angeles their home (Motel and Patten 2012b). Other important states of Cuban settlement include California (88,600), New Jersey (83,300), New York (70,800), and Texas (46,500).

Finally, while Cuban-Americans consistently registered and voted for the Republicans during the 1980s and 1990s, the influx of new immigrants and the growth of the second generation have resulted in a shift away from this single-minded political focus. Today, while 28 percent of Cubans say they consider themselves Republicans (a considerably higher percentage than for other Hispanics), another 20 percent are Democrats, with a full 27 percent considering themselves Independents (Pew Hispanic 2006). This indicates a growing division among Cuban émigrés—between the dwindling number of old guard exiles on the one hand, and the growing number of new immigrants on the other. The continued addition of at least 20,000 new immigrants directly from Cuba each year has constantly renewed the Cuban-born portion of the Cuban-American population. In fact, for the first time the 2010 Census found that a majority of Florida's 1.2 million Cubans arrived after 1990 (51.3% vs. 48.7% arriving before) (Leyva Martínez 2011). This shift was felt at the ballot box in the November 2012 elections when Florida broke late for Obama—who won a record percentage of the Cuban-American vote for a Democratic presidential candidate— and Miami elected its first ever Cuban-American Democrat, Joe García to Congress (Caputo 2012; Tamayo 2012).

Three Paradoxes of the Cuban-American Community in the United States: Exiles or Immigrants?

The consistent arrival of new Cuban immigrants along with the gradual increase in the size of the second generation competes with the demographic (as well as economic and political) strength of the pre-1980 exiles in determining the overall orientation and identity of the Cuban émigré community (Grenier and Pérez 2003). Even so, while *exile* identity and politics have predominated among the Cuban-American community historically, a new *immigrant* identity and politics has more recently emerged. However, it remains to be seen whether the newfound diversity of political opinion and policy approach within the Cuban exile community can overcome the three enduring paradoxes of Cuban-American life: (1) resistance to assimilation, (2) political intransigence, and (3) the legitimacy dilemma (Portes 2005).

In order to achieve success, immigrants usually feel the need to integrate into the mainstream of the host society. In contrast, Cubans remain proudly separate and have even created a distinct political and moral economy in South Florida (ibid.). That is, unlike virtually every other immigrant group, Cubans in Miami have rewritten the standard rule of U.S. immigration that says assimilation equals success. Instead of assimilating into the mainstream in order to succeed, they have largely redefined the mainstream by taking it over (in South Florida) and forcing others to acculturate to Cuban(-American) culture (Portes and Stepick 1993). As with Northeastern Jews, Cubans' tremendous socioeconomic and political success in the United States has been based not on assimilation, but predicated on the preservation of their ethnic social networks and a distinct ethnic identity. It remains to be seen, however, whether this resistance to assimilation is but a generational lag that will dissipate over time, especially after changes within the Cuban government puts a definitive end to Cubans' exile identity.

The second paradox is the focused, intransigent, and conservative orientation of Cuban-American politics. Over time in the host country strident political attitudes tend to mellow under the pressure of external influences. However, in the Cuban case, the historic exile leadership has remained an unbending foe both of the Castro government and of any U.S. policy approach other than absolute hostility and isolation. While this approach has earned Cuban-Americans the reputation of being extremists who are willfully out of touch with the post–Cold War world, it has served them well as perhaps the most successful immigrant/ethnic lobby in American political history. This Cuban-American political machine originated out of a common perceived experience of dispossession, expulsion, and betrayal. However, it was only consolidated beginning in 1980 with the election of President Ronald Reagan and the ascendance, in South Florida, of Miami businessman and lobbyist Jorge Más Canosa, the founder of the Cuban American National Foundation (CANF).

Modeling itself on the Pro-Israel Political Action Committee (PAC), the CANF came into being just as Cuban-Americans were gaining citizenship and voting in American elections for the first time. Given its laser-like focus on the issue of U.S.

LITTLE HAVANA AND HIALEAH, MIAMI, FLORIDA

Little Havana was long the geographical, cultural, and economic capital of Cuban Miami. In the past 20 years, however, it has been superseded by the neighboring suburb of Hialeah. At the same time, Little Havana has evolved into a redoubt of Cuban nostalgia filled with Cuban-themed book stores, retail outlets, and restaurants, even if it is now home to more Hondurans, Nicaraguans, and Guatemalans than Cubans. In fact, part of Little Havana has been renamed Little Managua after the Nicaraguan capital. Still, the geographic center of Little Havana is certainly the famous *Calle Ocho* (8th Street).

Hialeah's large Cuban population makes it the sixth largest city in Florida (if counted as separate from Metro Miami). Hialeah is also the U.S. city with the second highest percentage of people who speak Spanish at home (92% of its 225,000 population). Hialeah is home to what is perhaps the largest concentration of Cubans in the United States, with 75% of its population being of Cuban ancestry. Reflecting Cubans' tendency to identify as both white and Hispanic, the 2010 Census reported that 92.6% of Hialeah's residents listed their race as white, while 94.7% identified as Hispanic or Latino.

foreign policy toward Cuba under Reagan during the Cold War, the CANF could be counted on to line up block votes for both Democratic and Republican candidates and consistently generate campaign donations from its Cuban-American followers. In short, under the CANF's leadership the exile lobby had a simple, powerful, and extremely effective three-pronged strategy based on message, money, and votes. Its anti-Communist message was clearly consistent with U.S. foreign policy interests during the Cold War. No other political lobby had an interest in challenging its goals by funding dialogue-minded politicians. And no other group could deliver such disciplined, focused, and reliable voter turnout (Zamora 2005).

These abilities resulted in the CANF's success in having three Cuban-Americans elected to congress in the 1990s, two Republicans from South Florida (Representatives Ileana Ros-Lehtinen and Lincoln Díaz-Balart) and one Democrat from New Jersey (former representative and now Senator Robert Menéndez). After 2000, three other Cuban-Americans were elected to national office with the CANF's help, Representative Mario Díaz-Balart (Lincoln's younger brother), Senator Mel Martínez (both Florida Republicans), and Representative Albio Sires (Democrat-New Jersey). While the CANF's political influence has waned more recently in part due to disagreements within its ranks about the wisdom of maintaining its traditional hard-line stance on Cuba, Cuban-Americans have continued to enjoy great success at the ballot box. The 41-year-old child of Cuban émigrés, Marco Rubio, was elected to the U.S. Senate from Florida in a 2010 Cinderella campaign where he upset the state's sitting Republican governor in Charlie Crist. He did so with backing from the ultraconservative Tea-Party, using Crist's embrace of Obama and his policies against him (Rubio 2012).

This Tea-Party backed insurgency led to another child of Cuban émigrés being elected to the U.S. Senate in November 2012, the victor this time being the Harvard graduate Ted Cruz (Republican-Texas). In the same election, however, Florida voters replaced the disgraced Cuban-American Representative David Rivera with its first-ever Cuban-American Democrat, Representative Joe García. Having been defeated in the past by other Cuban-American Republicans, García is a leading representative of the emergent moderate faction within Florida's Cuban-American community as well as being a former president of the CANF under Más Canosa. His election will complicate the uniformity of the traditionally hard-line Cuban-American congressional caucus (Caputo 2012).

More surprising still was President Obama's showing among Florida's Cuban-American voters in the 2012 presidential elections. As expected, Obama easily carried the Hispanic vote nationally (71% to Mitt Romney's 27%) and in Florida (60% to 39%), with the strong support of the state's burgeoning Puerto Rican population. However, Obama also won the battleground state of Florida outright (50%–49.1%), and did so while perhaps winning the Cuban-American vote with 49 percent to Romney's 47 percent (Caputo 2012; Pew Hispanic 2012). While the actual outcome of the Cuban-American exit polls is in dispute—other pollsters gave Romney a clear majority of the Cuban-American vote in Florida, 59 percent to Obama's 41 percent—what is clear is that, at worst, in 2012 Obama outperformed all previous Democratic presidential candidates among Cuban-Americans. "In comparison," writes Juan Tamayo in the *Miami Herald*, "75 percent of Florida Cubans voted for the Republican presidential candidate in 2000, 71 percent in 2004 and 65 percent in 2008" (Tamayo 2012).

The final paradox is one of legitimacy. In short, while the Cuban-American political machine has successfully elected politicians and influenced (even at times dictated) U.S. policy toward Cuba, it increasingly suffers from a legitimacy crisis given the fact that its tactics of aggression, embargo, and isolation have been supremely unsuccessful at achieving regime change in Havana. In fact, if anything, it is likely that the CANF's past confrontational tactics have only fueled Castro's thirst for power and control, allowing him to stoke the coals of Cuban nationalism and manipulate fears of foreign invasion (Portes 1998, 2005). Indeed, one oft-cited irony of the historic Cuban exile community is that though they never came with the intention to stay, they have enjoyed unequalled success among Latinos at what they say they are not (immigrants) and continued failure at what they say they are (exiles). In the end, exiles only succeed if and when they can return triumphantly to their homeland (Grenier and Pérez 2003).

This paradox of legitimacy has gradually deepened during the late-1990s and into the 2000s as the interests of the exile lobby and the U.S. government began to diverge. In short, after the end of the Cold War the exile lobby's message began to lose its focus and come into conflict with U.S. interests. Moreover, both the U.S. farm and tourism lobbies began to challenge the generous political donations of the exile lobby, competing for the attention of U.S. politicians. Finally, as the Cuban-American population began to diversify with new immigrants (not exiles) arriving from Cuba by the hundreds of thousands, the exile lobby gradually lost its effectiveness at getting out a unified Cuban-American vote. Newcomers might share old-timers' rejection of socialism and the Castro dynasty, but they often differ markedly on the issues of family travel, remittances, and even the embargo itself—especially since they are far more likely to have close relatives back on the island with whom they insist on maintaining a relationship.

What had been the lobby's strengths, a unified message that coincided with U.S. interests, well-placed political donations with no competition, and command of disciplined voting bloc, began to unravel in 1999–2000 fatally undermining its effectiveness (Zamora 2005). Partially as a result of this paradox of legitimacy, the CANF experienced an internal debate over its traditional isolationist approach and identification with the Republican Party. This debate led to a rift within the organization and the departure of many CANF hard-liners, who formed the Cuban Liberty Council in 2001. Thus, are Cubans in America still exiles, and not immigrants? As with the Castro brothers' own legendary longevity in Havana, the exile identity is subject to "the biological solution" (death from old age). At the same time, Más Canosa's death in 1997, the Pope's visit in 1998, the outcome of the Elián González affair in 1999–2000 have combined with some negative fallout from new restrictions on remittances and family travel to Cuba since 2003, leading to the emergence of many new, more moderate voices and organizations within the Cuban-American community that are beginning to challenge the monolithic image of Cuban-Americans. Some of these more moderate, pro-engagement groups include the Cuban Committee for Democracy founded in 1993, the Cuban-American Alliance and Education Fund founded in the late 1990s, the Cuba Study Group founded in the early 2000s, ENCASA/US-CUBA (Emergency Network of Cuban American Scholars and Artists for Change in U.S.-Cuba Policy) founded in 2006, and CAFÉ (Cuban-Americans for Engagement) founded in 2012.

BIBLIOGRAPHY

Ackerman, Holly. 2005. "Los balseros: antes y ahora." *Encuentro de la Cultura Cubana*, 36: 131–141.

Bejerano, Margalit. 1993. "La inmigración a Cuba y la política migratoria de los EE.UU. (1902–1933)." Hebrew University of Jerusalem. *Estudios Interdisciplinarios de América Latina y el Caribe*, 4 (July–December), 2. http://www.tau.ac.il/eial/IV_2/bejarano.htm.

Blanco, Juan Antonio, Uva de Aragón, Jorge Domínguez, Jorge Duany, Carmelo Mesa-Lago, and Orlando Márquez. 2011. "The Cuban Diaspora in the 21st Century." Cuban Research Institute, Florida International University. http://casgroup.fiu.edu/news/docs/2554/1331179294_cuban_diaspora_in_the_21st_century.pdf

Caputo, Marc. 2012. "Poll: Obama Got Big Share of Cuban American Vote, Won Among Other Hispanics in Florida." *Miami Herald*, November 8. http://www.miamiherald.com/2012/11/08/3087889/poll-obama-got-big-share-of-cuban.html#storylink=cpy#storylink=cpy.

Castro, Fidel. 1980. "May Day Speech." Plaza de la Revolución, May 1. http://www.cuba.cu/gobierno/discursos/1980/esp/f010580e.html

Chardy, Alfonso. 2012. "Sharp Surge in Cuban Migrants Seeking to Reach US." *Miami Herald*, November 1. http://www.miamiherald.com/2012/11/01/3078386/sharp-surge-in-cuban-migrants.html.

Chardy, Alfonso, and Juan O. Tamayo. 2011. "Se duplica número de cubanos que llegan Estados Unidos." *El Nuevo Herald*, October 8. http://www.elnuevoherald.com/2011/10/08/v-fullstory/1040619/se-duplica-numero-de-cubanos-que.html.

Chardy, Alfonso, and Juan O. Tamayo. 2012. "Number of Cubans Trying to Enter U.S. Increases." *Miami Herald*, June 17. http://www.miamiherald.com/2012/06/17/2854846/record-number-of-cubans-try-to.html.

Conde, Yvonne. 2000. *Operation Pedro Pan: The Untold Exodus of 14,048 Cuban Children*. New York: Routledge.

De la Campa, Román. 2000. *Cuba on My Mind: Journeys to a Severed Nation*. New York: Verso.

Domínguez, Jorge I. 1992. "Cooperating with the Enemy? US Immigration policies toward Cuba." In Christopher Mitchell, ed., *Western Hemisphere Immigration and US Foreign Policy,* pp. 31–88. University Park, PA: Pennsylvania State University Press.

Duany, Jorge. 2005. "La migración cubana: tendencias actuales y proyecciones." *Encuentro de la Cultura Cubana* no. 36: 164–180.

Ennis, Sharon R., Merarys Ríos-Vargas, and Nora G. Albert. 2011. "The Hispanic Population: 2010." U.S. Census Brief, May. http://www.census.gov/prod/cen2010/briefs/c2010br-04.pdf.

González Yanci, Pilar, and Maria José Aguilera Arilla. 2002. "La inmigración cubana en España. Razones políticas y de sangre en la elección de destino." *Espacio, Tiempo y Forma, Serie VI*, Department of Geography of UNED, vol. 15, pp. 11–27. http://e-spacio.uned.es/fez/eserv.php?pid=bibliuned:ETFSerie6–3D16F873–95BB-0CBC-972F-73C1F74D9428&dsID=Documento.pdf.

Grenier, Guillermo J., and Lisando Pérez. 2003. *The Legacy of Exile: Cubans in the United States*. Boston, MA: Allyn and Bacon.

Henken, Ted. 2005. "Balseros, boteros y el bombo; persistencia de un trato migratorio especial." *Encuentro de la Cultura Cubana* no. 36: 142–163.

LeoGrande, William M. 1995. *The United States and Cuba after the Cold War: The 1994 Refugee Crisis*. Washington, DC: Institute for the Study of Diplomacy, School of Foreign Service, Georgetown University.

Leyva Martínez, Ivette. 2011. "Censo 2010: 1.8 millones de cubanos viven in EEUU." *Café Fuerte*, May 27. http://cafefuerte.com/miami/noticias-de-miami/sociedad/980-censo-2010-1-8-millones-de-cubanos-viven-en-estados-unidos.

Masud-Piloto, Félix. 2005. "Bienvenidos a Guantánamo." *Encuentro de la Cultura Cubana* no. 36: 21–30.

Merlín, María de las Mercedes. 1841. *Los esclavos en las colonias españolas*. Madrid: Imprenta de Alegría y Charlain.

Moreno Fraginals, Manuel. 1995. *Cuba España/España Cuba, historia común*. Barcelona: Editorial Grijalbo-Mondadori.

Motel, Seth, and Eileen Patten. 2012a. "Hispanics of Cuban Origin in the United States, 2010." *Pew Hispanic Center*, June 27. http://www.pewhispanic.org/files/2012/06/2010-Cuban-Factsheet.pdf.

Motel, Seth, and Eileen Patten. 2012b. "The Ten Largest Hispanic Origin Groups, 2010: Characteristics, Rankings, Top Counties." *Pew Hispanic Center*, June 27; updated, July 12. http://www.pewhispanic.org/files/2012/06/The-10-Largest-Hispanic-Origin-Groups.pdf.

National Archives. 1934. República de Cuba, Secretaría de Hacienda, Sección de Estadísticas, Inmigración y movimiento de pasajeros, Havana,1903–1930. Memorandum from C.R. Cameron, Washington, DC, 837.55/142, February 29.

OAS (Organization of American States). 1996. Inter-American Commission of Human Rights. Informe #47/96, Caso 11.436, Víctimas del barco remolcador "13 de marzo" vs. Cuba, October 16. http://www.cidh.oas.org/annualrep/96span/Cuba11436.htm.

Ojito Mirta. 2005. *Finding Mañana: A Memoir of the Cuban Exodus*. New York: Penguin Press.

Ortiz, Fernando. 1987. *Los negros esclavos*. Havana: Editorial de Ciencias Sociales.

Pedraza, Silvia. 2002. "Cuban Migrations to the United States." In Luis Martínez-Fernández, D. H. Figueredo, Louis A. Pérez, Jr., and Luis González, eds., *Encyclopedia of Cuba: People, History, Culture*. Westport, CT: Greenwood Press.

Pérez, Lisandro. 2000. "De Nueva York a Miami: El desarrollo demográfico de las comunidades cubanas en Estados Unidos." *Encuentro de la cultura cubana* 15: 13–23.

Pérez-Rey, Lisandro. 2004. "Beyond the Sea/Más allá del mar." Gato Films.

Pew Hispanic Center. 2006. "Cubans in the United States: A Profile," August 25. http://pwehispanic.org/files/factsheets/23.pdf.

Pew Hispanic Center. 2011. "Hispanics of Cuban Origin in the United States, 2009." May 26. http://pewhispanic.org/files/factsheets/73.pdf.

Pew Hispanic Center. 2012. "Latino Voters in the 2012 Election." November 7. http://www.pewhispanic.org/files/2012/11/2012_Latino_vote_exit_poll_analysis_final_11–07–12.pdf.

Pichardo, Hortensia. 1980. *Documentos para la historia de Cuba*. Multiple volumes. Havana: Editorial de Ciencias Sociales.

Portes, Alejandro. 1998. "Morning in Miami: A New Era for Cuban Americans." *American Prospect* 9, no. 38 (May–June): 28–32.

Portes, Alejandro. 2005. "The Cuban-American Political Machine: Reflections on Its Origins and Perpetuation." In Joseph S. Tulchin, Liliam Bobea, Mayra P. Espina Prieto, and Rafael Hernández, eds., *Changes in Cuban Society since the Nineties*, pp. 187–205. Washington, DC: Woodrow Wilson Center Report on the Americas no. 15.

Portes, Alejandro, and Alex Stepick. 1993. *City on the Edge: The Transformation of Miami.* Berkeley, CA: University of California Press.

Rubio, Marco. 2012. *An American Son: A Memoir.* New York: Sentinel.

Sheffer, Gabriel. 1986. *A New Field of Study: Modern Diasporas in International Politics.* London: Croom Helm.

Tamayo, Juan. 2012. "Did Obama or Romney Win the Cuban-American Vote?" *Miami Herald*, November 12. http://www.miamiherald.com/2012/11/12/3094299/winner-of-cuban-american-vote.html.

Torres, María de los Ángeles. 2004. *The Lost Apple: Operation Pedro Pan, Cuban Children in the U.S., and the Promise of a Better Future.* New York: Beacon Press.

Wasem, Ruth Ellen. 2009. "Cuban Migration to the United States: Policy and Trends." Washington, DC: Congressional Research Service, June 2. http://www.fas.org/sgp/crs/row/R40566.pdf.

Zamora, Antonio. 2005. "The Political Evolution of the Cuban-American Community of South Florida: 1959–2005." Paper prepared for the Wisconsin Symposium on Cuba, March 3–5.

Zayas, Manuel. 2012. "La Isla del nunca jamás." *Diario de Cuba*, January 17. http://www.diariodecuba.com/derechos-humanos/8952-la-isla-del-nunca-jamas.

The Media

Reinaldo Escobar

Cuban journalism began in 1790 with the appearance of the *Papel Periódico de La Habana* (The News of Havana). Except for a handful of short-lived informational pamphlets of relatively little importance, the *Papel Periódico* constituted Cuba's first newspaper and was published under the aegis of the renowned *Sociedad Económica de Amigos del País* (Economic Society of Friends of the Country). Even before 1812, the year in which freedom of the press was first declared in Cuba, a number of other periodicals had appeared in the island's capital including *El regañón de La Habana* (The Havana Nag), *El Criticón de La Habana* (The Havana Critic), and *El patriota americano* (The American Patriot), among others. At around the same time, *El amigo de los cubanos* (The Friend of the Cubans) appeared in Santiago de Cuba in 1805, followed shortly thereafter by *El espejo de Puerto Príncipe* (The Mirror), in Camagüey.

Many of Cuba's first newspapers openly advocated for the island's independence from Spain, including those published on the island as well as others published from exile. The most important publications from this era were *El Habanero*, founded by Félix. Varela and published in New York from 1824 to 1826; *La voz del pueblo cubano* (The Voice of the Cuban People), published clandestinely in Havana in just four editions all in 1852 (Marrero 1999; Monterrey 2002); and José Martí's *Patria* (Homeland), first published in New York in 1892. The title of Martí's *Patria* hearkened back to *La Patria Libre* (The Free Homeland), the very first paper he founded, in 1869, when he was just 16. *Patria* continued to be published through the end of 1898, well after Martí's death in 1895. Its last issue was number 522, published on December 31, 1898, commemorating the ending of the War of Independence and marking the beginning of a four-year U.S. military occupation of Cuba (Márquez 2012).

Cuba's "Republican" era (1902–1958) was rich in newspapers and magazines, and among dozens the most notable were *El País* (The Country), *Prensa Libre* (The Free Press), *Diario de la Marina* (Marina Daily), *Noticias de Hoy* (News of the Day)—which was a communist publication—*El Mundo* (The World), and *Bohemia*. In radio, the pioneer was the station PWX, founded in 1922. Only eight years later in 1930, there were already 61 stations, a figure proportionally higher than that which then existed in New York. What's more, at the time Cuba ranked fourth in the world in number of radio stations behind the United States, Canada, and Russia. Likewise, cinema news reels and television newscasts appeared on the island earlier than in many other parts of the world. Almost immediately after being launched in the United States, television arrived to Cuba in 1950 when URT-Channel 4 (*Unión Radio Televisión*) went on the air. It was the third television station in Latin America, followed later that same year by Channel 6. From the start of this rich tradition a diversity of views and the debate of controversial issues was a hallmark of the Cuban media. This had an essential impact on the formation of public opinion and on Cuba's political history. In November 1960, all newspapers, newswire services, and radio and television stations—except for the handful already aligned with the revolution—were nationalized by the government.

THE OFFICIAL VERSION

Today Cuban citizens have access to three national newspapers: *Granma*, published by the Central Committee of the PCC; *Juventud Rebelde* (Rebel Youth), published by the Union of Young Communists (UJC); and *Trabajadores* (Workers), published by the Cuban Workers Union (CTC). In each of Cuba's 15 provinces there is a provincial newspaper. The official price of all these papers is just 20 cents of a Cuban peso (about the equivalent of one U.S. cent). However, since their circulation is insufficient, there has long been a parallel informal market where retired people buy the newspapers in bulk at the cover price early each morning from Cuba's many newsstands and illegally resell each copy for one peso (about five cents).

The magazine *Bohemia*, founded over 80 years ago, is the only biweekly publication that covers general news. Other publications are in the tabloid format and specialize in specific themes, such as international news, *Orbe* (The Orb), cultural events, *La Gaceta* (The Gazette), and *El Caimán Barbudo* (The Bearded Caiman). Other more irregular publications cover sports, fashion, and technology. The magazines *Temas* (Themes) and *Cuba Socialista* (Socialist Cuba) are devoted to social, political, and ideological issues with a relatively high and nuanced intellectual level. However, they do so from a clearly partisan position in total alignment with the PCC. Other magazines of a more explicitly cultural nature retain a relative independence without being strictly official. These include the *Revista de la Biblioteca Nacional* (The National Library Magazine), *La Siempreviva* (The Evergreen), *La Calle del Medio* (Center Street), the University of Havana publication *Alma Mater*, and the more

Former reporter for the state newspaper Juventud Rebelde (Rebel Youth) and now an independent journalist and blogger, Reinaldo Escobar, holds up a copy of Cuba's national newspaper Granma, *published by the Central Committee of the Cuban Communist Party. The headline reads: "1987: 29th year of the Revolution, Yes, Now We Are Going to Build Socialism!" (Orlando Luis Pardo Lazo)*

theoretical and philosophical *Criterios* (Criteria). These are tolerated partly because of their limited reach and appeal and because of their normally harmless content.

There are three national television channels with varied programming plus two educational channels - a situation that improved somewhat recently with the appearance in Cuba of the Venezuelan-based network TeleSur. There are also the so-called provincial *telecentros* (tele-centers), all of which try to satisfy the viewers' demands. There are also five radio stations with a national reach and at least a provincial station in each province. While it is funded by the Cuban state, the island's media is far from being "public." Instead, the mass media is the private property of the only political party authorized by law, the PCC. Broadcast media outlets are "publicly" funded, but their editorial orientations, content, publication schedule, decisions about how much space to devote to one issue or another, and even the tone in which the news is reported or discussed by hosts, are all decided in the offices of the *Departamento de Orientación Revolucionaria* (Department of Revolutionary Orientation, DOR) of the PCC. The content of the information disseminated in the official media could be boiled down to the following statement: Cuba is the best of all possible worlds, and the rest of the planet is a permanent disaster.

These newspapers, magazines, and radio and television programs are justly deemed "official" not only because they are subject to control mechanisms that will be discussed later, but also because we can see at a glance that there is not a single line criticizing the government's performance. Instead, there is a nonstop drumbeat of praise and triumphalism. Generally speaking, official journalism avoids shameless lies, but does so by concealing or manipulating information. For example, when a group of countries votes in favor of a resolution condemning the Cuban government in Geneva, or when the United Nations points to problems with human rights on the island, the texts of such resolutions are never published on the island. Instead, if such news is reported at all, it is always with the forgone conclusion that that those who voted "against Cuba" did so by order of Washington. At the same time, when these same international organizations condemn the U.S. "blockade" of Cuba (as they frequently do), it makes front-page news.

Another example of this simplification and manipulation in the Cuban media is this: official journalists do not lie when they declare that there are no children without shoes in Cuba. But, at the same time, they knowingly hide the reality that all those shoes were bought at a price that does not correspond to the salary paid by the state to the parents of these children. Or that, in a good portion of the cases, money to buy the shoes was sent by a relative in Miami, or obtained by illegal means and therefore supposedly disapproved of by the state itself. On the other hand, official journalists do lie when they say, without showing any evidence, that someone who opposes the government is a "mercenary" employee of Washington, or that dissidents jailed for political reasons (and therefore "political prisoners") are only petty criminals justly deprived of their freedom.

Often, more subtle methods are adopted. Could an enraged news anchor of the National News on official state television be described as a liar when she blasts a particular barbershop for its prices, without alluding to the fact that a single bottle of soybean oil, unavailable in the national peso currency, is only sold in the state-run "dollar stores" at a price that greatly exceeds that of a haircut? From an ethical point of view, official journalists who believe in what they write hold their positions based on two basic arguments. First, they claim that the lack of freedom of expression is a consequence of the fact that the island is under siege by the world's largest imperial power, which has imposed a criminal blockade for over 50 years. A second common justification is that the achievements in health care, education, and the social safety net that Cuba showcases would not have been possible without the revolution, and that they would be lost if there were a political transition toward liberal democracy and a market economy. One might add that many of these individuals have given the best years of their lives to the revolution. Thus, it would be too traumatic and demoralizing for them to recognize that they have been on the wrong side of history all their lives.

Then there are the opportunists. These are the ones who sing public praises to the system, sure to applaud at all the right times. However, they secretly detest the system and hope in silence for a radical change. There are many who engage in this kind of hypocritical "*doble moral*" or duplicity, though it must be said that the press corps does not enjoy the kind of perks and material privileges that would justify such opportunism.

Until the late 1980s being a journalist could provide you with the possibility of obtaining a car, traveling abroad, or having the benefit of a house; but after the crisis that began in 1990 all that changed. Wages have risen slightly since the year 2000, but few journalists earn more than a monthly salary of 500 Cuban pesos, which is the equivalent of about $20. Many professionals in the media continue to cynically go through the motions because they like being journalists, with the concomitant social status that it affords them. Furthermore, their role as journalists grants them coveted access to the upper spheres of power which can bring them additional benefits. Others pretend simply because of the subtle but ever-present fear, knowing that if they were to write what they really thought they would end up expelled from their jobs, socially ostracized, and even risk imprisonment. Finally, there are those "old dogs" who cannot learn any "new tricks"; they have resigned themselves to the status quo because they cannot do anything else, nor can they imagine themselves working in another occupation to earn their daily bread.

The challenge of being an official journalist in Cuba has become more, not less, difficult over time because the regime continually demands more out of them. It is not enough to simply refrain from criticism. Even applauding the regime is not considered sufficient. It is necessary to applaud enthusiastically, and if possible with more enthusiasm each day. There is no point to the subtle tactic of trying to slip the critical ideas that the author really wants to express "between the lines." Those in control are experts at finding and punishing these hidden meanings.

MECHANISMS OF CONTROL

In Cuba, the mechanisms of control over the press function on four different levels. First, there is the aforementioned DOR of the Central Committee of the PCC. The DOR includes an ample working group devoted to analyzing and classifying all the news that is published in the country. They place permanent "trackers" on particular issues and authors. Based on this analysis—together with the particular interests of different origins coming from on high—a "thematic plan" is drawn up that stipulates which topics will and will not be addressed in the Cuban press, and in what form and intensity. This rigid control also extends to the music that is broadcast on Cuban radio stations, and the music videos, soap operas, and educational and scientific programs shown on Cuban television. Periodically, the directors of the news organizations meet to evaluate their compliance with this plan, which of course is mandatory.

A prime example of one particular theme systematically imposed on the Cuban media is the case of "the Cuban five." These are five undercover Interior Ministry agents—officially and exclusively referred to as "*los cinco héroes*" (the five heroes)—convicted of espionage in the United States and sentenced to long prison terms. When they were arrested in Miami in 1998, not a word was spoken or published about their plight in the Cuban national media. Only two years later when their trials began was the Cuban public bombarded with a nonstop official media campaign demanding their release. Of course, it was never made public that the so-called *Red Avispa* (Wasp Network), of which they were a part, originally had a dozen members, more than half of whom decided to cooperate with prosecutors.

It is also the DOR that appoints—after consultation at the highest levels of the regime—the directors of all media organizations as well as the heads of more specialized publications such as academic journals. This top-down control extends to national and provincial media organizations, municipal radio stations, specialized magazines, and so on. The DOR also deals directly with the Department of Information and Communication, where new journalists receive their academic training. It exercises control over the curriculum and is also involved in the selection of new students.

This award-winning photo from the first independent social photography contest "País de Pixeles" in 2011 captures two quite common if contrasting images in today's Cuba. A group of five men with apparently little to do stand and sit before a piece of political propaganda featuring the faces of the five Cuban intelligence agents arrested and charged with espionage in the United States in 1998. Four of them remain in U.S. federal prison today. The declaration reads: "Five Heroes of the Fatherland, Will Return!" (Luzbely Escobar)

The second mechanism of control involves a specific area of government. Each important ministry or institution has an outreach department that encourages journalists to do promotional work in their particular area, serving the interests of that sector. They are responsible for arranging visits to educational, production, or service centers. They are the ones who choose specific sites, where they enforce the "thematic plan" of the DOR, select people to be interviewed, and sometimes "create" scenes that are deemed appropriate to disseminate the message that they want to get out. These organizations—whose job is not to repress but to coordinate—are in charge of the journalists who specialize in their sector. They invite them to press conferences, meetings, annual budget meetings, and so on. They generate moral and material incentives and conduct annual or monthly assessments based on how they think the journalist has covered the information. These reports are essential because when the administration of each media outlet evaluates the work of each journalist, the results are used for salary rankings, promotions, and the award of distinctions.

The third mechanism of control is performed by the Ministry of Interior. In each media organization, there are individuals whose job is to "address" security.

They monitor all employees, taking special note of those who have a reputation for being "troublemakers." They also collect data on the nonprofessional activities of each writer, photographer, graphic designer, anchor, and administrator. More than controlling what is published (which they also do), these Interior Ministry agents watch what is said in the hallways and around the water cooler, monitor what kinds of questions reporters ask their interviewees (especially if they are foreigners), and note if they maintain contacts with dissidents or independent journalists.

The fourth mechanism of control is perhaps the most efficient and sophisticated of all. It is euphemistically called "self-censorship" and is the result of pressure exerted on the journalist by the various instruments described earlier. The state's fear of what an individual might say or write leads to censorship, while it is the fear of what the state might do to an individual that leads him or her to engage in self-censorship. It is so efficient, sophisticated, and powerful because it is both invisible and internal, functioning like a psychological barrier within each individual to a greater or lesser degree. Instead of policing every individual, the government has succeeded in getting each individual to police him or herself. As with the famous prison system, "Panopticon," dreamed up in 1785 by the English philosopher and social theorist Jeremy Bentham (the closest architectural embodiment of which is the now-abandoned *Presidio Modelo* built in Cuba on the Isle of Pines in the late 1920s under the president-turned-dictator Gerardo Machado), self-censorship derives its insidious power from convincing individuals that they are always under surveillance. This suspicion can easily lead to a chilling paranoia with the desired effect of forcing individuals to "choose to avoid trouble and modify their behavior in ways that are often subtle and even subconscious" (MacKinnon 2012: 80).

In the Cuban media, self-censorship is most often expressed in the actions, or more commonly the omissions of each journalist, making sure to always tread on safe ground and not come near (let alone cross) the invisible line of the permissible. For example, in his more than 30 years as head of the Cuban National Boxing Team, the now-retired head coach Alcides Segarra never received even the slightest criticism from sportswriters. How is that possible? Nobody knows for sure, but it is assumed that he must have enjoyed the personal sympathy of Fidel Castro, and that was enough. Likewise, a few days after the young and charismatic Roberto Robaina was suddenly replaced in his post as foreign minister without any satisfactory explanation, the Cuban head of state appeared before the television cameras for an unrelated event. However, despite the large group of Cuban journalists present, no one dared question the maximum leader Fidel Castro about it. There was no explicit prohibition, but it was clear to everyone: "don't go there." In fact, Cubans had to wait several years for the commander-in-chief to offer a public explanation in the form of a character assassination unrelated to the former minister's job performance.

For an official journalist who believes in what he writes, self-censorship is an act of political militancy. It is, to use the poetic words that a troubadour addicted to the regime might say, "the love-gag of an oath." He trusts what his comrades in the DOR tell him because they are the ones with all the necessary preparation and information to decide for him what can and what cannot be published. If he were asked to help his state security comrades with something related to the press, he would collaborate by writing up a report on a fellow journalist. Moreover, out of discipline, he regularly checks everything he writes with the disclosure department of the media outlet where he works.

On the other hand, journalists who work in the official press and who do not believe what they write must become professional pretenders. For them, self-censorship becomes a sign of professional ability; a way of showing their "talent and farsightedness" at guessing what is convenient to write or not. In this scenario, the restrictions imposed by the DOR are simply the "rules of the game" that must be followed and the comrade from state security becomes "the guy you have to be careful of." These kinds of journalists are also careful to maintain a good relationship with the disclosure department where they work. This is the case since a satisfactory work evaluation can come in handy around the time of National Journalist's Day, when bonuses such as banquets, gifts, and trips are awarded as material incentives.

Among the few positive developments in the world of official Cuban journalism since 2007 we should note the appearance of a letter-to-the-editor section every Friday in Cuba's national newspaper *Granma*. The publication of these letters has opened up interesting debates about many once-taboo topics, such as private self-employment, the growth of market forces, and other thorny issues. At the same time, of course, there is never even a whisper about clearly forbidden topics such as the hated restrictions on emigration, police abuse, and the general lack of civil liberties. The lesson, as the saying goes: "you can play with the chain, but not with the monkey."

Also of note is the fact that the First Conference of the PCC, held in early 2012 and coming on the heels of the 6th Party Congress in April 2011, gave the impression that the country's highest authorities understand that the press is boring and lacks credibility. This has led to the repeated calls to "suppress the harmful manifestations of secrecy" and to "banish self-censorship, mediocrity, effusive bureaucratic language, easy rhetoric, triumphalism, and banality." In the debates that took place within the Party Commission in charge of organizing the conference, the speakers seemed to enjoy openly criticizing the bureaucrats who prevented journalists from gaining access to the event and routinely deny them the information they need to report on the failure to meet production plans, as well as instances of malfeasance and fraud. However, the limits of this kind of criticism were crystal clear: nothing could be mentioned that would violate established party policy—including the one-party state and its historic leaders.

THE OTHER SIDE OF THE PAGE

Until the fall of socialism in Europe, Cuban translations of Russian, Polish, German, Bulgarian, Hungarian, Czech, Chinese, and Korean publications could be purchased at Cuban newsstands. But that time has passed. Up until 2006 news publications from Western Europe such as *El País*, *ABC*, *Le Monde*, *Paris Match*, and *Der Spiegel* were sold in some tourist shops and hotels. While these newspapers have all but disappeared from these exclusive outlets, even when they were available they were weeks out of date and sold at prices totally out of reach for the average Cuban. Although relatively widespread in Havana, satellite dishes and other UHF (ultra high frequency) systems able to pick up foreign television signals are illegal. The law also stipulates that any other antennas in use must be tuned exclusively to national channels and frequencies. Police operations aimed at detecting and removing these clandestine antennas are carried out with a huge deployment of resources reminiscent of scenes from science fiction films populated by nervous military officers squaring off against extraterrestrial beings.

Due to Cuba's proximity to the United States, American radio transmissions can often be picked up on the island, including the programming of Radio Martí, a U.S. government-funded station that transmits 24 hours-a-day especially for Cuba. The same is true for TV Martí, as well as for many other small radio stations run by Cuban exiles in South Florida. However, less than 20 percent of these hundreds of hours of broadcasting ever reach their intended listeners due to the Cuban government's sophisticated signal jamming along the entire length and breadth of the island. This situation has changed somewhat in the Internet age as much of Radio and TV Martí programing is also available via the website Martí Noticias. However, as discussed below, Internet access in Cuba remains extremely limited. This same jamming is applied to radio transmissions originating in Europe.

Finally, the Catholic Church produces a number of major publications, including *Palabra Nueva*, *Vitral*, and *Espacio Laical*, which are practically the only independent publications allowed to circulate—though in limited numbers—on the island. Though religious in scope, they are not exclusively so and include articles—often written by Cuban exiles—on social, economic, and political subjects with points of view not found in the official press. Given their moderate tone and their practice of addressing issues of great interest to Cuban readers, these publications have become greatly sought after by a public hungry for information and reasoned debate.

A number of other newsletters and magazines are printed in Cuba by alternative means and distributed under the most relentless persecution. Some of these are the publications of opposition parties while others come from groups of independent activists in the island's emerging civil society. Such publications have a circulation no more than a few 100 copies, which are read and passed clandestinely among friends and associates. While some of these are still printed on paper, it is increasingly common to find them posted on the web and circulated among Cubans on the island in various digital formats including thumb drives, CDs, or DVDs. Some of the better-known among these independent journals and "e-zines" are *Convivencia* (Coexistence), which is put together in the province of Pinar del Río. by a team of lay-Catholic civic activists led by Dagoberto Valdés (the former editor of the Catholic magazine *Vitral*); *Ácana*, which is produced by the alternative news agency Cubanacán Press in the province of Villa Clara; *Voces* (Voices), edited by the writer and blogger Orlando Luis Pardo Lazo in Havana; and the magazine *Primavera de Cuba* (Cuban Spring), which is written in its entirety by independent journalists residing on the island, but printed abroad and distributed on the island by various means including via regular mail.

Independent journalism is, by definition, the dissemination of information that the government actively censors or would censor if given the chance. It is difficult to chronicle the history of Cuban independent journalism because already in the 1980s there were a handful of projects that defined themselves only as "freelance." Then came the first self-consciously independent press agencies, such as *Cuba Press*, founded in 1995 by Raúl Rivero, and *Cuba Verdad*, established in 1997. Many of the pioneering journalists involved in those early projects ended up in prison as a result of the mass arrests of 2003 that became known as the Black Spring.

An independent journalist is normally not interested in repeating the coverage of an event as reported by the official press, and if he or she does cover the same event it is to offer an alternative point of view. The most recurrent theme in the independent press is the denunciation of arbitrary detentions, searches, and physical attacks made upon dissidents as well as reporting the abuses suffered by political prisoners. Corruption and state negligence are also frequent topics in the independent press. The most interesting articles are those that offer original analyses of economic issues, fresh perspectives on our recent past, and innovative proposals to solve some of our most pressing national problems.

Most people working as independent journalists are not graduates of the School of Information and Communications of the University of Havana. This is the case because, as explained earlier, the DOR participates in the selection of new students. Additionally, for many years admission to college has been restricted by strict ideological criteria, which can be summed up by the following slogan: "the university is for revolutionaries." It is true that some independent journalists barely know how to write a story, in the professional sense of the term. However, their big difference from and advantage over official journalists is that they are not subject to censorship nor are they forced to distort or hide information. To overcome their limitations, many of these journalists have taken different seminars and courses, including the ones offered regularly by the U.S. Interests Section in Havana, which has dozens of graduates.

Undoubtedly, among independent journalists there are partisan positions and it is not typical to find criticism of dissidents there. However, such an attitude is justified because the space available to them is so small that there is only space for criticism of the government. On the other hand, if independent journalism is conceived of as the counterpart to official journalism, it is condemned to not be impartial, because if it were it would conspire against an information equilibrium, at least to the degree that official journalism seeks to be objective.

Generally, independent journalists are connected to news agencies that serve as links between them and the newspapers and radio stations that publish their work and pay them. This opens up the controversial subject of money. No one, much less a journalist, can object to someone being paid for reporting the news. Moreover, when you find out how little an independent Cuban journalist receives for writing a story published abroad, the figure would provoke such pity and compassion that you'd want to sue the publisher for exploitation. But when you compare these payments with the average salary of professional Cuban journalists, then you can understand why, from the perspective of a state-controlled journalist, someone might accuse independent journalists of chasing after money, working as mercenaries "in the service of imperialism."

However, from a strictly rational point of view, what saves independent Cuban journalists from being seen, without exception, as docile employees of "empire," is the immeasurable risk they run in carrying out their work. Seen from this perspective, that is from a cost-benefit analysis, independent Cuban journalists would be the worst-paid mercenaries in the world, and are so poorly paid that it becomes absurd to call them mere mercenaries. This does not mean, however, that independent journalists cannot also be validly divided into at least two groups: Those who believe fervently in what they write and those who simulate their criticism.

From an ethical point of view, independent journalists who believe in what they write hold their positions based on two basic arguments. First, they claim that the lack of freedom imposed by the dictatorship is a mechanism to maintain its power, since allowing freedom of expression would cause the regime to collapse. The main conflict is not between Cuba and the United States, but between the Cuban government and the Cuban people. A second argument is that the much celebrated achievements in health, education, and social security are not nearly as solid, advantageous, or free as is assumed. Moreover, they argue that such achievements are far too small when one considers the high price of individual freedom that must be paid for them. One might add that these people have also given the best years of their lives—their youth—to the revolutionary cause, either as former protagonists in the cause or as its contemporary victims, and it would be too traumatic and demoralizing for them to accept that their children will eventually have to bear the same fate.

So, who are the opportunists among the independent journalists, and more generally within the opposition? First of all, we would have to set aside the State Security agents who have infiltrated their ranks, about whom it is not necessary to elaborate. Second, there are those who become dissidents as a means to emigrate, and are only building up their resumes of persecution in order to qualify for a refugee visa to the United States. Of course, the cynicism of this second group would make it hard to believe that they are die-hard revolutionaries passing as dissidents. They are simply emigrants seeking an easy path out of the country. All this is to say that among independent journalists there is no equivalent to the opportunistic official journalists described earlier: someone who is convinced that the system is the best, or at least that it is acceptable, and who becomes an independent journalist only for the money, or for some other advantage, or out of fear, or because of outside pressures. This kind of pretender, who writes the opposite of what he or she believes out of cowardice or opportunism, is only found among the ranks of official journalists.

Within the ranks of independent journalism we can only find, at most, the case of those who exaggerate, painting the internal situation with the most dire of tones, with the intention of making the story more attractive to the market, or perhaps with the more healthy purpose of calling attention to the problems exposed, but that's another thing altogether. Almost all of what is written by Cuba's independent press is published in the mass media outside the island, either on the Internet (on sites such as *Cubanet, Diario de Cuba, CubaEncuentro, Penúltimos Días, Café Fuerte*, and *Cubapress* among others), in Miami's Spanish language newspaper, *El Nuevo Herald*, or at *Martí Noticias*, or on another website, blog, or radio or television station abroad.

THE JUMP TO THE WEB

With regard to the Internet, we must begin with the fact that until the start of the quite timid reforms so far enacted under President Raúl Castro beginning in 2008, neither computers nor modems were sold to private individuals in Cuba. It was also expressly prohibited to introduce such equipment from abroad, even as a gift for a Cuban. Still today, there is no official Internet service for home users. The limited access that does exist is reserved for certain state institutions and a newly inaugurated chain of 118 cyber cafes with hourly prices equal to a Cuban worker's average weekly salary (US$5). Independent studies estimate that the rate of network connectivity in Cuba does not exceed 3 percent of the population, placing Cuba below even Haiti, which has a rate of 35 percent. An average Cuban citizen cannot walk into a public office to request a household Internet connection. This is a right reserved only for foreign residents on the island and for a handful of senior government officials.

Cuba does have an *Intra*-net, however, which is a network limited by the borders of the island, totally controlled by the state, and intended for the use of medical, scientific, and cultural institutions. More recently, the island saw the inauguration of its own online encyclopedia, called *EcuRed*, modeled after Wikipedia. However, users will find it extremely difficult to edit content. Cuba has also launched its own version of Facebook called *Red Social* (social network), which has the curious peculiarity of denying access from abroad. Access to the global Internet is extremely limited and frustratingly slow, with numerous sites which provide news about the country blocked. Some hotels provide Internet access—mainly intended for their foreign guests—at extremely high hard currency prices between $6 and $18 (6 to 15 convertible pesos, CUCs) per hour.

In December 2004, the digital magazine *Consenso* appeared, which constituted one of the first such cyber-publications produced entirely from within the country. It aimed to practice a critical, professional brand of journalism with a moderate tone that steered clear of both official propaganda and confrontational epithets. This space was later transformed into a portal of blogs under the name *Desde Cuba*, from whence was born the emblematic flagship of the alternative Cuban blogosphere, the blog "Generation Y" by Yoani Sánchez. The *Desde Cuba* portal has continued to

Turning the living room of their Nuevo Vedado apartment into a classroom, independent journalist Reinaldo Escobar (standing) and his wife blogger Yoani Sánchez (seated just to Escobar's left) hold periodic free workshops called "The Blogger Academy" for Cuba's growing community of citizen journalists. (Orlando Luis Pardo Lazo)

evolve, recently becoming a collective site known as *Voces Cubanas*, where more than 40 individual blogs are found. These blogs run the gamut of styles, tones, and themes, including everything from political denunciation to cultural chronicles, philosophical reflections, and even entertainment, sports, and kitchen recipes. Such a diverse, independent, and emergent Internet phenomenon represents a rupture in the long-standing government information monopoly over news emanating from Cuba to the world outside.

The choice of the Internet as a vehicle of expression and accessing news and information is not one of many options for Cuban journalists. Furthermore, it is all too clear that it is impossible to reach all the people using this path. However, it is quite paradoxically, the only crack left open, and it will remain so until the day that the Cuban media is no longer the exclusive preserve of a jealous ideology and the private property of a single party.

REFERENCES

MacKinnon, Rebecca. 2012. *The Consent of the Networked: The Worldwide Struggle for Internet Freedom*. New York: Basic Books.

Márquez, Alba. 2012. "Patria," March 14. http://www.cadenahabana.cu/2012/03/14/patria-2/

Marrero, Juan. 1999. *Dos Siglos de Periodismo en Cuba. Momentos, hechos y rostros*. Havana: Pablo de la Torriente Publishers.

Monterrey, Olvis Carlos. 2002. "Facciolo, La Voz del Pueblo Cubano y el anexionismo." *La Jiribilla* no. 115. http://www.lajiribilla.co.cu/2003/n115_07/fuenteviva.html

Internet, Social Media, and the Cuban Blogosphere

Yoani Sánchez

A 1.0 ISLAND IN A 2.0 WORLD

Cuba has the lowest rate of Internet connectivity of any country in the Western Hemisphere. Out of a total population of over 11 million people, just 2.9 million Cubans have access to the web (Frank 2012; ONE, 2012). However, even this already low penetration overestimates the true number of Cuban "internauts" since it includes those with access only to Cuba's limited national "intranet" along with those who occasionally use a national e-mail address ending in ".cu." There is no government or private office on the island where a Cuban citizen can go to purchase a household Internet connection. Such a connection is a privilege granted only to foreigners residing in Cuba, government officials, or trustworthy intellectuals ideologically aligned with the government (Freedom House 2012; Miroff 2011; Press 2011c, 2012a).

For those who do not fall into any of these categories, other alternatives are quite limited: turning to the black market to buy an illegal connection to the web, with the concomitant risk involved, or going to one of the few foreign embassies that provide Internet access to the public—an option not without its own level of risk of being labeled a traitor. Then there is the Internet access provided by a handful of exclusive Cuban hotels, a service primarily intended for their international guests. It has recently become possible for Cubans with hard currency to access these places. However, depending on the connection speed, an hour of surfing the web from a Cuban hotel can cost between $7 and $15 (US), the equivalent of between a third and an entire average monthly salary of a Cuban.

Finally, in June 2013, the Cuban government opened up 118 new Internet cafes across the island providing public access for the first time. When visiting one of these so-called *telepuntos*, one finds an air-conditioned room with three or four surprisingly fast computers. However, one also discovers a "walled garden" Internet interface called "*Nauta*" provided by the state telecom monopoly *Empresa de Telecomunicaciones de Cuba S.A.* (Telecommunications Company of Cuba, ETECSA), which prices access at US$5 an hour, far beyond the meager budgets of the vast majority of the population. Moreover, surfing the web reveals a number of blocked foreign sites including *CubaEncuentro, Cubanet*, and even Cuba's answer to *Craigslist*, known as *Revolico*. Fortunately, the blockade of "politically incorrect" sites is not total as other critical sites such as *Café Fuerte, Penúltimos Días, Diario de Cuba*, and *El País*, as well as the sites of Amnesty International and Reporters without Borders are indeed available. Most chilling, perhaps, is the fact that each user is required to show their ID card and sign a contract before seating themselves in front of a computer screen. The contract clearly stipulates that the service should not be used for "actions that can be considered . . . harmful or detrimental to public security."

Because of these obstacles we should not be surprised at the utterly anemic presence of Cuba in cyberspace, both in terms of the low number of Cubans online and the lack of intensity of their collective cyber activity. Nevertheless, in the past decade (2004–2013) there has been a significant growth in the number of web portals, blogs, and users of social networks from within the island. Still there is a great imbalance between the number of websites administered by state institutions and those run by independent Cuban citizens (Henken 2011). Cuba has yet to incorporate the world's newest mobile, interactive, and collaborative information and communication technologies with their intended real-time dynamism. For example, Cubans on the island are still unable to carry out a bank transaction via the web, reserve and purchase an airplane or train ticket from the comfort of the keyboard of their own computer, or even shop online. The few minutes of web 2.0 connection that some Cubans are able to afford each month are barely enough for them to check e-mail, chat with a friend or relative abroad, or search for a way off the island.

The fact that large-scale access to the Internet does not exist in Cuba has several explanations, some of which follow the official government discourse and others which are revealed by the island's obstinate reality. For a number of years, when critical voices rose to denounce the technological indigence that hung over the Cuban population, government spokesmen immediately reminded them about the restrictions imposed by the U.S. embargo against the largest island in the Greater Antilles. It is true that at that time Cuba was limited exclusively to a weak satellite connection (Valdés 2009a,

2009b). Commercial and financial constraints imposed by the United States prevented the island from accessing the already existing fiber-optic cables that pass very close to Cuban shores. Moreover, major Internet companies like Google and Microsoft have been instructed to disable access to many of its most useful services from within the island. These frustrating sanctions have been stepped up even as the U.S. Congress allocates upward of $20 million each year to "help break the information blockade" and "support the free flow of information" within the island and between it and the world outside (Miroff 2012). The clumsiness of a long line of Washington administrations had given the government of Fidel Castro—and now to that of his younger brother Raúl—the perfect pretext for keeping the country isolated from revolutionary global developments in information and communication technology.

With the support of this justification, the Cuban government has made clear its intent to find an independent and "sovereign" path to link the island to the technological landscape enjoyed by other nations in the region (Valdés 1997, 2001). In late 2007 the government announced its plan to connect Cuba to the Internet via a fiber-optic cable from Venezuela, a project that promised to increase by a factor of 3,000 the speed with which its 11 million inhabitants access the Internet (Hopkins 2011; ITU 2011). At the time, many pundits predicted that the days of Cubans feeling like Robinson Crusoe—stranded on an isolated island—would soon be over. But they were wrong.

HERE COMES THE CABLE!

By the beginning of 2011 the fiber-optic cable between the province of Santiago de Cuba and the Guaira region of Venezuela was finally installed. After three years of hearing the government herald such an ambitious undertaking—at an estimated cost of $72 million—Cuba's potential "internauts" anxiously awaited the new connection with great expectations. However, Cuban officials were quick to lower such expectations with the clarification that the priority for this new information and communication technology would be social access in spaces such as schools, youth computer clubs, universities, medical centers, libraries, and research centers. It then became clear that providing a domestic connection to the Internet to any citizen willing to pay for it did not factor into the plans of the Cuban Ministry of Computer Science and Telecommunications (Press 2012b; "Venezuela" 2012).

Instead of lowering the high connection prices in hotels or allowing Cuban citizens to pay for their own private household accounts, 2011–2012 has seen a drastic increase in government propaganda (both on state television and on the web itself) aimed at turning the Cuban Internet into a battlefield where it can better fight what it has called a "cyber-war." There has been a notable growth in official propaganda against the alternative Cuban blogosphere, as well as sustained attacks on exile news sites that had previously been completely blocked such as *Café Fuerte*, *Penúltimos Días*, *CubaEncuentro*, and *Diario de Cuba*, aimed at undermining their credibility.

The former state strategy of blocking entire blogs, websites, and portals on the island as was the case for three years (2008–2011) with the blogger portal *Voces Cubanas*—and especially the blog "Generation Y"—was now replaced with a new tactic. Censorship gave way to constant propaganda. Instead of making it impossible for

Cuba's "netizens" to access these alternative sites, now the government began to energetically combat them through innuendo, character assassination, and exaggerated claims that they are "puppets of foreign powers." According to a leaked internal Ministry of the Interior video featuring Eduardo Fontes—a self-styled cyber-revolutionary—the current government tactic consists of attempting to "beat the enemy at their own game" (Acosta and Israel 2011; Coral Negro 2011; Medel 2011; Tamayo 2009).

By mid-2011, it had become clear that something was wrong with the fiber-optic cable. Rumors began to circulate about a possible corruption scandal at ETECSA, the Cuban telecom company. The official press, run by the government and the Communist Party, has been silent so far about whether the costly cable is actually in operation or has been seriously damaged by mismanagement or the use of cheap material. Those who had expected a rapid activation of the cable that would result immediately in a bandwidth previously unknown on the island have been very frustrated. Cuba's entry into the world of Web 2.0 has been postponed once again. Of course, with such a technological delay comes damage to Cuba's professional development, economic updating, and even its civic progress. Every day that goes by without mass access to the Internet for the Cuban population results in years of backwardness in terms of economic and social development with a profound impact on the future of the nation.

Raúl Castro's government finds itself caught in a difficult dilemma, sometimes called the "dictator's dilemma." On the one hand, it could allow mass access to the Internet and accept the consequent loss of its information monopoly. On the other hand, it could reinforce the firewall that disconnects the island from the outside world and accept the resulting underdevelopment. Perhaps the delay in making the fiber-optic cable operational is due to the government's effort to replicate China's so-far successful defiance of the dictator's dilemma: a robust economy, a high-powered

---

THE CUBAN BLOGOSPHERE

Accessing the Internet in Cuba takes place in a context of polarization and suspicion, where Cuba's "internauts" find themselves blockaded by the U.S. embargo on the one hand and by the internal state blockade on Internet access on the other. Just 3 percent of the Cuban population has access to the World Wide Web. The Cuban government has attempted to isolate and alienate different bloggers from one another, mining the virtual space of social media with the same polarizing propaganda that it uses in the traditional media: "In a state of siege, dissidence is betrayal" and "If you are not a revolutionary, you must be a mercenary."

Coming out of this difficult context are Cuba's four most prominent blogger collectives, *Voces Cubanas*, *Havana Times*, *Bloggers Cuba*, and *La Joven Cuba*. Although each has its own history and personality, type of content, way to connect to the Internet, and editorial line, all confront similar challenges in establishing their legitimacy, maintaining their independence, and connecting with both a national and international readership in a polarized domestic context where access to the Internet remains extremely limited and where one's independence can easily be taken to mean you are a dissident.

(if vigilantly filtered) Internet, and an authoritarian state run by a business-minded communist party. Call it "networked authoritarianism," which has figured out how to make the PC (personal computer) compatible with the CP (Communist Party) (MacKinnon 2012; Morozov 2010; Goldsmith and Wu 2006).

For decades, an important element in the rigid ideological control of the Cuban population has been precisely the government's ability to manage the news and silence information about politically unseemly events, even ones that take place inside the country. A political system that has been based for so long on the censorship of information cannot easily survive the avalanche of free communication and the autonomy of its citizens to empower themselves through access to and the ability to create and circulate its own information. If censorship in Cuba has become a method of governing, opening the island up to the free flow of opinions could be a short-term death sentence for the aged and stagnant Cuban Revolution. However, as the other surviving authoritarian regimes such as Iran have shown, "Internet freedom" may empower and connect previously isolated netizens, but it may also facilitate government censorship, surveillance, and propaganda (Morozov 2010).

INTERNET WITHOUT INTERNET

Those who live in other latitudes have great difficulty grasping how some Cubans can share their opinions on the World Wide Web despite the high cost of Internet access and constant government censorship and surveillance. However, such observers are unaware of the ingenuity and creativity that characterizes a population that has lived for decades with chronic scarcities of all kinds in a system that lurches from crisis to crisis. Given such a situation, resilient Cubans have developed a repertoire of gallows humor that makes light of their often desperate, dire straits, and helps explain the technological miracle of Internet access in a place so disconnected. For example, during the worst years of the "special period" that ravaged Cuba in the years following the collapse of the Soviet Union in 1990, there appeared on the dinner tables of many Cuban homes a new recipe: *picadillo de carne sin carne* (ground beef without the beef). This mystery meat was usually a combination of ground plantain peels mixed with tomato sauce and a dash of spice. Given the normally avid appetite of the diners, the final recipe could easily pass for a plate of veal or beef.

If Cubans were able to overcome food shortages with such an inventive cuisine, it is no wonder that they have managed to navigate their lack of kilobytes with the same ingenuity. This is what has been referred to in today's Cuba as "*la Internet sin Internet*" (i.e., getting *on* the Internet, without access *to* the Internet). Such a feat is accomplished through the use of digital tools like flash drives, CDs, and DVDs onto which blog posts, articles from the international press, blocked television programs, inaccessible YouTube videos, and even entire websites, can be copied by those lucky enough to peek into cyberspace. Then they are shared with others in a kind of "hand-to-hand information combat." In this way, someone with access to the Internet can provide a kind of "transitive access" to the web to literally hundreds of others who have never been connected. Of course, this is a method that spreads information virally and exponentially, given the ease with which digital data can be copied, stored,

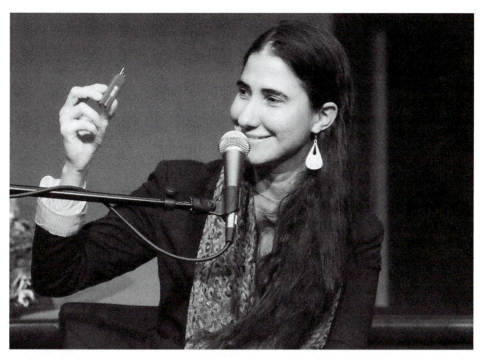

At the start of her first ever visit to the United States, on March 14, 2013, Cuban blogger and human rights activist Yoani Sánchez visited Columbia University's Journalism School to speak about the power of new information and communications technologies at breaking the "information blockade" within the island. She holds up a flash drive while saying that someday a monument should be built to it given its ubiquity as a means of sharing uncensored information. (Tracey Eaton)

and transferred, making it a "medium" of great efficiency and influence in today's Cuba (Hoffmann 2011; Miroff 2010b; Pardo Lazo 2009).

To publish and update websites, blogs, and accounts in the emergent world of social networks, Cubans also turn to this kind of collective ingenuity. In the case of a micro-blogging service like Twitter, for example, it is possible to send text messages (also known as SMS, or Short Message Service) that automatically appear on one's online timeline even if the user is completely disconnected from the web. Nevertheless, this kind of artificial web access is still severely limited by the high prices of instant messaging (IM) and the small size of the mobile phone market in Cuba. Although there has been exponential growth in cell phone use in Cuba since 2008 when public access was legalized, even the 1.5 million user threshold reached in 2012 is still the lowest rate in all of Latin America. It almost goes without saying that Cuban cell phones hail from a time before smart phones, such as the iPhone, Blackberry, or Android, none of which are fully operational in Cuba (Frank 2012; Miroff 2010a).

A single SMS message sent from Cuba abroad costs one CUC, the rough equivalent of a $1.20 (US). Meanwhile, the vast majority of Cubans are still paid in the national currency, CUP, which is worth 24 times less than the CUC. An average Cuban monthly salary is equivalent to 350 pesos, or 14.50 CUC (about US$16). This means that a simple Tweet or SMS greeting sent to a family member abroad costs

HOW TO CONNECT A CUBAN CELLPHONE TO TWITTER

Connect to the Internet and create a Twitter account. Add "Twitter" as a contact in your cell phone using the following number 11–944–762–480–0379. Then, send these four brief messages to the number: 1. start, 2. username, 3. password, 4. ok. Do not to leave spaces before or after the words or use any accent marks. Wait two minutes between each message. Each message will cost you $1. If you make an error you will have to start over again.

In the space for "username" put the name you plan to use on Twitter. Do the same with your password. Before beginning, be sure you have at least $5 credit on your cell phone. After sending these commands, compose a message in the form of a greeting to other Twitter users and ask a friend with Internet access to verify whether your greeting appeared. Now you can send SMSs of no more than 140 characters and have them appear on the Internet for any other Twitter user to read. You will not be able to read what others tweet, nor can you respond to a direct message, but at least this method can serve as a means of transmission.

the average Cuban almost 7 percent of their monthly salary. Who can afford such astronomical prices in Cuba?

The answer to such a question is complex, but it is worth the effort to offer a preliminary answer. For example, those who work in state corporations or joint ventures and receive a portion of their salary in hard currency can afford this luxury. Some of those who receive remittances from abroad and others who engage in the many illicit transactions in the ubiquitous Cuban black market often have enough disposable income for access to cellular technology. Then there are those who exhibit such ideological loyalty that they are entrusted with powerful bureaucratic positions that include a subsidized cell phone as one of the perks. There are also others such as Cuban technicians sent abroad on official missions, as well as some of the island's leading artists, musicians, and athletes, who are able to return from their international travels with enough cash to pay for access to technology.

More recently, given the expansion of self-employment, a special class of Cuban entrepreneurs has arisen on the island many of whom can easily afford cell phones. And finally, there are those who count on the friendship and solidarity of supporters, often anonymous, all around the world who voluntarily subsidize their access to costly information and communications technology. If none of these alternative pathways existed—some illegal and others ethically questionable—Cuba would be a mute island cut off from the cellular revolution.

In such an economically and politically distorted environment, Cuba's community of alternative bloggers and tweeps have bet on the twin virtues of independence and transparency. They have figured out how to post their messages to the world on the web from their Cuban cell phones and often send thanks out into cyberspace to their readers who refill their cellular credit accounts using sites like http://ezetop.com and http://recargasacuba.com. They are often able to get online, thanks to the support of friends and readers who help cover the high cost of Internet access in Cuban hotels or by turning to the Internet access provided—without ideological conditions—by a handful of foreign embassies in Havana. In this way, they help transform their solidarity into Tweets, opinions, and comments based on Cuban reality. They are left with a choice between this limited and risky option or that of remaining silent; forced to run the gauntlet between being labeled "lackeys" and "mercenaries," working for "the Yankee dollar," and the pain of forever keeping their mouths shut.

A PROFILE OF A CUBAN "INTERNAUT"

Any characterization of Cuban "internauts" (Internet users) must take into account the material base from which they manage to connect to cyberspace. This is what determines their independence, the topics they address in their posts, and the frequency with which they are able to publish. We can, nevertheless, take the risk of identifying three preliminary categories with the foreknowledge that describing something others would prefer to keep hidden is extremely difficult. In the strange and sui generis context that is today's Cuba, there are three clearly defined groups: those who connect from official institutions, making sure to avoid any "delicate" topics; those who go online in hotels or embassies, using these platforms as a kind of civic loudspeaker of denunciation; and finally there are the foot soldiers in the ideological battle over the World Wide Web who benefit from a high-speed broadband Internet access unthinkable to the average Cuban with which they can conduct their cyberwar against the revolution's enemies. A quick look at each of these groups will allow us to appreciate their capabilities and limitations.

The Institutionalists

However brave or talented some of these internauts may be, their writings are always conditioned by the ideological directives of their workplace or school. Even so, it would not be accurate to characterize everyone who uses an official connection as an "*oficialista*" (a government apologist or mouthpiece), because that would be falling into the same rigid and schematic definitions used in government propaganda. Among these individuals there are some who manage to break out of the state-imposed straightjacket, maintaining blogs or Twitter or Facebook accounts totally disconnected from the social and political reality in which they live. They are careful to stick to messages of a strictly social nature such as, "Hello to all my friends out there. . . . What a beautiful sunrise I saw this morning. . . . Too bad for those of you who don't have such a view of the sea before your eyes, huh? :-)." Others are a bit more daring—venturing into light criticisms, but knowing all the while that they cannot directly address taboo issues like the urgency of term limits, the need for freedom of expression, the precarious situation of human rights on the island, or the demand for a multiparty system.

The Ciber-cimarrones

These bloggers use the Internet as a tool of denunciation, as an SOS to their fellow Cubans and to the outside world, and as a way to bear witness to that part of Cuba which the official media hides. As a result, they are under constant attack from official propaganda and often find that their cell phones are disabled by Cuba's state monopoly telecom company, ETECSA, so that they are unable to report the news independently. Some of these *ciber-cimarrones* (cyber-escapees) connect to the web from foreign embassies, which offer such a service. They also frequently use the public areas of hotels with Internet service even if doing so too often can leave a hole in their pockets. If we were to analyze their texts, videos, and Tweets, we would find a mixture of calls for help, a chronicle of crime, and demands for more public spaces for free expression and association. Many of them come out of the world of dissidence, independent journalism, or civic activism. Their use of the great global web affords them a more immediate way to make known to the world what their lives are really like. It also serves them as a surprisingly effective protective shield whenever they are subject to state repression. Like the slaves that once fled Cuba's brutal plantations for the safety of hard-to-reach *palenques* (communities of escaped slaves), these digital *cimarrones* know that there is no going back to a life of silence. However, they also know that their kilobytes are an insufficient hideout to avoid punishment. They navigate as they dream and they share their opinions on the web in a way they have never been able to in their day-to-day lives (Henken 2010; Reporters without Borders 2006).

The Soldiers of the Web

These are Cuba's "fortunate sons"; web surfers who enjoy privileged access to the Internet and a regular state paycheck in exchange for their constant if normally redundant and unoriginal cyber-attacks against critics of the system. This might seem hard to imagine for Internet users in other parts of the world, but if we are attentive a few key questions come to mind: If these "revolutionaries" are really organic, independent defenders of the Cuban system, why is it that they fall silent on Twitter each evening when the workday ends? Why is it that so many of those who seem to enjoy attacking critics of the government lack the courage to show their faces, hiding behind the easy anonymity of a cyber-pseudonym? How is it that they are able to regularly publish information they could only have obtained from Cuba's intelligence service, the political police? If they are not organized and coordinated from on high, how is it that so many of them automatically begin using the exact same hashtag together on the same day at the same time? The fact is that on the Internet these militaristic strategies leave a clear trace. Amidst the spontaneity inherent in social networks, partisan postures are easy to detect (Coral Negro 2011; Press 2011a).

TWITTER AND FACEBOOK

The first mention made of social networks in Cuba's official press was to make clear that Twitter and Facebook were "technologies developed by the CIA." After that, even though Cuban newscasts occasionally mentioned Tweets favorable to the island's government, a shadow of suspicion, danger, and prohibition continues to hang over social media for many people. Nevertheless, something of its chirps, trills, and tweets echoes each day in the ears of more Cubans. The tweets that are sent out into the world from the cell phones of dozens of activists manage escape our island's insularity and travel to Cuban émigrés and others interested in our peculiar reality. They then send these brief news flashes back to Cuba. In that sense, Twitter is the boomerang many turn to, launching news into cyberspace abroad so that its echo is then heard in Cuba.

But there is still a lot to do. Cuba's blogosphere and Twittosphere remain hampered by their fragile, embryonic state. They are yet to function as an effective forum for social mobilization, much less focused and coordinated civic or political organization. Many observers have asked why they have not seen a "Cuban Spring" to match the revolutionary uprisings in the Middle East dubbed the "Arab Spring." The answer lies in the technological indigence that besets the country. Here people see their cell phones like hard-won forbidden fruits. After so much cost and frustration, they are reluctant to use them in ways that might lead to their being repossessed or deactivated.

Instead of stopping what has begun, setting aside our keypads, and returning to apathy, it should be remembered that each click made on a tiny gadget brings Cubans closer to a different kind of society. It is a more inclusive society where they will be able to navigate the web and Tweet from a domestic connection without being forced to pay with the costly currency of our docility. It is a society where "we the people" can access a microphone, a newspaper column, or a minute in front of the TV cameras to say our piece. Until that day comes, the chirps, trills, and tweets will continue to be few, but firm. And creativity will help discover new paths out of this "island of the disconnected" toward cyberspace.

BIBLIOGRAPHY

Acosta, Nelson, and Esteban Israel. 2011. "Cuba Unblocks Access to Controversial Blog." *Reuters*, February 8. http://ca.reuters.com/article/topNews/idCATRE7175YG20110208.

Coral Negro. 2011. "La ciber policía en Cuba" [The cyber police in Cuba]. Vimeo video, 53:08, posted by "Coral Negro," January 31. http://vimeo.com/19402730; English transcription: http://translatingcuba.com/?p=7111.

Frank, Marc. 2012. "More Cubans Have Local Intranet, Mobile Phones." *Reuters*, June 15. http://www.reuters.com/article/2012/06/15/net-us-cuba-telecommunications-idUSBRE85D14H20120615.

Freedom House. 2012. "Freedom on the Net, 2012—Cuba." http://www.freedomhouse.org/report/freedom-net/2012/cuba

Goldsmith, Jack and Tim Wu. 2006. *Who Controls the Internet? Illusions of a Borderless World.* Cambridge: Oxford University Press.

Henken, Ted. 2010. "En busca de la 'Generación Y': Yoani Sánchez, la blogosfera emergente y el periodismo ciudadano de la Cuba de hoy." pp. 201–242 in Beatriz Calvo Peña, ed., *Buena Vista Social Blog: Internet y libertad de expresión en Cuba*, Valencia: Aduana Vieja.

Henken, Ted. 2011. "Una cartografía de la blogósfera cubana: Entre 'oficialistas' y 'mercenarios'." *Nueva Sociedad* no. 235 (September–October): 90–109. http://www.nuso.org/upload/articu-los/3799_1.pdf.

Hoffmann, Burt. 2011. "Civil Society 2.0?: How the Internet Changes State-Society Relations in Authoritarian Regimes: The Case of Cuba." GIGA, The German Institute of Global and Area Studies Working Paper No. 156, January. http://www.giga-hamburg.de/dl/download.php?d=/content/publikationen/pdf/wp156_hoffmann.pdf.

Hopkins, Curt. 2011. "Cuba's Internet Capacity to Increase 3,000x." *ReadWriteWeb* (blog), February 13.

ITU (International Telecommunication Union). 2011. "ITU Hails Connectivity Boost for Cuba," news release, February 11. http://www.itu.int/net/pressoffice/press_releases/2011/CM03.aspx.

MacKinnon, Rebecca. 2012. *The Consent of the Networked: The Worldwide Struggle for Internet Freedom*. New York: Basic Books.

Medel, Monica. 2011. "Bloggers Celebrate as Cuba Unblocks their Sites." Journalism in the Americas Blog. http://knightcenter.utexas.edu/blog/bloggers-celebrate-cuba-unblocks-their-sites.

Miroff, Nick. 2010a. "Getting Cell Phones into Cuban Hands." *Global Post*, May 17. http://www.globalpost.com/dispatch/cuba/100514/cell-phone.

Miroff, Nick. 2010b. "Teaching Twitter in Havana." *Global Post*, April 22. http://www.globalpost.com/dispatch/education/100401/blogging-twitter-Sánchez.

Miroff, Nick. 2011. "In Cuba, Dial-Up Internet Is a Luxury." *National Public Radio*, December 14. http://www.npr.org/2011/12/14/143721874/in-cuba-dial-up-internet-is-a-luxury.

Miroff, Nick. 2012. "How the U.S. Keeps Cuba Off the Web." *Global Post*, June 27. http://www.globalpost.com/dispatch/news/regions/americas/cuba/120627/us-embargo-google-analytics-cuban-internet-access.

Morozov, Evgeny. 2010. *The Net Delusion: The Dark Side of Internet Freedom*. New York: Public Affairs.

ONE (Oficina Nacional de Estadisticas). June 2012. *Tecnología de la Información y la Comunicaciones en Cifras, Cuba 2011* [Information and Communication Technology, Cuba 2011] (Havana: ONE).

Pardo Lazo, Orlando Luis. 2009. "Guerrilla Blogging: A Virtual Democracy Against the Odds." *In These Times*, December 6. http://www.inthese-times.com/article/5215/inside_cuba_guerrilla_blogging/.

Press, Larry. 2011a. "Ecured is Not Open Like Wikipedia." The Internet in Cuba (blog), December 21. http://laredcubana.blogspot.com/2011/12/ecured-is-not-open-like-wikipedia.html.

Press, Larry. 2011b. "Cuban Internet: Past, Present, and Future." *Cuba in Transition*, vol. 21. Washington, DC: Association for the Study of the Cuban Economy (ASCE), Miami, Florida, August 5. http://som.csudh.edu/fac/lpress/record-ing/cuba/cuba.html.

Press, Larry. 2011c. "The State of the Internet in Cuba." January. http://som.csudh.edu/cis/lpress/cuba/chapters/lpdraft2.docx.

Press, Larry. 2012a. "Updated Cuban ICT statistics," The Internet in Cuba (blog), July 26. http://laredcubana.blogspot.com.es/2012/07/updated-cuban-ict-statistics.html.

Press, Larry. 2012b. "Hard Data on the Idle ALBA-1 Undersea Cable." The Internet in Cuba (blog), May 22. http://laredcubana.blogspot.com.es/2012/05/hard-data-on-idle-alba-1-undersea-cable.html.

Reporters without Borders. 2006. "Going Online in Cuba: Internet Under Surveillance." http://www.rsf.org/IMG/pdf/rapport_gb_md_1.pdf.

"Silenced During Papal Visit, Cuban Bloggers, Dissidents Speak Out (VIDEO)." 2012. *Hispanically Speaking News*, April 7. http://www.hispanicallyspeakingnews.com/noticitas-de-noticias/details/silenced-during-papal-visit-cuban-bloggers-dissidents-speak-out-video/15038/.

Tamayo, Juan O. 2009. "Cuba Fighting Blogs with Blogs." *Miami Herald*, December 13. http://www.miamiherald.com/2009/12/13/1380664/cuba-fighting-blogs-with-blogs.html.

Tamayo, Juan O. 2012. "Cuba Diverts Dissidents' Phone Numbers in Pope Crackdown," *Miami Herald*, March 30. http://www.miamiherald.com/2012/03/30/2723658/cubas-interior-ministry-left-fingerprint.html.

Valdés, Nelson P. 1997. "Cuba, the Internet, and U.S. Policy." *Georgetown Cuba Briefing Paper Series* no. 13, March.

Valdés, Nelson P. 2001. "Cuba and Information Technology." *Cuba-L Direct*, March, 2008 (originally published in 2001).

Valdés, Nelson P. 2009a. "About Bandwidth and Other Questions." *Progreso Weekly*, November 25.

Valdés, Nelson P. 2009b. "Cyber Cuba: The Internet, Broadband, and Foreign Policy." *Counterpunch*, November 19.

"Venezuela: Fiber-optic Cable to Cuba is Working." 2012. *Bloomberg Businessweek*, May 24. http://www.businessweek.com/ap/2012-05-24/venezuela-fiber-optic-cable-to-cuba-is-working.

Culture

INTRODUCTION

This chapter on culture highlights the extraordinarily broad and prolific cultural production that has emanated from Cuba during the 20th century. It chronicles the nation's cultural achievements in the arts with a particular focus on language, literature, art, dance and music, filmmaking and photography, cuisine, sports, and popular culture and customs. The chapter also contrasts the contradictory governmental policies of support and promotion of revolutionary art and culture on the one hand, with the repression of independent and critical art on the other. In the process, the authors highlight the emergence of a variety of independent cultural projects and the tentative creation of new more inclusive spaces of creation and dialogue in the dynamic, ongoing relationship between art and revolution.

Since Fidel Castro gave his 1961 speech, "Words to the Intellectuals," establishing the cryptic policy: "Within the revolution, everything; against the revolution, nothing," Cuba's artists have had to proceed with trepidation never knowing for sure what was within, what was without, and what was against the revolution. As a result, to paraphrase Cuban writer Antonio Benítez-Rojo, Cuban culture has long been doubly mediated by fear: the state's fear of the artist, resulting in censorship; and the artist's fear of the state, leading to self-censorship (Benítez-Rojo 1990).

Language and Literature

Miguel Iturria Savón and Ted A. Henken

LANGUAGE

Cubans speak Spanish, which as a phonetic language, is written as it is spoken. However, there is great variation across the Spanish-speaking world. For example, you can happily (though not very easily!) *coger una guagua* (catch a bus) in Cuba, but don't try to take a *guagua* in Bolivia or *coger* a bus in Mexico. In the first case, you might be arrested for kidnapping and in the second for indecent exposure! Despite this variation, native speakers of Spanish can be mutually understood almost anywhere in the Spanish-speaking world. Written Spanish is highly regular in its grammatical rules, syntax, and spelling. If you know even a little Spanish, you can make yourself understood in Cuba.

Most non-Spanish speakers are scared away from the language by having to learn the proper placement of stress and the use of written accents. However, the rules for stress in Spanish are actually quite simple and consistent. Learning the rules is important since words can change meaning based on stress and accent. For example, "*jugo*" means "juice," while "*jugó*" means "(he/she) played." Similarly, "*si*" means "if," while "*sí*" means "yes." If a word ends in a *vowel*, "*n*" or "*s*," the (natural) stress falls on the second-to-last syllable. Words with other endings (all consonants except "n" or "s") carry a (natural) stress on the final syllable. Any word that departs from this pair of rules must carry a written accent.

Common words with natural stress include "*comida*" (co-MI-da), "*hombre*" (OM-bre), "*vasos*" (VAS-os), "*mujer*" (mu-HAIR), and "*vivir*" (vi-VIR)—and thus none of these words carry a written accent, though all have a (natural) stress. Common words that must carry a written accent mark (often referred to as a *tilde*) include "*lámpara*" (LAM-pa-ra), "*árbol*" (AR-bol), and "*unión*" (un-i-ON). Incidentally, nearly all words ending in "*-ión*" in Spanish carry a written accent mark over the "*o*." Only vowels are given written accents since they separate Spanish words into different stressed and unstressed syllables. For example, "*co-MI-da*," carries no accent mark but has a natural stress on the second-to-last syllable. In contrast, "*lám-pa-ra*," breaks the rule so must carry a written accent on the third-to-last syllable, "*LAM*." Finally, single syllable words, such as "*si*" and "*sí*," mentioned earlier use accents to distinguish different meanings, not different sounds, since by definition single-syllable words cannot carry stress. Likewise, certain words used in interrogatory sentences, such as "*¿cuándo?*," "*¿cómo?*," or "*¿qué?*," are distinguished by a written accent mark from the same sounding words when they are used in declarative sentences: "*cuando*," "*como*," or "*que*."

Characteristics of Cuban Spanish

Despite such simple rules, understanding what Cubans are saying (especially when they are speaking with each other) can be a challenge. In Cuba, Spanish becomes a kind of fast-paced contact sport where informality, invention, wordplay, coquett-ishness, satire, mockery, and speed are all highly regarded qualities. In its spoken form, Cuban Spanish tends to be among the most difficult forms of the language to understand for an outsider. This derives from the accent, the speed, and the Cuban (and Caribbean) tendency to drop (or merely imply) entire syllables and to let one's voice fall at the end of each word so that the final syllable is often de-emphasized when not totally silent.

Cuban utterances tend to feature a marked rise in intonation with a sustained high-pitched climax before a rather sudden fall of intonation (often devoiced) at the end of a sentence. Perhaps the two best examples of this characteristic are, in fact, the two words most stereotypically associated with Cubans, "*chico*" (buddy) and "*caballero*" (friend, literally gentleman). Just as the use of "*che*" (hey or buddy) has become emblematic of Argentine speech, constant use of the terms "chico" (pronounced with a loud, rising "*CHI-*" and a contrasting, almost mute "-*co*") and "*caballero*" (with the "*lle*" stressed and lengthened and the final "*ro*" softened) are representative of the cadence and rhythm of Cuban Spanish in general.

Cubans love nicknames and use them lavishly. Any pronounced personal char-acteristic, it seems, will lead to an affectionate but often mocking *apodo* (nickname). These diminutive nicknames have tenacity and before long you will have close per-sonal friends whose real names you may not even know. Castro himself, often called simply as "Fidel" by Cubans, is just as often referred to by one of his many nick-names: "*El Comandante*" (The Commander), "*El Viejo*" (The Old Man), or "*El Ca-ballo*" (The Horse). Cubans are especially fond of nicknames that highlight a certain distinctive physical characteristic, and it is not uncommon to hear someone referred to in a way that might be cause for offense elsewhere: *Negrita* (Blacky), *Gordita* (Fatty), *Loqui* (Crazy), *El Chino* (The Chinaman), *El Gago* (The Stutterer), *Flaco* (skinny), or *El Cojo* (Limp).

There are innumerable "*cubanismos*" (words and idioms particular to Cuba) that distinguish Cuban slang and reflect the island's history, diverse cultural in-fluences, and current reality. Common cubanismos today include "*no es fácil*" (it ain't easy), "*ya tu sabe(s)*" (right on), and "*no cogas lucha*" (don't fight it). There is also the infamous, universal, and multipurpose Cuban expression, "*coño*," which though just four letters has innumerable variations, among which are the abbrevi-ated "*¡ñó!*," mentioned earlier, as well as the elongated "*¡ñooooooo!*" These *cuban-ismos* can be described as "short sentences drawn from long experience," and in Cuba have become almost an art form, known alternately as *refranes*, *adagios*, or when used for the purpose of catching a potential lover's eye, *piropos* (one-liners/come-ons). One common example of this last form is "*Oye linda, si cocinas como caminas, me como hásta la raspita*" (Hey beautiful, if you cook like you walk, I'll even eat the leftovers). Perhaps Cuban poet, patriot, and independence leader, José Martí was the most prolific inventor of these powerful phrases. His, of course, are much less *atrevido* but no less powerful or witty. Some of his more memo-rable refrains include "*La patria necesita sacrificios; Es ara y no pedestal*" (The fatherland needs our sacrifice; It is an altar not a pedestal); "*Preferible es no ser, a no ser sincero*" (It is preferable not to be, than not to be sincere); and "*El dogma que vive de autoridad, muere de crítica*" (The dogma that lives from authority, dies from criticism).

While there are literally thousands of busts of Cuban poet and independence leader José Martí in Cuba, the one pictured here is in a West New York, New Jersey park overlooking the Hudson River and Manhattan skyline. On his first ever visit to the New York Metropolitan area in May 2013, Cuban computer scientist, political activist, and You-Tube sensation Eliécer Ávila ponders the inscription below the bust, which reads: "La patria es ara no pedestal" (The fatherland is an altar not a pedestal). (Ted Henken)

A Mestizo *Language*

When the Spanish navigators briefly disembarked in Cuba in October 1492, and up to the beginning of the conquest of the island in 1511, the majority of the island spoke the insular Arawak language of the *Taínos*. Though this was the island's most extended and developed pre-Columbian culture, we know precious little about their language. After the conquest, the Queen of the Castile region of Spain spread Castilian (*castellano*, what we now call Spanish) as the official language in Cuba, ignoring all preexisting languages. While the Taíno language and civilization were quickly destroyed, a few tangible traces of their culture have survived. Some of these include their different kinds of structures like *bohíos* (palm huts) and *caneyes* (large sheds), as well as other terms which have been absorbed into Latin American Spanish (and American English), such as *tabaco* (tobacco), *barbacoa* (barbecue), *hamaca* (hammock), *canoa* (canoe), *cacique* (chieftain), *huracán* (hurricane), and *iguana* (Paz Pérez 1998). The Taíno names of numerous cities, natural regions, plants, and animals have also survived.

Cuban Spanish vividly reflects the many transculturized ethnic and geographical influences absorbed by the island over its more than 500-year history. In Cuba, the Spanish of European conquistadores, colonists, and immigrants, has been modified, enriched, and "Cubanified"—if you will—by Taínos, Africans, North Americans, and many others over such a long time and to such a degree that Cubans no longer speak standard Spanish, but what we might call "*Cubonix.*" The complex ethnic and cultural processes on the island fostered a linguistic *mestizaje*, as was the case in Brazil and Venezuela. Such circumstances differ from "transplanted societies," such as Argentina and Uruguay, as well as from predominately indigenous ones like Bolivia, Ecuador, Guatemala, and Peru, which continue to treasure and preserve the languages of their native peoples.

TAÍNO TOPONYMS, HYDRONYMS, AND ZOONYMS ARE ALIVE AND WELL

Although the Arawak/Taíno language is largely gone from Cuba, as much as 70 percent of Cuban place names used to this day are of native origin. Some examples are the cities of Baracoa, Bayamo, Camagüey, Guanabacoa, Guantánamo, Moa, and Mayarí; the villages Cajobabo, Guáimaro, Guamá, Guanabo, Manatí, Mayajigua, Sagua de Tánamo, Sibanicú, and Siboney; the rivers Arimao, Bacuranao, Bacunayagua, Bacunagua, Baconao, Caonao, Cojímar, Cuyaguateje, Hanabana, Jatibonico, Mayabeque, Sigua, and Saramaguacán; the valley of Yumurí; the mountains Nipe-Sagua, Guamuhaya, and Yateras; Guajaibón Peak; the Guaniguanico mountain range; Turiguanó Island; Guajaba Key; Los Taínos lagoon; Dayamajabo and Yarey beaches; Caguanes and Tabaco Points; the bays of Batabanó and Guacanayabo; and the peninsula of Guanahacabibes. Cuba's flora and fauna are no exception. The primordial names of some botanical and zoological species include yuca (manioc), guanábana, guayaba (guava), papaya, mamey, guayacán, and majagua. Birds with indigenous names include the tojosa, tocororo and colibrí; there are rodents such as the almiquí and jutía; as well as the following fish: the biajaca, guabina, and the guajacón.

Despite the great variation across Latin America and the Caribbean in Spanish phonology (sound), morphology (word structure), syntax (word order), and style (cadence and rhythm), there are two great language families in the region. One is "dynamic" (an Andalucía-influenced "trade-route Spanish" that includes the Caribbean and other lowland, coastal areas). The other is "static" (the "vice regal Spanish" of Mexico, Peru, and other interior highlands) (Davis 2002). This explains why the linguistic characteristics of Cuban Spanish are very similar to other areas connected to the slave trade and the mercantilist commodity trade route of the colonial period, such as the Dominican Republic and Puerto Rico as well as those coastal regions of Mexico (Vera Cruz), Colombia (Cartagena), and Ecuador (Esmeraldas), which share similar histories.

Like the Spanish spoken in these other regions, Cuban Spanish is the result of a true transculturation of a variety of ethno-linguistic influences, the strongest of which are Southern Spain (Andalucía) and the Canary Islands, West Africa (Yoruba, Bantu, Carabalies, Congolese, Lucumies, Mandingas, and as many as 20 other African ethno-linguistic groups), and the Arawak/Taíno. To these major constituent elements can be added three other less significant linguistic infusions: that of the French refugees who arrived in Santiago and Guantánamo fleeing the Haitian revolution (1791–1804); the more than 125,000 Chinese laborers who came to the island between the 1860s and the 1890s; and perhaps equal number of black migrant workers who came to labor in Cuba's cane fields during the first half of the 20th century, primarily from Jamaica and Haiti. A final addition to this already polyglot mixture arrived with the U.S. soldiers in 1898, American English. Surprisingly, there seems to have been little if any influence of the Russian language on Cuban Spanish, though an entire generation of Cuban students were taught the language and raised on *muñequitos rusos* (Russian cartoons). One exception to this rule is the use of the Russian term *nomenklatura* to refer to privileged members of the Communist Party hierarchy (Valdés Bernal 1994).

Examples of Africanisms common in everyday Cuban speech include *"asere"* (buddy), *"ecobio"* (friend), *"monina"* (friend), *"chévere"* (cool), *"¿Qué bolá?"* (What's up?), *"nagüe"* (buddy), *"fula"* (bad or money), *"iria"* or *"iriampo"* (food), and *"aché"* (spirit or soul force), as well as the many African words used in Cuban sacred rituals (e.g., *orisha*, meaning deity) and popular music. Perhaps the most commonly heard Africanism in Cuban Spanish is the expression, *"¿Qué bolá, asere?"* (What's up, buddy?), which originates in the sacred language of the Afro-Cuban secret society alternately called Abakuá or Ñáñigo (described in the section on Religion at the start of Chapter 5) who came from the Calabar region of Africa, thus the other common name for the ethnic group in Cuba, Carabalí.

While the majority of these Africanisms originate with the Nigerian-cordofana linguistic family of languages brought to Cuba by the Yoruba, the Bantu-speaking people of the Congo have also contributed a number of words to the Cuban lexicon, including two words intimately connected with dance music: *sandunga* (flirtatiousness or mischievousness) and *bemba* (lips, forever associated with Cuban singer Celia Cruz's version of the song "Bemba Colorá," Red Lips) (Valdés Acosta 2002). This popular Bantu word is also commonly used in Cuban Spanish when referring to the "rumor mill" (*radio bemba*) and in the popular expression, *"No te pongas esta bemba"* (Don't put on that sad/angry face). Other terms associated with specific musical genres include *rumba*, *conga*, and *mambo*, while some of the many African-termed percussion instruments include the tambor, chéqere, bongo, conga, tumbadora, and maraca (though this last one more likely comes from the Taíno). Many of these African words are recognizable in Cuban Spanish as they preserve the letter combinations *"mb"* (as in *bemba*, *rumba*, *mambo*, and *timba*) or *"ng"* (as in *conga*, *bongo*, *sandunga*, and *songo*).

The Africans also inadvertently contributed a number of Anglicisms to Cuban Spanish that they learned from English slave traders. Some of these include *fufú* (food—plantain mash), *tifi-tifi* (thief), *yari-yari* (yearn), and *luku-luku* (look). Aside from actual African-derived words, perhaps a deeper impact from the Yoruba and Bantu languages is evident in the informal, playful nature of Cuban speech. A related, if somewhat surprising influence on Cuban Spanish comes from the almost 60-year American presence on the island. There are a host of common Cuban words and even some expressions that have clear origins in standard American English of the first part of the 20th century. Examples include *"claxon"* (horn), *"blúmer"* (bloomers/panties), *"bróder"* (brother/buddy), *"restaurán"* (restaurant), *"vivaporú"* (Vicks Vapor Rub, more commonly heard in Miami), *"pulóver"* (t-shirt), *"fílin"* (feeling, an emotive genre of music), *"doile"* (doily or placemat), *"plo"* (plug), *"breiker"* (breaker), *"fei"* (face), *"cake"* (with the same meaning as in English, but pronounced like the letter "k"), *"noháu"* (know how), and *"sidecar"* (motorcycle sidecar) (Paz Pérez 1998), as well as many drinking, boxing, and baseball terms incorporated along with American leisure culture, such as, *"strike"* (straight up/neat), *"a la roca"* (on the rocks), *"jaibol"* (highball glass), *"lager"* (beer), *"shor"* (shorts), *"estrai"* (strike as in baseball), *"nocaut"* (knock out) *"ring"* (boxing ring), and *"jonrón"* (homerun).

Cubans are renowned among Latin Americans for their particular mode of dropping their voice at the end of phrases and even clipping words in half in order to communicate more quickly and with more personality and emotion. Like Andalusians, Dominicans, and Puerto Ricans, Cubans are also notoriously hungry for "Ss." Thus, perhaps the most distinctive characteristic of the sound of Cuban Spanish is the tendency to aspirate the "s" at the end of words. For example, "*los amigos*" suddenly becomes "*loh amigo*." Cubans also commonly clip off the final consonants of words. The letter "d" also often falls victim to this tendency, especially with the ending "-dad." This can be heard, for example, in the common use of the word "*cantidad*" at the end of a sentence to mean "very," "much," or "a lot," as in "*Me gustó cantidá*" (I liked it a lot) or "*Soy malo cantidá*" (I'm very bad).

The "*d*" is also often aspirated when Cubans use past participle constructions like "*-ado*." Perhaps the most famous example of this characteristic is found in Ernest Hemingway's *The Old Man and the Sea*, where the old Cuban fisherman Santiago, who has gone for so long without catching anything, is described as being "*salao*" (instead of the proper, "*salado*"), which literally means salty, but in Cuban and southern Spanish slang indicates "the worst kind of bad luck." This trait grows directly out of Andalusian Spanish where the vocabulary associated with the Roma (also known as gypsies, or *gitanos* in Spanish) and flamenco music and dance features terms like *tablao* (from *tablado* or stage), *cantaor* (from *cantador* or singer), and *bailaor* (from *bailador* or dancer).

A final pair of phonological tendencies in Cuban Spanish has to do with words that end with an "r." Often a final "r" is replaced by an "l" sound as in the word "*actuar*" (to act) becoming "*actual*" (current). Another modification sometimes made to words ending in "r" is most common among the rural, working class who generally shift the "r" to a "y" as when "*comer*" becomes "*comey*" or "*compadre*" becomes "*compay*." Thus, the stage name of the late "son" musician Francisco Repilado, *Compay Segundo*.

In terms of word structure, Cuba is *tú* territory ("you" familiar), eschewing the familiar *vos* (also meaning "you") that is used in parts of Central and South America. Moreover, Cubans rarely use the more formal pronoun *usted* ("you") even when addressing an elderly person or figure of authority. When employing a diminutive, Cubans frequently replace the more common "-*ito*" with "-*ico*." They say "*chiquitico*" (not *chiquito*) "*ratico*" (not *ratito*) and "*puntica*" (not *puntita*). Cubans also invert the word order (syntax) in many common phrases. For example, they often fail to reverse the verb-pronoun in interrogative sentences, saying "*¿Qué tú quieres?*" not *¿Qué quieres (tú)?*, a habit that may have originated through influence from English. Another common Cuban word inversion occurs in expressions using an initial '*más*' as a negative combination. Instead of the more standard "*nada más*" (nothing more) or "*nunca más*" (never again), Cubans are more likely to say "*más nada*" and "*más nunca*." Cubans are also more likely to use the word "*cantidad*" as an adjective, as in "*Está bueno cantidad*," instead of the standard "*Está muy bueno*" (It's very good).

A spiritual element related to spoken language is gestural language, expressed through motions and gestures that illustrate speech with actions and attitudes. Like the Spanish, Italians, and other Latin nations of the Mediterranean, the Cuban people communicate each idea with a gesture, be it facial, manual, corporal, or by combining them together. Of course, this Cuban trait was also influenced by a similar tradition of African gestural language.

In any event, during colonial times knowing Spanish constituted a way of climbing the socioeconomic and political ladder for immigrants of any origin, and an obvious way of showing adhesion to Spain and "*Hispanidad*" (Spanish culture) on the island. Those who spoke only Galician, Catalan, or Basque had to learn Spanish and make the transition from their mother tongue to the dominant language. This process often also involved a move from the bilingualism of one's children to the monolingualism of one's grandchildren, so that already by the third generation the ancestral language was lost. This linguistic succession began again with the cycles of immigration from the Spanish peninsula and the Canary Islands, especially for those coming from isolated rural areas where a local, native language predominated long before Castilian Spanish become a quasi-national language during the first half of the 20th century.

CUBAN LITERATURE: THE AVANT-GARDE VERSUS THE VANGUARD

Colonial Literature

It is nearly impossible to briefly summarize half a millennium of creative musings, from the journal of Christopher Columbus, moving through the primitive simplicity of the first Cuban improvising versifiers, historians, academic prose, the theater, the essay, the narrative, the poetic overabundance, and the writings advanced by printing houses and newspapers, which burst forth with the takeoff of Creole culture in the middle of the 18th century. After the conquest, works of literary value scarcely existed, except the allegations of Father Bartolomé de las Casas against the abuses of the conquest and the letters from Cuba's first governor, Diego Velázquez, informing the King of Castile about his tours across the island to found the first villas. Such documents, of course, precede Cuban literature properly speaking. Moreover, the colonizers made no attempt to understand and record the oral traditions of Cuba's aboriginal peoples.

In spite of the slow development of the island and the early departure of many of the colonizers to Mexico, Central America, Florida, and Peru, there remained an effort to create sacristies in the towns of the Indians, where they would be taught to speak, read, and write Spanish. In 1523 the Bishop of Santiago de Cuba created the charge of *Maestrescuela* (master school) to prepare the clergy for this undertaking. The Creole Miguel Velázquez, educated in Seville and Alcalá de Henaresy, acted as the first teacher between 1540 and 1544. A half-century later, Bishop Juan de la Cabeza Altamirano founded the Semanario Tridentino and inserted himself into the history and early literature of the island upon being kidnapped by the pirate Gilberto Girón and later rescued by a slave. This dramatic saga was set down in a fictionalized version by Silvestre de Balboa in his work *Espejo de Paciencia* (1608), the first written literary account on the island. Though written in the early 17th century, *Espejo de Paciencia* was not discovered until 1838 by the writer José A. Echeverría. In the lyrical tradition of Spain and epic Renaissance poetry, the book is a long narrative poem. Its plot is lineal and structured into cantos and incorporates real people (Instituto de Literatura y Lingüística 2002/2003).

As a genre, historiography is the daughter of the 18th century. In Cuba, it was through historical texts—with authors looking at the past to explain the evolution of the island—that Cuban literature got its start. To the elder priest, Onofre de Fonseca

(1648–1710), is owed the *Historia de la aparición milagrosa de Nuestra Señora de la Caridad del Cobre* (The History of the Miraculous Apparition of Our Lady of Charity, 1703), a laudatory pamphlet that tries to give historical credibility to a mythical tradition. A greater contribution is the *Carta de relación de la isla de Cuba y sus partidos* (Letter about the Island of Cuba and Its Times), with three stories about the governors of Havana, the bishops and the viceroys of Mexico, written by Antonio Zayas Bazán (1666–1748). The *habanero* José Martín Feliz de Arrate (1701–1765) wrote in modern style and was a known defender of the rights of the Creole elite. His work was a forerunner of the pro-independence essayists of the 19th century. Arrate represented the conscience of the Creole in opposition to the Spanish *peninsulares*, as well as promoting the concept of Cuba as *patria* (homeland)—later wholeheartedly embraced by José Martí.

During the first reformist period (1790–1820), as Spain allowed a limited economic opening in Cuba, Cuba tried to shake off its colonial drowsiness and incorporate itself into modernity. The American Revolution (1776–1783), the French Revolution (1789), the Haitian Revolution (1791–1804), and the occupation of Spain by Napoleon in 1808 all had an impact on the island and sowed the seeds of independence in Latin America (1810–1822). Cuban literature then came into its own, subject to the neoclassicism coming from Spain and the politics of the "enlightened despot," which promoted progress and culture and was personified by Governor Luis de las Casas Aragorri, founder of the *Papel Periódico de La Habana* in October 1790 and the *Real Sociedad Patriótica*. From 1820 to 1868 there was a transition to Romanticism, and in the three following decades *Modernismo* dawned.

Colonial literature also lived through journalism. The essay, its principal genre, had among its devotees the landowner Francisco de Arango y Parreño (1765–1837), ideologist and spokesman for the slave-owning bourgeoisie, and Father José Agustín Caballero (1762–1835). In their writings, each expressed the complexity of socio-economic and cultural relations in the transition from the economy of sailor-soldier military services to that of the sugar plantation, which demanded more slaves, in contradiction to the introduction of technical advances. Arango y Parreño, sometimes described as "the stateless statesman," expressed his economic liberalism in a clean and modern prose in his *Discourse on Havana Agriculture and Ways to Promote It*. In other thoughtful and pragmatic leaflets he advocated an autonomous government for Cuba. In contrast to the pragmatism of Arango, Caballero wrote in a more varied and philosophical prose. He demanded improvements in the living conditions of slaves and advocated—with his harangues and essays—the introduction of experimental science to the island's educational system. It was into this context that sailed the European explorer, naturalist, historian, and Proto-anthropologist Alexander von Humboldt, often thought of as the second "discoverer" of Cuba.

Throughout Cuban history, writers and intellectuals have coalesced into a series of intellectual and literary movements. After 1820, several writers emerged to address the triple struggle to achieve the abolition of slavery, win political independence from Spain, and form a distinctly Cuban national identity. The leading lights of this movement included the thinker Félix Varela (1787–1853)—successor to the ideology of Caballero—the poets José María Heredia (1803–1839), Gertrudis Gómez de Avellaneda (1814–1873), and the legendary José Martí (1853–1895), prose writer, journalist, poet, thinker, and independence leader. Varela and Heredia introduced

ALEXANDER VON HUMBOLDT (1769–1859) IN CUBA

Cubans sometimes say that while Columbus was the island's first "discoverer," the German naturalist Alexander von Humboldt was its second. Humboldt first visited the island in late November 1800. He returned in 1804 in order to carry out geological studies commissioned by Cuba's *Sociedad Económica de Amigos del País*. Humboldt's keen sense of observation, illustrated in his book-length essay, *The Island of Cuba*, allowed Cubans to see themselves through the critical gaze of a sympathetic foreigner for the first time. His portrait pleased the Cubans because it found a nationalist sentiment and hinted at the island's great, so far untapped potential.

Humboldt managed to arrive in Cuba just as it was becoming a sugar-producing, slave-based economy. He saw the economic potential of Cuba's vast interior, yet warned against expanding slavery which he considered "the greatest of all evils which have afflicted mankind." However, many of the same Creole aristocrats who had worked with him during his stay in Cuba staunchly disagreed, considering slavery the only way that Cuba could harness its formidable natural resources.

the image of the country from afar and the literature of exile, first developed by the essayist José Antonio Saco (1797–1879). Two other important 19th century literary figures who sought to advance these causes were Domingo del Monte (1804–1853) and Cirilo Villaverde (1812–1894).

Varela was a thinker with his own aesthetic, which he expressed in his essays on the transition from reform to independence, on the neoclassical criticism of the 18th century to the romantic and passionate 19th century, and on the concept of the Cuban Creole. By replacing Caballero as the chair of philosophy at the University of Havana, he countered scholasticism and introduced the experimental sciences stimulated by Bishop Espada y Landa. In 1821 he published his *Observations on the Political Constitution of the Spanish Monarchy*. As a Cuban representative to the Spanish Cortes in 1823, he revealed his radical thinking, so that upon the restoration of the absolutism of Ferdinand VII, he was forced to flee to the United States, where he lived in exile for the rest of his long life. In New York, in 1824, he founded the newspaper *El Habanero* and edited his *Misceláneas filosóficas*, the *Cartas a Elpidio*, and scores of articles, speeches, and letters. He also became known in New York as a leading cleric and fearless defender of the city's Irish immigrants.

José María Heredia, considered the first of Latin America's Romantic poets, was also Cuba's first poetic icon. Despite residing most of his life outside the island because his father was a Spanish government official, Cuba remained the center of his certainties, frustrations, and hopes. As a child, he shuttled with his father between Santiago de Cuba, where he was born, and Pensacola, Florida, Santo Domingo, Venezuela, and Mexico. As an adult in Mexico, he plunged into civil strife, serving as judge, prosecutor, legislator, minister, and journalist; while writing plays and polishing his book of verse, *Poesías*, published first in New York in 1825, and in an expanded edition in Toluca, Mexico in 1832.

Due to his pro-independence political activities, Heredia spent a good deal of his adult life in the United States and Mexico. After publicly renouncing his conspiratorial beliefs, he returned to Cuba in 1836 only to be met with the scorn of his former friends, including one former mentor, Domingo del Monte. Rebuffed, he returned to Mexico almost immediately and died there a few years later. His most emblematic poems established the recurrent theme of nostalgia for a lost *patria* (homeland) in Cuban literature. Among his most cited are the odes *En el Teocalli de Cholula* (1820), a reflection on the passage of time after viewing the ruins of an Aztec temple in Mexico; *A la estrella de Cuba* (To the Star of Cuba, 1823); and *Oda al Niágara* (1824), composed after visiting Niagara Falls. A novelized account of his peripatetic life was recently published as *La novela de mi vida* (The Novel of My Life, 2001), by one of Cuba's leading contemporary novelists, Leonardo Padura (2001, 2003b).

Domingo del Monte was the leader of the most important literary salon of 19th century Cuba, which served also as an important incubator of abolitionism and protonationalism. First from his home in Matanzas and later in Havana, Del Monte mentored an entire generation of Cuban intellectuals, writers, and abolitionists, many of whom called themselves "*delmontinos*" in his honor. Included among the writers who attended Del Monte's literary salon, or *tertulia*, were the novelist Cirilo Villaverde, the poet and former slave Juan Francisco Manzano, and Heredia. Due to his abolitionist activities and friendship with the British antislavery crusader David Turnbull, Del Monte was forced into exile himself in 1842. Thereafter, he was tried in absentia as part of the Escalera conspiracy and died in exile in Madrid.

Del Monte's role as the main intellectual force incubating Cuban protonationalism was furthered by his disciple Cirlio Villaverde. Like Del Monte, Villaverdre was forced to spend much of his life in exile due to the political content of his writings, especially his novel *Cecilia Valdés*, which has come to be celebrated as Cuba's "national" novel and founding myth. The novel, subsequently made into a play, operetta, and film, features a rivalry between sugar-planting and coffee-growing families set in the early decades of the 19th century. Also prominently featured is

JUAN FRANCISCO MANZANO (1797–1854)

The only memoir of slavery in Latin America actually written by a slave himself is Juan Francisco Manzano's *Poems by a Slave in the Island of Cuba, Recently Liberated* (1840). The book contains an autobiographical narrative and a series of poems. Though Manzano's childhood was fairly carefree, when he entered adolescence he experienced many of the degradations of slavery, being subject to harsh and often arbitrary punishments, many of which are recounted in his book. After escaping from slavery in Matanzas, Manzano came to Havana and eventually met the great writer and intellectual Domingo del Monte. With Del Monte's assistance Manzano continued publishing his poetic work and gained notoriety. It was actually due to Del Monte's urging and encouragement that Manzano wrote his autobiography. In 1844, Manzano was falsely accused in the Escalera conspiracy and jailed. Although he was cleared of any involvement and released in 1845, Manzano never wrote again.

a complicated cross-racial and cross-class romance between the star-crossed lovers, Cecilia, a free *mulata*, and Leonardo, a wealthy white planter (who turn out to be half-siblings). Though started in Cuba in 1839, the novel was not completed and published in its final form until 1882 in New York.

Together with Heredia, Gertrudis Gómez de Avellaneda, often referred to simply as "*La Avellaneda*," was one of the most important figures of 19th century Cuban Romanticism. A literary movement characterized by hostility toward Spanish rule in the Caribbean and support for independence in Spain's remaining colonies, the Cuban strain of Romanticism also featured a marked sense of protonationalism and a commitment to exposing the harsh social, political, and economic conditions as lived on the island. Though born in Camagüey to a Spanish father and a Cuban Creole mother, Avellaneda departed for Spain at 22 after rejecting an offer of a "good marriage" from a suitor. Her sonnet, *Al partir*, written upon going to Spain in 1836, is a cry of love and *cubanía* (Cubanness).

As a writer and thinker, *La Avellaneda* can be described as an abolitionist and protofeminist who enjoyed tremendous success in Madrid's literary circles as a playwright between the late 1830s and 1858. Her life on the Peninsula was a succession of creative goals and personal passions, far outside the norm of the patriarchal 19th century. To her dramas, comedies, stories, and two volumes of poetry she added a collection of love letters of human depth and feminine affirmation. In 1838 she debuted the tragedy *Leoncia*. She then published several novels and dramas.

Prior to her literary success, Avellaneda bore a child out of wedlock to her Spanish lover, the poet Gabriel García Tassara. The child later died and a subsequent marriage to another Spaniard ended after only three months when her new husband also died. Despite her strong literary qualifications, Avellaneda was denied membership in the Spanish *Academia* in 1853 because she was a woman. She returned to Cuba in 1859 with her second husband and remained there until 1864, during which time she wrote her *Álbum Cubano de lo Bueno y lo Bello* (Cuban Album of the Good and the Beautiful) and the novel, *El artista barquero* (The Boatman Artist). However, she is best known in Cuba for her early 1841 novel that attacked slavery, *Sab*.

Finally, apart from his constant political activities and writings on behalf of Cuban independence, Cuban patriot José Martí distinguished himself as one of the

---

CIRILO VILLAVERDE (1812–1894)

Abolitionist, independence agitator, and member of the progressive literary salon of Cuban intellectual Domingo del Monte, Cirilo Villaverde published many novels in Cuba but is most famous as the author of the 19th century classic Cuban novel, *Cecilia Valdés* (1839, 1882). In 1848 Villaverde was imprisoned in Cuba for conspiracy, but managed to escape and eventually went into exile in the United States in 1849. While in New York, Villaverde worked briefly as Venezuelan filibusterer Narciso López's secretary before becoming a Spanish teacher. He continued his conspiratorial activities and was able to return briefly to Cuba in 1858 where he contributed to various leading literary magazines. In 1868, he became actively involved in New York in support of the newly launched effort for Cuban independence.

leading journalists and literary figures in the Spanish-speaking world of his time. As a poet, Martí was a cofounder with Nicaraguan Rubén Darío of what was perhaps Latin America's first wholly unique literary movement, *Modernismo*. Though Martí only published two slim volumes of poetry during his lifetime, *Ismaelillo* (1882) and *Versos sencillos* (1891), together with Darío he revolutionized the way that poetry was written in American Spanish, in the same way that Walt Whitman or Edgar Allan Poe had done with poetry in American English. Two other volumes of Martí's poetry were published posthumously, *Versos libres* (1913) and *Flores del destierro* (1933). Finally, Martí was unequaled as a journalist and essayist. Though he wrote voluminously about every subject under the sun, perhaps his greatest journalistic achievement was as an observer of life in North America and its relationship to Latin America and Cuba. Usually written in a "letter to the editor" format for a wide group of leading Latin American newspapers, his many essays and dispatches in the series "*Escenas norteamericanas*" (North American Scenes), provided his many readers across the region with vivid analysis of the life, culture, and politics of the United States (Luis 2001; Martí 2002).

Literature of the Republic

After the turn of the 20th century, the exponents of historical and literary testimony exalted the heroic deeds of the independence leaders, while expressing their skepticism about the Republican political context. Among those scribbling warriors who blended the historical with the autobiographical and the anecdotal, the following stand out: the generals Enrique Collazo (1848–1921), author of *Cuba independiente* (1900), *Los americanos en Cuba* (1905) and *Cuba heroica* (1912); José Miró Argenter (1852–1925), who brought us his *Crónicas de la guerra* (1909); Bernabé Boza, author of *Mi diario de la guerra*, 1906, and Manuel Piedra Martell (1868–1954), who published *Mis primeros 30 años* in 1940, which is, of a literary value equal to that of Máximo Gómez's *Diario de Campaña* (Campaign Diary, 1868–1898), the most complete record of the island's epic of liberation. A completely different, more intimate and reflective sytle of writing is found in the many volumes of poetry and memoir penned by the accomplished writer and world traveler Dulce María Loynaz (1902–1997), whose long life parallels the ups and downs of 20th-century Cuba.

The protagonists of the war led the country until 1933, favored by the precariousness of Cuban philosophical and literary thought. They spread the myths about the independence heroes and North American intervention, decisive in the defeat of the Spanish army and the transition to the Republic. Cuba's new leaders were secular and liberal-minded, but overwhelmed by economic backwardness, warlordism, and tensions with the United States, symbolized by the Platt Amendment and the Reciprocity Treaty of 1902. These two hated documents unleashed disappointment, frustration, and inferiority complexes that have left a lasting mark on Cuba throughout the 20th century.

According to the Cuban essayist and historian Rafael Rojas (2006), contemporary Cuban culture is influenced by the island's transnational orbit (often caught in-between the geopolitical war games of the great powers), the appeal of utopias, and the doubts, melancholies, and anxieties that conceived of writing as a restitution for

DULCE MARÍA LOYNAZ (1902–1997)

Author of numerous books of poetry, prose, and memoir, Dulce María Loynaz began publishing poetry while still a teenager and published actively until 1960. In 1992, she was awarded the Cervantes Literary Prize by Spain. She traveled extensively in the United States and Europe in the 1920s and earned a degree in civil law in 1927. She continued her travels in the Middle East and Latin America, and in subsequent years was declared an honorary citizen of Spain's Canary Islands about which she wrote the book, *Un verano en Tenerife* (A Summer in Tenerife, 1958). She was a frequent contributor to literary magazines in Spain and Cuba, including *Social and Orígenes*. She was elected to membership in the *Real Academia Española de la Lengua* in 1968 and is best known for her books of poetry, *Juegos de agua* (1947) and *Poemas sin nombre* (1953), and her novel *Jardín* (1951). After a long literary silence, she began publishing again in the 1980s and 1990s, managing to publish more than six new books of poetry and memoir before she died at the age of 94 in her home in Vedado, Havana, in 1997.

national myths. Always hanging over the heads of Cuba's writers was the curse of the "unfinished revolution and the return of the Messiah," which led to a series of symbolic, redemptive, and heroic political platforms—liberal Republican, Catholic, and finally Marxist—each of which contested the intellectual hegemony of the country and saw in revolution the long-awaited return of the Messiah. This led to a number of simultaneous processes that included the renewal of music and the visual arts, which bear witness to ruptures caused by dictatorial leaders, who ushered in modernity but hastened the deaths and resurrections of the nation. All this was expressed in a succession of epochal transitions from the liberal Republic of 1902 to the democratic Republic of 1940, supplanted by the Marxist-Leninist regime in 1961. Marx's Cuba was itself was recast as Martí's communism in 1992, and again as an "updated" form of socialism after 2008, providing a convenient legitimizing narrative that obscures the past and censors the present (Bueno 1953).

The first literary and artistic movement to coalesce around a particular theme in an independent, Republican Cuba was known as *Afrocubanismo*. Lasting roughly from 1920 to 1940, it was like the Harlem Renaissance in its celebration of black art and culture. However, it was more apt than its New York counterpart to be led by white intellectuals, more politically radical, and more concerned with the project of building a national identity and culture independent from both Spain and the United States. Ironically, while the promoters of *Afrocubanismo* celebrated some aspects of black Cuban culture (especially in music and literature), a central characteristic of the movement was its ambivalence toward the more authentic expressions of Afro-Cuban culture that came from the street. For example, some of the movement's main protagonists, including the writer Alejo Carpentier, the painter Eduardo Abela, the popular musicians Ernesto Lecuona and Eliseo Grenet, and the classical composers Alejandro García Caturla and Amadeo Roldán, all white men who both took pride in and exhibited some embarrassment toward black-derived cultural forms (Moore 1997).

The leading light of *Afrocubanismo*, Alejo Carpentier (1904–1980), would go on to become one of Cuba's most distinguished novelists of the 20th century. Carpentier's early involvement in the radical anti-Machado politics of the late-1920s landed him in prison where he wrote the first version of what would later be published as his first novel, the Afro-Cuban themed *¡Ecue-Yamba-O!* (Praised Be the Lord!, 1933). During this period, Carpentier also began to collaborate with the Cuban composers Roldán and García Caturla putting together a series of concerts of "new music," culminating in the *Afrocubanismo* artistic movement.

The excitement of this moment is evident in Carpentier's breathless declaration in his 1946 book, *Music in Cuba*:

> [We] began to notice, that in Regla, on the other side of the bay, there were rhythms as complex and interesting as those created by Stravinsky to evoke the primitive rituals of pagan Russia. [. . .] The possibility of expressing what was local with a new conception of its values became ingrained in the minds of artists. [. . .] Suddenly, blacks were at the center of everything. [. . .] Thus, the Afro-Cuban tendency was born. (Carpentier 2001: 268–269)

Carpentier admits that in their effort to exasperate the old guard and establish a new, more authentically Cuban cultural identity, he and his colleagues had a tendency to exoticize Afro-Cuban culture with superficial stereotypes such as the "black man under palm trees drunk on the sun." Despite these immature flourishes, he asserts that "Afro-Cubanism was a necessary step in better comprehending certain poetic, musical, ethnic, and social factors that had suffused all contours of what it means to be uniquely Cuban" (Carpentier 2001: 269).

Cuban writer and diplomat Alejo Carpentier poses during a portrait session held on September 13, 1979 in Paris, France. (Ulf Andersen/Getty Images)

What distinguished Carpentier from the host of other progressive white Cuban intellectuals of his time was the life-altering and artistically fertile trip he made to Haiti in 1943. This trip allowed him to understand Cuban and Latin American culture in a deeper and more fantastic way, leading to his coinage of the term, "*lo real maravilloso*" (later popularized as "magical realism"). His most famous works from this period include *TheKingdom of this World* (1949) and *The Lost Steps* (1953), the last two of which he wrote in exile in Venezuela. Upon the triumph of the revolution, he returned to Cuba and was appointed Cuban ambassador to France. His later works include *The Chase* (1956), *Explosion in the Cathedral* (1962), and *Baroque Concert* (1974). In 1977, he was awarded Spain's Cervantes Prize. He completed his final novel, *The Harp and the Shadow* (1978), before succumbing to cancer in Paris in 1980.

Together with *Afrocubanismo*, 1920s Cuba saw a rupture with the "poetry of contests, literary institutions, and academies" of the past. In their place came a veritable boom in progressive political, artistic, and literary movements including the *Protesta de los trece* (Protest of the 13) and the establishment of the *Grupo Minorista*. These two movements turned Cuban culture decidedly away from European trends in art and literature, committing it instead to the defense of ethical values and intellectual activism. During the years of transition (1923–1927), boom (1927–1930), and dissolution of the vanguard (1930–1935), poetry, fiction, the essay, and—to a lesser extent—nonfiction were enriched, spread by what would become the period's leading literary magazine *Revista de Avance* (1927–1930). In a public protest against the corruption of the Zayas administration (1921–1925), a group of 13 writers, artists, and lawyers, including Rubén Martínez Villena, Jorge Mañach, Juan Marinello, and José A. Fernández de Castro, boycotted the Academy of Science in May of 1923. That same year a group of leftist nationalist writers and artists, which included some of the "13," began to meet in *tertulias* in cafés around Havana issuing increasingly

---

ALEJO CARPENTIER (1904–1980)

Born in Lausanne, Switzerland, before moving with his French father and Russian mother to Havana as an infant, Alejo Carpentier was among Cuba's leading 20th century novelists. At a young age, Carpentier moved to Paris where he studied music. He returned to Cuba and began studying architecture in 1921. However, he soon abandoned his studies and turned to journalism, working at a number of leading magazines of that era including *Social*, *Hispania*, and most notably *Carteles*, where he would remain a fixture until 1948. At this time, Carpentier also became involved in radical nationalist politics as a member of both the famous *Protesta de los trece* and the *Grupo Minorista* (1923). In 1927, he was one of the founders of the leading political and literary magazine of the period, *Revista de Avance* (1927–1930). Carpentier coined the term "*lo real maravilloso*" (later popularized as "magical realism"). His most important works include *Music in Cuba* (1946), *The Kingdom of this World* (1949), *The Lost Steps* (1953), *Explosion in the Cathedral* (1962), and *Baroque Concert* (1974).

strident calls for social, political, and cultural reform. Given their small number, they labeled themselves the *Grupo Minorista*.

In 1927, this group published a manifesto, written by Rubén Martínez Villena, in which it expressed its principles and goals including the economic independence of Cuba, an end to personalistic dictatorships, a revision of nationalist values, and an artistic renovation in music, literature, and painting. Those in the poetic vanguard included Mariano Brull, Federico de Ibarzábal, and the prolific Gustavo Sánchez Galarraga. Other important poets included the exquisite Eugenio Florit, the desolate Enrique Loynaz, the avant-garde José Z. Tallet, and the talented Nicolás Guillén. While not a formal organ of this group, *Revista de Avance*, published between 1927 and 1930, and edited by Carpentier, Mañach, and Marinello, was in many ways the voice of the progressive intellectual and artistic generation of the 1920s. Its voluntary closure in 1930 after the publication of its own anti-Machado manifesto was caused by the editors' rejection of a new law that would subject all media to government censorship (Martínez 1990).

Between 1936 and 1958, various competing artistic and literary vanguards were spread through competitions, publications, and magazines in Havana and other cities. During these years there was a fierce, if civilized, coexistence among three main irreconcilable trends that became so-called *"ciudades letradas orgánicas"* (organic literary movements). There was the Catholic trend led by José Lezama Lima, whose principal works were *Nadie Parecía*, *Verbum*, *Espuela de Plata* and the literary magazine *Orígenes* (1944–1956). Some of his collaborators in this endeavor were Medardo Vitier, Gastón Baquero, and Mercedes and Rosaura García Tudurí. The Communist tendency was expressed in the magazines *La Gaceta del Caribe* (1944) and *Nuestro Tiempo* (1954–1959) and led by the Marxist writers Juan Marinello, Carlos Rafael Rodríguez, Mirta Aguirre, Raúl Roa, José A. Portuondo, and Nicolás Guillén (who is described later). Lastly, the liberal movement produced the magazines *Diario de la Marina*, *Bohemia*, and *Ciclón* (1955–1959) and was represented by the prose of Jorge Mañach, Roberto Agramonte, Elías Entralgo, Humberto Piñera Llera, Rafael Esténger, and Francisco Ichazo.

The beginning of the poetic work of mulatto poet Nicolás Guillén (1902–1989) can also be traced to the sociopolitical upheaval and renovation of the 1920s and 1930s. In fact, Guillén was a guiding light of the emerging pan-Caribbean *"Negrista"* literary and cultural movement. In 1926, Guillén moved to Havana and began to dedicate himself full time to poetry and politics. During the late 1920s and early 1930s, he began to publish his poetry in some of Havana's leading magazines. His first book of poems, *Motivos de son*, which had first appeared in 1928 serialized in the newspaper *Diario de la Marina*, came out in book form in 1930 and was followed by *Sóngoro Cosongo* (1931) and *West Indies Ltd.* (1934).

This earliest stage of his work is concerned with portraying blacks as an essential element in Cuban national identity. As such, his poetry often shocked those who associated black culture with criminality and superstition. Instead, Guillén sought to write his poetry *"en negro de verdad,"* that is, he based his poetic voice on the natural rhythms of Afro-Cuban speech, while rejecting the exoticism that often accompanied even sympathetic portrayals of Afro-Cuban culture by whites. Guillén also befriended other non-Cuban writers who were engaged in similar work in their countries, including Langston Hughes in the United States and Jacques Roumain in Haiti.

By the mid-1930s, Guillén had begun to collaborate in the cultural activities of the Cuban Communist Party. In 1937, he traveled to Mexico and Spain as a representative of the party, attending a number of progressive writers' congresses in the company of the leading leftist Cuban writers Juan Marinello and Alejo Carpentier. It is during this period that he began to publish works of a more overtly political nature, including *Cantos para soldados y sones para turistas* (Songs for Soldiers and Sones for Tourists, 1937) and *España, poema en cuatro angustias y una esperanza* (Spain, Poem in Four Anguishes and One Hope, 1937).

Increasingly persecuted as a Communist in the late 1940s and early 1950s as the Cold War heated up, Guillén remained in exile after a 1953 trip to Chile, living between Latin America and Europe until 1959. After returning to Cuba, he was named president of the Cuban Union of Writers and Artists (UNEAC), and set to work on the poetry that would seal his reputation as one of Cuba's most vital and versatile poets. This stage of his career saw the publication of *Tengo* (I Have, 1964), a work that proudly celebrates the new lease on life that the revolution had given to the formerly downtrodden, especially blacks; *El gran zoo* (The Great Zoo, 1967); and *El diario que a diario* (The Daily Diary, 1972). Some, however, consider that his final position as a Communist bureaucrat and commissar tainted his reputation as a poet, since he—willingly or grudgingly—imposed an orthodox cultural line on others.

The last great Cuban literary movement prior to the arrival of the Cuban revolution was led by writer and intellectual José Lezama Lima (1910–1976) and took place in the pages of the literary magazine *Orígenes* (1944–1956). The most important and long lasting of a series of seven literary magazines published in Cuba between 1937 and 1959, *Orígenes* was different from the politically progressive literary journals that preceded it in that it largely eschewed sociopolitical commitments, placing aesthetics over politics. The journal was based on the ideal that art and poetry seek the origin of artistic being (thus its name) and that artists had a responsibility to disseminate this visionary ideal to other members of their society.

Like many educated Cuban men of his time, Lezama Lima earned a law degree and practiced his profession until the mid-1940s, but his true passion was literature to which he dedicated most of the rest of his life. Unlike other Cuban writers and intellectuals, he rarely traveled, never visited Europe or the United States, and only left his beloved Havana twice—once for a trip to Mexico in 1949 and again the following year to Jamaica. Prior to founding *Orígenes* in 1944, he was extremely active as an editor and literary critic, helping to found *Verbum* (1937) at the University of Havana Law School, *Espuela de Plata* (1939–1941), *Nadie Parecía* (1942–1943), and *Clavileño* (1943). The cofounder and principal funding source for *Orígenes* was José Rodríguez Feo, and the journal's principal collaborators included Virgilio Piñera, Eliseo Diego, Cintio Vitier, and Fina García Marruz, along with many of the leading painters of the *Vanguardista* movement, including Mario Carreño and René Portocarrero (Martínez 1994). *Orígenes* was forced to close in 1956 after Lezama Lima and Rodríguez Feo had a falling out over editorial policy. Often referred to as the Marcel Proust of the Caribbean, Lezama Lima was the intellectual leader of his generation. He is most remembered today as the founding editor of *Orígenes* and as the author of his masterwork, the novel *Paradiso* (Paradise, 1966).

JOSÉ LEZAMA LIMA (1910–1976)

Lezama Lima's style can be described as modern baroque in that it was sensuous, colorful, full of life, and playfully intellectual while at the same time being highly ornate and seriously classical in its concerns. After 1959, he enjoyed brief, if obligatory recognition being appointed director of the Literature and Publications Department of the National Council of Culture. He was also appointed one of six vice presidents of the UNEAC. However, his work was marginalized due to its nonpolitical bent and homosexual overtones. As a result, he lived and worked in virtual isolation for the last decade of his life. Apart from his most important novel, *Paradiso* (Paradise 1966), other major works include the book of poetry, *Muerte de Narciso* (Death of Narcissus, 1937); the collections of essays, *Analecta del reloj* (1953) and *La expresión americana* (1957); and the unfinished novel, *Oppiano Licario*, published posthumously in 1977 (Luis 2001).

Literature under the Revolution

Between 1959 and 1961, the previous tradition of competition and civil coexistence between liberal, Catholic, and Marxist literary movements was supplanted by unanimity. The protagonists of the Revolution overturned structures, social conventions, and the spontaneous advance of artistic and literary expression, imposing Marxism and populist voluntarism. The rising tension between culture and power passed through the mechanisms of state control, nullifying civil liberties and subjecting artistic creation to ideology from then on. The state monopoly over the Revolution established official structures of control such as the *Cuban Book Institute* and the UNEAC, which promote publication, confer literary prizes, and award writers with trips abroad while simultaneously reigning in works that cross an invisible but very real ideological line. This policy has generated as many adherents as opponents, silencing authors who refused to sing the praises of the New Man celebrated by the new ideology.

Throughout the revolutionary period there have been successive processes of collective acknowledgement of the victims of what is sometimes euphemistically referred to as the "*quinquenio gris*" (the gray five-year period of cultural repression that lasted from 1971 until 1976). While the list of victims is long and the punishments varied, the most prominent writers targeted for falling outside the revolutionary "parameters" (mockingly referred to as *los parametrados* in Cuba) were Reinaldo Arenas, Heberto Padilla, María Elena Cruz Varela, and Raúl Rivero. Others point out that the period of rigid ideological orthodoxy was of a much darker color and lasted quite a while longer (Coyula 2007).

There are also many "organic intellectuals" who admit that mistakes were perhaps made and excesses committed, but continue to extol the "Words to the Intellectuals" of the revolution's Maximum Leader (Fidel Castro): "Within the revolution, everything; against the revolution nothing." These faithful ones include Nicolás

Guillén, Cintio Vitier, Roberto Fernández Retamar, Lisandro Otero, and Abel Prieto. Of course, there is also a long list of prominent dissident writers, including Jorge Mañach, Gastón Baquero, Guillermo Cabrera Infante, Jesús Díaz, Manuel Díaz Martínez, and Manuel Moreno Fraginals, who have produced a prolific and varied literature of exile that reconstructs their imagined island (Vitier 1970).

In the 1960s, the search for an aesthetic language and formal structure for literature in a drastically different and unstable context forced writers to test the boundaries of freedom. Heberto Padilla's award-winning book of poetry, *Fuera del juego* (Out of the Game, 1968), is perhaps the most illustrative example of a critical-minded writer who took the risk of producing a work that deeply questioned revolutionary taboos. The work, its writer, and their fate—described later—provide a vivid portrait of the result when poetry is subject to slogans. Partially as a result of the Padilla debacle, in the 1970s the artistic scope of fiction declined under the so-called *quinquenio gris*. Memorable literature of artistic value largely disappeared save the work of writers like Eliseo Diego, Alejo Carpentier, and Miguel Collazo (Garrandés 2008).

In the 1980s, writers like Reinaldo Montero, Miguel Mejides, and Senel Paz were able to breathe life into their youthful characters who, finding themselves immersed in conflicts, are far from being clear-eyed and single-minded New Men with all the right answers. Instead, they are full of doubts about their surroundings, the times, and of course about sex and love. During the 1990s, Cuban literature rediscovered allegorical and symbolic worlds, brought to life by protagonists who bypass the numbing official discourse and bear witness to the reality of their individual lives. They also refused to avoid long-taboo subjects such as the fleeing of rafters, the multiplication of prostitutes and corrupt officials, and the spread of disenchantment like a social cancer. Perhaps the best illustration of the tension between literature and revolution in the late 20th century is the novel *Las iniciales de la tierra*, by Jesús Díaz. Three other books—all biographical testimonials—also attempt to speak a personal, often unpleasant truth to the power that only celebrates or condemns. These are *Informe contra mí mismo*, by Eliseo Alberto Diego, and *Dulces guerreros cubanos* and *Narcotráfico y tarea revolucionaria*, both by Norberto Fuentes. Finally, the critically acclaimed and quite popular work of writer Leonardo Padura stands out for its commitment to reintroducing Cubans (and readers around the world) to their own willfully muted and often tragic history through charming but all-too-human characters who speak, sweat, swear, and struggle in the present just like they do.

After 1959, the Cuban revolution initially opened up the field of culture and inspired an effervescence among artists of all stripes to participate in building a new revolutionary society allowing the avant-garde world of art to briefly come together with the world of the political vanguard (Franco 2002). However, unlike the case in cinema, Cuban writers have been much less able to successfully preserve their aesthetic autonomy and creative subjectivity in the face of the constant demands of revolutionary discipline and dogmatic austerity. The revolutionary goal of encouraging writers to produce politically "committed" art came up against a series of dilemmas not the least of which was the traditional value of artistic and critical subjectivity. That is, the line separating revolutionary art and culture from that of non- or counterrevolutionary art was never clear, leaving writers on their own to interpret the parameters of what was permissible, producing a legacy of censorship and self-censorship that continue to constrain Cuban literature today (Benítez-Rojo 1990; Dopico Black 1989).

It would seem that Fidel Castro's June 30, 1961 speech, "Words to the Intellectuals," which included the famous declaration, "Within the revolution, everything; against the revolution, nothing" (Castro 1961), established a cultural policy of inclusion, allowing autonomy and creative freedom to all writers and intellectuals as long as they were not *against* the revolution; that is, *counter*revolutionaries. However, in practice the vagueness and paternalism of this decree allowed it to be applied in a manner equivalent to: "You're either with us or against us." In short, being critical of, ambivalent toward, or outside the revolution was equated with being against it. In the tense context of the Cold War, the "necessity" for revolutionary unity always won out over the "luxury" of artistic subjectivity.

In the first few years of the revolution, the government established numerous cultural institutions and literary magazines and journals, including the international center of literary promotion and research *Casa de las Américas*, the previously mentioned UNEAC, the Cuban Film Institute (ICAIC), *Lunes de revolución* (a literary supplement to the newspaper *Revolución*), the cultural magazine *El Caimán Barbudo*, the youth oriented newspaper *Juventud Rebelde*, and the political and philosophical journal *Pensamiento Crítico*. Also during this period the government successfully focused its attention on the expansion of literacy, access to basic education, and transforming "high" culture from the exclusive realm of a privileged few to the right of all. In line with these laudable goals, in 1961 the government mobilized the population in a year-long effort to teach reading and writing to peasants in some of the most remote and neglected areas of the country in the legendary literacy campaign.

However, beginning around 1966 and culminating in the Padilla affair and First National Congress of Education and Culture of 1971, it became increasingly clear that "the idealized austerity of the guerrilla and the idealized simplicity of the peasant could be reconciled neither with the exuberance and excess of the aesthetic nor with the status of the writer as hero" (Franco 2002: 3). During these years, many of the aforementioned journals and magazines were closed down or co-opted by the state. Many valuable but revolutionary ambivalent literary works were ignored by the powerful new cultural apparatus—officially denounced, or banned outright. Finally, many leading writers were either dismissed from their official posts, imprisoned, or escaped into exile.

Easily, the most infamous instance of repression against a Cuban writer was the Padilla affair, a series of events that took place in Cuba between 1968 and 1971 throwing into relief the limits to artistic expression in revolutionary Cuba. Between 1959 and 1961, Heberto Padilla (1932–2000) collaborated with Cabrera Infante as a writer and critic for *Lunes*. In the mid-1960s, Padilla gave a positive review to Guillermo Cabrera Infante's novel *Three Trapped Tigers* (after Cabrera Infante had defected), while criticizing another novel written by Lisandro Otero, the secretary of the Cuban Writers' Union. The final episode of Padilla's troubles with the government began in 1968 when his book of poems *Fuera del juego* (Out of the Game) won the Writers' Union poetry prize. The book was eventually published, but the editors attached a denouncement of its content to the beginning given the critical nature of many of its poems. As a result, in 1971 Padilla was arrested and made to read a public confession of his crimes against the revolution. These events provoked an international incident with many erstwhile friends of Cuba signing an open letter of protest. After years of house arrest, Padilla was eventually allowed to go into exile in 1980 to the United States where he continued to write, including an autobiography, *Self Portrait of the Other* (1989), that recounts these events in detail.

The careers and distinct literary trajectories of two final writers, Jesús Díaz and Leonardo Padura, help illustrate the fact that during the late 1980s and especially since the 1990s Cuba's writers have struggled against bureaucratic inertia and ideological rigidity to open new spaces to express their criticisms. During his long and productive career, Jesús Díaz (1941–2002) was a successful novelist, critic, filmmaker, theater producer, and magazine editor. After 1959, Díaz studied international relations at the Ministry of Foreign Relations (1961–1962), worked in the Latin American section of the Cuban Institute of Friendship with the Peoples (1962), and joined the Philosophy Department of the University of Havana (1963–1971). In 1966 he received the prize for best short story collection from Casa de las Américas for his book, *Los años duros*. It was while at the University that he aided in the publication of the magazines *Juventud Rebelde* (1965–1966) and *El Caimán Barbudo* (1966–1967), of which he was the founding editor. During this period of his artistic and political life he identified closely with the revolution and became an active party militant. However, he soon discovered the limits to open debate within the revolution when the provocative Marxist philosophy journal *Pensamiento Crítico* (1967–1971), which he helped edit, was closed by the government.

In the late 1970s, Díaz began to actively cultivate ties with returning exiles who had favorable attitudes toward the revolution, an experience he chronicled in his book of interviews, *De la patria y el exilio*, and in the film, *55 Hermanos* (55 Brothers and Sisters). As a member of ICAIC, he directed dozens of documentaries and feature films in Cuba including his most successful, *Lejanía* (Distance: The Parting of the Ways, 1985). In the late 1980s, after a long literary silence, he published *Las*

GUILLERMO CABRERA INFANTE (1929–2005)

One of Cuba's most celebrated and original writers, Guillermo Cabrera Infante was born into a family of political activists who helped found Cuba's first Communist Party in the 1920s. However, he was attracted more to art and cinema than politics and became active in Havana's literary circles in the early 1950s, writing numerous film reviews and developing a lifelong addiction to Hollywood movies. He attended his first movie with his mother at the impressionable age of just 29 days. As a result, he liked to claim, "I was born with the silver screen in my mouth."

An early supporter of the revolution, he became the editor of *Lunes de Revolución* in 1959. One of the most significant, original, and widely read publications of its kind, *Lunes* lasted only a little more than two-and-a-half years before it was closed in the wake of controversy. In 1966 Cabrera Infante defected and moved to London, becoming a leading critic of the regime. He is most famous for his experimental novel, *Tres tristes tigres* (Three Trapped Tigers, 1967), which paints an elaborate picture of the glorious decadence of 1950s Havana nightlife.

iniciales de la tierra (The Earth's Initials, 1987), followed in 1991 with *Las palabras perdidas* (The Lost Words). Both books portrayed the ideological crisis of the artist within the revolution, a constant theme in almost all his works. Díaz went into exile in Spain in 1991 where he spent the rest of his life. While his work in Cuba was of vital importance, he is best remembered for his final novels written in exile in Madrid, including *Dime algo sobre Cuba* (Tell Me Something About Cuba, 1998) and for founding *Encuentro de la cultura cubana* in 1996, followed by its very popular companion website CubaEncuentro.com, before his untimely death in 2002 (Luis 2001).

Finally is the instructive case of Leonardo Padura, among the best and most successful of Cuba's contemporary writers. Born in 1955 just before the triumph of the revolution, Padura continues to live and write from his home in Havana. He is able to travel abroad freely and—despite initial obstacles in the early 1990s—all of his brutally honest and highly critical novels have been published in Cuban editions without a single word being censored. For example, his most recent novel, *El hombre que amaba a los perros* (The Man Who Loved Dogs, 2009), is a denunciation of the worst excesses of Soviet Communism under Stalin, many of which had repercussions in Cuba. The book describes the life of Ramón Mercader, the Spaniard who assassinated Soviet exile and critic León Trotsky with an ice pick on orders from the Kremlin. The novel also brings to life the true story of the final years that Mercader lived in anonymity in Cuba, thanks to an arrangement between the Soviet and Cuban governments.

Without a doubt, Padura is the most emblematic artist of a generation of fiction writers who have created a "literature of disenchantment," which expresses a feeling of defeat and a profound skepticism toward the revolutionary project. These writers

REINALDO ARENAS (1943–1990)

Born in Holguín in 1943, Reinaldo Arenas moved to Havana in 1962 and immediately launched a prolific, if often tragic literary career. While working in various cultural institutions, including the National Library and Casa de las Américas, Arenas began to publish prizewinning short stories in the UNEAC's literary competitions. Though his first books *Celestino antes del alba* (Celestino Before Dawn, 1967) and *El mundo alucinante* (Hallucinations, 1968) impressed the judges, their only slightly veiled criticisms of the government and open flaunting of his homosexuality landed Arenas on the government's blacklist. As a result, he was sent to the infamous UMAP work camps in the late 1960s and was repeatedly jailed during the 1970s. Forced to smuggle his work out of the country, Arenas became well known internationally while remaining a non-person in Cuba. He was finally able to escape on the Mariel boatlift in 1980 and is best known in the United States for the prolific outpouring of novels, political tracts, and autobiographical writings he wrote during the next 10 years. His most famous work is his fantastical autobiography *Antes que anochezca* (*Before Night Falls*, 1992), which he finished just before he died of AIDS in 1990 (Luis 2001).

Cuban writer Leonardo Padura participates at the inauguration of "Author's Week" at La Casa de las Americas in Havana, on November 27, 2012. Cuba's leading contemporary novelist, Padura has published literary criticism, music reviews, investigative journalism, screenplays, and novels. His recent work includes the historical novel, El hombre que amaba a los perros *(The Man Who Loved Dogs, 2011) and the screenplay for the 2012 film, "Seven Days in Havana." However, Padura is best known for his ongoing series of detective novels each of which is set in Havana, centering on the exploits of the aging anti-hero detective Mario Conde. (Alejandro Ernesto/epa/Corbis)*

began to publish their first works in the 1980s, always pushing up against the limits of what was acceptable. Although some of the members of this generation have gone into exile—such as the previously mentioned Jesús Díaz, as well as Eliseo Alberto, Amir Valle, Albilio Estévez, and Antonio José Ponte—Padura has not emigrated nor has he become a dissident. These writers, both at home and abroad, have forged a new space for critical, independent creation that reflects Cuba's current ideological and economic crisis. In their work, together with a recognition of some of the positive values and achievements of the revolution, there is a palpable sense of deception and loss. Furthermore, the 1990s economic crisis weakened the government to such an extent that it could no longer easily support—or control—artistic production. As a consequence, many writers, intellectuals, artists, and filmmakers have sought out foreign sponsorship and an international audience, freeing themselves from state dependence. This has also allowed them to take much greater risks, producing works fiercely critical of Cuban society while still "within the island," if not as clearly "within the revolution."

After graduating from the University of Havana in 1980 with a degree in Spanish Literature, Padura went to work as literary critic at the magazine *Caimán Barbudo*. Very soon, however, he found himself in hot water with the magazine's editors for what they called his "ideological problems." "Like almost all the members of my generation," he recalls with irony, "I was accused of having 'ideological problems,' as if a writer could live without having ideological problems." Nevertheless, he discovered that his ideological problems placed him in good literary company. Around the same time that he was expelled from *Caimán*, the magazine also refused to publish a short story by Cuban writer Senel Paz about student at a Cuban boarding school who commits suicide. Paz is the same author who would later write the important short story, "El lobo, el bosque y el hombre nuevo" (The Wolf, the Forest, and the New Man), on which the taboo-shattering Cuban film *Fresa y chocolate* (Strawberry and Chocolate) is based (Buckwalter-Arias 2003). The editors even rejected an article about John Lennon by none other than the renowned Colombian Nobel laureate—and close personal friend of Fidel Castro—Gabriel García Márquez.

Most absurd of all was the fact that Padura's banishment from *Caimán*—at the time a weekly magazine with a circulation of just 30,000—resulted in his being sent to work as a reporter for *Juventud Rebelde*. This bizarre "demotion" allowed him to expose many more readers to his ideologically suspect views since *Juventud* is a much more prominent newspaper run by the Union of Communist Youth (UJC) with a daily circulation at the time of 100,000 and a special Sunday edition of 250,000. During his six years as a journalist at the newspaper (1983–1989), Padura was able to develop a unique brand of investigative cultural and historical journalism.

Working as part of a special team of reporters—most of whom eventually joined the internal opposition, like journalist and blogger Reinaldo Escobar, or went into exile, like poet Raúl Rivero—Padura focused on rescuing the lost stories of people and places not typically found in official publications but which he considered essential to the unique culture and character of the island. These included the legendary king of Cuban pimps, Alberto Yarini (1882–1910), the history of Havana's Chinatown and its dwindling number of Chinese descendants, and many of prerevolutionary Cuba's most popular and influential musicians, a number of whom had since gone into exile and were subsequently erased from the island's official history.

Despite publishing critically acclaimed books of historical fiction such as the previously mentioned *El hombre* and *La novela de mi vida*, Padura is best known as the writer of a series of critically acclaimed crime novels that have also enjoyed great popular success at home and abroad. In the initial four books in the series, Padura almost single-handedly reinvented the genre of Cuban *noir*, breaking clearly with the rigid, uninspired, and didactic model of revolutionary crime novels promoted by the government during the 1970s and 1980s. Each of these novels chronicles a different season during the all-important year of rupture, 1989, in Havana, featuring the endearing and all-too-human police detective Mario Conde. Instead of uncritically celebrating the revolution's achievements and promoting the socialist ideology and the figure of the New Man, these novels—together with a pair of follow-ups that update Conde's story into the 21st century—focus on the degradation of a society in moral and material crisis.

"I had two fundamental purposes in writing these novels," Padura has explained. "First of all, I wanted to write literature. That is to say, I wasn't interested in writing crime novels, but in writing novels. And the second purpose was that these novels, which have the character of crime novels, not be anything like the crime novels that had been written in Cuba up to that moment" (De la Soledad 2006). The character most representative of this "disenchantment" in these novels is, of course, detective Conde himself—a hard-boiled antihero in the tradition of Raymond Chandler's Philip Marlowe and Dashiell Hammett's Sam Spade. "For Cuban readers," Padura recognizes, "Mario Conde has perhaps meant the possibility of seeing Cuban reality from a different angle. A pessimistic, disenchanted, ironic angle, allowing them to easily identify with the character" (ibid.). Representing a generation of lost illusions, Conde keeps the few things he still truly values on an altar: friendship, literature, loyalty, and decency. He no longer believes in the great, failed communal projects of the past, nor does he consider himself any kind of "revolutionary." Life has turned him into a skeptic, but he struggles mightily to preserve something of his youthful romanticism and rejects the cynicism that surrounds him.

Padura wrote his series of crime novels in the context of Cuba's so-called "special period." Caused in part by the exhaustion of Cuba's own rigid socialist economic model, the economic collapse was triggered by the sudden—and for Cuba unthinkable—disappearance of what had up to then been the revolution's primary economic and ideological support system, the Soviet Union. Ironically, the ensuing material and moral crisis that hit Cuba like a cyclone, beginning in 1989, led to the most fruitful stage in Padura's artistic career. In fact, he began writing *Pasado perfecto*, the first in his Cuban noir series, in that same year. As economic upheaval provoked new cleavages in Cuban society, writers like Padura took advantage of their modicum of newfound artistic autonomy and began dealing openly with a series of long-taboo themes that would have been inadmissible—even judged as counter-revolutionary—just a decade earlier. Exile, narcotics, prostitution, violence and delinquency, inequality, homosexuality, corruption, desperation, and suicide are the themes that populate the lives of Padura's characters.

When Padura entered the manuscript of this first novel in what would become his quartet of novels into the crime novel competition of Cuba's Ministry of the Interior in 1991, it was rejected. "They had no interest in promoting that kind of novel," Padura observed, because Conde did not fit into the facile mold of the revolutionary hero. Instead, he is "a man who is a bit disenchanted, skeptical, who defends himself with irony, and who has great loyalties and great phobias," making him inadmissible for Cuba's cultural orthodoxy. As a result, *Pasado perfecto* was initially published in Mexico. (Incidentally, the novel's playful title is a double entendre, which refers to the "past perfect" grammatical tense, as well as mocking the myth that the past 30 years of revolution had been perfect.) Still, the novel seems to have caused quite a stir among the Cuban jury because Padura found out later that "they had agreed his was indeed the best novel entered in the contest. As a result, they decided not to award the top prize to any novel that year" (De la Soledad 2006).

By 1994, when Padura was ready to publish the follow-up, *Vientos de cuaresma* (published in English as *Havana Gold*), he claims that Cuban publishers jumped at the chance to praise and publish it, even though this time around Conde "is revealed in all his sadness, his pessimism, his painful feelings about life and his merciless examination of the reality in which he lives" (ibid.). In fact, Padura recalls that authorities were more open to his second novel because one of the perhaps 100 copies of his first novel that managed to get into Cuba ended up in the hands of Abel Prieto, the minister of culture. Instead of denouncing its author, Prieto observed, "this is a necessary book that we have to publish in Cuba. It is necessary because it offers another vision of the Cuban crime novel, while being a work of literature at the same time" (ibid.). Thus, the UNEAC published the first novel together with the second in 1994 and have published editions of all Padura's subsequent work. Padura notes:

Readers will ask how is it possible that an author who lives, writes, and publishes in Cuba can talk so freely about the reality of life in Cuba and even criticize decisions of the authorities. But this is the truth. I live in Cuba, I write in Cuba, and my books have never been censored. On the contrary, they have all won important prizes and they are all read widely. What is certain is that, in the 1990s, the levels of tolerance increased. (Ibid.)

The case of Padura also illustrates that, despite the relative opening of new spaces for Cuban culture over the last 20 years, certain invisible but well-known parameters still exist for writers who live on the island. For example, although Padura's novels are among Cuba's most popular, their unvarnished reflection of the frustration and disenchantment of Cuban life has led to a virtual blackout of the writer and his work in the Communist Party–controlled mass media. Ironically, while he has done public readings and discussed his novels at universities around the world, Padura is never invited to lecture at Cuba's universities. While each of his novels typically generates scores of reviews abroad and is translated into as many languages, there are practically no reviews of them in the Cuban newspapers and magazines where he once worked. This despite the fact that *La neblina del ayer* (published in English as *Havana Fever*), his latest effort in his Conde crime series, won Cuba's National Literary Criticism Award for best novel in 2006. Even more contradictory is the fact that Padura was awarded the National Prize for Literature at the 2013 Havana Book Fair.

Furthermore, while it is true that his works have never been censored and all have appeared in Cuban editions, enabling wide access to them is clearly not in the interests of the cultural commissars in charge of book printing and distribution. As has been the case with politically incorrect foreign films like the Oscar winning German film, "The Lives of Others," or with domestic ones such as "Strawberry and Chocolate," "Guantanamera," or "Suite Habana"—which are typically given a single premiere and never shown publicly again—Padura's books are nearly impossible to find in the island's bookstores. The small number that are published sell out immediately— often even before arriving in stores—and are then passed from friend to friend like rare jewels, with their black market prices reaching as much as a month's salary.

Conclusion

As 2007 began, a new cultural controversy exploded into public view that illustrated once again how past cultural policies of the revolutionary government continue to define the terms of the ongoing and often heated debate over the proper balance between the artistic avant-garde and the political vanguard. However, this time around the indignant and vociferous public reaction of Cuba's leading intellectuals (both at home and abroad) seemed to indicate that some of the more repressive and arbitrary policies of the 1960s and 1970s would not be allowed to return. The crisis began on January 5 when the Cuban television programs *Impronta*, *Diálogo abierto*, and *La diferencia* each successively featured retrospective interviews with three figures responsible for designing and implementing the repressive cultural policies of the 1970s: Luis Pavón Tamayo, Armando Quesada, and Jorge Serguera, respectively. Because the interviews seemed to vindicate these figures and willfully ignore the deep scar their dogmatic, Stalinist policies left on Cuban culture, many of Cuba's leading intellectuals and writers protested publicly demanding an explanation and apology (Padura 2007).

What began as a series of e-mails shared among those writers and intellectuals soon began to spread via the Internet beyond Cuba, finally being addressed in a meeting between the leadership of the UNEAC and the Communist Party. Attempting to put an official end to the debate, these institutions published a partial explanation in the pages of *Granma* on January 18, under the cynical title, "The Cultural Policy of the Revolution is Irreversible." While the declaration made clear that the UNEAC shared the writers' indignation, the statement seemed more preoccupied with disqualifying certain exiled writers from the debate as "annexationists obviously working in the service of the enemy," than with openly addressing the present controversy or delving into a highly problematic past (Padura 2007: 6).

Despite the official attempt to quell the growing debate, the crisis snowballed into a series of public debates in late January and February 2007. Many participants in the debate sought to use this particular instance to make the point that the entire dark period of cultural repression that lasted between the late 1960s and 1976 (the *quinquenio gris*) had never been officially rectified, addressed, or even recognized as having taken place. Others contended that as bad as they were, the three officials in question had only implemented cultural policies conceived and approved by Castro. In an article chronicling the debate, Cuban journalist Dalia Acosta noted, "[M]any of those taking part in the e-mail exchange underscored the need to lift the veil of silence on that sad episode in history, and to study its causes and effects and recognize the mistakes made in order to prevent a repeat." Acosta also quoted Cuban writer Reynaldo González, 2002 National Literature Prize winner, who argued, "Errors are part of the past only if they are rectified" (Acosta 2007).

Expanding the debate further into the public realm, Cuban poet César López challenged attendees at Havana's International Book Fair in February 2007, by dedicating the event to "all Cuban creators," specifically singling out four blacklisted writers who died in exile still staunchly opposed to the policies of the Cuban government: Guillermo Cabrera Infante, Heberto Padilla, Reinaldo Arenas, and Jesús Díaz. Perhaps the best epitaph to this brief but significant episode was pronounced by Reynaldo González who told Acosta, "They have let the genie out of the bottle. And it will not go back in" (ibid.). Thus, the long fight by members of Cuba's avant-garde to open up and defend spaces of autonomous creation and critical debate during the toughest years of the 1980s and 1990s has made the outcome of this most recent controversy decidedly more positive for Cuban writers and artists, if still within the limits set by Castro long ago in his, "Words to the Intellectuals"—"Within the revolution, everything; against the revolution, nothing" (Castro 1961; Padura 2007).

REFERENCES

Acosta, Dalia. 2007. "Exorcising the Ghosts of the Past," *Inter Press Service News*, February 23. http://www.ipsnews.net/news.asp?idnews=36701.

Benítez Rojo, Antonio. 1990. "Comments on Georgina Dopico Black's 'The Limits of Expression: Intellectual Freedom in Post-revolutionary Cuba'." *Cuban Studies* 20: 171–174.

Buckwalter-Arias, James. 2003. "Sobrevivir el 'periodo especial': La suerte del 'hombre nuevo' y un cuento de Senel Paz." *Revista Iberoamericana* 69, no. 204: 710–714.

Bueno, Salvador. 1953. *Antología del cuento en Cuba (1902–1952)*. Havana: Ediciones Mirador.

Carpentier, Alejo. 2001. *Music in Cuba*. Minneapolis, MN: University of Minnesota Press.

Castro, Fidel. 1961. "Words to the Intellectuals: Castro's Speech to Intellectuals." FBIS report, June 30. http://lanic.utexas.edu/la/cb/cuba/castro/1961/19610630.

Coyula, Mario. 2007. "El Trinquenio Amargo y la ciudad distópica: autopsia de una utopia." In Desiderio Navarro, ed., *La política cultural del período revolucionario: Memoria y reflexión*. Havana: Criterios, Centro Teórico-Cultural. http://www.criterios.es/cicloquin queniogris.htm

Davis, Pablo Julián. 2002. "Cuban Spanish (Language)." In Luis Martínez-Fernández, D. H. Figueredo, Louis A. Pérez, Jr., and Luis González, eds., *Encyclopedia of Cuba: People, History, Culture*. Westport, CT: Greenwood Press.

De la Soledad, María. 2006. "In life, 'there is little worth believing in'," an exclusive interview with Cuban author Leonardo Padura Fuentes on the occasion of the release of his novel *La Neblina del Ayer*, *Progreso Weekly*, February 2–8. http://www.progresoweekly.com/index .php?progreso=art_culture&otherweek=1139032800.

Dopico-Black, Georgina. 1989. "The Limits of Expression: Intellectual Freedom in Postrevolutionary Cuba." *Cuban Studies* 19: 107–142.

Franco, Jean. 2002. *The Decline and Fall of the Lettered City: Latin America in the Cold War*. Cambridge: Harvard University Press.

Garrandés, Aiberto. 2008. *La ínsula fabulante: El cuento cubano en la Revolución (1959–2008)*. Havana: Editorial Letras Cubanas.

Instituto de Literatura y Lingüística. 2002/2003. *Historia de La Literatura Cubana, tomos I y II*. Havana: Editorial Letras Cubanas.

Luis, William. 2001. *Culture and Customs of Cuba*. Westport, CT: Greenwood Press.

Martí, José. 2002. *Selected Writings*.Translated by Esther Allen. New York: Penguin, 2002.

Martínez, Julio A. 1990. *Dictionary of Twentieth-Century Cuban Literature*. Westport, CT: Greenwood Press.

Martínez, Juan A. 1994. *Cuban Art and National Identity: The Vanguardia Painters, 1927–1950*. Gainesville: University Press of Florida.

Moore, Robin D. 1997. *Nationalizing Blackness: Afrocubanismo and Artistic Revolution in Havana, 1920–1940*. Pittsburgh: University of Pittsburgh Press.

Padura, Leonardo. 2001. *La novela de mi vida*. Havana: Ediciones Unión.

Padura, Leonardo. 2003a. *Faces of Salsa: A Spoken History of the Music*. Translated by Stephen J. Clark. Washington, DC: Smithsonian Books.

Padura, Leonardo. 2003b. *José María Heredia: La patria y la vida*. Havana: Ediciones Unión.

Padura, Leonardo. 2007. "La memoria y el olvido," *Cultura y Sociedad* 13, no. 1, Havana: Inter Press Service, January.

Paz Pérez, Carlos. 1998. *Diccionario cubano de habla popular y vulgar*. Miami: Agualarga.

Rojas, Rafael. 2006. *Tumbas sin sosiego: Revolución, disidencia y exilio del intelectual cubano*. Barcelona: Editorial Anagrama.

Valdés Acosta, Gema. 2002. *Los remanentes de las lenguas bantúes en Cuba*. Havana: La Fuente Viva, Fernando Ortiz Foundation.

Valdés Bernal, Sergio. 1994. *Inmigración y lengua nacional*. Havana: Editorial Academia.

Vitier, Cintio. 1970. *Lo cubano en la poesía*. Havana: Instituto Cubano del Libro.

Dance, Music, and Theater

Regina Coyula and Ted A. Henken

Cuba has developed and successfully exported a long succession of musical styles, popular dances, and infectious rhythms, many of which have gone on to conquer the Hemisphere and circle the globe. Both before the revolution and especially since, Cuba has also produced some of the world's best classical ballet dancers, many of whom now perform as members of the world's leading companies in New York, London, Moscow, and St. Petersburg. This section describes Cuban dance (classical, modern, folkloric, and popular); classical and especially popular music (likely Cuba's most well-known export); as well as Cuba's lesser-known but deeply rooted tradition of theater that has often acted as a vital link between Cuban literature—discussed earlier—and Cuban film—described in the following section.

DANCE

Classical Ballet

Havana has long attracted many of the world's leading artists, who have come to the island's capital city to perform in one of its many theaters. As such, the city has hosted international ballet troupes from time to time, even bringing stars such as Anna Pavlova. However, a home-grown, national ballet did not appear until October 28, 1948. On that day, at the Auditorium Theatre of Havana—today's Amadeo Roldán—the Ballet of Alicia Alonso was born. Although Alonso's Ballet company was eventually recognized as a national treasure and pioneer and renamed the National Ballet of Cuba upon the triumph of the revolution, when it was inaugurated in 1948 it had only 16 Cubans among its 40 members. Its founding was made possible thanks to three people who would leave an indelible mark on the history of this art form on the island: Alicia Alonzo (née Alicia Martínez del Hoyo) and the brothers Fernando and Alberto Alonso. Foreign dancers hailing from the *Ballet de la Sociedad Pro Arte Musical de La Habana* (among them Sonia Calero) and the Ballet Theatre of New York came together with local dancers to form a troupe that would go on in a few short decades to become one of the best companies in the world, setting in place a tradition of excellence (Cabrera 1989, 2000).

During the early years, the same misunderstandings, official neglect, hardships, and conflicts with the government of the time that characterized other cultural institutions confronted ballet. Only great effort and love for dance above all else allowed the company's founders to become trailblazers and put on shows in the most diverse places across the island. They were also invited to perform in the leading concert

In her prime Alicia Alonso was among the world's best classical ballet dancers, a prima ballerina assoluta. She went on to found the world-renowned National Ballet of Cuba, and still serves as its director even though she is partially blind and over 90 years old. (Palm/ RSCH/Redferns)

houses of the United States and Latin America. The Alicia Alonso Academy of Ballet was created in 1950, drawing on the Alonso family's meager resources along with financial support from the Federation of University Students and the more progressive sectors of the Cuban intelligentsia.

Alonso's troupe would soon begin to train a new generation of dancers, increasing the Cuban presence in the company, establishing a serious home-grown educational foundation. Elements borrowed from already existing schools of ballet were combined with the unique characteristics of Cuban culture, such as its native tradition of dance, its climate, the character of the people, and local idiosyncrasies, before finally giving birth to the *Escuela Cubana de Ballet*. Out of this tradition essential figures in the history of Cuban ballet soon emerged such as the so-called four jewels—Mirta Plá, Aurora Bosch, Loipa Araujo, and Josefina Méndez—as well as Ramona de Saá, Laura Alonso, Menia Martínez, Joaquín Banegas, and Adolfo Roval.

Between 1948 and 1956, the Alicia Alonso Academy of Ballet (by this time already renamed the Ballet of Cuba) began the hard work of disseminating ballet across the country as part of the island's national culture. The troupe also consolidated its own choreographic line, which included both classic and contemporary styles of dance. In 1956 the company lost the little state support it had had in part because it refused to play ball with the government of dictator Fulgencio Batista. After leading a tour across the country in protest, Alicia, Fernando, and Alonso suspended the company's activities but remained active as teachers. In 1959, Revolutionary Law 812 singled out ballet as a national art form, granting funding, institutional support, and official legitimacy to the newly renamed National Ballet of Cuba. Two years later, the troupe took on the task of creating the National School of Ballet, which since 1966 has been a virtually bottomless source of high-profile dancers such as Marta García, Ofelia González, Jorge Esquivel, Amparo Brito, Lázaro Carreño, Fernando Jhones, María Elena Llorente, Orlando Salgado, Rosario Suárez, Jorge Vega, Andrés Williams,

ALICIA ALONSO (1921–)

Alicia Martínez del Hoyo began her ballet career in 1931 at the newly formed *Escuela de Ballet de Pro-Arte Musical* in Havana. After marrying her dance partner Fernando Alonso at age 15, Alicia moved to New York and began performing on Broadway. She managed to have a long and successful career in New York and internationally despite being partially blinded by an eye defect at age 19. Her talent, charisma, discipline, and stamina has made her synonymous with modern classical Cuban ballet and she was also honored with the title of the world-class prima ballerina assoluta in her own right.

In 1948, Alonso returned to Havana in order to found Cuba's National Ballet Academy, which became the National Ballet of Cuba upon the triumph of the revolution in 1959. Although in her mid-50s, Alonso's career as a dancer, choreographer, and teacher reached its climax in Cuba in 1977 when her company debuted 10 new works across the island, reaching as many as 20,000 spectators. In that same year, Alonso performed her signature role in Giselle in the United States and Latin America to rave reviews. In 2002, Alonso was named UNESCO Goodwill Ambassador for her leading role in the development and popularization of classical ballet.

and José Zamorano. Standout members of the latest generation includes dancers of world-class caliber such as Carlos Acosta, Rolando Candia, Alihaydee Carreño, José Manuel Carreño, Xiomara Reyes, Viengsay Valdés, Sadayse Arencibia, Lienz Chang, and Lorna and Lorena Feijoó. Among choreographers, Gustavo Herrera, Alberto Méndez, and Iván Tenorio stand out (García 2003).

Modern Dance

The wide panorama of dance styles and traditions on the island has also included modern dance. In September 1959, Ramiro Guerra Sánchez—head of the newly created Department of Modern Dance of the National Theater of Cuba—issued a call for dancers to form a company inspired by the aesthetic approach Guerra had absorbed from his previous work with the master Martha Graham in New York, among other icons of modern dance. Guerra's idea was to capture through undulating dance and baroque expressionism the unique Antillean world reflected in the work of Cuban painters Wifredo Lam and René Portocarrero, literary masters Alejo Carpentier and Nicolás Guillén, and avant-garde musicians such as Amadeo Roldán and Alejandro García Caturla (Pajares 1993). In 1971, the company changed its name to National Dance of Cuba, and again in 1987 to Contemporary Dance of Cuba. It has an active repertory of more than 60 works, which seek to integrate the universal works of modern theater with the particular language of contemporary dance without ignoring Cuba's rich cultural heritage.

Cuba's Contemporary Dance company has accumulated wide critical recognition and numerous awards. Its dancers are graduates of Cuba's National School of Art, where they have learned to meld the techniques of modern dance with movements that originate in the parallel universe of African dance, a particularly rich source of creative and spiritual inspiration in Cuba. Such a combination of models gives Cuban modern dance its original and distinctive stamp. Some of the most popular pieces in the wide repertory of Cuban modern dance are "Michelangelo" and "Panorama," both by Victor Cuéllar. The former is born out of Cuba's shared culture with the rest of Latin America while the latter appropriates Cubans folk dances and reinterprets them with modern dance techniques. "Súlkary," "Okantomi," and "Otansí," created by the late star Cuban choreographer Eduardo Rivero Walker, are considered classic works of contemporary Cuban dance that draw on Cuba's African traditions. Outside the standard repertory of modern dance, but considered legendary and influential, are Ramiro Guerra's "Impromptu galante" and "Decálogo del Apocalipsis," the second of which has actually never been publically performed.

Folkloric Dance

Before 1959, Cuba had no institution dedicated to collecting the unique forms of music and dance that make up the island's folklore. Given the prejudice and neglect that existed toward all expressions of African culture on the island, Afro-Cuban folklore was especially unknown and undervalued - except of course among Afro-Cubans themselves who kept African derived chants, rhythms, and dances alive across many generations. Nevertheless, Cuba's most prominent ethnologists and ethnomusicologists such as Fernando Ortiz and Lydia Cabrera (both white) devoted much of their lives to the collection and study of Cuban folklore—with a special focus on Afro-Cuban music, dance, and spirituality. It is precisely their hard work that has allowed for the wide dissemination and celebration of Cuban folklore in all its aspects during the last half century. Ortiz published his first scientific works in 1906, followed by innumerable other publications over more than half a century, which, present the fundamental characteristics of Cuban folklore and make the first serious attempt to explain the formation of Cuba's complex ethnic composition.

In 1960, the National Theater of Cuba's Department of Folklore presented public shows that highlighted a broad range of the island's folklore for the first time. This gave birth to the idea of forming a dance company that would be dedicated exclusively to the preservation and celebration of Cuban folklore through dance performances. The National Folkloric Company (*Conjunto Folklórico Nacional*) has since been responsible for selecting those folk forms of true artistic value and arranging them according to the most modern theatrical demands. Founded in early 1962, the company's goal has been to rescue and rehabilitate the roots of the island's dance and music while not cheapening or betraying their popular essence.

In this way, Cuba has developed a style of Folk Art Theater of great theatrical and aesthetic effectiveness. Its founders and first performers were not classically trained dancers or musicians, but men and women of popular origins and occupations who had first learned these dances at home and preserved them through participation in family and community traditions. Among the many aspirants to join the *Conjunto*, a first group of 56 individuals was selected on the basis of their traditional knowledge and artistic skills. Among these, there were those with expertise in all Afro-Cuban folkloric forms, including Yoruba, Congo, Abakuá, and *rumba*. Subsequently, a company school was created for young people who were taught the basics of Cuba's folk dances, regardless of their individual family or ethnic backgrounds. Later, graduates of the National Schools of Art who specialized in folk dance joined the company enriching the professionalism and versatility of its performances.

The Rumba

Strictly speaking, the classic *rumba* can be described as a combination of vocals, percussion, and dance performed together in any one of three styles—the *yambú*, the *columbia*, or the *guaguancó*—often referred to as the "*rumba* complex." However, the term "*rumba*" itself can refer to this specific group of traditional music-dance performances or to a variety of other tropical musical forms and even social gatherings (*rumbear* is a Cuban-Spanish verb that means "to party"). Alejo Carpentier once famously quipped, "Everything can be labeled [a *rumba*]. [. . .] More than a genre, [it] represents an 'atmosphere' or feeling; [. . .] in Cuba there is no single '*rumba*,' but various '*rumbas*' [all] synonym[ous] for revelry, lascivious dance, carousing with loose women of the street" (quoted in Moore 1997: 169). It is perhaps for this reason that when *son* music was first marketed in the United States in the 1930s it was not labeled *son*, but the more Africanized, seductive "*rumba*," often misspelled, "*rhumba*") (Sublette 2004: 258).

Much like jazz, blues, and hip-hop in the United States, tango in Argentina, merengue in the Dominican Republic, samba in Brazil, and reggae in Jamaica, historically, the *rumba* was rejected by middle- and upper-class Cuban society as vulgar dances fit only for the black underclass. As such, it was constantly repressed by both colonial and Republican authorities. Nor has the revolutionary government been immune to this classist and Eurocentric attitude. In fact, during the 1960s and 1970s many battles were fought between promoters of Afro-Cuban musical styles and the socialist authorities over the provision of public spaces for the development and performance of *rumba* (Moore 1997: 169).

As a secular artistic expression with roots in sacred ritual, the *rumba* has a number of precursors. First, its form and purpose is surprisingly similar to the *areíto*, a sacred ceremony of Cuba's indigenous peoples that involved percussive music, communal dancing and singing, and the ritual consumption of tobacco and alcohol. Second, the Afro-Cuban *bembé* is an even more direct influence on the modern *rumba*. As an informal devotional event common to many Afro-Cuban religions in Cuba, the *bembé* is a ritual organized around music and dance performances in praise of the *orishas*. For this reason, a *bembé* is often casually referred to in Cuba today as a "*toque de santo*," that is, a festival where the rhythm that calls forth each *orisha* is ritually performed on the three sacred two-headed *batá* drums, the smallest *okónkolo* drum, the mid-sized *itótele* drum, and the largest "mother" drum, the *iyá*. During this devotional drumming ceremony, the lead singer, known as the *akpwon*, engages in a musical dialogue with the chorus, called the *ankorí* (Sweeney 2001). As with the *areíto*, during a *bembé* food and drink are ritually offered to the *orishas* and then consumed by participants at the conclusion of the ceremony. Other influences on the development of the *rumba* were the *yuka* and *makuta*, a pair of dances from the Congo commonly performed in 19th century Cuba, as well as the more aggressive *baile de maní*, a kind of blood-sport sometimes performed on Cuban slave plantations (Alén Rodríguez 1992; Sublette 2004: 258–262).

Rumba, however, is a secular dance/music complex that emerged in Cuba's western provinces of Havana and Matanzas in the mid-19th century. That is, the *rumba* is neither African nor Spanish, but a Cuban invention synthesized from both African and Hispanic elements. The *rumba* was developed by lower-class free black and poor white dockworkers and stevedores in the tenements (*solares*) and ports of Havana and Matanzas. Whichever of the three aforementioned types of *rumba* is being enacted, the performance amounts to a profane festival with each "song" and "dance" sharing a similar, very specific structure. All *rumbas* begin with an opening, nonsensical melodic fragment called a *diana*. While the *diana* has no "text" as such, it acts as an opening call that sets the musical tone instructing the chorus how to respond during the *rumba* that follows. It is likely that this element derives from the vocal wails common in the flamenco singing of Spanish Andalucía and the Canary Islands (themselves influenced by both gypsy music and the Moorish/Arabic chants common in medieval Spain) (Sublette 2004: 267).

Immediately after the *diana* comes the rhythmic sound of the *clave* (similar to the *son clave* - described later -, but done in 3–2 time), which continues to echo throughout the entire song. Now the "lead singer," called a *decimista*, begins an energetic call-and-response exchange with the accompanying chorus of voices that includes a *censor* (who provides the texts), a *clarina* (a female singer with a high voice), and a *tonista* (a *rumbero* with a good ear who acts as a listener and guide). A *rumba* usually begins with a relatively slow tempo, building up speed and energy as it progresses. This gradual strengthening normally takes up the first third of the song, at which time the *rumba* reaches an energetic climax and "breaks" (*se rompe la rumba*) (Sublette 2004: 267). At this point the entire performance enters a kind of controlled but ecstatic chaos where the chorus and various percussion instruments join in the fun.

The most important of these percussion instruments are the three *tumbadoras* (better known as "conga" drums when used in popular dance music). Inherited from a combination of the *cajones* (packing crates) used by dockworkers (and similar to the *cajón* used in flamenco music) and the *mula*, *caja*, and *cachimbo* used in the 19th century Congo *yuka* dance, these three drums are known as the *tumbadora conga*, the *salidor*, and the *quinto* in their modern incarnations. The *tumbadora conga* and the *salidor* are both low-pitched drums, which carry the rhythm of the *rumba*, while the *quinto* is a high-pitched drum used for "talking"—that is, communicating with the singer and dancers. In addition to the *clave* and these three *tumbadoras*, the *rumba* percussion section is completed by the *catá* (a *clave*-like instrument also known as the *guagua*, as in *guaguancó*), which locks together with the *clave* producing the *rumba*'s rhythmic structure (Sublette 2004: 266–267). As the three *tumbadoras* join in the *rumba*, with the *clave* and *catá* wailing away in the background, a complex three-way call-and-response interaction begins to take place between the *decimista*, the *quinto*, and the various dancers whose strangely stiff movements can suddenly turn smooth, seductive, graceful, and acrobatic.

As a dance, the *rumba* can take one of the three aforementioned basic forms, the *yambú*, *columbia*, and *guaguancó*, of which the *guaguancó*, a seductive couple dance, is easily the most common and influential on the way modern *salsa* is danced. Rarely danced today, the *yambú* is a mimetic dance that reenacts household chores as performed slowly by an elderly couple with the movements devoid of sexual content. In contrast, the *columbia* is an impossibly rapid, even convulsive dance, which involves the interaction of a group of male dancers in a kind of physical dialogue with the beat of the *quinto* drum and the voice of the *decimista*. The *columbia* also involves the high-speed handling of various props such as a machete, knife, bottle, glass of water, or plate (Sublette 2004: 268). As such, every movement of the *columbia* is designed to show off the dancers' skills and acrobatic abilities in competition with one another, with improvisation, speed, wit, and grace—the most highly prized qualities.

Finally, the *guaguancó* is a *rumba* danced by a couple at an intermediate speed involving an often explicit sexual pantomime of the interaction of a rooster and a hen. Playing hard-to-get, the female dancer uses a colored kerchief, which she occasionally drops to the ground and with which she feigns bashfulness and coquettishly hides her private regions from her dance partner. Meanwhile, the male dancer slyly moves ever closer to her waiting for his opportunity to pounce. Her moves to variously avoid, deflect, or reject his advances are known as the *botao* (from the Spanish *botado*, or "thrown out"), while his attempts at conquest are called the *vacunao* (from the Spanish *vacunado*, or "vaccinated"). The *guaguancó* concludes when the goal of the symbolic sexual possession of the female by the male dancer is achieved (Alén Rodríguez 1992; Sublette 2004: 271–272).

Of course, Cuba's folk art also includes dances and music of Spanish origin, such as peasant dances like the *zapateo*, the *caringa*, and the *zucu-zucu*. There are also the ballroom dances—described in greater detail in the following section—such as the *quadrille* (also called the *contradanza*), the *danzón*, the *mambo*, the *cha-cha-chá*, and the all-important *son*. Exhaustive studies have also been carried out on their origins and development and they have been subsequently incorporated into the *Conjunto*'s repertory. As with Afro-Cuban performances, the staging of these more Hispano-centric folkloric shows has been based on ethnographic research and performed by artists selected for their special knowledge of these dances, songs, and rhythms. In fact, many of these artists had previously worked under the direction of Fernando Ortiz and participated in the work of the Institute of Ethnology and Folklore. Without the invaluable experience of these organic practitioners, it would have been impossible to organize the *Conjunto* and stage its shows. The titles of some of their works reflect the wide range of styles that the *Conjunto* has preserved: the Yoruba cycle; *rumbas* and *comparsas*; the Congo and Abakuá cycles; royal Congos; and popular dances, *sons*, and *apalencados*, among others.

Apart from the National Ballet, the Contemporary Dance Company, and the *Conjunto*, the island is home to many other dance companies, including the Ballet of Camagüey, the Classical Ballet of Havana, *Retazos*, *Danza Abierta*, *Danza Combinatoria*, the Narciso Medina Studio Academy, the *Teatro de la Danza del Caribe* in Santiago de Cuba, Guantánamo's *Danza Libre*, Codanza of Holguín, Danza del Alma in Villa Clara, and Matanzas' Danza Espiral. Such is the variety and ubiquity of dance in Cuba today that the island is even home to a troupe that goes by the provocative name *Danza Voluminosa* given that its members are proudly obese.

Ballroom Dance

Even more important than the various "staged" dance styles described earlier, Cuba is home to a deep and widespread tradition of popular dance, sometimes referred to as "ballroom dance" (*bailes de salón*) even if they rarely take place in actual ballrooms. Nearly all popular Cuban music is dance music. Traditional peasant dances like the *zapateo* are danced in pairs face-to-face but without physical contact. Other dances with greater African influence such as the previously described *rumba* include solos (like the *columbia*), couple dances (such as the *guaguancó* and *yambú*), and group numbers that make space for soloists. Together with the *rumba*, the main predecessors of the *casino*—described later—are the *son* and the *danzón*, both of which were considered quite risqué in their time. Like the *casino*, they are couple dances in which the dance partners have physical and often intimate contact. In this same tradition are the *mambo* and the *cha-cha-chá*, each of which has its own choreography, as was the case with other more ephemeral dance styles such as the *mozambique* and the *pilón*, neither of which is danced today.

The *son* and the *rumba* are considered the first manifestations of traditional popular Cuban dance music. The *son* arose in eastern Cuba at the turn of the 19th century with the black *Habanero* composer and musician Ignacio Piñeiro being its most prominent early innovator and evangelist. Piñeiro's importance derives in part from a career that began with *rumba* but then flowered with the rise of *son*, first in Havana and then in the United States. During the early years of the 20th century as *son* began to circulate, the French origin *contradanza* was still quite popular in the ballrooms of the Haitian immigrant clubs in eastern Cuba. As a result, the *son* began to fuse together with the *contradanza* leading to the creation of the *danzón*, a third manifestation of traditional popular Cuban dance music. The *danzón*'s evolution and popularization was carried forward under the influence of the Havana orchestra *Arcaño y sus Maravillas*, which became famous in the 1930s and 1940s for its live shows that gave dancers a plethora of *danzones* to move to. (Today the *danzón* is rarely danced in Cuba but has gradually become one of the most popular dances in Mexico, especially in cities on the Caribbean coast like Vera Cruz). Finally, Enrique Jorrín, under the influence of the dancers of both the *danzón* and its faster-paced cousin, the *mambo*, made a key rhythmic modification that led to the creation of the slower and more refined *cha-cha-chá*, a fourth essential creation of Cuban dance music made popular during the first half of the 20th century.

Cuban popular music is danced in couples, and the most popular form of popular dance for the past half-century has been the *casino*, which features a multiplicity of complex variations on a basic syncopated or stutter step that allows the couple to show its skill and sensuality. For example, when dancing to *salsa* music (which is the popular name outside of Cuba of the musical genre that accompanies *casino* dancing - itself popularly referred to outside of Cuba as "*salsa*" dancing), each number features a *montuno* section, which is charged with a prolonged blast of rhythmic energy. At this point the couple will separate with each partner moving freely in an improvised, provocative riot of sensual thrusts and gyrations. Different styles of popular dance have come and gone as transient fads and fashion, but the *casino* stands out from the rest given its popular rootedness and versatility.

The origin of the *casino* is in the Cuban ballrooms of yesteryear, and before that, in the pre-classical dances of the European Renaissance. Numerous ballroom dances were introduced to Cuba from other countries as early as the 18th century, almost always entering through the port cities of Havana and Matanzas. These include the French *quadrille* (or *contradanza*), the minuet, the rigadoon, and the waltz. However, once they reached the island these highly formal and melodic European styles of dance underwent a process of adaptation, enabling their "creolization" into distinctly Cuban ballroom dances. This process gave birth to the *contradanza criolla* (the Creole quadrille), the *danza*, the *habanera*, and the *danzón*.

The *contradanza* contributed its basic step to all subsequent styles of Cuban ball-room dancing, which consists of a series of four alternating forward and backward steps. That basic choreographic essence survives in the *danza*, the *danzón*, the *son*, and the *casino* (or *salsa*). At the start of the 1950s, the first elements that would eventually make up the *casino* as the new style of Cuban ballroom dance began to gestate. Their main forums were the scores if not hundreds of recreational societies, clubs, and dance halls (also known as *casinos*) where the most popular bands of the era would play live.

The syncopated style of music known as the *son*—described in detail later—contributed substantially to the development of the *casino* dance style, especially in how its choreography mimics the rhythmic key (known as *la clave*) that is the unifying element of the *son*. This rhythmic key has the dancers take their basic step in time with the beat of *claves*, always keeping in mind the melody, otherwise known as dancing in *contratiempo* (i.e., in syncopation or on the offbeat). This link in the *son* between the rhythmic key, the melody, and the beat in relation to the basic step, became part of the *casino*, not only following the musical beats but also in the corporal movements and spatial designs of the dancers.

In 1956, the now popular phenomenon of creating a dancing circle of interdependent couples began. This circle of multiple pairs of dancers—itself known as a *rueda del casino*, or casino wheel—would follow the voice commands of a lead dancer so that they could all simultaneously perform the same steps and seamlessly exchange partners without ever missing a beat, losing the rhythm, or slowing the flow of the circle. This phenomenon was first observed in a popular dance hall known as the *Casino Club Deportivo*, where the young dancers liked it and began to imitate it elsewhere. As this dance style began to spread throughout the city and country, it would invariably be described with the phrases, "*vamos a hacer la rueda como en el Casino*" (let's do the wheel like they do in the Casino) or "*vamos a hacer la rueda del Casino*" (let's do the Casino wheel). Thus, even today Cubans rarely if ever speak of dancing "*salsa*," which is a term invented abroad to describe popular Cuban dancing as well as a general term for popular Cuban dance music itself. Instead, they speak of dancing *casino* or if it is in a group of coordinated interchanging couples, *rueda del casino*.

The *casino* is the latest Cuban ballroom dance created spontaneously by dancers themselves. In other words, it is a popular choreography born from the confluence of many diverse elements introduced in an almost unconscious evolutionary process by various ancestral groups. Today, it enjoys widespread dissemination not only within Cuba but also through out the entire world thanks to the boom of so-called *salsa* music over the past 40 years. The *casino*'s popularity as a dance style arises in part from the fact that it is a perfect complement to *salsa* music, and to the fact that it can be done in couples or casino wheels, based on the dancers' ability to improvise and on their choreographic skill. It also has the advantage that almost anyone can learn to "set the pace" or execute the varied and complex web of steps that have been incorporated into it over the years. Finally, like Cuban music itself—described in detail later—popular Cuban dance benefits from its astonishing capacity to absorb new choreographic influences while simultaneously diffusing itself into new dance styles as diverse as tap, swing, jazz, and hip-hop.

MUSIC

This section describes the development of a variety of Cuban musical genres with a focus on the 20th century. Some of these include *son* and *rumba*; *danzón*, *canción*, and *punto guajiro*; "*rhumba*,"*conga*, *mambo*, Latin jazz, and *cha-cha-chá*; *bolero*, *trova*, *nueva trova*, *songo*, *timba*, Cuban hip-hop, and of course, *salsa* itself, whose Cuban paternity is universally recognized by the mostly "Nuyorican" (New York Puerto Ricans) musicians who brought it into existence in New York City in the late 1960s. In presenting these various genres, our focus is on the two most unique and outstanding characteristics of Cuban music: absorption and diffusion (Padura 2006: 205). These two traits have allowed Cuban music to take on a multitude of diverse influences and cross borders to the United States and beyond, constantly reinventing itself while remaining both vital and authentically Cuban in the process. As famed Cuban anthropologist and ethnomusicologist Fernando Ortiz once observed, the *son*—the sine qua non of authentic Cuban "roots" music—was itself born of an impure yet quite fruitful "love affair between the African drum and the Spanish guitar" (Manuel with Bilby and Alrgey 2006).

Origins

Cuban music was born from the fusion of Spanish musical folklore and the innumerable African rhythms brought to Cuba by black slaves. A slight French influence was also added in the early years of the 19th century through Santiago de Cuba following the Haitian revolution. The phenomenal richness of Spanish folklore mixed together with the astounding vigor and complexity of African music creating an exuberant and explosive musical synthesis. While from a formal and harmonic point of view Cuban music has not been very innovative, it has produced a melodically and rhythmically overwhelming collection of sounds that have become familiar the world over.

The first notable compositions created on Cuban soil were the works of Esteban Salas (1725–1803) and Juan París (1759–1845). Of a liturgical and vocal character, these compositions were followed by others written for the symphony and the chamber. Such compositions were rooted exclusively in European musical traditions. It was not until the beginning of the 19th century that the first expressions of a music with a different, uniquely Cuban rhythm appeared. A *contradanza* by the title of "San Pascual Bailón" (anonymous, 1803) and the many *contradanzas* written by Manuel Saumell (1817–1870) are the first compositions that permit us to speak of a truly Cuban music, reflecting an authentically Creole sound. From this moment and out of this development the fertility and influence of Cuban music would be assured.

Already by the end of the 18th century this Spanish-African mixture had produced a danceable music with powerful popular roots that slowly but surely began to replace the European *danzas* at the parties of the Creole planter and merchant class. The 19th century witnessed the rapid evolution of this Creole dance music and can be heard in the works for piano by Manuel Saumell and Ignacio Cervantes (1847–1905) and in the compositions of Nicolás Ruiz Espadero (1832–1890). It was also during the 19th century that Cuba produced its first composers and instrumentalists of international renown, including the Afro-Cuban violinists Claudio José Domingo Brindis de Salas (1852–1911) and José White (1836–1912), author of the emblematic "Bella Cubana." The mulatto Brindis de Salas and White—a black man—each had triumphant national and international careers testifying to the transculturation of Cuban music already at this early stage and to the great power that their driving musical personalities had in overcoming the considerable racial and economic barriers of the time.

The wealth of Cuban music—principally the opulence of its rhythmic patterns—make it quite contagious. Styles of Cuban music that prefigure ragtime (itself a precursor of jazz) were introduced into the United States from the Caribbean by the Creole American composer Louis Moreau Gottschalk (1829–1869), who spread them from his musically fertile hometown of New Orleans. Even today many are still ignorant of the extensive influence of Cuban music in the development of jazz, and often Afro-Cuban rhythmic formulas are confused with those of jazz. Between 1920 and 1940, Cuba's *bolero, son, rumba,* and *conga* all travelled around the world, often stylized and commercialized under the catchy exotic name "rhumba" by leading U.S. recording companies and in scores of Hollywood movies. This led to the proliferation of Cuban-based dance music for a largely non-Cuban but growing and seemingly insatiable public. Composers of the caliber of Aaron Copland, Leonard Bernstein, and George Gershwin, all wrote works based on the rhythmic base of the *danzón, son,* and *rumba*.

Classical Music and Cuban Jazz

No less important—although less well known—is Cuba's so-called classical music. Among the most notable composers in this genre are Gonzalo Roig (1890–1970), with his well-known operetta *Cecilia Valdés,* and Ernesto Lecuona, with his own important collection of *zarzuelas*. In fact, many of Lecuona's best pieces for piano have since become world famous standards. The first two Cuban composers to embrace the revolutionary sonic techniques of Stravinsky and Bartók were Amadeo Roldán and Alejandro García Caturla. Their own rich and daring harmonic pallets, use of grand symphonic forms, and magnetic manipulation of orchestral power placed Cuban music within the tradition of universal contemporary art music for the first time (De la Vega 1990).

Inheritors of this musical vanguard—and under the influence of the Catalan composer José Ardévol—a number of Cuban composers later came together under the name *Grupo de Renovación Musical* (Group of Musical Renovation). Edgardo Martín, Harold Gramatges, and the important musicologist Argeliers León were members of this group. Julián Orbón and Aurelio de la Vega are two independent and original musicians within the tradition of Cuban art music. More contemporary still are the composers Leo Brouwer, Carlos Fariñas, Roberto Valero, Juan Piñera, and Sergio and José María Vitier, who are known above all for their compositions that accompany Cuban films.

During the 1950s another unique, experimental, and jazz-related musical movement known as "feeling" developed in Havana. Leading composers of this poetic, often romantic, *bolero*-like genre included Martha Valdés, César Portillo de la Luz, and José Antonio Méndez. The best-known interpreters of this deeply felt song movement were Olga Guillot (also known for her *boleros*), Elena Burke, and Omara Portuondo, who would perform with the bare, stripped-down accompaniment of a single guitar or perhaps a piano, allowing their soulful voices to give flight to their full expressive power. Finally, the global jazz scene counts more than a few Cubans among its established masters, including the late Bebo Valdés (father) and Chucho Valdés (son), Paquito D'Rivera, Gonzalo Rubalcaba, and the recent MacArthur "Genius" grantee Dafnis Prieto, who are potent trailblazers in the subgenre of Latin jazz (also called Afro-Cuban jazz).

Three other important Cuban innovators in the Latin jazz genre are Luciano "Chano" Pozo and the brothers-in-law Mario Bauzá and Frank Grillo, better known as "Machito." Though Pozo lived fast and died young, in his short 33-year life he was an influential musical innovator, percussionist, and composer who impacted the development of CuBop and Latin jazz in the United States. Having absorbed the African rhythms of his youth, Pozo began to gain notoriety in Cuba after 1940 for his performances at the famed Sans-Souci Cabaret in a show called "*Congo Pantera*." During the early 1940s he composed a series of *guaracha-rumbas* with playful Afro-Cuban names like "Blen-blen-blen," "Pin-pon-pan," "Ariñañara," and "Wachi-wara." After moving to the United States in 1946 and touring with Dizzy Gillespie's jazz ensemble, he was tragically killed in a Harlem bar in 1948 before he could reach his full potential or witness the far-reaching impact of his brief contribution to the development of Cuban music. He is perhaps best remembered today for the Latin jazz standard, "*Manteca*," which he cowrote with Gillespie in 1947.

Born in Tampa in 1912, where his father had been a tobacco worker, Machito (Francisco Raúl Gutiérrez Grillo, 1912–1984) moved to Havana with his family as a child. Machito is recognized, together with his brother-in-law Mario Barzá (1911–1993), as a godfather of Latin jazz, one of New York City's three original mambo kings, and a major inspiration for *salsa* music. These achievements all flowed from the fact that Machito led from 1940 until his death in 1984, the most influential Cuban band in the United States, *Machito and His Afro-Cubans*. Machito's career cannot be separated from that of his closest artistic collaborator and musical arranger, Mario Bauzá. Before joining forces with Machito, Bauzá had played with some of the best jazz musicians of 1930s New York, including Chick Webb, Ella Fitzgerald, Don Redman, Fletcher Henderson, and Cab Calloway. *Machito and His Afro-Cubans* was formed in 1940, when Bauzá left Calloway's jazz band to work with Dizzy Gillespie and Machito who had arrived in New York from Havana in 1937. In fact, Machito and Bauzá formed their band to create a fusion of the Afro-Cuban music they had grown up with in Cuba and the African-American jazz music they were surrounded by in New York (Roberts 1999).

The years following the revolutionary triumph back in Cuba were ones of upheaval and experimentation in Cuban jazz. Because of the revolutionary credentials and personal connections of the ICAIC's longtime director, the late Alfredo Guevara, the organization has enjoyed a bureaucratic latitude and relative creative autonomy unlike most other state institutions. This fact allowed classical guitarist Leo Brower to set up the *Grupo de Experimentación Sonora* (GES, Musical Experimentation Group) in 1969. Like many *nueva trova* singer-songwriters such as Silvio Rodríguez and Pablo Milanés, a host of aspiring young jazz musicians enjoyed

Circa 1940, Group portrait of Cuban-born Latin jazz singer and bandleader Machito (Francisco Raúl Gutiérrez Grillo, 1912–1984) holding maracas while leading his band the Afro-Cubans. The band's composer and arranger Mario Bauzá (1911–1993) is middle trumpet. (Frank Driggs Collection/Getty Images)

protection under the ICAIC's auspices. The GES produced soundtracks for Cuban cinema, promoted politically oriented songs, worked to protect and renew Cuban musical traditions, and provided a space for musical experimentation.

It was through the auspices of the GES that the *Orquesta Cubana de Música Moderna* (OCMM, Cuban Orchestra of Modern Music) was created in 1967. The core of this bureaucratically created supergroup had begun their musical odyssey in 1963, when pianist Jesús "Chucho" Valdés, guitarist Carlos Emilio Morales, and saxophonist Paquito D'Rivera took part in an experimental jazz orchestra known as *Teatro Musical de La Habana*. As a jazz ensemble called into existence by the decree of the National Council of Culture, the OCMM constantly suffered from bureaucratic obstacles that hindered the improvisational artistic spirit that music such as jazz is supposed to embody. As a result, these three musicians struggled constantly for creative autonomy during their tenure in the OCMM. Finally, in 1973 they broke off to form what would become Cuba's premier jazz band, *Irakere*. Although Valdés was able to gain a significant measure of autonomy in the formation of *Irakere*, he had to constantly maneuver bureaucratic obstacles following the band's inception. This kind of negotiation is especially evident in the band's dual repertoire. From the start, it sought to push the limits of experimentation and fusion in jazz and Afro-Cuban music, but it also successfully produced a stream of popular, danceable

---

JESÚS "CHUCHO" VALDÉS (1941–) AND IRAKERE

A key musician in the development of Jazz in Cuba and an important influence on the broader musical genre Latin jazz, Chucho Valdés is a virtuoso pianist equally fluent in classical, popular, and experimental jazz forms. The son of the great Cuban pianist Bebo Valdés, Chucho was cofounder and longtime leader of Cuba's most influential jazz fusion group *Irakere*. Apart from his impressive achievements as a bandleader and later as a solo artist (winning Grammies for each), Valdés' career is so important to the history of Cuban jazz because he continued the tradition started in the 1940s and 1950s by Armando Romeu and Mario Bauzá, and through his inspiration and influence allowed it to continue by collaborating with a series of jazz virtuosos who each went on to a stellar solo career, including Paquito D'Rivera, Arturo Sandoval, Orlando "Maraca" Valle, and José Luis Cortés "El Tosco."

---

music—a must for any Cuban band that wants to connect with the dancing Cuban public. This skill was also instrumental in allowing the group to stay alive for more than 30 years and spawn a series of virtuosos who themselves would go on to stellar solo careers and form a new generation of jazz fusion groups. The most prominent alumni of *Irakere* include Paquito D'Rivera and Arturo Sandoval (both of whom have since established themselves as leading "Latin Jazz" musicians in the United States), Valdés himself, as well as two of the most talented and innovative Cuban jazz fusion musicians of the 1990s, Orlando "Maraca" Valle and his group *Otra Visión* and the popular timba sensation José Luis "El Tosco" Cortés and his group *NG La Banda* (Acosta 2003).

PAQUITO D'RIVERA (FRANCISCO JESÚS RIVERA FIGUERAS, 1948–)

A jazz virtuoso on the alto and soprano saxophone as well as the clarinet, Paquito D'Rivera began his musical career at a young age due to the influence of his bandleader father, Tito Rivera. On the cutting edge of musical experimentation and jazz in Cuba from his youth, D'Rivera joined Chucho Valdés in 1963 as a member of the experimental jazz orchestra known as *Teatro Musical de La Habana*. He subsequently moved with Valdés to the *Orquesta Cubana de Música Moderna* in 1967, continuing on to form their own jazz band *Irakere* in 1973. D'Rivera fled Cuba in 1980, settling in New York City where he set to work producing a flurry of Latin jazz, jazz, and classical recordings of the highest quality. In 1988, Dizzy Gillespie invited him aboard as a charter member of the 15-piece United Nations Orchestra, which he took over in 1993 after Gillespie's death. He was honored with a Lifetime Achievement Award by Carnegie Hall in 1991 and won the first of many solo Grammys in 1996 for his recording, "Portraits of Cuba." In 2005, he was awarded the National Medal of Arts by President George W. Bush in an Oval Office ceremony.

The Son

Best compared to American Blues as Cuba's central and most widely influential musical genre, the *son* was essential to the development of all subsequent forms of popular Cuban dance music, but especially during the formative decades of the 1920s and 1930s. Preceded by the *changüí*, a very similar rustic, rhythmic music that originated in the mountains of Guantánamo in Cuba's Oriente, *son* also began its long life as relatively "simple" country music from the highlands around the Sierra Maestra played by wandering groups of musicians armed with maracas, a standard acoustic guitar, a *tres* (an acoustic guitar with three sets of double strings), a *güiro* (a dried, elongated calabash with ridges that are scraped with a stick), a set of bongo drums, and sometimes a *marimbula* (a "finger piano," or rudimentary bass instrument). The *claves*, a pair of hard wooden pegs, were added after the *son* arrived in Havana around 1910 (Sweeney 2001: 45–52). Carried to the capital city by young black army recruits from eastern Cuba, the *son* rapidly displaced the *danzón* and grew into the popular dance music of Cuba, later becoming the source of most forms of modern Latin American and Caribbean dance music.

After 1910, the entire vast history and innumerable genres of music on the island converged through the crystallization of *son* into a national musical style, producing a synthesis that for the first time posed an effective musical resolution to the age-old tension between classically inspired European ballroom music (such as the *contradanza*, *danza*, and *danzón*) and popular Afro-Cuban percussive styles emanating from the street (such as the *rumba*). In his book, *Music in Cuba* (2001), first published in Spanish in Cuba in 1945, Cuban writer Alejo Carpentier argues that "Thanks to the *son*, Afro-Cuban percussion, confined to the slave barracks and the dilapidated rooming houses of the slums, revealed its marvelous expressive resources, achieving universal status" (Carpentier 2001: 228).

Specifically, it was *son*'s African-inspired 2–3 "rhythmic key," known as the *clave*, that made it unique. "*Sin clave, no hay son*" (without *clave*, there is no *son*), is how Cuban musicians emphasize the sine qua non importance of the *clave* (though some Cuban musicians hold that the *clave*—both the instrument and the rhythm it plays—was adapted from *rumba* to the *son*). The powerful and penetrating rhythmic crack of the two wooden pegs (themselves called the *claves*) both distinguished the *son* from other types of Cuban music and allowed it to meld together the floating melodies and harmonies of European instruments based on strings and horns (especially the Spanish guitar) and the driving percussive rhythms and call and response vocals based on the African drum. Ethnomusicologist Ned Sublette's gloss of the term is helpful:

"The ships were held together not with nails but with wooden pegs, called *clavijas*, made of hard, dense wood that wouldn't rot when wet. [. . .] The word *clave* has several meanings in Spanish. [. . .] One of the meanings of the word is "key" [. . .]. Just as the hardwood *claves* once held ships together, when they are clicked together as instruments, the rhythm they play holds the melody line and percussion parts together. [. . .] So the *claves* locked the black and white together in song—the process of creolization in action." (Sublette 2004: 94–96)

Carpentier had previously made much the same point, focusing his attention on the *clave*'s ability to bring a variety of previously incompatible instruments together giving birth to a new, singular musical genre.

> The great revolution of ideas instigated by the *son*'s percussion was in giving us the sense of a polyrhythm subjected to a unity of time. Up until then, one spoke of the rhythm of the *contradanza*, the rhythm of the *guaracha*, the rhythms of the *danzón*. [. . .] The *son*, on the other hand, established new categories. Within a general tempo, each percussive element assumed an autonomous existence. (Carpentier 2001: 229)

Such is the omnivorous power and open nature of *son*, what Cuban ethnomusicologist Radamés Giró called, "a force capable of digesting everything it borrows" (Fernández 2000: 275), that it was later transformed, most famously by the composer and blind *tres* guitar player Arsenio Rodríguez and his *conjunto* orchestra in the late 1940s and 1950s, into the many different styles of Cuban dance music we know today: *son guaguancó, son montuno, son pregón, son afro, guaracha-son, guajiro-son, bolero-son*, and modern-day *salsa*—which is essentially *son* played with new musical arrangements, Caribbean and North American influences, a Latino/Latin American consciousness, and a New York urban sensibility.

Though the *son* is perhaps the most powerful symbol of Afro-Hispanic cultural fusion and Cuban nationalism, it was "re-Africanized" by Rodríguez in the late 1940s when he enriched its rhythmic base by introducing the piano, double trumpets, a stand-up base, and, most importantly, the conga drum (*tumbadora*) for the first time—creating the *conjunto* ensemble. These instrumental additions added a fiery dynamism to Rodríguez's musical arrangements that combined the musical world of the *son* septet with the swing of the North American jazz band (Sublette 2004).

Of Rodríguez's many musical innovations, perhaps his two most important were the *son guaguancó* (a version of the *son* that incorporated elements from the *rumba*, an even more Africanized Cuban urban musical genre) and the *son montuno*. The second of these styles had been played for years, being the final, more open-ended "jam" section of a *son* arrangement that followed the initial verse section (sometimes credited with leading to the creation of the wildly popular *mambo*). However, Rodríguez's *conjunto* breathed new life into the *montuno* by dividing it into sections that highlighted the horns, pumping more energy and excitement into it until it climaxed and "broke." This final *montuno* section, which Rodríguez renamed "*diablo*" (devil), was characterized by a cyclic, African-derived, formal structure, constant improvisation (with lyrics and instrumental solos), and a typically African call-and-response interaction between the main *sonero* (singer) with either the chorus or an instrumental soloist.

In his own highly original development of the *son montuno*, Benny Moré, a contemporary of Rodríguez and perhaps the most gifted Cuban *sonero* of the 20th century, clearly demonstrated the difference between "*cantar*" (singing) and "*sonear*" (the ability to improvise lyrics "in a manner that fits rhythmically and melodically with the accompanying *coro* [chorus] of the *son montuno*" (Fernández 2000: 269, 276)). This arrangement closely mimics the structure of a traditional *rumba* described earlier.

ARSENIO RODRÍGUEZ (1913–1970)

Born in Matanzas in 1913, as a child Arsenio Rodríguez was surrounded by Afro-Cuban *rumba* and Congolese spirituals. As a result, he developed early into a multi-instrumentalist, choosing the *tres* guitar as his main instrument. By the early 1930s he moved to Havana and began playing music profession-ally by 1935. Although less of a commercial success than his contemporaries Benny Moré, Pérez Prado, or Frank "Machito" Grillo, Rodríguez was the most important single figure of Cuban music in the 20th century. During the 1940s, Rodríguez became a prolific composer of *son*, *mambo*, and *bolero* music, as well as an influential and innovative bandleader. Now recognized as the individual most responsible for revolutionizing the way traditional Cuban *son* was played in 1940s Havana, Rodríguez made a series of daring innovations to the form by adding hard-hitting lyricism, a new instrumental format, and a more complex rhythmic structure. Nicknamed *"El ciego maravilloso"* due to his blindness, Rodríguez immigrated to the United States in the early 1950s. However, he never achieved popular success abroad and died in obscurity in Los Angles in 1972 just as *salsa* began to enjoy its greatest popular and commercial success.

After 1960, the *son*'s central importance in Cuban popular music waned. Still, the transformation of the *son* into the *songo* by the wildly popular dance band *Los Van Van* kept Cuban audiences dancing to the basic *clave* rhythm through a new series of modernizations, miscegenations, and mutations. Also, during the 1970s and 1980s a number of *son* "revival" groups, including *Sierra Maestra* and *Alalberto Álvarez y son 14*, succeeded in keeping classic *son* alive. In fact, it was *Sierra Maestra*'s bandleader, Juan de Marcos González, who was the main producer and musical arranger in Cuba behind the formation and worldwide success of the 1990s *son* revival sensations *Buena Vista Social Club* and the *Afro-Cuban All Stars* (Robinson 2004; Sweeney 2001).

As we learn in one of the opening scenes of Wim Wenders's Academy Award–nominated documentary film of the same name, the *Buena Vista Social Club* was one of many social dance clubs that blanketed the Havana of the 1940s and 1950s. The *Buena Vista* phenomenon, however, was the almost accidental making of a group of recordings—most of which were remakes of *sons*, *boleros*, and *guajiras* from the golden age of Cuban music—when the U.S. guitarist and roots music aficionado Ry Cooder arrived in Havana in 1996 together with producer Nick Gold. They had come intending to make a fusion recording between Cubans and a group of musicians from Mali who were unable to obtain visas in time. Making virtue of necessity, they quickly recruited a handful of once famous but now largely retired and forgotten old timers and—amid the crumbling facades of Havana—recorded and "rediscovered" these elderly yet virtuosic and photogenic musicians. The original group included vocalists Omara Portuondo and Ibrahim Ferrer, the pianist Rubén González, and—perhaps the best known, and eldest, of all—Compay Segundo. As of this writing, while a slightly reconfigured and rejuvenated version of the supergroup continues to record and tour the world, eight of the original members have died between 2000 and 2011, including Ferrer, González, and Segundo.

BENNY MORÉ (1919–1963)

Born Bartolomé Moré in the town of Santa Isabel de las Lajas, Cienfuegos, the Cuban vocal sensation better known as Benny Moré or "El Benny" first came to prominence while touring in Mexico. It was there that he took the advice of a friend who said that Bartolomé was a name fit more for a donkey than a musician. More than any other singer or performer, Moré came to embody the flash, charismatic genius, and magical synthesis that was Cuban popular dance music during the "boom" years of the genre, the 1940s and 1950s. Like his contemporary Arsenio Rodríguez, Moré excelled in multiple genres both as a composer and as a performer. He could sing a piercing *bolero* and suddenly shift gears into a high-energy, percussive *guaguancó* without missing a beat or compromising on the quality of either. However, unlike Rodríguez, Moré was a huge popular success and a legendary *sonero* (*son* vocalist) with his own orchestra, *La Banda Gigante*.

Crossover Success: From the Son to the Mambo, and Beyond

Together, the *son* and *rumba* form the backbone of all popular Cuban dance music. However, the *son* has been more successful than the *rumba* (through absorbing many of its characteristics) at achieving popular crossover success both in Cuba and abroad. This success at having, in the vivid phrase of Fernando Ortiz, "the dances of the rabble accepted by aristocrats in their palaces" was accomplished through an ambivalent process of "nationalizing blackness" (Moore 1997). In fact, as ethnomusicologist Robin Moore argues in his wonderfully insightful anthropology of the origins of modern Cuban music, *Nationalizing Blackness: Afrocubanismo and Artistic Revolution in Havana, 1920–1940*, a strange mix of pride and embarrassment accompanied the gradual embrace of *son* as Cuba's national music par excellence. During these pivotal 20 years, a host of mostly white, conservatory-trained Cuban composers and musicians, including Ernesto Lecuona, Amadeo Roldán, Alejandro García Caturla, Eliseo Grenet, Moisés Simons, the mulatta actress and vocalist Rita Montaner, and the black showman and composer Bola de Nieve ("Snowball"), participated in the simultaneous "purification," popularization, and universalization of the *son* first in Cuba and then abroad.

The career of black pianist Bola de Nieve especially highlights the irony of this ambivalent embrace of Afro-Cuban musical culture. Born Ignacio Villa in the Havana suburb of Guanabacoa, Bola became famous in Cuba for his highly original versions of the stylized *afros-son* of white composers. Being black himself, however, he was distinguished as the one-and-only successful Afro-Cuban performer of this *afrocubanista* salon music (Moore 1997: 137). Alternately derided for being a kind of Cuban Uncle Tom or celebrated as the incarnation of authentic *afro-son*, Bola de Nieve was neither. Instead, his unique position as a kind of translator of Afro-Cuban culture allowed him to simultaneously celebrate Afro-Cuban popular culture and parody the often simplistic renditions of it created for popular consumption by white composers.

According to Moore, Bola's signature self-parodying performances, "overtly reflect the tensions between racism, populism, and elitism so prevalent in Cuban works" of the 1930s (ibid.: 138). Bola's songs would typically poke fun at the figure of the *negro catedrático*, the humble Afro-Cuban who put on airs by dressing up and singing in English, Catalan, French, Italian, and Portuguese (sometimes within a single song). Indeed, his live shows have been called "mini-docudramas of Cuban social/racial everyday life" (Fernández 2000: 268). However, because of the effectiveness of his stage persona, it was never clear to his audience whether he was engaging in sophisticated mockery, humorous self-deprecation, or had internalized racist stereotypes.

The *mambo*'s origins are most commonly attributed to the brothers Orestes and Israel "Cachao" López who composed a *danzón* called "Mambo" in 1938 as members of Antonio Arcaño's orchestra. Arsenio Rodríguez, who often referred the final section of his *son montuno* as a *mambo* or *"diablo"* is also understood to be a key contributor to the birth of the genre. However, pianist, arranger, and bandleader Dámaso Pérez Prado is clearly the single figure most responsible for refining and popularizing the *mambo* into an internationally recognizable sound. Essentially, the mambo is a musical hybrid that was born in Cuba in the late 1930s and developed there during the 1940s. However, because it was considered too experimental even in Cuba, it had to wait almost 10 years for its eventual consolidation and popularization in Mexico, Latin America, and the United States between 1948 and 1953. Lyrically, the *mambo* is uninspiring as the texts of most numbers are comprised simply of the word "*mambo*" endlessly repeated and interchanged with shouts and loud grunt-like sounds such as "Ungh!" or "Dilo!" (an especially typical feature of Pérez Prado's recordings).

Often working in collaboration with *sonero* Benny Moré in Mexico in the late 1940s, Pérez Prado developed the *mambo* into a distinct style of Cuban dance music by adding vibrant, driving rhythms, a fast tempo and pulsating flow, blaring trumpets, and a signature reckless dissonance to his compositions. Though his compositions are often criticized by purists for their lack of the complex polyrhythms more common in the work of Machito's Afro-Cubans or Arsenio Rodríguez, Pérez Prado was an undeniable musical innovator who continued to create new rhythms and experiment with ambitious compositions throughout his long career. In fact, his performances openly embraced popular and commercial success, while never abandoning daring experimentation. He also was immensely popular with his audiences since his numbers invariably pushed dancers to the very limits of human endurance.

Pérez Prado was able to join forces at the height of his popularity with Benny Moré, allowing him to balance his angular, taut, and technical approach with Moré's more smooth, easygoing, and intuitive side (Sublette 2004). Nicknamed, *El bárbaro del ritmo* (the rhythm wizard), Moré first traveled to Mexico in 1945 with the band of *son* sensation Miguel Matamoros. However, he soon surpassed Matamoros first as a big-band singer and later as a bandleader himself. Moré left the *Conjunto Matamoros* to join Pérez Prado's *mambo* orchestra quickly becoming as popular as Pérez Prado himself. After a number of years of traveling back and forth between Cuba and Mexico, changing bands constantly, Moré finally formed what was to be the ultimate dance band in Cuban musical history, in many ways the culmination of the long evolution of Cuban popular dance music, *Benny Moré and his Banda Gigante*.

Though Moré had no formal musical training, he commanded this enormous orchestra with an exacting precision and typically Cuban flair, making the band's performances an unforgettable spectacle. During his rise to superstardom, he developed a signature style of singing, performing, and dressing that always included a wide-brimmed hat, cane, baggy pants, and long coat. As he sang and directed his orchestra, he often danced wildly across the stage in much the same way as James Brown, "The Godfather of Soul" would do later in the United States. Though less of a composer than a performer, before his death in 1963 from alcoholism, Moré composed a number of his own hit songs that have since become standards, including the smash hit and signature Moré number, "Castellano, que bueno baila usted," which he cowrote with his trombonist and arranger Generoso "El Tojo" Jiménez.

Cuban Music after 1959: Salsa, Nueva Trova, Songo, *and* Timba

The long series of Cuban dance crazes that had periodically overtaken the United States—from the *rumba*, to the *conga*, to the *mambo*, to the *cha-cha-chá*—came to an abrupt halt in the late 1950s (Pérez 1999). In those years, the upstart child of the blues that called itself rock and roll dealt a fatal blow to American social dancing and at the same time neutralized the crossover appeal of Cuban music in the United States. Simultaneously, Cold War hostility cast a dark shadow over the two-way musical collaboration between Cuba and the United States that had existed since the beginning of the 20th century. Cuban music and musicians in the United States suddenly found themselves cut off from their musical roots, and, unable to constantly reconnect and renew, were increasingly relegated to the margins of the American musical mainstream. Meanwhile, back in Cuba, new cultural policies that eradicated the economic backbone of the island's music industry— commercial record labels, tourism, hotels, casinos, and independently owned bars and night clubs—sent many leading musicians into permanent exile (Celia Cruz, Pérez Prado, Cachao, Arsenio Rodríguez) while others like Moré died before their time (Moore 2006). This series of cultural, economic, and geopolitical shock waves sounded the death knell to what had been the golden age of Cuban popular music (Padura 2003: 186).

Still, the second half of the 20th century saw four important, if quite different Cuban musical innovations: so-called *salsa*; *nueva trova*, a Cuban version of 1960s poetic protest music; *songo*, an updated version of the *son* popularized by the Cuban super group *Los Van Van*; and *timba*, the complex, even aggressive Cuban dance music that itself evolved out of the *songo* and became particularly popular amid the crisis and desperation of the 1990s. What is today referred to as *salsa* music was born during the 1970s and 1980s out of the uprooted Cuban rhythms circulating between New York, Miami, and Puerto Rico, among other locales, fusing together with jazz as well as with a variety of forms of Caribbean folk music, such as Puerto Rican *bomba* and *plena*. Due to the cultural isolation imposed by the U.S. embargo and the Cuban revolution, Cuban popular music on the island became stagnant as it ceased to be enriched through the incorporation of new influences. In fact, it was not until the visit of Venezuelan *salsero* Oscar de León to Cuba in the 1980s that Cubans began to rediscover and celebrate the Cuban musical roots of *salsa*.

CELIA CRUZ (1925–2003)

Probably the best-known and most widely loved Cuban female vocalist, or *sonera*, Celia Cruz first gained notoriety in Cuba after appearing on the radio in the 1940s, especially on the famous radio station 1010 (Radio Mil Diez). Her rise to stardom both in Cuba and abroad was especially important given her role as the one of the few female lead singers in Cuban dance music, a genre known for its bawdy macho lyrics and leading men. Soon thereafter in 1950, she joined the musical group *Sonora Matancera* as its lead singer touring around Cuba and across Latin America for the next 15 years. However, after defecting along with most of her band in 1960, she had a long, successful career in the United States becoming known as "the queen of *salsa*," since her powerful voice was one of the signature sounds of the 1970s *salsa* music phenomenon. Her death in 2003 prompted an outpouring of emotion both in Cuba and especially in the Cuban and Latin communities of Miami and the New York area where she lived.

This rediscovery led to an explosion of modern dance music on the island—under the names *salsa*, *songo*, and later *timba*—which though a latecomer to the international tropical dance music craze produced excellent musical results. While Celia Cruz became the indisputable queen of *salsa* abroad, a variety of styles of this Cuban dance music blossomed both on and off the island. Its most innovative Cuban interpreters at home have been *Los Van Van*, *Adalberto Álvarez y son 14*, and *NG La Banda*, while abroad the *Miami Sound Machine* and its lead singer and later solo artist Gloria Estefan along with Willy Chirino have been both popular and influential. Today on the island *timba* is the most common style of popular dance music, characterized by a rich musical mixture of a variety of modern, electronic, and traditional folk forms.

Salsa

The permanent exile of many of Cuba's leading musicians combined with the unprecedented surge of Caribbean immigration into New York City began to create a new mixture of urban musical styles based on the kernel of the Cuban *son* that had long since been internalized by Big Apple musicians and universalized throughout Latin America and the Caribbean. The result of this new mixture would simmer and mature underground during much of the 1960s only to burst forth in the late 1960s and 1970s as *salsa*. Partly for the same reasons of novelty and marketing that had previously given birth to Cuban music in the United States as "*rhumba*," *salsa* was unique in that it became identified as a pan-Latino banner of cultural pride not just for Cubans but also for Puerto Ricans, Colombians, Dominicans, Panamanians, and the host of other displaced Latin Americans and Caribbeans residing in *Nueva York* (Fernández 1994). For this reason, despite the initial rejection of the term as a simplistic and confusing commercial tag by many of its leading practitioners, *salsa* is an appropriate label for this new tropical urban sound in that it describes a synergic musical product that is more than the sum of its parts.

Just as the confusing commercial term *rhumba* was given to a wide variety of *son*-based rhythms once stateside, *salsa* is a catchall label that means different things to different people. First of all, *salsa* music shares much with its most important musical ancestor Cuban *son*, itself a "transculturalized" hybrid with its own rural sensibility. Thus, while *salsa* is clearly an appropriation of Cuban musical tradition, it is a truly "creative appropriation," the rightful heir to Cuban *son*, since it is "a miscegenation of the already *mestizo* Cuban *son*" (Padura 2003: 198). Many Latinos in the big cities of the United States celebrate *salsa* as their collective cultural patrimony and as a form of resistance to cultural assimilation and marginalization. In essence, it has become a sign of cultural heritage as "natural" as the equally constructed and problematic term "Hispanic." On the other hand, for a time many Cubans interpreted *salsa* as a cultural looting; "another instance of Yankee imperialism taking advantage of musical sources for purely commercial purposes" (Fernández 1994: 112).

For the sake of simplicity and in order to recognize its three central characteristics, it may be best to define *salsa* as Cuban music, played by Puerto Ricans, in New York City. That is, nearly all of the non-Cuban participants in the original *salsa* movement including Tito Puente, Dominican Johnny Pacheco, Eddie Palmieri, Willy Colón, and Panamanian Rubén Blades have recognized Cuba as the transcendent musical inspiration for the basic rhythms and arrangements of the *salsa* phenomenon. At the same time, upon this Cuban foundation was erected a sound that owes much to the traditional *Boricua* rhythms of *bomba* and *plena* given the overwhelming demographic presence of Puerto Ricans in New York City at the time *salsa* was brought into being.

Ironically, the *salsa* phenomenon did not come to fruition in Cuba's other capital, Miami, until the mid-1980s. However, it did so with a mainstream crossover success unmatched by perhaps any group before or since: Gloria Estefan and the *Miami Sound Machine*. After having fled Cuba with her family as a child, Gloria Fajardo met Emilio Estefan, then the musical director and percussionist of a Spanish-language group *The Miami Cuban Boys*, in the mid-1970s while attending a wedding. Called up on stage to sing with the group, Gloria eventually joined the group in 1976 under the new name *Miami Sound Machine*. Although the group played mostly Spanish-language numbers, recording four Spanish-language albums between 1981 and 1983, by 1984 they began to add English lyrics to their Cuban-based rhythms and immediately won great popular success with hit songs like "Dr. Beat" and "Conga." The band was one of the first and most successful groups in the United States to fuse Cuban rhythms with American rock, practically inventing what became known as the "Miami sound."

In the late 1980s, Gloria Estefan went solo, still backed by the *Miami Sound Machine*, and in the early 1990s Estefan reinvented herself once again, recording a number of albums in Spanish, including the powerful and evocative *Mi Tierra* (Epic 1993), for which she won a Grammy. Attesting to their resonance with Spanish-speaking fans the world over, these albums were wildly successful across Latin America and Spain, where *Mi Tierra* became the best-selling album of all time. Though often criticized by purists or those who disagree with her politics, Estefan's Spanish-language albums include a number of true musical gems, especially the stunning modern version of what can best be described as a *salsa/rumba/conga*, "Tradición," on *Mi Tierra*. A true tour de force, this track includes solo performances by a veritable hit parade of Cuban and Latin musicians such as Arturo Sandoval, Israel "Cachao" López, Paquito D'Rivera, and Tito Puente (López and Padura 1997).

Nueva Trova

With the end of Cuba's tourism industry and the subsequent disappearance of most of the country's live music venues, the state began to subsidize music schools and offer a systematic artistic education to many musicians for the first time. Music production was reorganized with new, noncommercial goals in mind. These included safeguarding the island's cultural roots and national traditions, promoting the education of amateur musicians in an effort to discover new talent, training professional musicians through upgrading Cuba's musical education system, and creating bureaucratic structures that would allow for musical experimentation. However, these goals quickly ran up against a number of obstacles including chronic shortages of musical equipment, the primacy of the ideological struggle over purely creative, aesthetic, or market criteria, and the rise of a new class of bureaucrats (most of whom were nonmusicians) who controlled funding and often arbitrarily withheld state support of any musical initiatives not clearly in line with revolutionary principles (Acosta 2003; Moore 2006).

For example, a new emphasis on the revival of "folk" traditions led to the creation of a number of "roots" groups including the previously mentioned *Conjunto Folklórico Nacional*. However, this laudable achievement was undermined by open discrimination against "popular" music such as big band *son*, *mambo*, or *rumba* orchestras equating them with the prostitution and decadence of the capitalist past. Even the past contributions of standard bearers of Cuban musical culture, such as Celia Cruz, Cachao, and Pérez Prado, were now officially considered Yankee corruptions of authentic Cuban culture and associated with vice, casinos, and organized crime (Guillermoprieto 2004). Thus, despite the revolution's laudable efforts in cultural promotion and musical education, it fell like a bucket of cold water on the musical world of 1950s Havana, filled as it was with lavish, lascivious cabarets and new luxury hotels, each with its own night club and casino. In fact, one of the reasons that Cuban popular music in general and jazz specifically suffered so much during the 1960s was that they were associated in the minds of many revolutionaries with the imperialist control of the island and especially its entertainment industry since at least the 1930s.

The revolution ushered in a series of "idiosyncratic" crackdowns on jazz by "extremist, opportunist, and Neanderthal" apparatchiks who ignorantly tried to portray jazz as "imperialist music," often unaware or incurious about its African-American roots (Acosta 2003). The transformation of Cuban society during the 1960s included the closure of most music venues and the elimination or nationalization of all bars, small privately owned clubs, bodegas, as well as the all-important "holes-in-the-wall" in the Revolutionary Offensive of 1968. Due to this disruption of the normal flow of social life and spontaneous musical exchange and innovation so essential in musical creation, 1968's ideological crackdown on the last vestiges of independent entrepreneurial space amounted to "the most disastrous year for Cuban popular music [. . .] whose negative consequences [Cuba is still] suffering thirty years later" (Acosta 2003: 202). Havana's famed nightlife show business, musical reviews, and the great tradition of marathon popular dances were left in ruins for at least the next 20 years.

At the same time, certain government cultural institutions including the ICAIC began to promote experimentation with new revolutionary and nationalistic forms of musical and film expression, including what became known as *nueva trova*, as well as a number of danceable "new rhythms" such as the *songo*, the *batanga*, the *mozambique*, and the *pilón*. After experiencing repression for its association with the "decadent" youth culture of the 1960s, *nueva trova* found a protected space and a public following in the early 1970s. The previously mentioned GES (*Grupo de Experimentación Sonora*) of the ICAIC, directed by Leo Brouwer, became its key incubator.

Best described as Cuban "protest" music performed by young Cuban singer-songwriters on acoustic guitars in the poetic and often political mold of Bob Dylan, *nueva trova* was also inspired by the politically progressive Latin American "new song" movement. As its name indicates, however, *nueva trova* was also a continuation of the island's own tradition of musical troubadours or *trova* first established at the start of the 20th century by musicians like Manuel Corona and Sindo Garay. To this was added some of the sounds and aesthetic concerns of beat poetry, folk, rock, and Brazilian *bossa nova*. The use of ethnic and electronic instruments was also common in *nueva trova*.

Unlike most other forms of Cuban music (but like its immediate Cuban predecessor, *vieja trova*), *nueva trova* is music more for the head and heart than for the hips and feet. Likewise, unlike the often raunchy, macho lyrics of the *rumba*, *son*, *mambo*, or *guaracha*, *nueva trova* approached the topic of love from a romantic, sentimental perspective. Calling it "protest" music, however, is a bit confusing in the Cuban context since a good portion *nueva trova* clearly celebrates the Cuban revolution and expresses solidarity with leftist, anti-imperialist struggles throughout Latin America. Given these political concerns, though some of the genre's leading musicians were harassed and even jailed before 1971, afterward they were increasingly identified both in Cuba and abroad as standard bearers of the revolution and international symbols of musical resistance and protest against U.S. military and cultural imperialism.

The clear leaders of the *nueva trova* movement are the singer-songwriters Silvio Rodríguez and Pablo Milanés. Rodriguez's deeply poetic lyrics have been committed to memory by many a Latin American and his voice is among the most recognizable of any in the Spanish language today. Among his most famous compositions are "Unicornio Azul," "La Era Está Pariendo un Corazón," and "¿Quién Fuera?" Minlanés' musical style is rich in harmonies, engaging melodies, and palpable symbolism. He is also an expert at integrating folkloric elements into his modern compositions. During the 1980s and 1990s, Milanés became instrumental in promoting many younger Cuban musicians through his foundation. Some of his better-known works include the political anthems, "A Santiago" and "Yo pisaré las calles nuevamente," as well as the romantic ballads, "El breve espacio en que no estás" and "Yolanda."

Other leading *nueva trova* singer-songwriters include Carlos Puebla (famous for his rustic odes to revolutionary leaders such as "Y en eso llegó Fidel" and the paean to Che Guevara, "Hasta Siempre"), Sara González, a kind of "official" protest singer, and the more independent and critical Pedro Luis Ferrer. Finally, since 1990 a new generation of singer-songwriters have emerged on the island often cultivating

PABLO MILANÉS (1943–)

Along with singer-songwriter Silvio Rodríguez, Pablo Milanés is one of the two singer-songwriters most responsible for popularizing a new synthesis of Cuban music that combined traditional *trova* (troubadour) music with the Cuban romantic *bolero*, and *canción* styles to produce *nueva trova*, or Cuban protest music. Milanés was born in Bayamo, a city in Cuba's old Oriente province, and as such was well-steeped in *son*, *bolero*, *feeling*, and *vieja trova* before he began to experiment with this new form. In fact, after a childhood spent performing with various groups in many musical styles, he composed what most critics consider to be the first piece of *nueva trova* music, "Mis 22 años" (My 22 Years), in 1965. While a vocal revolutionary, Milanés has never been an uncritical one. Since 2000, he has been particularly outspoken about the revolution's stifling of dissent. For example, when asked his opinion of a hunger strike by well-known dissident Guillermo Fariñas in a March 2010 interview, Milanés responded that repression of dissidents "must be condemned from a humanistic point of view." He continued, "ideas should be discussed or even combated, but not imprisoned" (Álvarez 2010).

a more critical stance vis-à-vis the government and infusing their songs with rock experimentation. Sometimes referred to as *novísima trova*, this movement's leader has been Carlos Varela with his 1990s anthem of generational frustration "Guillermo Tell" (William Tell). Also of note for its innovative musical "synthesis" of electronic music with instruments and chants from the Yoruba religious pantheon of *Santería* is the group *Síntesis*.

Other excellent artists in this tradition of musical fusion which benefit from institutional support—or at least tolerance—include *Interactivo*, *Buena Fe*, and *X Alfonso*. A final important band to emerge during the 1990s is the now defunct but musically innovative and influential *Habana Abierta*. This was a unique case of a group of island-based musicians—including Vanito Brown and Kelvis Ochoa—who traveled to Spain to tour and record an album, both of which were surprisingly successful given that they had no institutional backing from within the island. However, their music began to catch on among Cubans abroad, especially among the growing post-1995 Cuban population in Miami. This popularity abroad eventually led to the group's developing a following among Cuban youth on the island itself.

Songo *and* Timba

A third type of "new music" to emerge in Cuba after the revolution was the popular dance music that became known as *songo*. Most associated with Cuba's leading popular dance band, *Los Van Van*, *songo* is a musical fusion developed by the group's leader Juan Formell that successfully combines the rhythms and instrumentations of big band Cuban dance music of old with rock, jazz, funk, *bolero*, and in the 1990s, hip-hop. Formed in 1969 during the abortive nationwide struggle to harvest a record 10 million tons of sugarcane, *Los Van Van* has consistently ranked among Cuba's most popular musical groups in part because its rhythms are aimed at giving the people something to dance to and because the lyrics to its many, many songs directly relate to and comment with humor on the ironies and struggles of daily life as lived by Cubans under the revolution.

Neither revolutionary orthodox nor dissident, the most popular of *Los Van Van*'s songs take note of Cuban society's failings not with combativeness or aggression, but with a lighthearted irony that most Cubans share. *Los Van Van* constantly performs concerts in Cuba and around the world, having toured across Latin America, Europe, Africa, and even on rare occasions in the United States. Some of the most popular songs from the group's many albums are "Marilú," "Chirrín Chirrán," "Sandungera," "Soy todo," "El buey cansao," "Se acabó el querer," "La Habana no aguanta más," "Temba, Tumba, Timba," "Somos Cubanos," and "Muévete." Neither a traditional *son* conjunto nor a *salsa* band, *Los Van Van* has been in many ways Cuba's own original answer to American *salsa* music. During the 1990s, however, the original rhythms of *songo* have been modified by Cuban bandleaders under the influence of a variety of new national and international styles becoming *timba* in the process.

Originally a *rumba* term, *timba* is used today to denote modern Cuban dance music. While based on the basic rhythm of the *son* and similar to international *salsa*, *timba* incorporates influences from a wider variety of international and Cuban folk-loric sources. For example, jazz, rock, and funk are all clearly evident in most *timba* compositions, as are many styles of Afro-Cuban ritualistic music including *batá* drumming and authentic neighborhood *rumba*. Also, *timba* bands have incorporated American style drum-sets, synthesizers, and rapped vocals giving their numbers a more innovative, experimental, and modern feel than is typical of other Cuban dance music. Finally, *timba* is both unapologetically raw in its use of often vulgar street language and often harshly critical of the growing social and economic cleavages that have descended upon Cuba starting in the special period of the 1990s. As such, *timba* bands commonly celebrate the semilegal black market "inventions" of young Afro-Cubans from marginal neighborhoods in their lyrics. They also often demand respect for Afro-Cuban traditions of worship and rituals.

Timba "targets everything smacking of hypocrisy or of any variance between revolutionary discourse and reality," writes Maya Roy. "It does not wave the flag of revolt, but proclaims its wish that young people may be and may live as they see fit" (Roy 2002: 172). This hard urban edge has both given *timba* its unique flavor and provoked official criticism of it as over-the-top and disrespectful of authority. Also, because a *timba* ensemble normally incorporates a wide variety of instruments and singing styles, the music and lyrics are often dense and somewhat inaccessible to non-Cubans, making the successful marketing of the genre outside of Cuba difficult. While the most recent work of *Los Van Van* could easily fall into the *timba* mode, other singers and bands more representative of this new genre include Isaac Delgado, *NG La Banda, Manolín—El Médico de la Salsa*, and *La Charanga Habanera* (ibid.; Orovio 2004: 210; Perna 2005).

Cuban Music Today

The wide panorama of Cuban music in the 21st century includes most of the previously described genres; new urban music; a generally critical and even defiant strain of "underground" music (with the English word often used to describe it); along with hip-hop, rock, and even a Cuban version of *reggeatón* sometimes called *Cubatón*. Born in the United States in the 1970s, hip-hop and rap would never have irrupted in Cuba if not for the historical, cultural, and musical antecedent of *rumba*. Particularly important in melding this "American-made" urban, Afro-centric music and lifestyle with Cuba's own rich African heritage were the *rumba* styles known as *columbia*, *guaguancó*, and *guaracha*, given their similar vocal cadences, tough urban milieu, and defiant cultural and racial pride. The Ministry of Culture has repeatedly attempted to co-opt and control these more raw, organic, and defiant musical forms by creating state agencies for rap and rock. Thus, the relationship between the socialist government and these newer musical genres has been tense and often antagonistic, with self-censorship often the clear if unspoken price artists must pay in exchange for opportunities to perform and record their music and tour abroad.

While *timba* groups frequently incorporate rap modalities in their songs, a number of undiluted hip-hop groups have emerged on the island since 1995. An early pioneering Cuban hip-hop group (now based in France) is *Orishas*. As their name indicates, on their debut album, *A lo cubano*, they created a powerful and authentic synthesis of hip-hop and Afro-Cuban spirituality. They also successfully use the hip-hop technique of musical "sampling," paying homage in their songs to their musical forebears. This is especially evident in the nostalgia-filled song, "537 C-U-B-A," the musical structure of which is clearly based on Compay Segundo's "Chan Chan" (537 is the international telephone access code for the city of Havana). Other prominent

While many Cuban musicians engage in a constant low-level negotiation of censorship and self-censorship with the government in order to gain access to public, state-controlled spaces where they can perform or record their music, the proudly defiant punk rock group Porno para Ricardo (Porn for Richard) eschews such an approach. As a result, its lyrics are unadulterated political mockery and satire, but the group has been barred from performing in public on the island. It has also had to develop relationships abroad to record and distribute its music, a process made much easier with the Internet. The group's members include lead singer Gorki Águila, lead guitarist Ciro Díaz (seated), bassist William Retureta (far left), and drummer Renay Kairus (not pictured). (Orlando Luis Pardo Lazo)

hip-hop groups active in Cuba today include *Obsesión* and *Doble Filo*, who have joined forces to produce the collective *La Fabri-K* (The Cuban Hip-Hop Factory), whose brief U.S. tour was chronicled in the 2005 documentary film of the same name by Cuban-American filmmaker Lisandro Pérez-Rey (Acosta 2007; Fernández 2006; Lacey 2006; Robinson 2004; Seitz 2007).

Two other important Cuban hip-hop groups to emerge in the first decade of the 21st century are *Los Aldeanos* (the villagers) and *Eskuadrón Patriota* (patriot squadron), whose cutting lyrics reflect the deep frustration and alienation of many Cuban youth today. While far less raunchy than the standout Puerto Rican hip-hop duo known as *Calle 13*, these two groups are much like those world-famous "bards of Borinquen" in their verbal dexterity and antiestablishment politics. A final addition to the Cuban hip-hop movement is the innovative and deeply spiritual subgenre of "Free-Hop" associated with the multidisciplinary artist David D'Omni, who is a member of the experimental art collective Omni-Zona Franca, described in chapter 3. A rock/punk group with a more in-your-face and even proudly counterrevolutionary message is the band *Porno para Ricardo* (Porn for Richard). Led by the charismatic front man Gorki Águila, in honored punk tradition *Porno* has endured numerous legal battles as punishment for its vocal and often intentionally vulgar musical transgressions. These groups are not played on Cuba's radio stations nor have they been allowed to perform or record in state controlled venues (which are a state monopoly). However, they have gained both a national and international following by turning to digital technology to successfully record and market their music, often allowing fans free downloads over the Internet.

Finally, like the rest of the Spanish Caribbean, Cuban audiences and dancers have also been unable to resist the rhythmic pulse of the much-criticized *reggeatón*. In just a short time, Cuban *reggeatón* has rapidly gained a strong national fan base with a home-grown style known as *Cubatón* and stars such as Baby Lores, Eminencia Clásica, and Osmani *"la voz"* García. Though much of its boom in popularity has been at the expense of hip-hop—with which it has a mutual love-hate relationship—, Cuban *reggeatón* exists in both a "pure" form and in many more "pop" styles that sample the genre. Given its often simplistic musical arrangements and bawdy sexual references, *Cubatón* has recently come under official criticism and even occasional censorship. For example, García's 2011 mega hit "Chupi Chupi" (sucky sucky)—"a playful and unapologetically vulgar 'ode' to oral sex" (Biddle 2011)—was publicly criticized as "a threat to the soul of the nation" by Cuban Minister of Culture Abel Prieto and removed from contention for that year's people's choice Lucas Awards, which it was sure to have won (Cancio Isla 2011; Biddle 2011). However, given *reggaetón's* popularity among Cuban youth, it is doubtful that it will disappear from the current musical scene any time soon.

THEATER

Origins

Cuban theatrical culture began as a reflection of that found in colonial Spanish theater. Of particular importance were the theatrical celebrations dedicated to the

Christian Festival of Corpus Christi starting in Cuba as early as 1520, the oldest such theatrical performances in the Americas. These celebrations are also referred to as the "Festival of the Floats" given the presence of caravans that carried the farcical performers atop floats, accompanied by music, songs, and dances. Parallel to the Festival of Corpus Christi were the various theatrical manifestations of African culture in Cuba, the most prominent of which was the 19th century Afro-Cuban tradition of slaves being allowed to organize annual costumed parades in public known as *comparsas* during the January 6 celebration of Three Kings Day (also known as Epiphany, which commemorated the arrival of the Magi in Bethlehem).

Organized by Cuba's African-origin societies, known as *cabildos de nación*, these annual processions were quite extraordinary if the European observers who chronicled and graphically depicted them—such as the French artist and lithographer Frédéric Mialhe—are to be believed. As a part of the celebration of the birth of *el niño Jesús* (Baby Jesus), an unwritten Cuban rule would give the island's black slaves a single day of freedom, which they would celebrate with *comparsas* that shocked and amazed foreign observers. Mialhe's lithographs from 1848 show Afro-Cubans dressed in elaborate costumes of European royalty dancing through the streets of colonial Havana led by street bands playing maracas, pots, and drums. Observers from the period breathlessly reported the feigned "pomposity" and "majestic strut" with which thousands of slaves would parade by "dressed as kings from the Middle Ages, with red velvet jackets and magnificent crowns of golden paper." While seemingly out of control, these *comparsas* actually followed a strict and inexorable logic and choreography as they would start at dawn and cease precisely at the stroke of four in the afternoon each January 6, with the revelers required to exit the walled city at that time. Their festivities would continue beyond the city walls for the remainder of the day and into the night, with the oppressive slave order returning again at sun-up (Brunus 2012; Moore 1997; Ortega 2010).

The first Cuban play written for theater was *El príncipe jardinero y fingido Cloridano* (The Garden Prince and the Hypocritical Cloridano) written between 1730 and 1733 in Seville, Spain by Santiago de Pita y Borroto. An updated version of a previous stage opera by the Italian Giacinto A. Cigognini, this play references neither the character, customs, and idioms of the island's inhabitants nor the uniqueness of the island's flora and fauna. Instead, it is a rare example of Cuban rococo featuring a pleasant plot without distracting philosophical pretensions. Still, it is remembered today for its *joie-de-vivre*, gallant versification, and the assimilation of lexical and phonetic elements of the Americas. Also impressive are the sharp and humorous dialogues between its opposing characters in the style of Cervantes' Quijote (the Prince) and Sancho Panza (Lamparón). It is a typical story of the time about gentlemanly courtship and honor-bound heroes in a mythical, Edenic setting called "Tracia," as far from the Cuban reality as its author was from antiquity. However, there are overtones of *Cubanía* in the servants Flora, Narcisa, and Lamparón, which transform the master-servant relationship into a hidden source of mayhem and mockery, undermining social hierarchy.

When reading the play through the perspective of these characters, the comedy achieves a strangeness which is its true mark of naturalistic distinction. In fact, *choteo*, the cutting mockery so characteristic of Cuban humor, was born with this play. The work, then, far from being a typical sweet literary artifice is actually meant to be a joke; a mockery where the humble—the jokester servants—suddenly take on the vitality and strength of the popular and real. As if proving this, when the play was presented in Havana in 1791, it caused a great stir of criticism and outrage based on its scandalous inversion of the social order. However, the audience eventually recognized the work as the island's true offspring. As a result, today the play is considered not only Cuba's first dramatic text but also a foreshadowing of much of what was to come in popular Cuban theater.

Cuban Vernacular Theater

During the 19th century, the famed Francisco Covarrubias (1775–1850) inaugurated the tradition of Cuban vernacular theater with his light and farcical comic sketches such as *Tío Bartolo*, *El cómico de Ceiba Mocha*, and *El gracioso sofocado*. Often referred to as a "better actor than playwright," Covarrubias staged such invented stock characters as the *gallego* (literally meaning Galician but used as a derogatory term for any Spaniard) and the *negrito*, which was a falsely sophisticated black character always played by white actors for white audiences. Covarrubias took wide liberties with the dialect of his characters (thus the genre "vernacular" theater) and had his *gallegos* speak in an exaggerated mainland Spanish while his *negritos* spoke always in "*bozal*," a parody of the supposedly broken Spanish spoken by Afro-Cubans and especially recently arrived slaves.

Despite his often racist caricatures and the fact that the texts of his plays are almost completely lost today, Covarrubias' merit as a playwright is in his conscious undermining of the Spanish roots of the light comedy sketch. He achieved this by staging contemporary Cuban traits and customs, including popular music of the day in his sketches, and above all, by placing a rich, colloquial language in the mouths of his everyday characters. Covarrubias' passion for these day-in-the-life comic sketches and boilerplate Creole characters was deepened by the Spanish playwright Bartolomé J. Crespo y Borbón (1811–1871). Better known by his penname *Creto Gangá* (an allusion to his likeable but obedient and naïve *negro bozal* character), Crespo was associated with *La Compañía de Bufos de La Habana* (The Havana Buffo Theater Company). In the tradition of Covarrubias' vernacular theater, this troupe performed satirical works similar to U.S. vaudeville and Blackface Theater, featuring exaggerated theatrical portraits of Catalans, *guajiros*, *gallegos*, *negritos*, and the Chinese, in contrast to the more serious zarzuelas and foreign operas.

Havana, a City of Theaters

As the Cuban economy began to boom at the end of the 18th century, many new theaters sprang up across the capital city. The Coliseum Theater opened its doors in Havana on January 20, 1775, exhibiting the dramas and comedies of Spanish companies. Thirteen years later, after being renovated, the Coliseum was rechristened with the name "El Principal." It stood proudly as Cuba's premier temple of the dramatic arts for 70 years until its brilliant theatrical life was cut short by the hurricane of 1846. Despite this setback, many new theaters were opened in Havana during the course of the 19th century including some in improvised spaces, originally intended for other purposes. Such was the case of The Circus Theater, which was born in 1800 when an inventive businessman transformed a deactivated equestrian arena into a theater in the round located in the erstwhile *Campo de Marte* near today's *Jardines del Capitolio*.

Other Havana theaters included the *Diorama* (1827), the *Tacón* (1838), the *Payret* (1879), and the *Irijoa* (1884). Theaters were also erected in Cuba's other capital cities such as Matanzas, Santa Clara, Cienfuegos, Sancti Spíritus, Camagüey, and Santiago de Cuba. Named after Cuba's Spanish Captain General, Havana's sumptuous Tacón Theater was inaugurated on February 28, 1838, with a masked ball of some 7,000 attendees. At the time, it was ranked as one of the world's three best theaters. Soon thereafter, the Tacón's stage was conquered by the Italian opera and the Spanish operetta known as the Zarzuela. As large Spanish touring companies had the run of Havana's premier theater, Cuban artists had to seek refuge in the city's more modest and popular theaters.

The arrival of Romanticism ushered in an era of romantic playwrights. The *comedia* was consolidated based on the proliferation of light comic opera and *teatro bufo*, described earlier. Still other theaters were thrown up with many companies developing homegrown talent of the first order. All this transformed the city into an obligatory stop on the world theater circuit. The most distinguished Cuban playwrights of the time include José María Heredia, José Jacinto Milanés, Gertrudis Gómez de Avellaneda, and Joaquín Lorenzo Luaces. Though it lacked the necessary drama for the stage, José Martí's play *Abdala* was also written during these years launching one of the most illustrious literary careers of the era.

Located in a prime cultural, transportation, and tourism site along the Paseo del Prado, across the street from the Parque Central and just adjacent to the Capitolio (Capitol Building), the Gran Teatro de La Habana is home to various theatrical spaces including Sala Federico García Lorca and Sala José Lezama Lima. (Orlando Luis Pardo Lazo)

The Tacón Theater, launched when Cuba was still a Spanish colony, has been frequently restored and renamed. In 1905 on the heels of Cuba's independence, the island's first president Tomás Estrada Palma refused to purchase it as state patrimony. Instead, it became property of the *Centro Gallego*, a powerful immigrant organization, which renamed it the *Teatro Nacional* (National Theater). In 1915 it was renamed once again becoming the *Gran Teatro Nacional*. During the 1950s, it was redesigned as a movie theater, suffering severe damage to its acoustics as a result. In 1959, it was converted back into a theater for live drama and briefly renamed the Estrada Palma. However, in 1961, it was nationalized by the revolution and renamed simply the *Gran Teatro de La Habana*.

Just a single theatrical space would systematically present live works of theater between 1900 and 1935: the renowned *Teatro Alhambra*. Its longevity as a site for the dramatic arts is due to the fact that its typical theatrical fare, the popular *teatro bufo*, was exactly the genre that had been thoroughly consolidated during the 19th century. This showcase included elaborate day-in-the-life plays, everyday stock characters, colloquial language, parody, and the heavy use of music, dance, and humor in the storylines, all of which had been popular elements of Cuban vernacular theater. In the later part of the Republican period (1935–1958), the work of Virgilio Piñera, Cuba's most important playwright of the era, along with that of Carlos Felipe, Rolando Ferrer, and Paco Alfonso, became well known (Carrió 1992). Their plays represented a break from the past as they eschewed the ribald parody of the *bufo* genre for a more thoroughgoing psychological analysis of the conflicts within the alienated and asphyxiating world of the Cuban petty bourgeois family. From a dramaturgical perspective, this was an undeniable step forward as it elevated Cuba's theatrical language above everything that had come before and separated it from the severe limitations of vernacular theater without abandoning the search for *Cubanía* (Leal 1980).

Cuban Theater after 1959

Following the triumph of the Revolution in 1959, Cuban theater has passed through three easily distinguishable phases. The first lasted from 1959 until 1967, the year in which Cuba's First National Theater Conference was held. This period was characterized by an initial artistic effervescence in the early 1960s followed by a slow but inexorable reigning in of playwrights, directors, and actors under an increasingly rigid revolutionary orthodoxy. The second stage lasted from 1968 to 1978 and saw the establishment of the Ministry of Culture following the 1976 Socialist Constitution. The third stage started during in 1980 and continues until today. This most recent stage has seen a weakening of the state's ability to sponsor, and thus control cultural production, especially after the start of the special period in 1990.

Many of the writers who pursued the intimate psychological themes that characterized the theater of the final decades of prerevolutionary Cuba enthusiastically joined the new movement that saw its commitment to the collective as part of its artistic duty. The First National Theater Conference in 1967, however, revealed the deep social and artistic division that existed among playwrights. There were those who considered theater to be lagging behind the dramatic social transformations of the time, while others defended theater's duty to art and artistic subjectivity over and

ANTÓN ARRUFAT'S "SEVEN AGAINST THEBES"

Arrufat's play is based on a work of the same name by Aeschylus. It involves a sibling rivalry between Polynices and Eteocles, nephews of Creon king of Thebes. The brothers inherit the throne and decide to alternate power. However, Eteocles changes his mind and refuses to cede rule to his brother. Polynices goes into exile, returning to take Thebes as one of seven captains. After the brothers slay one another in the ensuing battle, Creon buries Eteocles but punishes Polynices by demanding that his body be left on the battlefield to rot. However, his sister Antigone defies that order.

Arrufat's version of the play was so incendiary in 1968 because of the parallels it drew between ancient Greece's Thebes and revolutionary Cuba. In Arrufat's play Polynices remarks to Creon, "I find repugnant what you represent/ infallible power and a steel hand," a statement that could not but be taken as a veiled criticism of Castro. Arrufat's sibling rivalry could also be interpreted as a stand-in for the fight over Cuba (Thebes) with Eteocles representing Cubans on the island and Polynices standing in for Cuban exiles, with the vengeful king Creon representing Castro (García 2007; Peters 2007).

above political and ideological partisanship. During this time, many plays considered at odds with revolutionary ideals were censored. The most notorious example was the play *Los siete contra Tebas* (Seven against Thebes) by Antón Arrufat. Despite the fact that it won the 1968 award for best play in the annual competition of Cuba's National Union of Writers and Artists, when published, the text included a note of official denunciation. Even worse, Arrufat was not allowed to publish again for almost 15 years during which time he was punished with the task of packing other people's books in the basement of a Marianao library. His controversial play was not produced theatrically in Cuba until almost 40 years later in 2007.

In 1971 the infamous National Conference of Education and Culture was held. It was seen by many as the official start of the darkest and most repressive period for culture under the revolution, sometimes referred to as the *quinquenio gris*, or gray five-year period. In fact, Castro's speech that closed the Conference as well as the final document it produced set down rigid and exclusive parameters regarding what would be considered "politically correct" under the revolution. Essentially, art—including theater—was to be made exclusively by and for revolutionaries. As an inevitable result, many distinguished intellectuals were marginalized for their work, their religious beliefs, or even their sexual orientation.

Perhaps more thoroughly than in other areas of art, the Cuban theater was shaken to its core by the establishment of this policy of "parameterization," which was nothing less than a form of legalized discrimination based on one's supposed deviation from the proper revolutionary attitude in political, religious, or sexual matters. As a consequence, many of Cuba's best actors, directors, and playwrights were left without work. Important theater groups were dissolved or reduced in size, while other more ideologically tractable groups were created in their place.

The only notable progress of that dark period was the creation of the Escambray Theater. There, a small group of experienced theater people set up shop in a remote mountain area in the middle of the country. Thanks to their talent and to the socio-cultural research they carried out in the area, they successfully developed an experiment in the so-called *Teatro de Relaciones*. This is a type of theater that promotes a social change by transforming the elitist logic of traditional theater through a commitment to the area's residents, their lives, and stories (Castañeda Borys 2008). As a result, the Escambray troupe enjoyed great acceptance and public participation among the rural residents of the area.

After the giant step backward that the 1971 Conference and its resolutions meant for Cuban culture, in 1976 the Ministry of Culture was created. This allowed for the creation of university degrees in the fine arts, including acting, theater, and drama from the Advanced Institute of Art (*Instituto Superior de Arte*, ISA). In contrast to the previous period, new works by young, critical-minded Cuban playwrights began to proliferate. However, fear of repression made the practice of self-censorship a common feature in many of their works. Still a number of particularly talented producers emerged at this time including Flora Lauten and her group Buendía and Victor Varela with his troupe that would perform in all kinds of nontheatrical spaces. Varela's bold work has shaken up the stayed theatrical, institutional, and political world of Cuban drama. His provocative independent performance of "The Fourth Wall" (1988), which appropriated the Grotowski method, went totally against the tradition of seeking official approval before mounting a show (Valiño 2002).

The Ballet Theater of Havana followed in Varela's steps by staging works that prioritized movement over text. At this time Cuban youth returned to the exciting experimentation that had defined the theater of the 1960s, turning to the inspiration of Jerzy Grotowski, Antonin Artaud, and the anthropological theater of Eugenio Barba. While this initiative was considered harmful by Cuba's political and cultural officials, audiences became directors' accomplices in their appreciation of what took place on stage. At this point, the theater groups with a stable payroll began to cede space to the more spontaneous and emergent groups of playwrights and actors in order to carry out new and more independent projects. However, the country was on the verge of its biggest economic crisis in history—known as the special period—and as a consequence, the state subsidy for the arts began to rapidly evaporate. This had the positive effect of allowing Cuban theater to operate with much greater independence from state institutions, but the downside of provoking a massive emigration of actors, authors, and directors.

Despite this loss of talent, today's theater panorama features a number of companies that survived the difficult years of the special period coming out stronger than before. Some of these troupes are *El Público*, *Buendía*, *El Ciervo Encantado*, and *Argos Theater*. Other groups have made innovations in Cuban musical theater by adding elements of traditional theater. Likewise, Cuban musicals themselves have begun to incorporate elements of Broadway but still lack a popular national hit with which to claim a space. There have also been efforts to consolidate lyric theater, promote comedies, and develop new versions of universal classics. Plays have also recently been staged that are adapted from other genres such as novels. Now there are also Cuban theater festivals dedicated exclusively to the monologue and to pantomime.

Finally, Camagüey hosts Cuba's National Theater Festival on an annual basis and the International Theater Festival every two years (Espinosa Domínguez 1992; Martínez Tabares 1993).

CONCLUSION

Throughout the revolutionary period, all forms of artistic creation and intellectual production have been marked by the censorship that began with Castro's 1961 speech at the National Library known as "Words to the Intellectuals," where he declared: "Within the Revolution, everything; against the Revolution, nothing" (Castro 1961). As a result, the pluralistic, universal, and extemporary manifestation—that is, art—was subordinated to the monolithic and particularistic ideology of the Revolution. From that moment forward, whoever failed to heed the dominant ideology imposed from high on was doomed to ostracism. This polarizing cultural policy has had a chilling effect on theater, film, poetry, fiction, and many other areas of artistic expression. It also led to the censorship of the documentary *PM* and the closure of the weekly literary supplement *Lunes de Revolución* in 1961 and the denunciation of the award-winning works "Out of the Game" by Heberto Padilla and "Seven against Thebes" by Antón Arrufat in 1968. While the power of the government to reward or punish Cuban artists based on their adherence to this exclusionary formula has weakened over the past 20 years, it continues to be felt today.

BIBLIOGRAPHY

Acosta, Dalia. 2007. "Hip Hop Sidelined but Still Rapping." *Inter Press Service News*, March 19. http://www.ipsnews.net/news.asp?idnews=36988.

Acosta, Leonardo. 2003. *Cubano Be, Cuban Bop: One Hundred Years of Jazz in Cuba*. Translated by Daniel S. Whitesell. Washington, DC: Smithsonian Books.

Alén Rodríguez, Olavo. 1992. *De lo Afrocubano a la Salsa: Géneros musicales de Cuba*. San Juan: Editorial Cubanacán.

Álvarez, Rafael J. 2010. " 'Quiero un cambio en Cuba cuanto antes,' entrevista a Pablo Milanés." *El Mundo*, March 13. http://www.elmundo.es/america/2010/03/13/cuba/1268442243 .html.

Biddle, Ellery. 2011. "Reggaeton Hit 'Chupi Chupi' Denounced by Authorities." *Global Voices Online*, December 7. http://globalvoicesonline.org/2011/12/07/cuba-reg gaeton-hit-chupi-chupi-denounced-by-authorities/.

Brunus, J. 2012. "The Art of Othering in Colonial Cuba." *Great is Truth Blog*, March 26. http://greatistruth.wordpress.com/2012/03/26/the-art-of-othering-in-colonial-cuba/.

Cabrera, Miguel. 1989. *Historia del Ballet Nacional de Cuba*. Havana: Editorial Letras Cubanas.

Cabrera, Miguel. 2000. "Una lección de medio siglo." *Revista Cuba en el Ballet*, Havana, January–April.

Cancio Isla, Wilfredo. 2011. "Cantante del 'Chupi Chupi' acusa de censor al ministro de Cultura." *Café Fuerte*, November 26. http://cafefuerte.com/cuba/noticias-de-cuba/ sociedad/1360-cantante-del-chupi-chupi-acusa-de-censor-al-ministro-de-cultura.

Carpentier, Alejo. 2001. *Music in Cuba*. Minneapolis, MN: University of Minnesota Press.

Carrió, Raquel. 1992. *Revista Tablas* #4, Havana.

Castañeda Borys, Alexis. 2008. "¿Es el teatro de relaciones una imagen viva de la comunidad?" *Iré a Santiago*, June 26.

Castro, Fidel. 1961. "Words to the Intellectuals: Castro's Speech to Intellectuals." FBIS report, June 30. http://lanic.utexas.edu/la/cb/cuba/castro/1961/19610630.

De la Vega, Aurelio. 1990. *Breve historia de la música cubana*. Northridge, CA: California State University at Northridge.

Espinosa Domínguez, Carlos. 1992. *Una dramaturgia escindida*. Madrid: Centro de documentación teatral.

Estefan, Gloria. 1993. "Mi Tierra." Sound recording, Epic.

Fernández, Ariel "Asho." 2006. Information, music, and videos provided the authors in interviews, lectures, and personal communication with Cuba hip-hop promoter and impresario Ariel "Asho" Fernández.

Fernández, Raúl A. 1994. "The Course of U.S. Cuban Music: Margin and Mainstream." *Cuban Studies* 24: 105–122.

Fernández, Raúl A. 2000. "The Musicalia of Twentieth-Century Cuban Popular Musicians." In *Cuba, the Elusive Nation: Interpretations of National Identity*. Damián Fernández and Madeline Cámara-Betancourt, eds., Gainesville, FL: University Press of Florida, 2000.

García, Edmundo. 2007. "Entrevista a Antón Arrufat." *La noche se mueve*, October 26. http://delpalenqueypara.blogspot.com/2007/11/entrevista-antn-arrufat-marat.html.

García, Kenia. 2003. "Enseñanza del ballet, apuntes para una historia." Doctoral thesis, Advanced Institute of Art, Havana, October.

Guillermoprieto, Alma. 2004. *Dancing with Cuba: A Memoir of the Revolution*. Translated by Esther Allen. New York: Pantheon Books.

Lacey, Marc. 2006. "Cuba's Rap Vanguard Reaches Beyond the Party Line," *New York Times*, December 15.

Leal, Rine. 1980. *Breve historia del teatro cubano*. Havana: Editorial Letras Cubanas.

López, Rigoberto, and Leonardo Padura. 1997. *Yo soy del son a la salsa*. RMM Filmworks.

Manuel, Peter, with Kenneth Bilby and Michael Alrgey. 2006. *Caribbean Currents: Caribbean Music from Rumba to Reggae* (revised and expanded edition). Philadelphia, PA: Temple University Press.

Martínez Tabares, Vivian. 1993. "Mirar atrás desde el siglo XXI." http://bibliotecavirtual.clacso.org.ar/libros/cuba.

Moore, Robin D. 2006. *Music and Revolution: Cultural Change in Socialist Cuba*. Berkeley, CA: University of California Press.

Moore, Robin D. 1997. *Nationalizing Blackness: Afrocubanismo and Artistic Revolution in Havana, 1920–1940*. Pittsburgh, PA: University of Pittsburgh Press.

Orovio, Helio. 2004 *Cuban Music from A to Z*. Durham: Duke University Press.

Ortega, Josefina. 2010. "Día de Reyes." *Cabaiguán.net*, January 6. http://www.cabaiguan.net/profiles/blogs/una-anecdota-de-el-dia-de.

Padura Fuentes, Leonardo. 2003. *Faces of Salsa: A Spoken History of the Music*. Translated by Stephen J. Clark. Washington, DC: Smithsonian Books.

Padura Fuentes, Leonardo. 2006. *Entre dos siglos*. Havana: Inter Press Service.

Pajares, Fidel. 1993. *Ramiro Guerra y la danza en Cuba*. Quito: Editorial casa de la Cultura.

Pérez, Louis A. 1999. *On Becoming Cuban: Identity, Nationality, and Culture*. Chapel Hill, NC: University of North Carolina Press.

Perna, Vincenzo. 2005. *Timba: The Sound of the Cuban Crisis*. Hampshire, England: Ashgate.

Peters Philip. 2007. "Seven Against Thebes." *The Cuban Triangle*, November 10. http://cuban triangle.blogspot.com/2007/11/seven-against-thebes.html

Roberts, John Storm. 1999. *The Latin Tinge: The Impact of Latin American Music on the United States* (second edition). New York: Oxford University Press.

Robinson, Eugene. 2004. *Last Dance in Havana: The Final Days of Fidel and the Start of the New Cuban Revolution*. New York: Free Press.

Roy, Maya. 2002. *Cuban Music: From Son and Rumba to the Buena Vista Social Club and Timba Cubana*. Princeton, NJ: Markus Wiener Publishers; London: Latin American Bureau.

Seitz, Matt Zoller. 2007. "Courage Through Rhymes: 'East of Havana'." *New York Times*, February 1.

Sublette, Ned. 2004. *Cuba and Its Music: From the First Drum to the Mambo*. Chicago: Chicago Review Press.

Sweeney, Philip. 2001. *The Rough Guide to Cuban Music*. London: Rough Guides.

Valiño, Omar. 2002. "Para una geografía ideológica del teatro cubano de los 80–90." *Anales de Literatura Hispanoamericana* #31, Mexico.

Cinema and Photography

Henry Constantín and Miriam Celaya

The invention of photography in 1839 suggested the possibility that the camera could capture such a rapid succession of pictures that images could reproduce true movement. This idea became a reality when the British photographer Eadweard Muybridge (1830–1904) first recorded a horse race as a photographic sequence by using a battery of 24 cameras, an invention that he patented in 1881. Shortly thereafter, Frenchman Etienne-Jules Marey invented a kind of photographic tube to capture birds in flight. Thomas Edison then devised a way to move rolls of film through a camera, and in 1889 the Frenchman Marey and the Englishman W. Freise-Greene invented the movie camera. However, December 28, 1895, is the date that marks the true beginning of film, when the brothers Louis and Auguste Lumière presented the cinematograph in France.

As with other technical advances, cinema arrived in Cuba almost immediately after being patented. In fact, the country's first public film exhibition took place in Havana in January 1897. The following month Gabriel Veyre, who represented the Lumière house of Paris in colonial Havana, filmed Cuba's first silent short. For our purposes, the subsequent history of Cuban cinema can be divided be into two broad periods: one following its inception at the close of the 19th century up until 1959–1960, and another extending from that date until the present. Likewise, the first period can be clearly divided between the era of silent film followed in the 1930s by the first sound films (Del Río and Díaz 2010; López 2005).

SILENT FILM

At the end of 1898, while the Spanish flag was still flying over Havana, the first film by a Cuban made its appearance. *El brujo desaparecido* (The Missing Witchdoctor) was its title and it was a short advertisement for a brewery made by José Casasús. In 1907, the fanatical and driven filmmaker Enrique Díaz Quesada filmed *Un duelo a orillas del Almendares* (a duel on the banks of the Almendares river), which was the first feature length Cuban film. By the time of his death from pneumonia on May 13, 1923, he had completed 16 other features, which comprised more than 40 percent of all films shot in Cuba during the silent period.

The break from the conservative influence of Spain and the deepening economic links with the United States facilitated the explosion of cinema both as a business enterprise and as a mass media phenomenon during the early years of the Republic. Many live drama theaters were rapidly transformed into movie houses, while new cinemas constantly opened their doors, with Havana's *Novedades* (Novelties) being the first. These state-of-the-art theaters were quick to deploy a veritable parade of new technologies and exhibition styles all brought in—like most of the films themselves—from France. At the same time, Cubans experimented with local methods such as the use of loudspeakers and *ruideros* (people hired to do live voice-overs and soundscapes for the films being displayed) (Del Río and Díaz 2010; López 2005).

SOUND FILM

In 1926, Warner Brothers introduced the sound system known as *Vitaphone*, which consisted of recording musical soundtracks and spoken texts on large discs that were synchronized with the action on the screen. Then in 1927 the company released Alan Crosland's *The Jazz Singer*, the world's first "talkie," starring the Russian-born showman Al Jolson, who enjoyed an immediate and unexpected success with audiences around the world. This signaled the end of the silent film era and caused the owners of movie theaters to race to update their equipment so that they could exhibit sound films. This technical leap marked a turning point in Cuban cinema with the appearance of the first sound films on the island in the early 1930s. One of the first was the 1932 *Maracas y bongó* (Maracas and Bongos) by Max Tosquella.

Over the next 25 years Cuba produced scores of films, most of which have all but disappeared from public memory. Some standouts include the Manolo Alonso films *Siete muertes a plazo fijo* (Seven Deaths Standing Still, 1950) and *Casta de roble* (Oak Caste, 1954), the latter is considered by both the public and critics alike as the best Cuban film of its era. Although director/producer Alonso was a controversial figure,

---

CUBAN FILMS IN EXILE

There is a long list of Cuban films made in exile that have never been shown publicly on the island. Among them are the documentaries *Conducta impropia* (Improper Conduct), *Nadie escuchaba* (Nobody Listened), and *8-A* all by Néstor Almendros. The first of these was codirected by Orlando Jiménez Leal, whose award-winning 1979 feature film *El Súper* (The Superintendent) has still not been exhibited in Cuba almost 35 years after its release. Other films that suffered a similar fate include *La Cuba de ayer* (Yesterday's Cuba) and *El milagro del éxodo* (The Miracle of the Exodus) by Manuel Alonso; *Campo minado* (Minefield) and *Espera* (Power Game) by Fausto Canel; and Andy García's nostalgic 2005 film *The Lost City*.

---

he was also a good filmmaker and arduous visual journalist. Less significant was *El romance del palmar* (Palm Grove Romance, 1938) by Ramón Peón, the film which launched the career of the renowned vocalist Rita Montaner. *La serpiente roja* (The Red Serpent, 1937) by Ernest Caparros and the silent film *La virgen de la Caridad* (The Virgin of Charity) also by Peón are virtually unknown today (Del Río and Díaz 2010; López 2005).

Cuban cinephiles are still waiting to see Néstor Almendros' short 1960 film *1958–1959*, which was considered "the best experimental film made by a Cuban" by the great writer and film critic Guillermo Cabrera Infante. Likewise, a pair of controversial films about José Martí, *La niña de Guatemala* (The Girl of Guatemala) and *La rosa blanca* (The White Rose), were never distributed after their debuts. Still, Cubans took to film with gusto, quickly transforming cinema into a central element of Cuba's cultural milieu. The growth was so rapid that by 1958 there were already 30 film circuits that linked together 170 theaters with a total capacity of 167,081 seats in some 519 movie halls, of which 340 had cinemascope projection technology.

FILMS AFTER 1959

The ICAIC *Takeover*

During the 1960s Cuban cinema took on a nearly universal sympathy with the revolution. At times, the films produced reflected a subtle indifference toward the revolutionary project—as was the case with the famous 1968 Tomás Gutiérrez Alea film *Memorias del subdesarrollo* (Memories of Underdevelopment)—but they never became overly critical nor could directors operate independently of the government. Tomás Gutiérrez Alea, Julio García Espinosa, and Santiago Álvarez are the three directors most responsible during this decade for pioneering the founding works of the state-run film institute, the Cuban Institute of Cinematographic Art and Industry (*Instituto Cubano del Arte e Industria Cinematográficos*), hereafter ICAIC or the Cuban Film Institute. Linked together from the prerevolutionary period through leftist political organizations, in the late 1950s García Espinosa and Gutiérrez Alea together produced the short film *El mégano* (The Charcoal Worker), which is a neorealist docudrama denouncing the misery of the Ciénaga de Zapata's charcoal workers and their families during the 1950s. In fact, after the film was debuted at the University of Havana, it was seized by Batista's police, who also took Espinosa in for questioning.

Their past political militancy gave these directors the standing to become the most emblematic filmmakers of the nascent political process that began in 1959. In fact, together with Álvarez, the three are often considered the revolution's "official" filmmakers, though García and Alea would always chafe at ideological control, managing to make popular films that also pushed the limits of what was acceptable throughout their long careers. At the end of 1960, this pair of still youthful directors separately produced two important films. Alea's *Historias de laRevolución* (Stories of the Revolution) was an epic, timely docudrama that recreated a series of key scenes from the 1950s armed struggle. Its heroic content gave it an immediate wide circulation on the island's many cinemas. García's *Cuba baila* (Cuba Dances), however, was only given a single screening in December 1960, before it had its formal premiere in April 1961. Unfortunately for the director, the launch of his excellent film coincided with the heady events of the Bay of Pigs invasion that same month making its focus on the island's popular dance traditions seem frivolous and out-of-touch. Nevertheless, both films are visibly influenced by the then fashionable Italian neorealist style. In fact, the cinematographer of Alea's *Historias* was the same Italian—Otello Martelli—who would later work on the classic *La dolce vita*.

In 1961, the intentional liquidation of the vast and diverse system of American and Cuban film distribution companies began. This process would last until 1965. Already in 1959, the Ministry of Recovery of Misappropriated Assets began taking steps in this regard under the pretext that it was recovering goods and properties acquired unscrupulously. The ICAIC took over the important role as sole film distributor, a legal monopoly established through Law 169, which named the Film Institute as responsible for producing and promoting Cuban domestic films in an organized and systematic fashion starting on March 25, 1959. Over the next two decades under the leadership of Castro's college friend, Alfredo Guevara, Cuba developed one of Latin America's most prolific and vital film industries, producing, distributing, and exhibiting films of aesthetic quality and intellectual content, if often simultaneously used as tools of propaganda. Under Guevara, the ICAIC successfully made 112 feature-length films, an astounding 900 documentaries, and more than 1,300 newsreels by 1983 (Luis 2001).

One reason that the ICAIC was often able to preserve both its relative autonomy and its aesthetic quality is that it has functioned over the years as a "quasi-autonomous nongovernmental organization." That is, unlike the press, radio, and television, which the state has made into deadening governmental mouthpieces, filmmaking in Cuba "came to occupy a unique cultural space as a major site of public discourse that at the same time enjoyed a de facto autonomy because of a privileged relation to the source of power and authority" (Chanan 2004: 17). The impeccable revolutionary credentials of longtime ICAIC director Alfredo Guevara and leading director Tomás Gutiérrez Alea, combined with their personal relationships with Fidel Castro, afforded them the space in which to develop a national cinema that answered to artistic and intellectual criteria without being forced to always and only spout a simplistic revolutionary line.

Despite the rigid monopoly control over film production and distribution exercised by the ICAIC after 1959, its creation as the state agency responsible for promoting national cinema is not as unprecedented as it may seem. In fact, in January 1955, under the notorious government of Fulgencio Batista, Law-Decree 2135 called into existence the *Instituto Nacional para el Fomento de la Industria Cinematográfica Cubana* (INFICC, or the National Institute for the Promotion of the Cuban Film Industry). Led by Manuel Alonso, an ambitious businessman and film promoter who had Batista's ear (and influence over his purse strings), the INFICC incurred enormous debts and seems to have misused its generous state subsidy. Still, it managed to make more films than what had been produced previously. Moreover, the INFICC deserves credit for not attempting to place the entire film industry under state control as would its successor agency, the ICAIC (Agramonte García 2006).

For its part, the INFICC inherited the assets of the *Comisión Ejecutiva para la Industria Cinematográfica* (the Executive Committee for the Film Industry, CEPLIC), which was also created by the Batista government in 1952. The CEPLIC itself was born out of a previous state boondoggle known as the *Patronato para el Fomento de la Industria Cinematográfica* (the Trust for the Development of the Film Industry, PFIC), which had emerged together with other legendary instances of corruption and graft out of the previous *Auténtico* administrations of Ramón Grau San Martín (1944–1948) and Carlos Prío Socarrás (1948–1952). It is in these tens of thousands of pesos originally allocated to film production by the Grau government that we find the seed of state sponsorship of the Cuban film industry. However, what has been unique to the revolutionary government is the absolute monopoly it rapidly achieved over all aspects of the film industry, as well as the placing of that monopoly at the service of the reigning political ideology (Lawson 1986).

PM *and Castro's "Words to the Intellectuals"*

The ICAIC was founded in March 1959 as part of the twin process of the nationalization of private property and the dissolution of civil society. Two years later, on May 12, 1961, Cuba's newly created Commission for the Study and Classification of Film banned a short, apparently innocuous film with the cryptic title *PM*. As its simple title hints, what was arguably the most problematic film in the history of Cuban cinema up to that point was little more than a noisy and seemingly naive short film documenting Havana nightlife in a cinéma vérité style, without dialogue or commentary. However, the film proved to be so problematic perhaps because the committed and self-sacrificing masses busy building socialism—so essential to official propaganda—were nowhere to be found. Instead, the film featured scores of joyful Cubans, bathed in the lights of bars and drunk on fun, music, and alcohol, far from the class struggle with no thought of the impending imperialist threat (the failed Bay of Pigs invasion had taken place just a month before in April 1961).

After an appeal by the film's directors, Orlando Jiménez Leal and Sabá Cabrera Infante, the Commission upheld the ban on the film on May 31, prohibiting its exhibition in any of the country's theaters, which were now under state control. Though *PM* had been filmed without ICAIC sponsorship, its censorship sparked an unusual commotion among the many Cuban artists and intellectuals who still sympathized with the revolution. This concern among the Cuban *avant-garde* was soon answered that same summer with a notorious and fatal speech by Fidel Castro, known ever after as "Words to the Intellectuals." Laying down a strict if quite cryptic line indicating the creative limits that would be placed on art and thought in Cuba, Castro intoned: "Within the Revolution, everything; against the Revolution, nothing."

Because it was a film made by Cubans who had participated in the fight against Batista and who had close relations with those in charge of government media at the time, the early banning of *PM* was the most notorious incident of censorship during these years. However, even before the *PM* incident, on November 16, 1960, the ICAIC's Board of Directors issued Resolution No. 119 prohibiting the public or private screening of 87 foreign films judged to be of "inferior technical and artistic quality, whose reactionary content and tendencies distort history and reality" (Cabrera Infante 2005).

Revolutionary Cinema

Historias de la Revolución, mentioned earlier, holds the distinction of being the first in a long line of films that make up what is considered Cuba's "official cinematography." Such a term has no precedent prior to 1960, since "official" films should always put a positive, even heroic spin on the ideas and achievements of the revolution. Examples of such films include *El joven rebelde* (The Young Rebel) (Julio García Espinosa, 1961), *Las doce sillas* (The Twelve Chairs) and *Los sobrevivientes* (The Survivors) (Tomás Gutiérrez Alea, 1962 and 1978, respectively), *Manuela*, *Lucía*, and *Cantata de Chile* (Humberto Solás, 1966, 1968, and 1975), *El hombre de Maisinicú*

TOMÁS GUTIÉRREZ ALEA

Better known as "Titón," Tomás Gutiérrez Alea (1928–1996) was the most acclaimed filmmaker of the revolutionary period. During his 50-year career, he made movies that were both entertaining and intellectually stimulating; "committed" to the revolution and critical of its errors; and that catered to Cuban idiosyncrasies, while also appealing to international audiences. In the late 1940s, Gutiérrez Alea became involved in the *Cine Club de la Habana*, later renamed *Cinemateca de Cuba*. After studying at Rome's *Centro Sperimentale de Cinematografía*, Titón made the short, neorealist film *El mégano* (The Charcoal Worker, 1954–1955) with Julio García Espinosa. After the Revolution, they collaborated again on the film *Esta tierra nuestra* (This Land of Ours, 1959). Starting in the 1960s, Gutiérrez Alea focused on feature films, producing a succession of movies of the highest artistic quality. These included the slapstick comedy, *La muerte de un burócrata* (Death of a Bureaucrat, 1966), the masterful meditation on indecision and alienation, *Memorias de subdesarrollo* (Memories of Underdevelopment, 1968), a slavery allegory, *La última cena* (The Last Supper, 1974), an examination of the clash between revolutionary orthodoxy and homosexuality, *Fresa y chocolate* (Strawberry and Chocolate, 1993), and the biting special period satire, *Guantanamera* (1995).

(The Man from Maisinicú) (Manuel Pérez Paredes, 1973), *De cierta manera* (In a Certain Way) (Sara Gómez, 1974), *Mella* (Enrique Pineda Barnet, 1975), *El brigadista* (The Brigadier) and *Guardafronteras* (The Border Guard) (Octavio Cortázar, 1977 and 1980), *Polvo rojo* (Red Dust) (Jesús Díaz, 1981), and at the close of this effusive period, the excellent and violent *Clandestinos* (The Underground) (Fernando Pérez, 1987) and *Caravana* (Caravan) (Rogelio París y Julio César Rodríguez, 1990).

While long out of vogue, the fervent and faithful cinematography of this period is reflected in a number of contemporary Cuban films, which—unlike the fine examples of *Clandestinos* and *Caravana*—tend toward apology and hero worship such as *Kangamba, Ciudad en rojo* (Red City), and *Sumbe*. The greatest merit of such "revolutionary" cinema was the opportunity it provided to a number of actors to further develop their skills, some of whom had already achieved stardom including Adela Legrá, Adolfo Llauradó, Raquel Revuelta, Eslinda Núñez, Sergio Corrieri, Reinaldo Miravalles, Luis Alberto Ramírez, Raúl Pomares, Mario Balmaseda, and Salvador Wood, among others. Some of the titles from that time have become part of the cultural memory of the nation, in part because they have circulated on television in endless reruns in a country where there was virtually no alternative for decades to the two state channels and the state-owned movie theaters.

This is the case of "The Brigadier," "The Border Guard," "Lucía," "Memories of Underdevelopment," and the documentary *Coffea Arábiga* (Nicolás Guillén Landrián, 1968). Gutiérrez Alea's 1968 masterwork, "Memories of Underdevelopment," was particularly important as it won its director wide popularity and critical acclaim for his complex portrait of an aloof intellectual who chooses to remain in Cuba after his bourgeois wife and family leave for the United States. Some of these films are also memorable for their aesthetic value or the acting skills of their casts, as is the case with Juan Padrón's animated feature series *Elpidio Valdés* (began in 1979) and Fernando Pérez's "The Underground." In 1960, Santiago Álvarez—the daring young pioneer of the Cuban propaganda newsreel—began to make a highly original and effective series of short documentary pastiches through his *Noticiero ICAIC Latinoamericano* (ICAIC Latin American Newsreels). There was nothing measured, academic, or neutral about these hard-hitting propaganda films. However, they possessed the undeniable originality and vitality of a master craftsman putting all his artistic skill at the service of a cause, the Cuban revolution. Thus, in-your-face films like *Now!* (1965), *Hanoi, martes 13* (1967), and *LBJ* (1968)—which were a frontal assault on the imperialism, militarism, and racism of the United States—had the ability to provoke indignant sympathy for a cause even in the most impassive spectator.

Cinema of the Marginal and Absurd

One of the problems of post-1959 Cuban cinema is that films made outside the ICAIC have been systematically excluded from both the theaters and television. Moreover, looking in the state-controlled mass media (newspapers, magazines, radio, television, etc.) for announcements or reviews of such films would be a fool's errand. And each time Cuba's cinema commissars have suspected filmmakers of straying too far from the party line their work has been banned from production and dissemination. This was the fate of Ramón Peón, Ernesto Caparrós, Fausto Canel, Orlando Jiménez

Leal, Manolo Alonso, Néstor Almendros, Sabá Cabrera Infante, Nicolás Guillén Landrián, Sergio Giral, Jesús Díaz, and Orlando Rojas, among others. Some of them have gone into exile as a result, while others can only find a place for their work in festivals or in the few limited spaces among the island's intellectual elite.

Starting almost imperceptibly in the mid-1980s, the ICAIC began to favor the production of comedies over the epic political dramas it had promoted up to that point. And though often light in content, these situational comedies were invariably seasoned with a subtle but quite dangerous dose of social criticism. Perhaps this was a reaction to the winds of change that began to blow in from the Soviet Union. It could have also been a way for filmmakers to capitalize on the relaxation of the repressive and dogmatic cultural policies of the 1970s, known as the *quinquenio gris* (or the gray period). There was also the jarring crisis of the Mariel boatlift in 1980. Finally, in 1982, the ICAIC was dealt a serious financial blow when its first-ever big budget film *Cecilia* (directed by Humberto Solás)—a free film adaptation of a founding work of Cuban literature—turned out to be a critical, popular, and financial flop. Critics were aghast at Solás' radical alterations to the plot of such a canonical work of Cuban culture and that, together with the huge financial loss that the film represented, led to the demotion of longtime ICAIC director Alfredo Guevara. After 23 years at the Film Institute's helm, Guevara was unceremoniously replaced by filmmaker Julio García Espinosa.

Following this debacle, the irony, absurdity, and mockery long absent from revolutionary Cuban film surfaced once again, as did plots that included the previously taboo topics of class, racial, and gender conflict. These were the ICAIC's most profitable years but—judging from what the critics had to say at the time—resulted in a crop of films with little artistic merit. Big hits during these years included *Se permuta* (House Swap) and *Plaff o demasiado miedo a la vida* (Plaff, or Too Afraid of Life) (Juan Carlos Tabío, 1983 and 1988, respectively), *Los pájaros tirándole a la escopeta* (The Birds Shooting at the Gun) (Rolando Díaz, 1984), *Una novia para David* (A Girlfriend for David) (Gerardo Chijona, 1985), the animated film *Vampiros en La Habana* (Vampires in Havana) (Juan Padrón, 1985), and *La bella del Alhambra* (The Beauty of the Alhambra) (Enrique Pineda Barnet, 1989) (Douglas 1996: 292–293). Obviously, the ICAIC was in tune with its new director, García Espinosa, who had directed *Aventuras de Juan Quin Quin* (The Adventures of Juan Quin Quin), which was a comedy of errors from 1967 that up until 1990 was the ICAIC's biggest box office success with 3.2 million tickets sold.

Alice in Wonderland

Gradually, as the pace of liberalization quickened in Eastern Europe, social criticism in Cuban movies of the 1980s became more heated until the innovative *Papeles secundarios* (Supporting Roles) (Orlando Rojas, 1989) arrived. This was followed shortly thereafter by a film as important as it was terrible, *Alicia en el pueblo de Maravillas* (Alice in Wonderland). A kind of cultural counterpart to the 1989 political-military imbroglio that led to the shocking trial and execution of the decorated Cuban General Arnaldo Ochoa, this 1990 film follows a young girl named Alice (played by actress Thais Valdés) to the obscure, allegorical land of "Maravillas"

(Wonder) where everything—including the name of the town itself—is exactly the opposite as advertised. Arriving in "Wonder-land" with the mission to teach theater to the town's residents, Alice only finds economic and spiritual misery, pessimism, lies, fear, and hopelessness, all of which seems to emanate like a true disease from the town's "Director" (played by Reinaldo Miravalles). Alice confronts the Director but eventually flees from the town in terror.

Directed by Daniel Díaz Torres and cowritten with Eduardo del Llano, the film set up an obvious parallel between the Director and Fidel Castro just after the culmination of the Ochoa affair and as a new major economic crisis cast its ominous shadow over the country. In such a charged atmosphere, this veiled but devastating criticism coming from the normally quite obedient ICAIC nearly resulted in its destruction. The official media—true to its pack mentality—began to mercilessly attack the film. Although it is far from being a great film by artistic standards, *Alicia* represents the very best of contemporary Cuban cinema in terms of its thematic audacity. It is also one of the most unvarnished and least metaphorical of the critical films made under the revolution, which is quite an achievement. In the end, the ICAIC was saved by the removal of García Espinosa and the reappointment of a tried-and-true ally of the country's commander-in-chief, Alfredo Guevara. He may not have been able to sell many tickets but he could be trusted to reign in potentially subversive films before they saw the light of day.

Alicia was screened only in a handful of theaters, always under tight surveillance, and still 22 years later has never been broadcast on state television. The fate of *Alicia* did not mean the end of all critical content in Cuban films. But it was the only and final time that a film so clearly pointed a mocking, accusatory finger at those responsible for the nation's disaster. It was also a rare public exposure of the manipulative and cynical methods the "Directors" use to preserve their power. After *Alicia*, the allegories and metaphors used in Cuban films to examine the country's social and political reality would be much more subtle. As for Alicia herself, while it is true that she confronted the Director and tried to change things, she ultimately fled, like so many other characters in Cuban cinematic history, including Diego the rebellious homosexual of the 1993 Gutiérrez Alea and Tabío film *Fresa y chocolate* (Strawberry and Chocolate), mentioned above.

The characters of Cuban cinema after 1990 are depressing. The revolutionary heroes able to stand up against the most powerful and ruthless enemies in order to change the world for the better gave way to characters full of doubt and confusion of every kind who barely survive as ethical subjects at all. The vast majority are alienated, hopeless, silent, and want to flee. When they do choose to stay, it is because of the desire or attraction they feel for another person (*Personal belongings*, by Alejandro Brugués, or *Fábula* [Fable], by Léster Hamlet), or because they want to antagonize those who told them to leave. In the best of cases, the characters are indifferent to their sociopolitical surroundings, even the normally idealistic young people. A notable exception, which will hopefully be the precedent for a new kind of antihero, is the recalcitrant Juan in the recent horror film "Juan of the Dead" (*Juan de los Muertos*, Alejandro Brugués, 2011) who opts to remain in an island flooded with ravenous zombies, instead of fleeing across the sea. Of course, this film is no horror flick at all but a bitingly satirical comedy that casts zombies as a powerful metaphor for Cuba's "undead" national civic life.

CUBAN CINEMA AS A CULTURAL EVENT

Despite the centralism and control that has characterized film production and exhibition under the revolution, filmmaking has managed to have a unique and unprecedented cultural impact. In 1979, the First International Festival of New Latin American Cinema took place, and has since become an annual cultural event for two weeks each December. The festival brings together scores of filmmakers and actors from around the world. It also has the added benefit of exposing Cuba's cinephile public to first-rate filmmaking from across the hemisphere and around the world at affordable prices, with each ticket costing only 2 pesos (the equivalent of just eight cents) (Díaz 2012). The artistic rigor and diversity of the hundreds of films exhibited over the past 34 years is undeniable. Moreover, in recent years a number of provocative Cuba-themed films made by foreign directors have been shown to rave reviews both at this Festival in Havana and later in Miami. Two examples are the feature *Una Noche* (One Night, 2012), a gritty tale of a young love triangle overlapping with a desperate attempt to emigrate by raft written and directed by newcomer Lucy Mulloy, and the 2011 documentary *Unfinished Spaces*, a powerful, evocative, and politically daring film directed by Alysa Nahmias and Benjamin Murray about Havana's Schools of Art, architectural marvels born out of the revolutionary fervor of the early 1960s, which were then abandoned for their supposed decadence and waste.

The success of the Havana Film Festival inspired the creation in 2000 of the similarly named Havana Film Festival in New York, a follow-up showing of many of the December films in a series of coordinated events each spring in The Big Apple. Carole Rosenberg and the American Friends of the Ludwig Foundation, one of Cuba's leading arts institutions, has run this event for the past 14 years. A recent alternative to the Havana Festival is the International Festival of Poor Cinema (*Festival Internacional del Cine Pobre*, FICP), which was founded by the late Cuban director

34TH ANNUAL INTERNATIONAL FESTIVAL OF NEW LATIN AMERICAN CINEMA

With 566 movies from 46 countries, the 34th Annual Havana Film Festival cast its enchanting spell over the city for the first two weeks of December 2012. The festival included talks by actors and directors, as well as concerts and tributes, all leading up to the awarding of the Grand Coral Prize to one of the 21 feature-length films in competition. Considered the island's most important cultural event, the festival featured 20 shorts, 21 first works, 23 documentaries, 27 animated films, 29 unproduced screen plays, and 21 movie posters. Though its official focus is on "New Latin American Cinema," in 2012 four non-Latin filmmakers were honored: the Japanese Kenji Misumi (1921–1975), the Frenchman Chris Marker (1921–2012), the Italian Michel Angelo Antonioni (1912–2007), and the Czech master animator Jan Svankmajer (1934–). One big surprise was "From Hollywood to Havana," a special line-up of American films presented by none other than U.S. Academy of Motion Picture Arts and Sciences president, Hawk Koch.

Humberto Solás (1941–2008) in the provincial town of Gibara in October 2003. Intended to highlight artistically rigorous films made for under $300,000, it quickly became another mandatory stop on the annual cycle of Cuban film festivals. After Solás' death in 2008, the festival was renamed the Humberto Solás International Festival of Poor Cinema, in honor of its founder.

Solás was a movie director, producer, and screenwriter whose film *Lucía* (1968) is considered one of the 10 most important films in Latin American history. Of course, he was the same filmmaker who made the previously described big-budget flop *Cecilia*. Solás achieved international recognition with *Un hombre de éxito* (A Successful Man, 1986), the first Cuban film to be nominated for the Academy Award for Best Foreign Language Film. He was also one of the founders of the Havana Film Festival and won Cuba's National Film Award in 2005. Using the FICP as a base, Solás called for the democratization and freedom of cinema enabling the voices and visions of young filmmakers and many marginalized communities to become part of the world's audiovisual heritage. Apart from its low-budget aesthetic, the FICP is based on the search for new, authentic narratives, a commitment to human welfare, and the freedom of expression. The peculiarity of placing a limit on the budgets of the films featured at the festival gives it a greater level of independence from the control and censorship of the ICAIC than is the case for other festivals. However, this autonomy has eroded since Solás' death in 2008, after which the festival has come under increasing pressure to conform, with especially harsh censorship in 2012.

Another recent addition to the annual Cuban film festival circuit is the Young Filmmakers Exhibition (*Muestra de Jóvenes Realizadores*) that takes place each spring in Havana under the of the auspices of the ICAIC. This innovative festival was led since its inception by noted Cuban filmmaker Fernando Pérez, director of classic films such as *Clandestinos* and *Suite Habana*. However, Pérez resigned his post in April 2012 due to repeated instances of ICAIC censorship over the films chosen for the festival. He also signed a petition defending the right of free expression (Pardo Lazo 2012). Pérez's resignation shocked many in Cuban film circles and led to a heated exchange of e-mails (mostly among young filmmakers themselves) showing their frustration and sadness at his absence as head of the Festival, given that many saw him both as a mentor and as the island's foremost living filmmaker. These e-mails can be found on what is perhaps the best Cuban film blog written on the island, *Cine cubano, la pupila insomne* (Cuban Cinema: The Unsleeping Eye), written by the critic Juan Antonio García Borrero.

Pérez resigned his position to avoid being complicit in what he saw as the unjust elimination from the festival of the documentary *Despertar* (Awakening), a film by Fernando Figueredo and Anthony Bubaire that chronicles the life and times of dreadlocked Cuban rapper Raudel Collazo. In the film, Collazo, whose stage name is *Escuadrón Patriota* (Patriot Squadron), performs songs that amount to "a generational howl against the institutionalized intolerance of the Cuban Revolution" (Pardo Lazo 2012). Previously, in the 2010 festival the similar film *Revolution* by Maykell Pedrero, which focused on the popular hip-hop duo *Los Aldeanos,* suffered a similar fate.

A worthy successor of Tomás Gutiérrez Alea, Fernando Pérez is the leading Cuban filmmaker of the past two decades and winner of Cuba's 2007 National Film Award. Aside from Gutiérrez Alea, Pérez's influences include the Cuban filmmakers Santiago Álvarez, Manuel Octavio Gómez, Manuel Herrera, Sergio Giral, and José Massip. International auteurs whose work can be found referenced in Pérez's films

---

RAUDEL COLLAZO, THE FILM *DESPERTAR*, AND THE SONG "DECADENCIA"

Raudel Collazo is best known for exposing the revolution's "decadence" in a powerful and unapologetic song of the same name. With lyrics like "Decadence, all of us, like robots, accepting the brain washing/Decadence, they've stripped us of everything, except our resistance," the song delivers a devastating critique of Cuban social and political reality. The video clip of the song has been viewed more than 180,000 times on YouTube (Collazo 2009). The filmmakers Fernando Figueredo and Anthony Bubaire made Collazo the subject of the banned documentary *Despertar*. However, the film's censorship only increased interest in it with Cubans sharing it by flash drive and viewing it on more computer screens than perhaps would ever have seen it on the silver screen (Nellis 2012; Pardo Lazo 2012). It did eventually open in a venue provided by the independent projects *Cine a toda Costa* (Film at Any Cost) and *Estado de SATS* (State of SATS). In fact, according to the independent Cuban blogger and photographer Orlando Luis Pardo Lazo, "Artists no longer depend on the whims of a caste of officials whose attitudes range from paternalism to despotism. There are [now] alternative mini-productions and an incipient underground market for distribution" (Nellis 2012; Pardo Lazo 2012; Rodríguez Y. 2011; Sánchez 2012b).

---

include Andrzej Wajda, Bernardo Bertolucci, and Alfred Hitchcock. Pérez began his career in the 1970s as a documentary filmmaker with *Crónica de una victoria* (Chronicle of a Victory, 1975)—codirected with the late Jesús Díaz—and *Omara* (1983)—a short biopic of Cuban bolero singer Omara Portuondo.

At the end of the 1980s, he turned to feature films with *Clandestinos* (The Underground, 1987), followed by *Hello Hemingway* (1990), *Madagascar* (1994), and *La Vida es Silbar* (Life is to Whistle 1998). Since 2000, he has experimented with wildly different styles. His films *Suite Habana* (2003), *Madrigal* (2006), and *Martí, el ojo del Canario* (Martí, the Eye of the Canary 2010) have each won international and domestic awards as well as critical acclaim. Though on very different topics, his films share a preoccupation with the city of Havana, the future that awaits its youth, and the search for inner freedom, truth, and love. Perhaps Pérez's most powerful, innovative, and heartfelt film to date is *Suite Habana*, his poetic, melancholic ode to the city and people of Havana. In it, Pérez manages to achieve the near-impossible feat of making a successful feature-length docudrama that almost completely dispenses with dialogue, while at the same time portraying the everyday struggles and joys in the lives of a series of real Cubans without embellishment, preaching, or spin (Scarpaci 2005).

CUBAN CINEMA TODAY

Filmmaking in Cuba suffers from the same grave problem that hampers nearly all other areas of life on the island: it is subject to a state monopoly. The ICAIC is only one of the branches of this monopoly. It is the state itself—the absolute administrator of all audiovisual production on the island—that ultimately produces the negative effects of the monopoly. However, as with every wall—seemingly solid and eternal—the Cuban state monopoly on the production of film, video, television, etc., has been slowly crumbling over the last 20 years. This weakening of state control is the result of an increase in the number of people with camcorders and other resources with which they can produce their own work. Additionally, foreign collaboration and co-production has made many other projects possible, while simultaneously mediating those projects to make them more palatable (and marketable) to foreign audiences.

Who is currently producing audiovisual content in Cuba? First, of course, there is the already mentioned ICAIC. Then, there is the Cuban Institute of Radio and Television (ICRT), which makes more than 90 percent of the content shown on Cuban television. Besides them, a number of other schools and institutes produce a truly abundant volume of audiovisual material little of which is given public distribution. Among these institutions are the International School of Film and Television (EICTV) and the School of Audiovisual Media (FAMCA) with their headquarters in Camagüey and Holguín, respectively, which were created by the University of the Arts to produce filmmakers. Other official entities include the Saíz Brothers Association, the Film Studios of the Armed Forces, and perhaps the most authentic and original cinematic project of all, *Televisión Serrana*. Although bureaucratically overseen by the ICRT, TV Serrana deserves special mention for its original and creative programming, which reflects the richness and diversity of rural life as lived by everyday Cubans in the foothills of the Sierra Maestra mountain range at the eastern end of the island.

There is also a long list of young directors and producers who make feature films and documentaries independently of the state. They include Humberto Padrón, Miguel Coyula, Jorge Molina, Esteban Insausti, Ian Padrón, Aram Vidal, Milena Almira, Ariagna Fajardo, Arturo Infante, Carlos Lechuga,

---

TV SERRANA

TV Serrana (TVS) was begun in 1993 under the leadership of the journalist and filmmaker Daniel Diez Castrillo. Initiated with UNESCO sponsorship and the collaboration of the National Association of Small Farmers (ANAP), it was conceived of as a way to reflect and defend the identity, values, and culture of the inhabitants of the Sierra Maestra, Cuba's most remote mountain range. Located in the community of San Pablo de Yao, the project aims to spread the knowledge of audiovisual media among the area's people so that they can be the authors of their own stories and use filmmaking to find solutions to communal problems and educate outsiders about their reality. Though founded by outsiders, today TVS's directors and producers were born and raised in the community and educated at the film school set up there by TVS. The founders of TVS knew they had to gain people's trust and "not act like colonizers who would steal their images and disappear" (Americas Media Initiative 2012). In order to do this, they had to live in the mountains together with its people, sharing their reality so they could help to accurately reflect it on film (C. Rodríguez 2011; TV Serrana 2011).

Ernesto Piña, Eliecer Jiménez Almeida, Pedro Luis Rodríguez, Léster Harbert Noguel, Juan Carlos Calahorra, Michel Pascual, Maryulis Alfonso, Yimit Ramírez, Carlos Machado Quintela, Gretel Medina, Adrián Replanski, Ricardo Miguel Hernández, Susana Barriga, Jessica Rodríguez, Sebastián Miló, Gustavo Pérez, and Yolyanko William, among others.

After the demise of the USSR, as cheaper means of filming began to slowly arrive on the island, potential filmmakers were able to overcome their dependence on the monolithic state institutions and film more with less limitations on content and style. Since then, the underground production of short films, documentaries, music videos—numbering in the dozens given their commercial appeal—cultural and artistic videos, and purely journalistic material has been slowly increasing. In much smaller numbers we find independent cartoons and feature films. A leading example of the independent production of Cuban short films is the 10-part series written and produced by Eduardo del Llano, all of which feature his character Nicanor O'Donnell (Del Llano 2012). *Monte Rouge*, a 15-minute short that incisively mocks and hilariously satirizes Cuban state security and its system of surveillance, is by far the most effective and a well-known short in this series (Scarpaci 2005).

One type of audiovisual content that until 2010 was exclusively produced by Cuban state television is production with political and social content. However, starting in 2011 short independent programs focusing on these long-taboo topics started to emerge, produced by various activists and filmmakers with shoestring budgets making use of digital technology to both record and distribute their shows. Three such projects stand out for their consistency, quality, and seriousness. First are the panels of debate and analysis hosted by the independent journalist Reinaldo Escobar under the name *Razones Ciudadanas*. Having produced a series of 12 shows during 2011 and 2012 on topics as diverse as "Racism," "Elections," "Economic Reforms," and "LGBT," this series is distributed on the island primarily by CD, DVD, and flash drives; however, the producers have also uploaded the entire series to YouTube and Vimeo, as well as making it available on a blog and a number of other sites (Razones Ciudadanas 2012). The project *Estado de SATS*, founded by Antonio G. Rodiles, follows a similar format and distribution strategy but is distinguished by hosting a wider variety of content, including debates, concerts, and interviews. SATS also stands out as a physical gathering space (the home of Rodiles) for a variety of independent projects of Cuba's emergent civil society (Estado de SATS 2012). Finally, in the spring of 2012 Eliécer Ávila, a former student of computer science who became famous after he publicly questioned the head of Cuba's National Assembly, Ricardo Alarcón, in a video that went viral on YouTube, began producing a series of thematic monologues under the title *Un cubano más* (Just Another Cuban). To date, his three short programs have addressed the press, politics, and citizenship respectively (Un Cubano Más 2012).

Because all movie theaters and television stations are state owned, and their owner—the Cuban Communist Party—greatly limits access to anything filmed outside of its control, the vast majority of this underground Cuban production, including that produced by Cubans abroad, only reaches the Cuban public thanks to CDs, DVDs, flash drives, and the underdeveloped but uncontrolled black market. Unfortunately, the extremely limited access and agonizingly slow speed of the Cuban Internet does not yet make it a viable alternative for large numbers of Cubans to view or download videos. These limited if marginally effective means of communication are not ideal because they make it virtually impossible for independent directors and producers to sell their products. Of course, none of this independent media is ever shown on Cuban television nor is it distributed to the mass public in the country's many cinemas, leaving independent filmmakers with contests and the festival circuit as their only option to earn back a portion of their investment. Moreover, this handful of independent Cuban directors and producers—which usually amounts to little more than a person, a camera, and a group of friends—have no legal status or recognition, making film production independent of the state in Cuba today quite precarious both economically and politically.

THE HISTORY OF CUBAN PHOTOGRAPHY

When the daguerreotype—the earliest ancestor of modern photography—was first introduced to the world in 1839, Cuba was still a Spanish colony but enjoyed a certain degree of economic prosperity due to its position as a sugar producer. Because of sugar, Cuba was the first Latin American country to introduce the railroad in 1873, doing so even before Spain. Thus, it should come as no surprise that photography— like cinema—came rather early to the island. According to the the newspaper *Noticioso y Lucero de La Habana*, Cuba's first daguerreotype was made in 1840 by Pedro Téllez Girón. Téllez was the son the the island's Captain General and obtained his modern image-capturing equipment directly from Paris. Soon thereafter, equipment to make daguerreotypes was sold in Havana leading to the island's first photographs and the start of the history of Cuban photography.

The first photographers to introduce and spread this new technological invention in Cuba were foreigners. The Spanish-Cuban Téllez Girón was followed by photographers from the United States, Canada, Italy, and France. The first photographic institution was also founded by the foreign daguerreotypist, George W. Halsey, an American who opened a studio on the roof of the *Real Colegio de Conocimientos Útiles* (Royal College of Useful Knowledge) in Old Havana in January 1841. It was the first public photo studio in all of Latin America at the time and its founding is commemorated today as the *Día del Fotógrafo Iberoamericano* (Ibero-American Photographer's Day). The second half of the 19th century saw the emergence of Cuba's first professional photographer, Esteban de Arteaga, who taught daguerreotyping and imported the necessary equipment and chemicals from Europe and the United States. He also specialized in portraits and landscapes. Gradually more Cuban photographers emerged, with some of them carrying their heavy and cumbersome equipment out into the countryside in order to take pictures of rural landscapes.

As photography spread, photographers began to chronicle important national events, such as fires, Masses, military parades, and other incidents of social interest, giving birth to documentary photography and photojournalism. A noteworthy picture—one of the most important of the time—was taken by the photographer Esteban Maestre on Saturday, August 8, 1863, of Cuba's then Captian General Domingo Dulce Garay and his cabinet as they posed at the ceremony commemorating the start of the demolition of the enormous wall that once surrounded Old Havana. This was the first time that a Cuban governor posed in public for a photographer with the scene being captured in an image for posterity. Havana was home to Cuba's first photography studios and the island was only the second country in the world to open a commercial photography gallery, doing so even before Paris where the technology was first invented. Soon, photography reached an ascendant state of development on the island, allowing it to play an important role in the country's social, political, and cultural life. The faces of the island's most aristocratic families were captured, as were many of the island's most famous plazas, monuments, buildings, and streets.

Following the latest artistic and technological innovations in the galleries of Madrid, New York, and Paris, the daguerreotype was soon replaced by newer, more manageable methods of photography in Havana's studios. Meanwhile, photojournalism and later photoengraving were able to transmit the striking images of the War of Independence to the entire world—and especially to the United States—with an uncanny immediacy that would have unimagined political ramifications. In this way, from its very origins Cuban photography became embedded in the island's most important historical developments. For example, the Spanish photographer José Gómez de la Carrera took a series of incomparable photographs of the War—and particularly Spanish general Valeriano Weyler's reconcentration campaign—that bore witness to its brutality and transmitted it to the entire world. These photographs are today part of the collection of Havana's José Martí National Library. Other equally valuable documentary images from that time are part of the permanent collections of the Library of Congress and Smithsonian Museum in Washington, DC.

As in other countries, Cuban photography developed as a response to the growing modern need for a communicative-informative and documentary-testimonial technology. Given its early development, high quality, and great variety of expressive styles, the tradition of Cuban photography is considered one of Latin America's richest, alongside work from Mexico, Brazil, and Argentina. Since its beginning it included topics as diverse as portraiture, landscapes, architecture, science, advertising, and social photography. There was also extensive development of the nude portrait along with other forms of aesthetic experimentation. During the first half of the 20th century, the rapid development of Cuban photography was accelerated by the constant introduction into the country of all manner of technical experimentation. The fact that the country was also awash at this time in every kind of publication—including books, magazines, catalogs, newspapers, movie posters, phone directories, etc.—along with the dramatic increase in commercial advertising, helped spur the development and diversification of Cuban photography.

CUBAN PHOTOGRAPHY AFTER 1959

The revolutionary takeover in 1959 and the profound social transformations that took place in the decades since also effected the destiny of Cuban photography. The first years were characterized by a veritable flood of images that reflected the dramatic sociopolitical upheaval that reached every corner of the national territory. The 1960s saw the predominance of an epic photography that chronicled the captivating force of the Cuban people and their guerrilla leaders. It was all but impossible for photographers to remain immune to the photogenic attraction of the emerging revolution, and scores of them eagerly embraced the opportunity to document an unfolding social process unique in the history of the hemisphere. This photographic vocation also included the graphic testimony of the aggressions suffered by the nation during the revolution's first years: the explosion of the French munitions vessel *La Coubre* in 1960, the Bay of Pigs invasion in 1961, the Cuban Missle Crisis in 1962, and various acts of sabotage, among others.

During the 1970s, this tendency of documenting the revolutionary process and its institutionalization continued. There was a marked emphasis on capturing snapshots of life that could celebrate the achievement of the revolution's ambitious economic plans, its many victories in sports, or innovations in culture and other fields. At the same time—without abandoning this epic style—some photographers took a more clearly artistic and naturalistic turn. New spaces were also established to teach the art of photography, always in line with strengthening the ruling socialist ideology. As was the case with every manifestation of the cultural and social life of the country, noncommercial photography was subordinated to politics, which hindered its development to a large degree.

The overriding tendency toward centralized government control together with an eagerness dictate the production and spread of images was reflected in the creation of institutes and organizations to bring photographers together based on their function. In this way, photojournalists were required to join the Union of Cuban Journalists (UPEC), art photographers were enlisted as members of the Union of Cuban Writers and Artists (UNEAC), and after going through a rigorous process of selection, photographers under 35 became members of the Saíz Brothers Association (AHS). At the same time, the Cuban Fund for the Photographic Image (FCIF) was created in the 1990s to gather all photographers into a single bureaucratic group. Of course, independent photographers lacked official legitimacy and were prohibited from showing their work in any gallery or publishing it in the official press, over which ruled a fierce censorship.

On the other hand, the material difficulties that were evident almost from the very beginning of the revolution slowed the promising development of amateur photography, which had enjoyed a great impetus in earlier decades and out of which emerged the island's best photographers. Film and photographic equipment became scarce and quite expensive given that the United States was the source of most such technological advances. As a result, Cuban photographers were forced to rely on the limited market and low quality products that originated in the socialist countries of Eastern Europe. However, the 1980s saw a period of consolidation of Cuban art photography. Many of the island's emerging photographers were educated in the schools of fine arts and thus came under the influence of the different schools of North American and European photography.

Despite rigid ideological control, the creation of state-sponsored institutions of photography wasn't without its positive effects. On the one hand, these institutions allowed for the education of invaluable photographers and the exhibition of their art. On the other hand, they promoted the conservation of Cuba's photographic patrimony. For example, the *Fototeca de Cuba*, founded in 1986 in Old Havana with the declared objective of becoming the "governing institution of Cuban photography," is a key cultural institution that serves simultaneously as an archive, a museum, and a gallery in which both Cuban and foreign photographers exhibit their craft. As such, it is home to an invaluable trove of iconographic memory of more than 160 years of Cuban photography with 21,000 photographs and more than 17,000 rare negatives, as well as an unparalleled collection of books, documents, magazines, and catalogs related to Cuban and universal photography. Much of the work of the island's leading photographers is catalogued and digitalized there to preserve the historic memory contained in their images. Each year the *Fototeca* hosts more than a dozen exhibitions, including the Photography Colloquium (started in 2006), conferences, and gatherings. Moreover, each November since 2008, the *Fototeca* hosts *Noviembre Fotográfico*, Havana's month-long celebration of the art of photography, which is coordinated with other cultural institutions and galleries across the city. Since 2005, this institution has published *Revista de Fotografía Cubana*, an annual review of the island's best photography.

In the 1990s a group of photographers with a more conceptual vision began to emerge. They have attempted to carry out a series of artistic photo essays that document life in a nonepic and nonjournalistic style. More recently, Cuba's new generation of photographers have taken advantage of digital technology to advance their craft. This digital turn is evident in both photojournalism and in the development of a new type of digital art with high creative standards. Given the almost unlimited possibilities that new computer and communication technologies offer, these photographers have captured and distributed images of some of Cuba's most important and controversial social events in real time without having to submit to the rigid ideological control of the past. This has allowed them to share images of long-hidden realities, debates, and conflicts, giving way to the emergence of a testimonial-type of photography, which is unapologetically confrontational and includes a clear social and political critique of Cuban reality.

Among the most distinguished Cuban photographers of the revolutionary period, the following stand out: Alberto Díaz Gutiérrez, aka Korda, Adonis Flores, Ernesto Fernández Nogueras (National Prize of Fine Arts, 2011), Osvaldo Salas, Raúl Corrales (National Prize of Fine Arts, 1996), and Roberto Salas. More recently, a younger generation of photographers has emerged, including René Peña, Marta María, Abigaíl González Piña, Eduardo Hernández Santos, Cirenaica Moreira, and Joaquín Blez Marcé, some of whom work semi-independently from state

KORDA

Cuba's best known photographer is Alberto Díaz Gutiérrez, aka Korda (1928–2001). His worldwide fame derives primarily from his iconic photo of a defiant Ernesto "Che" Guevara taken at the memorial service for the victims of the explosion of the French munitions ship *La Coubre* on March 5, 1960. The world's most reproduced image, Korda's photograph of Che, is considered by many critics to be one of the best portraits of all time. Largely self-taught, Korda was also a pioneer of Cuban underwater photography. In the early 1950s, he joined forces with fellow photographer Luis Pierce and established Korda studios where he worked as a commercial photographer between 1953 and 1968. Following 1959, Korda's work became closely identified with the revolution and the photographer eventually became Fidel Castro's personal photographer.

institutions. There is also a group of photographers who do freelance work for independent Cuban websites and blogs such as *Havana Times*. Some of these young photographers have their own photo blogs, as is the case with the writer and photographer Orlando Luis Pardo Lazo, who publishes his writings on his blog *Lunes de Post-Revolución* (Post-Revolution Mondays) and his vivid, inventive, and diverse photos both on his photoblog *Boring Home Utopics* and frequently accompanying the texts Yoani Sánchez posts on her pioneering blog, *Generation Y*. Both *Havana Times* and Pardo Lazo have also promoted the art of photography by sponsoring independent photo contests, with Pardo Lazo creating the website *País de Pixeles* (Land of Pixels) to showcase this work.

REFERENCES

Agramonte García, Arturo. 2006. "Manuel Alonso: 'El zar del cine cubano'," *Cubacine* no. 4 (October—December). http://www.cubacine.cult.cu/revistacinecubano/digital04/centro cap41.htm.

Americas Media Initiative. 2012. "About TV Serrana." http://americasmediainitiative.org/ about-tv-serrana. Accessed December 12.

Cabrera Infante, Guillermo. 2005. "G. Caín." *Un oficio del siglo XX*. Madrid, Alfaguara.

Chanan, Michael. 2004. *Cuban Cinema*. Minneapolis, MN: University of Minnesota Press.

Collazo, Raudel. 2009. "Decadencia." *YouTube*, September 6. http://www.youtube.com/ watch?v=6JGI-arwt-g.

Del Llano, Eduardo. 2012. "Nicanor O'Donnell." *Eduardo del Llano's Blog*. http://eduar dodelllano.wordpress.com/nicanor-o'donell/. Accessed December 12.

Del Río, Joel, and Marta Díaz. 2010. *Los cien caminos del cine cubano*. Havana: Ediciones ICAIC.

Díaz, Rigoberto. 2012. "Arranca el Festival de Cine de La Habana." *El Nuevo Herald*, December 5. http://www.elnuevoherald.com/2012/12/04/1357736/arranca-el-festival-de-cine-de.html.

Douglas, María Eulalia. 1996. *La tienda negra: El cine en Cuba* [1897–1900]. Havana: Cinemateca de Cuba.

Estado de SATS, 2012. http://www.estadodesats.com/. Accessed December 12.

Jiménez, Guillermo. 2008. *Los propietarios de Cuba, 1958*. Havana, Editorial de Ciencias Sociales.

Lawson, John Howard. 1986. *El proceso creador del filme*. Havana: Editorial Arte y Literatura.

López, Naito, ed. 2005. *Cronología del cine cubano*. Santiago de Cuba: Editorial Oriente.

Luis, William. 2001. *Culture and Customs of Cuba*. Westport, CT: Greenwood Press.

Nellis, Krystina. 2012. "Despertar Trailer." *Duendeism*, June 16. http://www.duendeism.com/ film/despertar-trailer/.

Pardo Lazo, Orlando Luis. 2012. "Despertar: No Censor, No Cry." *Sampsonia Way*, May 14. http://www.sampsoniaway.org/fearless-ink/2012/05/14/despertar-no-censor-no-cry/.

Razones Ciudadanas, 2012. http://vocescubanas.com/razonesciudadanas/. Accessed December 12.

Rodríguez, Carlos. 2011. "Cuba—Leonardo Padura, TV Serrana, Pedro Ruiz." *Nueva York*, Episode 97. August 16. http://www.youtube.com/watch?v=xH8mua3arFg&feature= player_embedded.

Rodríguez, Yusimi. 2011. Interview with Raudel Collazo: To Express My Ideas and Have Them Heard" (Parts I & II), *Havana Times*, February 15 and 18. http://www.havanatimes.org/?p=37846 and http://www.havanatimes.org/?p=38068.

Sánchez, Yoani. 2012a. "Havana's Annual Film Festival Returns." *Huffington Post*, December 4. http://www.huffingtonpost.com/yoani-sanchez/havanas-annual-film-festi_b_2241710.html.

Sánchez, Yoani. 2012b. "Despertar (Awakening)." *Generation Y*, April 22. http://www.desdecuba.com/generationy/?p=2952.

Scarpaci, Joseph L. 2005. "Recent Satire and Criticism in Cuban Film." *Journal of Latin American Geography* 4, no. 2: 137–140.

TV Serrana. 2011. "Who Are We?" *ICRT*, March 22. http://www.tvserrana.icrt.cu/index.php/qsomos.

Un Cubano Más, 2012. http://www.youtube.com/user/1cubanomas. Accessed December 12.

Cuisine

Maritza de los Ángeles Hidalgo-Gato Lima and Ted A. Henken

INTRODUCTION

While Cuban cuisine has much in common with that of other Caribbean islands, it is unique in many ways. Foreigners are often surprised that despite the fact that the *habanero* pepper takes its name from Cuba's capital, chili peppers and most other kinds of hot spices are notably absent from Cuban kitchens. For most Cubans, even black pepper is considered too spicy! (That is less true in *Oriente*, where centuries of influence from French and Haitian Creole cuisine have given the *orientales* a broader palate.) In place of hot spices, Cubans make constant and creative use of garlic, onions, cumin, oregano, and a concoction called *sofrito* (described later). As with language, Cuban cuisine has absorbed influences from Spain, Africa, its indigenous inhabitants, Haiti, and the United States. Paradoxically, despite being an island with many kinds of fish, lobster, and other seafood in abundant supply, Cubans tend to prefer meat, especially beef (when they can get it, which is rarely) and pork (which is more readily available), though chicken is also popular.

The Spanish and later the Chinese made rice a mainstay of the Cuban diet, along with beans (red and especially black) and the abundant variety of rooted vegetables indigenous to the island. Cubans also love sweets and tend to consume them in copious quantities. Ironically, whereas many foods are in short supply in today's Cuba, one visit to the legendary ice cream Mecca *La Coppelia* (known popularly as *la catedral del helado*, the "ice cream cathedral," with branches in Havana and Santiago) will teach you that when Cubans finally sit down to eat their *helado* after a lengthy wait in line, they do so with decadent abandon and unapologetic gluttony! Other Cuban desserts are made with either milk or fruit and contain lots of sugar, as does Cuban coffee (*café criollo*), which is usually brewed syrupy thick and drunk in tiny demitasse cups in the late afternoon as a pick-me-up with a kick, or in the morning

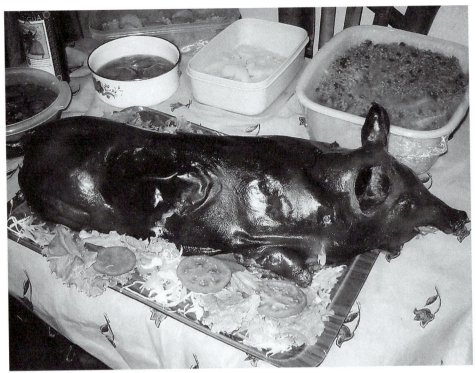

Cooking lechón asado *(roast pork) is much like a cross between the American traditions of Thanksgiving dinner and a backyard barbecue, with the same combination of family lore, secret recipes, macho posturing, and grill pride and envy. (Ted Henken)*

with steamed milk and served under the name *café con leche*, though *leche con café* might be a more appropriate title given that it is at least two parts milk and only one part coffee (Villapol 2002).

TYPICAL CUBAN CUISINE

A handful of dishes have become symbolic of Cuban cuisine. They are the main meat dishes: *lechón asado* (roasted pork/roast suckling pig), *ajiaco* (Cuban stew), *ropa vieja* (shredded beef, or literally "old clothes," surely one of the best names for a dish ever invented), and *picadillo* (ground beef/mincemeat). Three popular side dishes that normally accompany the aforementioned meat dishes are *frijoles negros* (black beans, always served with white rice), *moros y cristianos* (black beans mixed with rice, often referred to simply as *moros*, literally meaning "Moors and Christians," runner-up for best name of a Cuban dish), and *yuca con mojo* (cassava with garlic sauce).

Black beans prepared alone and served with white rice is distinct from the equally common *moros*. A popular variant of *moros* is *congrí oriental* ("dirty rice," sometimes written *congrís*). Typically, *moros* is eaten in western Cuba and features black beans, while *congrí* is more common in the east and contains red beans (*frijoles colorados*) and rice (though the terms are often used interchangeably). The gourmet chef of Cuban television, Nitza Villapol, suggests that the strange term *congrí*

LECHÓN ASADO (ROAST PORK/ROAST SUCKLING PIG)

The preparation of roast suckling pig is a daylong event, usually engaged in by the whole Cuban family on special occasions. It is the Cuban equivalent of the American Thanksgiving turkey, only a lot bigger, juicier, and tastier (though perhaps less healthy given the amount of pig fat involved). For Cubans abroad, *lechón* is typically prepared as the family meal (including aunts, uncles, grandparents, nephews, children, grandchildren, and a few brave or curious friends) on *Noche Buena* (Christmas Eve). In Cuba, this tradition has waned because of the de-emphasis of Christmas and the lack of access to entire piglets. Still, the cooking of a roast suckling pig is often at the center of all traditional country *fiestas* in Cuba. In fact, despite the scarcity of meat, Cubans continue to celebrate New Year's Eve in Cuba today by getting ahold of at least a small piece of *lechón* with which to ring in the New Year (García 2004; Villapol 2002).

---

originated from the popular Haitian Creole term for "beans and rice," *congó et riz* (Villapol 2002: 40). Other popular Cuban dishes include *arroz con pollo* (yellow rice with chicken), *croquetas* (croquets), and *casabe*. Called cassava bread in English, *casabe* is a yuca-based native Taíno food still eaten in eastern Cuba in the form of a starchy bread or cracker. Finally, there is *tamal en cazuela*, which—like its Mexican cousin—is made from ground kernels of corn wrapped in husks and steamed. Though Cuban *tamales* are seasoned with spices and sauces, and sometimes include meats or sweets, they are made without chili pepper.

A final addition to the Cuban palate, in scarce supply on the island today, arrived with the North Americans at the turn of the 19th century. These are the famed sandwiches, the *media noche* ("midnight") and the *cubano* ("Cuban sandwich"). Now ubiquitous in the delis of South Florida and New York City, these sandwiches became popular in Republican Cuba (1902–1958), along with the *frita*—Cuba's version of the American hamburger—as a quick way to fill up during a busy day or, better yet, late at night. In fact, the name "midnight" originated from the practice of wolfing down one of these succulent sandwiches after going out dancing or to one of Cuba's ubiquitous movie theaters. Filled with roast pork, boiled ham, Swiss cheese, pickles, and mustard, the *media noche* is served hot and slightly toasted on soft, sweet bread. The very similar *cubano* is not normally toasted and comes on Cuban bread or more properly on a French baguette (García 2004).

Additionally, Cubans have come up with innumerable ways to prepare *plátanos* (plantains, both ripe and green). There are *plátanos maduros fritos* (fried sweet plantains), *tostones* (cut into thick wedges, fried, mashed, and fried again, known as *patacones* elsewhere in the hemisphere and in eastern Cuba), *mariquitas* (thinly sliced and fried into crunchy chips), and *plátano en tentación* (long-cut roasted sweet plantains coated with sugar and cinnamon). Another important food group is the rooted vegetable (tuber), also prepared in a variety of ways. Usually boiled or fried, Cuba's many tuber varieties can all be smothered in the rich garlic sauce known as *mojo* mentioned earlier. The three most common roots are the *yuca* (cassava or manioc), *malanga* (taro root), and *boniato* (white sweet potato). Fruits, such as mango and papaya (known as *fruta bomba* in western Cuba), and vegetables, such as avocado and tomato, are also abundant.

Popular desserts include *flan* (caramel custard), *natilla de chocolate* (custard pudding with chocolate), *arroz con leche* (rice pudding), *pasta de guayaba con queso* (guava paste with cheese, sometimes called *timbita*), and cake (often extravagantly decorated with lots of icing). Cubans use the English word "cake" (pronounced Kay on the island), not the Spanish word *torta*, *tarta*, or *pastel*, used in other Spanish-speaking countries. During times of scarcity, especially in the early 1990s after the collapse of the Soviet Union, many Cuban dishes and desserts were recreated with a creativity and simplicity imposed by the times. One example of this is *pan con timba*, which is a simple piece of sweet guava paste between two slices of bread. There are also a number of popular Cuban pastries, most of which are derived from Spanish cuisine but which employ tropical ingredients more commonly found on the island. Some of these homemade sweets include *cascos de guayaba* (guava peels), *coco rallado en almíbar* (grated coconut in syrup), *boniatillo acaramelado* (sweet potato bathed in caramel), *raspadura* (sometimes referred to as panela in English, this delicacy is a solid cake of unrefined or brown cane sugar), *cucuruchos de boniatillo* (sweetened sweet potato peels), and coconut with pineapple.

TRADITIONAL CUBAN BEVERAGES

Cuba's famed espresso coffee comes in three varieties, *café criollo* (described earlier), *café con leche* (similar to French *café au lait* or Italian *caffe latte* and drunk in the mornings in a large coffee cup), and *café cortado* (a 50/50 mixture of *café criollo* and milk, drunk from a demitasse cup and usually referred to in Cuba simply as a *cortadito*). Coffee is ubiquitous even in the humblest of Cuban homes. It is customary,

---

HOW TO MAKE A CUBAN *MOJITO*

One of three signature Cuban cocktails, the *mojito* is a sweet, minty, citrus drink perfect for those hot summer nights. Similar to the bourbon-based mint julep popular in the U.S. South, the *mojito* is a refreshing rum-based cocktail that combines many ingredients native to Cuba. They include one ounce of fresh lime juice, two ounces of medium brown cane sugar, two ounces of high-quality white rum and a splash of dark rum, one cup of ice cubes, one ounce of club soda or lemonade, and a few sprigs of fresh *yerba buena*.

To prepare your *mojito*, wash and stem the mint leaves, reserving a few whole sprigs as a garnish. Combine the lime juice, *yerba buena*, and sugar in a glass. Crush the mixture well with a pestle—this extracts the tasty mint oils. Add the white rum and fill the glass with ice. Add the lime juice and stir until the sugar begins to dissolve. Just before serving, add the club soda (or lemonade) and top off the glass with a splash of dark rum. Stir gently. Garnish the glass with a sprig of *yerba buena* and serve with a straw (García 2004; Villapol 2002).

even obligatory to offer a small demitasse cup of strong and often syrupy sweet *café criollo* to visitors at one's home. It is also quite common for Cubans to have a cup of hot, strong, and bitter coffee as their only breakfast. Although Cuba was once an important producer and exporter of high-quality coffee, production has declined since 1990. Consequently, low-quality coffee is imported and mixed together with other ground beans and peas for distribution and sale at low, subsidized prices through the ration booklet. The resulting mixture is referred to popularly as *café de chícharo* and serves a similar purpose as the tradition of combining coffee with chicory common in New Orleans, Louisiana.

In his ongoing effort to revive and reform the Cuban economy, President Raúl Castro told the following story as part of a speech he gave to National Assembly delegates on December 19, 2010, proving that he has both a sense of humor and a pragmatic streak sorely lacking in his elder brother:

> After the U.S. war of aggression against Vietnam, the heroic and undefeated Vietnamese people asked us to teach them how to grow coffee, and there we went, and we taught and transferred our experience. Today Vietnam is the second-largest exporter of coffee in the world. And a Vietnamese official said to a Cuban colleague: "How is it possible that you taught us to grow coffee just the other day, and now you are buying coffee from us?" I don't know how the Cuban responded. Surely he said to him: "*El bloqueo*" [the U.S. embargo]. (quoted in Peters 2011)

Finally, Cuba boasts a number of original cocktails. Nearly all of them are rum-based, given the fact that the island is the producer of some of the world's best rum. As a result, at least three Cuban cocktails are well known and consumed avidly abroad, including the *daiquirí*, the *Cuba libre* (Cuban rum, cola, lime, and ice), and the *mojito*. Less well known off the island are the *añjeo* (aged rum taken straight or on the rocks), the *ron collins*, the *Mary Pickford*, and the *Cubanito* (Cuba's rum-based version of the Bloody Mary). There is also the *canchánchara* (a mix of bee honey and sugarcane *aguardiente*), which became popular among Cuban soldiers during the military campaigns of the 19th century independence wars.

HISTORY AND ANTECEDENTS OF CUBAN CUISINE

The different items in Cuba's cuisine can be divided between those native to the island and others brought in from outside. Many native elements are still used today, especially in rural areas. Food customs also vary across Cuba's different geographic and climactic regions. The combination of native and imported elements make up what is today Cuba's so-called Creole cuisine, that is homegrown food specific to the island and its culture, otherwise known as traditional food or *comida típicas*. According to Acela V. Matamoros Traba, the sociohistoric development of Cuban cuisine has taken place over three long stages: a pre-Columbian or native period, a colonial period that lasted until the end of the 19th century that led to the formation of Cuban Creole cuisine, and a contemporary period that includes various arriving ethnic groups in the late 19th and early 20th centuries (Matamoros Traba 2003). To this can be added the current revolutionary period, which saw a radical shift in culinary habits as in all other areas of Cuban life.

Native Foods

Cuba's most ancient indigenous people belonged to archaic cultures. They had very small populations with low levels of development and unstable conditions of survival. They were hunters and gatherers who stalked large rodents (such as the now extinct giant sloth) and collected a diverse array of roots and fruits. Other cultures that arrived on the island later specialized more in fishing and benefitted from a higher level of technical development in their fashioning of tools and utensils, making their adaptation and exploitation of the island's natural resources more successful. The final native group, the Taíno, was able to domesticate wild plants by practicing a rudimentary form of agriculture. They also made ceramic tools that allowed them to achieve a greater dietary variety. This last indigenous group was Cuba's most advanced and it is they who had direct contact with the Spanish, to whom they transmitted many of their culinary traditions still preserved to this day (Barcia, García, and Torres Cuevas 1994).

The principal remnant today of the Taíno indigenous diet is the cultivation of *yuca* (bitter cassava) to prepare *casabe* bread, their main sustenance. They also planted chili peppers, yams, and other crops. They supplemented their diets with river and sea fish, the hunting of wild birds, and other species, as well as the gathering of roots and fruits. The *casabe*, as well as *ajiaco*—a thick broth cooked with different kinds of tubers—has remained part of Cuban popular cuisine. Indigenous Cuban cuisine reflects a healthy and diverse diet that sustained the Spanish for many years. In fact, during the first years of colonization, Cuba's native people supplied Spanish ships with *casabe* during their stays in Havana's harbor. Research done by Cuban scholar Juárez Figueredo indicates that the legacy of Indo-Cuban cuisine goes well beyond the well-known *ajiaco* and *casabe:*

> Indigenous Cuban cuisine remains among Cubans. In Cuba, Columbus and his sailors learned for the first time about corn, cassava, peanuts, yams, pumpkin, chili peppers, the *yautía* (a type of wild malanga), among other plant foods, [from the Taíno]. The archipelago's animal richness included the *jutía* [a large rodent]. And its abundant fruits [included] the *chirimoya* [custard apple], the *guanábana* [soursop], the pineapple, the star apple, the *mamey*, the sugar apple, white coco plums, the guava, and the cashew apple. (Juárez Figueredo 2003)

Early Inherited and Creole Foods

The history of human migration has had a significant impact on Cuban cuisine involving immigrants primarily of American, European, African, and Asian origin. While many of today's stalwart Creole dishes started out as a simple and inexpensive way to "kill hunger," some have progressed over time turning into national delicacies worthy of "licking your fingers." Of the foods brought in by Spaniards, those that adapted the most to Cuba's weather were poultry, including hens, ducks, and pigeons. The Spanish also imported bigger animals, which were crucial for the economy and their diet, such as cattle, goats, pigs, and horses. The island's food crop species expanded when the Spanish introduced plant species both from Europe and the rest of the Americas, as well as from other parts of the world. These transplanted foods include sugarcane, potatoes, limes, mangoes, and oranges. This diverse array of foods led to a new diet among the island's inhabitants. Other native food items were taken up by the Spanish during the conquest and colonization process, including the previously mentioned *casabe* (which replaced European wheat due to the difficulty of importing wheat flour), as well as yams, corn, and yuca.

Traditional Creole cuisine has long played an important role in life on the island. The previously mentioned *lechón asado* (roast suckling pig) bathed in *mojo* sauce has become *de rigueur* at Cuban weddings or in the celebration of the birth of a child, while hot chocolate or *café con leche* are traditionally served during funerals. As such, Creole culinary tradition has become part of everyday life, playing a part in hospitality, friendship, reconciliations, meetings, brotherhoods, and the festivities celebrated by Cuban families and communities. Despite the ups and downs of each historic period and variations across different regions, Cuban cuisine has remained largely unchanged for most of the population. This shared tradition includes rice, corn flour, beans, boiled and fried roots, eggs, pork, goat, and chicken. Despite Cuba being an island, fish is surprisingly absent from Cuban diets except in specific fishing towns. Bread, dessert, and coffee are also common.

Other culinary habits have their origins in different religious traditions, especially those of European or African roots. The traditional Christmas Eve and New Year's Eve dinners—originating with Christianity—have become a national tradition shared by all social classes and religious persuasions. Such dinners always include *lechón, moros, yuca con mojo*, and *buñuelos*—sugarcoated balls of sweet fried dough. Similarly, the commemoration of All Souls' Day once called for the preparation of corn with a sprinkling of ashes. Each town's festival for its patron saint has traditionally included fairs that highlight each region's most typical dishes. Finally, during Holy Week and Easter, *agua loja* (a mixture of water, molasses, cinnamon, and ginger) is consumed as part of the processions for the African deities.

Immigrant Influences on Cuban Cuisine

Toward the end of the 17th century, the Haitian revolution sent a large number of settlers and their slaves to eastern Cuba. With them they brought their customs and French-derived culinary habits, which gradually became part of the cuisine of Oriente, just as it did in New Orleans where many of these same refugees eventually settled. A half a century later in 1847, a new type of immigration and pseudo-enslavement appeared in Cuba: indentured Chinese laborers. Many of these arrivals eventually went into business as petty tradesmen, while also dedicating themselves to the cultivation of vegetables. This gave birth to Cuba's cheap and renowned "Chinese diners," which dished out traditional Cantonese cuisine. Gradually fusing their culinary customs with the already established Cuban Creole cuisine, the new arrivals enriched and expanded the island's culinary tradition. Among the best known Chinese dishes still served in Cuba today are fried rice, chop suey, and the so-called *maripositas chinas* (Chinese butterflies, which are fried wontons with sweet and sour sauce). Chinese immigrants also influenced Cuban pastries and the making of fruit-flavored ice cream.

The economic, political, and social transformations that took place with the founding of the Cuban Republic in 1902 led to a significant increase in immigration to Cuba by Europeans and others in search of better living conditions. Led by immigrants from England, France, and Germany, as well as from Mexico, Puerto Rico, and the Yucatan peninsula, these arrivals also brought their culinary customs with them, which quickly became part of the island's Creole cuisine. These initial migrations grew thanks to World War I (1914–1917), which brought in thousands of Italian, Polish, French, Russian, Portuguese, Dutch, Lithuanian, Hungarian, and Romanian immigrants of all different social origins and class backgrounds. They too left their mark on the island's cuisine. To this expanding immigrant population were added new groups of Haitian and Jamaican laborers who settled primarily in Cuba's eastern provinces. They contributed techniques from French and English cooking, including the use of coconut milk, which is still present today in various Cuban dishes. A second Chinese migration came to Cuba in 1917, which—together with the arrival of a small wave of Japanese immigrants in 1920—was known as the "yellow invasion." The culinary traditions of these immigrants contributed a variety of foods to the Cuban palate, including raw fish, garden vegetables mixed with fish and meat, and leeks with pork, chicken, or fish.

Cuban Cuisine since the Revolution

With the revolutionary victory in 1959, the socioeconomic transformations that took place had a direct and radical impact on the culinary habits of everyone. The revolutionary period ushered in a massive, social, and collective type of diet. After links with the United States were severed, food markets had to find new sources for their supplies and they turned most naturally to the island's new commercial partners in Eastern Europe, especially the Soviet Union, Bulgaria, Czechoslovakia, and Romania. Over time, Italian dishes such as pizza, spaghetti, and other types of pasta also became popular.

At the same time, as food supplies became scarce, the state established a system of control and distribution of the island's food supplies through the so-called basic food basket, marking a milestone in Cuban culinary history. Though this measure began as a necessary emergency response to food scarcity in order to insure the basic nutrition of all, it expanded and became permanent over time. Regulated through the "ration booklet," which was established in 1962 and fixed dietary quotas for each member of a household, Cuba's system of rationing has waxed and waned over time in accordance with the country's economic standing. Of course, reliance on rationing often determines what foods can be prepared and when.

Although the monthly quotas of many products have been cut in recent years amid plans to eventually phase out the entire system itself, as of 2012 the ration book provided a monthly diet of 7 pounds of rice, several ounces of beans, 5 pounds of sugar, a quarter pound of oil, 10 eggs, 1 pound of chicken, 4 ounces of *chícharo* coffee, and a few other products such as pasta and cookies. Fish was once part of the "basic basket," but today is reserved for those with a doctor's prescription only. As a consequence, chicken has been substituted to replace the 11 ounces of fish that was previously distributed. Rationed milk is reserved for children under seven years of age and for those under doctor's orders. On the other hand, a single roll of 80 grams is allotted for each holder of a ration booklet per day.

Due to the severe limitations of the deep structural crisis of the Cuban economy, the prices of items not included in the rationing plan are extremely high. This has limited the ability of many households to prepare some of Cuba's most traditional dishes. Still, despite such chronic limitations and scarcities, Cuban Creole cuisine has yet to lose its essence. This is thanks in no small part to the perseverance and inventiveness of many Cuban mothers and grandmothers who have been forced to reinvent Cuban cuisine once again while preserving its traditional identity. They have done this by often resorting to recipes inherited from their great grandmothers, who themselves once performed veritable miracles in the preparation of foods in times of crisis. Truly incredible dishes have been created under these conditions, with inventive substitutions of ingredients coming out of the popular imagination of the island's cooks allowing for the preservation of the best of Cuban cuisine.

REFERENCES

Barcia, María del Carmen, Gloria García, and Eduardo Torres Cuevas. 1994. "Las comunidades aborígenes de Cuba." In Lourdes Domínguez, Jorge Febles, Alexis Raves, eds., *La Colonia*. Havana: Editora Política.

García, Alex. 2004. *In a Cuban Kitchen*. Philadelphia, PA: Running Press.

Juárez Figueredo, Héctor. 2003. "Aproximación a la cocina cubana." Havana: Escuela de Hotelería y Turismo de La Habana.

Matamoros Traba, Acela V. 2003. "Cocina Cubana: Platos tradicionales y nuevas creaciones." Havana: Biblioteca de Hotelería y Turismo de La Habana.

Peters, Philip. "Quotable," *The Cuban Triangle,* January 3, 2011. http://cubantriangle. blogspot.com/2011/01/quotable.html

Villapol, Nitza. 2002. *Cocina Cubana*. Havana: Editorial Científico-Técnica.

Art and Architecture

César Leal Jiménez

ART

Painting

Nicolás de la Escalera is recognized as Cuba's first painter. A mixed-race Creole, he painted murals in the parish church of Santa María del Rosario, built between 1760 and 1766. It is unclear whether he or the church's architect, José Perera, was also responsible for the island's first painted gold leaf wood altarpieces also featured in the church's interior. In any case, De la Escalera's work constitutes a descriptive representation of Cuban society during the late 18th century. He was a self-taught artist who learned his craft by copying the masters. His humble social origins prevented him from getting a solid education in the arts. Thus, Cuban painting—with its particular defining characteristics—was born at the end of the 18th century, a time when painting was considered more a trade than an art. Artists were mainly dedicated to painting landscapes and portraits, many of which today are part of the invaluable collection of the National Museum of Fine Arts of Havana.

While De la Escalera's art was focused primarily on religious subjects, Francisco Javier Báez (1748–1828) was a Cuban painter who expanded his thematic focus to include secular portraits, religious insignia, and even illustrations for cigar brands and their boxes. In fact, this last artistic activity became something of a cottage industry in Cuba with the elaborately decorated boxes eventually attaining worldwide recognition as much sought after collectors' items. Vicente Escobar also stands out among the colony's Creole painters. A descendant of Cuba's sizable free black population, Escobar was able to travel abroad to attain a classical education at the Academia San Fernando in Madrid. There he was named a painter of the Spanish Court. His portraits are characterized by their softness and hints of naivete. Without a doubt, Escobar was Cuba's most talented portrait artist of the colonial era given his uncanny ability to capture the true psychological essence of his subjects in his work.

In 1818, the French painter Juan Bautista Vermay established The Academy of San Alejandro. Vermay is also the artist who painted the triptych of murals that adorn the interior of the monument known as *El Templete* that commemorates the founding of Havana. San Alejandro is Cuba's premier academy of art, still open today almost 200 years after its founding. Many generations of Cuban painters have studied there, some of whom have achieved international renown. The Academy originally schooled its students in the tradition of romantic expressionism initiated by Esteban Chartrand, notable for its sentimental and idealized approach to nature. However, during its first century of existence, San Alejandro undervalued Cuban artists not including their work in its academic canon.

During the 19th century, Cuban painting was characterized by the preeminence of naturalism, mimetically reproducing the colors, proportions, light, shadow, and textures of the natural world. It also aimed at life-like reproductions with elaborate and carefully controlled brushstrokes. Paintings from this era also show a marked contrast between the background scene and the foreground subject, as well as a minimal use of bright colors or any polychromatic variation. A good portion of the artists educated at San Alejandro absorbed and reproduced this academic approach in their art. Some of the most notable examples of such formalism are the sculptors Teodoro Ramos Blanco and Florencio Gelabert. This school was also promoted in the central part of the island, with painters like Mariano Tobeñas and Oscar Fernández Morera being the best 19th century examples of such academic formalism.

It was not until 1925 that Cuban artists finally abandoned these mimetic techniques and began to reflect the modern concerns found in contemporary art elsewhere. This shift occurred when a group of painters who had been trained at San Alejandro grew frustrated with the limitations of their education and began to travel to Europe to broaden their artistic formation. Many of these artists came under the vigorous and renovating influence of the Paris School. The undisputable leader of this generation of 20th century Cuban artists, later becoming the most representative painter of what is known as the island's *vanguardista* generation, was Victor Manuel. Often considered rough and unrefined by the conservative and highly influential academic critics of the time, Manuel's work was eventually accepted by critics and artists alike as the most original and pioneering of all contemporary Cuban painting.

In 1927, many works of artists in this emerging *vanguardista* generation were exhibited in Havana. Together with Victor Manuel, the sculptor Juan José Sicre and painter Antonio Gattorno took part in this series of exhibitions. In May of that year, a memorable group exhibition that included these and other artists took place in the Cuban capital inaugurating what would become known as the so-called heroic period of Cuban art. Other fresh and innovative artists joined the *vanguardista* cause, including Carlos Enríquez whose work is filled with sensuality; Eduardo Abela, who created the iconic character "*El Bobo*" (The Dummy) during Gerardo Machado's dictatorship before moving on to subsequent periods, which are also considered part of Cuba's authentic national cannon today. There was also the groundbreaking work of the painter Fidelio Ponce de León who created a pictorial technique quite uncommon in Cuban painting of the time in which whites, browns, and sepias are key elements. Many of these artists, but especially the bold sculptor Enrique Moret, sought to reflect in their art some of the social and political transformations then taking place in Cuba. Unfortunately, these artists were forced to truly earn the title of *vanguardistas* since their work was neither critically understood nor financially supported by the gatekeepers of the island's art institutions of the time.

In 1937, Abela became the director of the *Estudio Libre de Pintura y Escultura* (Free Studio of Painting and Sculpture), an important school where the leading second generation of *vanguardista* painters Mariano Rodríguez and René Portocarrero taught. Like their predecessors, these artists both embraced and redefined national themes in their art and have since been much celebrated as national treasures. The reigning frustration of the island's oppressive political reality caused some of these artists to turn inward in search of creative peace, allowing them in turn to develop

WIFREDO LAM (1902–1982)

A leading member of the Cuban modernist *Vanguardia* movement, Wifredo Lam was of mixed Spanish, Chinese, and African heritage. First trained at the Academy of San Alejandro in Havana, Lam left for Europe in the early 1920s and lived for long periods in Spain and then, after the defeat of the Republican cause in 1938, in France where he befriended Picasso and became active in the cubist and surrealist movements. He was especially close to French surrealist writer André Breton, with whom he collaborated on a number of projects. Lam returned to Cuba in 1941, a journey that would have tremendous impact on his art.

His paintings began to reflect the vivid Cuban landscape, mixing tropical scenes with cubist influences from Picasso and his previous exposure to African sculpture. He also made creative use of Afro-Cuban deities, myths, and symbols in his paintings, producing a body of work best described as modern primitivism. After the war, Lam settled permanently in Paris. During his lifetime, he had many solo shows including a 1944 New York show where James Johnson, the director of Manhattan's Museum of Modern Art, bought Lam's painting *La jungla* (The Jungle, 1943) for the museum's permanent collection.

the formal elements of the *"criollismo pictórico"* (pictoral Creolism) style. This style is known for its representation of national elements such as the half-circle stained-glass window, iron balcony railings, roosters, typical Cuban interiors, and a diverse array of urban and rural landscapes.

The works of Mariano and Portocarrero evidence a marked tendency toward the baroque, the preeminence of color, and the use of loose brushstrokes. In 1963, the tireless Portocarrero was recognized with the Sombra International Prize at the Second São Paulo Biennial for his painting *La Ciudad* (The City). Another distinguished Cuban *vanguardista*, the painter Amelia Peláez, traveled throughout Europe and the United States in order to absorb the new concerns and techniques developed abroad. She was deeply influenced by Cubism, a sytle she later successfully adapted to the Cuban reality through the innovative representation of colonial interiors and national flora with a distinctive decorative flair. Other important *vanguardista* painters to exhibit their work in Havana's galleries during the 1950s include the imaginative abstract minimalist Luis Martínez Pedro and studied "Naif" painter Ernesto González Puig.

Wifredo Lam is perhaps the most internationally distinguished Cuban artist. Before the end of World War II, Lam had a lenghty and successful apprenticeship in Europe working under the guidance of such luminaries as Pablo Picasso. After the War, he returned to Cuba and began to spread what he had learned. However, not content to merely parrot the work of the European masters, Lam ingeniously combined his experiences abroad with the cultural influences of Cuba's—and his own—mixed African heritage. This reencounter with Cuban culture helped give his own work an original foundation, winning him an international following. The surrealist ideas and national themes often found in his work are perhaps best represented in his masterpiece *La Jungla* (The Jungle, 1943), now part of the collection of New York's Museum of Modern Art.

Painting after 1959

The level of creativity and originality in Cuban cultural expression expanded during the Republican period once the island's artists engaged with contemporary artistic, social, and political currents directly and critically. However, following an early burst of creative—even revolutionary—effervescence, the triumph of the Revolution itself marked an abrupt and abysmal reversal of fortune for any Cuban artistic expression that was not ideologically aligned with the new regime. The creation of official cultural institutions such as the National Council of Culture, among others, placed art at the service of the state and turned culture into political propaganda. Changes within the visual arts were a testimony to the larger sociopolitical changes taking place in the country as they were now enlisted in the process of raising the people's revolutionary consciousness (González Rojas 2012).

As the 1960s lent Cuban culture an epic and propagandistic aura, the visual arts were converted into a mouthpiece for the historic path of the revolution. As part of this new path, in 1962 Cuba broke ground on an architecturally breathtaking campus of national art schools—*las Escuelas Nacionales de Arte* (ENA)—constructed on the grounds of the former Havana Country Club. The ENA's pedagogical approach exposed Cuban students to an artistic education based on the aesthetic achievements and cultural movements that had flourished around the world during the 20th century. This was a time when a series of "primitive" art movements—such as "naïf," abstract, and pop art—all reached their peak. These movements all attempted to erase the traditional line between "high" and "low" art, embracing magical, irreverent, and popular elements. In Cuba, this led to a coming together of artists from different generations with similar creative interests. Veterans were promoted together with young artists, leading to the development of a variety of new and experimental expressive forms. Among the most distinguished Cuban artists to emerge during the heady decade of the 1960s were Carmelo González, Servando Cabrera Moreno, Ángel Acosta León, Antonia Eiriz, Fayad Jamis, Raúl Martínez, Juan Moreira, Umberto Peña, and Salvador Corratge.

During the 1970s there was an expansion of the artistic themes and languages used by Cuban's leading painters. The work of various artists from this period shows the clear influence of the leading currents in contemporary art, especially in expressionism and photorealism. Abstract art, both in its optic and kinetic aspects, achieved a surprising level of importance within Cuba's visual and cultural panorama. Distinguished artists who emerged during this decade include Pedro Pablo Oliva, Nelson Domínguez, Flora Fong, Roberto Fabelo, Gilberto Frómeta Fernández, Ever Fonseca, and Manuel Mendive. In the 1980s, the concept of a piece of artwork expanded beyond the traditional idea of an aesthetically pleasing object. Art installations became a popular new form of artistic expression during this decade as well, as they typically combined various visual genres and made innovative use of the island's exhibition spaces. This allowed artists to behave as theorists and critics of their own work. Also during these years, a number of experimental artistic movements attempted to take art out of the museums and into the street. This was done through the concept of mass popularity and participation, where any materials and expressive means were employed that would allow the artists reach their conceptual objectives. Artists of this time used strategies of immediacy, such as aggression, mockery, or direct references to popular culture in order to provoke audience participation. Among the many themes addressed by this generation of Cuban artists, the most common were art itself, sex, politics, institutions, religion, society, and popular culture.

Since 1990, Cuban painters have expanded further on the conceptual heritage of the 1980s generation, while shifting their focus back to more individual and traditional genres. These artists have also made use of new creative strategies such as cynicism, simulation, the hypocritical pose, and the desecration of images, icons, and values previously considered taboo, such as making ironic, artistic use of Communist Party newspaper, *Granma*, adapting the omnipresent image of José Martí, or even engaging in the playful manipulation of famous photos of revolutionary heroes like Che Guevara and Fidel Castro. In 1990 the young artist Ángel Delgado even staged a "happening" that featured the artist dragging his feet through an installation of thick white plaster of Paris and later defecating publicly onto an opened copy of *Granma*. This stunt earned Delgado a brief stay in prison, where he proceeded to make miniature sculptures from the bars of soap he was issued and small paintings that employed handkerchiefs as his only canvases.

With the collapse of the Soviet Union and the coming of the economic crisis known as the "special period," art began to focus more and more on the island's

MURAL PAINTING AND POSTER ART IN CUBA

Mural painting exploded in Cuba after 1959 with prominent works created for the National Schools of Art (ENA), *Casa de Las Américas*, the Habana Libre Hotel, and many hospitals and schools. The caricaturists Rafael Blanco, Eduardo Abela, Conrado W. Massaguer, and Juan David turned their art into a veritable national tradition by creating murals that reflected the social and political tumult of the times. This tradition of socially conscious popular mural art has been kept alive by José Luis Posada, René de la Nuez, Chago (Santiago Armada), and Arístides Hernández Guerrero (González Rojas 2012).

The artistic genres of engravings and lithographs flow from this socially conscious tradition and have been popular among many Cuban painters. Famous and influential artists working in this genre include Raúl Martínez, Umberto Peña, Tony Évora, Femez (José Gómez Fresquet), and Alfredo Roostgard, who gained notoriety through their masterful creation agitprop poster art for political mobilizations and the island's films and documentaries. Developed within state institutions like the OSPAAAL (Organization of Solidarity of the People of Asia, Africa, and Latin America) and the ICAIC (Cuban Film Institute), these works of art were aimed at inspiring solidarity with the cultural and political goals of the revolution.

precarious socioeconomic condition. Artists such as Abel Barroso and the multimedia-installation team known as *Los Carpinteros* (The Carpenters) have highlighted the reintroduction of elements of capitalism, including the "Yankee Dollar" and the inequalities and contradictions that the island's expanding tourism industry has exposed. Other artists like Sandra Ramos and Kcho (Alexis Leiva) have often focused on the themes of migration, nostalgia, displacement, and lost illusions.

These and other artists have also taken advantage of the Havana Biennial, which was launched in 1984, to showcase their work to the international art world. At the 10th Havana Biennial held in 2009, the bold and highly original experimental artist Tania Bruguera staged a performance piece at the Wifredo Lam Center for Contemporary Arts entitled "Tatlin's Whisper #6." The piece featured a live microphone set up in front of a podium inviting members of the public to say anything they liked for 1 minute each, during which time a white dove was placed on the speaker's right shoulder by actors dressed as soldiers. This was an obvious reference to one of Fidel Castro's most famous speeches given at the dawn of the revolution on January 8, 1959, when a white dove spontaneously perched upon his shoulder as he spoke.

During the 1990s and into the 21st century, many artists began to court galleries and buyers for their work in the international art market, relying increasingly on collectors and curators abroad. As a result, some artists have begun to paint with the international buyer in mind, producing finished and aesthetically pleasing works that contain messages that outsiders can easily understand. Still, Cuban visual arts today remain the repository of the diverse ethnic groups, religious traditions, political systems, and aesthetic conceptions that have influenced the arts throughout the history of the country. With the passage of time and the establishment of a national identity, a number of genuine Cuban cultural expressions have emerged that are now considered part of the canon of universal art.

ARCHITECTURE

Antecedents

At the beginning of the Spanish conquest in 1511, the Taínos were Cuba's dominant native culture. These island inhabitants produced a rustic architecture that—according to the Spanish chronicles—included four basic kinds of structures: *bohíos* (palm thatched huts), *caneyes* (log cabins), *barbacoas* (lofts for preserving food), and *bajareques* (mud huts). Though relatively simple in design and layout with little more than a single room, these constructions made intensive and ingenious use of natural elements such as tree limbs to erect the shells upon which would be laid swaths of branches for walls. Roofs were made of expertly arranged palm leaves—*yaguas de palmas*—which were in abundant supply on the semitropical island.

Of these native constructions, the *bohíos* remain today as the traditional structure *par excellence*, still common in many rural areas of the island. However, these have been updated and expanded, and now often include multiple rooms with various functions: living rooms, kitchens, dinning rooms, etc. Alternately, reconstituted *bohíos* are also featured attractions in Cuba's expanding tourism industry. *Bajareques* are also still found on the island, but are now commonly referred to as *vara en tierra* constructions, and used by peasants to store their crops. Finally, though the native *barbacoa* constructions are no longer in use, the word *barbacoa* is commonly employed in today's Cuba to refer to the split-level lofts improvised in many now-subdivided homes that had once featured high ceilings for the circulation of air.

At the beginning of the conquest, Spaniards often adopted the materials and construction techniques used by the natives because they were appropriate to the island's semitropical climate and the new settlers' meager resources. Nevertheless, Spaniards adapted them as much as possible to their own traditions and needs. Over time, as the Spanish conquest and colonization of the island proceeded an inexorable transformation took place in styles of construction as European—and particularly Spanish—architectural models were introduced. Of course, these models had to be adapted to the local characteristics of the island and its climate, thereby giving birth to what can be called a Cuban architectural tradition.

Cuban Architecture from Colonial Times to the Revolution

Given the island's many large natural bottleneck bays, most of Cuba's original urban settlements—such as Havana and Santiago—have been located at or near its major ports. In colonial times, these ports became the key for commercial relations between Spain and the rest of the Americas, later becoming the site of most of the island's massive defensive fortresses and still later the location of its most architecturally significant residences, museums, apartment buildings, tenement houses (known as *solares*), high-rises, and hotels. Moreover, Cuba's rainy, semitropical climate, harsh sun, and stifling heat have all conditioned Cuban architecture. The island's location in the path of the trade winds and being the target of frequent hurricanes have also influenced the way the island's architects have attempted to adapt their designs to Cuba's natural physical and meteorological environment.

After their arrival to the island in 1511, the Spanish conquistadors began to establish the first seven European *villas* (towns) on the island, including Baracoa (1512), Bayamo (1513), Trinidad (1514), Sancti Spíritus (1514), Havana (1514), Puerto Príncipe (1514—now called Camagüey), and Santiago (1515). After having been originally established at a less desirable location on the southern coast of the island in 1514, the city of *San Cristobal de La Habana* (Havana) was refounded at its present site adjacent to the Puerto de Carenas on the western bank of Havana Bay on November 16, 1519. It did not become Cuba's capital until more than a century later in 1621. Its becoming the seat of the island's government in that year was due largely to the new location's magnificent natural conditions that could protect the Spanish royal fleet and enable commerce with Spain. Thus, since the 17th century, Havana has easily been Cuba's most important port city and as such the premier site of most of the island's architectural styles and innovations.

Buildings with sloping roofs were the most common type of construction in Cuba during early colonial times given that they facilitated the collection of rainwater in specially constructed underground tanks given the fact that there were few other natural sources of freshwater. Construction techniques were adapted to the available materials, which generally included stone, clay, and wood. Initially, most homes featured a simple, functional layout of a single floor with an interior patio that helped to naturally ventilate and cool homes in Cuba's semitropical climate. Subsequently, the addition of a mezzanine and a second floor became common, with the interior patio now surrounded by galleries and corridors on different levels. These construction features, together with the presence of military engineers and master builders for the island's extensive defensive edifications, formed Cuba's colonial architecture that developed through the 19th century. As the 20th century approached, this style of architecture gradually fused with the Baroque and Neoclassical styles, with eclecticism and modern styles becoming more prominent during the 20th century.

Toward the end of the colonial period, a new architectural style known as Cuban Baroque emerged on the island that fused the traditional Baroque with Moorish elements (*mudéjar*). The best architectural representative of this style is perhaps the Cathedral of Havana. Cuban Baroque is characterized by its simplicity in comparison to the Spanish and American Baroque, also being less pompous and decorative than those styles. This difference is largely due to the organogenic nature of the island's construction material (a type of limestone called *jaimanita*) that is not suitable for sculpting. Porticoes were also built on the main homes of the Cuban Creole aristocracy and the Colonial Administrative buildings. This ubiquitous feature of Havana's colonial architecture—especially in *Habana Vieja*, as the colonial quarter is called today—were used as transition points between the interior and exterior areas, as well as providing necessary protection from the elements when passing from one building to another. This feature necessitated the inclusion of colonnades which protected passersby from the sun and the tropical heat and is a construction style employed by Cuban architects well into the 20th century.

With the sociopolitical changes that followed Cuban independence in 1902, including the economic boom-and-bust cycle known as the "dance of the millions," an eclectic architectural style developed on the island. Inspired by the legacy of the Neoclassical style, this eclectic style mixed in new French and American architectural

The construction of this Jesuit church began in 1748, but was halted when the Jesuit order was expelled from the Western Hemisphere. The church was eventually finished in 1776, becoming the city's Cathedral a year later. (Ted Henken)

elements. For example, the development of residential neighborhoods saw homes increasingly removed from the streets and sidewalks with the addition of fences, iron grills, and even walls along the home's perimeter to close it and its gardens off from the public. Grand avenues, such as the Avenue of the Presidents (also known as "G" Street) in Vedado and Fifth Avenue in Miramar, also began to appear, lined by ostentatious mansions and French style chalets.

Art Nouveau started in Belgium and France in 1895, rapidly becoming a popular international style before disappearing during World War I. It arrived in Cuba quite late and competed with the island's then reigning eclecticism. From a formal point of view, it featured curved lines, floral motifs, and made frequent use of wrought iron. Cuban Art Nouveau also made both practical and decorative use of glass, achieving great mastery in the production of lamps, glass doors and partitions, and stained-glass windows. Art Deco was introduced in Cuba in the early 1920s and developed through the 1940s. It was characterized by the use of geometrical shapes both in its architectural constructions and decorative designs. Late Art Deco style was often merged with modern architecture, a hybrid style often referred to as modern monumental. Taken to a simplistic extreme, this style took on a fascist influence and has been mocked by architecture critics under the epithet "brutalist." Finally, the 1950s saw the emergence of the new, North American rationalist style in Cuba. Combining a new aesthetic that merged a greater functionality of construction with an eye toward creating more comfortable interior spaces, this rationalist style can be seen in the many high-rise apartments that appeared throughout Havana, but especially in the city's Vedado neighborhood, in the 1950s. The Riviera and Havana Libre hotels (the second of which was originally named the Havana Hilton), as well as the massive Focsa building—one of the seven wonders of Cuban engineering—are prime examples of this architectural style.

Architecture during the Revolutionary Period

Following the triumph of the armed rebellion in 1959, Cuban architecture entered a dark period in which the development of and investment in urban areas was largely discontinued. There was also a destructive, supposedly socialist tendency to view the profession and art of architecture as a superfluous and even indulgent capitalist waste of resources. Many peasants were resettled in urban areas under the goal of providing them with modern housing along with its many comforts but with little awareness of the jarring change this might entail or of their ability to maintain their new living quarters. During the first decade of the revolution, the development of low-cost, easily constructed housing was promoted above all else. Buildings from this period are characterized by an extreme formal schematism, with little flexibility or awareness of geographical, aesthetic, or regional context.

As a result, very few examples from this period are considered works of architectural value. A magnificent exception are the National Schools of Art, designed by the Cuban architects Ricardo Porro and Roberto Gottardo with the Italian Vittorio Garatti. However, produced in a flurry of creative effervescence and revolutionary hope, these wondrous works of architectural art were just as quickly abandoned and condemned as wasteful extravagance (Loomis 2011; Nahmias and Murray 2011). Of course, the strong political and cultural influence of the Soviet Union, which reached their climax during the 1970s and 1980s, imposed a monotonous obsession for symmetry and space saving, together with a predilection for mass-produced, prefabricated materials.

In fact, during the 1970s prefabricated materials were employed in a vast array of architectural projects, including hotels, schools, hospitals, and public housing projects. As a result, a regrettable uniformity characterized these constructions breaking with the tradition where form would be determined by function and context. In an attempt to confront the growing housing deficit caused by the demographic explosion of these years, the so-called construction "micro-brigades" were launched. This was a government scheme aimed at building hundreds of thousands of housing units in a very short time enlisting the virtually free but unskilled labor of the future inhabitants themselves. Unfortunately, this and many other government housing projects had little awareness of or respect for the great aesthetic rigor of Cuba's architectural heritage. Perhaps the most representative architectural example of this period is the gargantuan Alamar project, a suburb located in far eastern Havana. This district is little more than an enormous prefabricated city of sleeping quarters with scores of gray low- and high-rise buildings chaotically distributed in a vast area unconnected to the rest of the city and cut off from many of the amenities that make life enjoyable such as transport hubs, concert halls, movie theaters, parks, and community networks and traditions.

A classic American car, predating the revolution but still running strong—thanks to the Cuban ability to "resolver" (resolve) problems and "inventar" (invent) ingenious solutions to myriad everyday obstacles—travels down San Lázaro street in the densely populated, working class neighborhood of Centro Habana. Unfortunately, the same cannot be said for Havana's housing stock, which shows the effects of years of neglect and disinvestment. (Orland Luis Pardo Lazo)

Following 1980, a deeper concern about the formal aspect of state constructions began to grow, reflecting a desire to re-embrace the uniqueness of Cuban architectural tradition. Thus, the decade was marked by a not-always-successful attempt to achieve greater harmony between the construction of new structures and the existing built and natural environment. Functional modernism and postmodern styles enjoyed a resurgence but were accompanied by a prevailing weakness in conceptual order and a lack a resources, accountability, and follow-through. This resulted in the frustration and waste of scores of abandoned construction projects littered about Cuba's cities. Following the collapse of the Soviet Union in the early 1990s, Cuba embraced tourism as an economic strategy giving rise to hundreds of modern luxury hotels intended for foreigners. While some attention has been given to restoring neglected colonial structures—especially under the guidance of City Historian Eusebio Leal in *Habana Vieja*—most tourism-related construction reflects the dominant trends in modern Western architecture at large, with massive iron-and-glass buildings that imitate the typical façade of skyscrapers. At the same time, a significant portion of the housing stock in many of the country's working class residential neighborhoods, such as *Centro Habana*, teeters somewhere between condemnation and collapse.

REFERENCES

González Rojas, Antonio Enrique. 2012. "Breve circunvolución a las dinámicas editoriales de la gráfica cubana," *Esquife: Revista de arte y literatura*, September 4. www.esquife.cult.cu.

Loomis, John. 2011. A *Revolution of Forms: Cuba's Forgotten Art Schools* (updated edition). Princeton, NJ: Princeton Architectural Press.

Nahmias, Alysa, and Benjamin Murray. 2011. *Unfinished Spaces*, Ajna Films, 86 min.

Popular Recreation and Sports

Rogelio Fabio Hurtado

It is often claimed that the early inhabitants of Cuba performed a recreational-religious activity that we remember today as *batos*. This is often cited as the most ancient ancestor of what has long been modern Cuba's national pastime, *la pelota* or baseball. In actuality, there are no specific references that Cuba's native peoples practiced a game even remotely similar to today's baseball. The early chronicles do refer to a ritual activity of a very different nature, which made use of a ball formed by vegetable resin that was passed between players hitting it with their shoulders, elbows, hips, and legs. This ball game was in fact widespread throughout Mezo-America, but did not involve the use of a bat or other blunt object. Like modern soccer—which is quickly gaining popularity in today's Cuba—it seems that this pre-Columbian ball game strictly forbade touching the ball with one's hands. Nevertheless, the island's popular imagination has fixed on the idea that baseball is a tradition rooted in ancient indigenous cultures that disappeared from Cuba during the Spanish conquest and colonization.

During the 400 years of Spanish colonial rule, betting games of chance such as cards, dice, and dominoes constituted the most common form of recreation used by those early adventurers, sailors, and men of fortune. The most popular dice games were *siló* and *cubilete* and the island's many varied card games included *monte* (mount), *burro* (donkey), and the still-popular *fañunga*, all introduced by Spain. By the 20th century, some American and English card games such as poker and the less popular bridge were played irregularly. It is said that one of the few still preserved autographs of the legendary Cuban chess player, José Raúl Capablanca, is dedicated to a Havana bridge club, a game the chess grandmaster also enjoyed. Today, perhaps the most popular and widespread gaming tradition in Cuba is dominoes, a board game in which four players do battle with a "double-nine" set of 55 dominoes which come in numbered pairs from zero to nine (unlike in Spain where a European 28-piece double-six set is used instead). Almost any gathering of family or friends includes a *mesa de dominó* (dominoes table), where pairs of players take turns playing together.

PASTIMES

Cockfighting

The introduction of cockfighting into Cuba is attributed to the *curros*, Spanish immigrants of Andalusian origin. In fact, the first official document that mentions it dates back to April 1737. So widespread was this kind of activity during the colonial era that Francisco Dionisio Vives, Cuba's Captain General, had his own *gallería* (gallery of fighting cocks). Nevertheless, cockfighting—as well as the wagers that it engenders—was banned by the captains General Miguel Tacón in 1835 and O'Donnell in 1844. Still, according to Cuban historian Hortensia Pichardo, "it was the most typical Cuban pastime, both in the countryside and in the towns" (1976:

334–336). In July 1909, during the administration of President José Miguel Gómez, the game was reauthorized under the newly independent republic. After 1959 it was prohibited once again, but neither then nor today has it been possible to permanently eradicate it given its rootedness as one of Cuba's oldest rural traditions.

The Lottery

Even more popular than cards, dice, or cockfighting is Cuba's lottery, which was the most widespread recreational activity during both the colonial period and the almost 60 years of the republic. It originated as part of town fairs as a way to raise money for local patron saint celebrations. It was a pastime of chance that was based on numbers, which involved the random selection of a series of balls out of a group numbered 1 through 90. A participant would pull the numbered balls out of a red sack and announce the lucky numbers to the other players, each of whom had their own numbered cards—as in American bingo—which they would progressively cover with kernels of corn or small buttons as numbers were called out. One could win with various combinations: the *pintas*, or the numbers in the four corners of the card; the *centro*, or getting two numbers in the center lines; or *tres bolas*, which won when a player covered any three numbers in a row. Similarly, *cuatro bolas* and the grand prize *cinco bolas* were given when four or five numbers were marked on any line of the card. If the players wished, an even bigger prize could be offered to whomever covered the top line of card. Given the small amount wagered, competitors would often spend many hours playing without a costly investment, making the lottery extremely popular among both women and the poor.

Serving simultaneously as entertainment and a form of gambling, the Cuban lottery was banned after 1959 even though it had long enjoyed broad popular support. For many years after that, it survived at the domestic level, played occasionally for low stakes among friends and family. Though now virtually extinct, the lottery has been superseded by the rapid growth of the *bolita*. This shift is not so much because the revolution has diminished the appeal of gambling among the population, but because *bolita* can be played with more discretion while also being more tempting given its much larger jackpots.

Additionally, in Cuba—as in Spain—there was a National Lottery authorized in 1909, with weekly drawings. It awarded three major jackpots, the so-called *Gordo* (fat prize) of 100,000 pesos, and two lesser prizes of 50,000 and 25,000 pesos respectively. Individual tickets could be divided up into 100 parts and resold to others who would be awarded proportionally if their number came up. During the republic, the National Lottery was a coveted cash cow of corruption and patronage and thus the subject of frequent scandals. After 1959, it was continued but under the auspices of the National Institute of Savings and Housing (INAV) and run by the trusted revolutionary, Pastorita Núñez González. While cash jackpots were maintained for a time, they were eventually replaced with prizes that included a program of construction of new apartment buildings in the *Reparto Camilo Cienfuegos* section of the housing developments in *Habana del Este*. The INAV was eventually swept aside in 1968 as part of the Revolutionary Offensive targeting the last vestiges of capitalist private ownership on the island.

Chess

The "game of kings" has a centuries-old tradition in Cuba. During the 19th century Havana played host to two world chess championships between famous European—often Russian—players of the era. Out of this fervid atmosphere emerged the great Cuban master José Raúl Capablanca y Graupera, the son of a colonial army officer. Sent in early youth to study engineering in the United States, he soon put aside his textbooks for the chessboard. His first precocious achievement took place while abroad, when he beat the leading North American chess player of the time, Frank Marshall, opening the doors for him to European tournaments of the first magnitude, where he could show his exceptional ability. In 1921, Capablanca won in Havana against the then world champion, Emmanuel Lasker of Germany. Capablanca held the world title until 1927, when the equally exceptional Alexandr Aleckine managed to snatch it away from him in Buenos Aires. Until his death, Capablanca remained one of the world's best players, though Aleckine never agreed to grant him a well-deserved rematch. He died in New York in 1941, and his subsequent wake in Havana's *Capitolio* has been unforgettably chronicled by Cuban writer Guillermo Cabrera Infante in his book *Mea Cuba*.

In the World Chess Olympiad in Buenos Aires (1939), Cuba finished in 11th place among 26 countries. The year before, Cuba won first place in the Central American and Caribbean Sports Games held in Panama. Chess continued to be a popular

Nearing its 50th year, the Capablanca Memorial Chess Tournament takes place each spring at Hotel Riviera on Havana's Malecón. This photo taken during a recent tournament shows a match between Cuban (left) and Russian players. (Orlando Luis Pardo Lazo)

pastime in Cuba during the 1940s. In the early 1950s, Grand Master Paul Keres visited Havana, where the Capablanca Chess Club organized tournaments and international meetings, including a showdown with an American club that included a still-young prodigy named Bobby Fischer. Among the leading intellectuals of Cuba's Popular Socialist Party (PSP), it was fashionable to master chess and teach it to one's children, being a game which the Soviet Union dominated.

This hallowed tradition was strengthened by the arrival to Cuba of the Argentine chess aficionado Ernesto "Che" Guevara, who once said that his first contact with the island was through his admiration of Capablanca. As president of the National Bank of Cuba, Guevara accepted the suggestion of the leading Cuban sportsman José Luis Barreras that the government finance the celebration in Havana of a world-class chess tournament. As a result, the First Capablanca Memorial Chess Tournament took place at the Hotel Habana Libre in 1962, attended by a veritable constellation of stars, including former world champion Vassily Smyslov and the future champion, Boris Spassky. However, the championship was won that year by the Polish-Argentine Miguel Najdorf, who clinched a dramatic last round game against the Cuban Eldis Cobo. Partly as a result of this tournament, chess fever spread across Cuba during the 1960s. Wherever you looked you would find a board with players, surrounded by curious onlookers.

SPORTS

In 1807 the Royal Patriotic Society of Havana took steps to introduce Johann Heinrich Pestalozzi's pedagogical ideas into the island. Pestalozzi (1746–1827) was a Swiss educational reformer and precursor of contemporary teaching methodology who gave great importance to physical education. In 1808, the Society sent Father Juan Bernardo O'Gaban to study these ideas in Europe. Upon his return to Cuba, O'Gaban introduced sports into Cuba's educational system, for which he is considered the father of physical education in Cuba. At this time, thanks to O'Gaban, the practice of basketball, boxing, and other sports began on the island. In 1839, Latin America's first gymnasium was erected in Havana, and by the end of the 19th century gymnastics was introduced in secondary education as a mandatory subject. During the Republican period (1902–1958), physical education was included in the curriculum of both urban and rural public schools. In 1928, the National Physical Education Institute was established, which graduated Cuba's first teachers with specific training in this field. However, an island-wide network aimed at effectively developing national system of sports was still lacking.

Baseball

Starting in the second half of the 19th century, young Cubans who studied in the United States began to introduce baseball to the island. *La pelota*, as Cubans refer to the sport, soon gained wide acceptance in part because it was associated with the modern United States and not the increasingly detested Spain, which exported *la corrida de toros* (bullfighting) to the Americas but which never took root in Cuba. It has long been held that Cuba's first baseball match took place on December 27, 1874, in

Matanzas at the *Palmar de Junco* field. However, according to anthropologist Félix Julio Alfonso the first game was actually played long before, on September 2, 1867, between youth from the *Comercio Habanero* and a group of North Americans residing in Cuba (Tembrás Arcia 2012).

The popularity of baseball continued to grow on the island since then. By 1888, the first Cuban League was founded, with a raging rivalry quickly developing between the two top teams, *Almendares* (in blue) and *Habana* (in red). Fans on opposing sides saw the *Almendares* team as a stand-in for the Cuban independence movement, while the "Reds" of *Habana* represented the Spanish loyalists in the popular imagination. This symbolic use of sports as an expression of political sentiment is a deep rooted Cuban tradition, only today it has taken on a regionalist character, with Havana's "Blue" *Industriales* the team associated with the New York Yankees (and thus the United States) and the Black Wasps of Santiago de Cuba seen as the team supported by the Castro brothers, who are both from Cuba's *Oriente* (or far eastern region).

There are literary chronicles that document epic baseball competitions organized during the 1890s. The Almendares/Habana rivalry was joined by famous showdowns between other teams such as *El Fe* and *Santa Clara*. The growing craze for the game was not restricted to Cuba's large cities. In fact, every small provincial town across the length of the island seemed to field its own respective club, usually sponsored by local civic organizations or businesses. In Havana and Matanzas—both port cities on the island's northern coast frequented by merchant ships from the United States—there were frequent matches between Cuban teams and ad hoc teams made up of the crews of the visiting vessels. Contact between the two countries via baseball became so commonplace during these years that it was Cuban tobacco workers living in Key West and Tampa—not North Americans—who founded the first baseball teams in South Florida.

With the occupation of the island by the U.S. military at the close of the 19th century, this previous exchange only intensified in both directions. Teams of Cuban players, initially both black and white, toured the East Coast of the United States playing against local teams—typically earning more victories than defeats—prevailing even against the top professional teams. These successful road trips earned Cuban baseball a well-deserved reputation for quality in the United States. In fact, many pro teams of the time, both in the Major Leagues and the segregated Negro Leagues, took on Cuban names as a mark of skill such as the "Cuban Stars" and "Cuban Giants." Ironically, endowing African-American players with a fictitious Cuban origin allowed them to avoid some of the racial discrimination that would otherwise have prevented them from playing in the Majors. For the all-white pro teams of the era, losing to Cubans—even if some of the players were Black—was preferable to losing to their black compatriots. There are even tales from this era of skilled African-American ball players who traveled to Cuba, learned some Spanish and obtained papers that identified them as the natives of the island, allowing them to return to the United States and be hired by Major League teams, as Cubans.

Postseason visits to Cuba by star-studded teams from the U.S. Major Leagues are also well documented, with them both winning and losing against their Cuban opponents. Cuban baseball lore is rife with stories about the Yankee slugger Babe Ruth, who failed to hit a homerun against Cuban pitcher the "*Diamante Negro*" (José de la Caridad Méndez). Legend has it that manager Joe McCarthy commented at the time that he would happily take the "Black Diamond" to the Majors only if he could paint him white. By the second decade of the 20th century, the first Cuban stars began to appear in the Big Show, including the pitcher Adolfo Luque and the outfielders Merito Acosta and Vicente "Tarzan" Estalella. While Luque and Acosta were white, Estalella was a very light skinned mulatto. All of them initially faced and eventually overcame the bigotry and hostility of American racists. Other major figures of these early years included Cristóbal Torriente, and years later, Martín "The Immortal" Dihigo. However, they were unable to reach their full potential due to impenetrable racism and discrimination of the time.

At the end of the 1940s when the baseball magnate Branch Rickey decided to break the color line, he needed to recruit a black player whose skill on the field could convince even the most virulent racists. This player also had to be of imposing size and patient enough to endure the insults the fans of opposing teams were sure to hurl at him. Ricky first thought of Silvio García, a 6-foot-tall Cuban slugger and shortstop. But when he asked García how he would react if a fan called him a "shitty nigger" to his face, he replied: "I'd pull out my knife and stab him." This anecdote explains why the ever-patient Jackie Robinson was chosen to break the color line instead. The first black Cuban to play in the Majors was not García but the great Orestes "Minnie" Miñoso, a native of Matanzas, who played for the Chicago White Sox.

During the 20th century, baseball became the sport of choice for Cubans. In the early decades amateur baseball prevailed, with figures like Sandalio Consuegra and the ancient Conrado Marrero, who pitched for the Washington Senators during the years of World War II. By the 1940s, pro ball had come to predominate, first at the Stadium of the Tropical Beer Brewery and after 1946 at the brand-new Grand Stadium of El Cerro, where the "Cuban League of Professional Base-Ball" was headquartered, with its four inaugural teams: *Havana*, *Almendares*, *Cienfuegos*, and *Marianao*. In practice, these teams functioned as unofficial farm teams for the U.S. Majors. That is, promising young prospects for the St. Louis Cardinals came down to play for *Habana*; the Cleveland Indians used *Almendares*; *Cienfuegos* tried out prospects for the Cincinnati Reds; and *Marianao* acted as a proving ground for the Detroit Tigers, the Chicago White Sox, and the New York Yankees.

The level of quality of the Cuban pro leagues surpassed that of the U.S. Triple A. This made it an inexpensive and ideal setting to forge the most promising rookies for the leading teams of the Major Leagues. For example, during the 1950s, the Grand Stadium of El Cerro hosted players like Kent Boyer, Bill Virdon, Jim Bunning, Willy Tasby, and Bob Shaw, among others, all of whom went on to lead successful careers in the Majors. In the mid-1950s, the famous impresario Bobby Maduro obtained a Triple-A franchise, allowing him to found the Cuban Sugar Kings, a team that grouped together Cuban, Dominican, Puerto Rican, and Venezuelan players, to play in the United States during the summer months since the Cuban season always took place during the winter. This team represented the joint aspirations of both Maduro and Cuban baseball fanatics, which was to break into the Big Leagues someday. Their motto during these years was: "One more step and we arrive."

With the coming of the revolution in 1959, nothing changed overnight. The national championship was interrupted for several days, and the American players who were in Cuba at the time enjoyed this as an unusual holiday. For example, the left-handed pitcher Tommy Lasorda, who played for *Almendares*, climbed into a jeep with red and black flag of the triumphant rebels and toured Havana. In the summer of that year, the Sugar Kings won the so-called Little World Series against a team from Minnesota-Saint Paul in the overflowing Grand Stadium of El Cerro with the revolutionary government's new prime minister, Fidel Castro, looking on. However, this honeymoon soon came to an end, as would also be the case with Cuba's professional boxing tradition.

Boxing

In 1959 Cuba had a very promising crop of young professional boxers, which allowed promoters to organize shows with three or four 10-round fights that filled the *Ciudad Deportiva* Coliseum. Among the standouts of that time were Urtiminio Ramos, the future world champion in the 126-pound category; José "Mantequilla" Nápoles, a world welterweight champion (146 pounds); the Spaniard José Legrá, who was a two-time world featherweight champion. Another champion was the native of Villa Clara, Bernanrdo Benny "Kid" Paret, who died later at the hands of the American Emil Griffith, in a celebrated Madison Square Garden bout. Other welterweight stars included the exceptional stylist Luís Manuel Rodríguez and the lefty jabber Florentino "Tres Toneles" Fernández, whose rematch against the Filipino Rocky Kalingo at the end of 1959 packed Cuba's Coliseum. There were also other very gifted boxers, such as the featherweights Douglas Vaillant and Ángel Robinson García, and the bantamweight Enrique Hitchmann. These fighters continued the tradition started by the likes of Eligio "Kid Chocolate" Sardiñas, Kid Tunero, Bill Black, and Kid Gavilán.

REVOLUTIONARY SPORTS

Following the creation in February 1960 of the National Institute of Sports and Recreation (INDER), all professional sports were outlawed by 1962, marking the dawn of the revolutionary era that continues today. Sporting activity was no longer controlled by various private and civil society organizations and passed into the hands of the state. Private profit gave way to political propaganda and the satisfaction of an unbounded national chauvinism. Sports could not escape the destruction of the old society in favor of a new one, which the majority of the population supposed would also be a better one.

Those connected to professional sports—athletes, coaches, promoters, etc.—were laid off. Most top athletes emigrated in search of the freedom and a market in which to develop their skills. Some coaches and technicians, especially in baseball and boxing, remained in Cuba and were employed by INDER to continue their work, including Alcides Segarra who for many years had been the head coach of the national boxing team. In baseball, figures such as Conrado Marrero, Gilberto Torres, Fermín Guerra, Pedro Almenares, Asdrúbal Baró, and Amado Ibáñez, also stayed in Cuba to become coaches of the island's up-and-coming athletes, whose traditional goal of joining the U.S. Major Leagues had become impossible given the political fracture between the two countries. These coaches were rewarded with an injection of necessary funds through INDER to develop a crop of top athletes who came to dominate regional and many international amateur competitions, such as the Central American Games, the Pan American Games, and the World Championships. This supremacy was particularly pronounced in baseball where Cuba's dominance would last for decades.

This success was famously celebrated by Cuba's Maximum Leader Fidel Castro as: "The victory of free baseball over slave baseball"; a phrase long used to prevent the island's top athletes in baseball, boxing, volleyball, and soccer from participating in professional leagues abroad. Great Cuban boxers emerged under this new amateur system including the heavyweight and multi-Olympic champion Teófilo Stevenson, whose much sought-after but now impossible bout against the great American pro Muhammad Ali die-hard fans are still playing out in their heads. INDER also produced the middleweight champions Emilio Correa, lightweights Adolfo Horta and Henry Regüeiferos, and welterweights Orlandito Martínez and Douglas Rodríguez, among many others. In the history of the revolutionary baseball, standout players have included the likes of José Antonio Huelga, Braudilio Vinent, Miguel Cuevas, Agustín Marquetti, Antonio Muñoz, Omar Linares, Antonio Pacheco, Orestes Kindelán, Pedro Luis Lazo, and Norge Luis Vera. However, Cuba's refusal to participate in the Caribbean Series and the suspension of the exchanges between Cuba and the United States has weakened the quality of Cuban baseball overall, a fact that has become increasingly evident since 2005 as Cuban teams have performed poorly and top athletes have defected on trips abroad.

It must be admitted that Cuba's state-controlled sports system has built first-class facilities throughout the island, both baseball stadiums and enclosed arenas for basketball, volleyball, and a host of other sports that were previously practically unknown on the island such as handball. Moreover, sports that were once the exclusive privilege of the wealthy, such as swimming and tennis, have been made available to any youth with the drive and talent to excel at them. Also thanks to the revolution, baseball spread to all parts of the country through the National Series of 90 games, which far surpassed the prerevolutionary pro league, which was limited to the capital city only. In 1963 the National School Games were born together with a national system of sports education, extending across almost the entire country. This system includes the Advanced Institute of Physical Culture and the International School of Sports and Physical Education, where both Cubans and students from dozens of underdeveloped countries have been provided with a high-quality sports education. Ironically, these luxuries were only possible under Fidel Castro's version of a totalitarian state controlled economic system, now being gradually dismantled and defunded by his younger brother Raúl. However, the system put in place under Fidel was supremely successful in ensuring that the socialist Revolution would obtain always more and better medals, which could serve as effective global propaganda for Cuba's socialist system.

However, the disappointing results of the First Baseball Classic (2006) and the Beijing summer Olympics (2008) were only confirmed in the Second Classic (2009) when the Cuban baseball team failed to make it to the finals, knocked out of competition in a pair of humiliating games against defending champions Japan in which they were unable to score a single run. This revealed the decline of Cuban baseball and of "revolutionary" Cuban sports in general. For example, while Cuba won a total of 27 medals in the 2004 Games in Athens, its medal total fell to 24 in the 2008 Beijing Summer Games, dropping again to just 14 in London's Summer Olympics in 2012. The cause of this decline lies in the systematic subordination of sports to political ideology and the totalitarian nature of the system itself, which has mobilized an unsustainable level of resources for the sake of achieving these symbolic if diminishing sports victories (Betancourt and Fuentes 2007).

Meanwhile, the Cuban athlete has been converted into a kind of gladiator representing the Cuban state at international competitions. Currently, there are special rewards in hard currency doled out to Cuban athletes to maintain the so-called glories of Cuban sports. This is a way, however diminished it may be, of paying them for their loyalty to the state. Of course, many young athletes with professional prospects in baseball, boxing, volleyball, and other sports have chosen to "stay behind" abroad while competing at international events. For example, between 2009 and 2011, Havana's *Industriales* baseball team lost a total of 10 of its top players. Likewise, the ranks of Cuba's boxing, volleyball, and soccer squads have all been reduced by recent high-profile "desertions," which is a loaded term used by the official press to classify all such athletes as "traitors to the homeland."

These athletes are prohibited from visiting the island and even from socializing with their former teammates during their travels abroad. Such is the case for the four players on Cuba's national soccer team who absconded just before playing in a World Cup qualifying match against Canada in October 2012. "I'm not a traitor," explained Maikel Chang Ramírez one of the players. "I just want to play soccer and advance professionally and economically, which are things I couldn't do in my country" (*Havana Times* 2012). In prerevolutionary Cuba it was always considered a worthy achievement for athletes shine abroad. This was the case for both chess master José Raúl Capablanca and fencer Ramón Font, whose victories were world class and largely achieved abroad. No one would have dared dispute their right to do so. This makes the opposite treatment of Cuban athletes after 1959 that much more glaring, underlining the fact that they are considered state property with their individual rights routinely ignored. Recent reforms under Raúl Castro, however, have hinted that the prohibition against Cuban athletes competing as professionals abroad may soon be lifted (Díaz Moreno 2013).

Basketball

Basketball was first played in Cuba in social and immigrant associations, as was the case with the Asturias Sporting Club (*Deportivo Asturias*). It was also played in the associations of the middle and upper classes, such as the Vedado Tennis Club, the Cubanaleco, the Miramar Yacht Club, and teams at the University of Havana. The basketball clubs grouped together under the so-called "Big Five" played an annual tournament, which was closely followed by the prerevolutionary press. While there were no international achievements during these years, basketball was included as part of the program of secondary and higher education. During his studies at the *Colegio de Belén* in Havana, Fidel Castro was fanatical about basketball and known to practice for hours at a time.

Upon the triumph of the revolution, José Llanusa Gobel was the lead player of the quintet who had previously represented Cuba in the first Pan American Games held in Mexico in 1955. This success allowed the Cuban basketball team to receive sufficient support to continue representing the island in international tournaments even as the prerevolutionary Big Five championships were discontinued. In a continental tournament held in Colombia in the early 1970s, the best Cuban team of all time—led by Jaime Davis, Pedro Chappé, and Miguelito Calderón—was able to defeat the U.S. team. Over the years, however, predictable "desertions" have eroded the level of Cuban basketball in both the men's and women's leagues. More recently, a national team has participated in the professional tournament held in Venezuela but with more grief than glory.

Volleyball

Volleyball was practiced prior to the Revolution, especially on the campuses of religious schools, in some recreation societies, and in a handful of Cuba's municipalities such as Jiguaní, in the east of the country. However, it never achieved mass appeal nor were there national tournaments as with basketball. After 1959, the level of the national team gradually rose, with the women's squad becoming one of the world's best from the 1970s onward. The men's team was also among the world's elite for many years but has struggled to remain competitive after periodically losing its best players to the professional Italian leagues, a situation that has not hurt the women's team. Although major volleyball matches occasionally manage to fill the Coliseum of Havana's *Ciudad Deportiva*, it is not a sport of mass appeal. Instead, it is promoted to field world-class teams of both sexes, a goal that has almost always been achieved. Among the sport's most notable stars are Mercedes "Mamita" Pérez, Alfredo Despaigne, Raúl Diago, and Orlando Samuels, now the coach of the men's national team. Also notable is Eugenio George, the mastermind coach behind the dominant women's national team, repeatedly named coach of the year by the International Federation of Volleyball.

Track and Field

As the oldest organized form of sport, track and field celebrated its first competition in Havana in 1905. Then in 1922, the *Federación Cubana de Atletismo* (Cuban Track and Field Federation) was created. This sport has produced many outstanding Cuban athletes both before and after 1959, including the Pan-American and Olympic champions Rafael Fortún, Enrique Figuerola, Alberto Juantorena, Carmen Trustée, Ana Fidelia Quirot, Zulia Calatayud, Anier García, Dayron Robles, Javier Sotomayor, Iván Pedroso, Yumileidi Cumbá, Maritza Martén, María Caridad Colón, and Osleidys Menéndez.

Fencing

Although fencing was used by Cuban independence war veterans as a weapon of attack and defense, it emerged as a sport between 1867 and 1868, when *La Sala de Armas del Casino Español* opened. In 1922 the Fencing Federation of Cuba was founded, and this same year the Cuban team defeated the U.S. team at the New York Athletic Club in all three categories of competition: foil, épée, and saber. Cuba featured athletes of the stature of Ramón Fonst, who scored victories in Paris against leading fencers at age 16 and was the Olympic champion at the 1900 Paris Games and again in St. Louis four years later. Another outstanding fencing champion was

Manuel Dionisio Díaz, who held the title in 1904 for individual saber. This fame attracted prominent fencers to Cuba in the early years of the century, multiplying the number of associations and auditoriums for practicing the sport.

Jaialai

Known in the first half of the 20th century as *Frontón Jaialay*, which referred to the Basque game of the pointed basket, Havana became one of the sport's strongholds in the Americas. In fact, Cuba's capital once had one of the largest jaialai courts in the world, the well-known *Frontón* on Lucena Street in Centro Habana. This court was later dedicated to other sports leading to its gradual deterioration. There was also another, smaller court, the Havana-Madrid on Belascoaín Street, which was popularly known as *La Bombonera*. Eradicated from Revolutionary Cuba for many years since it encouraged betting, jaialai reemerged in Cuba during the last decade of the 20th century as an elite sport, without betting or mass appeal. It is currently played on a series of courts adjacent to Havana's *Ciudad Deportiva*, built in 1991 expressly for its revival with the support of federations in Spain and Mexico.

Soccer

Despite having recently concluded its 97th national championship, Cuban *fútbol* (soccer) had long gone without recognition or noticeable success abroad. However, in recent years, Cuba has seen an explosion of interest in the sport, which now competes with baseball for aficionados. Many young Cubans follow the European and Latin American leagues closely, along with the exploits of famed stars like Lionel Messi or Cristiano Ronaldo, in part because the radio or television transmission of Major League Baseball is prohibited. Also, many Cubans have recently adopted both Barcelona and the Spanish national soccer teams as their own given those squads' amazing achievements in recent years. Finally, Cuba's national team recently won its first Caribbean Cup defeating Trinidad and Tobago 1–0 in December 2012, indicating the rising skill of Cuban soccer players (Evans 2012).

REFERENCES

Betancourt, Lázaro, and Basilio Fuentes. 2007. *Cuba y el mundo en los años olímpicos, 1924–2004*. Havana: Editorial Científico-Técnica.

Díaz Moreno, Rogelio Manuel. "Cuba Moves Towards Professional Sports," *Havana Times,* August 31, 2013. http://www.havanatimes.org/?p=98464

Evans, Simon. 2012. "Soccer-Cuba Win Their First Caribbean Cup." *Reuters*, December 16.

Havana Times. 2012. "Cuban Soccer Player Says He's No 'Traitor'," November 12.

Pichardo, Hortencia. 1976. *Documentos para la Historia de Cuba*. Volume II. Editorial Ciencias Sociales.

Tembrás Arcia, Rudens. 2012. "El Béisbol es patrimonio nacional de la nación." *Trabajadores*, March 26.

Popular Culture, Customs, and Traditions

Regina Coyula and Fernándo Dámaso

As a manifestation of culture, customs and traditions are rooted in the origins, history, and idiosyncrasies of a particular place and group of people. Cuba's is a "Creole" culture in the sense that it is the result of a unique and distinctive blend of principally Spanish and African elements, with other influences—such as Chinese—present to a lesser degree. This Creole character is also reflected in the fact that Cuban traditions are stamped with a particular local, island air that both connect it to and differentiate it from the customs and traditions of its various original parent cultures. In other words, Cuban popular culture is just as *mestizo* and syncretic as the folk religions, music, and ethnic mixture described previously, and for which the island is rightfully famous. Of course, over time the island's popular traditions have evolved in a dynamic relationship with the economic and political realities of each historical period. Some have been all but wiped out while others have survived by "hiding in plain sight," masking themselves as folklore or taking on politically acceptable façades only to reemerge when conditions allow. This fact demonstrates that the cultural memory of a people constitutes a spontaneous phenomenon that refuses to march to the beat of any particular ideological or political directive, but is rather the organic product of the spiritual life of a nation (Guanche 2011; Iglesia 1983).

The totalitarian nature of the current Cuban government has exercised an overwhelming influence on the cultural life of the nation for more than half a century. Cuba's diverse array of popular local traditions and cultural practices cannot but have been influenced by the often coercive and totalizing nature of the government in power. In many cases, the popular or religious origins of the island's traditions have been manipulated to bring them into line with the inflexible exigencies of the government's all-or-nothing political discourse. For example, while the celebration of Christmas was stigmatized and virtually outlawed for decades, after it was recently permitted, once again the government has insisted on referring to the holiday as a "recess for the anniversary of the Revolution," which was achieved on December 31, 1958. Moreover, the official cultural policy, "Within the Revolution, everything; outside of the Revolution, nothing," has had a powerful impact on the island's rich array of traditional festivities, censoring some and homogenizing others into near meaninglessness. Still other cultural traditions have been promoted through state funding and education. But in most cases, their popular rootedness and organic spontaneity has been diluted or completely eliminated in favor of top-down control and political cheerleading.

ORAL TRADITION

All peoples have a group of oral traditions that are transmitted from generation to generation and as such constitute an important element of their cultural identity. Cuba's national repertory of oral tradition is rich and diverse and includes tales, legends, fables, myths, poetic expressions such as *décimas*, and diverse forms of capturing the country's popular imagination such as omens (*agüeros*), incantations (*ensalmos*), and spells (*conjuros*). Tales come in many varieties such as magical, satirical, or educational; legends can include supernatural apparitions, sacred elements, or historical events; fables can be imparted in verse or in prose and have both Spanish and Sub-Saharan African origins; likewise, myths arise from all of Cuba's many religious traditions including Christianity, *Santería* (such as the *pataki* or histories of each of the *orishas*—deities—in the Yoruba pantheon), Palo Monte, the Abakúa societies, and the traditions of Arará, Gangá, and Vodou. The versatile Spanish poetic tradition of the *décima* continues to be practiced in Cuba—often to the accompaniment of a guitar—and can be used to impart one's feelings or philosophy of life, describe social customs or historic and political events, focus on family life or be full of humor and irony. Finally, omens come in all shapes and sizes including numbers, colors, days of the week, animals, kinds of food, plants, pregnancies, births, marriage, etc.; incantations are used to cure diseases in humans or animals alike; and spells can be cast on people, animals, or elements in the natural world (Armas Rigal 2004).

Throughout the 19th century and at the beginning of the 20th century, gatherings among friends, neighbors, and family members known as *tertulias* were a traditional form of entertainment. At these *tertulias* literary, philosophical, or political discussions often took place and storytelling and the playing various games was common. In rural areas, storytelling often included stories based on superstitions like the belief in ghosts or "spirits of the dead" (specters). Many of these traditions that were passed on orally became part of the local folklore in each provincial town or village. In premodern times before mass literacy and the spread of science, the belief in witchcraft and sorcery was common and often the topic of oral tradition. Even though certain

This beautiful, pure marble statue of Cuba's Patron Saint, Caridad del Cobre (The Virgin of Charity), and the "Three Juans" below her in a small boat, crowns the tomb of the Ricardo Martínez family in the veritable city of the dead, Colón Cemetery, in Havana's Vedado suburb. (Orlando Luis Pardo Lazo)

CARIDAD DEL COBRE, OSHÚN, *LOS TRES JUANES,* AND "PAPA" HEMINGWAY

Located near Cuba's second largest city, Santiago de Cuba, the old mining town of *El Cobre* ("copper") is famous for its simple basilica, which houses the icon of Cuba's patron saint, *Caridad del Cobre* (The Virgin of Charity). For this reason, *El Cobre* is Cuba's most sacred pilgrimage site. Though most Cubans are not practicing Catholics, the fact that *Caridad del Cobre* is associated with the Yoruba orisha *Ochún*—the goddess of both love and motherhood—makes the site doubly significant. Legend has it that in 1606 three fishermen, each one named Juan and each one an allegorical representative of Cuba's three main ethnic cultures, Indian, African, and Spanish, became lost at sea. They were saved when they came upon a wooden icon of the Virgin floating in the Bay of Nipe. As homage, the men carried the statue to the copper mine at *El Cobre.* Ever since, the site has pulled at the hearts and imaginations of Cubans, who continue to visit the basilica with their prayers and offerings. Even Ernest Hemingway, the American writer and longtime Cuba resident, had a devotion to *Cachita* (as the Virgin is nicknamed), leaving his 1954 Nobel prize medallion there as an offering.

---

sectors of the Cuban population continue to believe in these spiritist traditions and invest great time and energy in seeking out and placating supernatural powers or use amulets to guard against the "evil eye," the truth is that oral tradition based on these superstitions has been practically wiped out today. Some of these traditions have fallen out of favor due to the rising level of education of the Cuban population and others have been unable to adjust to the new revolutionary reality or been prohibited or even persecuted by the authorities. Some popular oral traditions have also disappeared as a result of technological advances—such as radio, television, film, and now the Internet—which have gradually displaced them at different times in the island's history (Victori Ramos 1999, 2000).

TRADITIONAL FESTIVALS

In Cuba there have long existed patron saint's days in various towns and cities, rural peasant festivals, major and minor carnivals, *parrandas* (sprees), *charangas* (brass band festivals), and numerous Afro-Cuban festivities. Popular traditional festivals have almost always been associated with the sacred ecclesiastical calendar of the Catholic Church, just as is the case in Spain and much of the rest of Latin America and the Spanish-speaking Caribbean. At the same time, many of the festivals have taken on a secular, profane, and folk or popular character embedding themselves in local culture and lore and becoming creolized and syncretized with other important cultural activities connected to traditional celebrations like carnival, peasant festivals, and Afro-Cuban traditions.

Patron saint's days started in Cuba with the beginning of the Spanish conquest and remained through the colonial period. They always included a procession followed by

A Cuban woman sits next to a statue of the Catholic Saint Lazarus, known in Cuba as San Lázaro, El Viejo *(the old man), or in his Afro-Cuban guise, Babalú-Ayé—the orisha or deity of illness. Dressed in sackcloth and carrying a cane or using crutches,* San Lázaro *is often accompanied by a pack of dogs and is especially venerated in the days leading up to December 17 during the pilgrimage to his national shrine, El Rincón, on the outskirts of Havana. (AP Photo/Franklin Reyes)*

a street fair alternately referred to as a *verbena*, *guateque*, or simply a *feria*, depending on local tradition. Among these celebrations, the most popular today are the Feast Days of Our Lady of Charity (*Caridad del Cobre*, the patron saint of Cuba itself), Saint Lazarus (*San Lázaro*), Our Lady of Candelaria, and Saint John the Baptist.

Many of these festivities became obsolete or went into hiding or hibernation after 1959 during a period of antagonism between the government and the Catholic Church. After the official adoption of atheism in the Cuban Constitution as part of the Marxist ideology which rejects any religious manifestation as "the opiate of the masses," all traditional religious festivities were abolished from Cuban public life and henceforth remained confined exclusively within churches. Thus, celebrations and festivals like Christmas, Holy Week and Easter, religious processions, and any other popular tradition related to religious belief were prohibited and often even persecuted for decades. Members of the Communist Party were expressly forbidden from attending church services or participating in celebrations of a religious nature. They were even prevented from baptizing their children. However, since the early 1990s when the Constitution was changed to make Cuba a "secular" instead of an officially "atheist" state, and especially after Pope John Paul's 1998 visit, the Catholic

EL RINCÓN—THE FEAST DAY OF SAN LÁZARO, AKA, BABALÚ-AYÉ

Cuba's annual celebration of the Feast Day of Saint Lazarus (*San Lázaro*) takes place on December 17 at a sanctuary named in his honor in *El Rincón* near Havana. Leading up to the feast day, tens of thousands of devotees of *San Lázaro*—the patron saint of the infirm and the imprisoned—make a pilgrimage there, some enacting sacrificial rites of penitence as they go in order to "pay" a promise to "*El Viejo*"—as many refer to *San Lázaro*—in return for a miracle cure. The popularity of this feast day is heightened by the fact that *San Lázaro* is syncretized with *Babalú-Ayé*, an Afro-Cuban deity also associated with disease and miraculous cures.

Two different Lazaruses are mentioned in the New Testament. One was the man that Jesus raised from the dead. However, Cubans who flock to *El Rincón* have in mind the "other" Lazarus from the parable about a rich man and a poor, sick man (Lazarus) who begged for scraps at the rich man's door while dogs licked his open wounds. It is he whom Cuban devotees send their prayers to as part of this key ritual ("El culto . . ." 2013; "La leyenda" 2013; Pugliese 2010; "Santuario . . ." 2013).

Church has gradually recovered limited public spaces in which it can celebrate its religious festivities.

Prohibitions against religious practice were not limited to the Catholic faith. Indeed, any expression of Afro-Cuban religiosity that went beyond mere folklore was repressed. In particular, Cuba's many Yoruba-origin *Santería* traditions—which simultaneously included with those of Catholic origin due to their syncretic nature—had to revert to the colonial practice of hiding-in-plain-sight in order to survive. Ironically, the revolution's approach toward these popular traditions of the island's largely marginalized black population was not much different than it had been under Spanish colonialism: they were considered little better than barbarism and criminality, backward and superstitious practices of the uneducated. However, their deep popular rootedness kept them alive within family circles and intimate social networks during these years.

Fortunately, since 1990 many of these African-origin traditions and festivities have reemerged in public spaces as government policy became more tolerant. Depending on the particular branch, tradition, or rite (*regla*) being followed, Cuba's African-derived religious festivities include the *bembé*, *toque de santo*, and *plantes*, among others. These rituals also include many different kinds of musical arrangements, a wide array of chants, and a rich tapestry of dances depending on the particular anniversary being celebrated and the specific *orisha* (deity) being invoked. Apart from the most commonly practiced form of Afro-Cuban ritual tradition known popularly as *Santería* but more properly called *regla de Ochá*, Cuba is also home to the Congo-origin tradition of *Palo Monte*; the unique dances, vestments, and rhythms of the Náñigo (or *diablito*, little devils) of the all-male *Abakuá* secret society; the traditions of *Arará*; and finally various blendings of *Santería* with *Palo Monte* and *Santería* with *Espiritismo*.

LOCAL AND PEASANT FESTIVALS

More than 300 traditional local festivals currently take place in Cuba annually. They typically preserve the main elements of tradition while also constantly incorporating new, more modern innovations. They remain in full force because they have learned to adapt to Cuba's sometimes abrupt social changes. These festivals include *guateques* (fairs), *parrandas*, *charangas*, and *fiestas de bandos* (a kind of tournament). A *guateque* is a traditional rural fair where peasant music is typically played, especially music with a notable Spanish and particularly Canary Islands influence. In past years, these *guateques* also included traditional dances like the *zapateo*, *caringa*, and *sucu-sucu*. Today, this more traditional music and dancing has been transformed by the incorporation of more contemporary elements. These celebrations also feature plenty of traditional foods and beverages, as well as various competitive games (Eli Rodríguez 1997; Ezquenazi Pérez 1999).

One notable attraction is an improvised challenge between two vocalists called a *controversia*. In these competitions, the poets or *versificadores* must compose verses on the spot that fit into the *décima* (a 10-part metric rhyme scheme of Spanish-origin) and are accompanied as they attempt to best each other by the music of an acoustic guitar, the Cuban *tres* guitar, or a *laúd* (lute), usually together with a percussion instrument. This prized talent of improvisation (known as *repentismo*) forms a key part of the musical tradition of Cuban peasants. Also, because of its descriptive, home-spun quality and its often inventive use of a mocking but good-natured humor, it has remained a solid part of Cuban tradition while also influencing various genres of more modern musical improvisation as preformed by the *sonero* (lead singer) in *son* or *salsa* music.

There are also traditional rural festivals with a very local character. Guantánamo gave birth to one of the most traditional forms of *son* music and dance called the *changüí*, a musical form originally present only in that area. Other peasant festivities found today in Cuba's *Oriente* derive from Haiti having been introduced to the island either following the Haitian revolution over 200 years ago or brought in much more recently by the temporary Haitian sugarcane workers who toiled in the harvests during the Republican period. Many Haitian workers put down roots and started families in eastern Cuba contributing their particular culture and characteristics to the region's traditions. For example, Cuba's *Oriente* is home to a number of ritual festivities related to vodou, an African-derived religious practice brought to Cuba from Haiti. However, as practiced in Cuba it has a more folkloric than religious flavor. Still, Cuba's Haitian-origin religious festivities exhibit one of two distinguishable branches: the *Bande-Rará* or the *Loá* festival (Armas Rigal 2002).

In the *fiestas de bandos* or tournaments—which have been long celebrated and are still alive today in a few countryside towns—competing teams are differentiated by wearing red or blue. The main competition involves various kinds of horsemanship, as well as the climbing of a greased pole. Some local festivities are so popular that they bring together the residents of various towns in a single celebration. On the other hand the *bailes de tambor* (drum dances) trace their origins back to the 19th century slave communities. For example, the *yuka* drum festival remains active and the *kinfuiti* drum festival has been revitalized recently in the area around Mariel, today part of Artemisa province.

Parrandas *and* Charangas

Although different from carnival (described later), Cuba's traditional *parrandas* and *charangas* also feature floats, behind which the crowd "rolls" (*arrolla*), dancing to the rhythm of the music as they parade down the street. In each town, these festivals are celebrated as a competition between two rival neighborhoods, each named for an animal that is traditionally associated with their place of origin. For example, during the *parranda* of the city of Sancti Spíritus, rival neighborhoods group together under the names "goats" or "toads," while in the *parranda* of Yaguajay the rival groups are "hawks" and "roosters." Cuba's most popular *parrandas* are those of Remedios in Villa Clara province, in Bejucal near Havana, as well as in Caibarién, Ciego de Ávila, Sancti Spíritus, and Yaguajay, all of which feature shows of fireworks in which rival neighborhoods compete. During these *parrandas*, town residents from rival neighborhoods compete against one another by decorating parts of the town and their elaborate floats, setting off fireworks, dressing in extravagant and colorful costumes, and playing music. The floats are decorated by all residents of the neighborhood from which they come and usually take on themes inspired by literature, film, or some other fictional or mythical story. The very similar and equally popular street celebrations known as *charangas* also originated in Bejucal, where they are still practiced (Santos Gracia 1999).

For the towns that maintain these *parranda* or *charanga* traditions, the entire year leading up to December 24 is spent preparing for these competitive festivals. While they originated with Christianity, any religious connotation has gradually dissipated over time with the festivals remaining as expressions par excellence of local popular culture. Starting at dusk on December 24 and lasting far into the night, these towns let their creativity overflow as residents erect gigantic floats festooned with multicolored lights, beneath a sea of exploding fireworks that rain down all night long as rival neighborhoods do battle. The floats are the most elaborate and anticipated part of these *parrandas*. Made painstakingly by hand by neighborhood residents, these floats are beautiful three-dimensional creations that turn fantasy into reality.

For many years, *parrandas* were spontaneous popular festivals. Even when the town councils and wealthy locals provided economic and logistical support, the organization of the festivities themselves, as well as the construction of the floats, and the decoration of the town square were all completed thanks to popular initiative and enthusiasm. In other words, *parrandas* have always reflected the particular identities of the towns that put them on. However, under the revolution, municipal governments have taken control of the festivals and organize their every detail through their own bureaucratic institutions, often diminishing the splendor and spontaneity of this tradition.

Holguín's Romerías de Mayo *and Cuba's Chinese-Origin Festivals*

Even though many Cuban towns celebrate their own *romería* festivals, Holguín's *Romerías de Mayo* are easily the island's best known and most elaborate. A *romería* is a religious pilgrimage and the word originates out of the tradition of Christian pilgrims traveling to Rome, the political and spiritual seat of the Catholic Church. However, as has been the case with nearly all of Cuba's festivals that have a religious origin, its *romerías* have become a popular and largely secular tradition. Holguín's *Romerías de Mayo* are not an exception with many of the activities having taken on a decidedly political bent. Moreover, while the *Romerías* include many cultural activities such as book presentations and readings, art expos, films festivals, and draws an increasingly international group of "pilgrims" who come to Cuba to participate, the only real pilgrimage or procession that takes place during the festival is an all-but-required group ascent to the crest of the *Loma de la Cruz* (Hill of the Cross) that overlooks the city. As its name implies, the hilltop features a large wooden cross that dates from the 1790s.

Cuba's traditional Chinese festivals are celebrated with a more local Creole character than are other similar festivals in other countries given the fact that the island has seen almost no new Chinese immigrants in the last half-century. This has led to the gradual transformation of Cuba's Chinese-origin customs in comparison with the original ones brought to the island in the second half of the 19th century by Chinese indentured workers. Still, despite the fact that Cuba's Chinese-origin population has declined and their descendants are mainly assimilated *mestizos*, there has been a resurgence in the celebration of traditional Chinese festivals such as the Lunar New Year in recent years. In fact, Havana is home to an extensive Chinatown, complete with numerous Chinese restaurants (some of which actually serve passable Chinese food), a massive Chinese gateway, and a number of remnant Chinese neighborhood associations, even if there are few actual Chinese left residing in the neighborhood. Each year, the district—which includes the obligatory street named *Dragones* (Dragons)—plays host to various street festivals featuring paper dragon parades and people dressed in traditional Chinese outfits. The rescue of some Chinese traditions enjoys official government support motivated in part by an attempt to appeal to tourists and by the deepening political and economic relationship between the Cuban and Chinese governments.

CUBAN CARNIVAL

Carnival is a traditional Cuban festival with roots in similar Spanish festivals that precede Lent, the traditional 40-day period of self-denial and fasting leading up to Easter. In fact, some say that the word carnival originates with the Latin *carne* (flesh or meat) and *vale* (farewell), denoting an over-the-top bacchanal celebration before saying farewell to the flesh for 40 days. Like centuries old Spanish and Italian carnival festivals, the Cuban tradition includes masking, floats, *comparsas* (krewes), and parades. As in much of the rest of the world, Havana's carnival was long celebrated during the last three days—a Sunday, Monday, and Tuesday (known as "Fat Tuesday" or *Mardi Gras* in Louisiana)—prior the start of Lent, which always begins on Ash Wednesday according to the ecclesiastical calendar. However, since the onset of the Cuban Revolution, Havana's carnival celebration has been moved to the late summer months to coincide with the July 26th political holiday and August vacations. Likewise carnival celebrations in the central and eastern provinces—and especially in the island's second city, Santiago de Cuba—take place at other times usually linked to each town's own patron saint's day. For example, Santiago has long held its carnival during the week leading up to July 25, the Feast of Saint James (himself also known as Santiago). This was the reason that Fidel Castro chose the following morning to attack the city's Moncada military barracks in 1953 giving birth to the name of his revolutionary group, the July 26th Movement.

Although carnival was celebrated during the colonial period, it was not until the Republican era that it became a mass phenomenon and was transformed into an extravagant spectacle. For example, during these years Havana's carnival featured a beauty pageant, which crowned one of its young participants as "carnival queen" (*estrella*) along with six others as her "ladies in waiting" (*luceros*). On each successive night of carnival they rode supreme atop the head float of the city's parade, amid firework displays and dance, music, and costume competitions among the carnival krewes that represented the city's various neighborhoods. The beauty pageant eventually disappeared from carnival by the late 1970s now officially considered a retrograde bourgeois tradition that degraded women. Today, Cuba's carnival celebrations are characterized by their joyful music based on a strong foundation of drumming (usually the *conga* or *tumbadora* drum) and piercing horns (the bugle or *corneta china*). Usually including large numbers of participants organized into various krewes and even greater masses of spectators, carnival is the most spectacular festival among Cuba's popular cultural traditions.

Havana's Carnival

Even though carnival is celebrated in all of the island's provinces, the most popular and famous annual celebrations take place in the country's two major cities, Havana and Santiago de Cuba. Havana's carnival has its roots in the Catholic celebrations held during the Feast of Corpus Christi on Maundy Thursday during Holy Week and the Epiphany on January 6 (*Día de los Reyes*, or Three Kings Day). *Día de los Reyes* was the single annual occasion when black slaves were allowed a day of freedom to organize collective marches during which they would repeat the chants and dances of their native lands. The dates of Havana's carnival have changed over time and many years ago the festival began to lose its religious character gradually becoming a popular festival instead.

After 1959, Havana carnival began to take on a decidedly political aura. The location of the celebration migrated from its traditional headquarters on the famed *Paseo del Prado* between *Centro Habana* and *Habana Vieja*, to a section of the seaside Malecón close to the start of *La Rampa*, where it is held today. Still, the tradition of organizing neighborhood *comparsas* or krewes holds strong. These are huge organized throngs of competing dancers that enact intricate choreographed sequences to the beat of a group of conga drums and the whistled signals of the lead choreographer. Havana's most traditional and famous *comparsas* are *Los Guaracheros de Regla*, *Los Marqueses de Atarés*, *El Alacrán*, and *Las Bolleras*. They hail from the city's different neighborhoods and continue a fierce and long-lasting rivalry to present the most eye-catching, complex, and organized dance spectacle during carnival.

Havana's carnival also features a tradition of huge, phantasmagoric dolls known as "Muñecones," which are costumed revelers on stilts wearing exaggerated and often grotesque masks that call to mind a diverse array of characters. Acrobats are also seen parading with the *comparsas*, carrying large multicolored pinwheels with they keep continually spinning in both hands. As opposed to Santiago's more participatory carnival, Havana's festival follows the tradition of separating the mostly passive audience from the floats and *comparsas* by setting up bleachers for them along the parade route. Still, recently an area adjacent to the parade has developed with food and beverage stands, as well as a large open-air dance floor with a DJ and occasional live music. One traditional part of Havana's carnival to have disappeared under the Revolution is the parade of convertible cars, trucks, and acrobatic police motorcycles that joined the parades interspersed with the more traditional *comparsas*.

Santiago's Carnival

Most of the traditions associated with the carnival of Santiago de Cuba originate in either the *tumba francesa* brought to the island by Haitian immigrants or the African *cabildos de nación* that once brought together African slaves with similar ethnic origins. Santiago's carnival is renowned for the power and intensity of its music and for the massive collective participation of residents of the city's many historic if humble neighborhoods. Another distinctive element are the massive, communal dances known as *Congas*, where there is almost no separation between the parading *comparsa* group and the thousands of neighborhood spectators. Instead, as the band of drummers snakes its way through the city's neighborhoods, they are joined in the street by thousands of dancers who all "*arrollar*" (roll) their way forward. In this particular *Conga* dance, the public seductively gyrates their hips and shoulders,

---

THE *CONGA* TRADITION IN THE BARRIOS OF SANTIAGO DE CUBA

Santiago de Cuba's *Conga* tradition dates back well over 200 years. The parades originate in the city's six popular *barrios* that can boast their own *comparsa* group: Los Hoyos, Paso Franco, Guayabito, San Agustín, San Pedrito, and Alto Pino. Each of these bands make "visitations" to the others' home turf to do musical battle during the month preceding the culmination of Carnival on July 25. The biggest of these parades—which is known to attract between 15,000 and 20,000 singing, dancing revelers—is known as the "Invasion" and is led by the most fearsome of these bands, *La Conga de Los Hoyos*.

This unique element of Santiago's carnival tradition is a complex manifestation of popular Afro-Cuban culture that incorporates a group of perhaps 20 *Conga* drummers, the piercing sound of the *corneta china* (bugle) that serves as the melodic voice of the surging band, and various other percussive instruments like claves and cow bells. Together with this are the many creative improvisational vocalists who invent catchy and often risqué or politically provocative chants that are then repeated by the massive chorus of revelers who surround the drummers as they make their way across the city (Blue Throat Productions 2012).

while simultaneously sliding their feet forward to the rhythm of the drums, metal percussion, and the distinctive *corneta china* (bugle), without ever raising them off the ground. Incidentally, though this sweaty mass phenomenon inspired the much more buttoned-up "conga line" found in many a wedding reception in the United States, it bears almost no resemblance to it. Instead, its closest cousin stateside is New Orleans' famed neighborhood tradition of the brass band "second line" parade—a veritable movable feast!

REFERENCES

Armas Rigal, Nieves. 2002. *Danzas populares tradicionales cubanas.* Havana: Centro Juan Marinello.

Armas Rigal, Nieves. 2004. *Los agüeros cubanos: Entre señales y vaticinios.* Havana: Centro Juan Marinello.

Blue Throat Productions. 2012. "Conga Series." http://www.bluethroatproductions.com/video/conga-series/.

De la Iglesia, Álvaro. 1983. *Tradiciones completas.* Havana: Editorial Letras Cubanas.

"El culto a San Lázaro." 2013. Lecturas, CiberCuba.com. Accessed on January 3. http://lecturas.cibercuba.com/lecturas/cultura/el_culto_a_san_lazaro.html.

Eli Rodríguez, Victoria. 1997. *Instrumentos de la música folclórico-popular de Cuba.* Havana: Editorial de Ciencias Sociales.

Ezquenazi Pérez, Marta. 1999. "Música popular tradicional." *Cultura popular tradicional cubana.* Havana: Editorial de Ciencias Sociales.

Guanche, Jesús. 2011. *Cultura popular tradicional cubana.* Havana: Editorial Adagio.

"La leyenda." 2013. The Rincón de San Lázaro Church. Catholic Church in America. Accessed on January 3. http://www.rincondesanlazaro.org/leyenda.php.

Pugliese, Alanna. 2010. "The Inaccurate Saint: Devotion to San Lázaro/Babalú Ayé in Cuban Culture in Miami, Florida," Goizueta Foundation Undergraduate Fellowship, September 3. http://www.library.miami.edu/chc/fellowships/2010/pdf/pugliesereport.pdf.

Santos Gracia, Caridad. 1999. "Danzas y bailes populares tradicionales," in *Cultura popular tradicional cubana.* Havana: Editorial de Ciencias Sociales.

"Santuario de San Lázaro. El Rincón." 2013. D'Cubanos—Cubanos en Mexico. Accessed on January 3. http://www.dcubanos.com/rinconcuba/santuario-de-san-lazaro-el-rincon.

Victori Ramos, María del Carmen. 1999. "Tradiciones orales," in *Cultura popular tradicional cubana.* Havana: Editorial de Ciencias Sociales.

Victori Ramos, María del Carmen. 2000. *Cuba, expresión literaria oral y actualidad.* Havana: Centro Juan Marinello.

CHAPTER 7

Contemporary Issues

Raúl Castro's Reforms: Two Steps Forward, One Step Back

Dimas Castellanos

Now more than five decades after taking power through armed revolution in 1959, the factors that made totalitarianism in Cuba possible have reached their limit. The populist measures imposed during the early 1960s—such as the literacy campaign and the urban and agrarian reforms—were accompanied by the rapid dismantling of civil society and a process of state takeover of the economy. This began in 1960 with foreign-owned companies and culminated in 1968 with the confiscation of the last 56,000 small service–related and manufacturing businesses in the so-called Revolutionary Offensive. Furthermore, the efforts to subordinate individual interests and autonomous groups of civil society to those of the state has led to disaster. The confluence of the breakdown of the current economic and political model, national stagnation, citizen discontent, external isolation, and the absence of viable alternatives have made conditions ripe for change.

On the one hand this has led to despair, apathy, endemic corruption, and mass exodus, while on the other hand there has been an emergence of new social, cultural, political, and economic factors. In this context, a sudden and unexpected provisional transfer of power took place from Fidel to Raúl Castro in August 2006. The fact that this transfer was carried out by the same forces that led the country into crisis in the first place meant that the order, depth, and pace of change were determined from within the power structure itself, explaining the effort to change the appearance and efficiency of the system while preserving its fundamentally totalitarian character. Only time will tell if Raúl's reforms amount to "change we can believe in" or little more than rearranging the chairs on the deck of the sinking ship of state. However, it is our contention that this unresolvable contradiction has doomed the government's reforms from the start. This still unfolding process has now gone through three phases under the leadership of President Raúl Castro.

PHASE ONE

On July 31, 2006, as the result of a serious, life-threatening intestinal illness, Fidel Castro—the historic "Maximum Leader" of the Cuban Revolution, first secretary of the Cuban Communist Party (PCC), president of the Council of State and Council of Ministers, and commander-in-chief of the Armed Forces—temporarily delegated his multiple responsibilities to seven party and government leaders. His younger brother Raúl Castro was named first secretary of the PCC, commander-in-chief of the military, and president of the Council of State. José Ramón Balaguer was tapped to head Cuba's renowned health system. Ramón Machado and Esteban Lazo were named as heads of the national and international education program, respectively, and Carlos Lage became the driving force behind the so-called *revolución energética*, a national energy saving program. Additionally, the funding directed to the national programs for health, education, and energy were to be controlled respectively by Carlos Lage, Francisco Soberón (president of Cuba's Central Bank), and Foreign Minister Felipe Pérez Roque. These appointments marked the beginning of Raúl's administration.

Within the first year of being named provisional president, Raúl made a number of speeches and declarations that forcefully called for "the need to introduce structural and conceptual changes." He also repeatedly mentioned his willingness to normalize relations with the United States—statements that raised many people's hopes and expectations. For example, in August 2006 he said, "We have always been ready to normalize relations with the United States on an equal footing." Then, on December 2 of that same year he reiterated, "We are willing to resolve the dispute at the negotiating table on the basis of independence, equality, reciprocity, non-interference, and respect." These statements show an awareness among at least a sector of the Party elite of the two major challenges faced by the country: the need for internal reforms and the resolution of disputes abroad. Furthermore, without directly pointing a finger at his predecessor, Raúl began to quietly dismantle politically provocative but nonproductive activities, including constant massive protest marches, interminable speeches, weekend deployment of voluntary laborers, and other politically motivated actions associated with Fidel's quixotic "Battle of Ideas." He also began to level strong criticisms at the country's notoriously inefficient agricultural industry.

In this same vein, on July 11, 2007 at the closing session of the National Assembly NA, it was suggested that "each province have its own builders, its own teachers, and its own police." There was criticism of the bloated state-sector labor force and of the related practice of artificially reducing unemployment to almost zero by over-hiring workers in order to demonstrate the supposed superiority of the Cuban system. Retired teachers and professors were called on to return to the classroom to replace the inadequate novice teacher program put in place by Fidel. It was also announced that unnecessary free services and excessive subsidies would be eliminated. Finally, there was a move to increase the amount of land under cultivation, which had precipitously dropped by 33 percent between 1998 and 2007. Later that same month, Raúl emphasized the vital importance of manufacturing products in Cuba to substitute those purchased abroad and acknowledged the fact that huge tracts of land have been overrun by the thorny and nearly ineradicable *marabú* weed, making idle land difficult to bring under production.

Subsequently, after being named president in spring 2008, Raúl began to eliminate what he referred to as "ridiculous prohibitions," allowing for the sale of computers, DVD-players, mobile phones, and other consumer electronics to the general public. He also allowed Cubans to stay in hotels once reserved for tourists and to rent cars in hard currency. The licensing of private food vendors was expanded as free worker cafeterias were shuttered. Former state-employed taxi drivers, barbers, and beauticians were transformed into free private agents, now allowed to rent out their former autos and places of business from the state and keep any earnings for themselves as profit. Regulations on the construction and repair of homes were relaxed and the sale of fruits and vegetables along the highways was allowed.

While significant, most of these pro-market reforms simply recognized and legalized practices that workers had long engaged in informally. Still, the most striking change was Decree-Law 259, which allowed for the greatly expanded leasing of idle land. Unfortunately, like many of Raúl's tentative reforms, this symbolically significant measure was insufficient and contradictory. While it acknowledged that food production was an issue of national security and recognized the state's demonstrated inability to produce it, the law left this land under exclusive state ownership, undercutting production incentives for farmers who were now legally transformed into little more than state-dependent share-croppers.

PHASE TWO

As a result of Fidel's deteriorating health, a "Message from the Commander-in-Chief" was published on February 19, 2008, in which he permanently gave up his numerous governmental positions. Five days later, on February 24, the NAPP elected Raúl Castro president of the Council of State, marking the start of the second phase of his administration and giving rise to a contradictory period of conjecture, hope, and raised expectations. Cubans thought they knew Raúl, but did they really? What could they expect from this circumspect military manager, so different in style from his elder brother? Would he be different in substance as well?

The fragmentation of power that had followed in the wake of Fidel Castro's July 2006 decree ended with Raúl's constitutional ascension to power. Soon thereafter both Carlos Lage and Felipe Pérez Roque—once favorites and close confidants of Fidel—were removed from their posts and kicked out of the PCC. They were then publicly condemned to ignominy for having been overly ambitious and enticed by "the honey of power." At the same time, others within the Party and especially the military were elevated to new positions of authority, including Machado Ventura, who became second secretary of the PCC and vice president of the Council of State, and Esteban Lazo, who kept his position as member of the Politburo.

This second phase began with the introduction of a series of measures that could be classified as a basic reform plan. It was limited to certain sectors of the economy and its goals could be outlined as follows:

1) to achieve a strong and efficient agricultural sector capable of feeding the population and reducing dependence on imported foods,
2) to make people aware of the need to work in order to live,
3) to firmly reject illegalities and other forms of corruption,
4) to reduce the state payrolls, which had ballooned to over a million excess workers, and
5) to jump start self-employment.

Along these same lines, during the second half of 2011 various decrees and resolutions were issued authorizing the private sale of automobiles; the buying, selling, exchange, and donation of private homes; a relaxation in rules governing home rentals; and the free sale of private agricultural products in the tourism industry. An initial effort was also made to provide credit to self-employed workers and small farmers, and past restrictions on migration to Havana from the countryside were relaxed.

Among other factors, this basic program of reform was limited by a peculiar kind of power-sharing arrangement where Cuba's new leader, Raúl Castro, publicly requested permission from the NAPP to consult with Fidel on major decisions. Furthermore, Fidel continued to participate in policy debates by periodically providing indirect criticism primarily focused on international issues through his published reflections and occasional public statements. The most critical point in this duality came in mid-2010 when Fidel made a series of unannounced public appearances. On July 11 he showed up at the National Center for Scientific Research and two days later he appeared at the Center for World Economic Research, where he ordered an urgent investigation into the nature of global power in the post–Cold War era. Then on July 15, he was seen at the National Aquarium, followed by an appearance the next day at the Ministry of Foreign Affairs, where he met with Cuba's overseas ambassadors. On July 25, the eve of the anniversary of the assault on the Moncada Barracks, he appeared in Artemisa dressed in military fatigues. On the following day, Cuba's most important revolutionary holiday, he celebrated the occasion with artists, intellectuals, members of Pastors for Peace, and other invited guests.

On August 7, at a special session of the NAPP, Fidel appeared once again to express his concerns about an eminent nuclear war and relations with the United States. In his impromptu address, he asserted that the world would be saved only if it accepted the logical arguments he was espousing. Referring to U.S. president Barack Obama, he said, "Perhaps he will not give the order if we can persuade him." Just prior to these querulous misadventures, Raúl Castro made the unprecedented announcement of the expansion of self-employment together with a drastic reduction in the state labor force. Then, without warning on August 13—Fidel's 84th birthday—six political prisoners were released, perhaps indicating internal contradictions within the government. What is significant about this second phase of Raúl Castro's administration is that the tentative but deepening economic reform measures, which were introduced in an unfavorable national and international economic context and which no country could sustain indefinitely, made it impossible to return to the stagnation of the past. Thus, the only solution—whether intended or not—was to continue moving forward with more reforms.

Finally, on September 8, 2010, the American journalist Jeffrey Goldberg posted details on his blog from a series of interviews he had done with Fidel Castro in late August, when Cuba's aging but newly active and vocal former leader invited him down to Havana to discuss a recent article Goldberg had written about Iran and Israel in *Atlantic* magazine. During a break in one of their marathon conversations about the Middle East, Goldberg wondered aloud whether Castro believed that the "Cuban model" was still something worth exporting to other countries as he had advocated in the past. Stunningly, the elder statesman responded with the quip, "The Cuban model doesn't even work for us anymore" (Goldberg 2010). As if an oracle, this statement preceded by only a few days the official announcement of the projected laying off of hundreds-of-thousands of state workers coupled with a major expansion of self-employment.

PHASE THREE

In November 2010, the PCC announced that the long-delayed Sixth Party Congress would be held in April 2011, publishing a lengthy set of "*Lineamientos*," a draft version of the Congress' "Economic and Social Policy Guidelines" to be reviewed and debated among the population in the months leading up to the April gathering. Both the gathering itself and the subsequent First National Party Conference in January 2012 would be defining events for Cuba's future. In his own report to the NAPP in December 2010, Raúl argued that self-employment (*trabajo por cuenta propia*) should become a "facilitating factor for the construction of socialism in Cuba." What he meant was that an expansion of the non-state, micro-enterprise sector—now with the ability to hire employees for the first time—could simultaneously increase the supply of goods and services to the public and provide them with greater employment opportunities, while also allowing the state to rid itself of the burden of directing activities with little strategic importance and concentrate on increasing efficiency and productivity in more economically fundamental areas. In order to do this, Raúl reasoned, "the party and government must first facilitate this form of work." However, he also called for a change in mentality saying that Party members must "not generate stigmas or prejudices against private entrepreneurs, much less demonize them. And for this," he concluded, "it is fundamental to change the negative views that more than a few of us hold toward this form of private work" (Peters 2010).

At the closing session of the Congress itself in April 2011, President Raúl Castro announced that the "updating" of the current economic model would take place gradually over the course of the next five years (2011–2016), scaling back his original, more ambitious pace of reform. He also acknowledged that, in spite of Decree-Law 259, there were still many thousands of undistributed hectares of idle land. He continued to call on the PCC to change its mentality and free itself from old dogmas and obsolete ways of thinking. At the same time, he made clear that he understood that his primary mission as president—and purpose in what remained of his life—was to defend, preserve, and continue to "perfect" socialism.

The outlines of a basic reform plan approved by acclamation at the Party conclave were codified in an updated version of the *Lineamientos* document. However, the new impetus to expand the "non-state sector" (the "private sector" was never mentioned) was constrained by the continued primacy of socialist system of central planning which sees state-run enterprises as the primary driving force of the economy. In fact, just a few days after the Party Congress had agreed to build a firewall between its political and administrative wings in each of its 15 provincial branches starting between May and July 2011, First Vice President Machado Ventura insisted publicly that "The party does not administer. That's fine, but it cannot lose control over its activists, no matter what positions they may occupy." He also demanded: "We have to know beforehand what each producer will plant and what he will harvest." Such statements were clearly intended to send the message that the economy would remain under the control of the Party over and above the interests of workers and farmers themselves, despite Raúl's insistence that the Party's mentality had to change.

Also, while recognizing the need to decentralize the decision-making process, separate the functions of Party from those of the State, and expand self-employment, the Congress refused to address the need for the rotation of political power. Raúl's reforms, however significant they may be relative to the past, have been limited to economic concerns, with the continued insistence that "only socialism can overcome the difficulties and preserve the gains of the Revolution." The Congress also failed to recognize the right of Cuban citizens to own and create small- and medium-sized enterprises, while simultaneously promoting foreign investment and the creation of joint ventures with foreign companies. These limitations transform the *Lineamientos* into an ambitious wish list and turn the reform process into little more than a PR campaign.

Still, these limitations do not completely annul the importance of the reform process. The recognition by the authorities of the need for changes and the introduction of measures that break quite dramatically with the rigidity and stagnation of the past are themselves provoking new contradictions in both the national and international context making a return to the past all but impossible. The crux of the problem lies in the fact that the rapid deterioration of the quality life, increasing despair, and a growing awareness that a change must come are moving much faster than the timid reforms themselves. Faced with this reality, there are two alternatives: Either the reforms are accelerated or the country approaches a chaotic and potentially violent solution, which has been regrettably all too common in Cuban history.

RESULTS OF THE THREE PHASES

By limiting the Sixth Party Congress to the economy, it was hoped that the Party Conference nine months later in January 2012 would focus on other basic issues given that the structural nature of Cuba's crisis calls for a comprehensive approach. However, the guiding plan for the Conference continued to ignore crucial problems. Limitations on the most basic political rights and civil liberties were left intact precisely at a time when the success of the reform package depends on the expansion of freedoms that would allow fuller citizen participation and provoke greater interest in the outcome of productive and intellectual activities. Beyond a declaration that top government officials would henceforth be limited to two terms of five years, there was not even a discussion of possible political or civil changes. Despite Raúl Castro's protestations to the contrary, this fundamental timidity reveals the incapacity of the Party to break with the orthodox ideologies of the past and undertake the necessary changes demanded by Cuba's current crisis.

A brief summary of the results of the main goals pursued in the five years since Raúl Castro became Cuba's president in 2008 follows. First, in spite of efforts to achieve *a strong and efficient agricultural sector capable of providing Cubans with enough to eat*, agricultural production fell by 4.2 percent in 2010. The cost of food imports rose from $1.5 billion in 2010 to $1.7 billion in 2011. The production of a wide variety of agricultural goods remains well below the levels reached more than 20 years ago in 1990 (ONE 2012).

Second, the goal of *making people realize that they need to work in order to live*—an issue closely associated with Cuba's bourgeoning black market, *illegalities, and other forms of corruption*—has gone nowhere. Instead, criminal activities have only increased as evidenced by the growing number of investigations and court cases that are ongoing (Rainsford 2012). In fact, along with economic inefficiency, corruption has now become a threat to national security. The government's response has been limited to stepping up repression, vigilance, and control. Ignoring the root causes of economic crime has made effectively addressing it impossible. In recent years, even the official state media—especially the newspaper *Juventud Rebelde*—has occasionally

---

THE LAND SHOULD BELONG TO THOSE WHO WORK IT—SOMEDAY, MAYBE . . .

The results of Decree-Law 259 aimed at distributing idle state land to peasants have been disappointing. There is still a lack of full freedom for private farmers to produce and sell their products on the open market. The state maintains its long-held *acopio* system, a monopoly on the purchase of these products at prices and conditions officially imposed. There is an unreasonably short usufruct period of just 10 years (though this can be renewed). An initial prohibition against building housing or other facilities on the granted land was thankfully rescinded. Finally, there continued to be a chronic lack of necessary supplies and farm implements with which to bring the long-idle and *marabú*-laden land under cultivation.

Moreover, the government—which has shown itself unable to produce successfully on its large state farms—has retained ownership rights to the land, while peasants who have enjoyed success in producing have had to settle for short-term usufruct rights only. While some of these obstacles were removed during 2012—allowing for inheritance rights, freer direct sales, and housing construction on farmland—the expected windfall in food production that would result from the distribution of more than a million hectares of idle land to private farmers has yet to materialize.

reported on the chronic price fixing, diversion of resources, theft, and robbery carried out daily by thousands and thousands of Cubans, including scandalous cases of high-ranking officials from state agencies who are now being tried in court. Nevertheless, the problem persists.

Third, the twin goals of *shrinking the state's bloated labor force and jump-starting microenterprise through an expansion of self-employment* have been partially achieved. However, they are moving forward much more slowly than initially projected due to the limitations that continue to block the full development of Cuba's entrepreneurial potential, preventing the non-state sector from absorbing the projected number of laid-off state workers. The project to reduce state payrolls, originally designed to move between 1.3 and 1.8 million state workers to the non-state sector, has not been met. It is estimated that 140,000 jobs were eliminated in 2011, while another 270,000 were originally slated for elimination in 2012. However, given the stagnation in the expansion of self-employment this goal was not achieved. This means that the layoffs in the past two years only amounted to about half of the original goal of 500,000 that had been set for April 2011. In fact, in the spring of 2012 the government recalibrated its targeted date, now setting the half-million layoffs goal for 2015.

Moreover, the government continues to limit self-employment to just 187 occupations—mainly subsistence-oriented, service sector jobs with little economic significance—and has refused to open the non-state sector up to professionals who wish to go into private practice. There is also a heavy tax burden that illogically penalizes those who hire more than five employees. And, although some efforts have been made to begin to provide credit to microentrepreneurs, a wholesale market for supplies at reasonable prices has yet to materialize. This explains why 68.3 percent of the licenses issued so far were given to those previously unemployed with another 15 percent going to retirees (Piñeiro-Harnecker 2012). Which is to say that of the almost 336,000 currently self-employed workers as of August 2013, more than 300,000 are people who were either already unemployed or retired, meaning that most came from the already existing informal economy, not from the state sector as intended. Thus, besides being unconstitutional—the constitution continues to stipulate that private entrepreneurs cannot profit from employing other workers—less than 20 percent of Cuba's newly self-employed workers were those laid-off from the state sector since fall 2010 (ibid.). All this explains the reason for the slowdown in the necessary overhaul of Cuba's labor market, extending to five years the reorganization that had initially been projected to take just three. In turn, this delay will make it impossible to increase productivity and raise wages in the state sector, which will prevent any significant increase in efficiency in the short term.

Fourth, Raúl's apparent initial willingness to *normalize relations with the United States* has not produced any substantial improvement in the U.S.-Cuba bilateral relationship. In his first term, President Barack Obama put in place a series of positive measures such as allowing unlimited travel by Cuban-Americans; the expansion of people-to-people visits to the island by academic, religious, and cultural groups; the routine granting of visas to most Cuban academics, musicians, and athletes; and the increased limit for remittances to $500 per quarter. These temporarily succeeded in reducing the level of confrontation and put the ball in Cuba's court. Cuba's response has been to insist on linking further, deeper economic and civic reforms to the resolution of the dispute with the United States and to unjustifiably bait the Cuban people with fear and paranoia of a new U.S. invasion always just on the horizon. For example, the planning document for the January 2012 Party Conference highlighted the external threat posed by the United States and called on all citizens to "continue giving full attention to preparations for the defense of the country."

The year 2011 concluded with a series of positive measures that were unfortunately laden with too many regulations, restrictions, and caveats to allow them to have any more than a marginal impact on the country's economy. For example, in September 2011 the long-awaited allowance of the sale of cars and private homes was decreed. Private farmers were also allowed to market their products more freely and establish sales contracts directly with tourism entities through agricultural cooperatives. Modifications in Cuba's banking regulations were made to allow them to offer credit and other banking services to the private sector for the first time. Finally, private entrepreneurs could now rent out space to and from state entities to facilitate business and—following the successful test cases of taxi drivers, barbers, and hair dressers—a number of new formerly state-controlled occupations such as carpenters, watchmakers, and a variety of repairmen, among others, were allowed to become free agents now leasing their stores and equipment from the state and legally pocketing any profits. Despite being a step in the right direction of greater enterprise freedom, the new measures apply mostly to small-scale services and subsistence occupations. They provide temporary respite for many but cannot pull the country out of its severe economic crisis.

In 2012 another series of positive measures was put into place including an income tax exemption through 2012 for businesses with up to five employees, an increase to 10,000 pesos as the amount of personal income for which no tax had to be paid, and a 5 percent credit for those who file their income tax returns early. In October, a momentous new migration reform law was finally published that would eliminate the hated exit permit and costly letter of invitation. It will also increase from 11 to 24 months the Cubans' ability to remain abroad without losing their residency rights. Since this measure only went into effect in mid-January 2013, it remains to be seen how it will impact the economy. However, it is bound to transform the traditional "escape hatch" of emigration into more of a "revolving door" of transnationalism.

December 2012 saw the publication of a new law allowing nonagricultural cooperatives for the first time and the issuance of a new tax law that could potentially lighten the tax burden on private sector. It is still too early to determine how these measures will be implemented, but initial pilot projects in more than 200 converted or newly created non-agricultural coops began operation in the summer of 2013. However, despite the appeal of these measures, they fail to address the essence of the country's crisis, which is the rigid adherence to an obsolete economic system and the continued lack of the most basic political rights and civil liberties. While Raúl's more pragmatic approach to the economy is a welcome respite from his brother's nonstop ideological campaigns and anticapitalist harangues, his reform package—like that implemented grudgingly by Fidel in the first half of the 1990s—seems aimed more at protecting the powerful and maintaining top-down control than at addressing the country's problems "for all and for the good of all," in the words of Cuban patriot José Martí.

THE REAL CAUSES

Cuba faces a profound structural crisis, which requires changes that are also truly structural in nature. The partial reforms enacted under President Raúl Castro have only revealed the urgent need to deepen and extend changes to include private and other forms of property, the formation of small- and medium-sized businesses, and the establishment of the rigorous rule of law where the rights and freedoms of all citizens are inviolable and not subject to a political or ideological litmus test. The goal of trying to preserve the failed socialist system of central planning as the principal route of economic development and the refusal to accept the need for diverse forms of ownership to play their proper roles in economic growth mean that the economy—the foundation for any takeoff—remains beholden to party and ideological interests, while citizen participation is absent. The failure of the totalitarian model has forced the Cuban government to adopt the very reforms that the Cuban people have introduced on their own at the fringes of the law in order to ensure their own survival. "Updating the model," as Raúl likes to euphemistically call his series of reforms, has been more an acknowledgement of the existing unworkable reality than the proactive introduction of an integral plan of economic growth born of a real desire for systemic change.

The uninspiring outcome of the First PCC Conference in January 2012 definitively revealed the current system to be unviable and incapable of reforming itself from the inside-out and the top-down. Its leaders have failed again and again to rise to the challenge of breaking with their ideological chains of the past that prevent the country from moving forward. But—to paraphrase Karl Marx—they have more to lose than their chains; they also fear losing their comfortable positions of power and influence. Their refusal to recognize a greater degree of civil liberties and political rights for the people has closed off the possibility of any real change. The long delay in announcing the migration reforms; their continued foot dragging in granting truly open access to the Internet and allowing the general public to benefit from the newly laid fiber optic cable from Venezuela; and their refusal to ratify into Cuban law the rights and freedoms outlined in the Universal Declaration of Human Rights, the Convention on Civil and Political Rights, and the Convention on Economic, Social, and Cultural Rights that the Cuban government pledged to support at the United Nations in 2008 are the principal causes for the current national catastrophe.

Time is running out. The fact that the government talks of moving forward slowly, steadily, and deliberately, *"sin prisa, pero sin pausa"* (without haste but without pause), only confirms the decision not to change anything that might threaten its grip on power. It may have once held all the power, but time is on the side of the people who are beginning to organize to assert their collective power. Despite the continued adverse conditions at the start of 2013, it should be emphasized that there is an increasing national consciousness in favor of change, with steady advances in both the hearts and minds of the people. This precludes any attempt to turn back the clock on the reforms already implemented, as has happened so many times before. There is a growing consensus both within the island and abroad for change, shared even among many within the current government despite the efforts of hardline elements to hinder the advance of reforms. This will facilitate further progress not just in the so-called economic "updating," but on the social and political front as well.

The Cuban government faces an insoluble contradiction: the incompatibility of the reforms with the conservation of the island's current economic and political system. From the kickoff of the reforms in July 2008 with Decree-Law 259 on the distribution of idle state land, to the September 2010 announcement of an overhaul in the self-employment legislation, to the November 2011 laws that permitted the sale of private homes and cars, to the Decree-Law 302 reforming Cuba's draconian migration regulations that took effect on January 14, 2013, to the extremely limited and costly Internet access points made available in June 2013, all legal changes enacted to date have been characterized by internal limitations, a lack of dynamism, and the inability to completely relinquish power and control over the Cuban people.

This significant series of still insufficient reforms has generated two tendencies within the regime: those who refuse to change anything and those who want to change some things. They both agree on saving the current system, but differ in the best way to achieve that goal. Raúl Castro, president of the Council of State for the five years since February 2008, and presumably his newly elected first vice president, the 53-year-old Miguel Díaz-Canel, lead the charge of those within the government in favor of changes. While both tendencies have supporters among the Cuban people, there is a growing third group who are convinced that the current system is impossible to reform or save. These people feel an urgency to change the system entirely instead of making piecemeal changes. This dilemma reveals the latent danger lurking behind the decidedly slow speed of the reforms.

From within the halls of power, it is impossible to enact reforms because the current government's main objective is to conserve its own power. Thus, Cuba's leaders find themselves trapped in a dilemma: They have to make changes because there is a growing social pressure for reform after so much talk of "updating the model."

Cuba's new vice president Miguel Díaz-Canel Bermúdez, right, listens to Cuba's president Raúl Castro during the closing session at the National Assembly in Havana, Cuba, February 24, 2013. Castro accepted a new five-year term that will be, he said, his last as Cuba's president and tapped rising star Díaz-Canel, 53, as vice president and first in the line of succession. (AP Photo/Ramon Espinosa)

If they move too slowly, the Cuban economy could completely collapse—especially now that Cuba's lifeline to Venezuela is in serious jeopardy with the death of Hugo Chávez. However, moving too fast could undermine their power base and the momentum of change could sweep them away. A good example of this dilemma was the recent appointment of the 53-year-old Miguel Díaz-Canel Bermúdez as Cuba's first vice president along with the announcement that henceforth top political officials, such as President Raúl Castro, would be limited to just two terms of five years in office. Despite Díaz-Canel's relative youthfulness, he was not elected democratically but tapped bureaucratically from within the existing power structure. Likewise, the imposition of term limits came only after Raúl Castro had already begun his second five-year term as president, following literally a lifetime of occupying the second most powerful political and military post in the country.

REFERENCES

Goldberg, Jeffrey. 2010. "Fidel: 'Cuban Model Doesn't Even Work For Us Anymore'." *The Atlantic*, September 8. http://www.theatlantic.com/international/archive/2010/09/fidel-cuban-model-doesnt-even-work-for-us-anymore/62602/.

ONE. 2012. *Oficina Nacional de Estadísticas* (Cuban National Bureau of Statistics). Annual Almanac. http://www.one.cu.

Peters, Philip. 2010. "Be a good communist, support your local entrepreneur." *The Cuban Triangle*, December 20. http://cubantriangle.blogspot.com/2010/12/be-good-communist-support-your-local.html.

Piñeiro-Harnecker, Camila. 2012."Non-state Enterprises in Cuba: Current Situation and Prospects." May. http://thecubaneconomy.com/articles/2012/09/camila-pineiro-harnecker-may-2012-non-state-enterprises-in-cuba-current-situation-and-prospects/.

Rainsford, Sarah. 2012. "Cuba Jails 12 Ex-Officials in Corruption Case." *BBC News*, August 12. http://www.bbc.co.uk/news/world-latin-america-19328953.

Agricultural Reforms

Dimas Castellanos

Cuba, a country with an ancient agricultural tradition, has suffered a drastic decline in production forcing it to import as much as 80 percent of the food it consumes from abroad. This is due to the government's often arbitrary willfulness under Fidel Castro, rigid centralization, state monopoly, the mismatch between wages paid to farmers and their cost of living, and the abolition of the market and the eradication of supply and demand. These different factors have inexorably produced a pronounced lack of interest in farming among the population, driving even those with a family agricultural tradition off the land. Cuba's agricultural collapse and dependence on imports has become a matter of national security. President Raúl Castro has publicly acknowledged the seriousness of the problem and introduced several reforms to address it. However, because the reforms are being implemented by the very same government that created the crisis in the first place, they were born subordinate to political ideology and the interests of those in power. This fact is reflected in the decision—against all logic and economic evidence—to retain the system of economic central planning in agriculture and the intention of extending it even to the non-state sector, such as private farms, agricultural co-ops, and the new usufruct program created in July 2008 by Decree-Law 259.

The main purpose of Decree-Law 259 was to make more than a million hectares of idle land available in usufruct to private farmers. The law brought a number of other changes to the island's agricultural sector, all of which were aimed at reducing the amount of unproductive land and giving farmers greater incentives to produce more. These changes included a modification in the *acopio* system, which had required farmers to sell most of their produce to the state at fixed prices, and a greater leeway in marketing products in the island's farmers' markets. There was also an effort to increase yields through the diversification, rotation, and poly-cultivation of crops. Bank loans have been made available and many past prohibitions have been lifted on hiring labor. Finally, there has been an effort to raise sugar production and increase derivatives from sugar cane, while many cane fields have been relocated bringing them closer to the processing plants. While all of these measures are necessary, they have been fraught with shortcomings, fears, and contradictions.

The lack of full economic rights, the refusal to allow farmers full ownership of the land they work, and the absence of a clear, integrated economic plan to guide the changes underway makes the government's declarations little more than a list of good intentions. However, the value in the half-hearted attempt to reform the system (as opposed to scrapping it) lies in the fact that these initial changes will provoke new interests, demands, and contradictions, which will themselves require the government to *reform the reforms*—making deeper and broader changes than it originally intended. And this in a difficult national and international economic and political context—especially with the recent death of Hugo Chávez—makes backtracking all but impossible.

The most far-reaching measure within the package of agricultural reforms is undoubtedly the land distribution scheme, which grants landless farmers up to 33 acres (*one caballería*) of idle state land and 99 acres (*three caballerías*) to those who already possess land each for a renewable 10-year period. However, the land is granted in usufruct only. That is, the state retains ownership rights to the property and continues to impose monopoly prices and conditions on the farmers. Moreover, until recently farmers were prohibited from erecting houses or other structures on these lands. Then there are other difficulties such as the high prices of farm implements and a generalized shortage of fertilizers, pesticides, herbicides, and fuel.

The meager results of these initial agricultural reforms have been expressed in the constant rise in the retail prices of foodstuffs and a growing dependency on expensive foreign imports. This has forced the government to consider new measures such as the allocation of more land to farmers than the law allows. This has been coupled with an expansion of the terms of tenancy beyond 10 years, the easing of the tax burden, and allowing farmers to build necessary structures on the land. Already in 2011, the high prices of farm implements were lowered and, more recently, direct sales of certain agricultural products to the tourism sector was authorized.

However, other, deeper reforms are urgently needed given the fact that living conditions are deteriorating faster than the reforms or food production can keep up. This state of crisis is abundantly evident in a brief look at the current state of four key agricultural products in which Cuba had long been a leader: sugar, coffee, rice, and cattle.

SUGAR

Cuba's most recent sugar harvests have typically yielded a paltry tonnage on par with that produced in the early years of the 20th century. For example, the 2011–2012 sugar harvest, officially slated to produce 1.45 million tons, had the same disappointing results as in the past despite having abundant state resources allocated to it. The result of all this is that the verdant, semitropical island of Cuba is forced to purchase 80 percent of its foodstuffs from abroad at steep international hard currency prices (ONE 2012). Many of the chronic obstacles in revolutionary agriculture were apparent once again including industrial breakdowns, operational disruptions, difficulties in the supply of sugar cane, inconsistent grinding, the aging of the raw material past its prime, and the shoddy repair of agricultural machinery. Moreover, late harvesting of sugar cane at 21 of the 46 mills, as well as a low grinding yield in seven of them which had been inactive for years caused problems. Other obstacles included the inadequate technical training of personnel and a utilization of just 60 percent of the potential grinding capacity of the mills. In the end, the harvest fell well short of already diminished expectations and was not completed on time (EFE 2012; Latin American Herald Tribune 2010).

THE FALL AND SEMIPRIVATIZATION OF CUBA'S SUGAR KINGDOM

Cuba's once mighty sugar industry experienced an unprecedented crisis during the 1990s, all but collapsing by 2002. The harvest dropped from 8.1 million tons in 1990 to a mere 4.3 million in 1993. Between 1989 and 2002, sugar's role in the composition of export trade dropped steadily from 73 to 32 percent, and by 2011 it accounted for just 5 percent of Cuba's foreign exchange earnings. Instead of reviving the industry, the government chose to "cut its losses" and fundamentally restructure it. In May 2002, Fidel Castro announced the closure of 71 of 156 mills, laying off a third of its workers, saying, "It's crazy to produce something that costs more to make than to import" (Peters 2003).

Cuba harvested just 2.2 million tons of sugar in 2003, the lowest tonnage of any harvest since 1933 (Mesa-Lago and Pérez-López 2005: 42, 66). More mills closed in 2003. As a result, the 2005 harvest produced just 1.3 million tons, the lowest yield since 1908 (Frank 2005). In mid-November 2011, the government announced the dissolution of the Ministry of Sugar (MINAZ), replacing it with the state-run holding company AZCUBA Business Group, which began administering the island's remaining 56 sugar mills (Frank 2011).

COFFEE AND RICE

As with sugar cane, in the late 18th century Cuba became the world's leading producer of coffee. That production began to decline after 1959 for some of the reasons already described. On December 18, 2010, Raúl Castro recognized the poor state of Cuban coffee production in his address to the National Assembly. "In the coming year," he warned, "we cannot afford to spend nearly $50 million importing coffee." Among the measures intended to reverse the decline of coffee harvests are the planting of new areas and varieties, replacing areas where aging varieties exceed 50 percent of the crop, increasing the prices paid to farmers, and an effort to repopulate some of the mountainous areas were the best Cuban coffee is grown. At present, the harvest figures speak for themselves: In the 1960–1961 harvest, 60,000 tons of coffee were produced in Cuba, while the 2010–2011 harvest yielded just 6,000 tons. With the new measures, the 2011–2012 harvest reached 7,100 tons—which represents an improvement but remains well below the levels achieved more than 50 years ago (ONE 2012).

Despite the new technologies introduced to improve rice farming in Cuba in recent decades, the government has been forced to import more than 400,000 tons of rice annually, representing 60 percent of national consumption. Because of this the country is forced to spend large amounts of hard currency on products that it should be perfectly capable of producing on the island. Recently, a new investment of $450 million aimed at improving national rice production through 2016 was announced. Unfortunately, similar efforts and investments have been made repeatedly in the past without achieving the desired results. This is due to the inherent inefficiency and lack of incentives of Cuba's inflexible state enterprise system.

CATTLE

As a result of ill-advised crossbreeding, the abandonment of pastures, and the invasive *marabú* weed, the parity that once existed between Cuba's human population and its head of cattle (sustained in the decade between 1958 and 1967) has been lost. Had that parity been maintained, the country would now have about 11 million head of cattle, instead of the less than 4 million it currently has. The government attributes this sharp decline to theft, illegal slaughter, the lack of imported feed, and droughts. As for milk, the backlog in production and sales to the state reached almost 4 million liters by the end of April 2012. Despite the fact that the price paid to farmers was increased to 2.53 pesos per liter in July 2007, production fell by 9.1 percent between 2010 and 2011. Moreover, in 2011 milk deliveries came in about 30 million liters under the established goal forcing the government to invest an additional $14 million to acquire it abroad. In all, 2011 milk production did not reach even half the level achieved in 1990, a trend which continued during 2012 (ONE 2012).

Despite increased investments, dozens of teaching and agricultural research schools, and thousands of engineers and technicians working to improve yields, Cuba's agricultural reforms have not risen to the challenge of the times. There is an evident lack of interest in farming among potential producers. Workers have little incentive because of the low wages paid in the sector. Owners lack entrepreneurial initiative due to the web of bureaucratic obstacles imposed upon them. They are often forced to buy their supplies on the black market and then sell to the state at bargain basement prices, and must then wait for months to be paid in a replay of the colonial era when tobacco sales were controlled by a royal legal monopoly. Therefore, despite increased prices paid by the state for milk, coffee, and beef, because farmers cannot market their products directly, many prefer to sell them clandestinely to middle men and avoid signing contracts with the state. This is the best proof that the partial reform of increasing prices—like the economic reform package in general—has not been deep and broad enough to turn Cuban agriculture around. All this translates into billions of dollars being wasted on buying foods abroad that Cuba is actually able to produce on its own (Frank 2012).

REFERENCES

EFE. 2012. "Cuba's Sugar Harvest Disappoints." *Fox News Latino*, May 29. http://latino .foxnews.com/latino/news/2012/05/29/cuba-sugar-harvest-disappoints/.

Frank, Marc. 2012. "Cuba Growing Less Food Than 5 Years Ago Despite Agriculture Reforms." *Reuters*, August 31. http://www.reuters.com/article/2012/08/31/cuba-food-idUSL2E8JVA UU20120831.

Latin American Herald Tribune. 2010. "Cuba's Sugar Harvest Worst in 105 Years." http:// www.laht.com/article.asp?CategoryId=14510&ArticleId=356545.

ONE. 2012. *Oficina Nacional de Estadísticas* (Cuban National Bureau of Statistics). Annual Almanac. http://www.one.cu.

Political Reforms and Rising Corruption

Marlene Azor Hernández

The Cuban political system is characterized by a highly centralized, vertical structure in which the higher levels dictate rules and procedures to the lower ones through a process of command and control as with any military structure, but with a highly personalized character within each level of decision making. This structure is a carbon copy of the political model that long-dominated the former Soviet Union and the rest of the so-called socialist bloc. The symbiotic relationship that exists between the state and the single legal political party in power, the Cuban Communist Party (PCC), reinforces the centralized and vertical nature of the system.

After the revolutionary government dismantled the various institutions of civil society that had existed prior to 1959, the population was quickly organized—also in a vertical, hierarchical manner—into a number of centrally controlled mass organizations. These included the Committees for the Defense of the Revolution, the Federation of Cuban Women, the National Association of Small Farmers, the Central Labor Union, the Union of Young Communists, the Communist Party, and the

Territorial Troops Militia. Others were organized according to professional criteria, such as writers and artists, journalists, economists, lawyers, etc. Even after more than half-a-century these organizations have not succeeded in achieving any room for ideological or operational autonomy from the state.

The party-state monopoly on the media (radio, television, and all print media) together with the island's notoriously slow, inaccessible, and expensive Internet connection have made it almost impossible for citizens to voice their demands for over half-a-century, effectively silencing any expression of public opinion that is at odds with the official one. Like its Eastern European counterparts, this governing model has celebrated citizens' social rights while systematically dismissing and violating their civil and political ones under the justification that such liberal democratic concerns are nothing more than meaningless "bourgeois" niceties. As a result, political and civil rights in Cuba—despite being enshrined in the Constitution—are subordinated to state-party leaders who take it upon themselves to decide which activities and rights are inalienable and which violate the goals of the "socialist" society and must be suppressed. This discretion extends to the application of civil liberties and criminal legislation as well, with such universally recognized rights and as property, association, assembly, mobility, and freedom of information and expression, being routinely violated by the state-party.

THE INNOVATIVE ASPECTS

With this as a necessary backdrop, the current government's political and civil reforms can be analyzed by examining the results of the two most important party gatherings in recent memory, the Sixth Congress of the Communist Party (April 2011) followed nine months later by the First Party Conference (January 2012). While not substantively different in procedure or outcome from previous meetings of the Party faithful, the April Congress stood out for the popular debate of its extensive agenda that took place across the island in the months preceding it. For the first time ever, both the preliminary agenda—known as the draft "Economic and Social Policy Guidelines," or "*Lineamientos*"—and the somewhat altered final version that came out of the meeting were published and made widely available at nominal cost. Equally important, the changes made between the two versions of this document, so important to the future of the country, were highlighted and minutely detailed so the public could see what was objected to and by how many, as well as what was altered, and why. Despite the fact that the data ultimately shared with the public had passed through an ideological filter, with as many as 50,000 complaints either ignored or left "under study," the publication of the final document was unprecedented ("*Lineamientos*" 2011).

The single major political change to come out of the two Party conclaves was the imposition of the first ever term limits on the highest offices of the state and the party, henceforth limited to two terms of five years. This change sets a clear "sunset" date on Raúl Castro's presidency. With his first term ending in February 2013, he has left himself a window of just five more years to establish his own legacy. Before this change, appointments in these and other offices were for life, unless interrupted by an official's fall from grace because of a specific political problem or—more frequently—due to corruption.

BREAD, BUTTER, AND A PASSPORT—CUBANS' TOP COMPLAINTS

The issues included in the original *Lineamientos* working document that drew the most concern from the population during the December 2010 to February 2011 debate that led up to the Congress are contained in just 12 of the more than 291 points covered in the document (the final document was expanded to 313 points). These 12 issues all relate directly to the challenges of everyday life: the population's lack of purchasing power to meet their basic needs (87,150 complaints), the deterioration of education and health services (40,391 opinions), the state of the transportation system (29,122 concerns), housing (23,945 views), and fuel for household use (22,599 opinions). This first tier of concerns raised by the population was followed by demand to allow the open sale of motor vehicles (13,816) and enact a migratory reform that would revoke the exit visa requirement and free foreign travel (11,195) (Chaguaceda and Azor Hernández 2011). All told, "more than 781,000 public suggestions were received from average citizens in 163,000 meetings held throughout the country" (Bilbao 2013).

Additionally, a first-ever separation of powers decree was established between the state administrative branch and the party leadership at both the provincial and municipal levels. Before this change, power was almost always concentrated in a single person at each level who simultaneously held both posts. Other important political and economic changes that came out of the Party gatherings include placing the Party in charge of implementing the approved policies on a projected schedule; an attempt to incorporate Cuba's microentrepreneurs into the single, state-controlled labor union, the CTC; the authorization of a limited market for the sale of private houses and cars; the lifting of restrictions on internal mobility; and the related and long demanded right to travel abroad without first obtaining prior government approval. This last reform was announced in October 2012 and took effect in mid-January 2013, and will be discussed in greater detail later.

THE LIMITATIONS OF THE REFORMS

The few civil and political reforms put in place thus far aim to respond to some of the citizens' most strident demands, while preserving the fundamental structures and functioning of state and party institutions. The intention is to inject some needed order into the island's dysfunctional economic and political model, while retaining that system's vertical structure and nondemocratic logic. This is the reason the government always insists on referring to their changes as "perfecting the socialist model" (changes within the same system) and not structural reforms (a change of the system itself). This is also why the new regulations are targeted at very specific (and limited) civil liberties—such as freedom of internal movement—and at legalizing many of the everyday economic practices that Cubans had long engaged in on the black market, such as the clandestine sale of cars and homes. Prior to the real estate reforms in November 2011, for example, Cuban homes changed hands through legal swaps, which almost always included under-the-table payments. This informal arrangement left the government with the inability to regulate the terms of the swap or collect any taxes from the exchange. This has now changed with the legalization of such transactions.

The buying and selling of private homes was legalized for the first time since the early 1960s with the 2011 Decree-Law 288. Under this new legislation, every citizen can own a maximum of two dwellings, a permanent residence and a vacation home. Additionally, inheritance rights for one's next of kin were expanded while the past practice of seizing the homes of all permanent émigrés has been eliminated. Prior to the new law, an emigrant's family would have to pay the full price of the property to the state once again in order to retain their rights to it—provided they could prove their right of inheritance and show that they lacked an alternate residence. Thus, the new law restores the right of personal real property, along with the right of exchanging it or ceding it to a family member. At the same time, the state has begun to levy a tax on the buying-selling or inheritance of such homes, set at 4 percent of the total value of the property.

Likewise, past regulations on the sale of motor vehicles were relaxed with Decree-Law 292 in September 2011. However, this change only applies to the buying-selling or donation of one of the many used vehicles from the 1950s through the 1980s still roaming the streets or resting in the garages of the country. The import and/or

In this April 19, 2013 photo, Estrella Díaz sits next to a homemade sign advertising her home for sale in Havana. A baffling, sometimes bizarre real estate market has emerged in the year and a half since President Raúl Castro legalized private home sales for the first time in five decades. The market still lacks a workable mortgage system, an easy means of advertising potential sales and, most important, a middle class with resources to buy. (AP Photo/Franklin Reyes)

purchase of new vehicles by Cuban citizens remains tightly controlled, while foreigners residing in Cuba do enjoy this right. The state retains its monopoly on the import and sale of new vehicles, which are allocated for official business or used in the country's tourism industry, while placing a 4 percent tax on all donations, purchases, and sales between private individuals. As with housing, in the past the state confiscated the cars of all émigrés. Now, these can be sold, donated, or inherited by their family. While both Decree-Law 288 and Decree-Law 292 represent an expansion of economic rights for the Cuban people, in many ways the state was forced to make this change by the long-standing reality where homes, vehicles, and many other consumer items were routinely bought and sold on the black market. Moreover, these new regulations do not restore full property rights in either case given the previously mentioned limitations on the purchase of new vehicles and the fact that the housing market continues to exclude Cuban citizens who live abroad from owning property.

Finally, in November 2011, Decree-Law 293 was issued relaxing previous restrictions on internal migration. Before that, Cubans whose official residence was in other provinces were prohibited from moving to Havana without government permission. While some important restrictions on free movement still remain, it is now possible for those with relatives living in the capital to become legal, permanent residents there as well. But again, this is more a bureaucratic change that legalizes the long-standing reality of irregular residence and clandestine migration within the country than a recognition of an inalienable right. Additionally, one of the most common complaints heard during the debates of the original *Lineamientos* document was against the requirement that Cubans obtain a costly exit visa and letter of invitation (roughly $300 for both on an average monthly salary of just $20) before being allowed to travel abroad. Many expected the April 2011 Party Congress or the later Party Conference in January 2012 to directly address this anachronistic violation of citizens' rights. However, such hopes were put on hold as the government remained silent on the matter nearly through the end of 2012.

Then, in October Decree-Law 302 was published repealing both the exit visa and the required letter of invitation. These and other changes in Cuba's migration laws took effect on January 14, 2013, turning what had been an escape hatch on a voyage of no return into a revolving door. Despite the potentially momentous nature of these changes, taken together Cuba's civil and political reforms do not imply a move toward the democratization of the political system, not even within the established state socialist structures. Instead, they are best interpreted as a partial and very narrowly focused liberalizations that respond to rising popular demand. In other words, liberalization does not necessarily mean democratization (Farber 2011).

THE PROBLEM OF CORRUPTION

In general, corruption takes place when public officials place their own interests above the interests of the common good, which they are duty bound to uphold. Anyone who benefits from the violation of a set of rules which they are responsible for enforcing commits an act of corruption (Hankiss 2006). In the case of Cuba, corruption became glaringly evident starting with the economic crisis of the 1990s known as the "special period." Nevertheless, its roots are deeply embedded in and nurtured by the centralized state socialist economic model that was forcefully implanted in Cuba during the second half of the 1970s.

A number of the specific features of state socialism make it "fertile ground" for the growth of black markets and an underground economy often linked to corrupt officials. Extensive price controls, the prohibition of private activity, extensive regulations and high taxes on any private activity, unsatisfied demand, impersonal state property under inadequate custody, the personal power of many government functionaries, and an acute need for many goods and services all create structural pressures, opportunities, and substantial rewards for corruption (Díaz Briquets and Pérez-López 2006).

Cuba's economic system suffers from nearly all the discussed characteristics making the problem of corruption particularly intractable (Azor Hernández 1996: 87–88). For example, directors of state enterprises—from the level of the enterprise itself to the upper levels, in a hierarchical structure of officials—are each appointed by those at the higher level. Selection criteria are primarily based on loyalty and ideology, not business expertise or professional qualifications. This is because efficiency and success is not measured by the reduction of costs, the introduction of new production methods or technologies, the amount or quality of production, or the entrepreneurial initiative to take maximum rational advantage of the resources, but on the mechanical achievement of production quotas. In fact, the goal of intentionally overfulfilling the often deliberately vague or low quotas is particularly common as it hides theft, waste, and inefficiency.

Another factor contributing to corruption is the impossibility of minutely controlling a diversified and complex economy. This inherent difficulty makes economic planning an exercise in overly general and imprecise estimation in order to standardize measurement. The interests of the bureaucrats are aimed at retaining their positions and gradually moving up in the bureaucratic hierarchy. To achieve this, they must faithfully fulfill the assigned plan and avoid conflicts and tensions in the branches they manage. Such a post provides its occupant a wide range of discretional perks not associated with his or her salary, but which provide access to an array of economic and social prerogatives and privileges such as special shopping, recreation, and medical care centers. Furthermore, the higher up they ascend in the so-called *nomenklatura* (bureaucratic hierarchy), the larger and better their prerogatives are.

Because of the reasons mentioned earlier, the standards of "good" economic management are not based on the rational and efficient use of resources, but instead on the particular "efficiency" with which the plan is accomplished—even when such a logic results in an overall economic inefficiency. In other words, the quality of the product is not determined by its success in the market. There are Cuban bureaucrats who request bigger budgets each year and hide the unused and depreciated stock of goods in their warehouses, since only the fulfillment of the preestablished plan will guarantee their job and preserve their social status. In turn, those who receive such deficient products into the supply chain are required to continue the production process with defective goods, only exacerbating the resultant waste in terms of the lack of durability and effectiveness of the final product. Amazingly, these problems do not stop the implementation of the plan, because standards are low, products are scarce, and there are no market competitors as in a mixed or market economy. The same thing happens with personal goods and services. There are few alternatives for consumption because virtually everything is produced and marketed by state companies run under the logic of the plan.

Despite holding all the cards, a state with monopolistic control does not produce goods with economic efficiency. This is due to problems inherent in such a system's organizational and operational structure. Not every type of planning has these faults, but monopolistic state planning does inevitably provoke them. Some of the unintended consequences of this kind of plan include waste, scarcity, overemployment, low productivity, and low wages barely adequate to cover basic needs. A monopolistic planned economy also indirectly encourages workers at all levels to divert resources from the state, the sole owner of goods, in order to survive. These stolen goods supply the black market.

Generalized scarcity, low wages, and widespread underground economic activity has also led—in the case of Cuba—to a "split" economy where the mass of the population is paid in the national peso currency (the Cuban Peso, or CUP), while foreign trade and tourism operates in hard currency (the convertible Peso, or CUC), which is roughly equivalent to the US dollar, that is, 24 times the value of the CUP. However, over time fewer and fewer necessary domestic products are available in CUPs, forcing the entire population to depend on CUCs in order to survive. This state of chronic material and financial penury also fuels low labor productivity in jobs that pay workers in CUPs and corruption as everyone is encouraged to use any position or influence they have to obtain hard currency. This corruption manifests itself at all levels given the lax oversight over state resources and the shared need of those entrusted with guarding them. Many higher-ups engage in major "white collar" crime aimed at personal enrichment, while everyday workers steal and divert resources as a means of survival.

This is the starting point of the reforms that the Sixth Party Congress (April 2011) intends to formalize and implement. However, the call for greater "order and control" intoned in the official discourse cannot be properly analyzed by studying the main Party documents since they lack a coherent overall strategy, a timeline, and clear direction for democratic change. From official speeches and interviews with those responsible in the office of the National Comptroller—which is part of the office of the Attorney General—two main lines of attack on corruption can be derived: the establishment of order throughout the entire system of production—which means complying with established laws—and a significant increase in the presence and power of the Comptroller General of the Republic, Gladys Bejerano.

In the first case, the intention to have strict adherence to the law faces the obstacle of the proliferation of laws, decrees, and resolutions promulgated for decades without regard to previous regulations or attention to any overall integrity and coherence. This means that before passing new laws against corruption, the first step should be to unify the existing legal statutes and decide which previous regulations should remain and which must be eliminated. However, as stated earlier, these aims clash with the current deeply embedded culture of illegality aimed at survival that predominates on the island, which has become routine after decades where theft and robbery ceased to be seen as crimes. In the second case, the power and authority of the Comptroller General has become well known with corporate audits carried out annually on both large- and medium-sized state enterprises. Gladys Bejerano, Cuba's newly appointed Comptroller General, pointed out the potential stumbling blocks in this process during a recent interview:

> In our planning for auditing and control, we try to make sure that a particular entity does not get audited more than once a year. . . . However, we still have entities that go more than two years without being audited even once due to lack of staff and other reasons. In addition, there are other situations, such as cases where three months after a successful audit, the police are tipped off and stop a vehicle carrying stolen goods from the very entity that just passed its audit. . . . In such cases, obviously we are forced to go back and investigate, corroborate, and develop the special report that will lead to criminal charges, with the auditor acting as an expert witness. (Rodríguez Gavilán 2012)

The work of control and the legal order to which they aspire will be ineffective if they are concentrated solely within centralized state organizations and limit themselves to mere law enforcement. Still sorely lacking are any institutions independent from the government that can act as a counterbalance to state and party power, such as a free press (the fourth estate) or labor unions. Also, since the root cause of much economic crime in Cuba is the inadequacy of peso salaries, corruption great and small will continue at least until wages rise well past their current below-subsistence levels. Moreover, the exclusive state monopoly on imports, production, and allocation, as well as the continued existence of the dual currency (CUPs and CUCs), conspire against efficiency and economic competitiveness despite the recent limited reform in favor of microenterprises (*cuentapropistas*) and the subsequent and as yet untested new law on nonagricultural cooperatives. In summary, the measures of state enterprise reorganization, stepped-up control, and greater enforcement of existing law enacted to date are still insufficient. The refusal to even entertain the need for structural changes in the current system of monopolistic central planning—which is the root cause of corruption in Cuba—mean that current efforts are unlikely to have any more than a marginal impact.

REFERENCES

Azor Hernández, Marlene. 1996."Las experiencias históricas del Socialismo de Estado." Department of Philosophy and History, University of Havana: Unpublished doctoral thesis, 87–88.

Bilbao, Tomas. 2013. "What Cuba's Reforms Tell Us About the Country's Leadership." *Georgetown Journal of International Affairs*, January 14.

Chaguaceda, Armando, and Marlene Azor Hernández. 2011."Cuba, política de participación y prácticas de autonomía: organización, acción y discurso." *Revista Crítica y Emancipación* 3, no. 6: 9–35.

Decree-Law 288. 2011. *Gaceta Oficial de la República de Cuba*. Ministerio de Justicia, November 2.

Decree-Law 292. 2011. *Gaceta Oficial de la República de Cuba*. Ministerio de Justicia, September 27.

Decree-Law 293. 2011. *Gaceta Oficial*. Ministerio de Justicia, November 16.

Díaz-Briquets, Sergio and Jorge Pérez-López. 2006. *Corruption in Cuba: Castro and Beyond.* Austin: University of Texas Press.

Farber, Samuel. 2011. *Cuba since the Revolution of 1959: A Critical Assessment.* Chicago: Haymarket Books.

Hankiss, Elemér. 2006. "La Corrupción." *Criterios Magazine*, Havana, no. 35, 249–285.

"*Lineamientos.*" 2011. "Información sobre el resultadodel Debate de los Lineamientos de la Política Económica y Social del Partido y la Revolución." *Sixth Congress of the Cuban Communist Party*, May.

Rodríguez Gavilán, Agnerys. 2012. Interview with Cuban official (Controladora General de la República) Gladys Bejerano. "Ningún acto de corrupción sucede en un día." *Juventud Rebelde*, February 18. http://www.juventudrebelde.cu/cuba/2012–02–18/ningun-acto-de-corrupcion-sucede-en-un-dia-2/.

Recent Cuban Elections

Armando Chaguaceda and Dayrom Gil

Between the triumph of the revolution in 1959 and the passage of the socialist Constitution in 1976, the Cuban government remained both legally and institutionally provisional. The Fundamental Law of 1959 eliminated representative democracy and its formal branches of government (Congress, Senate, and the periodic election of a president) and concentrated all executive and legislative powers in a cabinet (*Consejo de Ministros*) headed by the prime minister, Fidel Castro. The figure of the president remained but was appointed by the prime minister and stripped of any authority. Real governing power rested in the figure of the commander-in-chief—also Fidel Castro—who derived his authority from his role as the historic leader of the armed uprising that became the Cuban Revolution.

This government perceived itself, and was initially seen by its numerous followers, as a revolutionary democracy, legitimized by the armed struggle and justified by an ambitious program of material redistribution and social justice. In the long provisional period between 1959 and 1976, in the absence of elections, popular participation was radically restructured. A liberal democratic system made up of an ideologically diverse group of citizens invested with individual political rights and civil liberties was replaced by a mass of militants integrated into the revolutionary process and committed to the socialist project. This manifested itself in broad-based and all but obligatory participation in a wide array of mass organizations designed as transmission belts for decisions made by the Communist Party and the tasks assigned to them by the political leadership (Chaguaceda, Daubelcour, and González 2012; González Mederos, Viega, and Guanche 2012).

This type of mass participation essentially consisted of recommendation, acclamation, and implementation, but almost never included making decisions or holding the government accountable for its actions beyond certain very specific local processes. Thus, citizens' political rights and civil liberties were effectively reduced to being the grateful beneficiaries of the redistributive policies of the all-powerful state. With top administrative positions co-opted by figures appointed by the central government, solving the economic and social problems of each region required the direct intervention of the federal government, often micromanaged. This left local communities virtually powerless to manage or control their own affairs. And while this style of governing during the epic years of the 1960s benefited from the massive enthusiasm of a population as young as its leadership, grave errors, chronic inefficiency, and the lack of planning provoked the dire need to institutionalize the revolution under the Soviet model of governance, which was put into place in the mid-1970s.

In the 37 years between the passage of the current Constitution in 1976 and 2013, there have been 14 municipal elections and 5 elections for national representatives. The growing trend in null and blank votes—along with electoral absenteeism—seems to represent a dissent that is expressed within the limited mechanisms of the existing political system. From the very start, elections that followed the Constitutional institutionalization of socialism in 1976 showed almost impossibly high rates of participation. The constitutional referendum that year had a participation rate of 98 percent, with just 0.5 percent voided ballots and 0.8 percent blank ones. In the same year, 95.2 percent of voters participated in municipal elections. According to figures from the National Office of Statistics, between 1981 and 2000 electoral participation remained between 98.7 and 97.1 percent.

Such a high-level participation can be explained by several factors. One of them is the massive support for the revolutionary government, especially evident during the first three decades of its existence. However, there are other causes related to the particular characteristics of the electoral process itself and the sociopolitical order that sustains it. First, there was usually little that distinguished one candidate from another. Second, voting was easy, registration was automatic, there were no lines, and voting precincts were rarely more than a few meters from anyone's home. Third, not voting could stigmatize someone as a "counter-revolutionary." Voters were (and are, although less frequently today) visited door to door to see that they vote and there were intense campaigns in the state media calling for a "united" or strict party-line vote for the entire slate of candidates. Finally, despite the government's constant claims that each election is a referendum on its work to defend public welfare and national sovereignty, almost no national issues or "politics" are publicly debated in the run up to Cuban elections. This characteristic makes voting more a bureaucratic duty to be fulfilled and a symbolic show of loyalty to the revolution than a political exercise of citizen empowerment or a test of the government's or candidates' accountability.

In 2002 there was a slight drop in voter participation to 95.8 percent. Between 2002 and 2010, official figures indicate that the level of participation fluctuated between 95.8 and 96.7 percent. In the most recent elections in the fall of 2012, participation fell even further to 91.9 percent (Lee 2012). Blank and null votes also follow a similar trend. For example, in 2007 the combined sum of blank and annulled ballots was 7.21 percent, in 2010 that proportion rose to 8.89 percent, rising again to 9.3 percent in 2012 (August 2010; Granma 2010; Lee 2012). Furthermore, this trend of abstention crossed the symbolic 10 percent mark in the elections for National Assembly on February 4, 2013 in which only 89.68 percent of voters turned out at the polls—the lowest in many years. At the same time, the percentage of null and blank votes actually decreased to just 5.73 percent, making the total of "nonconformist" votes (the total of abstentions, null, and blank votes) 16.05 percent (Tamayo 2013). This shows that the combined total of abstentions, blank, and null votes has grown in recent years (from 10.27% in 2007 to 16.64% in 2012, and to 16.05% in 2013). However, this is not simply a numerical shift but also a change in the way Cubans express discontent. Moreover, such changes are not simply attributable to the incorporation of new voters and the elimination of others since there is not significant voter turnover in this relatively short period. Instead, there has been a qualitative change in the preferences and mentality of long-time voters.

We might attribute the increase in voter absenteeism in 2005 to the long-term results of the Fifth Party Congress of 1997, which scaled back the economic opening of the early 1990s and amounted to a recentralizing counterreform aimed at fighting Fidel Castro's so-called Battle of Ideas. However, the even more pronounced increase in absenteeism in 2012–2013 seems due to rising frustration over the results of policies under Raúl Castro's leadership since 2008, as expressed in the platforms of the Sixth Party Congress of 2011 and the National Party Conference of 2012. This time around, reforms raised expectations without fulfilling them, which could explain the open break represented by the increase in absenteeism. In contrast, the increase of the blank and null votes does seem to follow a continuous and growing trend in the years analyzed, which could correspond to exhaustion of the state-centered model of governance and the new awareness of the insignificance of the municipal elections among those who are still reluctant to openly abstain from voting.

Although we do not focus here on voting by province, the available data shows that Havana has been the area with the lowest levels of voter participation in all municipal elections, falling consistently two percentage points below the national average. It has also been the region with the lowest attendance in voting for representatives to the National Assembly. In 1998, 2003, and 2008, abstentions were again consistently between one and two percentage points below the national average. Results at the provincial level from the latest elections in the fall of 2012 have not yet been published, which could mean that Havana's electorate may have exceeded the symbolic level of 10 percent abstention. Moreover, the lowest level of support for any representative (*diputado*) to the National Assembly was the punishing 70.2 percent received by the first secretary of the Party in the special municipality of the Isle of Youth (*Cuba Encuentro* 2008). Perhaps as a result, she no longer appears as representative in the official website of the Assembly. A new secretary has also taken her place in the Party. However, there is no evidence of her being removed through a public process of a recall vote leading us to conclude that the decision to remove her must have come from on high, in violation of the rules of the electoral system.

The year 2012 provided another example of Party and central government interference in voting procedures. For example, the Party engaged in bullying and gerrymandering to prevent to reelection of the Las Tunas municipal delegate Sirley Ávila León (*Diario de Cuba* 2012). Other stories of electoral fraud were common, especially in order to prevent absenteeism. This included reports of the Party urging voters to vote on behalf of absentee family members. Such rumors have circulated in Cuba for years but recently the targets of such pressures have abandoned their past passive attitude and reported these problems to the international press (Suárez 2012). It is difficult to assess the impact of these complaints within the country, but their influence on voting trends should not be ruled out. Similarly, though the work of various opposition groups—both on the right and the new left—has had little influence on the national voting totals, it has likely influenced some to cast void or blank ballots or even to abstain from voting outright.

The trend described earlier of an increase in voided, blank, and absentee voting has not yet reached alarming levels for the government. In fact, Cuba's electoral system has even received recognition from various international agencies for its high levels of inclusion and participation. However, these agencies mistakenly apply to Cuba standards that have very different meanings in the free, fair, and competitive elections held elsewhere. While abstention, null, and blank votes do not necessarily translate to opposition, their rising numbers indicate an expansion in the lack of consensus, amounting to around one million people. Such levels of nonconsensus were previously unthinkable in Cuba: 16 percent of voters are not a small or insignificant group. In fact, in the hypothetical case that they could vote for other representatives and form their own block or party, they would make up 98 of the total 614 representatives in the National Assembly. Moreover, if we were to add to this 16 percent another 10 percent representing those Cubans who have emigrated and who continue to recognize the legitimacy of the government's elections—even if the Cuban government remains unique in the region in not allowing its émigrés to vote—we would be dealing with an electoral block of considerable political weight. In sum, one thing is clear from our analysis: this nonconformist block of voters represents a significant and growing minority whose silent acquiescence is less and less dependable.

REFERENCES

August, Arnold. 2010. "Los resultados de las Elecciones Municipales de Cuba: Notas iniciales." *Global Research*, May 27. http://www.globalresearch.ca/los-resultados-de-las-elecciones-municipales-de-cuba-notas-iniciales/?print=1.

Chaguaceda, Armando, Djanamé Daubelcour, and Lázaro González. 2012. "Community Participation in Cuba: Experiences from a Popular Council." *International Journal of Cuban Studies* 4, nos. 3 and 4, (December): 366–384.

Cuba Encuentro. 2008. "Raúl Castro recibió mayor respaldo que su hermano en los comicios del 20 de enero." January 31.

Diario de Cuba. 2012. "La delegada de Limones denuncia que las autoridades impidieron votar a una decena de sus electores." October 22.

Diario de Cuba. 2012. "Delegada del Poder Popular acude a la prensa extranjera, cansada de que el Gobierno la ignore." September 11.

González Mederos, Lenier, Roberto Viega, and Julio César Guanche. 2012. *Por un consenso para la democracia*. Espacio Laical Publications. http://www.espaciolaical.org/contens/publicacion/libro2/por%20un%20consenso%20para%20la%20democracia%20completo.pdf.

Granma. 2010. "Votó el 95,86% de los electores." April 30.

Lee, Susana. 2012. "Elegidos 13 mil 127 delegados en la primera vuelta." *Granma*, October 23. http://www.granma.cubaweb.cu/2012/10/23/nacional/artic09.html.

Suárez, Michel. 2012. "Castro celebra el bicentenario del 'gerrymandering'." *Diario de Cuba*, September 24.

Tamayo, Juan O. 2013. "Gobierno cubano emite cifras oficiales de participación en comicios parlamentarios." *El Nuevo Herald*, February 5.

Cuba's Demographic Crisis

Dimas Castellanos

"Cuba is a country trapped between a nativity rate like that of the first world and a level of emigration more typical of the third." —Yoani Sánchez, 2012

Although a declining birth rate combined with an aging population—what is known as a "demographic transition"—is normally a phenomenon found in developed, high-income countries, Cuba is currently experiencing just such a steady decline in births and an increase in life expectancy at birth. This is combined in the case of Cuba with economic underdevelopment, low incomes, and the permanent emigration of many of its young people. The interaction of these trends has led to a true demographic crisis on the island with a net loss in total population that will only worsen in the coming years.

For example, Cuba's National Office of Statistics (ONE) recently reported that the population decreased by 1,467 people between 2009 and 2010, giving the island a *negative* annual growth rate of 0.13 percent. Cuba's government is well aware of the impeding crisis associated with such negative population growth. Citing the aforementioned ONE numbers, Cuba's Communist Party–run national newspaper *Granma* featured a December 2010 headline warning that the island's population of 11.2 million, "will not reach 12 million," going on to admit that the country finds itself in a situation "unprecedented in developing societies in the absence of natural disasters, lethal epidemics, large-scale economic or political crises, or military conflagrations that could explain it" (Peters 2010).

Ironically, this crisis has been caused as much by the achievements of the revolution over the past half-century as by its failure to create a sustainable economic base and desirable employment for its educated young people who often opt to emigrate in search of better economic prospects. For example, Cuba's free and universally accessible health system has driven up life expectancy—from 59.8 years in 1960 to 77 years in 2009, similar to that of the many developed countries—while its policy of offering free and legal abortions has helped keep the birth rate low (ONE 2012). Likewise, women's access to free higher education and professional employment has helped the drive an already low birth rate even lower.

Like many other developing countries in the region, over the course of the 20th century Cuba's fertility rate declined from 2.8 children per woman in 1920 (already very low), to just 1.7 in 2009. This gives Cuba the lowest rate in Latin America, well below the 2.1 children per woman rate necessary to replace the population (Delgado Legón 2013; Rodríguez 2012). Also, unlike many developed countries with similarly low birth rates, Cuba has virtually no immigration with which to replenish its population. Thus, the systematic reduction of the fertility rate in conjunction with the steady increase in life expectancy have placed Cuba in an advanced stage of demographic transition.

Faced with this dilemma, the government included among its lengthy set of economic and social "guidelines" adopted at the Sixth Congress of the Party in April

2011 the need to "pay particular attention to the study and implementation of strategies in all sectors of society to address the high levels of aging in the population" (Delgado Legón 2013). Furthermore, Cuban vice president Marino Murillo—the man charged with implementing the "guidelines"—has left no doubt of the seriousness of the problem, saying in a speech to the National Assembly in August of 2012, ". . . the aging of the population no longer has a solution. It is going to happen and there is no way to stop it in the short term. Society must prepare for it" (Rodríguez 2012). By December 2012, the National Assembly set up a commission to study the related issues of population aging and the low birth rate.

Some important steps that have already been taken in recent years include increasing the retirement age by five years—from 55 to 60 for women and 60 to 65 for men—allowing retirees to return to work without losing their pensions, and expanding senior recreation facilities (Delgado Legón 2013). Other population management policies used with varying results in Asia and Europe have little applicability in Cuba, including providing economic incentives for childbearing, outlawing abortion, and attracting immigrants from poorer countries. Along with retaining more of its citizens by offering greater employment incentives (not by beefing up its detested obstacles to emigration), Cuba could implement policies that might attract some of its wealthy and educated émigrés to return or retire with their economic resources to the island. One step in the direction of reducing this "demographic hemorrhage" is certainly the reform of its antiquated migration law that took effect in January 2013 allowing greater circulation of the population in and out of the country (Dilla 2011).

The flight of Cubans abroad has been a distinguishing characteristic of the island's demography since 1959, prior to which it had been a historic immigrant-receiving country. While the outflow has been constant, there have been a number of critical moments of mass exodus from the country, including from the port of Camarioca (1965), the port of Mariel (1980), and directly to the United States during the rafter crisis or via Guantánamo Naval Base (1994–1995). These various waves, together with the extremely high levels of emigration since 1995, have placed an upwards of two million Cubans abroad, which is roughly equivalent to 18 percent of the island's population of 11.2 million. Moreover, in the most recent decade from 2001 to 2010, over 340,000 Cubans left the island permanently as part of a growing exodus that reached its highest annual level since the 1980 Mariel Boat Lift with 38,165 departures in 2010. This record was broken in 2011 when 39,263 Cubans departed (Peters 2012). Unfortunately for the island, those who leave are often the youngest, best educated, and most ambitious (Rodríguez 2012).

If current trends continue, and there is no indication that they will change, the island's population—which was 11,139,875 in 1998, just 11,177,743 in 2002, and seems to have peaked at 11,242,621 in 2009—will never reach 12 million. The consequence of this process is the inversion of the normal pyramidal structure of the population of developing countries (few elderly supported by many of working age, with still more minors entering the work force each year). In 2010, Cuba saw its segment of the population of children between birth and 14 years (17.4%) surpassed by that segment over 60 years (17.8%), with the proportion of seniors already exceeding that of children (*El Nuevo Herald* 2012). In fact, this proportion of elderly gives Cuba nearly double the regional over-60 rate of 9 percent, making the Cuban population one of the oldest in the Western Hemisphere. It is estimated that if Cuba continues along its current path, by 2035 fully one-third of its population will be over 60 (ibid.). Moreover, between 2015 and 2050, Cuba's population is likely to drop by between 1,557,000 and 2,300,000 people, while simultaneously seeing a growth of its elderly population by approximately 1,510,000 million people (Barros Díaz 2005: 56).

If we combine Cuba's inactive population of children and the elderly, and compare them with the active segment of the working age population (those 15–60 years old), we find an unsustainable relationship of dependency. In other words, the shrinking 64.8 percent of the population of working age will be increasingly unable to support the inactive and expanding 35.2 percent of the population (children and the elderly). Moreover, this dilemma is exacerbated in the case of Cuba given the fact that covering the growing costs of social security, health care, and the many other demands required by caring for an aging population demand precisely what is missing in Cuba: an efficient, productive economy. The only way to avoid the severe negative effects of this demographic crisis on the already low living standards of the Cuban population is a sustained increase in productivity and efficiency, something that will prove impossible under the current effort to merely "update the [current socialist] model" (*actualizar el modelo*), in the words of Raúl Castro. Moreover, there must be a concomitant radical reform in the island's migration policy, allowing the free exit and return of all Cubans with full rights, as existed in the past and as it exists—with rare exceptions—everywhere else in the world.

REFERENCES

Barros Díaz, Otilia. 2005. *Escenarios demográficos de la población cubana 2000–2050*. Havana: Editorial de Ciencias Sociales.

Delgado Legón, Elio. 2013. "Population Aging in Cuba." *Havana Times*, January 3.

Dilla, Haroldo. 2011. "Hemorragia demográfica: Los cubanos provienen o viven en una isla en proceso de despoblamiento." *Cuba Encuentro*, July 11.

El Nuevo Herald. 2012. "El 31% de los cubanos tendrá más de 60 años en 2030." September 10. http://www.elnuevoherald.com/2012/09/10/1297176/el-31-de-los-cubanos-tendra-mas.html#storylink=cpy.

ONE. 2012. *Oficina Nacional de Estadísticas* (Cuban National Bureau of Statistics). Annual Almanac. http://www.one.cu.

Peters, Philip. 2010. "Cuba's Aging Population." *The Cuban Triangle*, December 9.

Peters, Philip. 2012. *"Migration Policy Reform: Cuba Gets Started, U.S. Should Follow."* Arlington, VA: Lexington Institute.

Rodríguez, Andrea. 2012. "Cuba: un futuro de envejecimiento desafía la sostenibilidad económica." *El Nuevo Herald*, August 8. http://www.elnuevoherald.com/2012/08/07/v-print/1271467/cuba-un-futuro-de-envejecimiento.html#storylink=cpy.

Sánchez, Yoani. 2012. *Twitter*, August 22. https://twitter.com/yoanisanchez/status/2382885 42990745600

Recent Migration Reforms

Ted A. Henken

After years of rising anticipation and more than a few dashed hopes and false starts, the Cuban government announced its first major migration reform in 52 years in October 2012. Stressing that it was not acting under duress nor reacting to external pressure of any kind, Havana declared that "for the common will of the Cuban nation" (*Cuba Debate* 2012), as an exercise of its national sovereignty, and in an effort to "further normalize its relationship with the diaspora," it would henceforth no longer require citizens to request permission (via the *tarjeta blanca*, or exit visa) to leave the country, nor require them to first obtain a letter of invitation from someone in the country of destination (Cancio Isla 2012; *Granma* 2012). All they would need to travel abroad after January 14, 2013, when the new Decree-Law 302 would take effect, was a Cuban passport and a valid foreign visa (and of course the money to cover the costs of the trip itself).

While the fine print of the actual law does contain a number of restrictions and caveats (mostly contained in its Article 23) that make this reform less than the long-awaited recognition of citizens' inherent right to travel that was hoped for (Blanco and Dilla Alfonso 2012; Peters 2012), the change caught many Cubans by surprise as it repealed the 1961 statute (Law 989) that required the "nationalization through confiscation" of any real property and other assets of those who emigrate and cut by perhaps 80 percent the often prohibitive bureaucratic costs of traveling abroad (as an emigrant, tourist, or short-term traveler). Other important elements of the migration reform include the lengthening of the permitted time of residence abroad from 11 to 24 months without the forfeiture of one's residency rights and an end to the extremely high costs of extending one's stay abroad. Moreover, the 24-month migratory limit can now be extended indefinitely through application. Additionally, minor children are now allowed to travel abroad with the permission of their parents and can even gain permanent residence abroad while retaining Cuban residency (Dilla Alfonso 2012).

While the law did not restore Cuban émigrés' full citizenship rights to enter and leave their country of origin at will, it did create a legal path for them to regain their lost residency and the previous 30-day limit for their island visits was extended to 90 days (Cancio Isla 2012; Whitefield and Tamayo 2012). Additionally, it was later announced that the more than 100,000 Cubans who had emigrated "illegally" as rafters or defected while on trips abroad (including doctors and sports figures) would once again be allowed to visit their homeland provided that eight years had passed since their exit (Cancio Isla 2012; Peters 2012). To this was added the announcement that the island's doctors would *not* be prohibited from obtaining a passport as had widely been assumed since the law contains a special article designed to protect human capital and prevent brain drain in order "to preserve an educated work force for the economic, social, and technical-scientific development of the country" (Decree-Law 302). In sum, the reform "liberalizes the treatment of Cubans who wish to emigrate, who have emigrated and wish to return, or who wish to spend extended periods of time abroad" (Peters 2012: 3).

Some of the categories of those who are ineligible for passports under the new law are understandable and in line with international practice. For example, those undergoing legal proceedings, on parole, or eligible for military service can only obtain passports in special circumstances. However, this reasonable exception has already been used to deny passports to dissidents who had been released from prison but are still technically on parole, such as Ángel Moya and José Daniel Ferrer. Other restrictions against issuing passports listed in Article 23 are more chilling, including for "reasons of national defense and security" and the vague and potentially arbitrary "other reasons of public interest." Moreover, Article 23 unequivocally states that there remain some Cubans who are "inadmissible to the national territory" including those who "organize, stimulate, carry out, or participate in actions hostile to the political, economic, and social foundations of the Cuban State" (Decree-Law 302).

The wording of such stipulations is so vague that one has to wonder how broadly these exceptions will be invoked in practice. A hint came on the very first day at the new passport offices opened on January 14, 2013. Given that she had been denied an exit visa a record 20 previous times, the famed cyber-activist and blogger Yoani Sánchez made sure that she was at the very front of the line at her local immigration office to have her passport renewed that morning. However, this time around she reported via Twitter, "The official who saw me assured me that when I receive my passport I will be able to travel. I still can't believe it!" (Sánchez 2013a). Indeed, two weeks later Sánchez received her new passport and began a world tour in mid-February 2013 to, in her words, "learn and return" (Sánchez 2013b). While the Cuban government is taking a calculated risk in opening up its long-closed system

Independent Cuban blogger Yoani Sánchez has her documents checked at passport control before leaving Cuba to travel to Brazil and other countries at the José Martí International Airport in Havana, Cuba, Sunday, February 17, 2013. Sánchez is one of the Cuban dissidents who applied for passports to go overseas under recently enacted travel reform. Her request was granted in January 2013. On some 20 previous occasions, Sánchez had been denied the now eliminated exit visa that for decades was required of all islanders seeking to travel abroad. (AP Photo/ Franklin Reyes)

of migration with the potential loss of its authoritarian control and the emigration of tens of thousands of skilled personnel, it seems to be "betting on the idea that Cubans, given the freedom to travel and to return will indeed return in large numbers and bring important benefits to Cuba's economy" with them (Peters 2012: 1).

REFERENCES

Blanco, Juan Antonio and Haroldo Dilla Alfonso. 2012. "¡Habemus actualización migratoria! La cuestión migratoria no es una materia de permisos, sino de derechos." *Cuba Encuentro*, October 18. http://www.cubaencuentro.com/cuba/articulos/habemus-actualizacion-migratoria-280908.

Cancio Isla, Wilfredo. 2012. "Cuba anuncia reforma migratoria y elimina el permiso de salida del país." *Café Fuerte*, October 16.

Cuba Debate. 2012. "Por la voluntad común de la Nación Cubana." October 16.

Decree-Law 302. 2012. "Ley de Migración." *Gaceta Oficial*, October 16.

Dilla Alfonso, Haroldo. 2012. "Las encrucijadas de la política migratoria cubana." *Nueva Sociedad* 242 (November-December): 70–81.

Granma. 2012. "Actualiza Cuba su Política Migratoria." October 16.

Peters, Philip. 2012. *Migration Policy Reform: Cuba Gets Started, U.S. Should Follow*. Arlington, VA: Lexington Institute.

Sánchez, Yoani. 2013a. *Twitter*, January 14. https://twitter.com/yoanisanchez/status/290816894162841600.

Sánchez, Yoani. 2013b. *Twitter*, January 30. https://twitter.com/yoanisanchez/status/296758671583617024

Whitefield, Mimi and Juan Tamayo. 2012 "Will new Cuban migration policy really improve travel between U.S. and Cuba?" *The Miami Herald*, October 17.

Cuba's International Relations

Miriam Leiva

TWENTY-FIRST CENTURY RELATIONS BETWEEN CUBA AND THE UNITED STATES

Given their proximity, Cuba and the United States have been closely linked throughout their histories. Starting with the Spanish expeditions from Havana that discovered Florida in 1498, to John Quincy Adams' 1823 "ripe fruit" theory that assumed Cuba would eventually become a U.S. territory, to the U.S. entry in the Cuban War for Independence in 1898, to the Cuban revolution in 1959 and the subsequent U.S. embargo and emigration of more than a million of Cuba's citizens to the United States, the two countries have had a storied, intimate, and often antagonistic relationship. In fact, in his last annual message to Congress in 1898, U.S. president

William McKinley famously declared, "The new Cuba, yet to arise from the ashes of the past must needs be bound to us by ties of singular intimacy and strength, if its enduring welfare is to be assured" (Pérez 2003). More than 80 years later, the former U.S. diplomat Wayne Smith—who had done double duty working at the U.S. Embassy in Havana under Eisenhower in the early 1960s and again later in the late 1970s when President Carter reopened it as an Interest Section—made what was perhaps a more accurate observation when he wrote that "Cuba seems to have the same effect on American administrations as the full moon has on werewolves" (Smith 1988).

While there was some cooling of tensions between the two countries under the Clinton administration (1992–2000), relations became quite strained once again under President George W. Bush (2000–2008). For example, in May 2004 the Bush administration restricted the visits of Cuban-Americans to the island to just once every three years while also limiting their ability to send remittances to their relatives there. He even set up a federal body charged with writing a detailed plan for a future democratic Cuba in the "Commission for Assistance to a Free Cuba" and appointed an administration official with the dubious title of "Cuba transition coordinator." In 2009, Barack Obama lifted these bans, quietly did away with the commission and the transition coordinator, and began to facilitate religious, cultural, and academic exchanges aimed at empowering the Cuban people, reducing their economic dependence on the totalitarian state, and fomenting democratic ideas through people-to-people diplomacy.

Though since taking power in 2006 President Raúl Castro has repeatedly expressed a willingness to move toward the normalization of relations with the United States, his actions have shown otherwise. The best example of this mixed message was the late-2009 arrest of U.S. contractor Alan Gross who was accused of delivering equipment for satellite Internet access and cell phones to members of Cuba's small Jewish community. He was convicted and has remained in prison since then, so far serving more than three years of his 15-year sentence. The Cuban government has tried to suggest exchanging him for five Cuban prisoners convicted as spies in the United States, but this offer has been met with silence by Washington given its contention that the cases are not comparable.

Despite constant Cuban government propaganda about the damage it has suffered from the U.S. trade embargo, since 2001 the United States has become one of Cuba's main trading partners, mostly in food goods. It was already far and away the island's main source of remittances, with a stead growth in the numbers of Cuban-American visitors each year as well. At the same time, the embargo has failed to contribute to any change whatsoever in Cuba, only proving counterproductive for the interests of the United States. Moreover, Cuba is the only country in the world where the U.S. government does not allow its citizens to travel freely.

At the same time, the United States has welcomed and provided enviable opportunities and special legal treatment to Cuban immigrants, who with their descendants now number over 1.8 million people. While their departure has provided the Cuban government a convenient escape valve for unrest and dissent, today their knowledge, experience, and investments could help lift Cuba out of its current economic, political, and social crisis. Indeed, perhaps Cuba's January 2013 migration reform is aimed at encouraging just this kind of economic exchange and investment in the island by its many émigrés. The lifting of the travel ban against U.S. citizens by Congress would be a very positive step. Of course, there are many other areas where cooperation with

Jailed American U.S. Agency for International Development subcontractor Alan Gross, center, holds a sign as he poses for a photo with Rabbi Elie Abadie, right, and U.S. lawyer James L. Berenthal at the Finlay Military Hospital in Havana, November 27, 2012. Gross was arrested in December 2009. (AP Photo)

the United States—on the basis of mutual respect—could benefit the island such as drug enforcement, environmental protection, and cooperation on migration issues. Now in his second term and reelected with strong support from Cuban-Americans, President Obama has new options at his disposal to improve relations through executive order, but obviously appropriate reciprocal steps are required by the Cuban government, including the release of Alan Gross, a greater respect for human rights and civil liberties, and ending the constant harassment and arbitrary detention of members of Cuba's civil society.

SOCIALISM OF THE 21ST CENTURY: CUBA'S RELATIONS WITH VENEZUELA

Relations between Cuba and Venezuela also have a long history. In the first decade of the 20th century, diplomatic ties were established between the governments of the respective presidents, Tomás Estrada Palma and Cipriano Castro. Throughout the century, a back-and-forth migratory flow existed between the two countries, particularly during the dictatorship of Fulgencio Batista in the 1950s. Precisely for this reason, after the revolutionary government took power in Cuba, Fidel Castro's first foreign trip on January 23, 1959, was to Venezuela. Then, in November 1961, diplomatic relations were broken during the administration of Venezuelan president

Rómulo Betancourt, and from then on tensions deepened due to Cuba's support of guerrillas in Venezuela.

Diplomatic relations were restored in December 1974, but they suffered renewed tensions. First came the 1976 mid-air explosion onboard a *Cubana de Aviación* airplane which killed all the passengers, including the entire Cuban fencing team who was returning from a competition abroad. When investigations led to Luis Posada Carriles, Orlando Bosch, and other Cuban exile militants who had worked for Venezuelan intelligence agencies, bilateral relations suffered significantly. Later, relations were put on ice once again when former paratrooper Hugo Chávez received a hero's welcome upon his visit to Havana in December 1994 just two years after having participated in a military coup against Venezuelan president Andrés Pérez. These tensions were exacerbated by the support Fidel Castro provided to Hugo Chávez in winning Venezuela's 1998 presidential elections. Soon after Chávez took office, he and Castro signed a Comprehensive Cooperation Agreement, stipulating that Cuba would export goods and services (especially medical services) to Venezuela, while Venezuela would pay Havana with oil and its derivatives. This allowed the Cuban government to replace the subsidies it had lost with the disappearance of the Soviet Union and the socialist countries of Eastern Europe, helping it prolong its monopoly on power and reverse the initial reform measures it had been forced to introduce in the early 1990s.

When a coup attempt on April 12, 2002, jailed the Venezuelan president for two days, the support of the Cuban government—and particularly Fidel Castro's radio and television speeches from Havana—were instrumental in his return to power. That event solidified the integration project and led to an even deeper relationship between Castro's Cuba and Chávez's Venezuela. A new Energy Agreement with

Taken just outside the Cabaña Fortress on the east side of Havana's harbor during the annual International Book Fair, this photo features a broken down Fiat Polski, known affectionately in Cuba as a "Polaquito" for obvious reasons. The billboard in the background features the smiling face of the late Venezuelan president Hugo Chávez with the declaration: "We are going to make real the dream of Bolívar and Martí." (Orlando Luis Pardo Lazo)

Caracas was soon established which included the sale of 53,000 barrels of oil to Cuba per day (later increased to 92,000 barrels)—all under especially generous terms of financing. In April 2003, the first Cuban doctors arrived in Venezuela to work in health missions in poor neighborhoods known under the almost religious appellation *Misión Barrio Adentro*. In July of that same year, Cuban teachers began a literacy campaign in Venezuela modeled directly after Cuba's own successful campaign in 1961.

Finally, to celebrate the 10th anniversary of their first meeting, Castro and Chávez signed the so-called ALBA declaration (Agreement and Joint Declaration on the Application of the Bolivarian Alternative for Latin America and the Caribbean). Some Cuban officials were even quoted at the time as saying that Cuba now had two presidents, two flags, and that in the future would be known as a single country: "Cubazuela." While it is unlikely that many Cubans sympathize with such ideas, they are also aware that the island's economic crisis would be much worse if not for Venezuela's—and Chávez's—petrodollars. Moreover, thanks to the close relationship between the two countries, many Cubans have succeeded in getting relatively well-paying jobs in Venezuela—or even emigrating there—enabling them to significantly improve their standard of living, help their families back home, and sometimes use the country as a springboard to emigrate to the United States.

When Fidel Castro fell gravely ill on July 31, 2006, he was temporarily replaced by a team of seven officials, led by his brother General Raúl Castro, who until then had not been close to President Chávez. Chávez constantly celebrated Fidel Castro's hemispheric leadership and his stature as a role model for the Venezuelan president as he attempted to remake Venezuelan society in the image of Cuban state socialism. Ironically, this has taken place as Fidel himself teeters on the verge of death and while Raúl Castro has begun to institute "structural and conceptual changes" that move Cuba away from the state-centered model built by Fidel and admired with such adulation by Chávez.

In 2010, reciprocal trade in goods between the two countries amounted to $6 billion, with Cuban imports from Venezuela making up $4.3 billion of that total. Venezuela is currently Cuba's largest trading partner, both in the exchange of goods and services. At the same time, by 2011 there were some 44,000 Cuban technicians working in Venezuela, including doctors, paramedics, teachers, coaches, cultural attaches, and construction advisors. There were also an unknown number of security, intelligence, and high-up military officials. Moreover, in the larger framework of bilateral agreements and ALBA, Cuban personnel financed by Venezuela currently serve in Bolivia, Nicaragua, and Ecuador, as well as in other Caribbean countries and on other continents. The Cuban government pays for its vital oil imports and other goods from Venezuela with the services of these people, who only receive a fraction of the benefits that their labor makes possible.

However, after June 2011 the future of these key Venezuelan subsidies and the larger "special relationship" itself suddenly became very uncertain when Hugo Chávez discovered he had cancer, the specific characteristics of which have never been publicly disclosed. He underwent a repeated battery of operations, chemotherapy, and radiotherapy in Cuba, running the "Bolivarian" government from his Havana hospital bed and often sending his virtual commands back home via Twitter. His initial medical treatment in Cuba enabled him to temporarily recover enough to successfully win reelection for another term in October 2012. In December, however, he was forced to return to Cuba for another series of operations, making it impossible for him to be physically present at his own inauguration for a new term on January 10, 2012. Chávez died on March 5, 2013. Needless to say, this bizarre turn of events has called into question the continuance of the reciprocal solidarity and economic exchange between the two countries. Also, though Chávez won reelection with a solid majority in the October vote, he was contested for the first time by a charismatic candidate representing a united opposition. His chosen successor, Nicolás Maduro, was elected in a close and hotly contested election on April 14, 2013. However, it is doubtful that the Chávez-controlled state coffers—running quite low following the lavish social spending that led up to the October 2012 election—can be relied on to continue to so generously subsidize Cuba in the future (Corrales and Penfold 2010).

The political uncertainty faced by Venezuela together with Cuba's multifaceted crisis portend an uncertain future in the relations between the two countries not to mention their regional and international influence. The most sensible thing would be for the Cuban government to accelerate its reforms to at least begin to generate economic growth, while simultaneously diversifying its ties with other countries. Such a path would be greatly facilitated by parallel progress toward normalizing relations with the United States and an opening to the many Cubans living abroad that would allow them greater participation in the reconstruction of their homeland.

LIBERALIZATION WITHOUT DEMOCRATIZATION: CUBA'S RELATIONS WITH CHINA

To address the economic crisis and the possible loss of financial support from Venezuela, President Raúl Castro has sought to expand relations with other countries, and in 2009 he even visited some of them, though without achieving much success. Nevertheless, China and Vietnam have shown an interest in contributing to Cuba's economic reforms based on their own respective experiences in opening their economies to a kind of "market socialism," while successfully maintaining closed political systems. However, unlike the historic leaders of these two countries—Mao Zedong and Ho Chi Minh—who eventually disappeared from the political scene, Fidel Castro and the historic revolutionary leadership have only gradually stepped aside in Cuba. Moreover, despite his ambitious agenda of "updating" Cuba's socialist model, Raúl Castro has yet to prove himself a disciple of China's Deng Xiaoping who was fond of celebrating wealth, letting "a hundred flowers bloom, a hundred schools of thought contend," and of saying things like, "It matters not whether the cat is socialist or capitalist, if it catches mice then it is a good cat."

Relations between Cuba and these two Asian countries have had very peculiar characteristics. Vietnam received great support from the Cuban government during its war with the United States giving the two countries strong historical ties of solidarity. Meanwhile, Communist China, even when it was still internationally isolated, was recognized by the Cuban revolutionary government, which simultaneously broke diplomatic relations with Taiwan in September 1960. As roving ambassador without portfolio, Che Guevara visited China in 1961 to promote friendship and economic cooperation. Nevertheless, the following 30 years were touch-and-go given the "Sino-Soviet split"—the ongoing tensions between Beijing and Moscow, under whose orbit Cuba gravitated. When Cuba's special period began in the early-1990s due to the precipitous loss of Soviet subsidies, Fidel Castro quickly announced that one strategy of confronting the crisis would be through increased imports of Chinese goods, including hundreds of thousands of bicycles, hundreds of buses and locomotives, electric cookers, televisions, and refrigerators. Still, these Chinese products have not been accompanied by a steady supply of spare parts, possibly because of difficulties in payments by the Cuban government to Chinese companies for whom the bottom line goes hand in hand with socialist solidarity (Hearn 2009).

Still, bilateral trade between the two countries has risen to the point where China has become Cuba's second largest trading partner after Venezuela. In January 2010, trade reached almost two million dollars, more than half-a-million of which was Cuban exports. Likewise, China has begun to play a greater role in Cuba's bourgeoning tourist industry—building hotels and anticipating the arrival of ever greater numbers of newly wealthy Chinese tourists. There are also many initiatives of scientific and technical cooperation in the better cultivation of rice, soybeans, sorghum, and maize, along with the development of a solar energy industry on the sun-drenched island. Finally, in June 2011 the island saw the significant visit of China's vice president Xi Jinping, who became the general secretary of the Chinese Communist Party in 2012 and president of China itself in March 2013 when the National People's Congress convened.

During his stay in Cuba, 13 agreements were signed, with an emphasis on the expansion of economic cooperation between the companies *Unión Cubapetróleo* (CUPET) and China's National Petroleum Corporation, aimed at increased oil exploration in the Gulf of Mexico and an expansion in natural gas production at the Cienfuegos refinery. Additionally, a number of Cuban-Chinese joint venture companies in biotechnology and tourism are run out of China. However, unlike its relationship with Venezuela, Cuba's deepening relationship with China is based more on mutual economic and commercial benefits than on ideological solidarity or geopolitical strategy. Thus, Cuba's current inability to pay its debts, safeguard Chinese investments, or guarantee China a steady supply of export products make the relationship contingent at best.

REFERENCES

Corrales, Javier and Michael Penfold. 2010. *Dragon in the Tropics: Hugo Chávez and the Political Economy of Revolution in Venezuela.* Washington, D.C.: Brookings Institution Press.

Hearn, Adrian H. 2009. "China's Relations with Mexico and Cuba: A Study of Contrasts." *Pacific Rim Report*, No. 52, January. http://usf.usfca.edu/pac_rim/new/research/pacrim report/pacrimreport52.html.

Pérez, Jr. Louis A. 2003. *Cuba and the United States: Ties of Singular Intimacy.* Athens: University of Georgia Press.

Smith, Wayne S. 1988. *The Closest of Enemies: A Personal and Diplomatic History of the Castro Years.* New York: WW Norton and Company.

The Catholic Church, Dissidence, Civil Society, and Human Rights

Dimas Castellanos and Miriam Celaya

THE CATHOLIC CHURCH IN DIALOGUE WITH THE CUBAN GOVERNMENT

Between 2010 and 2012, the Cuban Catholic Church took on the role of mediator between the totalitarian government and the island's dissidents and political prisoners as represented by the *Damas de Blanco* (Ladies in White), moving from its past position of confrontation to one of dialogue. This was certainly not the first time in Cuba's history that the Church and its clergy acted as interlocutors. Father Pedro Agustín Morell intervened during the island's first mass slave uprising in 1731; Father Antonio María Claret acted as a mediator during the trial of Joaquín de Agüero and other patriots from Camaguey in 1851; Father Olallo José Valdés stood up against the Spanish army's attempt to intimidate and provoke their rebel rivals by publicly displaying of the dead body of independence leader Ignacio Agramonte in 1873; and Enrique Pérez Serantes famously intervened to save Fidel Castro's life after he was captured following his failed assault on the Moncada Barracks in 1953.

After seven years of nonstop struggle by the Ladies in White since 2003, the prolonged hunger strike of dissident Guillermo Fariñas, and sustained international criticism, the Church took on the role of mediator to negotiate the release of the remaining political prisoners from the Black Spring crackdown in 2003. While most dissidents quickly chose exile over continued imprisonment, others refused to be banished from their own country and insisted on remaining free inside Cuba to continue their fight. Of course, the government was brought to the negotiating table by its interest in winning favor with the European Union in order to eliminate the "common position" on Cuba, which conditions greater economic aid and trade on improvements in human rights. However, the results of the mediation remain insufficient. Legal proceedings that in the past resulted in long prison sentences have been replaced by extra-legal short-term detentions, constant harassment, threats, beatings, and supposedly spontaneous acts of mob repudiation. These initial efforts at mediation by the Church and its negotiations with the government will achieve lasting progress only when they result in a dialogue that includes all sectors of Cuba's diverse civil society (Booth and DeYoung 2010).

The Church hierarchy is aware of the government's critical situation, and therefore has followed a consistent strategy of giving in on some points in order to strengthen its hand in achieving others of greater importance. Such a strategy has its supporters and detractors, and has generated contradictions with some sectors of Cuba's emergent civil society. At present, the government's continued repression makes any process of further mediation impossible. However, the government's inability to indefinitely deny civil society its rightful role will lead—sooner rather than later—to structural changes in a process of negotiation where the Church will have an important place alongside a host of new actors.

THE VISIT OF POPE BENEDICT XVI, MARCH 2012

The official reason for Pope Benedict XVI's trip to Cuba in March 2012 was the celebration of the 400th anniversary of the first apparition of Cuba's patron saint, Our Lady of Charity of Cobre (*Nuestra Señora de Caridad de Cobre*). However, like the previous visit of Pope John Paul II in 1998, Benedict's arrival also had a political dimension that created great expectations. The Cuban government needed to send the world a sign of tolerance and respect for diversity. It also hoped to convince the Church to intercede on its behalf in the halls of global power to help alleviate the crisis that could result from potential loss of support from Venezuela, whether as a result of an eventual defeat of Hugo Chávez in the October 2012 presidential elections (he prevailed) or due to his death from his recurring cancer—which did indeed come to pass in March 2013. Upon his arrival, Benedict found in Cuba a stronger Catholic Church than the one that John Paul II had bolstered just 14 years before. Now it enjoyed more space for its ministry, had spread wider and deeper than in previous decades, and as a result has achieved greater social influence. At the same time, the influence of the ruling party over the people and even within the party's own rank and file has weakened significantly.

In this game of competing political interests, it would not be surprising for the Church to regain regular access to mass media, which has been impossible for half-a-century. The Church may also be permitted to renew its official involvement in the educational process. In fact, for years the Church has sponsored college-level courses on a variety of subjects taking place in religious centers throughout the country. The

Fourteen years after Pope John Paul II visited the country, Pope Benedict XVI made his first visit holding Mass in Havana's Plaza de la Revolución on March 28, 2012 following a similar event in Cuba's second city, Santiago de Cuba. (L'Osservatore Romano Vatican-Pool/Getty Images)

Church also holds annual events such as its "pedagogical week," which is attended by Catholic teachers who work in the national education system. Recently, the Church has inaugurated a new seminary and a business school in partnership with a Catholic university in Spain. Such interests were publicly expressed by Pope Benedict XVI during his visit to Havana: "We hope that soon will be the time when the Church is able to bring to the fields of learning the benefits of the mission entrusted to her by the Lord, which can never be neglected."

To avoid frictions with the authorities while also maintaining a safe distance from Cuba's own internal conflict, the Pope did not meet with dissidents during his visit. At the same time, he refused to say anything publicly that could be taken as support for the government, such as endorsing the release of the country's five agents held in U.S. prison. In the case of the U.S. embargo, he was diplomatic enough to condemn it in the same breath that he criticized the lack of freedoms in Cuba. Nevertheless, it is clear that neither the Pope nor any other external authority can do for Cubans what they must do for themselves. In the words of Benedict XVI himself: "Both Cuba and the world need changes, but they will only come if everyone is able to seek the truth and decide for themselves to take the path of love, sowing reconciliation and brotherhood" (Donadio and Burnett 2012).

DISSIDENCE AND CIVIL SOCIETY

Cuba is mired in a deep and long-term structural crisis the cause of which is the impracticality of its economic model and the lack of political will on the part of its current rulers. This situation dates back to the dismantling of Cuban civil society following the revolutionary triumph in 1959. Still more than half-a-century later, the Sixth Party Congress in April 2011, the First Party Conference in January 2012, and recent statements by government figures have only reconfirmed the conviction that the necessary "updating" of Cuba's socialist economic model will not be accompanied by any similar political opening. Currently, there exist numerous political opposition groups and other independent civic associations throughout the country, all of which lack legal recognition, placing their activities outside the law and facilitating repressive government action against them. Because such independent civic associations—whatever their varied nature or tendency—lack legal standing, those who spontaneously organize into such interest groups are automatically disqualified as counterrevolutionaries and grouped together into the diffuse category of dissidents.

Still, among these groups there are a handful of civic associations that enjoy relative tolerance from the government or benefit from a modicum of official recognition. One such group is the *Cofradía de la Negritud* (Black Brotherhood), which is a group of intellectuals who meet regularly to engage in debates, screen films, and hold exhibitions that analyze Cuba's racial history. A number of other independent leftist groups share a similar in-between status including a diverse group of revolutionary communists, Trotskyites, anarchists, and "libertarian socialists" (*socialistas libertarios*), who maintain various online bulletins such as the "SPD Bulletin" (*Socialismo Participativo y Democrático*) and the "Critical Observatory Bulletin" (*Boletín Observatorio Crítico*). They maintain a critical stance toward the current government, often accusing it—from the left—of being insufficiently socialist, mired in bureaucracy, and nondemocratic since it has traditionally concentrated power in just a few hands.

Members of these groups have recently reached out to other independent, alternative groups that make up Cuba's diverse and emergent civil society. Some of these contacts take place in the relatively open spaces recently won by the Catholic Church (such as the magazines *Espacio Laical, Palabra Nueva,* and *Convivencia*), while other contacts are with more defiant groups of independent bloggers, activists, and dissidents (such as the forum for debate provided by Antonio Rodiles and his project *Estado de SATS*). This network of civic associations is characterized primarily by its complete independence from the state and its members' expertise in certain professions such as law, economics, politics, or culture. Given the fear and mutual suspicion that characterizes non-state civic activity in Cuba and the lack of constitutional guarantees for freedom of association and assembly, contacts between these groups is a new phenomenon that is playing an important role in strengthening the civic and political formation of certain sectors of Cuban society.

While the main opposition groups to arise during the 1960s and 1970s were characterized by their failed attempt to spark an armed guerrilla uprising against the communist government, the most successful dissident groups of the 1980s and especially the 1990s have rejected violence and opted instead for what they call *la lucha cívica* (the civic struggle). They were aided by the fact that the collapse of the Soviet Union between 1989 and 1991 revealed the failure of the state socialist model. At the same time, Soviet premier Mikhail Gorbachev's policies of *perestroika* (political and economic restructuring) and *glasnost* (openness and transparency) began to slowly seep into many sectors of Cuba's intelligentsia and professional class. These changes also influenced the thinking of many ordinary Cubans who either considered the socialist model unsustainable or simply hoped for an economic opening that would allow them to prosper.

As a result, by the mid-1990s the island was home to over 100 active if often very small dissident groups, most of which came together under the *Concilio Cubano* (Cuban Council) coalition. Many of these groups have since disappeared or have been reconfigured forming new groups. This amounted to a revival of opposition movements in Cuba. Across the island numerous parties emerged, each with its own ideological leanings: Liberals, Christian Democrats, Social Democrats, and others most interested in pushing for the full recognition human rights. At the same time, independent journalists, independent libraries, and various clubs and civic groups with a wide range of demands and proposals began to proliferate as well. There are also opposition groups without a clear ideological definition or without concrete political projects, which generally establish alliances with the more recognized and politically organized groups.

The repression that dissidents have undergone at the hands of the authorities, the lack of avenues for free expression, and the absence of basic rights have all hindered the growth of political parties and independent dissident groups. These obstacles have also made it difficult for the population at large to access accurate information about political alternatives. Other limitations often arise from within the parties themselves, which in most cases have leaders who assume markedly sectarian or populist positions in a style similar to the very government that they seek to replace. Some even join the opposition as a way to emigrate to the United States as political refugees. In sum, opposition parties have largely failed to establish strong links between them to create a united or popular front against the government. However, the domestic dissident movement has played an important role in demonstrating that there is a growing and sustained movement opposed to the totalitarian government, while also publicly exposing the regime's violence and will to power.

While ideological differences and contrasting positions on crucial political issues—such as the embargo and relations with the United States—have led to conflict among various dissident groups, distancing them from the rest of society, in recent years some civic organizations have gained ground and positioned themselves to better influence the public. These groups usually stand out because they lack an inflexible vertical structure and hold no rigid ideological agenda. Instead, they take advantage of every possible alternative means of communication, dissemination, and contact to create spaces for serious and respectful debate and the formulation of realistic proposals for the future.

These emergent groups do not come together around a singular ideology but seek to build a consensus around their common claim to the exercise of full civil rights. Furthermore, they are characterized by their expression of a variety of independent projects, including publications such as the now defunct online magazines *Consenso* (Consensus), *Contodos* (With Everyone), or the new digital ventures *Voces* (Voices) and *Convivencia* (Coexistence); audiovisual projects such as *Razones Ciudadanas* (Citizen's Reasons); websites, including *Desde Cuba* (From Cuba), *Voces Cubanas* (Cuban Voices), *Havana Times*, other independent blogs and other, more overarching projects such as the Havana-based *Estado de SATS*, which features both a website and a physical space for its debates; and *Proyecto Convivencia* (Coexistence Project) which is directed by Dagoberto Valdés, grew out of the lay-Catholic magazine *Vitral*, and is located in Pinar del Río.

One especially unique project is the *Asociación Jurídica de Cuba* (AJC or Judicial Association of Cuba), which is based in the capital and has branches in several provinces. Founded by a group of lawyers, the AJC offers free legal advice to the public through consultations and via its own website. Finally, there is a growing set of alternative film, theater, music, and visual arts groups who develop rebellious artistic and cultural activities and have begun to communicate with one another in various ways. A standout in this area is the multidisciplinary art and poetry collective known as *Omni-Zona Franca*, which was born out of the massive housing project in Eastern Havana, Alamar. Similarly, other independent artistic groups such as *Alzar las Voces* (Raise Your Voices) project, various Hip-Hop groups, and graffiti artists, like *El Sexto*, have emerged in recent years to play an active role in Cuba's incipient civil society.

A weakness that has long existed both among the people at large and in the ranks of the dissident movement is their lack of a political culture and a civic education. In this sense, the alternative spaces for debate that have emerged in recent years have made it possible for Cubans of different tendencies to exchange ideas respectfully. All these point to the formation of true citizens—equally aware of their rights and responsibilities—and the resurgence of alternative civil society groups that deserve greater attention. Finally, Cuba has spawned a variety of other civic and human rights organizations, among the most prominent of which are the *Damas de Blanco* (Ladies in White) led by Berta Soler, the *Federación Latinoamericana de Mujeres*

Rurales (FLAMUR or the Latin American Federation of Rural Women), the *Comisión Cubana de Derechos Humanos y Reconciliación Nacional* (Cuban Commission for Human Rights and National Reconciliation) led by Elizardo Sánchez Santa Cruz, and the *Unión Patriótica de Cuba* (Patriotic Union of Cuba) headed by dissident José Daniel Ferrer.

HUMAN RIGHTS

The absence of human rights in Cuba constitutes the main obstacle to the solution of the country's structural crisis. The island's chronic economic backwardness, its widespread corruption, the generalized apathy and hopelessness among the population, the ongoing mass exodus of many of its youngest and brightest citizens, the accelerated aging of the population cannot be effectively addressed without the full and interested participation of Cubans themselves. This is because human rights and the full exercise of political rights and civil liberties are the foundation of a people's political, economic, and cultural participation in any modern society. The dismantling Cuban civil society and the elimination of the civil, political, and economic rights on which it is based, left society critically vulnerable to totalitarian control. The impact of this process was so severe that Cuba's debilitated civil society and retrograde political culture still suffer from the consequences more than half-a-century later (Amnesty International 2012).

The implementation of structural changes that would allow the nation to move beyond this state of affairs requires placing the Cuban people at the very center of the decision-making process, allowing them to participate directly in matters of national interest. While the road ahead for Cubans is an extremely perilous and complex one, the nation benefits from an enviable constitutional tradition dating back to the 19th century. This includes the key role played by the Cuban delegation in drafting the Universal Declaration of Human Rights in 1948. In fact, as described earlier, many of the elements contained in that Declaration had already been enshrined in Cuba's constitution of 1901, and expanded further in its 1940 Constitution. This tradition makes the lack of the recognition of human rights in today's Cuba especially absurd.

In fact, when Cuba held the presidency of the Non-Aligned Movement and was elected to serve on the Human Rights Council of the United Nations, the island's then foreign minister Felipe Pérez Roque was forced to publicly declare on December 10, 2007, that the government would soon sign various human rights treaties that were the body's foundation and had been in force since 1976, including the U.N. Covenant on Civil and Political Rights and the Covenant on Economic, Social, and Cultural Rights. However, after the island's representatives did in fact sign these agreements in New York on February 28, 2008, it put the island's government in a tenuous position. Since such agreements are binding, to actually ratify them back in Cuba would imply key changes to the country's laws, something incompatible with the nature of totalitarianism.

In this regard, a grassroots initiative launched in June 2012 called "Citizen Demand for Another Cuba" is noteworthy. Prepared by a group of independent Cuban activists, the petition cites Articles 3 and 63 of the current Cuban Constitution, which declare that "sovereignty resides in the people from whom all state power emanates"

"CITIZEN DEMAND FOR ANOTHER CUBA" (FRAGMENT)

As legitimate children of this island and an essential part of the nation, we feel a deep sorrow at the prolonged crisis in which we live and at the demonstrated inability of the current government to make fundamental changes. This obliges us to demand that the Cuban government immediately implement the Universal Declaration of Human Rights and ratify the U.N. Covenants on Civil and Political Rights and Economic, Social, and Cultural Rights, which it has already signed. This would ensure full respect for all citizens regardless of their political ideology and restore the right of dissent to the people. We consider such rights essential to the formation of a modern, free, and pluralistic Cuba. We are committed to a democratic transformation where everyone can share their views and contribute to their realization. We invite all Cubans inside and outside the island who identify with these demands to join this just and necessary petition. Our hope of being heard by the government is nearly exhausted, yet we have decided to set this demand before the authorities as an urgent recourse to achieve effective understanding. We refuse to accept institutional silence as a response to our demands.

and that "every citizen has the right to file grievances and make petitions to the authorities, and to receive pertinent responses in a timely manner, in accordance with the law." Then, citing the "demonstrated inability of the current government to make fundamental changes," the petitioners call on the government to be as good as its word and ratify the U.N. agreements it had previously signed. This petition, signed by scores of civil society activists, was then delivered to Cuba's National Assembly as a symbol of their determination to struggle for the fundamental changes that will allow a democratic transition on the island. This marked the kickoff of the ongoing *Por Otra Cuba* (For Another Cuba) campaign, which has since included various public events on the island, many of which have been met by repression and state-organized acts of mob violence.

Along the same lines, but with a broader reach, Cubans both at home and abroad launched the *Llamamiento urgente por una Cuba mejor y possible* (Urgent appeal for a better and more viable Cuba) in August 2012. Founded on their right to determine their own future through the full exercise of their freedoms, independence, and sovereignty, the signatories to the document called on all Cubans to avoid violent acts and bloodshed, particularly those directed at the defenseless. They call for a national dialogue in order to constructively take up the challenge presented by the current crisis. They also put forth a set of positive measures that can be immediately put into practice if and when there exists the political will to do so on the part of the government. In sum, the appeal sets forth a group of proposals whose starting point is the recognition of Cuban's fundamental human rights.

REFERENCES

Amnesty International. 2012. "Cuba—Routine Repression: Political Short-term Detentions and Harassment in Cuba." March 22. http://www.amnesty.org/en/library/asset/AMR25/007/2012/en/647943e7-b4eb-4d39-a5e3-ea061edb651c/amr250072012en.pdf.

Booth, William and Karen DeYoung. 2010. "Cuba to Release 52 Political Prisoners, Catholic Church Says." *Washington Post*, July 8. http://www.washingtonpost.com/wp-dyn/content/article/2010/07/07/AR2010070705265.html.

Donadio, Rachel and Victoria Burnett. 2012. "Raúl Castro Greets Pope Benedict at Start of Closely Watched Visit." *New York Times*, March 26. http://www.nytimes.com/2012/03/27/world/americas/pope-benedict-in-cuba-for-second-leg-of-latin-america-visit.html?pagewanted=all&_r=0.

Glossary

This section provides brief definitions or descriptions of common acronyms, terms, places, things, or phrases associated with Cuba. Special attention has been given to Spanish words that may have a particular meaning or resonance in Cuba. Key sources for the Afro-Cuban and music-related terms have been Cuban ethnomusicologist Helio Orovio's book *Cuban Music from A to Z* (Duke University Press, 2004) and Ned Sublette's *Cuba and Its Music: From the First Drum to the Mambo* (Chicago Review Press, 2004). Christopher P. Baker's *Moon Handbook: Cuba* (Avalon, 2006) has also been very helpful.

Abakuá   An all-male Afro-Cuban secret society whose members are known as *Ñáñigos*. Descending from the leopard societies of the Calabar region of Africa, they are also known by their ethnic name, *Carabalí*.

Aché   An African-*Yoruba* word used in *Santería*, which means "spirit" or "soul force."

Afrocubanismo   A Cuban cultural movement that emerged between 1920 and 1940 similar to the Harlem Renaissance.

Ajiaco   A traditional Cuban stew that derives its distinctive flavor from the variety of ingredients it contains. The word is often used to describe the mixture of ingredients that make up Cuba's unique ethnicity and culture as well.

ANAP   *Asociación Nacional de Agricultores Pequeños* (National Association of Small Farmers).

Añjeo   Aged rum usually taken straight or on the rocks.

Annexationism   A movement that emerged during the second half of the 19th century in Cuba and the United States that sought to incorporate the island into the U.S. political order either as a slave state or as a U.S. territory.

El apóstol   A popular, reverential title used to refer to Cuban poet and independence leader José Martí.

Arawak   The parent indigenous group that was the source of Cuba's *Taíno*.

Areíto   A *Taíno* ceremony that included music, dancing, and the call-and-response retelling of tales.

Asere   An African-origin word popularized by *Abakuá* members and commonly used among Cuban youth today to mean "buddy" or "friend." It is often heard as part of the popular expression: "*¿Qué bolá, asere?*" Or "What's up, buddy?" (see *ecobio*).

Auténtico Party   A political party founded in the 1940s by Ramón Grau San Martín, who served as Cuban president from 1944 to 1948. The party's full name was *Partido Revolucionario Cubano—Auténtico* (PRC-A), named in honor of the party founded in 1892 by José Martí (see PRC).

Autonomist Party   A Cuban political party founded in the second half of the 19th century with the aim of achieving political autonomy, while still remaining a formal dependency of Spain.

Babalú-Ayé   An Afro-Cuban *orisha* associated with sickness and syncretized with the Catholic Saint Lazarus (see *El Rincón*).

Bajareques   Mud hut structures used by the *Taínos*.

Balsero   Meaning "rafter" from the Spanish word *balsa* or "raft." The term *balsero* is associated with the Cuban rafter exodus of the early 1990s when tens of thousands of desperate migrants set themselves afloat on marginally seaworthy craft in an attempt to reach the United States.

Barbacoa   Originally a *Taíno* term for a loft for preserving food. Today, the term can refer to a style of cooking food (barbecue) or to split-level constructions within preexisting homes or apartments, increasingly common in Cuba due to lack of new housing.

Barbudo   Literally meaning "bearded," this term was popularly used to describe guerrilla fighters.

Batá drums   The word *batá* is *Yoruba* for "drum" and such drums are believed to contain a living spirit or *fundamento*. These sacred drums are always played in a set of three. Each drum is gendered (male or female), two headed, and played in one's lap in very specific patterns as a way of calling out to the *orishas*.

Batey   A "company town" adjacent to a sugar mill. Also used to describe the central plaza of such a town. The term is originally derived from the term *Taínos* used for their central plazas.

Battle of Ideas   A political mobilization led by Fidel Castro roughly between 1999 and 2006, when he stepped down from power. It involved a recentralization of government oversight, the scaling back of economic reforms, the public celebration of revolutionary consciousness (see *conciencia*), and a crackdown on economic crime and corruption.

Bay of Pigs   (*Bahía de Cochinos*) A bay on the southwest coast of Cuba where a U.S.-backed force of Cuban exiles failed in their attempt to overthrow the revolution in mid-April 1961 (see *Brigade 2506*). The abortive invasion is usually referred to in Spanish as *Girón*, in reference to the beach where the primary battle was fought (see *Playa Girón*).

La Bayamesa The name of a song composed in 1868 by Perucho Figueredo, which celebrates an early uprising in the town of Bayamo and gave its words and melody to the Cuban national anthem.

La beca The colloquial name given to Cuba's system of countryside boarding schools, also known as *la escuela al campo*.

Bemba An African-derived colloquial term for "lips," forever associated with Cuban singer Celia Cruz's version of the song *Bemba Colorá*, or "Red Lips." Also, commonly used in Cuban Spanish when referring to "word of mouth" of the "rumor mill" (*radio bemba*).

Bembé An informal festival celebrated for the enjoyment of the *Yoruba orishas*. Such festivals usually feature spirit possession and the playing of specialized *bembé* drums.

Bloqueo Meaning "blockade," this is the preferred term used by the Cuban government to refer to the U.S. embargo.

Bohío A hut with a thatched palm roof used by Cuba's *Taínos* and still commonly found in Cuba's rural areas.

Bongó An Afro-Cuban percussion instrument used by *son* trios consisting of two small gendered drums of slightly different size joined together by a piece of wood.

Boniato A white sweet potato used as a staple in the Cuban diet, alternately known as a *batata*, a Cuban sweet potato, or a white yam.

Botellas Sinecures (easy, well-paying government job) given as patronage to political supporters during the years of the Cuban Republic (1902–1958).

Brigade 2506 The exile invasion force that attempted to spark an overthrow of the revolutionary government in April 1961 (see Bay of Pigs).

Brigadista A term that can refer to members or the 1961 Bay of Pigs invasion force, Brigade 2506, or alternately to members of the youth literacy campaign who were active across the island that summer as part of the Conrado Benítez Literacy Brigade.

Brothers to the Rescue Known as *Hermanos al Rescate* in Spanish, this is a group of Cuban-American pilots led by José Basulto that ran search and rescue missions in the Straits of Florida in the 1990s aimed at locating stranded Cuban rafters (see *balsero*). In 1996 two of their civilian planes were shot down by the Cuban military over international airspace after their repeated penetration of Cuban airspace to drop leaflets on the island.

Brujería A derogatory term for witchcraft or black magic, related to the terms *bruja* "witch" and *brujo* "witchdoctor."

Cabildo de nación African ethnic associations created in Cuba as early as the late 16th century and based on the Spanish tradition of *cofradías* or religious brotherhoods. *Cabildos* were organized by slaves and free people of color belonging to the same African ethnic group.

Cacique A *Taíno* word for an indigenous chieftain, also used colloquially to mean "boss."

CAME *Consejo de Ayuda Mutua Económica* (Council for Mutual Economic Assistance), known in English as COMECON or CMEA, this abbreviation refers to the Soviet bloc trade organization that existed from 1949 to 1991, which Cuba joined in 1972.

Caney Meaning "log cabin" in the indigenous *Taíno* language, there is also a town named *El Caney* near Santiago de Cuba and a Cuban rum produced under the brand name Caney.

CANF The Cuban American National Foundation, one of the leading Cuban exile organizations in the United States founded in 1981 by Jorge Mas Canosa.

Carabalí A term used in Cuba to refer to the African ethnic group originating in the Efik and Efo groups of the Cross River region in Nigeria called the Calabar (see *Abakuá*).

Caribs One of the dominant indigenous groups present in the Lesser Antilles at the time of the conquest. They gave their name to the Caribbean.

Caridad del Cobre Our Lady of Charity of Cobre, Cuba's patron saint (see *Ochún*).

Casabe A dry bread or cracker cake made from the *yuca* root (known as manioc or cassava in English). It was a staple of the *Taíno* diet and is still consumed today in Cuba and other Caribbean islands.

Caserío A hamlet or group of small country houses.

Casino The original name used in Cuba in the late 1930s for the fast-paced couple dance that was later rebranded *salsa* in the United States. Cubans continue to refer to such salsa dancing as *bailando casino*. The term is related to a more choreographically complex group "wheel" dance known as *rueda de casino*.

Caudillo A military or political "strongman" who rules more through physical might and personal charisma than through bureaucratic or democratic channels.

CDRs *Comités para la Defensa de la Revolución* (Committees for the Defense of the Revolution). Neighborhood-based vigilance networks aimed at guarding against subversion and counterrevolutionary activity.

Central A term used in Cuba for a sugar mill and refinery usually located at the "center" of a sugarcane plantation (see *ingenio*).

Changó The Afro-Cuban *orisha* or deity associated with fire, lightening, and thunder, and syncretized with Santa Barbara.

Changüí One of the oldest variants of Cuban son that originated in Guantánamo.

Charanga A musical ensemble that first emerged at the turn of the 19th century playing *danzones*, later becoming associated with the *cha-cha-chá* in the 1950s. Typical instrumentation includes a flute, violin, piano, double bass, *paila* (Creole tympani), and *güiro* (gourd scraper), later augmented with the *conga* drum and two other violins.

Chéquere A percussion instrument made from a large, dry, hollowed-out gourd encased in a net of beads. Also spelled *chekeré*.

Chévere An African word from the *Efik* people of Nigeria used throughout Latin America to mean "cool."

Choteo Cuba's unique brand of irreverent mockery or satire, intended to undercut and question authority.

Cimarrón An escaped slave. When a *cimarrón* joined forces to live with other "run-aways" in community, such communities were called *palenques* and their members *apalencados*.

CIMEX Cuban Import-Export Corporation, Cuba's largest commercial enterprise.

Los cinco These are "the five" Cuban intelligence agents alternately referred to as "spies" or "heroes," who have been imprisoned in the United States for espionage since the mid-1990s. One of these has since returned to Cuba.

Clave A pair of hard wooden sticks used to keep the basic 3–2 or 2–3 rhythmic foundation of *son* and *rumba*, respectively. The rhythm itself is also called the *clave*.

Coartación The practice of allowing slaves to purchase their own freedom, known as "manumission" in English.

Cohiba The *Taíno* word for tobacco, now the brand name of the most sought-after Cuban-made cigar.

Colono A Cuban term for a small-scale sugar farmer.

Comandante Meaning "commander," this is one of Fidel Castro's most common nicknames, as in *Comandante en Jefe* (Commander in Chief). The term is also the military equivalent to a major, the highest rank awarded in Cuba's rebel army.

Comino The Spanish word for "cumin," a key ingredient in Cuban cuisine.

Comintern An acronym for the "Communist International," which was an international communist organization headquartered in the Soviet Union. Also known as the "Third International," it existed between 1919 and 1943, when it was officially dissolved by Joseph Stalin.

Commission for Assistance to a Free Cuba A working group set up by the Bush administration in 2004, it produced a pair of lengthy and detailed reports on aiding Cuba in its transition to democratic rule.

Comparsa de Carnival A neighborhood street parade that takes place during carnival season, accompanied by *conga* drums, chants, marching, dancing, and the bugle-like *coroneta china*.

Compay A colloquial abbreviation of the word *compadre* often used as a nickname as in the stage name of the late *son* musician Francisco Repilado, aka, *Compay Segundo*.

Conciencia Revolutionary consciousness, often used in the early years of the revolution to rally the Cuban people behind state-defined political goals and production quotas.

Concilio cubano A coalition of over 130 dissident organizations formed in 1995 and dedicated to the proposition that a democratic transition in Cuba can be brought about by peaceful means.

Conga A colloquial term for the *tumbadora* drum, used originally in *rumba* but later a common instrument in most popular dance bands. This kind of drum is also a fixture of "conga lines" or *comparsa* parades (see *tumbadora*).

Congo The name of the Cuban ethnic group originating in the African Congo and responsible for introducing the spiritual practice known as *Palo* or *Palo Mayombe* to the island.

Congrí oriental A popular variant of *moros* or "dirty rice." Sometimes written *congrís*, the term originated from the popular Haitian Creole term for "beans and rice," *congó et riz*.

Coño An all-purpose Cuban exclamation that can express surprise, anger, or even happiness.

Controversia A form of sung poetry where two poets or *repentistas* try to outdo one another with their inventive braggadocio.

Conuco The name given to the small gardens cultivated by the *Taíno*.

Corneta china A bugle-like instrument used in *conga* parades (see *comparsa de carnival*).

Council of Ministers A governmental body that comprises the Cuban cabinet.

Council of State The most powerful governmental body in Cuba exercising de facto rule.

Criollo A word meaning "Creole" in English, it was originally used to distinguish those born of Spanish parents on the island of Cuba (and throughout Spanish America) from the Spanish-born *peninsulares*. Today it denotes anything or anyone native to or typically Cuban.

Croquetas "Croquettes," a common Cuban snack made from breaded and fried ground chicken or ham.

CTC *Central de Trabajadores Cubanos*, the abbreviation for Cuba's single labor union.

Cuba libre A term popularized at the end of the 19th century to celebrate the fight for independence from Spain or a "free Cuba." It is also the name of one of the most popular Cuban cocktails made from the mixture of Cuban rum, Coca-Cola, lime juice, and ice.

Cuban Adjustment Act A U.S. law passed in 1966 intended to facilitate the regularization of the immigration status of hundreds of thousands of Cuban immigrants who had arrived in the country by irregular means following the revolution. The Act is partly responsible for the continued existence of special treatment for Cuban arrivals, also known as the "wet foot/dry foot" policy.

Cuban Democracy Act A law passed in 1992 under the leadership of U.S. Congressman Robert Torricelli (also known as the Torricelli Law), which hardened the U.S. embargo by prohibiting foreign-based subsidiaries of U.S. companies from trading with Cuba.

Cuban Missile Crisis The 13-day international standoff in October 1962 between U.S. president Kennedy and Soviet premier Khrushchev following the discovery of Soviet ballistic missile sites on the island of Cuba. Known in Cuba as *La crisis de octubre* (The October Crisis).

Cuban Revolutionary Council The "government in waiting" formed with U.S. government support in early 1961 prior to the Bay of Pigs invasion.

Cubanía A term that captures the essence of being Cuban or "Cuban-ness," also known as *cubanidad*.

Cubano The colloquial term for a "Cuban sandwich." Now ubiquitous in the delis of South Florida and New York City, such sandwiches were popular in Republican Cuba (1902–1958), but are hard to find on the island today.

CUC *Cubano convertible* ("Convertible Cuban Peso"), this is the Cuban currency pegged to the value of the U.S. dollar and worth roughly 24 times the value of the island's national currency, the Cuban peso, or CUP.

Cuentapropista "Self-employed worker," from the legal term given to micro-entrepreneurs or "own account" workers in Cuba, and derived from the Spanish term for self-employment, *trabajo por cuenta propia*.

CUJAE *Ciudad Universitaria José Antonio Echeverría* (José Antonio Echeverría University), Cuba's principal technical and engineering university located in Havana. Sometimes also referred to as the ISPJAE (*Instituto Superior Politécnico José Antonio Echeverría*), or the José Antonio Echeverría Polytechnic University.

CUP The "Cuban peso," or national currency (*moneda nacional*), which is the currency all state workers—the vast majority of workers—are paid in (see CUC).

Daiquirí A Cuban cocktail made with crushed ice, rum, lime juice, and sugar, named after a coastal town near Santiago de Cuba where the drink was invented in 1898 by the American Jennings Cox.

Damas de Blanco An organization—known as the "Ladies in White" in English—founded by the wives, mothers, and daughters of 75 dissidents and independent journalists arrested and sentenced to long prison terms during the Black Spring of 2003.

Dance of the Millions A period of economic upheaval in Cuba between 1920 and 1921 when the price of sugar first rose—leading to millions of dollars to be made over night—and then precipitously fell resulting in the loss of millions. This cycle of economic "boom" and "bust" is sometimes referred to in Cuba as periods of *vacas gordas* (fat cows) followed by *vacas flacas* (skinny cows).

Décima The basis of a great deal of *música guajira* (country music), this 10-line poetic form of Spanish origin follows a strict rhyme scheme called an *espinela*, A-B-B-A-A-C-C-D-D-C.

La Demajagua The name of the sugar plantation owned by Carlos Manuel de Céspedes where he freed his slaves and declared independence on October 10, 1868 (see *Grito de Yara*).

Diana The nonsensical vocalization that begins a *rumba*.

Directorio revolucionario estudiantil (13 de marzo) The "Student Revolutionary Directorate" (DRE) was an anti-Batista student group founded in 1956 and led by the president of the University Student's Federation (*Federación Estudiantil Universitaria*), José Antonio Echevarría, until his death in an attack on the presidential palace on March 13, 1957.

Divisa A term meaning "hard currency" or the U.S. dollar.

Doble moral A commonplace term used to capture the "double standard" or duplicity that many Cubans follow, feigning belief in revolutionary rhetoric in public while disavowing such belief in private.

Ecobio An Afro-Cuban term used by members of the *Abakuá* spiritual tradition to refer to fellow members or "brothers" (see *asere*).

EJT *Ejercito Juvenil de Trabajo* (Youth Labor Army), the youth wing of Cuba's Revolutionary Armed Forces (FAR), sometimes employed in economically productive tasks such as agriculture.

Elegguá   One of the most popular the *Yoruba* derived Afro-Cuban deities, this *orisha* is the keeper of the crossroads and must be saluted before addressing any other deity.

Las ENA   *Escuelas Nacionales de Arte* (National Art Schools), a group of five architecturally breathtaking art schools established in the early 1960s on the grounds of the former Havana Country Club in the Cubanacán district of Western Havana (now collectively known as the *Instituto Superior de Arte*, ISA).

Encomienda   A system of land and labor grants used in the early colonization of Cuba that dispossessed the *Taíno* of their ancestral lands and approximated slavery. Such grants ostensibly required grantees, known as *encomenderos*, to care for and Christianize their indigenous laborers, a task they seldom took seriously.

La Escalera   A slave-led independence conspiracy that led to a bloody wave of repression between 1841 and 1844, which included torturing suspected conspirators on *la escalera* (the ladder) until they died or confessed.

Espiritismo   A spiritual practice popular in the Spanish-speaking Caribbean and Brazil based on the teachings of the 19th-century French educator and writer Allan Kardec.

Factoría   A mercantilist tobacco system established in Cuba by Spain between 1717 and 1723 that provoked armed revolts from Cuba's *vegueros*, or tobacco growers.

FAR   *Fuerzas Armadas Revolucionarias* (Revolutionary Armed Forces), the official name of the Cuban military bureaucratically organized under the MINFAR, or the Ministry of the Revolutionary Armed Forces.

FEU   *Federación Estudiantil Universitaria* (University Student Federation), Cuba's mass organization that groups together university students.

Flan   Caramel custard, a popular Cuban dessert.

La Flota   The Spanish treasure fleet that sailed from Havana back to the mother country in a defensive convoy each year during the 16th and 17th centuries.

FMC   *Federación de Mujeres Cubanas* (Federation of Cuban Women), the mass organization that groups together Cuban women, led for more than 40 years by Vilma Espín, wife of President Raúl Castro, until her death in 2007. Its members are known as *federadas*.

Foco   A small group or "focus" of guerrilla fighters.

Freedom flights   The name given to the wave of Cuban emigration lasting from 1965 until 1973, which took place through regularly scheduled flights from Cuba to the United States.

Fula   A colloquial Cuban word meaning "money," "bad," or "stupid."

GAESA   *Grupo de Administración Empresarial, S.A.* (Enterprise Management Group, Inc.), the holding company for the Cuban Armed Forces.

Gao   A word of gypsy origin used colloquially in Cuba to mean house or home, as in "*Voy p'al gao*" (I'm going home).

Granma   The name of the American-owned yacht purchased in Mexico by Fidel Castro and used to invade Cuba and begin the revolution in late November 1956.

The name Granma has since been given to the province where the rebels came ashore and to the island's official Communist Party newspaper.

Grito de Baire The cry that began Cuba's final war for independence on February 24, 1895.

Grito de Yara A day following his declaration of independence on October 10, 1868, Carlos Manuel de Céspedes attempted to take the nearby town of Yara, where he issued the *Grito de Yara* (Cry of Yara) beginning the Ten Year's War, Cuba's first war for independence from Spain (see *La Demajugua*).

Guagua A colloquial Cuban term meaning "bus."

Guaguancó The most well-known form of *rumba*, featuring a seductive couple dance.

Guajiro The Cuban equivalent of a farmer or *campesino*, sometimes used to denote rustic simplicity or alternatively rural pride.

Guanahacabibes The name of the narrow peninsula at the western-most extreme of the island of Cuba with Cabo San Antonio at its tip. The pre-Columbian indigenous group with the similar name, *Guanajatabeys*, called this area home.

Guerra Chiquita "Little War," the name of the short inconclusive war (1879–1880), which followed the 1868–1878 Ten Years War.

Guerrilla In Spanish this term refers to a group of armed insurgents. A single member of a *guerrilla* is known in Spanish as a *guerrillero*.

Gusano An insulting label meaning "worm" commonly used in Cuba in the 1970s and 1980s for anyone who opposed the government.

Habana Vieja "Old Havana," the oldest, colonial section of today's metropolis, once completely surrounded by a protective wall.

Helms–Burton A bill passed by U.S. Congress in 1996 and signed into law by President Bill Clinton following the shoot down of two civilian Brothers to the Rescue planes by the Cuban military. It codifies the U.S. embargo into law and punishes third countries who do business with Cuba. Also known as the "Libertad" Act.

Históricos A colloquial term used in Cuba to refer to the 1950s guerrilla fighters who later took on leading roles in the revolutionary government, remaining in their posts indefinitely.

ICAIC *Instituto cubano de artes e industrias cinematográficos*, Cuba's state-financed "Film Institute," which has long exercised monopoly control of the production and distribution of films on the island.

Ingenio A term coined at the end of the 19th century to denote the more powerful, mechanized sugar mills that replaced the previous ones that ran on manual power (see *central*).

Inventar "To invent," a colloquial term used frequently since 1990 to describe the tenacious inventiveness with which Cubans find ways to survive during the economic crisis known as the "special period" (see *resolver*).

Iria or iriampo African-derived colloquial words for "food."

ISA *Instituto Superior de Arte* (Advanced Institute of Art) (see *Las ENA*).

Jinetera   A female seeking foreign male company for economic or other gains often in exchange for sex.

Jinetero   A male hustler who hassles tourists in search of a score.

La Joven Cuba   A clandestine armed revolutionary organization led by Antonio Guiteras formed after the fall of the revolutionary government of 100 days in early 1934. It ceased to operate when he was killed in a firefight in 1935. A blog started by three grad-students from the University of Matanzas in 2010 was also named *La Joven Cuba* in Guiteras' honor.

Latifundia   A large tract of land owned by a single person, family, or company.

Lechón asado   Roasted pork/roast suckling pig, a Cuban delicacy often served on Christmas Eve or New Year's Eve.

Libreta   The ration booklet.

Lineamientos   Officially called the *Lineamientos de la política económica y social*, these are a set of 313 economic and social "Guidelines" adopted in April 2011 at the Sixth Congress of the Cuban Communist Party.

Luchar   To struggle, a term commonly used to describe the difficulty of daily life.

Lukumí   Another name for the Afro-Cuban *Yoruba* people who introduced *Regla de Ochá*, popularly known as *Santería*, to Cuba. The term originates with the *Yoruba* greeting *Olukumi*, meaning "my friend."

M-26-7   *El Movimiento 26 de Julio* (The 26th of July Movement), the revolutionary movement led by Fidel Castro that began with an abortive attack on the *Moncada* garrison on July 26, 1953.

Machismo   The cult of male dominance, superiority, and virility. Related to the term *machista*, or a male chauvinist.

Malecón   The long seaside street, promenade, and retaining wall built at the turn of the 19th century by American engineers that runs along the northern coast of Havana. It has become one of the most often photographed and iconic emblems of the capital city.

Mambí(ses)   The collective name given to Cuban rebels in their revolutionary struggle against Spain at the end of the 19th century.

Mambo   A high energy Cuban dance music developed out of the *danzón*, *cha-cha-chá*, and *son* by the musicians and composers Israel "Chacao" and Orestes López, Arsenio Rodríguez, and Dámaso Pérez Prado in the 1940s and 1950s.

Manigua   A colloquial Cuban term for a swampy tropical forest.

Máquina   A classic, prerevolutionary American car, also referred to as an *almendrón* (big almond).

Marabú   A thorny bush with an extensive root system that has taken over many idle lands in Cuba making the expansion of independent agriculture difficult.

Maracas   A term likely originating with the *Taíno*, *maracas* are a percussive instrument made from a pair of small, dried gourds filled with seeds, attached to wooden sticks, and used in *son* and other music.

Marianismo   The celebration of a woman's traditionally subservient, nurturing role.

Mariel Boatlift   A massive exodus of 125,000 people from the port city of Mariel, west of Havana, to the United States over a six-month period in the summer of 1980.

MCL   *Movimiento Cristiano de Liberación* (Christian Liberation Movement), a civic and religious opposition movement led by Oswaldo Payá until his death in the summer of 2012 (see *Varela Project*).

Mestizaje   A term used to describe the racial and ethnic mixture common among Cubans. While elsewhere in the Americas the term *mestizo/mestiza* is often applied only to persons of mixed indigenous and European heritage, in Cuba it can also describe those with a mixture of African and European ancestry (see *mulato/mulata*).

Militantes del partido   Members of the Cuban Communist Party (see PPC).

MININT   *Ministerio del Interior* (Ministry of the Interior), the Cuban ministry responsible for internal security and citizen surveillance.

Misión Barrio Adentro   "Inner-city missions," Cuban staffed health missions set up in poor Venezuelan neighborhoods under the presidency of Hugo Chávez.

Mítines de repudio   The macabre strategy of repressing dissidents and deterring potential émigrés by subjecting them to violent public acts of repudiation, also called *actos de repudio*.

MLCs   *Mercados libres campesinos*, farmer's markets legalized from the late 1970s to the mid-1980s. They were reintroduced again in the early 1990s under the name *mercados agropecuarios* or *agros* (agricultural markets) for short.

MNR   *Milicias Nacionales Revolucionarios* (National Revolutionary Militias), a nonprofessional corps of citizen-soldiers that enlists a good portion of the population under the defense strategy of the so-called war of all the people (*guerra de todo el pueblo*)

Mogotes   Massive limestone hills and outcroppings located in the Valley of Viñales in the Cuban province of Pinar del Río.

Mojito   A signature Cuban cocktail that includes mint leaves (*yerba buena*), sugar, lime, soda water, and white rum.

Mojo   A thick white sauce made from ground garlic cloves usually served over *yuca*.

Moncada   The name of the army garrison that was targeted by Fidel Castro's revolutionary movement on July 26, 1953 (see M-26-7).

Mudéjar   An Moorish architectural style reminiscent of the construction styles of the southern Spanish province of Andalucía and northern Morocco.

Mulato/Mulata   A term for someone of mixed African and European ancestry (see *mestizo/mestiza*).

Nagüe   A Cuban slang term used in the eastern part of the island to mean "buddy" or "friend."

NAPP   *Asamblea Nacional de Poder Popular* (National Assembly of People's Power), Cuba's Parliament.

Negros curros   Free blacks who emigrated from Seville to Cuba in the 1500s. Their flamboyant style of dress lives on in the large ruffled sleeves and pants narrow at the waist but wide at the legs.

NICTs   New Information and Communications Technologies.

Nomenklatura   A term borrowed from Russian to refer to privileged members of the Communist Party hierarchy.

NAM   The Non-Aligned Movement, a group of countries aligned neither with the United States nor the Soviet Union during the Cold War. Ironically, in 1979 Castro elected the president of the NAM despite Cuba's close links with the USSR.

OAS   The Organization of American States.

Obatalá   The distant and white-clad creator deity of the *Yoruba* pantheon.

Ochún   The *Yoruba* goddess of love, syncretized with *Nuestra Señora de Caridad de Cobre* (Our Lady of Charity), Cuba's patron saint. Colloquially referred to as *Cachita*.

ONE   *Oficina Nacional de Estadísticas* (Cuba's National Bureau of Statistics).

Operación Pedro Pan   Operation Peter Pan, a program that brought more than 14,000 unaccompanied children from Cuba to the United States through the collaboration of the U.S. government and the Catholic church due to their parents' fears of losing them to communism.

OPJM   *Organización de Pioneros José Martí* (The José Martí Pioneer Organization), the mass organization that groups together all elementary children in Cuba.

Las ORI   *Las Organizaciones Revolucionarias Integradas* (The Integrated Revolutionary Organizations), formed in the early 1960s, *Las ORI* was an early forerunner of the *PCC*.

Oriente   The name of Cuba's easternmost province before it was divided into five smaller provinces in the mid-1970s. However, Cubans continue to refer to the east as *Oriente*, and easterners as *orientales* (see *palestinos*).

Orisha   A word used in Cuba to refer to African deities or *santos* (saints).

Ortodoxo Party   A Cuban political party founded by Eduardo Chibás in the late 1940s in a protest against the rising corruption of the Auténtico Party. Its full name was *Partido del Pueblo Cubano—Ortodoxo*. Fidel Castro was an early party member.

Paladar   Literally meaning "palate," this is the popular name for the home-grown private restaurants that have become a fixture on the Cuban landscape since the mid-1990s.

Palenque   A long-term community of escaped slaves (*cimarrones* or *apalencados*) located in difficult to reach places.

Palestinos   Literally meaning "Palestinian," the term is often used in Cuba to refer to migrants to Havana from the eastern part of the island (see *Oriente* and *orientales*).

Palo   (*Palo Monte* or *Palo Mayombe*), the spiritual tradition practiced by the Afro-Cuban ethnic group known as *Congo*.

Parametrados   A term that refers to the many artists and writers who did not fit into the revolution's narrow cultural "parameters" and were effectively banished from publishing or holding any public role as an intellectual during the 1970s and 1980s (see *quinquenio gris*).

PCC   *Partido Comunista de Cuba* (Cuban Communist Party).

Peninsular   A term used during colonial times to denote someone who was born in Spain (on the Iberian Peninsula) as opposed to a *Criollo* (Creole) born in Cuba.

Pentarquía   The "Pentarchy" was a short-lived, five-member ruling coalition that held governmental power after the resignation of President Gerardo Machado in the summer of 1933.

PIC   *Partido Independiente de Color* (Independent Party of Color), dating from the very early years of the republic until it was wiped out in a bloody government crackdown in 1912.

Picadillo   A key dish in the Cuban diet featuring white rice, ground beef, olive oil, onions, peppers, olives, raisins, and tomato sauce.

Pico Turquino   Cuba's highest peak located atop the Sierra Maestra mountain range in the province of Santiago de Cuba.

Plátanos   The Cuban diet is rife with "plantains," both ripe (*maduros*) and green (*verdes*). There are *plátanos maduros fritos* (fried sweet plantains), *tostones* (cut into thick wedges, fried, mashed, and fried again), *mariquitas* (thinly sliced and fried into crunchy chips), among other styles.

Platt Amendment   In force on the island from 1902 until 1934, this was a U.S.-imposed amendment to the Cuban Constitution of 1902 that required the new nation to grant the United States the right to intervene in Cuba's internal affairs as the price for ending its military occupation.

Playa Girón   This is the name of the beach where the failed Bay of Pigs invasion took place.

PNR   *Policía Nacional Revolucionaria* (National Revolutionary Police).

Polimita   A tiny colorful mollusk found only in the town of Baracoa in Guantánamo Province.

PRC   *Partido Revolucionario Cubano* (Cuban Revolutionary Party), the party founded in Key West in 1892 by José Martí as a way of coordinating the civil and military forces necessary to win independence from Spain.

PSP   *Partido Socialista Popular* (Popular Socialist Party), the name used by Cuba's Communist Party during the 1940s and 1950s.

Puro   A colloquial term for a fine, export-quality cigar.

PURS   *Partido Unido de la Revolución Socialista* (United Party of the Socialist Revolution), an interim political organization following the formation of *Las ORI* and prior to the founding of the *PCC* in 1965.

Quinquenio gris   A span of 15–20 years during the 1970s and 1980s euphemistically referred to as the "grey five-year period" when the government's cultural policies were especially repressive (see *parametrados*).

Lo real maravilloso   A literary style popularly known in English as "magical realism" and associated with the "boom" in Latin American literature between the 1960s and the 1980s. The original term and style is most associated with Cuban writer Alejo Carpentier and his novel *El reino de este mundo* (*The Kingdom of This World*, 1949).

Reconcentración   A brutal policy instituted in 1896 by Spanish General Valeriano Weyler of separating Cuba's civilian population from the rebels by "concentrating" them in towns unprepared to house or feed them, resulting in mass starvation and death.

Rectification Campaign   A brief period between 1986 and 1990 when Fidel Castro reversed previous economic openings as a way to guard against a Cuban version of Soviet *perestroika*.

Regla de Ochá   The proper name for the Afro-Cuban spiritual practice popularly known as *Santería*, introduced to Cuba by *Yoruba* slaves from Nigeria (see *Yoruba*).

Resolver   Meaning "to resolve" or "solve," this popular term captures a wide range of creative, often illegal solutions to everyday problems (see *inventar*).

Revolutionary Offensive   A 1968 move to close down or take over the island's more than 50,000 remaining small private businesses.

El Rincón   The name of the town on the outskirts of Havana where pilgrims go every December to pay "promises" and give homage to *San Lázaro*, the patron saint of the sick (see *Babalú-Ayé*).

Ropa vieja   Shredded beef, or literally, "old clothes."

Rumba   Also known as the "rumba complex," this is a secular, communitarian style of collective dance, drumming, and singing that mixes both African and European elements. The three most common forms of *rumba* are *guaguancó*, *columbia*, and *yambú*.

Salsa   The popular name given to a host of Cuban-derived musical styles that were reconfigured abroad, mainly in New York City by Puerto Ricans and others, in the 1960s and 1970s. It is a musical hybrid of Cuban *son* and *rumba*, with elements of Puerto Rican *bomba* and *plena*.

Sandunga   An Afro-Cuban term meaning mischievousness or flirtatiousness.

San Lázaro   (see *Babalú-Ayé* and *El Rincón*).

Santería   The popular, catch-all name for a host of complex Afro-Cuban spiritual practices, the most dominant of which is *Regla de Ochá*.

SDPE   *Sistema de Perfeccionamiento Empresarial*, Cuba's "System of Enterprise Improvement" pioneered in its military-run companies.

Self-employment   *Trabajo por cuenta propia*, a 1993 reform that allowed Cubans to gain licenses in 117 trades and micro-enterprises. This experiment was significantly expanded by Raúl Castro starting in the fall of 2010 (see *cuentapropista*).

Siboney   (also written Ciboney), these were Cuba's indigenous costal cave dwellers who once populated the western extreme of the island.

SMEs   Small- and medium-sized enterprises.

Socio-lismo   A playful combination of the word *socio* ("friend" or "associate") with *socialismo* ("socialism"), indicating that in Cuba there exists a parallel system of access to goods and status based on who you know.

Sofrito   A basic ingredient of many Cuban dishes, a *sofrito* is a combination of aromatic ingredients such as peppers, onions, cumin, garlic, bay leaf, oregano, and salt, which have been cut in very small pieces, and slowly sautéed in oil for 15–30 minutes.

Solar   The Cuban word for an overcrowded tenement, usually with a central common area open to the sky.

Son The classic form of Cuban music, which forms the rhythmic basis for most other styles of modern popular dance music. *Son* originated in *Oriente* as a rustic country music played by trios that combined a *tres* guitar, *maracas*, a *güiro*, and the *bongó* drums. It seems its rhythmic key, the *clave* sticks, were added when it arrived in Havana around 1910, after which its instrumentation expanded further to include violins, trumpets, conga drums, and the piano in larger *conjuntos*, sextets, and septets.

Songo A type of popular Cuban dance music created by the group *Los Van Van*—and in particular its second drummer José Luis Quintana *"Changuito"*—in the early 1970s.

The Special Period An era of deep economic and existential crisis in Cuba that began in 1990 partly as a result of the collapse of the USSR.

Taíno The indigenous group that inhabited much of the island of Cuba at the time of the Spanish conquest.

Talibanes A slang term that refers to policy hardliners within the Cuban government.

Tambor Drum.

Teatro Bufo Also referred to as *bufo habanero*, this musical-theatrical form, similar to Vaudeville, is characterized by a light, humorous plot line and exaggerated portraits of stock characters including the *gallego* (Spaniard), the *negro* (a black Cuban), and the *mulata* (a mixed-race woman).

Teller Amendment Added to the U.S. Congressional Joint Resolution authorizing President William McKinley to use military force in Cuba in 1898, the amendment forswore annexation and promised to leave "control of the island to its people."

Tertulia An informal gathering at which art, culture, and literature are shared and discussed.

Tiempo muerto The "dead time" that typically leaves sugar workers unemployed between annual harvests.

Timba The style of dance music most popular in Cuba during the 1980s and 1990s. *Timba* differs from the more well-known *salsa* in that it tends to incorporate a wider variety of influences such as jazz, rock, funk, and local Afro-Cuban folkloric styles as well.

Trabajo voluntario "Volunteer labor" was long a staple of the consciousness raising and labor mobilization strategy of the revolutionary government, but has been increasingly phased out under Raúl Castro's stewardship of the economy since 2006.

Transculturation A term coined by Cuban anthropologist Fernando Ortiz, this is the complex process that takes place when various cultures come together to form something distinct.

Tres A guitar featuring three (*tres*) sets of double strings often used in *son* trios.

Tumba francesa A style of music and dance brought to eastern Cuba at the turn of the 18th century during the Haitian Revolution.

Tumbadora The proper name for the so-called *conga* drum (see *conga*).

UBPCs *Unidades Básicas de Producción Cooperativa* (Basic Units of Cooperative Production), a type of agricultural cooperative launched in Cuba during the 1990s.

UJC *Unión de Jóvenes Comunistas* (Union of Young Communists).

UMAP Camps *Unidades Militares de Ayuda a la Producción* (Military Units to Aid Production), Lasting from 1965 to 1968, these camps were established to use hard agricultural labor to re-educate "anti-social elements," including nonconformists, homosexuals, and the religious.

UNEAC *Unión de Escritores y Artistas Cubanos* (Union of Cuban Writers and Artists).

U.S. Interests Section (USIS) The diplomatic representation of the United States in Cuba. Officially a "section" of the Swiss Embassy.

Vacas gordas/vacas flacas "Fat cows/skinny cows" (see Dance of the Millions).

Varela Project Named for the 19th century Cuban Priest Félix Varela, the Varela Project was engineered by the late Cuban dissident Oswaldo Payá and his Christian Liberation Movement (MCL). Its aim was to call for a referendum on the country's one-party system, win amnesty for political prisoners, and achieve the rights to freedom of speech and association, among others.

El Vedado Once a vast farm where it was "prohibited" (*vedado*) to build, *El Vedado* is now a centrally located, upscale Havana neighborhood.

Vegueros Tobacco growers. Their plots of land where they cultivate their crop are called *vegas*.

"Vergüenza contra dinero" The official slogan of the Orthodox Party popularized by its leader Eduardo Chibás during the late 1940s and early 1950s.

Voto unido Also known as *"votar por todos,"* this is the PPC mobilization prior to elections calling on all patriots to vote for the entire list of nominees as a single slate.

Yemayá The *Yoruba* goddesses of the sea, identified with the Catholic Virgin of Regla.

Yoruba The dominant Afro-Cuban ethnic, cultural, and religious group of Nigerian origin (see *Regla de Ochá* and *Santería*).

Yuca A root vegetable (tuber) important in the Cuban diet (see *casabe* and *mojo*).

Yuma Cuban slang for the United States (*La Yuma*), or for a North American or foreigner in general (*el* or *un yuma*).

Zafra Cuban term meaning "sugar harvest," as in *La gran zafra*, "The great sugar harvest," the failed effort to harvest 10 million tons of sugarcane in 1970.

Facts and Figures

TABLES A1–A7: BASIC FACTS AND FIGURES

TABLE A1. Country Info

Location	An archipelago consisting of two main islands and approximately 1,600 tiny islets in the Caribbean Sea. Florida lies about 90 miles to the north, the Bahamas are to the northeast, Haiti is to the east, Jamaica lies to the south, Mexico is to the west, and the Gulf of Mexico lies to the northwest.
Official Name	República de Cuba (Republic of Cuba)
Local Name	Cúba
Government	Communist state
Capital	La Habana (Havana)
Weights and Measures	Metric system, with U.S. and Spanish variations.
Time Zone	Same as U.S. Eastern Standard
Currency	Cuban peso
Head of State	President Raúl Castro
Head of Government	President Raúl Castro
Legislature	National Assembly of People's Power
Major Political Parties	Cuban Communist Party

Sources: ABC-CLIO World Geography database; CIA World Factbook (https://www.cia.gov/library/publications/the-world-factbook); UNESCO

TABLE A2. Demographics

Population	11,075,244 (2012 est.)
Population by Age:	(2012 est.)
0–14	17.0%
15–64	71.0%
65+	12.0%
Median Age:	(2012 est.)
Total	38.9 years
Males	38.0 years
Females	39.7 years
Population Growth Rate	0.115% (2012 est.)
Population Density	259 people per square mile (2012 est.)
Infant Mortality Rate	4.83 deaths per 1,000 live births (2012 est.)
Ethnic Groups	Mulatto (51%), White (37%), Black (11%)
Religions	Roman Catholic (nominal, about 85%), Protestant, *Santería*
Majority Language	Spanish
Other Languages	Haitian Creole, Catalan, others spoken by immigrant groups
Life Expectancy (Average)	77.8 years (2012 est.)
Fertility Rate	1.45 children per woman (2012 est.)

TABLE A3. Geography

Land Area	42,803 square Miles
Arable Land	28.0%
Irrigated Land	3,360 square Miles (2003)
Coastline	2,321 miles
Natural Hazards	East coast is subject to hurricanes from August to November, droughts
Environmental Problems	Air and water pollution; biodiversity loss; deforestation
Major Agricultural Products	Sugar, tobacco, citrus, coffee, rice, potatoes, beans; livestock
Natural Resources	Cobalt, nickel, iron ore, chromium, copper, salt, timber, silica, petroleum, arable land
Land Use	32.5% arable land; 3.8% permanent crops; 23.9% permanent meadows and pastures; 25.7% forest land; 14% other
Climate	Tropical, with a dry period from November to April and a rainy season between May and October. Average annual rainfall is 54 inches and average annual temperature is 77°F

TABLE A4. Economy

GDP	$57.5 billion (2010 est.)
GDP per Capita	$5,190 (2010 est.)
GDP by Sector	Agriculture—4%; industry—20.8%; services—75.2% (2011 est.)
Exchange Rate	0.9847 Cuban pesos = $1 USD (2011)
Labor Force	Agriculture—20%; industry—19.4%; services—60.6% (2005 est.)
Unemployment	1.4% (2011 est.)
Major Industries	Sugar, petroleum, tobacco, construction, nickel, steel, cement, agricultural machinery, pharmaceuticals
Leading Companies	Cubatabaco, ETECSA (telecommunications), Cupet (petroleum), Central Bank of Cuba (all state owned).
Electricity Production	16.88 billion kWh (2010 est.)
Electricity Consumption	14.65 billion kWh (2009 est.)
Exports	$6.347 billion (2011 est.)
Export Goods	Sugar, nickel, tobacco, fish, medical products, citrus, coffee
Imports	$13.26 billion (2011 est.)
Import Goods	Petroleum, food, machinery and equipment, chemicals
Current Account Balance	$328.4 million (2011 est.)

TABLE A5. Communications and Transportation

Telephone Lines	1.193 million (2011)
Mobile Phones	1.315 million (2011)
Internet Users	1.606 million (2009)
Roads	37,815 miles (2009)
Railroads	5,343 miles (2006) (about half of rail lines used by sugar plantations)
Airports	86 (2010)

TABLE A6. Military

Defense Spending (% of GDP)	3.8% (2006 est.)
Active Armed Forces	49,000 (2010 est.)
Manpower Fit for Military Service	2,446,131 males; 2,375,590 females (2010 est.)
Military Service	Compulsory two-year service obligation; both sexes subject to military service

TABLE A7. Education

School System	Starting at age six, students attend six years of primary school, followed by three years of early secondary school. Students may then continue for three years at a technical secondary school or for three years in an academic pre-university program.
Education Expenditures (% of GDP)	13.6% (2008)
Average Years Spent in School	16 (2010)
Students per Teacher, Primary School	9 (2009)
Primary School-Age Children Enrolled in Primary School	804,799 (2011)
Enrollment in Tertiary Education	800,873 (2009)
Literacy	99.8% (2005 est.)

TABLE B. Demographic Indicators, 2010

Resident Population	11,241,161
Women	5,612,165
Men	5,628,996
Annual Growth Rate (for every 1,000 inhabitants)	−0.2
Live Births (for every 1,000 inhabitants)	127,746
Deaths (for every 1,000 inhabitants)	91,048
Birth Rate (for every 1,000 inhabitants)	11.4
Fertility Rate (number of children per woman)	1.69
Death Rate (for every 1,000 inhabitants)	8.1
Population 60 Years of Age or Older (% of total)	17.8
Life Expectancy at Birth (years)	79.1
Skin Color (%)	
White	65.5
Black	9.7
Mixed (*mestizos* or *mulatos*)	24.8

Sources: Statistical Abstract of Cuba, 2011 and Economic and Social Panorama of Cuba 2010, National Bureau of Statistics (ONE)

TABLE C. Geography: Detailed Data

Political and Administrative Division	
Provinces	15
Special Municipality	1
Municipalities	167
Official Language	Spanish
Relative Humidity	81.0
Average Temperature	25.0
Average Annual Rainfall	1,287.0
Land Area	109,884.01
Island of Cuba	107,464.74
Isle of Youth	2,419.27
Adjacent Keys	3,126.41
Longitude of Coasts	5,746
North Coast	3,208.0
South Coast	2,537.0
Distances (km)	1,256.2
Widest Point	191.0
Narrowest Point	31.0
Highest Elevation (m)—Turquino Peak, Sierra Maestra Mountains	1,947.0
Longest River (km)—Cauto	343.0
Major Caves (km)	
Gran Caverna de Santo Tomás, Pinar del Río	45.0
Majaguas—Canteras, Pinar del Río	36.0
Los Perdidos, Pinar del Río	18.0
Closest Foreign Countries (km)	
Bahamas, Separated by the Old Bahamas Channel:	21.0
Haiti, Separated by the Windward Passage	77.0
Jamaica, Separated by the Strait of Columbus	140.0
The United States (Key West), Separated by the Florida Straits	150.0
Mexico, Separated by the Yucatan Straits	210.0

Source: National Bureau of Statistics, Republic of Cuba, 2012

TABLE D1. Economy: Basic Economic Indicators, 2005–2011

Concept	2005	2006	2007	2008	2009	2010	2011
Growth in Gross Domestic Product (%)	11.2	12.1	7.3	4.1	1.4	2.4	2.7
Economically Active Population (thousands)	4,816	4,847	4,956	5,028	5,159	5,113	5,175
Employed Population (thousands)	4,723	4,755	4,867	4,948	5,072	4,985	5,010
Unemployment Rate (%)	1.5	1.9	1.8	1.6	1.7	2.5	3.2
Average Monthly Salary (Pesos/CUP)	330	387	408	415	429	448	458
Average Monthly Pension (Pesos/CUP)	179	192	194	236	241	245	255
Budget Deficit as % of GDP	–4.6	–3.2	–3.2	–6.5	–4.8	–3.6	–3.8
Fixed Capital Formation as % of GDP	8.9	10.4	9.7	10.8	9.8	8.9	?
Exchange Rate (USD × Pesos/CUC)	1.08	1.08	1.08	1.08	1.08	1.08	1.0
Exchange Rate (CUP × CUC)	24	24	24	24	24	24	24

Source: National Bureau of Statistics, Republic of Cuba, 2012

TABLE D2. Economy: International Exchange of Goods and Services, 2005–2010 (at current prices)

	Unit: Millions of Pesos					
	2005	2006	2007	2008	2009	2010
Export of Goods and Services	8,963	9,869	11,918	12,506	10,642	14,258
Export of Goods	2,412	3,202	3,966	3,940	2,879	4,598
Export of Services	6,551	6,667	7,952	8,566	7,763	9,660
Import of Goods and Services	7,823	9,744	10,333	14,806	9,565	11,358
Import of Goods	7,647	9,533	10,118	14,312	8,910	10,647
Import of Services	175	211	215	494	656	711
Total Balance	1,140	126	1,585	–2,300	1,077	2,900
Balance of Goods	–5,235	–6,330	–6,152	–10,372	–6,031	–6,049
Balance of Services	6,375	6,456	7,737	8,073	7,107	8,949

Source: Statistical Abstract of Cuba, 2010, National Bureau of Statistics, Republic of Cuba

TABLE D3. Economy: Comparison between Main Products and Services, 1990 and 2010

Product/Service (%)	Unit	1990	2010	2010/1990
Sugar	Thousands of Tons	8,444.7	1,200.0*	14.2
Tobacco	Thousands of Tons	37.1	20.5	55.2
Citrus	Thousands of Tons	1,015.8	345.0	34.0
Coffee	Thousands of Tons	17.6	6.0	34.1
Pork	Thousands of Tons	126.4	261.0	206.4
Beef	Thousands of Tons	272.4	127.0	46.6
Poultry	Thousands of Tons	133.8	43.1	32.2
Cow Milk	Thousands of Tons	1,034.4	629.5	60.8
Tubers and Roots	Thousands of Tons	702.2	1,515.0	215.7
Vegetables	Thousands of Tons	484.2	2,141.0	442.1
Rice	Thousands of Tons	473.6	454.4	96.0
Corn	Thousands of Tons	65.0	324.5	499.2
Beans	Thousands of Tons	12.0	80.4	670.0
Other Fruits	Thousands of Tons	219.0	762.0	348.0
Fish	Thousands of Tons	149.1	43.2	29.0
Eggs	Thousands of Units	2,726.5	2,430.0	89.1
Cattle	Thousands of Heads	4,802.0	3,992.0	83.1
Soap	Thousands of Tons	41.6	36.0	86.5
Nickel and Cobalt	Thousands of Tons	41.1	70.1[#]	170.5
Oil Extraction	Thousands of Tons	670.9	3,024.8	450.8
Corrugated Rebar	Thousands of Tons	252.5	96.1	38.0
Cement	Thousands of Tons	3,288.8	1,631.4	49.6
Gas Extraction	Thousands of Cubic Meters	33.7	1,072.5	3,182.4
Electricity	Giga-watt Hours	15,024.7	17,395.5	115.8
Cigars	Millions of Units	318.4	375.6	118.0
Cement Blocks	Millions of Units	98.2	49.7	50.6
Bricks	Millions of Units	124.2	26.8	21.5
Tires	Thousands of Units	373.1	54.4	15.4
Housing	Single Family Units	36,326	73,901	93.3
Passengers Transported	Millions	2,721.2	1,589.5	58.4
Bus		2,522.2	888.8	35.2
Train		25.9	8.0	31.0
Cargo Transported	Millions of Tons	96.9	47.6	49.1
Truck		70.8	37.7	53.2
Train		15.1	8.4	55.6
Arrivals of visitors	Thousands	340.3	2,532.0	744.0
Tourist rooms available	Thousands	30.2	65.0	215.2

*An estimate due to lack of official statistics.
#For 2009.
Source: Annual Reports of the National Bureau of Statics of Cuba (ONE), 2012

TABLE D4. Economy: Growth Rate of Cuba's Gross Domestic Product (GDP), 1990–2009

Year	Annual Growth Rate (%)	Year	Annual Growth Rate (%)
1990	−2.9	2001	3.0
1991	−10.7	2002	1.5*
1992	−11.7	2003	2.6*
1993	−14.9	2004	8.0*
1994	0.7	2005	11.2*
1995	2.5	2006	12.1*
1996	7.8	2007	7.3*
1997	2.5	2008	4.1*
1998	1.2	2009	1.4*
1999	6.2	2010	2.4
2000	5.6	2011	2.7

*Growth rates after 2002 are not strictly comparable to those for earlier years because of changes to computation methodology, which include the value of free social services. *Sources:* Mesa-Lago 2005; Mesa-Lago and Pérez-López 2005; Pérez-López 2006; Pérez-López 2011: 33–34

Mesa-Lago, Carmelo. (2005) "The Cuban Economy in 2004–2005," pp. 1–18, *Cuba in Transition* Vol. 15.

Mesa-Lago, Carmelo, and Jorge Pérez-López. (2005) *Cuba's Aborted Reform: Socioeconomic Effects, International Comparisons, and Transition Policies.* Gainesville: University Press of Florida.

Pérez-López, Jorge. (2006) "The Cuban Economy in 2005–2006: The End of the Special Period?" *Cuba in Transition* 16, pp. 1–13. Washington: Association for the Study of the Cuban Economy.

Pérez-López, Jorge. (2011) "The Global Financial Crisis and Cuba's External Sector," pp. 31–49 in *The Cuban Economy: Recent Trends*, edited by José Raúl Perales. Washington, DC: Woodrow Wilson Center Reports on the Americas, No. 28, Woodrow Wilson Center for Scholars, Latin America Program (July). http://www.wilsoncenter.org/sites/default/files/WWC_LAP_RoA_%2328.pdf

TABLE **D5.**   Self-Employment Licenses, 1995–2012

Year	Number of Self-Employment Licenses (thousands)
1995	138.1
1996	120.0
1997	129.2
1998	112.9
1999	156.6
2000	153.3
2001	152.3
2002	152.9
2003	151.0
2004	166.7
2005	169.4
2006	152.6
2007	138.4
2008	141.6
2009	143.8
2010	218.0
2011	328.0
2012	380.0
2013	436.0

Source: Vidal Alejandro and Pérez Villanueva, April 2012; Rodríguez 2013

Rodríguez, José Alejandro (2013). "Aumenta el trabajo por cuenta propia," Juventud Rebelde, August 16.

Vidal Alejandro, Pavel and Omar Everleny Pérez Villanueva (2012). "Apertura al cuentapropismo y la microempresa, una pieza clave del ajuste structural," pp. 41–52 in *Miradas a la economía cubana: El proceso de actualización*, edited by Pavel Vidal Alejandro and Omar Everleny Pérez Villanueva. Havana: Editorial Caminos.

TABLE **E.**   Information and Communication Technology

Concept	2006	2007	2008	2009	2010	2011
Number of Computers (thousands)	430.0	509.0	630.0	700.0	724.0	783.0
Those Connected to the Web	258.0	330.0	400.0	455.0	434.4	469.8
Number of Internet Users (thousands)	1,250	1,310	1,450	1,600	1,790	2,610
Personal Computers/1,000 Inhabitants	38	45	56	62	64	70
Internet Users/1,000 Inhabitants	111	117	129	142	159	232
Domains Registered under ".cu"	1,389	1,431	2,168	2,331	2,225	2,285
Cellular Telephone Accounts (thousands)	152.7	198.3	330.0	621.2	1,003	1,315
Cellular Telephone Coverage (%)	71.0	77.2	75.8	77.5	78.0	78.1

Source: Ministry of Information and Communications, Republic of Cuba

TABLE F. Military: The Economic Role of Cuba's Military Leadership

---

Maj. Luis Alberto Rodríguez López-Callejas (mid-50s)—Head of GAESA

*Married to President Raúl Castro's eldest daughtér Déborah

Maj. Gen. Ulises Rosales del Toro (70)—Head of MINAZ/AZCUBA Business Group

*One of six Vice Presidents of the Council of Ministers

*Member of the Central Committee of the PCC

*Former head of GAESA

Col. Manuel Marrero Cruz (49)—Minister of Tourism

*Former chairman of the Gaviota Corporation

Col. Héctor Oroza Busutín—Head of CIMEX (*Comercio Interior, Mercado Exterior*), Cuba's major import-export company

Col. Armando Pérez Betancourt—Head of implementation of the Enterprise Improvement System (*perfeccionamiento empresarial*) from the FAR to the economy as a while

Col. Roberto Ignacio González Planas—Minister of Information Technology and Communications

Gen. Oscar Basulto Torres—Head of Habanos S.A., a joint venture marketing Cuban cigars abroad

Gen. Ramón Martínez Echevarría—President Institute of Civil Aeronautics of Cuba

Gen. Guillermo Garcia Frías—Director of National Program for Protection of Flora and Fauna

*Member of the Council of State

*Former Minister of Transportation

Source: Cuba Transition Project, Institute for Cuban and Cuban-American Studies, University of Miami, http://ctp.iccas.miami.edu/

TABLE G. Military: The Political Role of Cuba's Military Leadership

---

Gen. Raúl Castro (82)—Commander in Chief of the Revolutionary Armed Forces

*President of the Council of State

*Prime Minister of the Council of Ministers

*First Secretary of the Central Committee of Cuban Communist Party

Gen. Leopoldo Cintra Frías (72)—Minister of the FAR

*Member of the Council of State

*Member of the Council of Ministers

*Member of the Politburo and Central Committee

*Previously served as head of the Western Army.

José Ramón Machado Ventura (83)—First Vice President of the Council of State

*First Vice President of the Council of Ministers

*Second Secretary of the PCC; member of Secretariat, Politburo, and Central Committee

*Former Minister of Public Health (1960–1968)

Gen. Ramiro Valdés (80)—*Comandante* of the Revolution

*Vice President of the Council of State

*One of six Vice Presidents of the Council of Ministers

(*continued*)

TABLE G.   Military: The Political Role of Cuba's Military Leadership (*continued*)

*Member of the Executive Commission, Politburo, and Central Committee of the PCC

*Directs *Grupo de Electrónica de Cuba*, a computer and electronics importer

*Former Minister of Information and Communications

Gen. Alvaro López Miera (68)—First Vice Minister of the FAR

*Member of the Council of State

*Member of the Politburo and Central Committee of the PCC

*Former Chief of the General Staff of the FAR

Gen. Antonio Enrique Lussón Batlle (82)—One of six Vice Presidents of the Council of Ministers

*Member of Central Committee of the PCC

*Chief of Special Forces for the FAR

*Former Minister of Transportation, Merchant Marine, and Ports (1970–1980)

Col. Alejandro Castro Espín (mid-50s)—Special advisor to the President on national security

*Only son of Raúl Castro

Brig. Gen. Darío Delgado—Attorney General

Lt. Gen. Ramón Espinosa Martín (73)—Vice Minister of the FAR

*Member of Politburo and Central Committee of the PCC

*Former Division General and Chief of Eastern Army

Gen. Joaquín Quinta Solá (73)—Vice Minister of the FAR

*Member of the Central Committee of the PCC

*Former Division General and Chief of Central Army

Gen. Leonardo Andollo Valdés (67)—Second Chief, Estado Mayor General, FAR

*Member of Central Committee of the PCC

Gen. José Carrillo Gómez (61)—Member of the Political Directorate of the FAR

*Member of the Central Committee of the PCC

Source: Cuba Transition Project, Institute for Cuban and Cuban-American Studies, University of Miami, http://ctp.iccas.miami.edu/

TABLE H.   The Leadership of the Ministry of the Interior

Gen. Abelardo Colomé Ibarra (74)—Minister of the Interior (MININT)

*Vice President of the Council of State

*Member of the Council of Ministers

*Member of the Politburo and Central Committee of the PCC

Gen. Carlos Hernández Gondín (73)—First Vice Minister, Chief of High Command, MININT

*Member of the Central Committee of the PCC

Gen. Romántico Sotomayor García (73)—Vice Minister of Political Directorate, MININT

*Member of the Central Committee of the PCC

*Former Chief of the PNR (Revolutionary National Police)

Gen. José Julián Milián Pino (68)—Vice Minister of Internal Order, MININT

*Member of the Central Committee of the PCC

Source: Cuba Transition Project, Institute for Cuban and Cuban-American Studies, University of Miami, http://ctp.iccas.miami.edu/

TABLE I.   General Educational Indicators

Concept	2006/2007	2007/2008	2008/2009	2009/2010	2010/2011	2011/2012
Schools	12,355	12,314	12,166	11,308	9,964	9,673
Teaching Staff	280,603	289,279	298,687	303,348	316,118	298,508
Initial Enrollment	2,978,845	3,081,117	2,974,939	2,727,442	2,425,186	2,193,312
Graduates	640,347	639,691	673,234	609,434	554,830	—
Scholarships	487,625	468,117	414,905	297,669	202,310	169,866
Semi-interns	982,113	961,629	959,915	986,069	935,323	908,940

Source: Annual Reports of the National Bureau of Statics of Cuba (ONE), 2012

TABLE J.   Provincial Land Area, Population, and Relative Population Density, 2011

	Land Area		Resident Population		Density
	Total (km²)	% of total	Total	% of total	persons/km²
Cuba	**109,884.01**	**100.0**	**11,247,925**	**100.0**	**102.4**
Pinar del Río	8,883.74	8.1	591,931	5.3	66.6
Artemisa	4,003.24	3.6	507,304	4.5	126.7
La Habana	728.26	0.7	2,130,431	18.9	2,925.4
Mayabeque	3,743.81	3.4	380,274	3.4	101.6
Matanzas	11,791.82	10.7	696,528	6.2	59.1
Villa Clara	8,411.81	7.7	797,721	7.1	94.8
Cienfuegos	4,188.61	3.8	408,824	3.6	97.6
Sancti Spíritus	6,777.28	6.2	466,106	4.1	68.8
Ciego de Ávila	6,971.64	6.3	426,738	3.8	61.2
Camagüey	15,386.16	14.0	778,646	6.9	50.6
Las Tunas	6,592.66	6.0	540,016	4.8	81.9
Holguín	9,215.72	8.4	1,038,093	9.2	112.6
Granma	8,374.24	7.6	838,203	7.5	100.1
Santiago de Cuba	6,227.78	5.7	1,048,870	9.3	168.4
Guantánamo	6,167.97	5.6	511,781	4.6	83.0
Isla de la Juventud	2,419.27	2.2	86,459	0.8	35.7

Source: Annual Reports of the National Bureau of Statics of Cuba (ONE), 2012

TABLE K. Freedom House Rankings: Civil Liberties, Political Rights, and Press and Web Freedom

	2011	2012
Political and Civil Rights		
Civil Liberties	6	6
Political Rights	7	7
Rank*	6.5/Not Free	6.5/Not Free
Press Freedom		
Legal Environment (0–30)	30	29
Political Environment (0–40)	34	34
Economic Environment (0–30)	28	28
Press Freedom Score (0–100)*	92/Not Free	91/Not Free
Internet Freedom		
Obstacles to Access (0–25)	24	24
Limits on Content (0–35)	30	29
Violation of User Rights (0–40)	33	33
Internet Freedom Score (0–100)*	87/Not Free	86/Not Free
Internet Penetration	1–3%	5%
Web 2.0 Applications Blocked	Yes	Yes
Notable Political Censorship	Yes	Yes
Bloggers/ICT Users Arrested	Yes	Yes

*Note: On the scale of Civil Liberties and Political Rights, 0 = most free and 7 = least free; on the scales of Press Freedom and Internet Freedom, 0 = most free and 100 = least free. (Source: Freedom House, 2012 ad 2013)

TABLE L.   Cuban Presidents and U.S. Military Governors, 1899–2013

1899 (Jan.)	American general John R. Brooke
1899 (Dec.)	American general Leonard Wood
1902	Gen. Tomás Estrada Palma
1906 (Sept.)	Provisional U.S. governor William Howard Taft
1906 (Oct.)	Provisional U.S. governor Charles E. Magoon
1909	Gen. José Miguel Gómez
1913	Gen. Mario García Menocal (United States intervenes to protect 1916 reelection)
1921	Alfredo Zayas (governs with the oversight of U.S. envoy Enoch Crowder)
1925	Gen. Gerardo Machado (ousted in August 1933)
1933 (Aug.)	Carlos Manuel de Céspedes
1933 (Sept. 3)	Five-man junta (*pentarquía*) (led by Dr. Ramón Grau San Martín)
1933 (Sept. 10)	Dr. Ramón Grau San Martín (ousted by Fulgencio Batista)
1934 (Jan. 16)	Carlos Hevia (appointed and controlled by Fulgencio Batista)
1934 (Jan. 17)	Manuel Márquez Sterling (" ")
1934 (Jan. 18)	Col. Carlos Mendieta (" ")
1935 (Mar.)	José Antonio Barnet (" ")
1936 (May)	Miguel Mariano Gómez (" ")
1936 (Dec. 24)	Federico Laredo Bru (" ")
1940	Fulgencio Batista
1944	Dr. Ramón Grau San Martín
1948	Dr. Carlos Prío Socarrás
1952	Fulgencio Batista (assumes presidency after a military coup)
1959 (Jan.)	Manuel Urrutia (appointed by Fidel Castro)
1959 (July)	Dr. Osvaldo Dorticós (appointed by Fidel Castro)
1975	Fidel Castro
2006 (July 31)	Raúl Castro (assumes provisional presidency during Fidel Castro's illness)
2008 (Feb. 24)	Raúl Castro elected president of Cuba (Fidel Castro retires)
2013 (Feb.)	Raúl Castro reelected to second term of five years (institutes two-term limit)

Source: Thomas 1998

TABLE M. Principal Causes of Death and Rates (per 100,000 inhabitants)

Concept	2010	2011
Heart Disease	211.8	197.5
Malignant Tumors	197.5	193.6
Stroke	86.9	76.9
Influenza and Pneumonia	47.5	48.7
Accidents	42.0	41.5
Chronic Respiratory Disease	28.6	30.9
Arteriolosclerosis	24.5	22.6
Diabetes	23.5	19.9
Self-Inflected Wounds	13.7	13.5
Cirrhosis and Other Chronic Liver Disease	10.7	9.4

Source: Annual Reports of the National Bureau of Statics of Cuba (ONE), 2012

TABLE N. Access to Medical Professionals

Concept	2010	2011
Doctors	76,506	78,622
Family Doctors	36,478	34,738
Dentists	12,144	12,793
Inhabitants per Doctor	147	143
Inhabitants per Dentist	925	878
Consultations	97,611	100,813
Medical	78,961	81,050
Dental	18,650	19,763

Source: Ministry of Public Health, Republic of Cuba, 2012

TABLE O. Infant Mortality Rate and Rate of Low Birth Weight

	2006	2007	2008	2009	2010	2011
Infant Mortality Rate (per 1,000 live births)	5.3	5.3	4.7	4.8	4.5	4.9
Rate of Low Birth Weight (per 100 live births)	5.4	5.2	5.1	5.1	5.4	5.3

Source: Annual Reports of the National Bureau of Statics of Cuba (ONE), 2012

TABLE P. Status of Women, 2011

Concept	Percentage
Female Enrollment	
Primary	48.8
High School	48.2
University	61.0
Female Graduates in Technical and Professional Teaching	35.6
Female Graduates in Higher Education	62.8
Rate of Women's Economic Activity	60.1
Women Working as Professionals and Technicians	63.0
Female Administrators	36.7
Female Deputies in the XI National Assembly	43.3
Female Delegates in the Provincial Assemblies	40.6
Female Delegates in the Municipal Assemblies	33.4

Source: Annual Reports of the National Bureau of Statics of Cuba (ONE), 2012

TABLE Q1. Resident Population and Rate of Population Growth

Year	Population	Growth Rate (per 1,000 inhabitants)
1955	6,445,944	20.3
1960	7,077,190	14.2
1965	7,907,113	24.9
1970	8,603,165	13.3
1975	9,365,972	14.4
1980	9,693,907	−6.2
1985	10,138,642	10.8
1990	10,662,148	11.1
1995	10,947,119	3.1
2000	11,146,203	3.0
2005	11,243,836	0.2
2010	11,241,161	−0.1
Projections		
2015	11,220,354	−0.3
2020	11,190,082	−0.7
2025	11,029,033	−2.9

Source: Annual Reports of the National Bureau of Statics of Cuba (ONE), 2012

TABLE Q2. Evolution of the Age Structure (in %) of the Cuban Population, 1953–2025

Year	Total	0–14	15–59	60 and Older
1953	100	36.2	56.9	6.9
1970	100	36.9	54.0	9.1
1981	100	30.3	58.8	10.9
2003	100	20.1	64.9	15.0
2004	100	19.6	65.0	15.4
2005	100	19.0	65.3	15.7
2006	100	18.4	65.6	15.9
2008	100	11.4	71.6	17.0
2009	100	17.4	65.2	17.4
2010	100	17.3	64.9	17.8
2011	100	17.2	64.7	18.1
Projections				
2015	100	15.7	64.8	19.5
2020	100	14.6	63.7	21.6
2025	100	14.3	59.6	26.1

Source: Annual Reports of the National Bureau of Statics of Cuba (ONE), 2012

TABLE **R.**   Sugar Production, 1989–2006

Year	Millions of Metric Tons
1989	8.12
1990	8.12
1991	7.62
1992	7.01
1993	4.25
1994	4.08
1995	3.26
1996	4.45
1997	4.32
1998	3.29
1999	3.87
2000	4.05
2001	3.75
2002	3.61
2003	2.3
2004	2.5
2005	1.3
2006	1.2
2007	1.2
2008	1.6
2009	1.5
2010	1.2
2011	1.6

Source: Mesa-Lago 2005; National Office of Statistics 2012; Peters 2003; Ritter 2006

Mesa-Lago, Carmelo. 2005. "The Cuban Economy in 2004–2005," pp. 1–18, *Cuba in Transition* Vol. 15. Washington, DC: Association for the Study of the Cuban Economy.

National Office of Statistics (ONE). 2011. *Anuario Estadístico de Cuba (AEC)*, 2012. http://www.cubagob.cu/ingles/otras_info/estadisticas.htm

Peters, Philip. 2003. "Cutting Losses: Cuba Downsizes Its Sugar Industry." Lexington Institute, December. http://lexington.server278.com/docs/cuba1.pdf.

Ritter, Arch. 2006. "Cuba's Economic Re-Orientation." Paper presented at the Bildner Center conference, "Cuba: In Transition? Pathways to Renewal, Long-Term Development and Global Reintegration," March 30–31. http://web.gc.cuny.edu/bildnercenter/cuba/documents/CITBookFMpdfbychapter_000.pdf.

TABLE S.   Tourism: Visitors and Countries of Origin, 1989–2011

Year	Visitors (thousands)	10 Leading Source Countries, 2011 (thousands)	
1989	275	Canada	1,002.3
1990	340	United Kingdom	175.8
1991	424	Italy	110.4
1992	461	Spain	101.6
1993	546	Germany	95.1
1994	619	France	94.4
1995	746	Russia	78.5
1996	1,004	Mexico	76.3
1997	1,170	Argentina	76.0
1998	1,416	United States	73.6
1999	1,603		
2000	1,774		
2001	1,774		
2002	1,668		
2003	1,900		
2004	2,049		
2005	2,319		
2006	2,221		
2007	2,152		
2008	2,348		
2009	2,430		
2010	2,532		
2011	2,716		

Source: National Office of Statistics 2012; Peters 2002; Pérez-López 2006; Pérez-López and Díaz-Briquets 2011

National Office of Statistics (ONE). 2011. *Anuario Estadístico de Cuba (AEC)*. http://www.cubagob.cu/ingles/otras_info/estadisticas.htm

Pérez-López, Jorge. 2006. "The Cuban Economy in 2005–2006: The End of the Special Period?" *Cuba in Transition* 16, pp. 1–13. Washington, DC: Association for the Study of the Cuban Economy.

Pérez-López, Jorge and Sergio Díaz-Briquets. 2011. "The Diaspora and Cuba's Tourism Sector." *Cuba in Transition*, Vol. 21, pp. 314–325, Washington, DC: Association for the Study of the Cuban Economy. http://www.ascecuba.org/publications/proceedings/volume21/pdfs/perezlopezdiazbriquets.pdf.

Peters, Philip. 2002. "International Tourism: The New Engine of the Cuban Economy." Lexington Institute, December. http://lexington.server278.com/docs/cuba3.pdf.

TABLE T1. Migration—Cubans Obtaining Legal Permanent Resident (LPR) Status in the United States, 1960–2011

Year(s)	Total Number
1960–1969	202,030
1970–1979	256,497
1980–1989	132,552
1990–1999	159,037
2000	17,897
2001	25,832
2002*	28,182
2003*	9,262
2004*	20,488
2005*	36,261
2006*	45,614
2007*	29,104
2008*	49,500
2009*	38,954
2010*	33,372
2011*	36,261

*Between 2002 and 2011, 327,008 Cubans have become legal permanent residents, more than in any previous decade.
Sources: Peters 2012; Department of Homeland Security

Peters, Philip. 2012. "Migration Policy Reform: Cuba Gets Started, U.S. Should Follow." Arlington, VA: Lexington Institute, December. http://www.lexingtoninstitute.org/library/resources/documents/Cuba/ResearchProducts/CubanMigration.pdf

TABLE T2. Migration—Cuban Refugees and Asylees Admitted to the United States, 2007–2011

	Cuban Refugees	% of All Refugee Admissions	Cuban Asylees Admissions	% of All Asylee
2011	2,920	5.19	34	0.14
2010	4,818	6.57	33	0.16
2009	4,800	6.43	42	0.19
2008	4,177	6.94	87	0.38
2007	2,922	6.05	69	0.27

Sources: Peters 2012; Fiscal year data from State Department and Department of Homeland Security

Peters, Philip. 2012. "Migration Policy Reform: Cuba Gets Started, U.S. Should Follow." Arlington, VA: Lexington Institute, December. http://www.lexingtoninstitute.org/library/resources/documents/Cuba/ResearchProducts/CubanMigration.pdf

TABLE T3. Migration—Emigration from Cuba* (selected years), 1970–2011

Year	Net Emigration	Per Thousand Population
1965	18,003	2.3
1970	56,404	6.6
1975	2,891	0.3
1980	141,742	14.6
1985	8,164	0.8
1990	5,352	0.5
1995	33,648	3.1
2000	29,322	2.6
2005	33,348	3.0
2006	35,276	3.1
2007	32,811	2.9
2008	36,903	3.3
2009	36,564	3.3
2010	38,165	3.4
2011	39,263	3.5

*Net emigration is the annual excess of emigrants over immigrants to all destinations, not only to the United States.
Sources: Peters 2012; Data from Cuba's National Office of Statistics

Peters, Philip. 2012. "Migration Policy Reform: Cuba Gets Started, U.S. Should Follow." Arlington, VA: Lexington Institute, December. http://www.lexingtoninstitute.org/library/resources/documents/Cuba/ResearchProducts/CubanMigration.pdf

TABLE T4. Migration—Illegal Immigration from Cuba, Successful and Attempted, 2000–2012

Year	I. Arrivals by Sea (South Florida)	II. Intercepted (at sea)	III. Arrivals at Land Border
2000	1,820	1,000	
2001	2,406	777	
2002	1,335	666	
2003	1,072	1,555	
2004	995	1,225	
2005	2,530	2,712	11,524 (7,267 via Mexico)
2006	3,075	2,810	13,405 (8,639)
2007	3,914	2,868	13,840 (9,566)
2008	2,915	2,216	11,146 (10,030)
2009	637	799	7,803 (5,893)
2010	409	422	6,286 (5,570)
2011	685	985	7,051 (5,937)
2012*	354	1,261	9,191 (8,273)

*2012 figures for 11 months only.
Sources: Peters 2012; Fiscal year data from Homeland Security agencies compiled by Cafe-Fuerte.com

Peters, Philip. 2012. "Migration Policy Reform: Cuba Gets Started, U.S. Should Follow." Arlington, VA: Lexington Institute, December. http://www.lexingtoninstitute.org/library/resources/documents/Cuba/ResearchProducts/CubanMigration.pdf

Major Cuban Holidays and Festivals

Holidays celebrated in today's Cuba reflect a combination of Catholic, African, nationalistic, and revolutionary influences. For example, while Christmas celebrations have recently reappeared after a long ban by the government, traditional New Year's celebrations have been combined with political pageantry recognizing the triumph of the revolution on **January 1**, 1959. Furthermore, the country's most important national holiday is celebrated on **July 26**, commemorating Fidel Castro's failed attempt to overtake the Moncada army barracks in Santiago on that date in 1953. Each year, Cuban cities compete to be the site of this national celebration, which includes marches, revolutionary pageantry, and—in years past—a three- to four-hour speech by Castro. President Raúl Castro has discontinued this tradition, keeping his comments to under an hour and even sometimes ceding the podium to another keynote speaker. This holiday coincides with the end of the traditional, week-long **Santiago Carnival** celebration, which predates the revolution and has its origins in a syncretic mixture of Catholic saint day processions, African *orisha* ceremonies, and French-Haitian traditions brought from Haiti at the turn of the 18th century. Other parts of Cuba also celebrate **pre-Lenten Carnival** in February.

In exile, of course, January 1 is not celebrated as a patriotic holiday, and July 26 is not celebrated at all. Instead, some exiles celebrate **May 20**, commemorating the day in 1902 when Cuba became independent. Given that U.S. tutelage over Cuba lasted until 1934, others have mocked May 20 as amounting to a disgraceful "dependence" day. The U.S. government has developed the habit of announcing new policy measures against Cuba on May 20, in order to win favor with the exile community. Also popular among Cuban-Americans is the traditional family gathering and celebration on Christmas Eve, known as ***Noche Buena***. Despite this ongoing split, nearly all Cubans can agree to celebrate **October 10**, commemorating the day in 1868 when Carlos Manuel de Céspedes let forth the Grito de Yara, beginning the first war for independence.

Though not taking place every year, May and June often feature the ***Bienal de Artes Plásticas de La Habana*** (**Havana Arts Biennial**), a rich gathering of Cuban and international painters, sculptors, and other kinds of graphic artists.

Feast of *Caridad del Cobre* (The Virgin of Charity, or *Oshún*), September 8: On this day, many Cubans make a special pilgrimage to the town of Cobre, outside of Santiago de Cuba. *Caridad del Cobre*, Cuba's patron saint, is also honored as Oshún (a Yoruba deity) by adherents of santería on this day.

The ***Festival Internacional del Nuevo Cine Latinoamericano*** (**The International Festival of New Latin American Cinema**) and the **Jazz Plaza Festival** both take place in Havana each December drawing large national and international artists and spectators.

Feast of *San Lázaro* (*Babalú-Ayé*), December 17, is the occasion of a massive annual pilgrimage by those who have made promises to *San Lázaro* (*Babalú-Ayé*). Taking place on the outskirts of Havana in the small chapel known as *El Rincón*, this pilgrimage is a true feast for the eyes as thousands of people walk, crawl, or drag themselves to this spot over the course of a three-day period. In fact, while the final point on the pilgrimage is a Catholic church, few of the pilgrims are in fact practicing Catholics. As such, *El Rincón* is an ideal place in which to witness the convergence of Cuba's many syncretic belief systems, including Catholicism, spiritism, santería, and communism, as well as the consumerism and commercialism evidenced by the throng of street vendors administering to the spiritual and physical needs of the many pilgrims.

Other important national or religious holidays or feast days celebrated in Cuba include:

El Día de los Reyes (Three Kings Day), January 6: This is traditionally the date when Afro-Cuban organizations were given permission to parade through the streets in *comparsas* and sing their songs.

***La Feria Internacional de Libro* (International Book Fair), February**: This is one of Havana's premier cultural events, lasting almost an entire month and headquartered at El Morro Castle and La Cabaña Fortress on the east side of Havana Bay.

May Day, May 1: This is the international day dedicated to recognizing the contribution laborers make to society. In communist countries like Cuba, May Day is celebrated with parades, speeches, and rallies. Although most people are off work, many are required (or at least encouraged) to attend political rallies.

Country-Related Organizations

The primary purpose of this directory is to help build bridges between Cuba, its people, and the outside world—especially the United States. Having traveled to the island more than 15 times since 1997, I (Ted Henken) have had the privilege of meeting people (including the coeditors, Miriam Celaya and Dimas Castellanos, and most of the authors of this book) and working with institutions on the island (both within the government and, more commonly, independent of it) who have much to teach (and are always hungry to learn from) the world outside. These individuals and institutions have normally received this curious and pesky *yuma* (North American) with graciousness and generosity, sharing their wealth of ideas, experiences, and information on a basis of mutual respect and reciprocity. It is hoped that this directory can facilitate this kind of fruitful dialogue and collaboration between Cuba and the world beyond its shores in the future.

The directory is organized into the following 10 thematic sections: Education/Academic; Government, Nongovernmental Organizations (NGOs), and Think Tanks; Business and Economics; Art and Culture; Democracy and Human Rights; Diaspora and Exile Organizations; Travel and Tourism; Religion; News Sources; and Blogs. Within each section, we have listed organizations and websites in order of importance, not alphabetically. Thus, inclusion on this list (or exclusion from it) should not be taken as an endorsement (or repudiation) of any particular organization or viewpoint. Each entry includes a title, web address, brief description, contact name and e-mail, and address and phone/fax number (if available). We have tried as much as possible to list well-established organizations that represent a wide variety of political and ideological perspectives.

EDUCATIONAL/ACADEMIC

Latin American Network Information Center (LANIC)

http://lanic.utexas.edu/la/cb/cuba/

Description: Likely the best maintained, most extensive, and up-to-date list of links on Cuba, this site includes a useful collection of Castro's speeches from 1959 through 1996 compiled and translated into English by the Foreign Broadcast Information Service (FBIS).

Contact: Kent Norsworthy, Digital Scholarship Coordinator
E-mail: kentn@mail.utexas.edu,
Address: Latin American Network Information Center–LANIC
Teresa Lozano Long Institute of Latin American Studies
1 University Station D0800 Austin, Texas 78712

Latin American and Latino Studies Program at the University of Indiana

http://www.latinamericanstudies.org/cuba.htm

Description: A site with well-organized and up-to-date information on Cuba and extensive Cuba-related links.

Contact: Antonio Rafael de la Cova, Latino Studies, Indiana University

Cuban Research Institute (CRI), Florida International University

http://cri.fiu.edu/

Description: The CRI's mission is to disseminate knowledge on Cuba and Cuban-Americans. The institute builds on the university's wealth of Cuba experts and has developed strong relationships with scholars in Cuba through a variety of academic exchange programs. The CRI also holds a major multidisciplinary conference on Cuban studies every 18 months.

Contact: Jorge Duany, Director
E-mail: jduany@gmail.com
Address: University Park, DM 363, Miami, FL 33199
Telephone: (305) 348-1991; Fax: (305) 348-3593

Institute for Cuban and Cuban-American Studies, University of Miami

http://www.miami.edu/iccas/

Description: ICCAS is a center for research and study of a wide range of Cuban and Cuban-American topics. Its website contains many useful research reports and links on Cuba and its diaspora.

Contact: Jaime Suchlicki
E-mail: iccas@miami.edu
Address: PO Box 248174, 1531 Brescia Ave., Coral Gables, FL 33124-3010
Telephone: (305) 284-2822; Fax: (305) 284-4406, (305) 284-4875

Bildner Center for Western Hemisphere Studies, Cuba Program

http://web.gc.cuny.edu/bildnercenter/cuba/index.shtml
Description: The Bildner Center's Cuba Project is a collaborative effort to study changes in Cuban politics, economics, culture, and society. The Cuba Project works with other academic and policy-oriented institutions to promote dialogue between academics, policy makers, business and news media figures, as well as students from various countries and disciplines. The project holds monthly seminars and a major international conference every two years.

Contact: Mauricio Font, Director
E-mail: bildner@gc.cuny.edu; cubaproject@gc.cuny.edu
Address: Cuba Project, Bildner Center for Western Hemisphere Studies, The Graduate Center, CUNY, 365 Fifth Avenue, Suite 5209, New York, NY 10016
Telephone: (212) 817-2096; Fax: (212) 817-1540

Cuban and Caribbean Studies Institute, Tulane University

http://cuba.tulane.edu/
Description: The Cuban and Caribbean Studies Institute evolved out of several years of sustained effort in developing relations with Cuban counterpart organizations for the purposes of academic collaboration and exchange, curricular development, cultural enrichment, and international development and dialogue. The institute organizes lectures, performances, and courses aimed at promoting academic and cultural exchange between Cuba and the United States.

Contact: Ana M. López
E-mail: cuba@tulane.edu
Address: Caroline Richardson Building, New Orleans, LA 70118-5698
Telephone: (504) 862-8629; Fax: (504) 862-8678

The David Rockefeller Center for Latin American Studies, Harvard University

http://drclas.fas.harvard.edu/cuba
Description: The David Rockefeller Center for Latin American Studies (DRCLAS) seeks to continue, consolidate, and extend its program of scientific and scholarly exchanges with Cuba. The Cuban Studies Program departs from two basic premises. First, restoring and enhancing cooperation between the U.S. and Cuban academic communities can play a significant role in promoting peaceful changes within and between our

two countries. Second, strengthening and establishing institutional ties promotes inter-action and collaboration among current and future intellectual and opinion leaders and catalyzes positive changes in Cuban and U.S. perspectives and government policies.

Contact: Lorena Barberia, Program Associate; Yadira Rivera, Program Coordinator
E-mail: drc_cuba@fas.harvard.edu; barberia@fas.harvard.edu
Address: David Rockefeller Center for Latin American Studies, Harvard University
61 Kirkland Street, Cambridge, MA 02138
Telephone: (617) 495-9749; Fax: (617) 496-2802

International Institute for the Study of Cuba

http://cubastudies.org/

The International Institute for the Study of Cuba is an initiative by a team of U.K.-based academics, specialists, and consultants with the object of providing an in-depth and focused appraisal of the Cuban "Social Experience." The Institute is a membership association, open to all who share the aims and objectives. Its primary goal is to support and ensure the continued publication of the *International Journal of Cuban Studies* and to organize educational and academic events that disseminate research on Cuba, in particular its history, culture, and scientific achievements.

Contact: Stephen Wilkinson
E-mail: s.wilkinson@cubastudies.org
Address: P.O. Box 1406 Tring, Herts, UK HP23 9AT
Telephone: +44 (0)795-638-1640

History of Cuba.com

http://historyofcuba.com/

Description: The mission of this site is to provide a clear and detailed journey through the themes, concepts, people, and ideas that make up Cuban history. The site features many useful features, including a general index of people and events, a detailed timetable of Cuban history, a comprehensive bibliography of works on Cuba, a list of links and resources, and an appropriately titled author's blog entitled simply "Cuba on My Mind."

Contact: Jerry A. Sierra
E-mail: ja378sierra@rcn.com

Educational and Academic Institutions in Cuba

The José Martí National Library (Biblioteca Nacional de Cuba, José Martí)

http://www.bnjm.cu/

Description: The National Library hosts researchers from the United States as well as school librarians who have participated in professional exchanges and have attended conferences on topics related to the Cuban library system.

Contact: Siomara Carrillo
E-mail: bnjm@jm.lib.cult.cu
Address: Ave. Independencia and 20 de Mayo, Plaza de la Revolución, A.P. 6881, Havana, Cuba
Telephone: (537) 855-5442 through 5449; Fax: (537) 881-6224/833-5938

José Martí Studies Center (Centro de Estudios Martianos)

http://www.josemarti.cu/
Description: This research center is dedicated to carrying out studies and publishing work related to the life and writings of Cuban patriot José Martí. Center researchers have frequently participated in academic exchanges and often organize international conferences and lectures.

Contact: Reinio Díaz Triana
E-mail: jmarti@cubarte.cult.cu
Address: 807 Calzada at 4th Street, Vedado, C.P. 10400, Havana, Cuba
Telephone: (537) 855-2298; Fax: (537) 833-3721

Center for the Study of the Cuban Economy (Centro de Estudios de la Economía Cubana)

http://www.ceec.uh.cu/
Description: Perhaps the leading economic academic institution in the country, the *Centro de Estudios de la Economía Cubana* (CEEC) exists under the auspices of the University of Havana and is dedicated to the study and development of the Cuban economy and entrepreneurial management through teaching, research, training, and consulting directly with businesses.

Contact: Omar Everleny Pérez Villanueva
E-mail: yordan@ceec.uh.cu; jorge@ceec.uh.cu
Address: Ave 41 # 707 esquina 9na, Miramar, Playa, La Habana, Cuba
Telephone: 209-05-63; 202-13-91

Center for the Study of the United States (Centro de Estudios sobre Estados Unidos)

http://www.uh.cu/centros/ceseu/index.htm
Description: The CESEU was recently renamed *El Centro de Estudios Hemisféricos y sobre Estados Unidos* (The Center of Hemispheric and United States Studies.

Contact: Soraya Castro Mariño, Esteban Morales
E-mail: cehseu@rect.uh.cu
Address: 1421 33d Street, between 14th and 18th Avenues, Miramar, C.P. 11600, Havana, Cuba
Telephone: (537) 203-8541, 203-5807; Fax: (537) 302-2350

Center for Psychological and Sociological Research
(Centro de Investigaciones Psicológicas y Sociológicas)

http://www.cips.cu/

Description: CIPS is Cuba's foremost sociological and psychological research center focusing on changes in Cuban society.

Contact: María Isabel Domínguez García, Director
E-mail: cips@ceniai.inf.cu
Address: 15th Street at Ave. B, Vedado, Plaza, Havana, Cuba
Telephone: (537) 833-5366, (537) 830-1451; Fax: (537) 830-6554

The University of Havana

http://www.uh.cu/

Description: The University of Havana offers various Spanish language and Cuban culture courses to foreigners throughout the year. Courses are often combined with recreational activities and taught at various levels, from one to three weeks.

Contact: Ileana Dopico
E-mail: dpg@comuh.uh.cu
Address: Edificio del Rectorado, San Lázaro and L Streets, Vedado, Havana, Cuba
Telephone: (537) 832-4245, 870-8490, 878-6200; Fax: (537) 833-5737

Government, NGOs, and Think Tanks

Cuban Government Organizations and Sites

Official Site of the Cuban Government

http://www.cubagob.cu/ (in English: http://www.cubagob.cu/ingles/default.htm)

Castro Speech Database

http://www.cuba.cu/gobierno/discursos/index.html
   http://www.cuba.cu/gobierno/rauldiscursos/index2.html

Description: Many of Fidel and Raúl Castro's public statements from 1959 to the present, as compiled by the Cuban government. Available in Spanish, with translations into English, French, and many other languages.

National Center for Sex Education (CENESEX)

http://www.cenesex.sld.cu/

Description: The Cuban Center of Sex Education is dedicated to research and understanding of sexual diversity. CENESEX is a teaching, research, and welfare institution in the area of human sexuality.

Contact: Mariela Castro Espín, Director
E-mail: cenesex@infomed.sld.cu
Address: 460 10th Street, between 21st and 19th Aves., Vedado, Plaza, C.P. 10400, Havana, Cuba
Telephone: (537) 855-2528, 832-5464; Fax: 830-2295

Cuban Interests Section, Washington, DC

http://www.cubadiplomatica.cu/sicw/EN/Mission/InterestsSection.aspx
Description: Official site of the Cuban Interests Section in Washington, DC

Contact: Ambassador Jorge A. Bolaños Suarez
E-mail: secconscuba@worldnet.att.net; Información1@sicuw.org
Address: Embassy of Switzerland, Cuban Interests Section, 2630 16th St., NW, Washington, DC 20009
Telephone: (202) 797-8518, 797-8507, 797-8609, 797-8610

Cuban Mission to the United Nations, New York

http://www.cubadiplomatica.cu/onu/EN/Home.aspx
Description: The official website of the Cuban Mission to the United Nations.

E-mail: publicrelations@cubanmission.com
Address: 315 Lexington Avenue, New York, NY 10016
Telephone: (212) 689-7215; Fax: (212) 689-9073

U.S. Government Organizations and Sites

Office of Foreign Assets Control (OFAC)

http://www.ustreas.gov/offices/enforcement/ofac/programs/cuba/cuba.shtml
Description: Part of the U.S. Treasury Department, OFAC is responsible for obstructing economic relations with countries deemed to be enemies of the United States, Cuba among them.

Address: OFAC, U.S. Treasury Department, 909 Southeast First Ave. #736, Miami, FL 33131
Telephone: (305) 810-5140, (202) 747-5225

U.S. Department of State, Cuba Page

http://www.state.gov/p/wha/ci/cu/
Description: Cuba page of the U.S. State Department website. It contains links to fact sheets, press releases, reports, and more. The U.S. policy as presented in the reports can be summarized as "encouraging democratic and economic reforms, supporting the

development of civil society, promoting respect for human rights, and supporting the Cuban people. The U.S. Government continues to take steps to reach out to the Cuban people in support of their desire to freely determine their country's future."

U.S. Interests Section

http://havana.usint.gov/

Description: The U.S. Interests Section's functions are similar to those of any U.S. government mission abroad: consular services, a political and economic section, a public diplomacy program, and refugee processing unique to Cuba. The objectives of the Interests Section in Cuba is to promote a peaceful transition to a democratic system based on the rule of law, individual human rights, and open economic and communication systems.

Current Chief of Mission: Mr. John Caulfield (began service in September 2011)
Address: Calzada between L and M Streets, Vedado, Havana, Cuba
Telephone: (537) 833-3551; Emergency: (537) 833-3026; Fax: (537) 833-3700

CIA Fact Book, Cuba

https://www.cia.gov/library/publications/the-world-factbook/geos/cu.html
Description: U.S. Central Intelligence Agency "Fact Book" on Cuba.

Independent Research and Public Policy Institutions

Estado de SATS

http://www.estadodesats.com/en/

Description: State of SATS project hopes to create a plural space for participation and debate, where open and frank debate takes place. The project sponsors panel discussions, forums, and other events that are filmed and broadcast on the Internet. Opinions or points of view expressed on this site by individual participants do not necessarily represent the position of the rest of contributors.

Contact: Antonio G. Rodiles
E-mail: Antonio@estadodesats.com
Address: 4606 First Avenue, between 46 and 60, Miramar, Playa, Havana
Telephone: (535) 371-6460

Lexington Institute—Cuban Politics and Economy

http://www.lexingtoninstitute.org/cuba/

Description: The Lexington Institute is a nonprofit, nonpartisan public policy research organization based in Arlington, Virginia. Its Cuba program aims to provide readable, original research on Cuba's economy and analysis of developments in

Cuba, U.S.-Cuba relations, and U.S. policy toward Cuba. The Lexington Institute's resident expert on Cuba, Philip Peters, recently left to form his own organization, the Cuba Research Center (http://www.us-crc.org/).

Contact: Philip Peters
E-mail: info@us-crc.org
Address: 113 S. Columbus Street, Suite 100,
Alexandria, VA 22314
Telephone: (703) 257-3607

Cubasource (FOCAL)

http://www.cubasource.org/index_e.asp
Description: Though disbanded in 2010, Cubasource was a web-based information system on Cuba produced by the Canadian Foundation for the Americas (FOCAL). Its valuable reports are still available on the web. It was created to facilitate the exchange of information related to Cuba's international relations and the political, social, and economic trends and challenges facing the island, and to stimulate and facilitate constructive and informed research and discussion of these issues within Canada and internationally.

Contact: Cristina Warren, Program Director
E-mail: cwarren@focal.ca

The Cuba Study Group

http://www.cubastudygroup.org/
Description: The Cuba Study Group is a nonprofit, nonpartisan organization, comprised of Cuban business and community leaders who share a common vision of a democratic Cuba. The group makes policy recommendations that promote a peaceful regime change in Cuba and lead to democracy, an open society, a market-based system, respect for human rights, and national reunification. The group's website features a wealth of useful information and links.

Contact: Tomás Bilbao, Executive Director; Carlos Saladrigas, Co-Chair
E-mail: tomas.bilbao@CubaStudyGroup.org
Address: Washington: 611 Pennsylvania Ave., SE #208, Washington, DC 20003
Miami: 5900 Bird Road, Miami, FL 33155
Telephone: (202) 544-5088; Fax: (202) 315-3271
Miami: (305) 668-5437; Fax: (305) 668-5410

National Security Archive, Cuba Archive

http://www.gwu.edu/~nsarchiv/index.html
Description: An independent, nongovernmental research institute and library located at George Washington University, the archive collects and publishes declassified

documents obtained through the Freedom of Information Act (FOIA). The archive also serves as a repository of government records on a wide range of topics pertaining to the national security, foreign intelligence, and economic policies of the United States.

Contact: Thomas S. Blanton and Peter Kornbluh
E-mail: nsarchiv@gwu.edu
Address: National Security Archive, Suite 701, Gelman Library, George Washington University, 2130 H Street, NW, Washington, DC 20037
Telephone: (202) 994-7000; Fax: (202) 994-7005

Council on Foreign Relations (CFR)

http://www.cfr.org/region/cuba/ri213
Description: The CFR hosts a Cuba and U.S.-Cuba Relations Roundtable in Washington, DC, that addresses such issues as the status of the U.S. military base at Guantánamo Bay and the implications of Cuba's resuming normal trade relations with the United States. The CFR has also assembled an independent, bipartisan task force that produced the 2001 report "US-Cuban Relations in the 21st Century: A Follow-On Chairman's Report."

Contact: Julia E. Sweig
E-mail: jsweig@cfr.org
Address: 1779 Massachusetts Ave. NW, Washington, DC 20036
Telephone: (202) 518-3410; Fax: (202) 986-2984

Latin America Working Group

http://www.lawg.org/
Description: The Latin America Working Group's goal is to end the U.S. embargo against Cuba in order to benefit the people of both countries.

Contact: Mavis Anderson and Claire Rodríguez
E-mail: manderson@lawg.org; lawg@lawg.org
Address: 424 C Street, NE, Washington, DC 20002
Telephone: (202) 546-7010; Fax: (202) 543-7647

Washington Office on Latin America (WOLA), Cuba Project

http://www.wola.org/program/cuba
Description: WOLA's Cuba program encourages U.S. policy-makers to normalize relations with Cuba. WOLA is committed to advancing human rights, democratic institutions, citizen participation, and equitable economic development in Latin America. WOLA's views are nicely summarized in its recent online publication "A Time for Change: Rethinking US-Cuba Policy."

Contact: Geoff Thale, Program Director
E-mail: gthale@wola.org, wola@wola.org
Address: 1630 Connecticut Ave NW, Suite 200, Washington, DC 20009-1053
Telephone: (202) 797-2171; Fax: (202) 797-2172

Center for International Policy, Cuba Program

http://www.ciponline.org/cuba/index.htm
Description: The CIP Cuba program opposes the current containment policy toward Cuba and seeks a policy that will be productive in terms of real interests and objectives. Areas of policy focus of CIP's Cuba Program include terrorism, travel, and trade. The CIP website also contains an extensive and up-to-date list of useful Cuba links.

Contact: Wayne Smith
E-mail: cip@ciponline.org
Address: 1717 Massachusetts Avenue NW, Suite 801, Washington, DC 20036
Telephone: (202) 232-3317; Fax: (202) 232-3440

Center for Democracy in the Americas (CDA)

http://www.democracyinamericas.org/cuba/
Description: CDA is dedicated to changing U.S. policy toward Cuba by ending the ban on travel by Americans to the island and lifting the U.S. embargo against Cuba. Every Friday afternoon through its blog Cuba Central (http://cubacentral.wordpress.com/), the CDA publishes a comprehensive review of developments on the island and in U.S.-Cuba relations.

Contact: Sarah Stephens

E-mail: sstephens@democracyinamericas.org
Address: P.O. Box 53106, Washington, D.C. 20009

BUSINESS AND ECONOMICS

Association for the Study of the Cuban Economy (ASCE)

http://www.ascecuba.org/
Description: ASCE is a nonpartisan, nonpolitical organization inaugurated in 1990 to analyze the transformations taking place in the Cuban economy. ASCE publishes a compendium of papers, *Cuba in Transition*, drawn from its annual conference, available in PDF format on its website.

Contact: Ted A. Henken, President
E-mail: asce@ascecuba.org
Address: P.O. Box 28267, Washington, DC 20038-8267

The Cuba Center, Ohio Northern University

http://www.onu.edu/cuba/

Description: The Center for Cuban Business Studies conducts Cuban business and policy research, executes educational and advisory projects, and serves as a network of Cuba policy experts. Its various projects aim to facilitate interdisciplinary collaboration focused on Cuba.

Contact: Terry Keiser, Executive Director
E-mail: t-keiser@onu.edu
Address: 525 South Main Street, Ada, Ohio 45810
Telephone: 419-772-2325; Fax: 419-772-2330

Cuban Agricultural Research Program, University of Florida

Institute of Food and Agricultural Sciences

http://www.fred.ifas.ufl.edu/cubanag/index.php

Description: This research program produces economic analyses of Cuba's agricultural sector and assessments of the potential challenges and opportunities for the state of Florida and U.S. agriculture in the event of a normalization of relations with Cuba.

Contact: William A. Messina, Jr.
E-mail: WAMessina@mail.ifas.ufl.edu
University of Florida, Institute of Food and Agricultural Sciences, Food & Resource Economics Department
P.O. Box 110240, Gainesville, Florida 32611-0240
Telephone: (352) 392-1826, Ext. 308; Fax: (352) 846-0988

USA*Engage

http://www.usaengage.org/

Description: This organization lobbies against unilateral economic sanctions and seeks to open up opportunities for free trade with Cuba.

USA*Engage is a coalition of businesses, agriculture groups, and trade associations working to promote the benefits of U.S. engagement abroad and educate the public about the ineffectiveness of unilateral economic foreign policy sanctions. USA*Engage believes that positively engaging other societies through diplomacy, multilateral cooperation, the presence of American organizations, the best practices of American companies, and humanitarian exchanges better advances U.S. objectives than punitive unilateral economic sanctions.

Contact: Richard Sawaya, Director
E-mail: usaengage@nftc.org
Address: 1625 K Street, NW, Suite 200, Washington, DC 20006
Telephone: 202-887-0278; Fax: 202-452-8160

U.S.-Cuba Trade Association

http://www.uscuba.org/

Description: The U.S.-Cuba Trade Association is a membership-based, nonprofit organization based in Washington, DC, that works on behalf of its U.S. business members to protect, expand, and increase the current trade and potential for future business between the United States and Cuba.

Contact: Kirby Jones, President
E-mail: alacuba@aol.com
Address: 2300 M Street NW, Suite 800, Washington, DC 20037
Telephone: (301) 520-4297

CubaNews

http://www.cubanews.com/

Description: Founded in 1993, CubaNews is a leading source of business information on Cuba. CubaNews publishes a monthly newsletter with business-related reports from the island and assessments of changes in U.S. policy affecting U.S.-Cuba trade and business opportunities.

Contact: Larry Luxner, Editor
E-mail: larry@luxner.com; info@cubanews.com
Address: P.O. BOX 566346, Miami, Fl 33256-6346
Telephone: (305) 393-8760; Fax: (305) 670-2290

ART AND CULTURE

Cuban Ministry of Culture

http://www.min.cult.cu/

Description: An institution of the central administration of the Cuban government created in 1976, the Ministry of Culture is charged with directing, orienting, controlling, and carrying out the cultural policies of the government. Its aim is to guarantee the defense, preservation, and enrichment of the cultural patrimony of Cuba.

Contact: Rafael Bernal, Minister of Culture
E-mail: atencion@min.cult.cu
Address: 2nd Street, between 11th and 13th Avenues, Vedado, C.P. 10400, Plaza, Havana, Cuba

Cubarte, The Ministry of Culture's Portal to Cuban Culture

http://www.cubarte.cult.cu/paginas/index.php

Description: This is the official portal for Cuban culture. It has extensive information and links to most of Cuba's cultural institutions.

E-mail: comercial@webcubarte.cult.cu
Address: 251 Fourth Street, between 11th and 13th Avenues, Vedado, Havana
Telephone: 838-2223

UNEAC, Association of Cuban Writers and Artists

http://www.uneac.org.cu/

Description: The UNEAC (*Unión de Escritores y Artistas Cubanos*) is the official administrative and cultural center for all Cuban writers and artists. It publishes the magazine *Unión* and holds literary competitions, among many other cultural activities. UNEAC describes itself as "a social, cultural, professional, and non-governmental organization."

Contact: Carlos Martí Brenes
E-mail: uneac@cubarte.cult.cu
Address: 354 17th Street, between G and H, Vedado, C.P. 10400,
Havana, Cuba
Telephone: (537) 832-4551; Fax: (537) 833-3158

ICAIC, Cuban Film Institute

http://www.cubacine.cult.cu/

Description: The ICAIC (*El Instituto Cubano de Arte e Industria Cinematográficos*) was founded on March 24, 1959 and has the mission of producing, distributing, exhibiting, promoting, and conserving audiovisual materials produced in Cuba, principally films and documentaries.

Contact: Omar González
E-mail: presidenciaicaic@icaic.cu
Address: 1155 23rd Street, between 10th and 12th Avenues, C.P. 10400, Plaza, Havana, Cuba
Telephone: (537) 855-2859

International Festival of New Latin American Cinema

http://www.habanafilmfestival.com/

Description: Starting in December 1979, Cuba began hosting a Latin American film festival, bringing together the best of new cinema from around the hemisphere. Each December, Havana comes alive with the activities of this festival, which takes place in the city's many theaters.

Contact: Iván Giroud, Director
E-mail: festival@festival.icaic.cu

Casa de las Américas

http://www.casa.cult.cu/

Description: Dedicated to the promotion and study of culture and the arts since its founding in the early 1960s, the Casa provides a space for various forms of art and holds international literary competitions for writers of many different genres. Casa also works to disseminate the works of artists, writers, and musicians from Cuba, Latin America, and the Caribbean. The Casa also houses a literary research center and a center dedicated to the study of the Caribbean.

Contact: Roberto Fernández Retamar
E-mail: casa@cubarte.cult.cu; casa@casa.cult.cu
Address: 3rd Street at #52 G, C.P. 10400, Vedado, Havana, Cuba
Telephone: (537) 855-2706; Fax: (537) 833-4554

Casa del Caribe

Description: The Casa del Caribe is a meeting place for those dedicated to the study of the Caribbean. It is also the host for the annual international convention, Festival del Caribe.

Contact: Julián Mateo Tornés, Rafael Duharte, and Joel James
Address: 154 13th Street at 8th Avenue, C.P. 90400, Reparto Vista Alegre, Santiago, Cuba
Telephone: (53-266) 4-2285; Fax: (53-266) 4-2387

Advanced Institute of Art (ISA)

http://www.isa.cult.cu/

Description: The ISA is Cuba's most advanced school for the arts.

Contact: Raquel Mendieta
Address: 778th Street between 9th and 11th Avenues, Casa 910, Miramar, Playa, Havana, Cuba
Telephone: (537) 303-3652; Fax: (537) 303-3659

Juan Marinello Center for Research on Cuban Culture

http://www.perfiles.cult.cu/bloque.php?padre=2&bloque=3

Description: The Juan Marinello Research Center is dedicated to promoting Cuban culture both on the island and abroad. It works extensively with a wide array of researchers in Cuba and from abroad and periodically holds seminars on cultural and intellectual themes.

Contact: María Victoria Prado Ramírez
E-mail: cidcc@cubarte.cult.cu

Address: 63 Boyeros between Bruzón and Lugareño, C.P. 10600, Plaza, Havana, Cuba
Telephone: (537) 857-5770; Fax: (537) 877-5196

Wifredo Lam Contemporary Art Center

http://www.wlam.cu/

Description: The Lam center is devoted to the study and dissemination of the work of Wifredo Lam and other Cuban modernists of the Vanguardia movement. It also promotes the art of other contemporary painters and compiles information on developments in the field of the visual arts in Cuba. It is also the main body responsible for organizing the Havana Biennial, a major art exhibition that takes place periodically in Havana, attracting artists from around the world.

Contact: Dominica Ojeda Diez
E-mail: wlam@cubarte.cult.cu
Address: 22 San Ignacio Street at Empedrado, C.P. 10100, Habana Vieja, Havana, Cuba
Telephone: (537) 861-3419; Fax: (537) 833-8477

Fernando Ortiz Foundation

http://www.ffo.cult.cu/

Description: One of the leading historical and anthropological institutions in Cuba, the Fundaciónis a repository of information and experts on research into Cuban history, music, and Afro-Cuban culture. It strives to disseminate the thought and work of Fernando Ortiz and sponsors various conferences, seminars, and publications.

Contact: Miguel Barnet Lanza
E-mail: uhlha@unesco.org
Address: 160 L Street at 27A, Plaza, Vedado, Havana, Cuba
Telephone: (537) 832-4334; Fax: (537) 830-0623

Art-Havana

http://www.art-havana.com/

Description: Art-Havana has been promoting Cuban contemporary art since 1999. Groups from museums, art centers, as well as individual collectors have visited Havana through Art-Havana. Art-Havana offers historian-guided city tours, museum and gallery visits, as well as visits to the studios of the most important contemporary Cuban artists.

Contact: Rolando Milián, Director (in the United States)
New Haven, CT 06511

E-mail: rgmilian@art-havana.com
Telephone: (203) 980-7564; (203) 415-1506
Contact: Juan Pedro Sarracino, Co-Manager/Art-Curator
E-mail: contact@Art-Havana.com

Galeria Servando

https://www.facebook.com/servandoartgallery
Description: One of Havana's leading contemporary art galleries with a very professional and friendly staff. They have rotating exhibitions and good contacts with the artists themselves.

E-mail: galeriaservando@icaic.cu; servando@galeriascubanas.com
Address: 23rd Street between 10th and 12th Avenues, ICAIC Building, Vedado, Havana, Cuba
Telephone: (537) 833-9599

Temas *Magazine*

http://www.temas.cult.cu/
Description: Published since 1995 and online since 2002, *Temas* is the leading contemporary sociocultural journal published in Cuba today. It publishes articles on art, music, literature, the social sciences, political theory, and ideology. The editorial board is composed of Rafael Hernández, Alfredo Prieto, Natalia Bolívar, Rufo Caballero, Mario Coyula, Mayra Espina, Jorge Ibarra, Nelson P. Valdés, Oscar Zanetti, and Piero Gleijeses, among others. *Temas* also sponsors a monthly panel discussion and debate that takes place on the last Thursday of each month at the auditorium of the "Fresa y Chocolate" Café of the ICAIC, dubbed "Último Jueves."

Contact: Rafael Hernández; Alfredo Prieto
Email: temas@icaic.cu
Address: 1155 23rd St., 5th floor, between 10th and 12th Aves., C.P. 10400, Vedado, Havana
Telefax: (537) 855-3010, 830-4759, 855-3650 (Ext. 233)

Omni-Zona Franca

http://omnifestivalpoesiasinfin.blogspot.com/
Description: Led by multidisciplinary artists, Luis Eligio, Amaury Pacheco, David D'Omni, this group of poets, artists, and musicians is based in the massive government housing project of Alamar, east of Havana and exists outside of state cultural institutions. They host an annual December poetry and performance festival known as "*Poesia Sin Fin*" (Endless Poetry).

Center for Cuban Studies/Cuban Art Space/Cuba
Update, New York

http://www.cubanartspace.net/gallery/index.php
http://www.cubaupdate.org/
Description: The Center for Cuban Studies is a nonprofit educational institution located in New York City that promotes knowledge of Cuban culture and society with an emphasis on the achievements of the Cuban Revolution. Open since 1972, one of its aims is to end the U.S. embargo and achieve normalization in relations between Cuba and the United States. It sponsors various trips to Cuba for licensable professionals.

Contact: Sandra Levinson
E-mail: cubanctr@igc.org
Address: 231 W 29th St #401, New York, NY 10001
Telephone: (212) 242-0559; Fax: (212) 242-1937

Cuban Cinema Classics (CCC),
University of William and Mary

http://www.cubancinemaclassics.org/Cuban_Cinema_Classics.html
Description: CCC presents a showcase of Cuba's award-winning revolutionary documentaries. The initiative was established to address the difficulty of obtaining Cuban documentaries with English subtitles for educational and cultural purposes in the United States. CCC distributes the documentaries to colleges and universities, media arts centers, museums, and other agencies.

Contact: Ann Marie Stock
E-mail: orders@cubancinemaclassics.org
Address: Cuban Cinema Classics, 104 Wakerobin Rd., Williamsburg, VA 23185
Telephone: (571) 242-4297

Cuban Poster Art Project of Docs Populi (Documents for the Public)

http://www.docspopuli.org/CubaPosters.html
Description: Docs Populi documents and disseminates late 20th century political poster art, including that of postrevolutionary Cuba.

Contact: Lincoln Cushing
E-mail: lcushing@igc.org; lcushing@docspopuli.org
Address: 822 Santa Barbara Road, Berkeley, CA 94707
Telephone: (510) 528-7161

Related Sites: http://www.lib.berkeley.edu/~lcushing/Home.html; http://libr.org/pl/15_Cushing.html

Afro Cuba Research Institute

http://www.afrocuba.org

Description: The Afro Cuba Research Institute is a research group that studies and promotes Afro-Cuban traditions. It also publishes the *Afrocuba Journal* and conducts the Palo Monte program of cultural academic exchange between Cuba and the United States, founded in Matanzas, Cuba, in 1976.

Contact: Jorge Luis Rodríguez, Director; María Esther Ortiz, Editor
E-mail: Director@afrocuba.org; Ortiz@Afrocuba.org
Address: P.O. Box 26688, Los Angeles, CA 90026
Telephone: (323) 662-3750

Afro-Cuba Web

http://www.afrocubaweb.com

Description: This web page is dedicated to promoting recognition and research of the African cultures in Cuba.

E-mail: acw@afrocubaweb.com
Address: P.O. Box 1054, Arlington, MA 02474

CubaNOLA Collective

http://www.cubanola.org/

Description: CubaNOLA Collective brings together musicians, artists, scholars, and tradition bearers to explore and expand the ties between the musical, artistic, and cultural heritages of Cuba and New Orleans, Louisiana. The organization sees Cuba and New Orleans as cultural hubs for the Caribbean and Gulf South regions and builds relationships between artists and communities through performances, artist collaborations, educational programs, heritage tours, and documentaries.

Contact: Ariana Hall
E-mail: ariana@cubanola.org

Ludwig Foundation of Cuba and American Friends of the Ludwig Foundation

http://www.aflfc.org/

Description: The American Friends of the Ludwig Foundation of Cuba (AFLFC) is a leading organization in the United States fostering cultural exchange between American and Cuban artists and art professionals. Its partnership with the Ludwig Foundation of Cuba (LFC), a nongovernmental, nonprofit art and cultural institution in Havana, has enabled it to maintain ties with the art community of Cuba.

E-mail: info@aflfc.org
Address: 3 East 69th Street SR2, New York, NY 10021
Telephone: (212) 628-3494; Fax: (212) 628-4969

The Havana Film Festival New York

http://www.hffny.com
Description: The Havana Film Festival New York (HFFNY) collaborates with Havana's International Festival of New Latin American Cinema to introduce its audience to prominent and emerging filmmakers by showcasing the latest award-winning films and classics from and about Latin America, the Caribbean, and the U.S. Latino community.

Contact: Carole Rosenberg, Executive Director
E-mail: cr@aflfc.org

DEMOCRACY AND HUMAN RIGHTS

Cuban Commission for Human Rights and National Reconciliation, CCDHRN (La Comisión Cubana de Derechos Humanos y Reconciliación Nacional)

http://observacuba.org/
Description: The CCDHRN is one of Cuba's oldest human rights organizations. It tracks violations of human rights and issues periodic reports on arbitrary detentions, arrests, and imprisonment.

Contact: Elizardo Sánchez Santacruz
Address: 3014 21st Street, between 30th and 34th Avenues, Playa, Havana, Cuba

Observatorio Cubano de Derechos Humanos (OCDH, The Cuban Observatory of Human Rights)

http://observacuba.org/
Description: Working closely with the CCDHRN, the OCDH is a nonprofit organization founded in Madrid in 2009 by former political prisoners from the Black Spring of 2003 and members of the *Damas de Blanco*. Its objective is to transform Cuba into a democratic state and demand the respect for human rights on the island. To that end, it has created an ongoing project of systematic documentation, denunciation, diffusion, and publication of the violations of fundamental rights of Cuban citizens.

Contact: Elena Larrinaga de Luis
Phone: (53-7) 203-8584

Damas de Blanco *(Ladies in White)*

http://www.damasdeblanco.com/

Description: The *Damas de Blanco* came into being spontaneously in April 2003 in response to the imprisonment of their family members. Today they constitute a group of women of diverse creeds and ideologies from all across the island of Cuba. United initially to demand the release of their loved ones, they continue to fight for an end to arbitrary detentions and the respect for full political rights and civil liberties for all Cubans.

Contact: Berta Soler
E-mail: info@DamasdeBlanco.com
Address: 2525 20th Street, between 25 and 27, Pedro Betancourt, Matanzas

Unión Patriótica de Cuba
(UNPACU, Cuban Patriotic Union)

http://www.unpacu.org/

The Cuban Patriotic Union is a civic organization born out of the experience of repression that engages in a pacific but firm struggle against the violation of civic liberties in Cuba. At the start of 2013, the UNPACU recently joined forces with FANTU (*Foro Antitotalitario Unido*), another leading human rights organization on the island.

Contacts in Cuba: José Daniel Ferrer, Guillermo Fariñas, and Félix Navarro
Telephone: (53) 53-14-6740
International contacts: Luis Enrique Ferrer, United States
Telephone: (786) 304-6303; (786) 553-1666
E-mail: unpacu@gmail.com; luisenriqueferrer@gmail.com
Twitter: José Daniel Ferrer—@jdanielferrer (http://twitter.com/#!/jdanielferrer)
YouTube Channel: http://www.youtube.com/user/unpacu

Hablemos Press Information Center *(CIHPRESS)*

http://www.cihpress.com/

Description: The *Centro de Información Hablemos Press* (CIHPRESS) is a nonprofit Cuban nongovernmental organization founded on February 3, 2009, by a group of independent journalists and human rights activists with the purpose of reporting on human rights abuses in Cuba.

Contact: Roberto de Jesús Guerra Pérez
E-mail: robersm2007@gmail.com
Address: 394 Calle Santa Marta, Apt. 3 (altos), between Franco and Subirana, Centro Habana, Havana
Telephone: 879-9331; (5) 319-6927

Christian Liberation Movement (MLC)

http://www.oswaldopaya.org/es/

Description: Founded in 1988 by a group of lay Catholics led by Oswaldo Payá Sardiñas, the Christian Liberation Movement is best known for the Varela Project. The Varela Project seeks to start a civic dialogue, open up Cuba's political system, defend and promote respect for civil, economic, and human rights, and achieve national reconciliation through peaceful means. The MLC does not accept aid from the U.S. government and opposes the embargo.

Contact: Francisco De Armas, International Representative
E-mail:info@oswaldopaya.org
Telephone: (305) 285-7970

Freedom House, Cuba

http://www.freedomhouse.org/country/cuba

Description: The Cuba Programs of Freedom House seek to promote a peaceful transition to democracy in the island. Their strategy includes the distribution of publications and support for Cuban prodemocracy organizations and activists. Freedom House also publishes three annual "freedom" reports on countries around the world, including Cuba: "Freedom in the World," "Freedom of the Press," and "Freedom on the Net."

Contact: Daniel Calingaert and Viviana Giacaman
E-mail: press@freedomhouse.org; program@freedomhouse.org
Address: 1301 Connecticut Ave. NW, 6th Fl., Washington, DC 20036
120 Wall Street, 26th Fl., New York, NY 10005

Human Rights Watch/Americas, Cuba Page

http://www.hrw.org/americas/cuba

Description: A recent report from HRW on Cuba begins with the following summary: "Cuba remains a Latin American anomaly: an undemocratic government that represses nearly all forms of political dissent. President Fidel Castro's government continues to enforce political conformity using criminal prosecutions, long- and short-term detentions, mob harassment, police warnings, surveillance, house arrests, travel restrictions, and politically-motivated dismissals from employment. The end result is that Cubans are systematically denied basic rights to free expression, association, assembly, privacy, movement, and due process of law."

Contact: José Miguel Vivanco, Daniel Wilkinson, and Nik Steinberg
E-mail: wilkind@hrw.org; steinbn@hrw.org;
Address: 350 Fifth Avenue, 34th Floor, New York, NY 10118-3299
Telephone: (212) 290-4700

Amnesty International

http://www.amnesty.org/en/region/cuba

Description: Amnesty International (AI) tracks and documents human and civil rights violations around the world, issuing periodic "urgent actions" in order to call attention to violations of human rights in specific countries. AI also names "prisoners of conscience" when individuals who have neither used nor advocated violence are unjustly imprisoned.

Address: 1 Easton Street, London, WC1X 0DW, UK
Telephone: (+44-20) 7413-5500; Fax: (+44-20) 7956-1157
Twitter: *@Amnestyonline*

Center for a Free Cuba

http://www.cubacenter.org/

Description: The Center for a Free Cuba is an independent, nonpartisan institution dedicated to promoting human rights and a transition to democracy and the rule of law on the island. Established in November 1997, the center gathers and disseminates information about Cuba and Cubans to the news media, NGOs, and the international community. The center also assists the people of Cuba through its information outreach and humanitarian programs on the island.

Contact: Frank Calzón
E-mail: Freecuba@cubacenter.org
Address: 1000 Vermont Ave NW, Suite 300?Washington, DC 20005
Telephone: (202) 463-8430; Fax: (202) 463-8412

DIASPORA AND EXILE ORGANIZATIONS

Cuban American National Foundation (CANF)

http://www.canf.org/

Description: The Cuban American National Foundation (CANF) is a nonprofit organization dedicated to advancing freedom and democracy in Cuba. Established in Florida in 1981, CANF is the largest Cuban organization in exile, representing a cross section of the Cuban exile community. CANF supports a nonviolent transition to a pluralistic, market-based democracy grounded in the rule of law and the protection of human, social, political, and economic rights.

Contact: Mariela Ferretti

E-mail: hq@canf.org; canfnet@icanect.net
Address: P.O. Box 440069, Miami, FL 33144-9926
Telephone: (305) 592-7768; Fax: (305) 592-7889

Cuban Liberty Council (CLC)

http://consejoporlalibertaddecuba.org/

Description: Formed in 2001 after a split with the Cuban American National Foundation (CANF), the Cuban Liberty Council (CLC) is a nonprofit organization committed to promoting liberty and democracy in Cuba.

E-mail: cubanliberty@gmail.com
Address: 3663 SW 8 St, Suite 210, Miami, FL. 33135
Telephone: (305) 441-0313; Fax: (305) 441-0318

Encasa/US-Cuba

http://www.encasa-us-cuba.org/

Description: As the name indicates, the Emergency Network of Cuban American Scholars and Artists for Change in U.S.-Cuba Policy (ENCASA/US-CUBA) opposes current U.S. policy toward Cuba with special focus on the embargo, the restriction of family contacts, and the elimination of most opportunities for academic exchange. Formed in 2006, ENCASA seeks to break down the monolithic image of a uniformly hard-line Cuban-American community.

Contact: Rubén G. Rumbaut, Professor of Sociology and Co-Director
E-mail: encasa-us-cuba@runbox.com; rrumbaut@uci.edu
Address: Center for Research on Immigration, Population, and Public Policy, 3151 Social Science Plaza, University of California, Irvine, Irvine, CA 92697
Telephone: (949) 824-2495; Fax: (949) 824-4717

CAFÉ—Cuban-Americans for Engagement

http://www.cafeporcuba.com/

Description: CAFÉ comprises Cuban-Americans who seek to reflect the diversity of the Cuban diaspora and promote a better relationship between the United States and Cuba, based on the principles of exchange, engagement, and the normalization of relations between the two countries.

Contact: María Isabel Alfonso
E-mail: malfonso@sjcny.edu; concafeporcuba@gmail.com
Telephone: (786) 529-5123

Roots of Hope (Raices de Esperanza)

http://www.raicesdeesperanza.org/

Description: Roots of Hope is a network of more than 3,000 students and young professionals across the United States and abroad focused on empowering Cuban youth. It seeks to inspire young people to care about Cuba and proactively support young people on the island. Founded in 2003 by college students, today Roots encompasses a dynamic and diverse group of young leaders throughout the United States with students at more than 55 universities and young professionals in Boston, New York, Washington, DC, Los Angeles, Chicago, and Miami. The organization is guided by three basic principles: *amor*, *amistad*, and *esperanza* (love, friendship, and hope).

Contact: Raúl Moas
E-mail: info@raicesdeesperanza.org
Address: P.O. Box 260486, Miami, FL 33126
Telephone: (305) 735-1868

TRAVEL AND TOURISM

HavanaTur

http://www.havanatur.cu/
Description: City of Havana official tourism site.

E-mail: eduardoj@cimex.com.cu
Address: Sierra Maestra Building, 1st Street, between 0 and 2, Miramar, Playa, Havana, Cuba
Telephone: (537) 203-9770; Fax: (537) 204-2877

Marazul Charters

http://www.marazulcharters.com/
Description: The leading U.S.-based tourism agency catering to travel to Cuba, with two offices in New Jersey and three in greater Miami. Its website has abundant information on U.S. travel restrictions and links to the U.S. Treasury Department's Office of Foreign Assets Control—the entity responsible for licensing travel to Cuba.

Contact: Mayra Alonso and Hilda Diaz
4100 Park Avenue, Tower Plaza Mall, Weehawken, NJ 07086
Telephone: (201) 319-3900; Fax: (201) 319-9009

RELIGIOUS

Convivencia *Magazine*

http://www.convivenciacuba.es/
Description: An independent sociocultural publication of lay Catholic activists Pinar del Río. Led by Dagoberto Valdés, *Convivencia* is run by the same editorial board that had published the pioneering magazine *Vitral* until spring 2007. *Convivencia* also publishes a blog under the title Intramuros (http://convivenciacuba.es/

intramuros/). The publications seek to provide an integrated framework with which to revitalize the values of human freedom and community solidarity with an eye toward rebuilding Cuban civil society.

Contact: Dagoberto Valdés Hernández, Director
E-mail: redaccion@convivenciacuba.es; convivencia@convivenciacuba.es

Espacio Laical *Magazine*

http://espaciolaical.org/
Description: *Espacio Laical* (Lay Space) is a printed and digital magazine of social communication published by the Father Félix Varela Cultural Center of the Arch-Diocese of Havana. Its objective is to offer a Christian reading of Cuban society in dialogue with other perspectives through gatherings where there is space for everyone.

Contact: Roberto Veiga González and Lenier González Mederos
E-mail: info@espaciolaical.org
Address: Casa Laical, Teniente Rey between Bernaza and Villegas, Habana Vieja, CP 10100.

Palabra Nueva *Magazine*

http://www.palabranueva.net/
Description: Founded in April 1992, *Palabra Nueva* (New Word) is the magazine of the Arch-Diocese of Havana. Its aim is to respond to the call of Pope John Paul II to carry out a "new evangelization" within Cuban society. While primarily aimed at Cuban Catholics, the magazine addresses topics of interest to all Cubans including the economy, culture, sports, social sciences, and of course religion.

Contact: Orlando Márquez Hidalgo, Founder and Director
Address: Arzobispado de La Habana, Calle Habana No. 152 corner with Chacón, Habana Vieja, CP 10100
Telephone: (53-7) 862-4000; (53-7) 862-4008; (53-7) 862-4009

Caritas

http://www.caritas.org/worldmap/latin_america/cuba.html
Description: Caritas Cuba works through Cuba's 11 dioceses as one of the few independent nongovernmental organizations active there. Its programs include numerous soup kitchens and health-related projects. Caritas Cuba also focuses on two of Cuba's most vulnerable groups: the elderly and children with learning difficulties.

Contact: Ms. Maritza Sánchez, Director
Email: maritza@iglesiacatolica.cu
Address: Caritas Cubana, Calle D #512, Vedado, Ciudad Habana, Cuba
Telephone: (53-7) 83-33099; Fax: (53-7) 83-33048

Christian Center for Reflection and Dialogue (CCRD)

http://ccrd.org/

Description: A Protestant church with an active agenda of social outreach located in the city of Cárdenas. The CCRD publishes an online newsletter and organizes a variety of workshops.

Contact: Rev. Raimundo García Franco, Executive Director
E-mail: ccrd@enet.cu; franco@enet.cu
Address: 1210 Céspedes, between 25th and 26th, C.P. 42100, Cárdenas, Matanzas, Cuba
Telephone: (53-45) 52-2923, (53-45) 52-1710; Fax: (53-45) 52-1000

Martin Luther King Memorial Center

http://www.cmlk.org/

Description: A progressive, ecumenical religious organization dedicated to Cuban socialism and to the spread of a liberationist and context-specific theology through popular education.

Contact: Daisy Rojas
E-mail: rinternac@mlking.sld.cu; solidaridad@cmlk.co.cu; ihrr@columbus.rr.com
Address: 9609 53rd Ave., between 96th and 98th Streets, C.P. 11400, Marianao 14, Havana
Telephone: (537) 820-3940, 820-9741; Fax: (537) 827-2959, 833-2959

The Cuban Jewish Community
(La Comunidad Hebrea de Cuba)

http://www.chcuba.org/english/

Description: This is the primary Jewish community center and charity of Cuba. It has extensive contacts in Israel and with Jewish communities in the United States.

Contact: Dr. José Miller
E-mail: patronato_ort@enet.cu; beth_shalom@enet.cu
Address: I Street at 13th Avenue, Vedado, Havana, Cuba
Telephone: (537) 832-8953; Fax (537) 833-3778

Yoruba Cultural Association of Cuba
(Asociación Cultural Yoruba de Cuba)

http://www.cubayoruba.cult.cu/

Description: The Yoruba Cultural Association of Cuba has as its driving purpose the preservation, study, and promotion of the Yoruba cultural traditions in Cuba.

Contact: Antonio Castañeda Márquez, President
Address: 456 Gervasio, between Zanja and San José, Apartado 1, Centro
Habana, Havana, Cuba
Telephone: (537) 879-6948

NEWS SOURCES

Granma International *in English*

http://www.granma.cu/ingles/index.html
Description: International English version of Cuba's national newspaper, published by the Cuban Communist Party.

Juventud Rebelde *in English (The Newspaper of the Young Communist League)*

http://www.juventudrebelde.co.cu/
Description: International English edition of the national newspaper of Cuban youth.

Cuba Debate *in English*

http://en.cubadebate.cu/
Description: With the slogan "*Contra el terrorismo mediático*" (against media terrorism), *Cuba Debate* is Cuba's official "alternative" web-based portal aimed at sounding the alarm about "campaigns of defamation against Cuba."

Café Fuerte

http://cafefuerte.com/
Description: *Café Fuerte* (Strong Coffee) is a Miami-based website that provides original, balanced, and high-quality news and information about Cuba and Miami.

Cuba Encuentro

http://www.cubaencuentro.com/
Description: Once the site of the Cuban cultural journal *Encuentrode la Cultura Cubana* (Madrid), this is now the online news site CubaEncuentro.com, one of the best sources of news and information (in Spanish) on Cuba today.

Contact: Annabelle Rodríguez, President
E-mail: info@cubaencuentro.com

Diario de Cuba

http://www.diariodecuba.com/

Description: When the online portal CubaEncuentro.com split in December 2009, a number of its younger journalists decided to start this excellent site for news and information about Cuba.

Contact: Pablo Díaz Espi

Miami Herald

http://www.miamiherald.com/

Description: Miami's major daily newspaper with extensive coverage of Cuba-related issues.

El Nuevo Herald

http://www.elnuevoherald.com/

Description: The Spanish-language publication of the *Miami Herald*. This version of the paper often has more sustained and in-depth coverage of Cuba.

CubaNet News

http://www.cubanet.org/

Description: CubaNet is committed to fostering a free press in Cuba. The website acts as a clearinghouse of news on Cuba, with an emphasis on news directly from Cuba by independent journalists and a focus on human and economic rights.

Contact: Hugo Landa, Director
E-mail: CNRedaccion@aol.com
Address: CubaNet News, Inc., 145 Madeira Ave., Suite 207, Coral Gables, FL 33134
Telephone: (305) 774-1887; Fax: (305) 567-9687

CubaVerdad

http://www.cubaverdad.org

Description: This site is dedicated to human rights in Cuba and contains links to important news, reports, websites, and data. CubaVerdad also provides a free digest of a wide selection of articles from the international press about Cuba. The site also features an e-group with an archive of over 29,000 Cuba-related news articles: http://groups.yahoo.com/group.CubaVerdad/.

E-mail: admin@cubaverdad.org; CubaVerdad@yahoogroups.com

Cuba News Yahoo List

http://groups.yahoo.com/group/CubaNews/

Description: This syndication service seeks to bring to the attention of people concerned with Cuba a wide range of news and information about the island, the Cuban community abroad, Cuba's international relations, and related topics. The list is moderated by Walter Lippmann, an author, editor, and Cuba solidarity activist based in Los Angeles, California.

THE CUBAN BLOGOSPHERE

Blogs Written from Cuba

Generation Y—http://generacionyen.wordpress.com/
Author: Yoani Sánchez

Voces Cubanas—http://vocescubanas.com/ (a portal hosting a variety of Cuban bloggers)
Administrator: M. J. Porter

Translating Cuba—http://translatingcuba.com/ (an English translation of the previous site)
Administrator: M. J. Porter

Sin EVAsión/Without EVAsion—http://sinevasionen.wordpress.com/
Author: Miriam Celaya

El Blog de Dimas—http://dimasblogen.wordpress.com/
Author: Dimas Castellanos

Lunes de Post-Revolución—http://orlandolunes.wordpress.com/
Author: Orlando Luis Pardo Lazo

Boring Home Utopics—http://vocescubanas.com/boringhomeutopics/
Author: Orlando Luis Pardo Lazo

Desde La Habana—http://www.desdelahabana.net/
Authors: Ivan García, Laritza Diversent, and Tania Quintero

Havana Times—http://www.havanatimes.org/
Editor: Circles Robinson

La Joven Cuba—http://lajovencuba.wordpress.com/
Authors: Roberto G. Peralo, Harold Cárdenas Lema, and Osmany Sánchez

Observatorio Critico—http://observatoriocriticodesdecuba.wordpress.com/
Collective of authors

Cartas Desde Cuba—http://www.bbc.co.uk/blogs/mundo/cartas_desde_cuba/
Author: Fernando Ravsberg

Cuban Legal Advisor—http://leyesdelaritzaen.wordpress.com/
Authors: Laritza Diversent and Yaremis Flores

La Polémica Digital—http://espaciodeelaine.wordpress.com/
Author: Elaine Díaz Rodríguez

Paquito, El de Cuba—http://paquitoeldecuba.wordpress.com/
Author: Francisco Rodríguez Cruz

Bubusopia—http://bubusopia.blogspot.com/
Authors: Rogelio M. Díaz Moreno and Yasmín S. Portales Machado

Blogs Written from Outside of Cuba

Penúltimos Días—http://www.penultimosdias.com/
Author: Ernesto Hernández Busto

The Cuban Triangle—http://cubantriangle.blogspot.com/
Author: Philip Peters

The Cuban Economy—http://thecubaneconomy.com/
Author: Archibald Ritter

Along the Malecón—http://alongthemalecon.blogspot.com/
Author: Tracey Eaton

El Yuma—http://elyuma.blogspot.com/
Author: Ted A. Henken

The Internet in Cuba—http://laredcubana.blogspot.com/
Author: Larry Press

Babalú Blog—http://babalublog.com/
Authors: Val Prieto and Alberto de la Cruz

Capital Hill Cubans—http://www.capitolhillcubans.com/
Author: Maurcio Claver-Carone

Annotated Bibliography

GENERAL WORKS

Understanding the life and thought of José Martí is essential as a basis for understanding Cuban history, politics, culture, and society. However, digesting the multivolume collected works in Spanish is a challenge for even the most ambitious and talented Cubaphile. Luckily, Esther Allen has done a stellar job of editing and translating some of the most relevant of his sometimes dense and always penetrating poetry, letters, journal entries, and essays, in *José Martí: Selected Writings* (Penguin, 2002). Also published in 2002 is the first ever two-volume English language *Encyclopedia of Cuba: People, History, Culture* (Greenwood Press). Edited by Luis Martínez-Fernández, D. H. Figueredo, Louis A. Pérez, Jr., and Luis González, this essential collection of brief but informative entries on Cuba's history, politics, and culture is a gold mine of information on the island written by leading scholars both on the island and abroad.

A number of major anthologies on Cuba have been published during the last 25 years. Aviva Chomsky, Barry Car, and Pamela Maria Smorkaloff have edited *The Cuba Reader: History, Culture, Politics* (Duke University Press, 2003). This 700-page text contains an excellent and deftly edited collection of mostly primary materials arranged in eight chronological sections. Highlights of the reader include classic essays by Bartolomé de Las Casas, Fernando Ortiz, Manuel Moreno Fraginals, José Antonio Saco, José Martí, Miguel Barnet, Oscar Lewis, Che Guevara, Fidel Castro, Alejandro Portes, and Haroldo Dilla, as well as poetry and prose from leading Cuban authors including Juan Francisco Manzano, Gómez de Avellaneda, Nicolás Guillén, Alejo Carpentier, Reinaldo Arenas, Heberto Padilla, Nancy Morejón, and Roberto Fernández. A useful companion volume to the Chomsky, Car, and Smorkaloff

Cuba Reader is Chomsky's brief but surprisingly comprehensive *History of the Cuban Revolution* (John Wiley and Sons, 2011). Approaching Cuba's revolutionary experiment with third-world socialism from a decidedly sympathetic, progressive, and anti-imperialist standpoint, Chomsky does not shy away from airing the revolution's dirty laundry even if she places most of the blame for its troubles squarely at the feet of its more powerful neighbor to the north. Now in its 11th edition, *Cuban Communism, 1959–2003* (Transaction Publishers, 2003) is focused on the economic, military, social, and political aspects of the revolution. Editors Irving Louis Horowitz and Jaime Suchlicki have recently added new readings under the heading "Transition to Civil Society," making the book especially useful to comparativists.

Philip Brenner, William M. LeoGrande, Donna Rich, and Daniel Seigel edited the excellent *Cuba Reader: The Making of a Revolutionary Society* (Grove Press, 1989) almost 25 years ago. While some parts of it are dated, its more sympathetic approach to the socialist experiment is a nice complement to Horowitz and Suchlicki's more hard-edged collection. Especially enlightening are the essays by Cuban poet and social scientist Lourdes Casal. Brenner and LeoGrande, along with John M. Kirk and Marguerite Jiménez, released an updated reader focused on the special period, entitled, *Cuba Today: A Twenty-First Century Reader* (Rowman and Littlefield, 2007) and—given the momentous changes on the island over the last six years—are planning on publishing a new reader in 2013–2014. One final recent, well-written, and data-rich reference book on Cuba is *Cuba: A Country Study* (Federal Research Division, Library of Congress, 2002). Now in its fourth edition, edited and with an excellent introduction by Rex Hudson, this critical compendium of up-to-date information on the island includes sections on history, society, economics, political institutions, and the military, each penned by leaders in their fields.

CHAPTER 1: GEOGRAPHY

Some of the most underestimated but also most useful and information-packed resources on Cuban geography are the many guidebooks covering the island destination that have recently flooded the market. Few other resources combine readability with detailed facts and up-to-date information on seemingly everything under the sun. The best are *Moon Handbooks* (Christopher P. Baker, Avalon Travel Publishing, multiple years) and *Lonely Planet* (various authors, Lonely Planet Publications, multiple years). For comprehensive coverage, accurate, respectful reportage, and sheer readability, these two guides can't be beaten. Baker's 750-page guide manages to be truly encyclopedic without ever being boring and is the leader in the field. A bit more digestible is the 2006 Lonely Planet edition by Brendan Sainsbury, weighing in at just under 500 pages.

Also, the following classic works on sugar and slavery in the Caribbean with an emphasis on 19th-century Cuba all contain valuable geographic information and are highly recommended. The classic Cuban text on the island's allegorical battle between tobacco and sugar, *Cuban Counterpoint: Tobacco and Sugar* (Duke University Press, 1995), was written by Fernando Ortiz and originally published in Spanish in 1940. This new edition has been expertly translated by Harriet de Onís, with a fantastic introduction by Fernando Coronil. After Ortiz, perhaps Cuban historian

Manuel Moreno Fraginals's *Sugarmill: The Socioeconomic Complex of Sugar in Cuba, 1760–1860* (Monthly Review Press, 1976) is the next most important study of the socioeconomic impact that the sugar/slave nexus had on 19th-century Cuban society. This book was recently reissued by the Catalan publisher Crítica, under its original title in Spanish, *El ingenio: Complejo económico social cubano del azúcar* (2001).

German explorer and intellectual Alexander von Humboldt first visited Cuba in 1800 and later penned one of the classic political studies of the Spanish colony, *Ensayo político sobre la isla de Cuba*, first published in 1826 as part of a larger work chronicling his travels throughout the Americas. His study has recently been reissued by Markus Wiener Publishers in a new critical edition, entitled, *Island of Cuba: A Political Essay* (2001), produced under the guidance of historians Luis Fernández Martínez and Frank Argote-Freyre, and translated by Shelley Frisch. Likewise, the previously mentioned two-volume *Encyclopedia of Cuba: People, History, Culture* (Greenwood Press, 2002), edited by Luis Martínez-Fernández, et al., contains much useful geographical information, as does Martínez-Fernández's insightful essay "Geography, Will It Absolve Cuba?" published in *History Compass* 2:1, pp. 1–21, 2004.

CHAPTER 2: HISTORY

By far, the clearest, most easily digestible, yet eminently serious and scholarly one-volume history of the island is *Cuba: A Short History*. Published by Cambridge University Press in 1993, this book is excerpted from Cambridge's multivolume *Cambridge History of Latin America*. Edited by Leslie Bethell, this slim book is under 200 pages and includes chronological chapters from the eminent scholars Hugh Thomas, Luis E. Aguilar, Louis A. Perez, Jr., and Jorge I. Domínguez. For anyone wanting to dig deeper into Cuban history, the various books written by these same authors are an excellent guide and reference. First is Hugh Thomas's mammoth 1,700-page *Cuba or the Pursuit of Freedom* (revised ed., DaCapo Press, 1998). Despite its enormous size, this book covers just 200 years of Cuban history (1762–1962) and as such does so in intricate and tantalizing detail. Thomas is a true master historian who can breathe life into the seemingly mundane just as well as he can tease apart the intricacies of the explosion of the USS *Maine* in 1898 or the events surrounding the failed Bay of Pigs invasion in 1961. Likewise, Cuban-American historian Luis E. Aguilar adeptly places the 1959 revolution in its proper historical context by walking us through the failed revolution of 1933 in his *Cuba, 1933: Prologue to Revolution* (Cornell University Press, 1972).

The most prolific historian writing in English today on Cuba is without doubt Louis A. Pérez, Jr. Among his many very fine books on Cuba's history, his general overview *Cuba: Between Reform and Revolution* (now in its 4th ed., Oxford University Press, 2011) is perhaps the best to begin with. Besides being a fact-filled and entertaining general history, the book makes a clear, consistent, and convincing argument linking the Cuban revolution of today to the country's history of frustrated attempts at independence and sovereignty. It also includes an incomparable annotated bibliography of an enormous amount of source material on Cuba that could be a book unto itself. Pérez has also published an excellent historical study of

U.S.-Cuban relations, entitled *Cuba and the United States: Ties of Singular Intimacy* (University of Georgia Press, 1990). Finally, Jorge I. Domínguez has set the standard for institutional analysis of socialist Cuba in his detailed and critical-minded history of the island's 20th-century politics, *Cuba: Order and Revolution* (Harvard University Press, 1978).

Also worth noting are journalist Richard Gott's *Cuba: A New History* (Yale University Press, 2004). A longtime itinerant journalist reporting from across Latin America since the 1960s, Gott has produced a quite comprehensive, readable, and fresh new history of Cuba. His book is especially good at recounting specific episodes from Afro-Cuban history, including the Aponte conspiracy, the *Escalera* massacre, and the 1912 "race war," as well as chronicling Cuba's hugely influential involvement in the African wars in Ethiopia and especially Angola. Marifeli Pérez-Stable has written what is perhaps the clearest and most convincing historical sociology of the Cuban Revolution in her *Cuban Revolution: Origins, Course, and Legacy* (2nd ed., Oxford University Press, 1999).

The Cuban War for Independence that began in 1895, leading to the so-called Spanish-American War of 1898, has produced a voluminous historical literature. Perhaps the most comprehensive and useful work that treats this period of Cuba's history is Benjamin R. Beede's *War of 1898 and U.S. Interventions 1898–1934: An Encyclopedia* (Garland Publishing, 1994). More than the War of 1898 itself, this high-quality reference work includes entries on the various U.S. military occupations of the island, all the major military and political personalities on the various sides, as well as entries on the many U.S. interventions both in the Caribbean and in the Pacific that followed the invasion of Cuba in 1898. Louis A. Pérez, Jr., has set a new standard in critical historiography and national memory with his powerful and original *War of 1898: The United States and Cuba in History and Historiography* (University of North Carolina Press, 1998). This slim volume is anything but slight, as it takes on 100 years of scholarship on the war using a fresh, critical approach that questions many of the basic assumptions that led the United States to war and the basic lessons that we took from it as a nation.

There are perhaps no more fertile years for Cuba in terms of personal memoir and scholarly analysis than those between Batista's coup in 1952 and the Cuban Missile Crisis just over 10 years later in October 1962. The political scientist Samuel Farber has written a detailed and original reappraisal of the events of those years in his *Origins of the Cuban Revolution Reconsidered* (University of North Carolina Press, 2006). Also groundbreaking in terms of its focus on the long-neglected internal battle between the two wings of Castro's 26th of July Movement is Julia E. Sweig's *Inside the Cuban Revolution: Fidel Castro and the Urban Underground* (Harvard University Press, 2002). Two other important studies of that same period are Jules Benjamin's *United States and the Origins of the Cuban Revolution: An Empire of Liberty in an Age of National Liberation* (Princeton University Press, 1990) and Thomas G. Paterson's *Contesting Castro: The United States and the Triumph of the Cuban Revolution* (Oxford University Press, 1994). Finally, Thomas C. Wright's *Latin America in the Era of the Cuban Revolution* (Praeger, 1991) is a more broad based study of the impact the Cuban Revolution had on the hemisphere as a whole. His book is especially useful in understanding how a successful revolution in Cuba provoked a violent backlash across the region that changed the nature of the U.S. relationship with the nations of Latin America. Wright's revised edition (Praeger, 2001) has new material on the impact of the fall of the Soviet Union on the image and influence of the Cuban model for the hemisphere.

Literally hundreds of personal and political memoirs have been written in Spanish by the Cuban participants on the various sides of the revolution. Although few of these have yet been translated into English, there are many fascinating firsthand accounts of the events of the revolution as witnessed by Americans. With different roles and often wildly differing political interpretations of the events, some of these observers include *The New York Times* correspondents R. Hart Phillips and Herbert L. Matthews; U.S. diplomats Earl E. T. Smith, Philip Bonsal, and Wayne Smith; and U.S. attorney general Robert F. Kennedy. The author who originally published under the byline R. Hart Phillips was actually *Ruby* Hart Phillips, who had originally accompanied her journalist husband to Cuba as *The New York Times* photographer. After his untimely death, she became the *Times*'s chief correspondent in the country, remaining at that post from 1933 until 1961, when she was jailed and then unceremoniously thrown out of the country. Among her various memoirs about her time in Cuba are the excellent *Cuban Sideshow* (Cuban Press, 1935) and the riveting *Cuba: Island of Paradox* (McDowell Obolensky, 1959). This last book was republished under the title *The Cuban Dilemma* in 1962, with a new section on what Phillips saw as the tragedy of the revolution.

Ironically, trying to avoid having her press credentials revoked by Batista, in early 1957, Phillips brought in the then-famous editorial writer and foreign correspondent Herbert L. Matthews to make a rendezvous with Castro, and as it turned out with destiny, in the Sierra Maestra mountain range. Unlike Phillips, Matthews became quickly enamored with Castro and his seemingly righteous revolutionary cause. After publishing a series of historic articles that proved Castro to be alive and introducing him to the world, Matthews had a falling out with the newspaper over what it saw as his lack of objectivity. However, Matthews maintained to the end of his life, in his various books on Cuba, that Castro's intentions were genuine and the revolution was legitimate. These books include *The Cuban Story* (G. Braziller, 1961), *Fidel Castro* (Simon and Schuster, 1969), and *Revolution in Cuba: An Essay in Understanding* (Scribner, 1975). The entire fascinating tale has been retold recently by *Times* correspondent Anthony DePalma in his own book on the Matthews saga, *The Man Who Invented Fidel: Castro, Cuba, and Herbert L. Matthews of the New York Times* (Public Affairs, 2006).

Even more fascinating for aficionados of diplomatic intrigue are three memoirs written by three very different chief representatives of U.S. interests in Cuba. Like U.S. ambassador Arthur Gardner before him, Ambassador Earl Smith went to Cuba in 1957 as a Republican political appointee with no experience of foreign service and no knowledge of Spanish. As the title of his bitter memoir, *The Fourth Floor: An Account of the Castro Communist Revolution* (Random House, 1962), clearly indicates, Smith was convinced from early on that Castro had always been a communist and that his revolutionary group, the 26th of July Movement, was deeply infiltrated by communists. In the book, Smith maintains that not only was Castro a communist and the "Fourth Floor" (lower-level State Department officials) knew it, but incredibly they preferred him to Batista. From his primary briefing on Cuba by none other than *Times* correspondent Herbert Matthews, to his antagonistic relations with both the U.S. embassy staff and Washington State Department officials, Smith seemed to be always on the defensive.

Although Wayne Smith was never an official ambassador to Cuba, his position as a State Department analyst in Washington and a political officer in the Havana embassy between 1957 and 1961 gave him an intimate perspective from which to view the breakdown of U.S.-Cuban relations during that period. Furthermore, Smith was the first chief of the U.S. Interest Section (the diplomatic equivalent of an ambassador) when the embassy was reopened, nominally as a section of the Swiss embassy, in 1978. While Earl Smith blames the breakdown in U.S.-Cuban relations on the "liberal" State Department's unwillingness to support a weakening president (Batista), Wayne Smith argues in his own account, *The Closest of Enemies: A Personal and Diplomatic Account of U.S.-Cuban Relations since 1957* (W. W. Norton, 1987), that the breakdown was due to the ineptness of an inexperienced ambassador and the ignorance, overconfidence, and neglect of President Eisenhower and Secretary Dulles. A final valuable diplomatic memoir covering this period of U.S.-Cuban relations was published in 1971 by former ambassador Philip Bonsal. In his well-informed and evenhanded book, *Cuba, Castro and the United States* (University of Pittsburgh Press), Bonsal shows a clear understanding of Cuba's long history of frustrated attempts to gain true sovereignty and independence. He also is critical of the U.S. government's ignorance of this frustration, especially among people who should have known better, such as President Eisenhower. At the same time, in his detailed recounting of the crucial events between January 1959 and January 1961, the two years during which he served as U.S. ambassador, he argues that his many good-faith efforts to come to terms with Castro were repeatedly (and he thinks, purposefully) ignored.

When taking office in the early months of 1961, John F. Kennedy not only inherited a growing Cuba problem (diplomatic relations were broken in January 1961) but also found himself saddled with a plan for an exile invasion of Cuba that he reluctantly, and regretfully, allowed to go forward in April 1961. The best reflection on these events is *Politics of Illusion: The Bay of Pigs Invasion Reexamined*, edited by James G. Blight and Peter Kornbluh (Lynne Rienner, 1998). The book is essentially an edited transcript of a revealing conference held in May 1996, which featured scholars, former members of the Kennedy White House, the State and Defense Departments, the CIA, and the Kremlin, along with former members of the Cuban opposition and invasion force, Brigade 2506. The book also includes an extensive appendix of maps, chronologies, and a number of key declassified documents.

President Kennedy's failed invasion and embarrassment at the Bay of Pigs led directly, if ironically, to his redemption as an authoritative and level-headed leader during the "thirteen days" of the Cuban Missile Crisis of October 1962. The essential events of those tension-filled two weeks are expertly recounted by Robert F. Kennedy, one of the principal actors in the episode, in his *Thirteen Days: A Memoir of the Cuban Missile Crisis* (Mentor, 1968). One of the sources for the 2000 Roger Donaldson/Kevin Costner film of the same name, Kennedy's book is a study in brinksmanship and of the difficulty of avoiding group-think in crisis situations. The Cuban side of the story is told by Cuba's former UN ambassador Carlos Lechuga in his memoir, *In the Eye of the Storm: Castro, Khrushchev, Kennedy and the Missile Crisis* (Ocean Press, 1995). Aleksandr Fursenko and Timothy J. Naftali made expert use of exclusive access to the Soviet archives to tell the story from the perspective of the USSR in their book, *One Hell of a Gamble: Khrushchev, Castro, and Kennedy, 1958–1964* (W. W. Norton and Co., 1997). A final useful resource on the events of those heady days in October 1962 is the compilation of declassified documents and participant interviews and memoirs published under the title *The Cuban Missile Crisis, 1962: A National Security Archive Documents Reader*, edited by Laurence Chang and Peter Kornbluh (W. W. Norton and Co., 1999). The National Security Archive has made other declassified documents related to Cuba available on its website: http://www .gwu.edu/~nsarchiv/nsa/cuba_mis_cri/index.htm.

Although he finished it more than 20 years ago, the biography of Fidel Castro by *The New York Times* reporter Tad Szulc remains the best. It was published in 1986 by Avon Books under the title *Fidel: A Critical Portrait* and is readily available in most book stores. Also of note is the more recent biography by Robert E. Quirk, *Fidel Castro* (W. W. Norton and Company, 1995). Though not exactly a biography, *Cuba Confidential: Love and Vengeance in Miami and Havana* (Random House, 2002) is a fascinating character study of the "family feud" that has raged for more than 40 years between Fidel and his Miami enemies (and relatives). Written by investigative reporter Ann Louise Bardach, the book includes loads of original reporting and interviews by leaders on both sides of the conflict with information on the Elián González affair and an exclusive interview with Castro enemy and terror suspect Luis Posada Carriles. More recently, Bardach has resurrected an out-of-print and never-before translated collection of 21 letters Castro wrote to his supporters while in prison on the Isla of Pines in the mid-1950s. Complete with a new introduction by Bardach, the full text of each letter (both in Spanish and English), and a new epilogue by the original publisher and recipient of the majority of the letters, Luis Conte Agüero, this valuable book is *The Prison Letters of Fidel Castro* (Nation Books, 2007). Finally, Bardach has continued writing about the Castro family saga, the elder Castro's nearly fatal illness, and the unending machinations of Cuban exiles to do him in with her newest book *Without Fidel: A Death Foretold in Miami, Havana and Washington* (Scribners, 2009).

Also valuable is the recent 800-page extended interview and conversational biography of Castro published by the European intellectual and Castro supporter, Ignacio Ramonet, *Cien horas con Fidel* (2nd ed., Havana: Consejo de Estado, 2006). The fruit of many more than the 100 hours of the title, this book provides intimate access to Castro in the twilight of his life. First published in the spring of 2006, the second edition is said to benefit from Castro's meticulous corrections and revisions done during the summer of 2006 in the lead up to his provisional stepping down from power. For this reason, the book contains what are perhaps Castro's final sustained reflections, explanations, and justifications of a life of revolutionary power. The book is being published outside of Cuba under the title, *Fidel Castro: Biografía a dos voces* (Random House Mondadori, Debate) and will come out in an English translation by Penguin in the fall of 2007 under the title, *Castro: My Life*. A final recent study of the life of Fidel Castro, in tandem with a rare glimpse into the life and personality of his brother Raúl, is former CIA analyst Brian Latell's *After Fidel: The Inside Story of Castro's Regime and Cuba's Next Leader* (Palgrave Macmillan, 2005).

Since Ernesto "Che" Guevara's body was uncovered along with those of his comrades-at-arms, buried in a shallow grave on an abandoned airstrip in Valle Grande,

Bolivia, in 1997, the world's bookstores have been flooded with biographies and assessments of the life and thought of the Argentine-Cuban revolutionary. The three most comprehensive biographies based on original research and new interviews with those who knew him best are John Lee Anderson's *Che Guevara: A Revolutionary Life* (Grove Press, 1997), Jorge G. Castañeda's *Compañero: The Life and Death of Che Guevara* (Vintage, 1997), and Paco Ignacio Taibo II's *Guevara, Also Known as Che* (St. Martin's Griffin, 1999). The first of these is more than 700 pages long but reads like a novel and is the most comprehensive and balanced of the three. Mexican diplomat intellectual Castañeda's well-researched volume provoked howls of criticism from the Cuban government, which could be interpreted as a vote of confidence or a condemnation, depending on one's politics. Taibo's is by far the most sympathetic of the three.

Finally, if you're interested in reading some of Guevara's own prolific writings, many of his most important essays have been collected by Rolando E. Bonachea and Nelson P. Valdés in their edited volume *Ché: Selected Writings of Ernesto Guevara* (MIT Press, 1972). Similarly, Melbourne-based Ocean Press has recently issued the collection *Che Guevara Reader: Writings on Politics and Revolution* (2003). Ocean Press has also recently rereleased Guevara's *Motorcycle Diaries* (2004) to accompany the new Walter Salles film of the same name, as well as reediting Guevara's other reflections on his guerrilla adventures, *The Bolivian Diary: The Authorized Edition* (2005) and *Reminiscences of the Cuban Revolutionary War: The Authorized and Revised Edition* (2005). Not to be missed, of course, is the book perhaps most associated with Guevara, his how-to manual on revolutionary struggle, *Guerrilla Warfare* (University of Nebraska Press, 1985), edited by Brian Loveman and Thomas M. Davies.

CHAPTER 3: POLITICS AND GOVERNMENT

The institutionalization of the Cuban Revolution first during the 1970s under the new constitution, the newly reorganized Cuban Communist Party, and the Cuban military, and later during the late 1980s and early 1990s, is analyzed very well by Jorge I. Domínguez in his contributions to two works mentioned earlier, "Government and Politics" in *Cuba: A Country Study* (Library of Congress, 2002), and "Cuba since 1959" in *Cuba: A Short History* (Cambridge, 1993). More extended and detailed analysis is available in his *Cuba: Order and Revolution* (Harvard University Press, 1978). Phyllis Walker also does an excellent job of picking apart the sometimes dense history of Cuba's military and state security apparatus in her own chapter on national security in *Cuba: A Country Study* (Library of Congress, 2002). Finally, Domínguez's Cuban colleague and sometimes collaborator, Rafael Hernández, has collected a number of his own penetrating essays on civil and cultural change in Cuba under the revolution in his recently translated book, *Looking at Cuba: Essays on Culture and Civil Society* (University Press of Florida, 2003).

Two outstanding recent collections of essays on the significant challenges facing Cuban society and state institutions are available in the edited volumes *Changes in Cuban Society since the Nineties* (Woodrow Wilson Center, 2005) and *Cuban Socialism in a New Century: Adversity, Survival, and Renewal* (University Press of Florida, 2004). The first of these volumes was edited by a diverse group of authors including

Joseph S. Tulchin, Liliam Bobea, Mayra P. Espina Prieto, and Rafael Hernández, and includes contributions from leading Cuban scholars both on the island and abroad. Likewise, the other volume, edited by Max Azicri and Elise Deal, collects many penetrating essays by leading scholars both on and off the island on subjects as diverse as religion, the Cuban Communist Party, elections, presidential succession, the military, migration, and international relations. Also of note is Azicri's own book chronicling the survival of Cuban socialism during the crisis of the 1990s, *Cuba Today and Tomorrow: Reinventing Socialism* (University Press of Florida, 2000).

Finally, though they work from diverse ideological assumptions and come to sometimes wildly differing conclusions about the nature of Cuban society and polity, the following authors all clearly and critically explain the inner workings of Cuban socialism. They are Carollee Bengelsdorf, in her study of Cuba's experiment in democratic socialism, *The Problem of Democracy in Cuba: Between Vision and Reality* (Oxford University Press, 1994); Peter Roman, in his detailed and updated analysis of the functioning of Cuba's National Assembly, *People's Power: Cuba's Experience with Representative Government* (Rowman and Littlefield, 2003); Javier Corrales, in his penetrating article "The Gatekeeper State: Limited Economic Reforms and Regime Survival in Cuba, 1989–2002," published in *Latin American Research Review* 39, no. 2 (June 2004): 35–65; Haroldo Dilla Alfonso and Philip Oxhorn, in their original and well-informed essay "The Virtues and Misfortunes of Civil Society in Cuba," published in *Latin American Perspectives* 29, no. 4 (July 2002): 11–30; Mark Falcoff in his book, *Cuba, The Morning After: Confronting Castro's Legacy* (American Enterprise Institute, 2003); and Carlos Alberto Montaner in his many books on Castro and Cuban communism including, *Cuba hoy: La lenta muerte del castrosmo* (Ediciones Universal, 1996).

CHAPTER 4: ECONOMICS

Since Cuba entered an unprecedented economic crisis starting in 1988, which was immeasurably exacerbated by the fall of the Soviet Union and eventual cutoff of all preferential Soviet trade and aid, scholars from many different ideological (and geographical) positions have published books analyzing what went wrong and what could be done to remedy the situation. The first major book by a group of Cuban economists working within the system (then as members of a Cuban think tank, the Center for the Study of the Americas, CEA) to analyze the economic collapse and suggest ways to "restructure" the Cuban economy, while retaining its "socialist" character, was *Cuba: Restructuring the Economy—A Contribution to the Debate* by Julio Carranza Valdés, Luís Gutiérrez Urdaneta, and Pedro Monreal González. Originally published in 1995 in Cuba, the 1998 English edition was published by the Institute of Latin American Studies in London. A final helpful analysis of the economic and social changes that Cuba has undergone during Castro's tenure is available in *Back from the Future: Cuba under Castro* (Princeton University Press, 1994) by sociologist Susan Eva Eckstein.

In the United States, the Cuban economists Carmelo Mesa-Lago and Jorge Pérez-López (working both together and separately) have done more than any others to advance the study of the Cuban economy. While much of their excellent work on Cuba came out well before 1990, four important works published since then are Pérez-López's original study of Cuba's underground economy, *Cuba's Second Economy: From Behind the Scenes to Center Stage* (Transaction, 1995); Mesa-Lago's systematic, historical comparison of Cuba's development strategy under socialism with that of two other very different regional economies, *Market, Socialist, and Mixed Economies: Comparative Policy and Performance—Chile, Cuba, and Costa Rica* (Johns Hopkins University Press, 2000); their coauthored book *Cuba's Aborted Reform: Socioeconomic Effects, International Comparisons, and Transition Policies* (University Press of Florida, 2005); which was followed this year by their new collaboration, *Cuba under Raúl Castro: Assessing the Reforms* (Lynne Reinner, 2013), which asks: What led to the dramatic social and economic reforms introduced by Raúl Castro and how effective have those reforms been?

Two recent collections of economic analysis on Cuba can be found in the edited volumes *The Cuban Economy at the Start of the Twenty-First Century* (Harvard University, 2004) and *The Cuban Economy* (University of Pittsburgh Press, 2004). The first of these was coedited by Harvard professor Jorge I. Domínguez, along with Cuban economist Omar Everleny Pérez Villanueva and Harvard scholar Lorena Barberia. It is unique among studies of the Cuban economy in that it successfully combines work done by leading economists and sociologists in Cuba with other essays written by North American scholars. The second collection, edited by Archibald R. M. Ritter, Canada's leading expert on the Cuban economy, has a clearly written overview of the macro- and micro-developments in the Cuban economy during the 1990s written by the editor, along with an eclectic and provocative selection of articles by leaders in the field. Also of note, though likely hard to find at this point, is Ritter's 1974 book on socialist Cuba's development trajectory up to that point, *The Economic Development of Revolutionary Cuba: Strategy and Performance* (Praeger).

Two final books that focus in detail on the crisis and survival of the Cuban economy after 1990 are Ana Julia Jatar-Hausmann's *The Cuban Way: Capitalism, Communism, and Confrontation* (Kumarian, 1999) and Oscar Espinosa Chepe's *Cuba: revolución o involución* (Aduana Vieja, 2007). The first of these is a concise but penetrating overview of the Cuban economy and U.S.-Cuban relations with a special focus on the split between the grassroots, and often illegal, form of capitalism *a la cubana* ubiquitous on the streets of Havana and the "bigger-is-better" capitalism practiced between the government and foreign investors. The second book is a comprehensive collection of articles by Cuba's leading independent economist who served 19 months of a 20-year sentence between 2003 and 2004 for his unauthorized activities. Released in November 2004 due to his failing health, he has been recognized by Amnesty International as a "prisoner of conscience."

CHAPTER 5: SOCIETY

The two leading scholars of religion in Cuba and its diaspora are likely Margaret E. Crahan and Miguel A. de la Torre. While Crahan focuses more on the sociopolitical role of religion in Cuban society under the revolution in her edited volume *Religion, Culture, and Society: The Case of Cuba* (Woodrow Wilson Center, 2003), Miguel A. de la Torre has studied the role of religion as an inspirational force for counterrevolutionary activity in the Cuban-American community in the United States in his book *La Lucha for Cuba: Religion and Politics on the Streets of Miami* (University of California Press, 2003). De la Torre has also recently published a book, *Santería: The Beliefs and Rituals of a Growing Religion in America* (W. B. Eerdmans, 2004). In Cuba, the leading scholar of church-state relations is sociologist Aurelio Alonso, author of *Iglesia y política en Cuba revolucionaria* (Havana, Editorial de Ciencias Sociales, 1997). A more openly critical voice coming from inside the Catholic church (but from within the laity) is that of Dagoberto Valdés, former director of *Vitral* magazine and author of the collection, *Cuba: Libertad y responsibilidad (desafíos y proyectos)* (Ediciones Universal, 2005).

The four best historical, sociological studies of the "exceptionalism" of the Cuban community in the United States and its role in the formulation of a hard-line U.S. policy toward Castro are Guillermo J. Grenier's and Lisando Pérez's concise volume *The Legacy of Exile: Cubans in the United States* (Allyn & Bacon, 2003); Alejandro Portes's and Alex Stepick's historical and demographic analysis of the transformation of Miami into the "Capital of Latin America," *City on the Edge* (University of California Press, 1994); Silvia Pedraza's historical, demographic, and political comparison of the fates of Cubans and Mexicans in the United States, *Political and Economic Migrants in America* (University of Texas Press, 1985); and María Cristina García's *Havana USA* (University of California Press, 1996). Also of interest are *Latin Journey: Cuban and Mexican Immigrants in the United States* (University of California Press, 1985) by Alejandro Portes and Robert L. Bach, and *Political Disaffection in Cuba's Revolution and Exodus* (Cambridge University Press, 2007) recently published by Silvia Pedraza.

Other important, original, and incisive analyses of the Cuban diaspora in the United States include Gustavo Pérez Firmat's study of Cuban-American identity and popular culture, *Life on the Hyphen: The Cuban-American Way* (University of Texas Press, 1994); Joan Didion's excellent extended essay *Miami* (Simon and Schuster, 1987); and Jesús Arboleya's sociopolitical analysis of the history of the ongoing effort in South Florida to overthrow the Castro government, *The Cuban Counterrevolution* (Ohio University Press, 2000). Three other enlightening personal memoirs written by Cuban-Americans are Gustavo Pérez Firmat's *Next Year in Cuba: A Cubano's Coming of Age in America* (Anchor Books, 1995); Román de la Campa's *Cuba on My Mind: Journeys to a Severed Nation* (Verso, 2000); and Mirta Ojito's riveting recent account of the Mariel boatlift 25 years later, *Finding Mañana: A Memoir of a Cuban Exodus* (Penguin Press, 2005). Finally, of special note is journalist Tom Gjelten's history of the Bacardi family, the Bacardi brand, and the ongoing legal struggle between the originally Cuban and now multinational spirits company and the Cuban government, *Bacardi and the Long Fight for Cuba: The Biography of a Cause* (Penguin, 2008).

Books on sexuality, race, and ethnicity under the revolution have been especially strong. The most important works on sexuality and sexual politics include Ian Lumsden's *Machos, Maricones, and Gays: Cuba and Homosexuality* (Temple University Press, 1996) and Lois M. Smith and Alfred Padula's *Sex and Revolution: Women in Socialist Cuba* (Oxford University Press, 1996). For more on gender and sexuality, also see the work of Cuban historian Julio César González Pagés, including his *En busca de un espacio: Historia de mujeres en Cuba* (Havana, Editorial de Ciencias

Sociales, 2003), *Por andar vestida de hombre*, (Editorial de la Mujer, 2011), and *Macho, varón y masculino*, (Editorial de la Mujer, 2011). By far the most comprehensive and authoritative study of racial politics in Cuba during the 20th century is Alejandro de la Fuente's A *Nation for All: Race, Inequality, and Politics in Twentieth-Century Cuba* (University of North Carolina Press, 2001). Other useful and important books on racial identity in Cuba are the two volumes put together by Pedro Pérez Sarduy and Jean Stubs, *Afro-Cuban Voices: On Race and Identity in Contemporary Cuba* (University Press of Florida, 2000) and *AfroCuba: An Anthology of Cuban Writing on Race, Politics, and Culture* (Ocean Press, 1993). The most recent analysis of the revolutionary government's achievements in the area of racial equality is Mark Q. Sawyer's *Racial Politics in Post-Revolutionary Cuba* (Cambridge University Press, 2006).

CHAPTER 6: CULTURE

Recent investigations into Cuban identity, culture, and society have been as widespread as they have been penetrating. Here I will first present four more general surveys of Cuban national identity and culture, before going into a more detailed description of the most important works on religion; the Cuban diaspora; sexuality, race, and ethnicity; music and dance; art and architecture; and cinema and literature. The two leading analyses of Cuban national identity published in recent years are Louis A. Pérez's monumental *On Becoming Cuban: Identity, Nationality, and Culture* (University of North Carolina Press, 1999) and *Cuba, The Elusive Nation: Interpretations of National Identity* (University Press of Florida, 2000) edited by Damián Fernández and Madeline Cámara-Betancourt. While Pérez's work is an exhaustive analysis of the formation of Cuban national identity between 1850 and 1950 with special emphasis on the penetration and absorption of U.S. cultural influences in that process, the volume edited by Fernández and Cámara-Betancourt is a collection of essays on various themes including music, art, literature, and the Cuban diaspora. Damián Fernández has also published a slim but highly original monograph on the informal, personal nature of Cuban political culture, entitled *Cuba and the Politics of Passion* (University of Texas Press, 2000).

Two other important general surveys of Cuban culture are William Luis's *Culture and Customs of Cuba* (Greenwood Press, 2001) and the book of interviews by Canadian academic John M. Kirk and Cuban novelist and journalist Leonardo Padura Fuentes, *Culture and the Cuban Revolution: Conversations in Havana* (University Press of Florida, 2001). While Luis's volume is especially strong on the history and development of Cuban literature, cinema, and art, the Kirk and Padura Fuentes collection is more focused on the protagonists of Cuban culture working today in the areas of music, poetry, and cinema. Additionally, Mauricio A. Font and Alfonso W. Quiroz have recently edited two valuable collections of essays on Cuban history, politics, and culture. The first is entitled, *Cuban Counterpoints: The Legacy of Fernando Ortiz* (Lexington Books, 2005) and the second is *The Cuban Republic and José Martí* (Lexington Books, 2006).

Given Cuba's central role in the development and diffusion of popular dance music across the world during most of the 20th century, there has been an outpouring of books in recent years attempting to chronicle and analyze this phenomenon. Perhaps the most comprehensive and accessible to nonspecialists is Ned Sublette's fantastic *Cuba and Its Music: From the First Drum to the Mambo* (Chicago Review Press, 2004). Sublette, a musician, former coproducer of the public radio program *Afropop Worldwide*, and cofounder of the record label Qbadisc, which brought a cornucopia of contemporary Cuban music to the United States in the early 1990s, is a wizard with the details of Cuba's vast music history, which he manages to weave together in a spellbinding way. A bit more scholarly and focused on particular time periods are Robin D. Moore's two recent groundbreaking books on the history and development of Cuban music during the 20th century, *Music and Revolution: Cultural Change in Socialist Cuba* (University of California Press, 2006) and *Nationalizing Blackness: Afrocubanismo and Artistic Revolution in Havana, 1920–1940* (University of Pittsburgh Press, 1997). Also very useful is the recently revised and updated edition of *Caribbean Currents: Caribbean Music from Rumba to Reggae* (Temple University Press, 2006) by Peter Manuel with Kenneth Bilby and Michael Largey.

For those who read Spanish, any of the treasure trove of books on the history and development of Cuban music by Cristóbal Díaz Ayala is a good place to start, including *Cuando salí de la Habana (1898–1997): Cien años de música cubana por el mundo* (Ediciones Universal, 1998), his most recent, *Los contrapuntos de la música cubana* (Editorial Callejón, 2006), and his magnum opus, *Música cubana del areyto al rap cubano* (4th ed., Ediciones Universal, 2003). An earlier edition of this book has been translated into English as *The Roots of Salsa: A History of Cuban Music* (Excelsior Music Publishing, 2002). Useful and original books by other leading Cuban journalists and ethnomusicologists include Leonardo Acosta's *Cubano Be, Cuban Bop: One Hundred Years of Jazz in Cuba* (Smithsonian Books, 2003); Olavo Alén Rodríguez's *De lo Afrocubano a la Salsa: Géneros musicales de Cuba* (Editorial Cubanacán, 1992); Helio Orovio's dictionary, *Cuban Music from A to Z* (Duke University Press, 2004); Leonardo Padura's book of interviews with Cuban and Caribbean music greats, *Faces of Salsa: A Spoken History of the Music* (Smithsonian Books, 2003); and the anthology, *Panorama de la música popular cubana* (Editorial Letras Cubanas, 1995), edited by Radamés Giro, which includes articles by Cuban musicologists Argeliers León and Leonardo Acosta and musicians Emilio Grenet, Rosendo Ruiz, Jr., and Noel Nicola.

The recent cache of all things Cuban has led to a glut in the market of beautifully photographed but none too deep coffee-table books highlighting Havana's many architectural and natural wonders. Luckily there are also a number of more serious studies of the history, photography, and architecture of the country's capital city. The leader in this field is surely the coauthored book on Havana by Joseph L. Scarpaci, Roberto Serge, and Mario Coyula, *Havana: Two Faces of the Antillean Metropolis* (University of North Carolina Press, 2003). Now in its second edition, the book is the only English-language history of the city that also has chapters describing urban planning, architecture, public policy, and the many current social and economic challenges facing this most beautiful of cities. A more recent chronicle of the storied history of Cuba's capital is the engrossing, *History of Havana* (Palgrave Macmillan, 2006), coauthored by the North American novelist and translator Dick Cluster and the Cuban editor and political scientist Rafael Hernández. A good visual guide to accompany these books, as well as any architecture-lover's handbook on the buildings of modern Havana, is Eduardo Luis Rodríguez's *Havana Guide: Modern Architecture, 1925–1965* (Princeton Architectural Press, 2000). Another fantastically photographed architectural history of the city is the elegant *Havana: History and Architecture of a Romantic City* (Monacelli Press, 2000) by María Luisa Lobo Montalvo.

Two other excellent books of photography and essays are *Cuba: Going Back* (University of Texas at Austin, 1997) by Tony Mendoza and *Cuba on the Verge: An Island in Transition* (Bulfinch Press, 2003), edited by Terry McCoy, with an introduction by William Kennedy and an epilogue by Arthur Miller. This second book showcases the work of leading Cuban and American writers, journalists, and photographers including writers Antonio José Ponte, Abilio Estévez, Reina María Rodríguez, Nancy Morejón, Mayra Montero, Susan Orlean, Abelardo Estorino, Ana Menéndez, Jon Lee Anderson, Achy Obejas, Cristina García, and Pablo Medina, and photographers Manuel Piña, Abigail González, Abelardo Morell, and Carlos Caraicoa. Another important contribution to the history of Cuban architecture and photography is John Loomis's judiciously written and breathtakingly photographed book on the birth, short life, abandonment, and slow death of Cuba's architecturally revolutionary National Art Schools, *Revolution of Forms: Cuba's Forgotten Art Schools* (Princeton Architectural Press, 1999), recently re-released in 2011 in an updated edition.

The best two books on 20th-century Cuban art are Juan A. Martínez's *Cuban Art and National Identity: The Vanguardia Painters, 1927–1950* (University Press of Florida, 1994), which covers Cuban modernism, and Luis Camnitzer's *New Art of Cuba* (University of Texas Press, 1994), which chronicles art during the revolutionary period with an emphasis on the 1980s. Although Cuban film has distinguished itself as one of the leading forms of art under the revolution, there are few serious English-language studies of the form. The only book-length study currently available is Michael Chanan's *Cuban Cinema* (University of Minnesota Press, 2004). Luckily, this much revised and augmented edition of Chanan's 1985 *Cuban Image: Cinema and Cultural Politics in Cuba* (BFI Publishing) is a tour de force that chronicles many of the achievements of ICAIC (the Cuban Film Institute), while providing rich, nuanced descriptions of the periodic controversies to beset Cuba's revolutionary film industry. If you read Spanish, Juan Antonio García Borrero's *Guía crítica del cine cubano de ficción* (Editorial Arte y Literatura, 2001) will be an indispensible guide.

Cuban literature (both on the island and in exile) has attracted many critical assessments and scholarly analyses, among which two books can serve as a solid introduction. The first is the groundbreaking study of Cuban and Caribbean literature by Antonio Benítez-Rojo, *The Repeating Island: The Caribbean and the Postmodern Perspective* (Duke University Press, 1992). The second is Isabel Álvarez Borland's accessible introduction to the literature of the Cuban diaspora, *Cuban-American Literature of Exile: From Person to Persona* (University Press of Virginia, 1998). Another recent book that focuses on the development of the Cuban crime novel with a special emphasis on the work of contemporary Cuban novelist Leonardo Padura Fuentes is *Detective Fiction in Cuban Society and Culture* (Peter Lang Publishers, 2006) by Stephen Wilkinson. There are also a number of collections of Cuban literature (novels, poetry, essays, and short stories) translated into English. A few good introductions are the anthropologist Ruth Behar's collection, *Bridges to Cuba/Puentes a Cuba* (University of Michigan Press, 1995), Cuban-American novelist Cristina García's collection *¡Cubanísimo! The Vintage Book of Contemporary Cuban Literature* (Vintage Books, 2002), Jacqueline Loss and Esther Whitfield's *New Short Fiction from Cuba* (Northwestern University Press, 2007), and *Havana Noir* (Akashic, 2007) expertly edited and translated by Cuban-American novelist Achy Obejas. Obejas also recently translated the first work of up-and-coming Cuban novelist Wendy Guerra, *Everyone Leaves* (AmazonCrossing, 2012). Of course, there are also the many, many works of fiction and poetry written by the Cuban authors discussed in the literature section of chapter 6, including Alejo Carpentier, Nicolás Guillén, Roberto Fernández Retamar, Guillermo Cabrera Infante, Dulce María Loynaz, Heberto Padilla, Reinaldo Arenas, and Leonardo Padura.

Finally, though it has yet to find itself translated into English, the single best book I have ever read about Cuban culture under the revolution, indeed about the Cuban revolutionary period in general, is Eliseo Alberto's *Informe contra mí mismo* (Alfaguara, 1996). A highly personal, provocative exposé of the manipulative strategy of turning the entire country into government informants, the book's title roughly translates as "secret report against myself." The book also serves as a kind of midlife memoir and critical reflection on Cuban culture and governmental repression. The author, who lives in exile in Mexico City and is known to his friends as *Lichi*, also wrote the screenplay for the movie *Guantanamera* and is a member of one of the leading families of Cuban culture (son of poet Eliseo Diego).

The best place in the United States to find books on Cuban Spanish (and on many other Cuban-related topics) has long been the Miami-based bookstore and publishing house *Ediciones Universal*. Though their collection of books about Cuba in Spanish is unsurpassed, they recently succumbed to the crisis in the publishing industry and perhaps to the gradual replacement of the exile population with a Cuban-American immigrant and second-generation population that prefers to read books in English and not necessarily about Cuba! Still, Ediciones Universal provided two of the books most helpful in writing the section on language: Carlos Paz Pérez's *Diccionario cubano de habla popular y vulgar* (Agualarga, 1998) and José Sánchez-Boudy's *Diccionario mayor de cubanismos* (Ediciones Universal, 1999). Also helpful in understanding the nuances of Cuban syntax and phonology is Pablo Julián Davis's entry "Cuban Spanish (Language)" in the aforementioned *Encyclopedia of Cuba: People, History, Culture* (Greenwood Press, 2002). Finally, Cuba's Fernando Ortiz Foundation publishes *La Fuente Viva*, a new series of monographs focusing on specific areas of Cuban culture. Included among them is Gema Valdés Acosta's *Los remanentes de las lenguas bantúes en Cuba* (2002). Helpful in preparing the section on Cuban cuisine were Alex García's *In a Cuban Kitchen* (Running Press, 2004) and the incomparable Nitza Villapol's *Cocina cubana* (Editorial Científico-Técnica, 2002).

CHAPTER 7: CONTEMPORARY ISSUES

Over the past decade, but especially during 2012, Philip Peters has issued a flurry of insightful, information-packed research reports published by The Lexington Institute, a Washington, DC, think tank, assessing the progress to date of Cuba's economic reforms. All available for free in PDF format, the latest of these brief but extremely useful reports are "A Viewer's Guide to Cuba's Economic Reforms" (May 23, 2012);

"Cuba's Entrepreneurs: Foundation of a New Private Sector" (July 31, 2012); "Reforming Cuban Agriculture: Unfinished Business" (October 31, 2012); and "Migration Policy Reform: Cuba Gets Started, U.S. Should Follow" (December 6, 2012). Peters recently left The Lexington Institute, however, and started his own independent organization named the Cuba Research Center (http://www.us-crc.org/), where his newer publications are available.

Political scientist Samuel Farber's new book, *Cuba since the Revolution of 1959: A Critical Assessment* (Haymarket Books, 2011), is a comprehensively researched, up-to-date, and quite devastating assessment of the last 53 years of the revolution in power. In fact, the book should be called "a devastating assessment," not a "critical" one, although it is both critical in its analysis and devastating in its conclusions and recommendations (from the left). The book starts with two chapters on politics (domestic and international) and two on economics (development policy and labor policy), but the later chapters on Afro-Cubans (Chapter 5), gender politics and sexuality (Chapter 6), and an amazingly fair and comprehensive final chapter entitled, "Dissidents and Critics—from Right to Left" (Chapter 7) are especially original in their analysis of the revolution's failure to meet the just demands of each of these groups. The book concludes with a hard-hitting reflection aimed primarily at progressive supporters of (and apologists for) the regime on the many ways that the Cuban systems falls well short of being a "socialist democracy." It also has a useful and incisive epilogue where Farber critiques the direction and scope of Raúl Castro's economic reforms. Whereas other critics (such as Mesa-Lago and Pérez-López mentioned earlier) often argue that the reforms "do not go far enough," Farber says that they are going "in the wrong direction." Instead, he recommends "worker self-management, equality, and a democratization of the Cuban political system and society as a whole."

A final book well worth mentioning (and reading) is *Havana Real: One Woman Fights to Tell the Truth about Cuba Today*, a translation by M.J. Porter of a compendium of blog posts written by the young, female blogger Yoani Sánchez between 2007 and 2010 in her blog *Generation Y*. This pioneering blogger (with millions of hits a month on her site) and Twitter-user (she currently has over half-a-million followers) is as valiant as she is talented, combining in her blog (and in the book) the three qualities that have made her a force to be reckoned with both as a writer and as a human rights activist: brevity, constancy, and personality. That is, her entries are never more than a few paragraphs long; she never lets more than a few days pass before adding a new post; and her use of the day-in-the life vignette has the power to draw in a mass readership tired of long-winded political harangues and impenetrable intellectual treatises.

VIDEOS, DOCUMENTARIES, AND FEATURE FILMS

Cuban Music

¿De dónde son los cantantes? (1976): Luis Felipe Bernaza (32 min.)—Made in Cuba, this is a documentary about the famous Santiago "son" group Trio Matamoros.

The Routes/Roots of Rhythm (1984): Howard Dratch (55 min.)—Narrated and hosted by Harry Belafonte, this is a chronological documentary history of the

African roots of Cuban popular music, including son, rumba, Latin jazz, and salsa.

Machito: A Latin Jazz Legacy (1987): Carlos Ortiz (58 min.)—Bio pic of Latin Jazz great Frank "Machito" Grillo, lead man and cofounder of Machito's Afro Cubans.

Aché Moyuba Orisha (1990): Cristina Gonzalez (42 min.)—An excellent documentary film about Cuban *Santería* made in Cuba.

La última rumba de Papá Montero (1992): Octavio Cortázar (57 min.)—This cross between a documentary and filmic re-creation of the investigation of the mysterious death of the famous *rumbero* Papá Montero features examples of the various rumba styles as well as interviews with some of Cuba's leading ethnomusicologists.

Voices of the Orishas (1994): Alvaro Pérez Betancourt (37 min.)—A documentary that chronicles Cuba's Yoruba heritage and traditions.

Yo soy, del son a la salsa (I Am, From Son to Salsa, 1997): Rigoberto Mercado (100 min.)—With a screenplay written by leading Cuban novelist Leonardo Padura and narration provided by Cuban salsa sensation Issac Delgado, this film provides a documentary overview of 100 years of Cuban popular music at home and abroad.

Zafiros: Locura Azul (The Zafiros: Blue Madness, 1997): Manuel Herrera (115 min.)—A rare Cuba-U.S. coproduction, this film is a musical homage and biography of the early 1960s Cuban vocal group *Los Zafiros* (The Sapphires), a Cuban version of the Platters.

Cinco joyas de la música cubana (Five Jewels of Cuban Music, 1998): Luis Felipe Bernaza, Oscar Valdés, and Constante Diego (95 min.)—Five short documentaries on Ignacio Piñeiro, María Teresa Vera, Ernesto Lecuona, Benny Moré, and Bola de Nieve.

Buena Vista Social Club (1999): Wim Wenders (105 min.)—A documentary on Cuban "son" music featuring the stars of the original Buena Vista Social Club album.

Calle 54 (2000): Fernando Trueba (105 min.)—A film featuring performances of some of the "living legends" of Latin jazz, including Cachao, Paquito D'Rivera, and Chucho Valdés.

For Love or Country (2000): Joseph Sargent (120 min.)—Bio pic of Latin jazz trumpeter Arturo Sandoval, featuring Andy García in the lead role.

La Fabri-K: The Cuban Hip-Hop Factory (2005): Lisandro Pérez-Rey (64 min.)—A documentary film about two of the leading Cuban hip-hop groups.

La Tropical (2002): David Turnley (90 min.)—Set at the (in)famous open-air Havana club of the title, this sophisticated documentary is a vibrant tribute to the central but complex place music and dancing play in the lives of everyday Cubans.

Cuban Hip Hop All Stars (2004): Joshua Bee Alafia (60 min.)—A film that collects videos of some of Cuba's leading hip-hop groups.

Rumba en La Habana con Yoruba Andabo (2005): José Luis Lobato (103 min.)—A DVD that is perfect for classroom use as it includes performances of the many different kinds of sacred and profane Afro-Cuban music and dance.

Habana Blues (2005): Benito Zambrano (110 min.)—The classic tale of two kids from the barrio with big dreams of musical stardom who face the dilemma of getting exactly what they have long been wishing for—a recording contract—that will take them to Spain and away from everything and everyone they know and love.

East of Havana (2006): Jauretsi Saizarbitoria and Emilia Menocal (82 min.)—A taut tale of the underworld of Cuban hip-hop and the difficulties of navigating between artistic integrity and government bureaucracy.

El Benny (2006): Jorge Luis Sánchez (132 min.)—A bio pic of the great Cuban crooner Benny Moré.

Emigration and Exile

El Super (1979): Leon Ichaso and Orlando Jimenez Leal (90 min.)—A Cuban exile in New York City works as a building superintendent but yearns for his lost homeland.

90 Miles (2001): Juan Carlos Zaldívar (75 min.)—A filmmaker's return trip to his homeland.

Balseros (Rafters, 2002): Carlos Bosch and Josep Maria Domènech (120 min.)—This documentary film follows seven Cubans who risk it all to start over in the United States.

Adio Kerida (Good-bye Dear Love, 2002): Ruth Behar (82 min.)—U.S. Anthropologist Ruth Behar returns to her native Cuba to profile the remnant of the Sephardic Jewish community there and trace her own family's journey to the United States as Cuban-Jewish exiles.

Beyond the Sea (2003): Lisandro Pérez-Rey (80 min.)—A history of the Mariel boatlift.

Viva Cuba (2005): Juan Carlos Cremata (80 min.)—A poignant film that follows the wanderings of two Cuban runaway children as they make their way across the island in search of one's long-lost father.

The Lost City (2006): Andy García (143 min.)—A music-filled film about the end of an era in Cuba and the start of the revolution as experienced by a family torn apart by politics.

Homosexuality

Improper Conduct (1984): Néstor Almendros and Orlando Jiménez Leal (112 min.)—A documentary chronicling the treatment of homosexuals under the Cuban Revolution.

Fresa y chocolate (Strawberry and Chocolate, 1994): Tomás Gutiérrez Alea and Juan Carlos Tabío (108 min.)—The poignant story of a friendship between a cultured homosexual and a square party militant, and the lessons that they teach each other.

Before Night Falls (2000): Julian Schnabel (133 min.)—The film version of the fantastical autobiography of Cuban writer, dissident, and exile Reinaldo Arenas.

Cuban Women

Lucía (1968): Humberto Solás (160 min.)—This important, but overly long and melodramatic film chronicles the tumultuous lives of three Cuban women during three different periods in the country's history (1895, 1932, and the 1960s).

De cierta manera (One Way or Another, 1974): Sara Gómez (79 min.)—The only feature-length film by this acclaimed Cuban documentary filmmaker, this film blurs the lines between the two forms as it describes the construction of a new neighborhood.

Retrato de Teresa (Portrait of Teresa, 1979): Pastor Vega (103 min.)—Cuban cinema's most unflinching look at machismo, this film presents Teresa, a "new woman" who struggles to fulfill simultaneously her duties as a mother, wife, worker, and revolutionary.

María Antonia (1990): Sergio Giral (111 min.)—The story of María Antonia, a mulata who lives in a Havana slum of the 1950s, and struggles with life, love, and santería.

Mujer transparente (Transparent Woman, 1993): Mario Crespo, Ana Rodríguez, Mayra Segura, Mayra Vilasis, Hector Veitia (82 min.)—This five-part film, each part directed by a different filmmaker, explores different facets of contemporary Cuban womanhood.

¿Quién diablos es Yuliet? (Who the Hell Is Juliette?, 1997): Carlos Marcovich (90 min.)—This film (or is it a documentary?) is about a streetwise Cuban teenager and sometime prostitute who is orphaned by her father's immigration and her mother's suicide.

Cuban Women: Branded by Paradise (1999): Mari Rodríguez Ichaso (113 min.)—This documentary chronicles the impact of the revolution on a number of exiled women, including singer Celia Cruz, novelist Zoé Valdés, and poet María Elena Cruz Varela.

Politics, Polemics, and Personalities

Soy Cuba (I Am Cuba, 1964): Mikhail Kalatosov (141 min.)—A clearly propagandistic condemnation/celebration of the "before" and "after" of the revolution, this Soviet-made film also paints a cinematographically brilliant picture of Cuba.

Alicia en el pueblo de las maravillas (Alice in Wonderland, 1990): Daniel Díaz Torres (94 min.)—Banned in Cuba after the briefest of openings, this film parodies the absurdities of life in a town named Maravillas (Wonders), where people are sent to be redeemed.

Azúcar amarga (Bitter Sugar, 1996): Leon Ichaso (102 min.)—A portrait of the daily struggles and bitter contradictions of life in Cuba in the early 1990s as lived by one family.

El Che: Investigating a Legend (1997): Maurice Dugowson (83 min.)—A riveting, revealing documentary portrait of Ernesto "Che" Guevara and his role in the Cuban Revolution.

Thirteen Days (2000): Roger Donaldson (145 min.)—Based in part on the book of the same name by Robert F. Kennedy, this film focuses on the tense decision-making process in the White House during the Cuban Missile Crisis of October 1962.

Fidel (2001): Estela Bravo (91 min.)—A revealing, if sympathetic, bio pic of the Cuban leader.

Comandante (2003, 99 min.) and *Looking for Fidel* (2004, 57 min.): Oliver Stone—The controversial pair of made-for-TV HBO films focusing on the personality of Fidel Castro. The first, more sympathetic, *Comandante*, was pulled from circulation in the United States after Castro cracked down on hijackers and dissidents in the spring of 2003. The second, *Looking for Fidel*, is a more tough-minded interview with Castro about Cuba's human rights record. Incidentally, Stone was fined by the U.S. government for illegally traveling to Cuba to make these films.

The Motorcycle Diaries (2004): Walter Salles (128 min.)—Based on Ernesto "Che" Guevara's early diaries and staring Gael García Bernal, this beautifully filmed movie covers the future revolutionary's coming of age on a journey across the South American continent.

Monte Rouge (2004): Eduardo del Llano (15 min.)—This independent short film pokes fun at the often dreary realities of Cuban life, starting with government spying and hypocrisy. It was filmed with a borrowed camera on a $500 budget and distributed underground in Cuba.

He Who Hits First, Hits Twice: The Urgent Film of Santiago Álvarez (2005): Santiago Álvarez and Travis Wilkerson (147 min.)—This compilation of some of the best "propaganda art films" from renowned Cuban director Santiago Álvarez selected by U.S. filmmaker Travis Wilkerson includes seven films originally released between 1965 and 1973: *Now* (1965, 5 min.), *Cerro Pelado* (1966, 34 min.), *Hanoi Martes13* (1967, 38 min.), *Hasta La Victoria Siempre (LBJ)* (1968, 18 min.), *79 Primaveras* (1969, 25 min.), *El Sueno del Pongo* (1970, 11 min.), and *El Tigre Saltó y Mató, Pero Morirá . . . Morirá . . .* (1973, 16 min.). The 2-DVD set also includes a film portrait of Álvarez by Wilkerson, entitled *Accelerated Underdevelopment*.

Habana: Arte nuevo de hacer ruinas (2005/2006): Florian Borchmeyer and Matthias Hentschler (86 min.)—This film is a German-made portrait of the inhabited ruins of Havana and their strange blend of magic and demolition. It follows five real-life Havana residents, capturing the final moments of their lives in the buildings they inhabit before they are renovated—or simply collapse altogether.

Páginas del diario de Mauricio (2006): Manuel Pérez (135 min.)—On a September day in 2000, as the Sydney Olympics begin, a solitary Cuban man commemorates his 60th birthday by remembering key moments from the last 12 years of his life, a time of deep personal, political, economic, social upheaval both for him and for his island nation.

Revolución: Five Visions (2006): Nicole Cattell (57 min.)—A breathtakingly photographed documentary film about five very different, but each very genuine, Cuban photographers as they struggle to chronicle the epic of revolutionary Cuba.

Cuban Mysteries: An Interview with Leonardo Padura (2006): Claudia Ferman (30 min.)—An extended interview with Cuba's leading novelist, Leonardo Padura, interspersed with scenes from some of his recent crime novels set in Havana.

By Tomás Gutiérrez Alea

La muerte de un burócrata (The Death of a Bureaucrat, 1966, 85 min.): When an honored worker is buried with his ID card, his wife discovers that she cannot get her pension unless she figures out a way to get it back.

Memorias del subdesarrollo (Memories of Underdevelopment, 1968, 97 min.): When his wife and family leave for Miami, Sergio, a formerly wealthy aspiring writer, decides to stay behind in the new Cuba but can't quite come to embrace the revolution.

La última cena (The Last Supper, 1976, 120 min.): Set in the 1790s, just after the Haitian revolution, a naive plantation owner decides to reenact Christ's last supper by serving his slaves a meal, but they take their newfound Christian brotherhood seriously and revolt.

Fresa y chocolate (Strawberry and Chocolate, 1994)—See description earlier.

Guantanamera (1995, 105 min.): Codirected with Juan Carlos Tabío, this is the story of what happens when an aging diva from Guantánamo dies unexpectedly while visiting her home town. The rest of the movie is a hilarious farce chronicling the endless bureaucratic maneuvering needed to transport her body back to Havana for burial.

By Fernando Pérez

Madagascar (1994, 50 min.): A teenage girl looks for meaning in a world gone mad and a city in ruins.

La vida es silbar (Life Is to Whistle, 1998, 106 min.): Three characters in present-day Havana must overcome their fears in order to live a fuller, freer life.

Suite Habana (2003, 84 min.): Shot almost entirely without dialogue, this film is a sad but proud tribute to the city of Havana and its resourceful, tenacious inhabitants. It provoked both controversy and tearful standing ovations when it was debuted in Cuba.

El madrigal (2007): In the style of American filmmaker David Lynch, this film plays with the conventions of cinema by presenting a story within a story, while refusing to clarify which of the two is fact and which is fiction.

El ojo del canario (2010): The story of the young years of Cuba's national hero, José Martí.

Recent Releases and Contemporary Issues

Juan of the Dead (2011): Alejandro Brugués (92 min.)—When a group of slackers faces off against an army of zombies, the government claims the living dead are a bunch of counterrevolutionaries.

Habanastation (2011): Ian Padrón (95 min.)—Ostensibly a children's film, this picture exposes the emerging inequalities in Cuban society as experienced by two very different young revolutionary pioneers.

Seven Days in Havana (2012): Laurent Cantet, Benicio Del Toro, Julio Medem, Elia Suleiman, Juan Carlos Tabío, Pablo Trapero, and Gaspar Noé (129 min.)—Written largely by leading Cuban novelist Leonardo Padura and directed in turn by each of the previously mentioned international directors, this film chronicles seven consecutive days in the life of the city of Havana.

Unfinished Spaces (2011): Benjamin Murray and Alysa Nahmias (86 min.)—A visually arresting chronicle of the storied history of Cuba's once beautiful and long-neglected National Schools of Art.

Chico & Rita (2010): Toño Errando, Javier Mariscal, and Fernando Trueba (94 min.)—A rich and deeply imagined animated recreation of the glory days of Cuban popular dance music.

Forbidden Voices (2012): Barbara Miller (95 min.)—With the subtitle, "How to start a revolution with a laptop," this film chronicles the daily struggles of three young female bloggers, Iran's Farnaz Seifi, China's Zeng Jinyan, and Cuba's Yoani Sánchez.

La película de Ana (2012): Daniel Díaz Torres (157 min.)—The story of an unsuccessful actress who decides to make a documentary about prostitution in which she herself costars.

Despertar (2012): Ricardo Figueredo and Anthony Bubaire—A chronicle of the daily life and struggles of the Cuban rapper Raudel Collazo (aka, *Escuadrón Patriota*) shot in his hometown of Güines.

Una noche (2012): Lucy Mulloy (89 min.)—This film follows the trials of three young Cubans who opt to leave Cuban on a raft in search of brighter horizons in the United States. While visiting the U.S. to attend New York City's Tribeca Film Festival, in which the film emerged as a major award winner, two of the film's three protagonists defected on a stopover in Miami, making life stranger than fiction indeed. Stranger still, a year later the couple (who had played fraternal twins in the movie) turned up at a screening of the film in Miami, now living together with twins of their own on the way.

DISCOGRAPHY OF CUBAN MUSIC

Readers can see Ned Sublette's *Cuba and Its Music: From the First Drum to the Mambo* (Chicago Review Press, 2004) for a clear, entertaining social history of Cuban music up to the early 1950s. A good beginner's guides to the many groups, albums, and genres of Cuban music are Philip Sweeney's *Rough Guide to Cuban*

Music (Rough Guides, 2001), and the more scholarly Cuban musical dictionary by Helio Orovio recently translated into English, *Cuban Music from A to Z* (Duke University Press, 2004).

Compilations: Various Artists and Various Genres

Yo Soy, Del Son a la Salsa (2 CDs), RMM Filmworks Soundtrack, 1997.

Cuba, I Am Time (4 CDs), Blue Jakel Entertainment, 1997.

Official Retrospective of Cuban Music (4 CDs), Center for the Investigation and Development of Cuban Music, Tonga Productions/Salsa Blanca, 1999.

100 Canciones Cubanas del Milenio" (4 CDs), Alma Latina, 2000.

Rarezas del siglo, Vols. I and II, produced by Helio Orovio, EGREM and UNEAC, 2001.

Cuban Instrumental and Classical Music: Contradanza, Danzón, Etc.

Rotterdam Conservatory Orquesta Típica, *Cuba: Contradanzas and Danzones*, Nimbus, 1996.

Ernesto Lecuona, *The Ultimate Collection: Lecuona Plays Lecuona*, BMG Music, 1997.

Various Artists, *The Cuban Danzón: Before There Was Jazz, 1906–1929*, Arhollie, 1999.

Bola de Nieve, *Bola de Nieve*, Egrem/Nuevos Medios, 2003.

Son

Trio Matamoros, *The Legendary Trio Matamoros*, Tumbao, Cuban Classics, 1992.

Arsenio Rodríguez y su Conjunto, *Dundunbanza, 1946–1951*, Tumbao Cuban Classics, 1994.

Buena Vista Social Club, *Buena Vista Social Club*, World Circut/Nonesuch, 1997.

Afro-Cuban All-Stars, A *Toda Cuba le Gusta*, World Circut/Nonesuch, 1997.

Polo Montañez, *Guajiro Natural*, Lusafrica, 2000.

Vieja Trova Santiaguera, *Dominó*, Virgin Records, 2000.

Benny Moré, *Canto a mi Cuba*, EGREM, 2004.

Rumba

Lydia Cabrera and Josefina Tarafa, *Havana, Cuba, ca. 1957: Rhythms and Songs for the Orishas*, Smithsonian Folkways Recordings, 2001.

Lydia Cabrera and Josefina Tarafa, *Matanzas, Cuba, ca. 1957: Afro-Cuban Sacred Music from the Countryside*, Smithsonian Folkways Recordings, 2001.

Los Muñequitos de Matanzas, *Rumba de Corazón—50 Aniversario*, Bis Music, 2002.

Mambo

¡Cubanismo!, *Mardi Gras Mambo*, Hannibal Records/Rycodisk, 2000.

Benny Moré y Dámaso Pérez Prado, *30 exitos (30 Hits)*, Orfeon, 2001.

Cha-cha-chá

Orquesta América with Félix Reina and Richard Egües, *Cha-cha-chá-son*, Tumi Cuban, 2004.

Latin Jazz (Afro-Cuban Jazz)

Gonzalo Rubalcaba, *Gonzalo Rubalcaba*, EGREM, 1995.

Maraca y Otra Visión, *Habana mía*, OK records/Caribe Productions, 1998.

Calle 54—Music from the Miramax Motion Picture, Blue Note Records, 2001.

Chano Pozo with Dizzy Gillespie, *The Real Birth of CuBop: Manteca*, Tumbao, 2001.

Machito and His Afro-Cubans, *Ritmo Caliente*, Proper Records, 2002.

Bebo Valdés and Diego El Cigala, *Lágrimas Negras*, RCA Victor, 2003.

Chucho Valdés, *Chucho's Steps*, Four Quarters Entertainment, 2010.

Dafnis Prieto, *Proverb Trio*, Dafnison Music, 2012.

Salsa

Willie Colón and Rubén Blades, *Metiendo Mano*, Fania Records, 1977.

Willie Colón and Rubén Blades, *Siembra*, Fania Records, 1978.

Rubén Blades y Seis del Solar, *Buscando América*, Electra, 1984.

Fania All-Stars, *Hot Sweat: The Best of Fania All-Stars Live*, Vampisoul, 2005.

Celia Cruz and Johnny Pacheco, *Celia and Johnny*, Fania Records, 2006.

Gloria Estefan, *Mi Tierra*, Epic, 1993.

Timba—Modern Cuban Dance Music

Manolín, El Medico de la Salsa, *Para mi gente*, Milan, 1996.

Los Van Van, *Llegó . . . Van Van (Van Van Is Here)*, Havana Caliente/Atlantic, 1999.

Issac Delgado, *Malecón*, Bis Music, 2000.

David Calzado y su Charanga Habanera, *Soy Cubano, Soy Popular*, EGREM, 2004.

Bolero/Fílin (Feeling)

Olga Guillot, *La Reina de Boleros: Sus 22 Mejores Boleros*, Gema Records, 1995.

Armando Garzón with the Quinteto Oriente, *Boleros*, CoraSon Records, 1996.

Bebo Valdés and Diego Cigala, *Lágrimas Negras*, RCA, 2003.

La Lupe, *La Lupe es la reina*, Fania Records, 2006.

Vieja Trova

Los Compadres Original, *Epoca de oro del duo*, EGREM, 1996, Sonodisc, 2000.

María Teresa Vera, *La embajadora de la canción de ataño*, EGREM, 2002.

Nueva Trova

Silvio Rodríguez, *Canciones Urgentes, Los Grandes Éxitos*, Luaka Bop, 2000.

Pablo Milanés, *Como un campo de maíz*, Epic Records, 2005.

Pedro Luis Ferrer, *Rústico*, La Escondida Records, 2005.

Cuban Rock (Novísima Trova)

Carlos Varela, *Carlos Varela en vivo*, Bis Music, 1993.

Habana Abierta, *24 Horas*, Ariol, 1999.

Buena Fe, *Dejame Entrar*, EGREM, 2002.

Boris Larramendi, *La cibertimba y al bárbaro*, Bandcamp, 2013.

Cuban Hip-Hop

Orishas, *A lo cubano*, Universal Latino, 2000.

Various Artists, *Cuban Hip Hop All Stars*, Papaya Records, 2001.

Los Aldeanos, *Los guerreros de la tinta*, self produced, 2010.

Omni-Zona Franca, *Alamar Express*, self produced, 2010.

David D'Omni, *Free Hop*, self produced, 2011.

Escuadrón Patriota, *La nueva filosofia de lucha*, self produced, 2012.

Thematic Index

Note: Page numbers in italics indicate maps, tables, photos, and boxes.

Economy

Index

Note: Page numbers in italics indicate maps, tables, photos, and boxes.

About the Authors and Contributors

Ted A. Henken, Ph.D., is an associate professor in the Departments of Sociology and Anthropology and Black and Latino Studies at Baruch College, City University of New York. He is the current president of the Association for the Study of the Cuban Economy (2012–2014). His published works include ABC-CLIO's *Cuba: A Global Studies Handbook* (2008), a forthcoming monograph on public policy and micro-enterprise in revolutionary Cuba co-authored with Archibald R.M. Ritter, as well as articles on Cuba in various anthologies and the academic journals *Cuban Studies*, *Cuban Affairs*, *Latin American Research Review*, *Latino Studies*, *Cuba in Transition*, *Encuentro de la Cultura Cubana*, and *Nueva Sociedad*. Henken also writes about contemporary Cuba on his blog, *El Yuma* (http://elyuma.blogspot.com/) and is frequently interviewed about Cuba by major international media including *The New York Times*, *NPR*, *CNN*, *CNBC*, *BBC*, *AP*, *Reuters*, *The Christian Science Monitor*, *The Miami Herald*, *Univision*, *Telemundo*, *NTN24*, and *Martí Noticias*. Henken holds a doctorate in Latin American Studies from Tulane University. You can follow him on Twitter at @ElYuma.

Miriam Celaya González earned her bachelor's degree in art history from the University of Havana and did graduate work in anthropology at the University of Havana and the Cuban Academy of Sciences, where she worked as an archeologist between 1984 and 2005. She has also worked as a professor of Spanish language and literature and lectured on Cuban history, archeology, and anthropology at the University of Havana, the Advanced Institute of Industrial Design (ISDI), and the National Center of Restoration and Museology (CENCREM). She has published articles about native Cuban art and archeology in various cultural and scientific journals. She currently works as an independent journalist, regularly publishing articles in *Diario de*

Cuba, *Convivencia*, and *Voces* magazine, and was a cofounder of the independent digital magazine *Consenso* (2004–2007). She is also the author of *Sin EVAsión* (http://sinevasionen.wordpress.com/), one of Cuba's best-known blogs.

Dimas C. Castellanos Martí earned his bachelor's degree in political science from the University of Havana in 1975 and a degree in Theology from Havana's Advanced Institute of Biblical and Theological Studies in 2006. He has taught Marxist philosophy at the University of Havana. Currently an independent journalist, Castellanos writes for the digital publications *Diario de Cuba*, *Convivencia*, and *Voces* magazine. He also publishes his own blog, *El Blog de Dimas* (http://desdecuba.com/dimas/) and has won numerous journalism awards for his work. Castellanos has presented academic papers in the United States and Europe, including "Birth and Death of Civil Society in Cuba," at the Institute of Latin America of the University of Berlin and at the Department of Sociology of the University of La Laguna, Tenerife, Spain (2009). He is also a member of the Florida-based Cuban Studies Institute.

Armando Chaguaceda holds a doctorate in political science and has worked in various Cuban and Mexican universities and institutes as a professor of history and political science. His research focuses on Latin American popular social and political movements, with a particular emphasis on Cuba and Venezuela.

Oscar Espinosa Chepe holds a degree in economics from the University of Havana. In the 1960s, after serving as an economic advisor to Fidel Castro, he was sent to do agricultural work due to his heterodox economic ideas. Later, he served Cuba as an economic counselor in Eastern Europe and at the Cuban Central Bank. In the early 1990s he was accused of being a counterrevolutionary and relieved of all official positions. He has continued to work as an independent journalist and economist since then. In 2003, along with 74 other dissidents, he was arrested and sentenced to 20 years in prison but released on temporary medical parole in November 2004 after serving 20 months. He has published his analyses of the Cuban economy in many academic journals and international newspapers, including *Cuba in Transition*, *Encuentro de la Cultura Cubana*, *El País*, *The Miami Herald*, *ABC*, and the *Fohla de Sao Paulo*. In 2003, he published the book *Crónica de un desastre* (Chronicle of a Disaster) in Spain. This was followed in 2007 by *Cuba, revolución o involución?* (Cuba: Revolution or Involution?) and in 2011 by *Cambios en Cuba: pocos, limitados y tardíos* (Changes in Cuba: Few, Limited, and Late). He is Cuba's most renowned independent economist.

Henry Constantín is an independent journalist, blogger (*www.vocecubanas.reportesdeviajes.com*), and prizewinning writer and photographer. Due to his political ideas and activities he has been expelled from the journalism schools of the University of Oriente and Las Villas, and from the School of Audiovisual Communications of the *Instituto Superior de Arte*.

Regina Coyula has a degree in history from the University of Havana and worked for many years in Cuba's Ministry of the Interior. Currently, she blogs at the site *La mala letra* (http://lamalaletra.wordpress.com/).

Fernándo Dámaso is a retired member of the Cuban Armed Forces and currently works in public relations.

Reinaldo Escobar has a degree in journalism from the University of Havana and worked as a reporter for the newspaper *Juventud Rebelde* until 1988. Since then he has been an independent journalist and blogger. He is the host of the independent video series *Razones Ciudadanas*.

Dayrom Gil is a Cuban writer who lives in Brazil.

Marlene Azor Hernández is a sociologist and graduate student at the *Universidad Autónoma Metropolitana* in Mexico City where she is pursuing her Ph.D. in Social Science and Humanities. She was a professor in the Department of Philosophy and History of the University of Havana for 17 years, as well as a visiting professor at the University of Paris VIII, Saint Denis, France.

Maritza de los Ángeles Hidalgo-Gato Lima holds a degree in history from the University of Havana and has a master's degree in historical, regional, and local Studies. She has worked as museum curator and historical investigator. Her research focuses on Cuban traditions and cultural identity.

Rogelio Fabio Hurtado is a poet. He also holds a degree in journalism and works as an independent journalist. He has published two books of poetry and another book about the presence in Cuba of the Order of the Brothers of Saint John of God.

César Leal Jiménez holds degrees in journalism and art, and works as an artist. In his paintings, drawings, and lithographs, he explores social, cultural, and political subjects. He has taught at the San Alejandro School of Fine Arts, the Superior Institute of Art, and the National School of Design. Some of his work is part of the permanent exhibition of the Cuban National Museum of Art.

Miriam Leiva holds a degree in international relations. One of the founders of the Ladies in White, she was an active member of the group until 2008. As an independent journalist, she has published in *Slate*, the *International Herald Tribune*, *Salon*, *The Miami Herald*, *El Nuevo Herald*, and *ABC* She and her husband, Oscar Espinosa Chepe, also maintain their journalism at the blog *Reconciliación Cubana* (http://reconciliacioncubana.wordpress.com/).

Orlando Luis Pardo Lazo holds a bachelor's degree in biochemistry from the University of Havana School of Biology (1994). Since 2000, he has worked as a freelance artist, photographer, journalist, blogger, and social activist, while also publishing five books of short stories. He has edited several independent Cuban digital magazines including *The Revolution Evening Post* (2006–2008) and *Voces* (2010–2012). He has lectured on civil activism and new media at Princeton University, Brown University, and New York University, among others. He runs the photo blog *Boring Home Utopics* (*vocescubanas.com/boringhomeutopics*) and organized the first freelance documentary photo contest in Cuba *País de Píxeles* (2011–2012) (*vocescuba-*

nas.com/paisdepixeles). His photographs have been published in *El caimán barbudo* (Cuba), *Letras Libres* (Mexico), *The Root* (US), and *Veja* (Brasil). Most recently, his photography was featured on *The New York Times' Lens* blog (http://lens.blogs. nytimes.com/2013/04/03/blogging-a-bridge-from-havana/).

Yoani Sánchez earned a degree in philology from the University of Havana in 2000. She began her blog, *Generación Y*, in April 2007 and currently receives more than 15 million hits per month. She was awarded Spain's prestigious Ortega y Gasset prize in 2008 and Columbia University's Maria Moors Cabot award in 2009, both for digital journalism. She has published articles in *El País*, *The New York Times*, *The Washington Post*, and lectured at numerous universities in the United States, Spain, Germany, and many other countries. She has published two books, one a collection of her blog posts and the other a how-to bloggers' manual. She is also Cuba's leading Twitter user with over half-a-million followers.

Miguel Iturria Savón holds a degree in history and has published widely on Cuban literature, film, and fine arts. He is the author of various books of history and culture including *Memoria documental de los vascos en Cuba*, *Españoles en la cultura cubana*, and *Miradas cubanas sobre García Lorca*.

Wilfredo Vallín holds a degree in law and is the president of the Cuban Legal Association. He is an independent lawyer in Havana where he practices law.